SIGHT AND THE ANCIENT SENSES

What did ancient Greeks and Romans "see" when they saw? How did Graeco-Roman theories of seeing shape classical art, literature and philosophy? And how does such thinking relate to the "senses in antiquity", as well as to more modern western theoretical frameworks?

Sight and the Ancient Senses examines the sense that Greek and Roman antiquity theorized above all others. Approaching vision from a range of different thematic angles, the book provides the first thorough introduction to concepts of "seeing" in ancient philosophy, science, literature, rhetoric and art. At the same time, this anthology of specially commissioned chapters relates ideas about sight to ancient debates about other modes of sensory perception.

The volume brings together a range of interdisciplinary perspectives to deliver a broad and balanced coverage of its subject. Contributors explore the cultural, social and intellectual backdrops that gave rise to ancient theories of seeing, from Archaic Greece through to the advent of Christianity in late antiquity. The book also reaches beyond its Graeco-Roman framework, demonstrating how ancient ideas have influenced the *longue durée* of western sensory thinking. Richly illustrated throughout, including a section of colour plates, *Sight and the Ancient Senses* will be an invaluable resource for students and scholars alike – among classicists, as well as within the emerging field of sensory history.

Michael Squire is Reader in Classical Art at King's College London, and has held research fellowships at Berlin, Cambridge, Cologne, Harvard, Munich and Stanford. Previous books include *Image and Text in Graeco-Roman Antiquity* (2009), *The Art of the Body: Antiquity and its Legacy* (2011) and *The Iliad in a Nutshell: Visualizing Epic on the Tabulae Iliacae* (2011).

THE SENSES IN ANTIQUITY

Series editors: Mark Bradley, University of Nottingham, and
Shane Butler, Johns Hopkins University

Like us, ancient Greeks and Romans came to know and understand their world through their senses. Yet it has long been recognized that the world the ancients perceived, and the senses through which they channelled this information, could operate differently from the patterns and processes of perception in the modern world. This series explores the relationship between perception, knowledge and understanding in the literature, philosophy, history, language and culture of ancient Greece and Rome.

Published

Synesthesia and the Ancient Senses
Edited by Shane Butler and Alex Purves

Smell and the Ancient Senses
Edited by Mark Bradley

Sight and the Ancient Senses
Edited by Michael Squire

Forthcoming
Sound and the Ancient Senses
Taste and the Ancient Senses
Touch and the Ancient Senses

SIGHT AND THE ANCIENT SENSES

Edited by
Michael Squire

Routledge
Taylor & Francis Group
LONDON AND NEW YORK

First published 2016
by Routledge
2 Park Square, Milton Park, Abingdon, Oxon OX14 4RN

and by Routledge
711 Third Avenue, New York, NY 10017

Routledge is an imprint of the Taylor & Francis Group, an informa business

© 2016 Michael Squire for selection and editorial matter; individual contributions, the contributors

The right of Michael Squire to be identified as the author of the editorial material, and of the authors for their individual chapters, has been asserted in accordance with sections 77 and 78 of the Copyright, Designs and Patents Act 1988.

All rights reserved. No part of this book may be reprinted or reproduced or utilised in any form or by any electronic, mechanical, or other means, now known or hereafter invented, including photocopying and recording, or in any information storage or retrieval system, without permission in writing from the publishers.

Trademark notice: Product or corporate names may be trademarks or registered trademarks, and are used only for identification and explanation without intent to infringe.

British Library Cataloguing-in-Publication Data
A catalogue record for this book is available from the British Library

Library of Congress Cataloging-in-Publication Data
Names: Squire, Michael.Title: Sight and the ancient senses / edited by Michael Squire.
Description: Milton Park, Abingdon, Oxon : Routledge, 2016. | Series: The senses in antiquity | Includes bibliographical references and index.
Identifiers: LCCN 2015023167| ISBN 9781844658657 (hardback : alkaline paper) |
ISBN 9781844658664 (paperback : alkaline paper) | ISBN 9781315719238 (e-book)
Subjects: LCSH: Civilization, Classical. | Vision–Social aspects–Greece–History–To 1500. | Vision–Social aspects–Rome–History. | Visual perception–Social aspects–Greece–History–To 1500. | Visual perception–Social aspects–Rome–History–To 1500. | Senses and sensation–Social aspects–Greece–History–To 1500. | Senses and sensation–Social aspects–Rome–History.
Classification: LCC DE60 .S54 2016 | DDC 152.140938–dc23
LC record available at http://lccn.loc.gov/2015023167

ISBN: 978-1-84465-865-7 (hbk)
ISBN: 978-1-84465-866-4 (pbk)
ISBN: 978-1-315-71923-8 (ebk)

Typeset in Sabon
by Wearset Ltd, Boldon, Tyne and Wear

Printed and bound in Great Britain by
TJ International Ltd, Padstow, Cornwall

CONTENTS

List of illustations vii
List of contributors xi
Acknowledgements xiii

Introductory reflections: making sense of ancient sight 1
MICHAEL SQUIRE

1 Sight and the Presocratics: approaches to visual perception in
   early Greek philosophy 36
   KELLI RUDOLPH

2 Sight and the philosophy of vision in Classical Greece:
   Democritus, Plato and Aristotle 54
   ANDREA NIGHTINGALE

3 Sight and the perspectives of mathematics: the limits of ancient
   optics 68
   REVIEL NETZ & MICHAEL SQUIRE

4 Sight and reflexivity: theorizing vision in Greek vase-painting 85
   JONAS GRETHLEIN

5 Sight and painting: optical theory and pictorial poetics in
   Classical Greek art 107
   JEREMY TANNER

6 Sight and light: reified gazes and looking artefacts in the Greek
   cultural imagination 123
   RUTH BIELFELDT

7 Sight and death: seeing the dead through ancient eyes 143
   SUSANNE TURNER

CONTENTS

8 Sight and the gods: on the desire to see naked nymphs   161
   VERITY PLATT

9 Sight and memory: the visual art of Roman mnemonics   180
   JAŚ ELSNER & MICHAEL SQUIRE

10 Sight and insight: theorizing vision, emotion and imagination in
   ancient rhetoric   205
   RUTH WEBB

11 Sight and Christianity: early Christian attitudes to seeing   220
   JANE HEATH

12 Sight and blindness: the mask of Thamyris   237
   LYNDSAY COO

13 Sight in retrospective: the afterlife of ancient optics   249
   A. MARK SMITH

   Bibliography   263
   Index   306

ILLUSTRATIONS

Plates

1. Fragment of an Apulian krater from Tarentum, *ca.* 360–350 BCE
2. Reconstruction drawing of the same fragment
3. Detail of a funerary shrine on an Apulian volute-krater by the Helm Painter, last quarter of the fourth century BCE
4. Painted wooden votive tablet from Pitsa, sixth century BCE
5. Watercolour reconstruction of the Great Tomb at Lefkadia, late fourth century BCE
6. Painted metopes depicting a centauromachy from the Great Tomb at Lefkadia
7. Centauromachy metope from the Great Tomb at Lefkadia
8. Warrior: detail of the fresco paintings from the Great Tomb at Lefkadia
9. Hermes: detail of the fresco paintings from the Great Tomb at Lefkadia
10. Aeacus: detail of the fresco paintings from the Great Tomb at Lefkadia
11. Rhadamanthus: detail of the fresco paintings from the Great Tomb at Lefkadia

Figures

I.1	Attic red-figure *alabastron* showing a seated woman looking at her reflection in a mirror, *ca.* 500 BCE	6
I.2	Detail of a "Third Style" wall-painting of Narcissus staring at his reflection, from the north wall of *cubiculum* 6 in the Casa di Marco Lucrezio Fronto (Pompeii V.4,a)	7
I.3	Marble funerary stele of Orchomenos, signed by "Alxenor of Naxos", early fifth century BCE	11
I.4	Painted marble "eye" from the prow of an Athenian trireme, discovered in the Piraeus' Zea harbour, probably late fifth century BCE	20
I.5	Votive offering dedicated to Asclepius by Praxias (on behalf of his wife), from the south slope of the Acropolis in Athens, *ca.* 350 BCE	21

ILLUSTRATIONS

I.6	Floor mosaic of an eye under attack by dwarfs and animals, from the "House of the Evil Eye" outside Antioch, second century CE	22
I.7	"Archinos" marble relief from the sanctuary of Amphiaraos at Oropos in Attica, first half of the fourth century	23
I.8	Pair of eyes (made from bronze, marble, frit, quartz and obsidian) for inserting into a bronze statue, probably fifth century BCE	24
I.9	Chian "Wild Goat Style" phallus cup (with added plaster), with a pair of eyes painted on the glans, last quarter of the seventh century BCE	27
I.10	Floor mosaic from the threshold of the Basilica Hilariana on Rome's Caelian hill, probably second century CE: an eye is stabbed by a spear, surrounded by a group of animal attackers	29
I.11	Detail of an incantation from a Roman-Egyptian "magical papyrus" in the British Library, fourth century CE	30
3.1	Modern reconstruction diagram based on chapter 21 of Euclid's *Optics*	75
4.1	Jean-Baptiste-Siméon Chardin, *Soap Bubbles*, 1733–4	86
4.2	Attic black-figure *olpē* by the Amasis Painter, *ca.* 550–500 BCE	87
4.3	Attic red-figure "eye-cup" (Type A) by the Hischylus Potter, *ca.* 525 BCE	88
4.4	Detail of a Protoattic black-figure amphora by the Polyphemus Painter, *ca.* 670–660 BCE	91
4.5	Protoattic black-figure amphora by the Polyphemus Painter, *ca.* 670–660 BCE	92
4.6	Attic black-figure *skyphos* by the Theseus Painter, *ca.* 525–475 BCE	95
4.7	Pseudo-Chalcidian black-figure amphora, *ca.* 520 BCE	96
4.8	South Italian bell-krater by the Tarporley Painter, *ca.* 400–385 BCE	98
4.9	Apulian red-figure *pelikē* by the Tarporley Painter, *ca.* 380–370 BCE	99
4.10	Attic red-figure calyx-krater by Euphronios, *ca.* 525–475 BCE	101
4.11	Attic black-figure "eye-cup" (Type A) by the Lysippides Painter, *ca.* 525 BCE	103
4.12	Attic black-figure "eye-cup" (Type A) by the Cambridge Painter, *ca.* 520 BCE	105
6.1	Attic red-figure eye-cup attributed to the Nikosthenes Painter, *ca.* 520–510 BCE	127
6.2	Attic wheel-made clay lamp, *ca.* 475–25 BCE	132
6.3	Attic wheel-made clay lamp with two nozzles, *ca.* 400–375 BCE	133
6.4	Attic black-figure neck-amphora, showing Atlas (?) carrying the universe, *ca.* 510–500 BCE	134
6.5	Attic white-ground bobbin from the Athenian Agora showing Helios with chariot, *ca.* 480–470 BCE	135
6.6	Attic red-figure *pyxis* ("lid"), showing either Helios and Selene or Nyx and Eos, *ca.* 430 BCE	136
6.7	Attic red-figure *pyxis*, *ca.* 430 BCE (as seen from the side)	137
6.8	Attic red-figure *pyxis*, *ca.* 430 BCE (bottom)	137
6.9	Attic black-figure eye-cup attributed to the Nikosthenes Painter, *ca.* 520 BCE	138

ILLUSTRATIONS

6.10	Interior tondo of the same Attic black-figure eye-cup attributed to the Nikosthenes Painter, *ca.* 520 BCE	138
6.11	Attic red-figure bell-krater attributed to the Dinos Painter, showing Eros depilating a woman with a lamp, *ca.* 430–420 BCE	141
7.1	Black-figure Attic funerary *pinax* from Cape Kolias, attributed to the Sappho Painter, *ca.* 500 BCE	147
7.2	Marble funerary stele from Attica, *ca.* 375–350 BCE	152
7.3	Marble "Ilissos stele" from Athens, *ca.* 350–330 BCE	153
7.4	"Badminton sarcophagus" with scene of Dionysus and the Seasons, *ca.* 260–270 CE	155
7.5	Plaster cast of the limestone pediment with Medusa, Pegasus and Chrysaor from the Temple of Artemis on Corfu, *ca.* 580 BCE	158
7.6	Wall-painting showing Perseus and Andromeda with the head of Medusa, from the Casa del Vaticinio di Cassandra (Pompeii, VI.10.2), late first century BCE	159
8.1	Inscription from Aquae Flavianae, Algeria, second century CE	162
8.2	Front of a marble sarcophagus depicting Hylas and the Nymphs, installed in Rome's Palazzo Mattei, early third century CE	166
8.3	Votive altar from the sanctuary of Asclepius at Pergamon, second century CE (*in situ*). The translated inscription reads "To Taras: G[aius] Julius Nabus, Senator, dedicated this altar according to a vision seen in a dream"	174
8.4	Mosaic depicting Diana bathing with her nymphs, from the House of Venus at Volubilis in Morocco (*in situ*), early third century CE	176
8.5	Votive relief dedicated by "Archandros to the nymphs [and Pan]": from the sanctuary of Asclepius at Athens, *ca.* 425–400 BCE	178
8.6	Votive stele of the nymphs from Arcadia, inscribed *Nymphān* ("Of the Nymphs"), *ca.* 300 BCE. Tegea	178
9.1	Early Hadrianic marble funerary altar of T. Statilius Aper, *ca.* 120 CE	184
9.2	"Fourth Style" panel-painting from the north wall of *triclinium* 38 in the Casa dei Dioscuri (Pompeii VI.9.6,7 = Baldassare 1993: 894, no. 65)	194
9.3	Nineteenth-century reproduction drawing of a "Fourth Style" panel-painting from the west wall of *triclinium* 38 in the Casa dei Dioscuri (Pompeii VI.9.6,7 = Baldassare 1993: 896, no. 68)	195
9.4	Nineteenth-century reproduction drawing of a "Fourth Style" panel-painting from the east wall of *triclinium* 49 in the Casa dei Dioscuri (Pompeii VI.9.6,7 = Baldassare 1993: 951, no. 177)	196
9.5	Nineteenth-century reproduction drawing of a "Fourth Style" panel-painting from the south wall of *triclinium* 49 in the Casa dei Dioscuri (Pompeii VI.9.6,7 = Baldassare 1993: 952, no. 179)	197
9.6	Nineteenth-century reproduction drawing of a "Fourth Style" panel-painting from the north wall of *oecus* 17 in the Casa dei Capitelli Colorati (Pompeii VII.4.31,51 = Baldassare 1996: 1017, no. 27)	198
9.7	"Fourth Style" panel-painting from the west wall of *oecus* 17, Casa dei Capitelli Colorati (Pompeii VII.4.31,51 = Baldassare 1996: 1020, no. 30)	199

ILLUSTRATIONS

9.8	Nineteenth-century reproduction drawing of a "Fourth Style" panel-painting from the east wall of *oecus* 17, Casa dei Capitelli Colorati (Pompeii VII.4.31,51 = Baldassare 1996: 1024, no. 37)	200
9.9	"Fourth Style" panel-painting from the north wall of *exedra* 22 in the Casa dei Capitelli Colorati (Pompeii VII.4.31,51 = Baldassare 1996: 1040, no. 59)	201
9.10	Nineteenth-century reproduction drawing of a "Fourth Style" panel-painting from the south wall of *oecus* 24 in the Casa dei Capitelli Colorati (Pompeii VII.4.31,51 = Baldassare 1996: 1049, no. 72)	202
11.1	Drawing of the "Alexamenos graffito" from the Palatine Hill in Rome, most likely from the third century CE: the scrawled text reads *Alexamenos sebate theon* ("Alexamenos worships [his] god")	232
12.1	Detail of an Attic red-figure *hydria* attributed to the Group of Polygnotus, *ca.* 440–420 BCE	240
13.1	The eye according to Alhacen, based on his description in the first book of *De aspectibus* (*ca.* 1030 CE)	257
13.2	Two reflections from arc XD and one from arc EF; diagram after a passage in the fifth book of Alhacen's *De aspectibus* (*ca.* 1030 CE)	259
13.3	One reflection only, from arc EF; diagram after a passage in the fifth book of Alhacen's *De aspectibus* (*ca.* 1030 CE)	259

CONTRIBUTORS

Ruth Bielfeldt teaches classical archaeology at Harvard University, where she is Harris K. Weston Associate Professor of the Humanities. Research interests include visual narrative in Roman funerary art, Hellenistic urbanism and the cultural life of "things". She is the author of *Orestes auf Römischen Sarkophagen* (2005), and has edited *Ding und Mensch in der Antike: Gegenwart und Vergegenwärtigung* (2014).

Lyndsay Coo is Lecturer in Greek Language and Literature at the University of Bristol, and previously held a Junior Research Fellowship at Trinity College, Cambridge. She is currently completing a commentary on selected fragmentary plays of Sophocles.

Jaś Elsner is Humfrey Payne Senior Research Fellow in Classical Archaeology and Art at Corpus Christi College in Oxford, and Visiting Professor at the University of Chicago. He has published widely on classical, late antique and Byzantine visual culture.

Jonas Grethlein is Professor of Greek Literature at Heidelberg University. His recent publications include *The Greeks and their Past* (2010) and *Experience and Teleology in Ancient Historiography* (2013).

Jane Heath is Lecturer in the New Testament at Durham University, and currently holds an Alexander-von-Humboldt Research Fellowship in church history and classical literature at the Humboldt-Universität zu Berlin. She is author of *Paul's Visual Piety: The Metamorphosis of the Beholder* (2013).

Reviel Netz is Professor of Classics at Stanford, with a special interest in the history of pre-modern mathematics, literacy, cognitive history and visual culture. He is the author of numerous books on Greek mathematics, as well as a commentary on the works of Archimedes.

Andrea Nightingale is Professor of Classics at Stanford University. She has published widely on ancient philosophy and thought, including books on *Genres in Dialogue: Plato and the Construct of Philosophy* (2000), *Spectacles of Truth: Theoria in its Cultural Context* (2004) and *Once out of Nature: Augustine on Time and the Body* (2011).

Verity Platt is Associate Professor of Classics and History of Art at Cornell University. She is the author of *Facing the Gods: Epiphany and Representation in*

CONTRIBUTORS

Graeco-Roman Art, Literature and Religion (2011), and of numerous articles on ancient art and literature.

Kelli Rudolph is Lecturer in Classics and Philosophy at the University of Kent, where she works primarily on ancient philosophy. She has research interests in Presocratic and Hellenistic philosophy, as well as in ancient theories of sensation. She is the editor of the forthcoming *Taste and the Ancient Senses* volume in this series.

A. Mark Smith is Curators' Professor of History at the University of Missouri, Columbia. He has written on various aspects of ancient, mediaeval and early modern optics and visual theory. Foremost among these publications is his eight-volume critical edition and translation of Alhacen's *De aspectibus*, which has appeared in instalments between 2001 and 2010.

Michael Squire is Reader in Classical Art at King's College London. He has a special research interest in the interaction between ancient visual and verbal modes of representation, and is currently working on ideas of vision in the Elder Philostratus' *Imagines*.

Jeremy Tanner is Professor of Classical and Comparative Art at the Institute of Archaeology, University College London. His main interests lie in the history of classical art, as well as in the sociology and historiography of art more generally; his article on "Michael Baxandall and the Sociological Interpretation of Art" won the Sage Prize for *Cultural Sociology* in 2011.

Susanne Turner is Curator of the Cambridge Museum of Classical Archaeology. She has a particular interest in viewing, death and the body (especially in the context of Attic grave stelai); her current work focusses on viewing the gods in Greek temple contexts.

Ruth Webb is Professor of Greek Language and Literature at the Université Lille 3 and a member of the Unité Mixte de Recherche 8163, "Savoirs, textes, langage". Her main field of research has centred around mental images in ancient rhetoric and literature; she has also published works on ancient ecphrasis and late antique theatre.

ACKNOWLEDGEMENTS

Sight and the Ancient Senses is the result of a long and sustained academic collaboration: sincere thanks to all the contributors for their enthusiasm, above all for responding to one another (and to the editor) with such diligence and patience. Inevitably, perhaps, the final book has had to proceed without all the chapters that were originally commissioned: in particular, we hope that the article by Helen Morales (on "sight and power") will materialize in some other form, and much look forward to learning from it.

A number of people have been instrumental in transforming this project from abstract *eidos* into concrete materiality. Three editorial debts deserve particular mention. First, we are grateful to Mark Bradley and Shane Butler (editors of the "Senses in Antiquity" series), as well as to the two anonymous readers, not least for their rigorous comments on earlier chapter-drafts. Second, a special thanks to the press – above all to Tristan Palmer and Lola Harre at Acumen and Routledge, as well as to Hazel Johannessen and Kate Short (the book's eagle-eyed copy-editors) and Matthew Gibbons (its designer). Third, I am grateful to the Leverhulme Trust and Internationales Kolleg-Morphomata at the Universität zu Köln: the book may have appeared a little later than originally envisaged, but that it appears at all is due to the research leave that they funded between 2014 and 2016.

Finally, a word of personal thanks to the Usual Suspects: above all to my family and friends – especially Jaś Elsner, Verity Platt and my colleagues in the Department of Classics at King's College London; last but never least, I am grateful to Christopher Whitton.

INTRODUCTORY REFLECTIONS
Making sense of ancient sight

Michael Squire

ἄν μ' ἐσίδῃς, καὶ ἐγὼ σέ. σὺ μὲν βλεφάροισι δέδορκας,
 ἀλλ' ἐγὼ οὐ βλεφάροις· οὐ γὰρ ἔχω βλέφαρα.
ἄν δ' ἐθέλῃς, λαλέω φωνῆς δίχα· σοὶ γὰρ ὑπάρχει
 φωνή, ἐμοὶ δὲ μάτην χείλε' ἀνοιγόμενα.

If you look at me, I also look at you. You look with eyes,
but I without eyes – because I have no eyes.
Were you to wish, I speak, albeit without a voice: for you have a
voice, but I have lips that open in vain.

Sight and the Ancient Senses explores the sense that Graeco-Roman antiquity theorized above all others: that of visual perception. We open it with a riddle – an anonymous epigram from the fourteenth book of the *Greek Anthology* (*Palatine Anthology* 14.56). As the poem's title confirms (*Eis eisoptron*), this object that looks when looked at, and which silently speaks upon being spoken to, is a mirror. Yet by addressing the reader-viewer, and by playing knowingly upon epigraphic conventions of inscribing objects with a "ventriloquist" first-person voice, the mirror's ephemeral visual reflection is here made to speak. Thanks to the poet's self-reflective verbal intervention, the object of sight is turned into not only a speaking citation, but also a monumentalized visual subject: it has been bestowed with the capacity for speech that images (*qua* images) lack.[1]

Whatever else we make of the poem, its decidedly self-reflexive view of viewing makes for an appropriate epigraph to our volume. On the one hand, the epigram speaks of the extraordinary intellectual energy with which Greek and Roman antiquity reflected upon the phenomenon of seeing, no less than that of being seen: it holds up a mirror to a culture obsessed with the sensory semantics of sight, and one which would shape the entire trajectory of subsequent western thinking about the senses.[2] On the other hand, the epigram's very talk of reflectiveness reminds us, right

---

1 On the underlying pictorial-poetic games of sight and sound here – resonating as they do with Hellenistic critical traditions (especially in the context of epigrams on artworks) – see e.g. Gutzwiller (2002); Petrovic (2005); Meyer (2007); Männlein-Robert (2007a; 2007b); Tueller (2008); Squire (2010a).
2 Lindberg (1976: 1–17) still offers the most accessible short introduction to ancient ideas about sight, now supplemented by Darrigol (2012: esp. 1–15): both books are useful for setting those ideas

from the outset, of our own refracted perspectives. From a physiological viewpoint, ancient Greek and Roman eyes functioned as ours do today: for all our cultural remove from antiquity, modern science assures us that the workings of the human eye rely upon the same processing of reflected light and neurological communication with the brain.[3] And yet the ways in which that process was envisaged (and hence empirically experienced) were markedly different. However much we may long to "see as others saw",[4] we necessarily look to ancient seeing through the prismatic lens of our own cultural conditioning. Like the elusive mirage of our riddlesome mirror-poem, the sense of ancient sight is at once tantalizingly accessible and hopelessly distant: look as we may, it is our own eyes that we must see/see through/see looking back at us. However studiously we read such literary reflections on sight, moreover, ancient words can never reproduce the sensory experience of past seeing.[5]

This fundamental problem lies at the heart of the emerging field of "sensory history" (and is of course a familiar refrain in Routledge's "Senses in Antiquity" series).[6] But when it comes to vision specifically, the dilemma seems particularly

---

within a longer western history (up to the seventeenth and nineteenth centuries respectively); compare also the sketch of "theoretical approaches to vision" in Wade & Swanston (2013: 78–107). On Greek views of sight, G. Simon (1988) remains the fundamental work (translated into German as Simon 1992); cf. e.g. Beare (1906: 9–92); Mugler (1964) (on the Greek vocabulary of sight and seeing); Frontisi-Ducroux (1995) (above all on the reciprocity of Greek vision: "le *voir* n'étant pas séparé de *l'être vu*", 20); Morales (2004: esp. 8–35); Villard (2005); Blundell *et al.* (2013) (surveying the substantial bibliography, and introducing a special journal issue on "vision and viewing in ancient Greece"); A. M. Smith (2015) (above all on ancient "optical" traditions). Also important on changing Greek "discourses of viewing ... within a history of the construction of a viewing subject" is the work of Simon Goldhill (Goldhill 1996: 26); cf. e.g. Goldhill (1994; 1998; 2000a; 2000b; 2001). On Roman ideas about sight, above all from an art-historical viewpoint, Elsner (1995) remains key, while some of the author's other ground-breaking articles on "Roman eyes" are collected in Elsner (2007b); cf. e.g. Rizzini (1998); Bartsch (2000; 2006: esp. 58–67); Fredrick (2002) (introducing a landmark volume on the "Roman gaze"); Neis (2013: 27–40) (on "late-antique visual theory"). Frank (2000) and Jane Heath (2013b) are especially useful on late antique/early Christian views of sight; the classic analysis here remains Riegl (1901). For the ways in which ancient thinking about vision has shaped the entire subsequent western sensory economy, the key volume remains Jay (1993); cf. e.g. Jonas (1982); Levin (1993); and the essays in Brennan & Jay (1996).

3 On the essential "modernity" of this scientific discovery, see below, pp. 15–16 (on Johannes Kepler's confirmation of retinal imaging), as well as the chapters by Netz & Squire and Smith (this volume). There is a vast literature on the science of visual perception. For some different introductions, see Hubel (1988); Gregory (1998); Wade (1998); Hubel & Wiesel (2005); Livingstone (2013); Wade & Swanston (2013); J. Harris (2014: 59–145).

4 The phrase is taken from the subtitle of an influential volume on "visuality before and beyond the Renaissance": Nelson (2000).

5 On the problems (as indeed advantages) of reconstructing the history of the senses from texts, see Howes (2005: esp. 57).

6 On the senses as "a product of place and, especially, time" (M. M. Smith 2007: 3) – and hence a subject for combined anthropological and historical enquiry – see e.g. Howes (1991; 2003; 2005); Classen (1993); Geurts (2002); Jay (2011); Howes & Classen (2014) (arguing that "the ways we use our senses, and the ways we create and understand the sensory world, are shaped by culture", 1). Compare also the earlier pioneering work of van Hoorn (1972), and most recently Constance Classen's five-volume *Cultural History of the Senses* series, published by Bloomsbury (in which Toner 2014 offers a "cultural history of the senses in antiquity"). On the ancient senses specifically, the most important recent revisionist analysis is Porter (2010), discussing "visual experience" at 405–50, while also challenging "a modern division of the senses and the labors of form" (2; cf. 406).

acute. Again and again – from museums and galleries, to archaeological heritage sites and visual reconstructions – we find sight being exploited as a sensational means of bridging the present's remove from the past. Whether we think of our shared natural landscapes, or else of manufactured historical objects, our sense of sight is harnessed to the hope of actually "seeing" the past: unlike so many of the ephemeral smells and sounds of history, its visual stimuli appear to travel tardis-like across time, forging an immediate sensory connection between "antiquity" and "modernity" (however we define those poles).[7]

Given the importance of such themes for approaching historical visual materials, it is perhaps unsurprising that they have received particular attention within the discipline of art history, above all over the last 30 years. With the explosion of interest in "visual culture" – a phenomenon that has gone hand-in-hand with the so-called "visual turn" of the late twentieth and early twenty-first centuries[8] – art historians have been especially interested in the divergent ways in which different cultures have gone about the act of looking.[9] This is not just a question of adjusting cultural perspectives in order to understand the logic of historical texts. Because the past also bestows us with objects and images – materials that lend themselves to our visual experiencing in the present – it is imperative to think about both similarities and divergences between dominant "ways of seeing" in the modern western world and those of other times and places.[10] The subsequent quest to reconstruct the "period eye" of past cultures has taken on a sort of (postcolonial) anthropological flavour:[11] while it can be all too easy to assume that the sense of seeing is a transhistorical and transcultural absolute, visual culture studies have emphasized the relativity of visual perception. We are back once again with the opening reflections of our Greek

---

7   The most influential analysis of such "eyewitnessing" within the disciplinary field of history remains Burke (2001). For one recent attempt to rewrite our (text-derived) cultural histories of Classical Greece by looking to Greek visual stimuli, see R. Osborne (2011). "Visual images do not offer insights into different aspects of the past", R. Osborne (2011: 17) argues; "they offer different insights into those same aspects of the past about which historians already write on the basis of text". For a salient critique of Osborne's method, see Elsner (2015), problematizing the assumption (as indeed scholarly objective) of "seeing" through ancient Greek eyes.

8   For the term, associated with the "media age" and poststructuralist/postmodern critical turns, see W. J. T. Mitchell (1994: 11–34); compare Boehm (1995: 13) on the "iconic turn".

9   For some introductions to the field of "visual culture" and its disciplinary relationship to "art history", see Bryson *et al.* (1994), along with e.g. Mirzoeff (1999); Bal (2003); Herbert (2003); Cherry (2004). The best compendium (complete with 149 influential essays and extracts) is Morra & Smith (2006); for an additional anthology of twentieth- and twenty-first-century writings, oriented around "visual sense" specifically ("vision and sight as something sensorially integrated, embodied and experienced", 3), see Edwards & Bhaumik (2008b). It is worth emphasizing here that this late twentieth-century "visual cultural" turn has a much longer scholarly history – not least in e.g. Wölfflin (1932: 237 – first published in German in 1915), espousing the need for a "history" of vision (cf. Bredekamp 2003). It was nonetheless reinvigorated in response to scholarship on Gestalt theory and the psychology of sight – above all, the work of Rudolf Arnheim, Richard Gregory and Richard Wollheim (cf. Squire 2009: 79–83).

10 On "ways of seeing", the key intervention was Berger (1972), accompanying a celebrated BBC television series; cf. Barthes (1981: 12: "I want a history of looking").

11 For the term "period eye", see Baxandall (1972: 29–30). More generally on underlying modes of "retrieval art history", see Gaskell (1991) (coining this phrase on 182); compare Holly (1996) on the whole problem of "past looking". For the project of *Bildanthropologie*, see Belting (2011b).

epigraph: although historical objects may appear as actual apparitions of the past – "blurring the line between past and present", as sites and sights "where the gazes of both can meet" (in the words of Michael Camille)[12] – they offer neither direct nor unmediated access to past seeing. Like it or not, what and how we see must depend upon preconceptions about what "seeing" entails.[13]

One of the most influential articulations of these issues came in Hal Foster's delineation of "vision" and "visuality", spurring a landmark edited volume of 1988.[14] By "vision", Foster hints at the essential physiology of seeing – that innate process by which human beings (at once like and unlike other animals) process visual information. But "visuality", Foster argued, works along different lines, leading away from empirical sense perception and into the discursive field of cultural and social history:[15]

> The difference between the terms [vision and visuality] signals a difference within the visual – between the mechanism of sight and its historical techniques, between the datum of vision and its discursive determinations – a difference, many differences, among how we see, how we are able, allowed or made to see, and how we see this seeing or the unseen therein.

Foster is careful to avoid too strict a "nature"/"culture" division here ("vision is social and historical too", he writes, just as "visuality involves the body and psyche").[16] But the resulting dichotomy is nonetheless premised upon a fundamental distinction: where Foster's talk of "vision" tends towards absolute universals of sense perception, his notion of "visuality" aims to categorize those varied cultural peculiarities of a particular "scopic regime";[17] if "vision" points more towards cross-cultural constants, "visuality" refers above all to the variables of a given visual culture.[18]

The inevitable problem with such delineations comes in determining which aspects of (visual) sensory experience to assign to each of these two self-standing categories.[19] While, for example, all manner of studies have concentrated on the

---

12 Camille (1996: 7).
13 For the importance of the point in theorizing Imperial Greek ideas of seeing, see Goldhill (2000a), developed in Goldhill (2001): "The act of viewing itself is always (to be) constructed in a socially and intellectually specific way, which requires (historical) analysis" (2000a: 70).
14 H. Foster (1988b). The intellectual debt, of course, is to Michel Foucault's distinction between "sex" and "sexuality", the one a "pre-given datum", the other a "simultaneously discursive and institutional formation": Foucault (1980: 210).
15 H. Foster (1988a: ix). Cf. Bryson (1988: 91–2): "Between subject and object is inserted the entire sum of discourses which make up visuality, that cultural construct, and make visuality different from vision, the notion of unmediated visual experience".
16 H. Foster (1988a: ix).
17 For the language of "scopic regime", see Metz (1974).
18 In classicist circles, one of the most productive arenas for playing out such debates has been that of colour perception: although such questions have not usually been related to the broader art-historical bibliography, to what extent does the perception of colour belong to "vision" or to "visuality"? For a polychrome introductory discussion (and introductory bibliographic guide), see Bradley (2013), with references to Bradley (2009); cf. the important art-historical discussion of Gage (1993).
19 Cf. Jay (1993: 3–4), commenting on the work of John Gibson, especially Gibson (1979).

dynamics of the "gaze" – above all in the field of psychoanalysis, not least in the wake of Jacques Lacan's pioneering work[20] – debates still run rife about whether we should be talking here in transhistorical terms (that is, conceptualizing it as part of "vision"), or whether to do so is to impose the cultural parameters of modern "visualities" back onto past cultures. In recent years, new neurocognitive research has weighed in on such debates, using complex brain-scanning experiments in an attempt to make scientific sense of human sight; indeed, some of the most stimulating (albeit highly controversial) work within recent art history has tried to forge connections between visual processing of the brain and the history of image-making.[21] Such cognitive scientific approaches to art history and visual perception are still in their infancy.[22] If we can be sure of one thing, though, it is that human visual perception is culturally plastic, defying any straightforward nature/nurture dichotomy. Both "how" and "what" we see are conditioned by our surroundings, and adaptable to them.[23]

Thankfully, perhaps, contributors to the present book do not attempt to solve all these problems. Our aim is instead more focussed in historical scope: to explore ancient Greek and Roman ideas about sensory seeing from a range of different disciplinary angles. That polyphony of different voices – and kaleidoscopic range of visual perspectives – is fundamental to our project. Perhaps more than any of the other ancient senses explored in the "Senses in Antiquity" series, the theme of sight requires us to work not only between divergent sorts of texts, but also between different types of media. Although all too often approached in blinkered disciplinary isolation (with scholars turning a blind or censorious eye to materials beyond their

---

20 Cf. especially Lacan (1977: 74–90) – giving rise to a series of influential feminist critiques on the essentialist "phallocentricism" of the gaze (none more so than Mulvey 2009: 14–39, first published as Mulvey 1975). For a recent review of scholarship on the gaze and its applicability to Greek and Roman literature (especially epic), see Lovatt (2013: esp. 1–28).

21 I restrict myself here to just two influential attempts to explain the history of art through neuroscience: first, Zeki (1999), arguing that "the function of art and the function of the visual brain are one and the same…; hence by knowing more about the workings of the brain in general and the visual brain in particular, one might be able to develop the outlines of a theory of aesthetics that is biologically based", 1); and second, Onians (2007), attempting a much longer cultural history of such "neuroarthistory". Compare also the recent contributions of e.g. Livingstone (2013) and Hackett (2014) (on the neuroscience of painted perspective). Such cognitive approaches have been harnessed to recent scholarly attempts to challenge the cultural relativity of human experience, positing a more "universalist" approach: for one key intervention, see K. Silverman (2009).

22 One thinks here of ongoing attempts to integrate visual perception within the larger quest for artificial intelligence: see Ings (2007: 264–85), along most recently with Pizlio et al. (2014).

23 It is well known, for example, that illiterate populations do not develop the same degree of myopia as their literate counterparts; likewise, there is some evidence that British children develop more short-sightedness during term-time than while away from school in the summer vacation. For a general introduction to the "adaptable eye", see Ings (2007: 102–27); cf. Gregory (1998: esp. 150–1) (on cultural factors moulding the anthropological perception of space, "related to distance cues as available in the environment", 151). On the problems of this vision/visuality dichotomy from the perspective of ancient Greek "seeing", see also Bassi (2005: esp. 2–3). The classic art-historical account of seeing as a culturally loaded "symbolic" system (centred around the question of perspective) is Panofsky (1991, first published in German in 1927); cf. Gombrich (1960), along with Tanner's discussion in this volume; compare also e.g. Wartofsky (1979: 314), concluding that "human vision is itself an artifact, produced by other artifacts, namely pictures".

Figure I.1 Attic red-figure *alabastron* showing a seated woman looking at her reflection in a mirror, *ca.* 500 BCE. Athens, Piraeus Museum: inv. 6255 (photograph by the author).

particular expertise), making sense of ancient seeing calls for interdisciplinary collaboration: it brings together (among others) literary critics, philosophers and archaeologists, as well as historians of art, medicine and mathematics.

Once again, our opening epigraph demonstrates the point with particular aplomb, reflecting as it does not only on the intellectual speculations of literary and philosophical texts, but also on the *material* sights of antiquity. Wherever we look, we find Greek and Roman images reflecting a related sort of self-reflexivity about the subjectivity of mirrored seeing – from actual mirrors that set their polished sides against engraved mythological scenes of seeing, through fifth-century Attic vase-paintings that have us look at someone viewing (Figure I.1), to Roman paintings of the doomed Narcissus gazing longingly at his own mirrored image (Figure I.2; cf. Figure 9.3).[24] One of the challenges in approaching ancient sight is its pervasive

---

24 On ancient mirror-image representations, see Grethlein (this volume), along with e.g. Balensiefen (1990); Frontisi-Ducroux & Vernant (1997); Bartsch (2006); Elsner (2007b: 132–76); R. Taylor (2008). On the myth of Narcissus, see below, n.96.

Figure I.2 Detail of a "Third Style" wall-painting of Narcissus staring at his reflection, from the north wall of *cubiculum* 6 in the Casa di Marco Lucrezio Fronto (Pompeii V.4,a) (photograph: Alinari/Art Resource, New York).

seeping into so many different cultural arenas. Yet to have any hope of understanding past seeing means bringing together different disciplinary viewpoints: it is necessary not only to read such lettered poems against other texts, but also to view them against the actual sights of the ancient sensory world.[25]

As explained below ("Eyeing up the book", pp. 30–5), our objective in this volume is therefore to offer a new preliminary and provocative overview of sight and ancient senses – one that, while by no means panoramic, nonetheless aims to spur new sorts of interdisciplinary connections. Before outlining the volume's structure and rationale, the remainder of this introduction offers two broader preliminary reflections. The first tackles the innocuous-looking "and" that connects "sight and the ancient senses", exploring not just the place of seeing within ancient frameworks

---

[25] More generally on the ways in which "Greek painting and the art ... of optics started out together" here, cf. Summers (2007: 16–42, quotation from 16). The point is developed by Tanner (this volume).

of sensory perception, but also the ways in which ideas about sight shaped ancient epistemologies of cognitive understanding. In the second section, I then turn to ancient thinking about the human eye specifically, articulating a key cultural difference between modern (that is, post-seventeenth-century) scientific ideas about seeing and ancient ideas of the embodied eye. As the following chapters make clear, "ancient sight" is something of a misnomer here: Greek and Roman materials offer a disjointed range of different materials, testifying to ideas about seeing that change over time, as well as to divergent conceptual frameworks even in one and the same chronological period.[26] And yet, at least from a twenty-first-century perspective, one of the most striking aspects of ancient sight is antiquity's insistence upon the active nature of seeing. "If you look at me, I also look at you", as our opening epigram puts it: within the Graeco-Roman imaginary, and across a remarkably long timespan, to see was to enter upon a dynamic, reciprocal and mutually implicative relationship with the thing seen.

The eyes have it?

What sort of place, then, did sight have within Greek and Roman ideas about sensory perception, empirical knowledge and rational cognition? Before tackling that question head-on, allow me to preface my comments by saying something about the broader "Senses in Antiquity" project and its relationship to the book in hand. One of the most stimulating aspects of this series (as articulated in Shane Butler's and Alex Purves' opening 2013 volume on *Synaesthesia and the Ancient Senses*, and more recently developed in Mark Bradley's 2015 volume on *Smell and the Ancient Senses*) is its self-declared "resistance to hierarchies of the senses ... especially those which place vision at the top and disassociate it from other senses".[27] In the associated rallying cry to "move 'beyond the visual paradigm' in order to offer a synaesthetic reading of the ancient world", the series has similarly re-evaluated not just antiquity's perceived "ocularcentrism" (that is, its hierarchical privileging of sight over the other senses), but also the "narrowing conception of the work of reading". Since "the visual paradigm [has] thus revealed itself to be primarily a hermeneutic one", as Butler and Purves conclude, "its vision is that of a reader who reads in order to know": "what we seek to recapture ... is the reader who reads not just to make sense but also *in order* to sense".[28]

So how might a volume specifically dedicated to *Sight and the Ancient Senses* fit within that larger "Senses in Antiquity" remit? Like other titles, this book will be deeply sensitive to "synaesthetic" verges: one of our recurrent themes, for example, concerns how ancient seeing could "cross" sensory lines – whether by conceptualizing sight in relation to touch, or else by debating how "listening" might bring about

---

26 For one scholarly rallying cry to segregate "Roman" ideas about seeing from the "Greek", see the provocations of Fredrick (2002), with response in Morales (2004: 31, n.128): when it comes to the gaze, Fredrick insists, "Rome cannot be collapsed with Greece to support an argument in favor of social constructionism or essentialism" (2002: 24).
27 See Butler & Purves (2013b); Bradley (2015b). Quotation from Butler & Purves (2013a: 2).
28 Quotations from Butler & Purves (2013a: 2–3) – although the italics are my own.

"seeing".[29] As in other series volumes, our objective is also to question the range of ideas that (what we label) ancient "sight" encompassed: rather than simply impose modern ideas back onto ancient models, we aim to showcase the complex and interwoven relationships between at once similar and different cultural histories of "seeing".[30] No less important are ideas about the interrelations between "seeing" and "reading". Readers are by necessity viewers, of course. And yet – as ancient authors (and we might add ancient artists) recurrently remind us – viewing is an activity at once related to but fundamentally different from reading.[31]

More challenging, perhaps, is the associated "anti-ocularcentric" rallying cry: for how should a book expressly dedicated to sight respond to the charge of looking *beyond* its cultural privileging? I should perhaps be upfront here: for in my view, at least, such rhetoric risks blinding us to ancient historical ideas about both what the senses are – or perhaps better, what they *were*. For all our common anxiety about the anachronistic, shut-down prompts of hermeneutics (a point championed most forcefully in recent years by Jim Porter),[32] and despite our shared understanding of sensory perception (whether visual, olfactory, tactile, gustatory or aural) as something irreducible to "knowledge", there is something to be said for resisting the recent resistance to the visual paradigm. Like it or not (and there are many good reasons for *not* liking it), classical ideas about the senses recurrently start from an assumption of sight's supremacy: this was not just a question of explicit and rationalized hierarchy; rather, as we shall see, ideas about sight themselves gave rise to frameworks for "theorizing" the senses (and indeed perception, knowledge and understanding) *tout court*.

The point deserves emphasis right from the outset. One of the things this volume and series sets out to do is to consider attitudes to the senses in the ancient world. Yet fundamental to that historical understanding, I would argue, is a dominant cultural assumption about sight's centrality. Now, we may wish, on whatever ideological grounds, that this were not the case. Indeed, we may regret how such cultural models have so forcefully directed the (anthropologically speaking, wholly peculiar!) "ocularcentric" course of western cultural thinking.[33] But resist as we may, to over-

---

29 Cf. below, pp. 16–18 – as well as the contributions in this volume by Tanner, Turner and Webb.
30 For the point, see especially Porter (2013), with references to the key contribution of Porter (2010). Porter argues that when it comes to sight in antiquity – as indeed the other ancient senses – "seeing" cannot be distinguished from other sensory experiences ("we should acknowledge that the ancients were in fact virtuosos of *syn-aesthetics*", 20). As a revisionist critique, Porter's intervention offers a timely reminder of the (potential) multi-modal "plurality" of ancient sensory experience. As the comments in the following pages argue, however, this should not obscure the very concrete delineation of (and syncretic comparison between) different sensory modes, nor do I think we can simply pin the delineation of five senses onto some "Aristotelian" paradigm.
31 For my own thinking on the subject – in the context of one of late Roman antiquity's most complex and undervalued poets and artists – see Squire (2015a) (with references to the broader bibliography).
32 See especially Porter (2010: esp. 1–21), attempting to "unearth the materialist and sensualist predecessors to Plato and Aristotle" (4); if "aesthetic and empirical experience go hand in hand, as they only can", Porter argues, "recognizing that they do helps enlarge the scope of inquiry to anyone interested in broadening the frames of reference concerning aesthetic questions in antiquity on offer today" (6).
33 On the history of western ocularcentrism – and the subsequent imbuing of its "hegemonic role in the

look this situation would be historic(istic)ally disingenuous: whether we celebrate antiquity's celebration of the eye or challenge its enduring influence, it would be intellectually dishonest to deny this cultural scenario. Indeed, if we are to have any hope of getting *beyond* the visual paradigm, I for one think we have to work with (if not within) it: to probe how ideas about sight could in turn shape – as indeed challenge – attitudes to the senses as a collective.

The supremacy of sight within the classical cultural imaginary stretches back right to the very beginnings of Greek literature. Even in the earliest works of Greek poetry and philosophy, we find the sense of sight being used to define what it meant to be a sentient, subjective being. In the Homeric epics, the idea of "seeing the light of the sun" was synonymous with being alive (no less than with being seen),[34] just as – most famously in the eleventh book of the *Odyssey* – the realm of the dead was imagined as an unseen and unseeing world of darkness.[35] As Susanne Turner discusses in this volume, Greek and Roman funerary monuments likewise exploited the thematics of seeing to speculate about the relationships between the living and the dead. An early fifth-century BCE Greek grave relief nicely demonstrates the point (Figure I.3). Below the image of an old man offering a locust to his dog, the end of the hexameter instruction addresses its viewers in the second person, "but look!" (ἀλλ' ἐσίδεσ[θε]): it is the very ability to see, we might say, that defines what it means to be a living viewer as opposed to the depicted dead.[36] On much later Roman funerary monuments too, the stakes of seeing came to be visually thematized, and nowhere more so than in the context of Roman sarcophagi: as monuments that at once rendered the corpse present and occluded it behind the reliefs of its "flesh-eating" frame, sarcophagi often surrounded their vision of the dead with ideas about sight.[37]

If the sense of seeing defined what it meant to be a living subject, it was also quickly understood to trump other forms of sensory perception.[38] Our opening

---

modern era" "with a profound suspicion", above all in the modern and postmodern French critical tradition (14) – see Jay (1993); for the call that sensory history should get beyond that visual hegemony, see M. M. Smith (2007: 19–39). By no means all scholars have accepted the "ocularcentric" view of antiquity: cf. e.g. Ivins (1946) for one attempt to approach Greek culture (and Greek art in particular) as more oriented to the "haptic" than to the straightforwardly "ocular", along with Platt & Squire (forthcoming a).

34 For the point, see Turner and Bielfeldt (this volume). One example comes in Homer *Odyssey* 4.539–40 (οὐδέ νύ μοι κῆρ | ἤθελ᾽ ἔτι ζώειν καὶ ὁρᾶν φάος ἠελίοιο, "nor had my heart the desire any longer to live and to behold the light of the sun"). For discussions, cf. Frontisi-Ducroux (1986a: 208) and R. Osborne (1988) (on Archaic Greek death as the state of becoming "unseeing and unseen", 4).

35 Cf. Turner (this volume) on death and the sense of sight – along with touch – in the eleventh book of the *Odyssey*; compare also Grethlein's discussion of the "Eleusis amphora" (Figures 4.4–5), and Tanner's analysis of the Macedonian Tomb at Lefkadia (Plates 5–11). More generally on the Homeric phenomenology of seeing, the key work is Prier (1989). It is worth noting the impact Homeric associations between sight and wonder (*thauma*) would have on the Greek cultural imaginary – not only influencing the course of Greek philosophy, but also, as Neer (2010) argues, in driving the "naturalistic" developments of Archaic and Classical Greek art.

36 On this early fifth-century relief – signed by "Alxenor of Naxos" but found at Orchomenos in Boeotia – see Jeffrey (1961: 304, n.12) along with e.g. A. Stewart (1990: 23, 68) and Kansteiner *et al.* (2014: 1.564, no. 656).

37 On the thematics of seeing on Roman sarcophagi, see Platt (2012), along with Platt (2011: 335–93), both with detailed references; cf. also Turner's discussion in this volume.

38 Cf. e.g. Jay (1993: 21–33) (with bibliographic survey), along with Summers (1987: esp. 54–62).

Figure I.3 Marble funerary stele of Orchomenos, signed by "Alxenor of Naxos", early fifth century BCE. Athens, National Archaeological Museum: inv. 39 (photograph by the author).

epigraph has already introduced a long-standing ancient analogy between images for seeing and sounds for hearing – one that stretches back to Simonides' analogy between poetry as "talking painting" and painting as "silent poetry" in the early fifth century BCE.[39] Coupled with this perceived parallelism of visual and aural stimuli, though, was an idea that sights were more persuasive than sounds. According to the later testimony of Polybius, it was the Archaic Greek philosopher Heraclitus who coined the aphorism that eyes make for more reliable witnesses than ears.[40] Yet, already in the fifth and fourth centuries BCE, we find the adage repeated in all manner of contexts – from Candaules' persuading of Gyges to see his wife naked in Herodotus' *Histories* (since "men trust their ears less than their eyes", Herodotus 1.8.1),[41] to Socrates' venturing to visit the prostitute Theodote in Xenophon's *Memorabilia* ("we had better go and see ... for what beggars verbal expression cannot be learned from hearsay", 3.11.1).[42] Of course, as the following chapters emphasize, different Greek and Roman philosophical schools would conceive of sight in very different ways. Yet throughout the *longue durée* of antiquity we find a residual sense of sight's sensory hegemony: in his discussion of memory, for example, Aristotle writes that "sight is the most highly developed perceptive sense" (ἡ ὄψις μάλιστα αἴσθησίς ἐστι, *On the Soul* 3.3, 429a),[43] just as, in the first century BCE, Cicero explains his own system of visual memory in terms of a long-standing maxim that "of all our senses, the sense of sight is the sharpest" (*acerrimum autem ex omnibus sensibus esse sensum uidendi*: *On the Orator* 2.357).[44] Among the most forceful articulations of such thinking is Varro's attempt to explain the etymology of the common Latin verb for seeing in the first century BCE (*On the Latin Language* 6.80): "'I see' (*uideo*) comes from 'sight' (*uisus*), that is from 'force' (*uis*)", Varro concludes; "for the greatest of the five senses is in the eyes" (*uideo a uisu, id a ui: quinque enim sensuum maximus in oculis*).[45]

Countless other discussions could be marshalled to demonstrate sight's privileged place within ancient thinking about the senses, and from all manner of different

---

39 = Simonides frg. 190b Bergk (Plutarch, *Moralia* 346f): cf. A. Carson (1992); Sprigath (2004); Männlein-Robert (2007b: 20-2).
40 As quoted in Polybius 12.27 (ὀφθαλμοὶ τῶν ὤτων ἀκριβέστεροι μάρτυρες = DK 22 B101a): cf. Beare (1906: 89–90) for numerous later parallels, along with Rivier (1975) on Xenophanes. More generally on Presocratic attitudes to vision, see Rudolph (this volume).
41 Cf. Hartog (1988: 260–309), esp. 262–3 (noting parallels with e.g. Herodotus 2.29, 2.99, 156, 4.16); Morales (2004: 9–10); Cairns (2005: 127); Purves (2013: 40–41). More generally on the importance of autopsy in ancient historiography, see Nenci (1953); Schepens (1975); Bassi (2005: esp. 17–26); compare also Heath (this volume), on the influence of the topos not only in the Christian gospels, but also in Paul's writings.
42 For the episode, see especially Goldhill (1998), with further comments in Tanner (this volume).
43 Still more explicit is the opening of Aristotle's *Metaphysics* on our collective esteem for the senses (ἡ τῶν αἰσθήσεων ἀγάπησις), and above all others that of the eyes (καὶ μάλιστα τῶν ἄλλων ἡ διὰ τῶν ὀμμάτων) – "not only with a view to action, but even when no action is contemplated we prefer sight, generally speaking, to all the other senses", Aristotle continues (οὐ γὰρ μόνον ἵνα πράττωμεν ἀλλὰ καὶ μηθὲν μέλλοντες πράττειν τὸ ὁρᾶν αἱρούμεθα ἀντὶ πάντων ὡς εἰπεῖν τῶν ἄλλων, *Metaphysics* 980a). On Aristotelian ideas about vision, see Nightingale (this volume), along with the subsequent comments in the chapters by e.g. Netz & Squire, Tanner and Smith.
44 For discussion of the topos within ancient mnemonics, see Elsner & Squire (this volume).
45 Cf. Fredrick (2002: esp. 1–3).

cultural contexts, time periods and genres. But to engage in such inter-sensory rivalries would be to overlook a more fundamental point. For the sense of sight was itself exploited to provide ancient thinkers with their essential framework for approaching the epistemological project of philosophy: it was around the idea of *seeing* that the whole question of sensory and cognitive perception came to be understood. That visually oriented paradigm of knowledge, moreover, would set the course for the entire subsequent western intellectual history of approaching the senses.[46]

As many commentators have pointed out, this connection between sight and understanding is already embedded in Greek languages of "seeing" and "knowing", sharing as they do a common etymological stem. According to the Greek vocabulary of "seeing" (which finds a correlation with numerous other Indo-European languages), the state of knowing (*oida*, "I know") is both linguistically and conceptually inseparable from the experience of seeing for oneself (*idesthai*, "to behold").[47] However abstract and immaterial they may seem, philosophical "ideas" – at least within the framework of ancient Greek – were likewise premised upon theories of sight: what we would label the "brain" was frequently likened to a sort of inner visual organ – the "mind's eye" of the soul.[48] No less pertinent is the talk – in English, as in ancient Greek – of "theorizing" the senses in the first place. For us, of course, "theory" denotes an abstract set of rational thoughts and suppositions. According to its ancient Greek etymology, however, this very terminology once again betrays a debt to the sense of seeing, derived from the idea of *theōria* (from the Greek verb *theein*, "to see"), from which ancient "theatre" also stems.[49] The point cannot be overstated: where Michael Baxandall famously declared that seeing is necessarily a "theory-laden activity",[50] we might say that, in antiquity, theories of sense perception were themselves laden with ideas about seeing. The same holds true of Latin terminologies, providing the linguistic basis of so many modern European languages today: to cite just one example, our own language of "perception" attests to the Latin association between visually "observing" (*specere*) and mentally "discerning" (*perspicere*).[51]

---

46 Cf. Jonas (1982), with discussion in Jay (1993: 24–6); for the underlying connections between "sight and insight" in ancient thinking, see Webb (this volume), along with the chapters by Nightingale, Heath and Coo. On western philosophy's subsequent reliance on discourses of vision (and the various academic challenges of the nineteenth and twentieth centuries), see the essays in Levin (1997); cf. Levin (1988).
47 See most recently Giuman (2013: 2–4), along with Coo in this volume. Compare Blundell *et al.* (2013: 11): "the cognitive metaphor that understanding is seeing is encoded in the forms of the verb itself"; as the authors also note (comparing e.g. Mark Johnson 1987: 107–9), "the metaphor is not uniquely Greek, but it may still be quintessentially so"; cf. Tyler (1984).
48 Cf. Nightingale (this volume). As Blundell *et al* (2013: 11–12) point out, the image here of the "mind's eye" goes back to the works of Gorgias and Plato: cf. Gorgias, *Helen* 13 (*tois tēs doxēs ommasin*); Plato, *Symposium* 219a (*tēs dianoias opsis*), *Republic* 533d (*to tēs psuchēs omma*), *Sophist* 254a (*tēs psuchēs ommata*). More generally on the Platonic language of *eidos*, see e.g. Herrmann (2007); Platt (2014).
49 As Aristotle puts it, one cannot think without an image (*On Memory* 449b; cf. *On the Soul*, 3.3, 427b). On the related etymological roots of "theatre" as a place for "seeing", see Coo (this volume).
50 Baxandall (1985: 107) (analysing the paintings of Piero della Francesca).
51 The clearest articulation of the sentiment (in the early fifth century CE) comes in Augustine, *On the Trinity* 11.9.16: *uisiones enim duae sunt, una sentientis, altera cogitantis* ("Sights are of two kinds

No ancient thinker better – or indeed more influentially – encapsulates this complex nexus of ideas about "seeing" and "knowing" than Plato in the fourth century BCE. The corpus of works attributed to Plato in fact showcases a remarkable array of differing (and indeed in some sense contradictory) attitudes towards sight. As is well known, however, Plato was highly sceptical of the senses, and nowhere more so than when it came to the sense of seeing.[52] "The greatest and most esteemed realities have no manufactured image that humans can visually see", as Plato has a character put it to Socrates in his *Statesman* (τοῖς δ' αὖ μεγίστοις οὖσι καὶ τιμιωτάτοις οὐκ ἔστιν εἴδωλον οὐδὲν πρὸς ἀνθρώπους εἰργασμένον ἐναργῶς, 286a). Because the noblest and greatest truths are immaterial (literally, "bodiless" – *ta asōmata*), they necessarily call for the rational power of language (*logon ... dunaton*); it is for this same reason, the passage continues, that Socratic dialogue itself proceeds by way of discursive, verbal conversation (*ta nun legomena*, 286a), appealing to intellectual cognition rather than to the senses.[53] As Plato's theory of the "Forms" (*Eidē*) makes clear, most famously in the tenth book of the *Republic*, Platonic ideas about knowledge consequently champion the intellectual realm of *logos* (literally "speech", but also thereby "reason") over the material semblances of earthly *eidōla* ("semblances").[54] Crucially, moreover, Plato's crusade wages intellectual war not only on the tyranny of the senses, but also on mimetic visual imagery in particular: if material forms are inherently deceptive, hoodwinking the mind through the senses (and above all the sense of sight), man-made images prove doubly deceptive – they are debased visual imitations of phenomenal imitations that are themselves removed from the immaterial realm of truth.[55]

Whatever else we make of the Platonic position, it is worth noting the underlying scopic paradox. As Andrea Nightingale has explained, Plato's theories of knowledge rely here on a fundamental contradiction: for all his outright dismissals of seeing, the sense of sight nonetheless pervades every aspect of Platonic theories of knowing and understanding.[56] Yes, Plato might attempt to turn the equation between "seeing" and "knowing" on its head. Yet the very language of Platonic philosophy is premised upon an association between the two.[57] Just as Platonic ideas of knowing are couched in the language of sight, Plato likewise exploits the ritualized encounter with a cult statue (*theōria* in Greek) to envision his epistemological epiphany of metaphysical truths (and nowhere more strikingly than in the *Phaedrus*).[58] One need

---

   – one of sensory perception, the other of thought"); for the earlier Greek archaeology of Augustine's thinking, as well as its Judaeo-Christian influences and impact on later mediaeval concepts of allegory, see Akbari (2004: esp. 3–7).
52 See Nightingale (this volume), with further comments in Tanner's chapter.
53 On this and related passages, cf. Keuls (1978a: 119–25).
54 On Platonic ideas of the *eidōlon*, see Nightingale and Tanner (this volume), along with Platt (2014). On the Judaeo-Christian reception of such ideas about *logos* – most famously in the opening of John's gospel – see Heath (this volume).
55 One of the best introductions here remains Lodge (1953); cf. e.g. Janaway (1995); Halliwell (2002).
56 Nightingale (2004); cf. Halliwell (2002: 37–147); Herrmann (2013).
57 Cf. Nightingale (2004: 1–39): "The fourth-century philosophers differed quite strongly in their epistemological, psychological, ethical, and political theories. Yet all believe that wisdom takes the form of 'seeing' truth" (7).
58 Cf. Nightingale (2004: 36): "This model [*of theōria*] provided the terminology and narrative structure

only think back to Plato's notion of ideal "Forms" (*eidē*) to appreciate the point: while contrasting "true" intellectual seeing with sight as sensory perception, Plato nonetheless relies on a visual metaphor, whereby even immaterial truths take on a physical appearance.[59] No less revealing are Plato's perpetual explanations of his anti-sensory stance through visual metaphors (most famously in his allegory of the cave in the seventh book of the *Republic*).[60] Even – or perhaps especially – among antiquity's most overtly anti-sensory thinkers, the epistemology of rational understanding falls back on ideas (and indeed on broader cultural ideologies) of sight and seeing.

Subsequent chapters will return to the Platonic view of visual sensory perception, and not least its complex revisions in the hands of Plato's immediate successors. One important prefatory aspect for all the chapters that follow, however, is that antiquity lacked any singular, culturally dominant model for explaining the mechanics of sight.[61] From a modern perspective, this failure of consensus calls for a particular leap of cultural imagining. Ever since Johannes Kepler's 1604 famous analogy between the dissected eye of a cow and the *camera obscura* – and thanks above all to René Descartes' 1637 treatise on *La Dioptrique* (with its emphasis on the psychological processing of vision)[62] – modern science has been able to fall back on an established "normative" narrative of sight. We can talk of reflections of light, the refractions of the pupil, the projections onto the retina and neurological channellings (through the optic nerve between eye and brain). For all their intellectual, philosophical and cultural subscription to the importance of seeing, by contrast, Greek and Roman thinkers could not rely on any such single view. As a field of intellectual enquiry, the very subject of seeing fell between divergent sorts of intellectual and cultural projects, from the Hellenistic and Roman Imperial Greek "optics" of Euclid, Hero and Ptolemy (between the early third century BCE and second century CE), to Artemidorus' discussions of dream-apparitions in his second-century CE *Oneirocritica* and the Elder Philostratus' *Imagines*.[63] Perhaps nowhere is this conceptual

---

that Plato used in his foundational accounts of theoretical philosophy"; on the *Phaedrus* specifically, cf. Nightingale (2004: 157–68), along with Palmer (1999: esp. 17–30) on the Presocratic debts to Parmenides. As Elsner (1995: 90–3) notes, a related argument can be made of later Neoplatonists – not least Plotinus in the third century CE. More generally on the importance of divine epiphany for making sense of sight in antiquity, see Platt's chapter in this volume (with detailed bibliography).

59 Cf. E. A. Havelock (1963: 268): as Havelock concludes, it is little wonder that Plato did "not always succeed in shielding himself rigorously against this visual contamination".
60 Cf. Nightingale (2004: 94–138).
61 Cf. Morales (2004: 34), on the "whole spectrum of ways in which vision is perceived and represented in ancient culture", along with G. Simon (2003: 9–10). The key analysis is G. Simon (1988); cf. Darrigol (2012: 1–15) on Greek theorists' "highly diverse views on optics … [depending] on their broader philosophical outlook and on the weight they gave to the popular belief in a visual fire" (15).
62 See Smith (this volume). More generally on "la rupture cartésienne", see G. Simon (2003: 223–41, esp. 240–1), along with G. Simon (1988: 11–20); cf. Darrigol (2012: 26–49) (with bibliographic survey). On the "uncertainty and unreliability" of vision as a trope of the Renaissance and Reformation – that is, *before* the scientific breakthroughs of the seventeenth and eighteenth centuries – note the sparklingly broad-ranging analysis of Clark (2007: esp. 1–8), now supplemented by the essays in Melion & Wandel (2010).
63 See the chapters by Netz & Squire, Platt and Webb (this volume). Cf. e.g. Bartsch (1989: 80–108);

remove more conspicuous than in the context of ancient medical writings, among them a surviving Hippocratic treatise *On Sight*. While some ancient writers talk of "ducts" between the head and eye, ancient medicine largely understood ophthalmological disease in terms of the proper flux of internal bodily fluids: the most common recommended medical treatment consequently involves purging the head of excess moisture – and thereby facilitating the "proper" channelling of internal humours.[64]

As for the actual mechanics of sight, different Greek and Roman schools of thought championed divergent conceptual models.[65] Crucial here are two generic theories about how vision operates, which modern scholars have labelled "extramissionist" and "intromissionist" respectively. According to the first "extramissive", "extramissionist" or "emissionist" theory, the sense of sight was understood to emanate from fiery rays actively cast out from the eye, travelling to the thing seen. We find the theory reflected not only in early Greek poetry, but also among the early Pythagoreans (as well as in later optical treatises, including those by Euclid, Alcmaeon of Croton and Ptolemy, not to mention the works of Galen in the second century CE).[66] At the other extreme was the "intromissive" or "intromissionist" position. This is the theory developed by the atomists (including Leucippus and Democritus in the fifth century), who understood visible objects as emanating atom-thick replicas (*eidōla*) that moved through space and impacted upon the eye; it was also the preferred model of the Epicureans, and not least Lucretius in the first century BCE.[67] Between these two extremes were a myriad of more "interactionist" positions – from Plato's discussion in the *Timaeus* (45b–c), to Stoic ideas about the flow of a *pneuma* of air and fire (something emitted from the eye which touched the viewed object and then returned to the viewing subject, "stamping" its impression in the mind).

While numerous contributors return to these theories in their various thematic chapters,[68] two overriding points are worth emphasizing from the outset. First, in the absence of any single dominant model (and the hegemony of modern scientific perspectives), the mechanics of seeing were always open to reinterpretation: the way in which one envisioned sight depended upon one's subscription to a larger philosophical school – and hence upon one's intellectual view of the world.[69] Second, and no less importantly, these different models tend to visualize vision – albeit to larger and lesser degrees – in expressly haptic terms. Rather than work in sensory isolation,

---

Palazzini (1996); Cox Miller (1994); Newby (2009); Squire (2013a).
64 For a translation and commentary, see Craik (2006: 3–106); cf. Blundell *et al* (2013: 14–15).
65 The clearest explanation is A. M. Smith (1996: 21–3), in the context of Euclid's *Optics*; cf. the chapters by Rudolph and Nightingale (this volume), along with Lindberg (1976: 1–17); Rakoczy (1996: 19–37) (with summary on 272). Beare (1906: 9–92) still offers a useful account of the "ancient Greek psychology of vision" more generally, situating ideas about sight against those concerning the other senses.
66 Cf. Blundell *et al* (2013: 35, n.28), along with the chapters by Rudolph, Bielfeldt and Smith in this volume.
67 Cf. Bartsch (2006: 59–64) (with earlier bibliography), along with the chapters by Rudolph and Nightingale in this volume.
68 See the chapters in this volume by (among others) Rudolph, Nightingale, Bielfeldt, Turner and Smith.
69 For the point, see especially Nightingale (this volume).

the sense of sight falls back on a literal and metaphorical idea of touch. As the Hellenistic Greek astronomer Hipparchus put it (defending the extramissionist position), the eye acts like a "visual hand", its rays making tangible contact with the things visually encountered; in a favourite Stoic analogy, the *pneuma* emitted from the eye likewise "feels" its way in expressly tactile terms, just as a blind man uses a cane to "see".[70]

Such sensory interconnections between sight and other senses are important. Where this "Senses in Antiquity" series isolates five senses, treating each in turn, ancient thinkers were acutely sensitive to the synaesthetic cross-overs.[71] In the case of vision, ancient philosophers made much of the supposed capacity to "see" even those stimuli that outwardly seemed to appeal to the other senses. The idea goes back at least to Plato and Aristotle in the fourth century BCE, and to the quality of what came to be labelled *enargeia* (visual "vividness").[72] In the hands of later thinkers (influenced by Stoic theories in particular), *enargeia* would prove fundamental to ideas of *phantasia* (a sort of cognitive "impression" – albeit sometimes misleadingly translated as "imagination"):[73] *enargeia* was understood as the quality that enabled visual impressions to be formed in the mind's eye – even without the intervention of physical seeing. It was a theory of seeing that seeped into all manner of different cultural arenas. Within the field of later Hellenistic Greek and Roman rhetoric, for example, the feat of bringing about "seeing" through "hearing" came to be championed as central to the project of effective oratorical persuasion. For Quintilian in the first century CE, the Greek notion of *phantasiai* (translated into Latin as *uisiones*) is defined as the "means by which images of absent things are represented to the mind's eye"; it enabled listening audiences to "seem to have those [visions] before their eyes and have them present" (*ut eas cernere oculis ac praesentis habere uideamur*: *Training of the Orator* 6.29–30).[74] In the Greek *Progymnasmata* (schoolboy "handbooks" of rhetoric, dating from between the first and fifth centuries CE), we find the process duly explained and associated with the phenomenon of *ekphrasis* (literally, a "speaking out"): "*ekphrasis* is a descriptive speech which vividly

---

70 For Hipparchus' analogy, see Diels (1879: 404); on the Stoic "cane analogy", see Lindberg (1976: 9–11) (on Galen, *On the Doctrines of Hippocrates and Plato* 7.7). As A. M. Smith (1996: 21) puts it, "Whatever their specific differences, all Greek theories of vision share in common the fundamental premise that without physical contact between eye and visible object vision cannot occur". For the importance of touch to ancient ideas about vision, see e.g. G. Simon (2003: 65–9, esp. 66–7); Giuman (2013: 18–22); Platt & Squire (forthcoming a); cf. more generally Deonna (1965: 70–8).

71 On "synaesthesia and the ancient senses", see the essays in Butler & Purves (2013b).

72 On *enargeia*, and its relationship to *phantasia*, see Webb's chapter in this volume, along with e.g. Zanker (1981); Otto (2009); Webb (2009a: 87–130).

73 There is a very substantial bibliography on philosophies of *phantasia*, and especially their Stoic appropriations. Some of the most important contributions include M. Frede (1983: 65–93); A. Silverman (1991); Annas (1992); Zagdoun (2000); Barnouw (2002); Männlein-Robert (2003); cf. Rosenmeyer (1986); Watson (1988); Manieri (1998); Benediktson (2000: 162–88); Serra (2007); Webb (2009a: 107–30; Sheppard (2014). According to "Stoic" theories of vision, as M. Frede (1983: 67) puts it, "to see something … is to have a certain kind of thought generated in a certain way".

74 See Webb (2009a); cf. Lausberg (1998: 359–66, nos. 810–21) on *euidentia*. More generally on "visualization" in Roman rhetoric, see the chapters by Elsner & Squire and Webb (this volume), along with e.g. I. Henderson (1991); Vasaly (1993); Scholz (1998); Chinn (2007).

(*enargōs*) brings about seeing through hearing", as one such definition puts it (ἔκφρασίς ἐστι λόγος περιηγηματικὸς ἐναργῶς ὑπ' ὄψιν ἄγων τὸ δηλούμενον).[75]

As Ruth Webb explores in this volume, passages like these testify to widespread rhetorical ideas about seeing. But they also demonstrate an idea of sight as a sense that could reach beyond what was physically visible: if words can bring about visions, they might do so (at least according to rhetorical theory) in no less "visual" ways than material images. The topos proved central within ancient literary criticism too.[76] Although working through the verbal medium of words not images, for example, Homeric poetry was championed for its supposed "visual" qualities: it was on this basis that one *scholion* declared Homer's description of the baby Astyanax encountering his father (*Iliad* 6.467) as being so full of *enargeia* that it enables audiences not only to hear the scene, but also to see it.[77] Relishing the irony of the poet's blindness, Cicero likewise declares of Homeric poetry that we actually "view his work not as poetry but as picture" (*at eius picturam non poësin uidemus*: *Tusculan Disputations* 5.114).[78]

Such framing of one sense ("hearing") in terms of another ("seeing") returns us to the supreme intellectual capital of sight within the ancient sensory economy: given the endemic associations between "seeing" and "knowing", it was perhaps inevitable that the most powerful aural stimuli were understood to be those that appealed to the eyes rather than just to the ears. At the same time, it is worth emphasizing that the eyes were not always thought to convince. Alongside the championing of visual sensibility, we also find sight being expressly challenged, questioned and problematized. Just as sight could persuade, visual appearances could also be prone to leading viewers astray.[79] We have already mentioned Plato's censuring of the visual senses. But other thinkers likewise pondered the delusions of visual stimuli, noting their capacity to dupe and hoodwink (whether through mirage reflections, refractions in water or else recessions in space). If, as we have said, Varro could trace the etymology of "sight" (*uisus*) from the Latin word for "force" (*uis*), later Roman writers reversed the thinking: for the Younger Seneca in the first century CE, for example, the abundance of demonstrable optical illusions attested to the *infirma uis* ("ineffectual power") of seeing (*Natural Questions* 1.3.7). From the very beginnings

---

[75] Theon, *Progymnasmata* 118.7 (= Patillon & Bolognesi 1997: 66). The most insightful recent discussion of ecphrasis in the *Progymnasmata* is Webb (2009a) (complete with an appendix of the most important passages at 197–211); on the much older and literary archaeology of such thinking – stretching back to Homer's description of the shield of Achilles in *Iliad* 18 – see Squire (2013b).

[76] Cf. Nünlist (2009: 153–5, 194–8) (discussing numerous examples from the Greek scholia); cf. Rispoli (1984); Meijering (1987: 14–18, 29–52).

[77] Schol. bT on *Iliad* 6.467 (= Erbse 1969–88: 2.210): ταῦτα δὲ τὰ ἔπη οὕτως ἐστὶν ἐναργείας μεστά, ὅτι οὐ μόνον ἀκούεται τὰ πράγματα, ἀλλὰ καὶ ὁρᾶται ("These lines are so full of *enargeia* because the events are not only heard but also seen"). For the Elder Philostratus' sophisticated play with the topos – in the context of ecphrastic *verbal* descriptions of a gallery of *visual* paintings – see Squire & Elsner (forthcoming) on *Imagines* 1.1.

[78] As John Keats puts it in his poem *To Homer*, "there is triple sight in blindness keen". Compare e.g. Dionysius of Halicarnassus, *The Art of Rhetoric* 20; pseudo-Longinus, *On the Sublime* 15.2; Lucian, *Imagines* 8; pseudo-Plutarch, *Life of Homer* 216. For the literary critical topos, cf. Squire (2011a: 337–55), along with Zeitlin (2001).

[79] On the denigration of sight – and above all man-made images – in ancient thought, see Pekáry (2002).

of Greek literature (and not least in the Homeric epics), seeing could be associated with the sense of *thauma*, provoking "wonder", "marvel" and "astonishment" through the eyes of the onlooker (later translated through the Latin verb *mirari*).[80] Precisely because of their power to "amaze", however, wondrous *thaumata* and *miracula* could also deceive: "nothing is more fallacious than our eyesight", as Seneca concludes (*nihil esse acie nostra fallacius*: *Natural Questions* 1.3.9).[81]

The embodied eye

So far in this introduction, I have concentrated on the phenomenon and phenomenology of sight within broader Greek and Roman ideas about sense perception and cognition. At this stage, I want to turn briefly to ancient concepts of the eye itself. For one of the most important intellectual differences between "ancient" and "modern", post seventeenth-century views of vision lies in its degree of "embodiedness" – its corporeal implications for understanding the human subject. For Kepler and Descartes, as we have said, the analogy between the human eye and the *camera obscura* allowed sight to be conceptualized in disembodied terms: the science of seeing could not only be explained in relation to the pupil-lens and screen-like retina, but also be re-enacted in technological turn.[82] But where the discoveries of modern science tended to refract sight into a passive physical, physiological and psychological phenomenon – as something, like Kepler's dissected eye of a cow, that could be explained in "de-sensitized" isolation from the viewing body[83] – antiquity approached the act of viewing as a much more active process: to see, as indeed to be seen, was to engage in a complex two-way relationship, and one attributed with various far-reaching consequences.[84]

---

80 For the thinking, see especially Prier (1989); Vernant (1991: esp. 164–85); Neer (2010: esp. 57–69); cf. Platt (this volume). On the literary importance of the topos within Greek and Latin ecphrastic responses to artworks, see Gutzwiller (2002), along with Squire (2013b: esp. 159, 162–3, with further bibliography).
81 On Seneca's ideas about vision here and elsewhere, see N. Gross (1989: 41–56); Bartsch (2006: 183–229).
82 Cf. e.g. van Hoorn (1972: 150–206) ("Descartes' theory of perception is a mechanistic one", 150); Lindberg (1976: 202) (on the significance of Kepler's labelling the inverted retinal image as *picture*: "for this is the first genuine instance in the history of visual theory of a real optical image within the eye – a picture, having an existence independent of the observer, formed by the focussing of all available rays on a surface"). One might also note here antiquity's essential lack of so-called "exosomatic" devices to expand the human capacity to see – not just spectacles, but also telescopes, microscopes and cameras: for the term, see Innis (1984: 67), and on the history, see e.g. Ilardi (2007), along with the classic analyses of Crary (1991; 1999); on the evidence for the use of lenses in Graeco-Roman antiquity, see Plantzos (1997).
83 On this distinction, see especially Alpers (1983: 26–45), discussing the importance of Kepler's discoveries for approaching Dutch art of the seventeenth century: "it is a dead eye, and the model of vision, or of painting if you will, is a passive one" (36).
84 See especially Bielfeldt (this volume). For the best introduction to the "Dominanz des aktiven Auges" in antiquity, see Rakoczy (1996: 19–37): "Sowohl was die Funktion des Auges betrifft als auch das Zustandekommen des Sehens läuft die antike Auffassung der modernen diametral entgegen" (19). As Prier (1989: esp. 25–117) makes clear, such thinking about the reciprocity of sight harks back to Homer, and not least the Homeric language of *thauma idesthai* ("a wonder to behold"): the structural relationship between seeing and being seen is already located in the Homeric language of

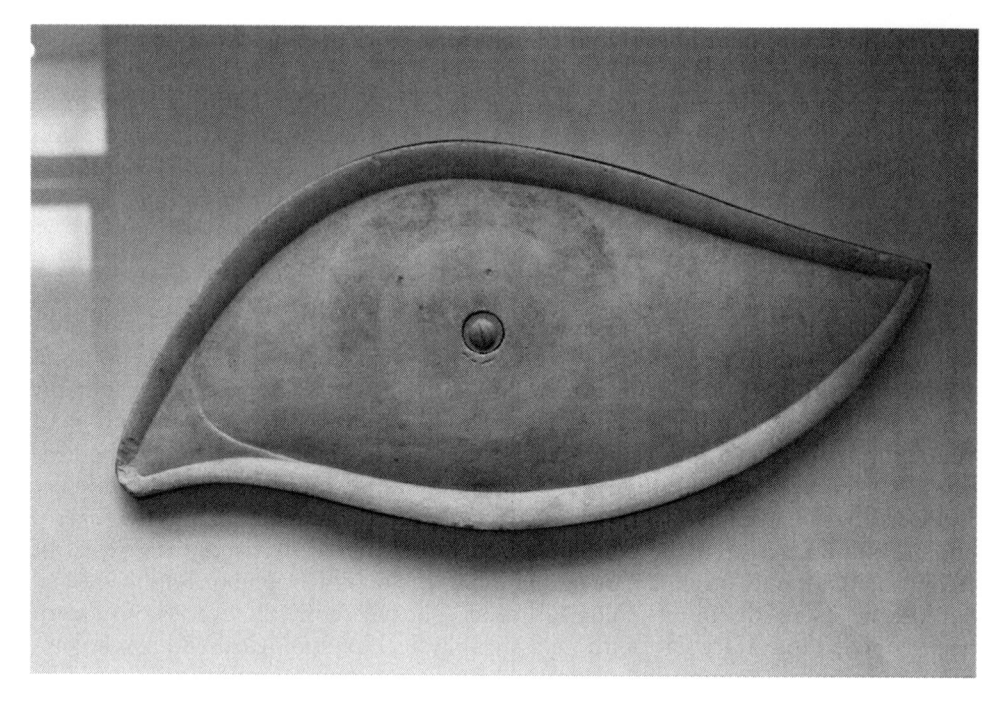

Figure I.4 Painted marble "eye" from the prow of an Athenian trireme, discovered in the Piraeus' Zea harbour, probably late fifth century BCE. Athens, Piraeus Museum: inv. 3465–2674 (photograph by the author).

The active agency of the eye helps us to make sense of its visual proliferation on all manner of ancient artefacts.[85] As isolated patterns, or else figurative designs within make-believe "masks" (effectively "worn" when a drinker raises his vessel to the face), painted eyes recur as a particularly popular motif on sixth-century BCE Attic black-figure drinking-cups (cf. Figures 4.3, 4.12, 6.1, 6.9).[86] Eyes were also a standard naval adornment on the prows of Greek trireme ships (e.g. Figure I.4),[87] and in Greek and Roman healing sanctuaries moulded images of eyes recur alongside other isolated body-parts as the single most common subject (testimony at once to the proliferation of ancient medical conditions compromising eyesight, and to the powerful role played by epiphanic visions in bringing about recovery: e.g. Figure

---

seeing, and not least the phenomenological nuances of the middle form (*idesthai*). On the symbolism of the "eye" more generally – with special reference to Graeco-Roman antiquity, but from a broad anthropological approach – the classic work remains Deonna (1965).
85 See especially Steinhart (1995).
86 Cf. the discussions in this volume by Grethlein and Bielfeldt. Among numerous recent publications, see Rivière-Adonon (2011) (with survey of earlier bibliography – and noting some 2,225 examples between 540 and 485 BCE); I have been unable to consult Moser von Filseck (1996). On literal masks – and their rendering of the eyes – in the Greek theatre, see Coo (this volume).
87 Cf. Morrison *et al.* (2000: 148–9, n.22), along with Saatoglu-Paliadele (1978). The most detailed analysis of such naval *ophthalmoi* is now D. N. Carson (2009): Figure I.4 is discussed by D. N. Carson (2009: 350, no. 4), with references to the earlier bibliography.

Figure I.5 Votive offering dedicated to Asclepius by Praxias (on behalf of his wife), from the south slope of the Acropolis in Athens, *ca.* 350 BCE. Athens, Acropolis Museum: inv. 15244 (photograph reproduced by kind permission of the Archiv, Institut für Klassische Archäologie und Museum Klassischer Abgüsse, Ludwig-Maximilians-Universität, Munich).

Figure I.6 Floor mosaic of an eye under attack by dwarfs and animals, from the "House of the Evil Eye" outside Antioch, second century CE (© Gianni Dagli Orti/The Art Archive at Art Resource, New York).

I.5).⁸⁸ Sometimes, we find ancient images isolating a single eye as privileged visual subject: numerous Roman mosaics – such as the one that lent its name to the "House of the Evil Eye" outside Antioch (Figure I.6) – give visual form to the so-called "evil eye", portraying it under attack by an army of animals and human weapons.⁸⁹ At other times, we find images exploiting eyes to raise broader questions about the active agency of the viewed object. In a much-discussed votive relief dedicated by a certain Archinos to the god Amphiaraos in a healing sanctuary at Oropos during the first half of the fourth century (Figure I.7), for example, we find a pair of eyes integrated

---

88 On sight and epiphany, see Platt's chapter (this volume), along with Platt (2011; forthcoming); cf. Petsalis-Diomidis (2006; 2010: 271–5) and Petridou (2013) on the visual importance of healing votive offerings, along with Hughes (2008) on the significance of their somatic "fragmentation". Specifically on Figure I.5 – a fourth-century BCE votive from Athens, dedicated to Asclepius by Praxias on behalf of his wife, and incorporating a marble face fragment with inlaid eyes (encased in a *poros* limestone frame) – see Salta (2012: esp. 108–17).
89 On the "evil eye", see below, pp. 26–30; on this particular mosaic, see Clarke (2007: 64–7).

Figure I.7 "Archinos" marble relief from the sanctuary of Amphiaraos at Oropos in Attica, first half of the fourth century. Athens, National Archaeological Museum: inv. 3369 (© Vanni Archive/Art Resource, New York).

within the object's upper frame. On the one hand, we see here Amphiaraos healing Archinos' shoulder (both by way of a direct divine intervention on the left, and via the snake-bite administered to Archinos on the right – portrayed sleeping under an object that recalls the four-square form of the relief before us); on the other hand, this relief purports to look back at the people who look upon it, in some sense embodying that epiphanic power which had brought about Archinos' recovery.[90]

While images like these attest to the symbolic significance of eyes in antiquity, playing with the promise of inanimate objects being made to "see", their representational status made them fundamentally different from the viewing eyes of

---

90 On the relief (Athens, National Archaeological Museum: inv. 3369), see R. Osborne (1998: 211–12); Petsalis-Diomidis (2006); Platt (2011: 44–8); cf. Platt's chapter in this volume.

Figure I.8 Pair of eyes (made from bronze, marble, frit, quartz and obsidian) for inserting into a bronze statue, probably fifth century BCE. New York, Metropolitan Museum of Art: inv. 1991.11.3a,b (© The Metropolitan Museum of Art/Art Resource, New York).

their human beholder. We know that ancient bronze sculpture paid particular attention to the eyes of its subjects, inlaying the hollow sockets with carefully crafted eye-balls – rendering the white surrounds, irises and sparkling pupil of the eye in (for example) glass-paste, coloured quartz and black obsidian (Figure I.8).[91] But however mimetically convincing such sculpted eyes might seem, real eyes were understood in relation to the bodily whole. Aristotle emphasizes the point in a passage of his *On Meteorology*. Each part of the body, Aristotle argues, is determined around its particular human function: if the eye is consequently defined by its capacity to see, it follows that an eye that cannot see is an eye in name alone – "like a dead corpse or a stone effigy" (*On Meteorology* 4.11, 390a). "Were the eye a living creature, its soul would be its vision, for this is the substance in the sense of formula of the eye", as Aristotle elsewhere puts it; "but the eye is the matter of vision, and if vision fails there is no eye, except in an equivocal sense, as for instance a stone or painted eye" (*On the Soul* 2.1, 412b).

Aristotle gives voice here to a key mode of thinking both about the eye and the associated sense of seeing. An eye that does not see – whether the represented eye of a painting or sculpture, or (in our terms) the one laid out on a modern dissection table – is, at least for Aristotle, no eye at all. Not only does the very notion of sight imply an active and dynamic relationship, but that relationship also defines the seeing subject in turn. This embodied aspect of sight has important repercussions. Regardless of whether one subscribed to intromissionist or extramissionist theories

---

91 Cf. Mattusch (1988: 182–4). A single inscription seems to preserve the Latin name for the specialized sculptor of such eyes (*oculariarius*: CIL 6.9402; cf. Calabi Limentani 1958: 173, no. 175).

of vision, to look upon something was itself to interact with it – and to allow the viewed object to interact with the onlooker in turn. Ancient myths probed this underlying reciprocity of sight – with tales of lethal visions (like the sight of the Gorgon Medusa), or else of divine apparitions that resulted in blindness, mutilation or death (Actaeon looking at the naked Artemis, Tiresias seeing Athena, or else Zeus appearing to Semele).[92] But such thinking about seeing also informs some of antiquity's (to our eyes) stranger stories about visions that *do* things to their beholders. Among countless examples, one might remember Heliodorus' tale as to how a black Ethiopian queen (Persinna) came to give birth to a white daughter (Chariclea, the protagonist of Heliodorus' second- or third-century CE novel, the *Aethiopica*): at the moment of conception, we are told, Persinna happened to be looking at a portrait of a naked, white Andromeda, and the visual impression duly reproduced itself in the embryo that would grow into the white-skinned Chariclea (*Aethiopica* 10.14).[93] Again and again, we find the act of seeing something envisioned as a two-way process: to see is to expose oneself to external visual forces, and forces that could themselves impact upon the body of the beholder.

One of the clearest ways in which the active and reciprocal nature of seeing came to be theorized was in relation to explanations of sexual desire. According to a familiar Greek pun (extending back to at least the dramatist Agathon in the late fifth century BCE), the act of "loving" someone (*eran*) was begotten from the act of "looking upon" him or her (*esoran*).[94] Antiquity's most famous account of this interconnection comes in Plato's *Phaedrus*. Sexual desire, Plato has Socrates explain, derives from the extramissionist look of the lover upon the beloved. Emanating from the viewer's eyes, the gaze hits upon an object of beauty and then passes back to the eyes so as to stimulate the soul; "he neither knows what has happened to him, nor can he even say what it is, but like a man who has caught an eye-disease from someone he can give no account of it, and is unaware that he is seeing himself in his lover as if in a mirror" (*Phaedrus* 255).[95]

As always, such accounts of vision and desire could be harnessed to ancient myth

---

92 On the Gorgon, see especially Vernant (1991: 111–38, 1998: esp. 31–8); Mack (2002); Giuman (2013: esp. 59–67), along with the contributions by Grethlein and Turner (this volume); more generally on divine epiphanies, see Platt (2011) – along with her chapter in this volume.

93 On the phenomenon (nicely labelled the "Andromeda effect"), see Reeve (1989). More generally on the sense of sight as a particularly pervasive theme in Imperial Greek novels, see Goldhill (2001), along with Morales (2004) (on Achilles Tatius as "the most eye-intense of all of the novelists", 12). It is also worth noting here that, just as seeing something could affect a change in the viewing subject, so too could a viewing subject be understood to bring about a change in the object viewed: cf. Cairns (2011: 40), discussing Aristotle, *On Dreams* 495b–60a (on the effects of a menstruating woman looking into a mirror).

94 For the association, see especially Walker (1993) (in the context of the Elder Philostratus' *Love-Letters*, and discussing the Agathon citation (= frg. 29 Nauck) at 132): "for the ancient mind, 'desiring' is intimately connected with 'seeing' ". Compare also Ogle (1920); Calame (1992: esp. 19–23); Cline (1972: esp. 267–78); Cairns (2011); Blundell et al (2013: 17–19). For Christian subversions of the *oran*/*eran* association – especially in reports of Thecla's *agapē* for St Paul – see Heath (this volume).

95 For discussions, see Halperin (1986) and Cairns (2013), along with Nightingale (this volume); on the passage's subsequent influence, above all in Second Sophistic literature, see Trapp (1990) and Webb (this volume). For the relationship between Platonic theories of visually mediated *erōs* and the visual imagery of Attic painted pottery, see Frontisi-Ducroux (1996).

in order to probe the relations between desiring visual subject and desired visual object – nowhere more so than in the story of Narcissus, whose fatal error was to gaze longingly at his own literal reflection.[96] Revealingly, we also find the longings of love provide an aetiology of the very origins of visual imagery (in the Elder Pliny's story about Butades' daughter sketching an outline around the shadow of her beloved: *Natural History* 35.15, 152).[97] The point to emphasize here, however, is the implication of seeing within the construction of interpersonal relationships. So powerful were these sensory interminglings of visual rays that the very act of sight could be conceptualized as a sort of corporeal copulation: sex itself becomes a re-enactment of the prototypical mingling of the look between lover and beloved.[98] By extension, the eroticized relationship between viewer and viewed could be understood in gendered terms. The acts of seeing on the one hand, and of being seen on the other, were bound up with ideas not only about sexual desire, but also thereby about relations between the masculine and the feminine: not for nothing is the penetrating gaze of the eye so often likened to the invasive force of the phallus (cf. Figure I.9).[99]

Perhaps nowhere is the dynamic reciprocal force of sight more conspicuous than in ancient thinking about the "evil eye".[100] The idea of evil forces emanating from the eyes – cast out from the pupils so as to inflict devastating harm on the intended victim – is in fact widely attested across the globe.[101] While Greek and Roman terminologies for such "bewitching" (*baskania/fascinatio*) did not term the phenomenon around the "eye" specifically, they were nonetheless explicit about the ocular mechanics. According to Plutarch, whose second-century CE *Table-Talk* provides one of

---

96 The most famous rendition of the story comes in Ovid, *Metamorphoses* 3.402–510, where it is related back to a longer set of philosophical ideas about love, subjectivity and sight; cf. Frontisi-Ducroux & Vernant (1997: 225–30); Hardie (2002: 143–72); Elsner (2007b: 132–76); R. Taylor (2008: esp. 64–77).
97 On the story and its significance, see most recently Naas (2011), along with Stoichita (1997: 11–41) and Bettini (1999: esp. 7–9).
98 See e.g. Goldhill (2001: 168–72) on Achilles Tatius 1.9.4 ("Achilles Tatius, with sly wit and brilliant manipulation of the possibilities of the technical language of vision and desire, rewrites the penetrating and longing gaze as a kind of copulation", 169); cf. Morales (2004: esp. 30–5).
99 The classic account of ocular "phallocentricism" in the modern western world (focussed around cinema) is Mulvey (1975, republished as 2009: 14–39): "in their traditional exhibitionist role women are simultaneously looked at and displayed, with their appearance coded for strong visual and erotic impact so that they can be said to connote *to-be-looked-at-ness*" (1975: 11); cf. e.g. Berger (1972: 45–64) and Irigaray (1985: esp. 25–6). On the applicability of such models to the ancient world, see e.g. Fredrick (2002), along with Morales (2004: 29–32, esp. 31, n.128). On ancient associations between the eye and the phallus, see e.g. Johns (1982: 61–76); Barton (1993: 95–8); Frontisi-Ducroux (1996).
100 For a concise introduction to the most pertinent ancient passages, see Ogden (2009: 222–6, nos. 192–6, with discussion at 224); cf. Barton (1993: 91–106); Schlesier (1994); Rakoczy (1996: 39–226); Cairns (2005: 140–2); Giuman (2013); Lovatt (2013: 328–34) (discussing the etymological relationship between *inuidia* and *uidere*). On the evil eye as a visual subject in all manner of different types of ancient objects, see Dunbabin & Dickie (1983: esp. 19–27), along with Chiara Pilo's "appendice iconografica" in Giuman (2013: 143–9); on the Judaeo-Christian reception of such ideas, see Dickie (1995); Rakoczy (1996: 216–26).
101 For an introduction, see Dundes (1981) and Potts (1982: esp. 5–16); further bibliography can be found in Rakoczy (1996: 3, n.5).

Figure I.9 Chian "Wild Goat Style" phallus cup (with added plaster), with a pair of eyes painted on the glans, last quarter of the seventh century BCE. London, British Museum: inv 1888,0601.496.a–c (© Trustees of the British Museum).

our most detailed discussions (*Moralia* 680a–683b), such "bewitching" was bound up with the sense of "envy" (*phthonos*).[102] "Vision, as something swift in movement and conveyed by a medium that gives off a fiery radiance, diffuses an amazing power so that mankind both experiences and produces many effects through it", Plutarch explains (πολυκίνητος γὰρ ἡ ὄψις οὖσα μετὰ πνεύματος αὐγὴν ἀφιέντος πυρώδη θαυμαστήν τινα διασπείρει δύναμιν, ὥστε πολλὰ καὶ πάσχειν καὶ ποιεῖν δι' αὐτῆς τὸν ἄνθρωπον, *Moralia* 681a). It follows that, just as the sense of seeing a beloved inflicts wounds on the lover (and in much more powerful ways than either touching or hearing him), envy can be communicated through the eyes (*Moralia* 681e–f):

---

102 Cf. Dickie (1991) and Rakoczy (1996: 186–205, 205–13) on Heliodorus, *Aethiopica* 3.7.

> When those so possessed by envy let their eyes fall upon people, and when these eyes (which are situated adjacently to the soul and draw evil from it) assail those people as if with poisoned missiles (ὥσπερ πεφαρμαγμένα βέλη), it is not at all paradoxical or incredible, I think, that they should have an effect on those whom they look upon.

Ocular "missiles" like the ones described by Plutarch feature in earlier literary accounts of sorcery, and not least in Apollonius' third-century BCE epic, the *Argonautica*. According to Apollonius, Medea could destroy the bronze figure of Talus merely by "adopting a mind bent on harm" (θεμένη δὲ κακὸν νόον, *Argonautica* 4.1669) and emitting from her eye "destructive phantoms" aimed at her assailant (ἀίδηλα | δείκηλα, *Argonautica* 4.1671–2); "she bewitched the bronze eyes of Talus with her hate-filled stares" (ἐχθοδοποῖσιν | ὄμμασι χαλκείοιο Τάλω ἐμέγηρεν ὀπωπάς, *Argonautica* 4.1669–70).[103]

Such thinking about "bewitching" returns us to the eye's imagined ability to do things to others. But it also underscores the idea of the eye as embodied agent, intrinsically connected to the will and intentions of the viewing subject. So powerful were the invidious gazes of others as to spur the production of protective amulets for warding off the evil eye, as indeed other installations to combat its malevolent force (e.g. Figure I.10; cf. Figure I.6).[104] We also sometimes find the image of the eye featuring in ancient spells and magical incantations. A fourth-century CE papyrus from Roman Egypt provides a nice example, instructing the user to carve a hammer from the specially prepared wood of a gallows and incant a particular spell (itself consisting of two pyramids of letters sandwiched between the image of an eye: Figure I.11); "may the thief's eye (*ophthalmos*) be struck as vigorously as I strike the eye with this hammer", the text continues, "and may it become inflamed until it reveals (*mēnusēi*) him".[105] Although (as so often with such "magical" papyri) the logic is somewhat obscure, the spell seems to literalize the notion of the evil eye in order to reveal the identity of a thief: an imaginary eye is used as a channelling device, and one that – by impacting upon the thief's real eyes – will make the thief visible in turn.

Allow me to tie together my discussion with one final reflection. As we have said, antiquity theorized the eye as an embodied entity, something that mediated actively between a viewing subject and the world around them. But, as the magical spell cited above makes clear, eyes could also themselves prove revelatory. If the eye was understood to look outwards, it also allowed others to look in, making visible the viewing

---

[103] For discussions, see Rakoczy (1996: 155–69); Buxton (2000); Powers (2002); and most recently Lovatt (2013: 334–6). As Lovatt notes, "it is no coincidence that Medea is a woman and a barbarian" (335): such ocular power seems to have been conceptualized as a particularly "feminine" trait, and one associated with barbarian women in particular. In his discussion of the evil eye, the Elder Pliny recounts reports by Isigonus, Nymphodorus and Apollinites of tribes from Africa and Bitiae with two pupils in their eyes (*Natural History* 7.16–18). Pliny adds that Cicero also states "that the glance of all women everywhere is injurious if they have double pupils".
[104] Cf. Bartsch (2006: 115–82, esp. 138–52). On Figure I.10 specifically, see Blake (1936: 158–9); the accompanying inscription can be found in *Corpus Inscriptionum Latinarum* (CIL) 6.30973.
[105] For the text (= *Papyri Graecae Magicae* 5.70–96), see Preisendanz & Heinrichs (1973: 1.184–5, with introduction on 180–1); for an English translation, see Betz (1992: 102).

INTRODUCTORY REFLECTIONS

Figure I.10 Floor mosaic from the threshold of the Basilica Hilariana on Rome's Caelian hill, probably second century CE: an eye is stabbed by a spear, surrounded by a group of animal attackers (photograph reproduced by kind permission of the Archiv, Institut für Klassische Archäologie und Museum Klassischer Abgüsse, Ludwig-Maximilians-Universität, Munich).

subject's inner thoughts, emotions and characteristics.[106] Right from the beginnings of the Greek literary tradition, we find Homeric poetry focussing on the outward gaze of epic protagonists, and nowhere more so than when it came to the blazing eyes of fiery anger.[107] Later philosophers developed the underlying idea in the claim that the eyes are the "window" of the soul: within the face (the Greek *prosōpon* – that is, the bodily site from which we look onto others and are ourselves looked upon),[108] the eyes were conceptualized as mediating between our inner self and others. In order to depict the invisible nature of the soul, as the celebrated fifth-century BCE painter Parrhasius and

---

106 Cf. e.g. Cairns (2005; 2011); Blundell *et al* (2013: 16–18); compare also Barton (2002) on shame and the eyes.
107 See Bielfeldt (this volume). Compare Lonsdale (1989); Blundell *et al* (2013: 37, n.63); Lovatt (2013: esp. 311–24).
108 Cf. Frontisi-Ducroux (1995: 19): the Greek term *prosōpon* pertains both to the "face" and to a "mask", raising fascinating questions of how objects could be "embodied" by looking "through" them; on such "masks"/"faces", and their importance for thinking about ancient vision; compare Coo and Grethlein (this volume).

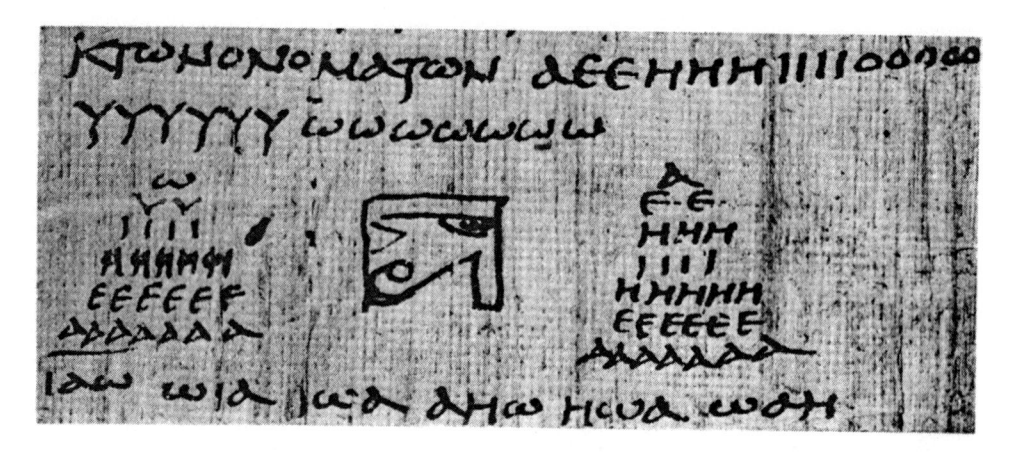

Figure I.11 Detail of an incantation from a Roman-Egyptian "magical papyrus" in the British Library, fourth century CE. London, British Library: inv. Pap. 46 (photograph reproduced by kind permission of Jacco Dielemann).

Socrates discuss in Xenophon's *Memorabilia*, painters must consequently focus on a subject's gaze (*to blepein*), concentrating on his *eyes* (*ta ommata*, *Memorabilia* 3.10).[109] From this perspective, it is perhaps little wonder that ancient physiognomic treatises privileged the look of the eyes above all other characteristics: "no other part of the body reveals more of the spirit of every animal – but particularly of men", as the Elder Pliny puts it (*Natural History* 11.145).[110] There is perhaps no better encapsulation of the reciprocal nature of ancient sight: eyes were not just something that facilitated sight, but were also a site of significance in their own right – for seeing *and* for being seen.[111]

Eyeing up the book

Sight and the Ancient Senses cannot aspire to treat every aspect of Greek and Roman visual thinking, nor does it survey all the different ways in which sight came to be theorized in classical art, literature, philosophy, medicine and science. In line with

---

[109] Again and again, the eyes emerge as a dominant topos in Greek and Roman criticism on painting: as the Elder Philostratus puts it, differentiating between the art of sculpture and painting, painting "permits the observer to recognize the look of the man who is made and now of the man who is sorrowing or rejoicing" (καὶ βλέμμα γιγνώσκει ἄλλο μὲν τοῦ μεμηνότος, ἄλλο δὲ τοῦ ἀλγοῦντος ἢ χαίροντος, *Imagines* praef. 2: on the passage, see Primavesi & Giuliani 2012: 57–61). Particularly revealing here is the series of Greek epigrams on Timomachus' painting of Medea (*Planudean Anthology* 135–43), which characterize Medea's *ēthos* in relation to the "look" of her eyes (e.g. *Planudean Anthology*. 138.2, 139.4, 140.1, 143.2): cf. Gutzwiller (2004); Gurd (2008: esp. 316–18).

[110] Cf. Cairns (2005: 127, with full bibliography on 144–5, nn.16–19): "the fact that they [ancient physiognomic writers] devote more of their energies to eye-sigs than to any other testifies to the importance of looking, eye-contact, and face-to-face orientation in social interaction". On the importance of the eyes to Polemon's *Physiognomy*, see Elsner (2007a); cf. Gleason (1995: esp. 55–81) and Rizzini (1999) on the importance of eyes for effective oratorical delivery in Rome.

[111] Cf. Barton (1993: 93–4), comparing Quintilian, *Training of the Orator* 11.3.75.

the other "Senses in Antiquity" volumes, our foremost aim has instead been to initiate new conversations – between contributors, certainly, but also (we hope) with others outside our circle. In bringing together different specialists, one objective has been to ask how different disciplinary perspectives might converge (as indeed diverge) in making sense of ancient sight. But another has been to engage scholars from beyond the frog-pond of classical studies: despite our historicist interest in Graeco-Roman antiquity specifically, our collective aim is to probe not just what sight *was*, but also what it *is* (or might be).

With that aim in mind, the book's chapters have been conceived thematically, striking a balance between broad survey (orienting readers around specific subjects) and decisive intervention (opening up new fields of enquiry). In chronological terms, "antiquity" is defined in deliberately broadbrush terms, from Archaic Greece right through to the mid-first millennium CE (and indeed beyond): while some chapters focus on particular chronological periods (e.g. Tanner on the fourth century BCE and Heath on Judaeo-Christian ideas between the first and fourth centuries CE), others break free from fettered periodization, veering diachronically across the *longue durée* (e.g. Netz & Squire, Turner, Platt). Just as the volume tackles a long timeline, so too does it encompass a broad geography. Authors were given relatively free rein here, choosing whether to discuss their theme in either "Greek" or "Roman" terms, or indeed to combine both. Some chapters likewise stretch beyond the Graeco-Roman Mediterranean altogether, thinking about the combined Judaic and classical thinking behind Christian attitudes to sight (Heath), for example, or charting the rich pickings of Greek theorists by Arabic mathematicians at the turn of the first to second millennium (Smith).

Although the many cross-references between chapters mean that they can be read in various configurations, an editor's job is to devise a "table of contents" and explain its sequential rationale. In laying out the volume, I have kept one eye on chronology (so that chapters generally progress from Archaic Greece through to late antique Rome). The other eye, however, has looked out for specific overlaps and connections.

The thinking holds particularly true for the following three contributions by Kelli Rudolph, Andrea Nightingale and Reviel Netz & Michael Squire. Dealing respectively with Presocratic thinking about sight, Classical Greek philosophies of vision and subsequent Graeco-Roman traditions of mathematical optics, these chapters lay out some of the theoretical underpinnings that underpin later chapters. They also progress from Archaic to Hellenistic (and indeed Roman Imperial) Greece. Of course, a stricter chronological guide might have begun with Homeric poetry (something to which subsequent contributors – for example, Grethlein, Turner and Bielfeldt – return). By beginning with philosophical traditions, however, the first three chapters set out to emphasize – from the very beginnings of Greek philosophy, and right from the outset of our project – the sheer plurality of ways in which sight came to be conceptualized and explained.

The point comes to the fore in Rudolph's chapter. In her discussion of "sight and the Presocratics", Rudolph surveys how some of Greek antiquity's earliest philosophers attempted to make sense of seeing (with particular reference to Alcmaeon, Anaxagoras, Empedocles and Democritus). For all their different takes on the mechanics of vision in the sixth and fifth centuries BCE – whether privileging extramissionist theories oriented around the viewing subject, or intromissionist models centred on the viewed object – what is striking about these Presocratic thinkers, Rudolph explains, is their common mode of theorizing sight around replication: it is the object's capacity for second-degree representation (or "image formation") that matters. In returning to Democritus, Andrea Nightingale's chapter starts with the philosopher with whom Rudolph ends. Yet Nightingale's discussion of "sight and the philosophy of vision" also posits some important shifts between pre- and post-Socratic Greek traditions. By comparing the ways in which Democritus, Plato and Aristotle approached literal and metaphorical "seeing" in the late fifth and fourth centuries BCE, Nightingale probes the connections between different theories of sight and different models of envisaging the world: since to "see" is to posit a particular relationship between the physical universe and the subjective "mind's eye" of the soul, philosophers could exploit sight to define broader divergences in philosophical outlook.

Where Rudolph and Nightingale both focus on "philosophical" texts, Reviel Netz & Michael Squire's chapter on "sight and the perspectives of mathematics" surveys the field of ancient optics (above all in the wake of Aristotle). Charting what we know about this field, and situating ancient optics within the broader pursuits of philosophy and mathematics, Netz & Squire analyse the contributions of particular thinkers between the fourth century BCE and second century CE. But they also ask why, given the radical innovations of these theorists, mathematical theories of optics did not gain greater traction in antiquity. Prefiguring Smith's analysis in the final chapter, as well as Tanner's discussions of painterly perspective, Netz & Squire argue that ancient optical treatises had much greater impact through later mediaeval Arabic translations than they ever did in the Greek and Roman worlds.

The chapters by Rudolph, Nightingale and Netz & Squire begin with theory – and with texts. But how do philosophical ideas about "sight and the ancient senses" relate to actual objects seen? That question resurfaces throughout the following chapters, yet it proves especially germane to the following contributions by Jonas Grethlein, Jeremy Tanner, Susanne Turner and Ruth Bielfeldt. While these four chapters generally stick with Greek materials, their innovation lies in pitting textually mediated reflections against extant images and objects. Ideas and ideologies of vision were not just the preserve of some disengaged philosophical mode: theoretical thinking was instead reflected, constructed and debated through visual material themselves.

This issue of "visual mediation" lies at the core of Grethlein's chapter on "sight and reflexivity". Greek painted pottery, Grethlein argues, probed the sensory stakes of sight in particularly self-conscious ways: not only do vase-painters offer poignant visual commentaries on vision, they do so on objects that were knowingly designed for visual engagement. Where Grethlein concentrates on the visual rendition of mythological stories centred around sight (above all, the blinding of Polyphemus and the petrifying stare of the Gorgon Medusa), Jeremy Tanner's chapter on "sight and painting" returns squarely to Greek philosophical, scientific and optical texts, investigating their relationships with Classical Greek art. For Tanner, the development of Greek painting between the fifth and fourth centuries BCE at once reflects and develops wider intellectual developments about vision. As his discussions of *skēnographia* (theatrical "scene-painting") and *skiagraphia* ("shadow-painting") make clear, Classical Greek debates about seeing emerge from a complex interplay of artistic practice, philosophy and optical theory.

A related approach underscores the chapters by Bielfeldt and Turner, dealing respectively with "sight and light" and "sight and death". In Graeco-Roman antiquity, as these introductory reflections have already noted, life was deemed synonymous with looking upon (and indeed being looked upon by) the sun. Tanner's discussion of *skiagraphia* ends with a related point (in the context of the Great Tomb at Lefkadia): namely, that to be dead was to inhabit a world that was – if not quite invisible – at least in the "shadows". Bielfeldt and Turner demonstrate how these ideas informed different sorts of visual cultural objects. In returning to Greek philosophy (especially the Presocratic philosophers discussed by Rudolph), Bielfeldt sheds light on the active agency of one particular group of objects: lamps. Centring her analysis around Praxagora's address to a lamp in the prologue of Aristophanes' *Women of the Thesmophoria* (while also drawing parallels with contemporary lamps and other man-made artefacts), her chapter investigates these objects as miniature manifestations of "Sun" on the one hand, and as light-emitting "eyes" to see and be seen on the other. Where Bielfeldt explores ideas of sight in the earthly realm, Turner heads to the underworld – and to thematics of "seeing" the dead. In Greek and Roman antiquity, Turner explains, the sense of sight could negotiate both the ontological status of the deceased and their capacity to be experienced by the living. Her chapter demonstrates how funerary rituals could make the dead visually present, as well as the role of myth in probing the structural relationships between living, seeing and dying. Ultimately, though, this cultural historical backdrop allows us to look at visual objects with new eyes: on Greek stelai, as on Roman sarcophagi, Turner argues, the ambiguous visual presence of the dead figures their bodily absence. For Turner, the dead emerge as entities to be sensed, certainly, but nonetheless lying beyond the parameters of mortal sensory perception.

In shuttling across the Greek and Roman worlds, Turner likewise sets the scene for the following three chapters (by Verity Platt, Jaś Elsner & Michael Squire and Ruth Webb). While thematically structured and diachronic in perspective, these three chapters are grounded in Republican and Imperial Roman case studies. They also showcase the intensity with which Roman ideas about sight looked back to earlier Greek theoretical paradigms.

Verity Platt begins by tackling "sight and the gods", and more specifically a second-century CE Latin inscription from Roman Algeria. Interrogating the inscription's combined erotic and epiphanic claim to have seen (*uidi*) the nymphs "naked" (*nudas ... nymphas*), Platt shows how visual encounters with the divine could complicate cultural paradigms of vision, and in both the Greek and Roman worlds alike. To "see" the gods (like "seeing" the dead) was to test the physical, ethical and epistemological limits of human sight: by challenging the relationship between sense-perception and conceptual knowledge, divine epiphanies probed the role of subjective imagination in shaping visual experience. Jaś Elsner & Michael Squire's analysis of "sight and memory" examine more pragmatic concerns. Although the connection between seeing and remembering harks back to Greek philosophy (and above all Aristotle), Roman rhetoricians are shown to have rationalized and taught such associations explicitly. Writers like Cicero and Quintilian testify to a remarkably "visual" way of conceptualizing verbal language. But, as Elsner & Squire demonstrate in the context of Campanian painting, their structural approach to visual experience is equally pertinent to the "language" of Roman art itself. Ruth

Webb's chapter on "sight and insight" likewise remains in the field of Roman and Imperial Greek ("Second Sophistic") rhetoric. This time, though, the focus is on the trope of "imagination" – that is, the capacity of a speaker/author to render a scene "visible" in the mind's eye of the audience/reader. Exploring a variety of texts (ranging from discussions of *ekphrasis* in the Greek *Progymnasmata* to St Augustine's "mental image" of Carthage), Webb relates such literary and literary critical discussions to philosophical paradigms of seeing, experiencing and knowing; in doing so, she also turns to longer-standing Stoic traditions of approaching vision in terms of "cognitive impression" (*phantasia*).

In line with other volumes in the "Senses in Antiquity" series, the final three chapters (by Jane Heath, Lyndsay Coo and A. Mark Smith) widen the book's critical gaze, exploring ancient ideas about sight in relation first to Judaeo-Christianity, second to the loss of sensory seeing and third to the longer legacy of western critical thinking. In her analysis of "sight and Christianity", Heath shows how the theological innovations of Judaeo-Christianity crystallized around literal and metaphorical vision during the first three centuries after Jesus' death. "Seeing" was fundamental to narrative accounts of Christ's resurrection, posing key theological questions about the nature of the Judaeo-Christian God; likewise, sight was exploited to define the core qualities of Christian faith (discussed in relation to Christian "love", or *agapē*, and Christian suffering). As Heath explains, such attitudes were not only informed by Judaic and classical ideas of epiphanic vision (discussed in the volume by Verity Platt), but also steeped in Stoic ideas about seeing and knowing (as analysed by Ruth Webb). Heath's closing comments about *lack* of sight (those "who have eyes but do not see": Mark 8:18) also form a bridge with Coo's chapter on "sight and blindness". Numerous Greek and Roman mythological figures were renowned for their loss of sight, Coo notes; right from the beginnings of Greek literature, moreover, blindness was associated with poetic insight and other supersensory qualities (in the *Odyssey*'s figure of Demodocus, for example, and later in biographical traditions concerning Homer himself). Coo structures her analysis around the literary history of Thamyris, a figure whose blindness is already mentioned in the second book of Homer's *Iliad*. By charting Thamyris' subsequent dramatic afterlife, though, Coo explores the semantics of "blindness" in the context of the Classical Greek theatre (the *theatron* – that is, a space for "seeing"). The very negation of sight brings into focus the range of physical, intellectual and metaphorical ideas associated with seeing. No less importantly, dramatic explorations of such themes raise questions about sight's role within the larger sensorium of ancient Greek theatre.

Charged with the unenviable task of discussing "sight in retrospective", Smith rounds off the book from a different perspective. His chapter returns to some of the classical authors discussed by other contributors (among them Plato, Aristotle, Euclid, Galen and Ptolemy). Here, though, the concern is with the different ways in which ancient texts were refashioned (or, as Smith puts it, "resynthesized") by later thinkers. On the one hand, Smith surveys Arabic translations of ancient Greek treatises between the ninth and eleventh centuries. On the other, he shows how, through subsequent Latin translations, and in collaboration with other Roman texts preserved by mediaeval scribes, the Arabic works of Avicenna, Alhacen and others influenced western mediaeval thought. Such creative "translations" of Greek optical works certainly refracted their earlier Greek sources. But they nonetheless helped introduce these back into a western intellectual arena – with explosive effects in late mediaeval and Renaissance philosophy, art and science.

Appropriately, perhaps, the book therefore ends with the latent "antiquity" of *Sight and the Ancient Senses*. After all, to talk of the "ancient senses" is to raise the question of antitype – to ask when, where and how we should situate a rift with "modernity". As we have already noted, one particularly important moment here comes in the seventeenth century. It was only in the seventeenth century – specifically, in the wake of Johannes Kepler's experiments in retinal imaging – that long-standing ancient debates between extramissionists and intromissionists could finally be put to rest. In drawing out the point, Smith's conclusion looks back full circle to Rudolph's discussion of Presocratic philosophers at the beginning of the book. But it also looks forward to distinctly "modern" paradigms of science and philosophy: in the work of Descartes, Kepler's experiments gave rise to a wholly different mode of approaching mind in dichotomous isolation from the body. If this resulted in an intellectual re-configuration of sight, it also caused an epistemological reimagining of the senses *tout court*.

My track through the book in the preceding paragraphs is offered as just one possible pathway. While each individual chapter has been commissioned as a self-standing article, our collective aim has been to make chapters talk with one another and to the other articles within the six-volume "Senses in Antiquity" project. Just as the body amounts to more than its single sensory organs, so does our book (like the series to which it belongs) aspire to something greater than the sum of its parts.

We are only too aware, of course, that some aspects of *Sight and the Ancient Senses* are better represented than others (e.g. power and the gaze, gendered dynamics, "love at first sight", Roman spectacle); inevitably in a project like this one, certain subjects, topics and individuals are conspicuously underplayed (architecture, medical treatments, Epicurean philosophy, Lucretius and numerous other Latin poets and prose authors – to mention but a few). Because the book cannot aim at an exhaustive overview, we make no apology for this. But we do hope that others will follow in our image: if they generate further reflections, as the riddlesome mirage of my epigraph puts it, "our lips have not opened in vain"…

1

SIGHT AND THE PRESOCRATICS
Approaches to visual perception in early Greek philosophy

Kelli Rudolph

This chapter introduces the earliest Greek philosophical thinking about the eye, visual perception and its relationship to sensory knowledge more generally. It deals with the so-called "Presocratic" tradition – that is, with philosophers between the early sixth and late fifth centuries BCE.[1] My aim is twofold: first, to explore the interconnected explanations used by these early thinkers to make sense of seeing in the Archaic and early Classical Greek world; and second, to show how the earliest traditions set a course for the subsequent development of theorizing "sight and the ancient senses". The two chapters that immediately follow take up this chronological structure: on the one hand, Andrea Nightingale charts the intellectual history of conceptualizing sight in later Classical philosophical traditions (focussing on Plato and Aristotle); on the other hand, Reviel Netz & Michael Squire move from (what we label) Greek "philosophy" to "science", probing the subsequent field of "optics" in the Greek and Roman worlds.

Presocratic theories of vision start out from a set of fundamental assumptions about the components of sight. Yet, as we shall see, their thinking results in a variety of approaches to the visual process. In what follows, I categorize these theories under three broad headings: first, those which understand vision as something akin to a form of reflection; second, those that approach vision as an "intromissionist" process, in which images or effluences from an external object enter the eye; and third, various "extramissionist" ideas about vision, whereby rays from the eye stream towards visible objects. In each case, early Greek philosophers adopt arguments from analogy to explain the origin of things and the processes of nature, adapting those arguments to suit a visual context.[2] To explain how vision occurs, Presocratic thinkers draw on a combination of common experiences, ranging from reflections in water or seal impressions in wax, to novel developments in painting, such as "shadow-painting" (*skiagraphia*)

---

1 For broader studies of the Presocratics, see Barnes (1982); Kirk *et al.* (2005); Long (1999); Warren (2007). For general discussions of early Greek perceptual and optical theories, see also Beare (1906); Park (1999: 3–76); Darrigol (2012: 1–14). In this chapter, I use the abbreviation "DK" to refer to Diels & Kranz (1951–2); references to Theophrastus, *On the Senses* refer to the edition in Diels (1879). All translations are my own unless otherwise stated.
2 See Lloyd (1966: 164–93) and Kamtekar (2009).

and "scene-painting" (*skēnographia*).³ Such explanations reveal an intimate connection between philosophical and artistic approaches to the problems of representation at the end of the sixth and during the fifth century BCE. For philosophers, such concerns are marked explicitly by attempts to explain variations in the accuracy and reliability of sight.

Although my primary interest in what follows centres on early Greek theories of sight and the reasoning and arguments used to establish them, it is nonetheless important to emphasize the contexts within which these ideas both arose and have come down to modern readers, since in its earliest form philosophy encompassed what today are the separate fields of physics, biology, psychology, theology and politics (to name a few). After outlining the difficulties we face when attempting to reconstruct Presocratic theories about the senses in the chapter's first section, I then turn to Alcmaeon (*fl.* 500–450 BCE) and Anaxagoras (500–428/7 BCE), who both liken vision to reflection. As I demonstrate, this development represents a break from the extramissionist accounts of the earlier poetic tradition, in which a ray leaves the eye and alights upon an object. In the third section of the chapter, I move to the intellectual innovations of Empedocles (*ca.* 495–435 BCE), often associated with an intromissionist theory of sight, involving emanations leaving an object and entering the perceiver's eye. For Empedocles these emanations arise from the interaction of light and darkness in the elemental form of fire and water. Finally, I turn to the last of the Presocratics – a younger contemporary of Socrates named Democritus (*ca.* 460–370 BCE), who combines elements of earlier theories in order to relate vision to the environmental factors that separate us from the objects we see. In many ways, Democritus' complex visual theory is the culmination of the philosophical concerns about variation in the visual experience in early Greek philosophy. As Andrea Nightingale explores in the following chapter, moreover, Democritus' approach also sets the scene for Classical Greek ideas about sight and the senses – and, by extension, the longer history of western intellectual thinking.

Reconstructing "Presocratic philosophy"

While numerous theories of perception emerge between the beginning of the sixth and the end of the fifth centuries BCE, this chapter focusses on those we label "Presocratic". This is a modern classification that largely follows the Platonic and Aristotelian accounts of Greek intellectual development insofar as it refers to those thinkers whose work does not show the influence of Socrates or "Socratic" thinking.⁴ Such an approach inevitably leaves aside theories put forward by doctors, poets and those

---

3 On which see Tanner (this volume); cf. Keuls (1975; 1978a; 1978b); White (1956); Pollitt (1974; 2015); Rouveret (1989); Summers (2007: 16–42).

4 This modern classification was established by Hermann Diels' seminal *Die Fragmente Vorsokratiker*, first published in 1903. The revised edition (Diels & Kranz 1951-2) is still the standard scholarly source for Presocratic philosophy. "Presocratic" was meant to demarcate those thinkers with interests in cosmology and physical questions, rather than the moral questions associated with Socrates; it is not primarily a chronological distinction, since the last of these thinkers were Socrates' (and in some instances even Plato's) contemporaries. See Mansfeld (1986); Nightingale (1995); Long (1999: 1–21); Warren (2007: 1–21).

teachers of rhetoric and politics that Plato pejoratively refers to as the "sophists". However, it brings together a group of thinkers who abandon mythological explanations and who are primarily concerned with giving real causal explanations for the origins and processes of nature; it is in this sense that we call such thinking "philosophy".

As with many of the authors from this period, the views of Presocratic philosophers are hard to interpret. In part, this is because the remains of their works are themselves fragmentary. Yet even when we have the author's own words, the terminology is often difficult to understand, since comparative uses are sometimes nonexistent or unhelpful. In the past, scholars tended to focus on reconstructing the exact words of these thinkers insofar as they could be extracted as direct quotations from our sources.[5] Current trends in Presocratic scholarship now also emphasize the reports and the contexts within which quotations are embedded, in order to elucidate elements of Presocratic thought for which direct quotations do not survive. This latter approach is especially valuable to anyone interested in theories of perception, since we are almost entirely reliant on reports, or *testimonia*, of earlier opinions preserved in the works of much later – usually Aristotelian – authors, who may have had access to the Presocratic texts themselves. Thus, Theophrastus (*ca.* 372–287 BCE) will figure as an important interlocutor throughout this chapter, not only because his treatise *On the Senses* provides the lens through which later "doxographical" writers view Presocratic theories of perception, but also because he is among our earliest critical sources for Presocratic theories of perception.[6]

Presocratic theorizing about the senses arises within the context of all-encompassing theories about the world and the place of humanity within it. Because these thinkers were concerned broadly with questions about the origin and nature of things, their inquiries extend to questions about mathematics and the movement of the planets, biology and the formation and structure of human and animal bodies, ethics and the nature of the gods, metaphysics, i.e. the place of matter, form and structure in the world, as well as the nature of explanation and human understanding, what we call epistemology. Thus, the areas of study that today are separated into the fields of philosophy, science and medicine were in antiquity closely linked. We will see the extent to which these areas of inquiry overlap in the theories of vision we find in Alcmaeon and Anaxagoras, Empedocles and Democritus.

---

5 Diels distinguishes between fragments (labelled "B"), which he identifies as extracts of "original" words or phrases from the Presocratics, and *testimonia* (labelled "A"), namely reports of Presocratic theories preserved in later sources. When referring to Presocratic fragments, scholars still largely use Diels' system, citing the chapter number, source type and entry number (so that, for example, "DK 68 A1" refers to Democritus (68), report (A), first entry (1)).

6 See Baltussen (2000; 2015). "Doxography" is also a modern term, referring to works that collect together the opinions of earlier thinkers on various topics or questions. Aristotle initiates this approach, insisting that philosophical investigation start with *endoxa* – the tested opinions of others. See Mansfeld (1986; 1999); Mansfeld & Runia (1997; 2009; 2010); Runia (2008).

Sight and reflections in Alcmaeon (*fl.* 500–450 BCE) and Anaxagoras (500–428/7 BCE)

Alcmaeon of Croton, one of the earliest Greek theorists to consider human physiology, was active between 500 and 450 BCE. Like all Presocratics, he was writing before the emergence of clear disciplinary distinctions between philosophy, science and medicine.[7] Alcmaeon is the first to suggest the central role of the brain for thought: on the basis of the connection between the eye and the optical nerve, he argues that the senses were connected to the brain via channels or pores.[8] So far as we know, Alcmaeon is also the first to theorize the cause of sight. Although his own writings do not survive, Theophrastus reports his opinion as follows:[9]

> ὀφθαλμοὺς δὲ ὁρᾶν διὰ τοῦ πέριξ ὕδατος. ὅτι δ' ἔχει πῦρ δῆλον εἶναι· πληγέντος γὰρ ἐκλάμπειν. ὁρᾶν δὲ τῷ στίλβοντι καὶ τῷ διαφανεῖ, ὅταν ἀντιφαίνῃ, καὶ ὅσον ἂν καθαρώτερον ᾖ μᾶλλον.

> The eyes see through the surrounding water. That the eye has fire is clear, for when struck, the fire shines out. Vision is due to the gleaming (i.e. the transparent), whenever it reflects; to whatever extent it [i.e. the reflection] is more clear, seeing is better.

Alcmaeon's account of the fire in the eye incorporates traditional notions of vision found in poetry. The eye was considered – from the very earliest Greek writings known to us – to be an active, fire-emitting organ, akin to the all-seeing sun. We find this thinking, for example, in the *Homeric Hymns* and in Pindar, where the sun's ray (*aktis*) is referred to as the "mother of eyes".[10] In many of our earliest sources, including Homer and Hesiod, the eye is active, with rays that beam forth or flash fire.[11] The "fiery eye" is such a powerful trope that it is a mainstay in both poetic and technical (philosophic and medical) accounts of vision throughout the Archaic and Classical periods.[12]

Alcmaeon's account combines this poetic representation of the fiery eye with details culled from everyday observation. Although seemingly simple, the resulting explanation shows close observation of the eye.[13] Alcmaeon describes the surrounding water, which is presumably the lachrymal fluid that keeps our eyes clean and lubricated. Additionally, he gives details of the observation of the pupil, on the

---

7 See Mansfeld (1975); Perilli (2001).
8 See Lloyd (1991: 164–93); Lo Presti (2009); Andriopoulos (2014).
9 Theophrastus, *On the Senses* 26.1–4 (= DK 24 A5). On Theophrastus' reliability as a source, see Baltussen (2000); cf. McDiarmid (1953); Long (1996b).
10 Cf. *Homeric Hymn to Demeter* 70; *Homeric Hymn to Helios* 9–11; Sophocles, *Trachiniae* 606; Pindar, *Paean Ode* 9 frg. 52k.1–2 Snell-Maehler. See the chapters in this volume by Bielfeldt, Turner and Coo – as well as Squire's introduction – for the notion that seeing defines what it is to be alive.
11 Cf. Homer, *Iliad* 1.101, 14.341, 19.12; *Odyssey* 4.150, 19.446; Hesiod, *Theogony* 826–7; *Homeric Hymn to Hermes* 45, 415.
12 See, for example, Sophocles, *Ajax* 69; Plato, *Timaeus* 45b–46a (with discussion by Cairns 2011). Cf. Nightingale's and Bielfeldt's chapters in this volume.
13 See Beare (1906: 12) for the suggestion that the optical theory described in the Hippocratic, *On Fleshes* (8.584–615 L) is that of Alcmaeon.

gleaming surface of which an image is reflected. Moreover, as is clear from the passage above, Alcmaeon reports the outcome of an experimental prodding of the eye as a demonstration of its internal fire.[14] It is these observations that set Alcmaeon's account apart as the first attempt at an empirical theory of vision. However, we must ask to what extent Alcmaeon is justified in his conclusion that "vision is due to the gleaming, whenever it reflects", and in his judgement that sight is better when the reflection in the surface is clearer.

Setting aside Theophrastus' later peripatetic gloss of gleaming (*stilbos*) as transparent (*diaphanēs*), it is clear that Alcmaeon is describing the mirror-like qualities of the eye, since the ancient Greek term *stilbos* is used regularly to describe highly reflective surfaces like those of water, oil or metal.[15] Like these objects, the eye throws back reflections, but such reflection is only called "vision" when the image itself is *seen in* (the literal meaning of the Greek, *emphasis*) the eye. Alcmaeon may here be attempting to explain why we have difficulty seeing in the dark, since dark objects are not as easily reflected in the pupil of the eye as light objects.

Alcmaeon further delimits sight by stipulating the conditions for the success of the visual act. Since "vision" in the Theophrastus passage cited above refers to the process of seeing, it is either the purity (*katharōteros*) of the gleaming (*stilbos*) or the clarity (*katharōteros*) of the reflection (*emphasis*) that makes vision better (*mallon*).[16] Although both interpretative options are possible, from the context we know that Alcmaeon's real concern is with the formation of a visual reflection. Thus, it is most likely that he referred to the clarity (*katharōteros*) of the reflection in the sheen of the eye as the mark of better (*mallon*) vision, as I have translated it above.

The final evaluative claim about what makes vision better has two significant implications for our understanding of early Greek visual theories. First, Alcmaeon expresses a judgement that suggests that vision can fall below some standard in its clarity or purity. Thus, from its very beginning, philosophical theories of vision attempt to account for variation in the clarity of sight. Second, the mechanics of vision on this account do not mention an object of vision per se. Instead, the focus is on the process of forming a reflection in a gleaming surface. So far as we know, Alcmaeon never specifies what the reflection itself is or how it is formed in the perceiver. Perhaps he assumes it is obvious or that the eye reflects the whole of the scene before us. The reflection theory of vision is a definitive break from the fiery rays emitted from the eyes in Greek poetry, and while Alcmaeon still focusses on an active process, the eye loses its agency and begins to take on the role of a receptacle. Such an approach to vision also opens the way for scepticism about how the senses put us in touch with things as they really are, because what we perceive visually –

---

14 Although he could not have known the cause, physiologically, when one prods the eyeball in the dark, flashes of light appear due to the retinal stimulation that results from the blow.

15 See Homer, *Iliad* 18.596; Plato, *Timaeus* 60a5–7; Aristotle, *On Meteorology* 370a13–9; Aristophanes, *Peace* 567. For connections between the notion of gleaming and visible renderings of the gods, see Neer (2010: 104–41) and Platt (2011: 77–123) – as well as Platt (this volume).

16 The final clause is missing an explicit subject, so it is difficult to know precisely what the antecedent referent of the comparatives "clearer" (*katharōteros*) and "better" (*mallon*) might be. It is almost certain that the *mallon* refers back to the infinitive subject "vision". The sentence is grammatically neater if the two comparatives refer to the same antecedent, but here that makes the sentence tautologous.

the visual reflection – is a step removed from the objects themselves. Even in the seemingly sparse report of Alcmaeon's theory we have (1) a general theory of vision; (2) clear evidence of an attempt to empirically verify a traditional account through observation; and (3) a sense that there is variation in the success of the visual process. These general considerations will recur throughout our investigation of early philosophical theories of vision.

Alcmaeon does not provide an account of how the reflection forms, but Anaxagoras, his near contemporary, has a slightly more lucid approach. Anaxagoras, from the Ionian city of Clazomenae, was the first of the Presocratic philosophers to work in Athens. He was well known among the Athenian elite for his cosmological opinions, his theory that in "everything there is a portion of everything" and the idea that mind (*nous*) controls all things.[17] We find references to Anaxagoras in the plays of Sophocles, Euripides and Aristophanes, and he had important connections with Pericles, which may have partially motivated the charge of impiety that led to Anaxagoras' exile in 436/7 BCE.[18] Theophrastus reports Anaxagoras' view that colours are visibly reflected in one another, with the strong (bright) colours better reflected in the weak (dark),[19] "which is why he holds that the visual organ is the same colour as night, and that light is the cause of the visual reflection".[20] But, Theophrastus concludes in his critique, if this were the case, then lifeless things like water and bronze – or for that matter colours – would possess the power of sight.[21] Anaxagoras also attributes a role to the "fine and lustrous membranes" of the eye, a sign that the construction of the eye itself has an explanatory role in his visual theory. However, as we might expect from Aristotle's brightest pupil, Theophrastus also criticizes even this aspect, saying that some sighted animals (such as crustaceans with hard eyes or fish) have unreflecting eyes. Moreover, he echoes Aristotle in arguing that if reflection were the cause of vision, then lifeless things – like water and bronze – would possess the power of sight.

In Anaxagoras we find references to colour as the object of sight, a theme which was absent in our evidence from Alcmaeon. Moreover, Anaxagoras is among those Presocratics who question the reliability of the senses. In DK 59 B21, Anaxagoras, speaking about the senses, says that "we are unable to distinguish the truth [of them] because of their lack of strength".[22] Sextus Empiricus, our source for this quotation, adds an additional detail about Anaxagoras' thinking (*Against the Mathematicians* 7.90–1):

τίθησί τε πίστιν αὐτῶν τῆς ἀπιστίας τὴν παρὰ μικρὸν τῶν χρωμάτων ἐξαλλαγήν·
εἰ γὰρ δύο λάβοιμεν χρώματα, μέλαν καὶ λευκόν, εἶτα ἐκ θατέρου εἰς θάτερον

---

17 On Anaxagoras, see Curd (2007) and Warren (2007: 119–34). Anaxagoras spells out his cosmogony at DK 59 B1, his theory of "everything in everything" at DK 59 B11 (cf. DK 59 B4 and B8), and the causal agency of *nous* at DK 59 B12.
18 See Barnes (1982: 305–6).
19 See Aristotle, *On Sense and the Sensible* 440a, where the technique of layering darker over lighter colours is described.
20 Theophrastus, *On the Senses* 37.4–5: διὸ καὶ τὴν ὄψιν ὁμόχρων ποιεῖ τῇ νυκτὶ καὶ τὸ φῶς αἴτιον τῆς ἐμφάσεως.
21 Theophrastus, *On the Senses* 36.
22 DK 59 B21: οὐ δυνατοί ἐσμεν κρίνειν τ'ἀληθές.

κατὰ σταγόνα παρεκχέοιμεν, οὐ δυνήσεται ἡ ὄψις διακρίνειν τὰς παρὰ μικρὸν μεταβολὰς καίπερ πρὸς τὴν φύσιν ὑποκειμένας.

[Anaxagoras] establishes, as evidence of their unreliability, the small changes that occur between colours when we take two, black and white, and pour one out into the other drop by drop. Sight will be unable to distinguish the small changes even though they underlie the nature of things.

Anaxagoras' evidence both substantiates his claim about the weakness of the senses and highlights their limitations without making the further sceptical claim that we should distrust them. While it may be beyond the distinguishing powers of the senses to detect minute and gradual changes, nonetheless, Anaxagoras famously asserts that what appears to us (*phainomena*) is "a glimpse of things unseen".[23] His point is that human vision, while incapable of making fine distinctions regarding minute changes in colour, nonetheless provides us glimpses of latent truths.[24] The mere fact that we can mix a small amount of white into black paint with no observable difference in the black is said to reveal truths about his claims that there is a bit of everything in everything and that predominance determines the character of a thing.[25] Thus, in Anaxagoras, too, we find a general account of vision that makes use of natural observations to substantiate broader claims. However, unlike Alcmaeon, Anaxagoras is not concerned with the *variability* of visual accuracy, but instead with vision's capacity to perceive minute differences *reliably*.

The reflection theory of vision that we find in Alcmaeon and Anaxagoras would become the standard account of vision. Theophrastus tells us that "the opinion about the visible reflection is somewhat common, for almost everyone explains vision thus: the visible reflection (*emphasis*) arises in the eyes".[26] When denigrating this theory, Aristotle tends to use the term *anaklasis*, meaning "beaming back", instead of *emphasis*. The difference in terminology suggests that for the early theorists it is the presence of an image in the eye, rather than its reflection back to the external observer, that is the cause of vision. If we, therefore, set aside the focus on "beaming back" reflections and instead focus on their "imaging in" surfaces, we can see why reflection is an important metaphor in early Greek visual theories.

The reflection theory of vision is tied at its point of origin very closely with wetness, which usually appears in its elemental form as water in philosophical contexts. References to the importance of water for sight are associated with most early

---

23 DK 59 B21a = Sextus Empiricus, *Against the Mathematicians* 7.140. See Lloyd (1966: 338–41) and Barnes (1982: 540–1); compare also the testimony about Democritus presented in DK 68 B125.
24 According to Theophrastus (*On the Senses* 29–30), Anaxagoras supposes the size of the sense organ to determine its perceptual capacity – which is why he claimed that large animals hear loud noises best, whereas small animals are best at hearing small sounds. Theophrastus himself rightly objects to this theory (*On the Senses* 34–5). See Baltussen (2015: 36–7) on the way organ size influences Anaxagoras' theory of smell.
25 See Warren (2007: 129–30). The weakness of human sight to distinguish the minute changes also acts as a counterargument to those who might claim that the senses do not reveal the truth of Anaxagoras' claims.
26 Theophrastus, *On the Senses* 36.1–2: περὶ δὲ τῆς ἐμφάσεως κοινή τίς ἐστιν ἡ δόξα· σχεδὸν γὰρ οἱ πολλοὶ τὸ ὁρᾶν οὕτως ὑπολαμβάνουσι διὰ τὴν γινομένην ἐν τοῖς ὀφθαλμοῖς ἔμφασιν.

technical accounts of vision.[27] Some scholars see in this a slavish commitment to elemental explanations,[28] but it need be nothing more than the fact that wet substances like water and oil are excellent reflecting surfaces. Still pools, even more than a polished metal mirror, would provide an ideal reflective surface for viewing not merely oneself, but also the wider world.[29] Moreover, although I may see my own reflection in your eye, from your perspective, your eyes observe a larger scene.[30] The correspondence between observation of reflections in nature and in the eyes of another presumably spurred the first thoughts about how vision occurs.

Reflections, whether in water, oil or mirrors are also obviously tied to the problems of accurate representation.[31] In these cases there is no lens or filter that alters the image reflected back to the viewer. Such reflecting surfaces represent whatever is put in front of them and, in this respect, the metaphor of reflection is a good one for getting an accurate sense of the world. It is, perhaps, precisely for these reasons that the mirror is held up as the symbol of knowledge – both of the self[32] and of the divine.[33] The surfaces of water, oil and polished metal may be distorted, but they nonetheless represent objects unmediated by another agent; the objects themselves are the cause of the image, insofar as their mere presence in front of a reflecting surface is sufficient for the appearance of the image. Although light conditions and the angles of refraction determine the clarity of the image reflected in such surfaces, even in relatively dim conditions water and oil, at least, remain reflective. For these early theorists, we can assume that what sets the eye apart from the likes of water and oil is the stability of its reflecting surface and its supposed internal source of light. This simplistic approach to the reflection theory, then, suggests that the image reflected in the eye accurately depicts the reality of the physical world.

The reflection theory, however, is superficial: a reflection lies only on the eye's surface, and it is not clear how the perceiver herself registers the visual reflections. Theophrastus elliptically recalls that for Alcmaeon "all the senses are connected

---

27 [Hippocrates], *On Fleshes* 17 8.606 L.
28 Beare (1906) is among the first to highlight this tendency.
29 Reflections in pools may very well explain the origin of the term *anaklasis*. Catoptrics does not appear to be of interest in these early theories, although it becomes important to Plato, Aristotle, Euclid and their successors (see Netz & Squire, this volume).
30 It becomes immediately obvious to the observer who sees herself in another's eye that, unlike ordinary reflections, the eye reflects the self in miniature: the point is also noted by Plato (*Alcibiades* 132e–133a).
31 On mirrors and mirror metaphors in ancient literature, see especially Bartsch (2006); cf. Goldberg (1985); Balensiefen (1990); Konersmann (1991); Jonsson (1995); A. Stewart (1996); Frontisi-Ducroux & Vernant (1997). Compare McCarty (1989) and G. Simon (2003) on the nature, material and properties of ancient mirrors, along with the discussions by Squire and Grethlein (this volume).
32 Compare Bias (DK 10 A73), one of antiquity's so-called "seven sages", who recommends looking into a mirror as a moral corrective. Cf. Diogenes Laertius 2.3; Plutarch, *Advice to Bride and Groom* 141d; Apuleius, *Apology* 15.8–15 (crediting Socrates with the notion that gazing in a mirror leads to self-knowledge). For the relation between reflection and self-knowledge in ancient philosophy, see Jonsson (1995) and Bartsch (2006).
33 Evidence for the importance of reflection in religious ritual can be found in e.g. Aristophanes, *Acharnians* 1128; Pausanias 7.21.12–13, 3.25.8; Lucian, *True Histories* 1.26; Apuleius, *Apology* 13. Cf. also Halliday (1913) and Delatte (1932) on ancient lekanomancy and katoptromancy. For the relation between reflection and divinity, see Seaford (2005); Elsner (2007b); Platt (2011).

somehow to the brain", but what the nature of this connection might be and how visible images are registered, remembered or processed remains unclear.[34] It may be that Alcmaeon saw no need to posit a homunculus sitting behind the eyes viewing the world, because for him, and perhaps for most of the Presocratics, the imaging of the world on the eye *just is* visual perception.

Another problem for the reflection theory is the loss of dimensionality. In reflections – whether in bronze, water or the eye – three-dimensional objects lose their depth in a two-dimensional representation. Such alterations call into question the accuracy of the reflection as a portrayal of reality. Theophrastus raises similar concerns about the precision of this model for vision, particularly when it comes to questions of the relation between objects and the reflected images of them.[35] In so doing, he stands in a long tradition, alongside Plato and the Sceptics, which questions the reliability of sight for knowledge.[36] Perhaps it was in response to the inadequacies of the visible reflection theory to address such questions that a new approach was introduced – that of the emanation from an object that entered the eye.

Sight, emanations and colour in Empedocles (*ca.* 495–435 BCE)

The emanation theory of vision provides a more sophisticated approach to the problems of sight than the earlier reflection account because it explains how information from an object reaches the eye of the perceiver. This intromissionist theory – in which something streams from an object and enters the perceiver's eye – makes vision a "contact" sense.

The earliest emanation theory of antiquity is that of Empedocles of Akragas. A philosopher, physician and poet active in southern Italy, Empedocles was a contemporary of Anaxagoras.[37] His philosophical and scientific theories figure prominently in the works of Plato and Aristotle and heavily influenced the Epicurean poet Lucretius.[38] Written in dactylic hexameter, Empedocles' work is part of the long tradition of Greek didactic poetry.[39] Empedocles highlights the importance of the soul, its immortality and the way in which a *daimōn* (that is, a god-like spirit), defiled by an act committed under the influence of Strife, journeys back to a state of purity through a series of reincarnations. Empedocles also explains the formation of the cosmos from the four material elements (fire, air, water and earth) acted upon by the two eternal and equal opposing forces of Love and Strife. It is in connection with his theory of world formation that Empedocles also postulates the generation of living

---

34 See Andriopoulos (2014).
35 Theophrastus, *On the Senses* 36.3–5.
36 Reflections sit notoriously low on Plato's divided line (*Republic* 510e–511a): in the *Sophist* (266a–e), as elsewhere, Plato likens such things to the mimetic arts.
37 Tracing lines of influence among the Presocratics is difficult. It is enough for our purposes to note that Empedocles and Anaxagoras, working around the same time, may have shared cultural experiences that influenced their philosophical positions. See Barnes (1982: 306–7).
38 On Empedocles' influence on Lucretius, see Sedley (1998).
39 Scholars traditionally consider Empedocles' writings to consist of two poems, entitled *On Nature* and *Purifications*. The recently edited Empedoclean fragments of the Strasbourg manuscript suggest that these are parts of a single poem. The single-poem hypothesis is, however, still controversial. See Martin & Primavesi (1999); C. Osborne (2000); Curd (2001).

things, first from separate, distinct limbs, then from combinations of them until finally "whole-nature" forms arise and individuals are then born from one another.[40] It is presumably in the context of delineating the nature of living things that he set out his theory of vision.

Some scholars credit Empedocles with a combined theory of vision, which includes the intromissionist effluences streaming off an object with the extramissionist theory of light passing out of the eye. This long-standing interpretation is due mainly to Empedocles' poetic comparison of the eye to a lantern:[41]

> And just as when someone planning a journey through the stormy night prepares a lamp, a flame of blazing fire, fitting to it lantern-sides as shields against the various winds, and these scatter the blowing winds' breath, but the finer part of the light leaps out and shines across the threshold with its unyielding beams; so at that time did she bring to birth the round-faced eye, primeval fire wrapped in membranes and in delicate garments. These held back the sea of water that flowed around, but the fine part of the fire penetrated to the outside.

The general consensus of scholarly opinion regarding Empedocles' visual theory has been nicely summarized by David Park:[42]

> An object gives off rays that carry information about its surface. To read this information, the eye projects forward a narrow *visual ray* that somehow feels the object's radiation and returns through the pupil into the sensitive part of the eye, where it creates an image in the mind. The visual ray is like a long finger projecting from the eye and sight is a kind of touch.

However, David Sedley has shown that such interpretations are the result of an Aristotelian conflation of the opinions of Plato on the one hand, and of Empedocles on the other.[43] Instead, an analysis of the actual Empedoclean evidence reveals not only that Empedocles had "turned the old belief about fire in the eye into a handy explanation of the role of light in vision",[44] but also that he located the seeing process at the surface of the eye, where water outside the eye, i.e. the lachrymal fluid, and fire from the internal passages of the eye coalesce. For Empedocles, then, there is no "long finger projecting from the eye". Rather, objects give off effluences that emanate towards the eye. The effluences of colours from objects are commensurate

---

40 DK 31 A72, B57, B59, B61–2.
41 DK 31 B84, translation Sedley (1992: 21): ὡς δ' ὅτε τις πρόοδον νοέων ὡπλίσσατο λύχνον | χειμερίην διὰ νύκτα, πυρὸς σέλας αἰθομένοιο, | ἅψας παντοίων ἀνέμων λαμπτῆρας ἀμοργούς, | οἵ τ' ἀνέμων μὲν πνεῦμα διασκιδνᾶσιν ἀέντων, | φῶς δ' ἔξω διαθρῶισκον, ὅσον ταναώτερον ἦεν, | λάμπεσκεν κατὰ βηλὸν ἀτειρέσιν ἀκτίνεσσιν· | ὣς δὲ τότ' ἐν μήνιγξιν ἐεργμένον ὠγύγιον πῦρ | λεπτῇσιν <τ'> ὀθόνῃσι λοχάζετο κύκλοπα κούρην, | <αἳ> χοάνῃσι δίαντα τετρήατο θεσπεσίῃσιν· | αἱ δ' ὕδατος μὲν βένθος ἀπέστεγον ἀμφιναέντος, | πῦρ δ' ἔξω δίιεσκον, ὅσον ταναώτερον ἦεν. Cf. Theophrastus, *On the Senses* 7, with Bielfeldt (this volume).
42 Park (1999).
43 See Sedley (1992).
44 Sedley (1992: 26).

with and so enter the pores of the eyes. Black effluences "fit into" the passages of water and white effluences "fit into" those of fire.[45] This is how the effluences cumulatively build up a picture on the eye's surface and how seeing occurs. Thus, what we find is that Empedocles' theory of vision is more concerned with the interplay of lightness and darkness cast off from objects than it is in the interaction of the perceiver and the object.

A theory of colour as an interplay of light and dark is the primary focus of Empedocles' theory. Such an approach is both more theoretical and more detailed than earlier reflection theories of vision. Rather than whole scenes being the object of vision, colour – conceived along a light–dark spectrum – now becomes the focus for sight. For Empedocles, the specific colour of an object depends on the mathematical ratio of the fire and water elements, which along with air and earth, constitute the object itself. Thus, the colour of an object depends on this proportion of dark water and bright fire.[46] For example, Empedocles explains how red blood and red flesh both contain equal proportions of all of the elements.[47] The result is that red occupies the middle point on his colour spectrum, since it has equal measures of fire and water. Aristotle, reporting Empedocles' explanation of eye colour, explains how grey-blue eyes contain more fire and dark eyes contain more water, which further substantiates the view that colour differences are dictated by the ratio of elemental fire to water.[48] Thus, for Empedocles, white and black sit on a continuum, with other colours falling somewhere between the two extremes.

The emphasis on colour in Empedocles' theory is central to subsequent Greek theorizing about vision. According to Plato (*Meno* 76c4–76d5) and Theophrastus (*On the Senses* 7), Empedocles' visual theory makes colour, not objects, the proper object of sight. Although we may say that we see an apple, according to Empedocles what we really see is its colour. As the effluence comes into contact with the eye, the organ of sight is equipped only to process the ratio of watery and fiery particles that "fit" into it. Thus, what we see is the colour of the apple – the ratio of watery and fiery particles – rather than the apple itself.

Empedocles' account highlights one of the essential connections between the development of Greek painting and optics.[49] Unlike Alcmaeon, who accepts the poetic conception of fire within the eye, Empedocles' fiery eye is largely metaphorical. Observations about the interplay of light and dark are found in his descriptions of colour formation and the metaphors of vision, and he seems to incorporate these

---

[45] For the association of fire with the colour white, see DK 31 B96, B21. For the association of water with the colour black, see DK 31 B94 for that of water with black. This summary of Empedocles' theory of colour is largely based on Ierodiakonou (2005).

[46] Ierodiakonou (2005: 19–20) addresses the extent to which juxtaposition of white and black particles generates the spectrum of colours we experience. For an overview of ancient theories of colour, see Bradley (2009: esp. 56–86).

[47] DK 31 B21.1–6, B98, A78, A86 (= Theophrastus, *On the Senses* 10).

[48] Aristotle, *On the Generation of Animals* 779b15–20 and *Problems* 910a12–15. Although Empedocles' account of the rainbow (DK 31 B50) does not contain any reference to the formation of the colours seen, it may have been clear to him and other ancient theorists that the colours arise in some way from the interaction of the light from the sun and the water of the rain: cf. Aristotle, *On Sense and the Sensible* 439b18, 440a10–12; *On Meteorology* 374a7–8.

[49] For the development of optics in antiquity, see Netz & Squire (this volume).

into his understanding of light and shadow into his visual theory. Indeed, Empedocles' explanation of visual appearances is closely related to the artist's desire to render appearances in his medium. Philosopher and painter alike attempt to define the visible in terms of light, dark and colour. In addition to his physical account of fitting colours together, Empedocles also likens the cosmogonic process to the painting of a scene:[50]

> Just as when painters embellish votive offerings, those men with expertise, who are well taught by wisdom, when they have taken up in their hands many-coloured paints mixed in harmony – some more, others less – from these, the painters arrange forms resembling all things, producing trees, men and women, beasts, birds, water-nourished fish and immortal gods, greatest in honour. Thus, do not let trickery overcome your mind, that the source for mortals is from some other place, however many countless things have become clear. Rather, know these things distinctly, having heard the account from a god.

In this passage, Empedocles likens the capacity of Love to create a world from four elements to the work of skilled painters who, from a small number of colours, are able to depict the whole of the natural world. The painting metaphor suits Empedocles' cosmology because painting captures the world of experience in a medium that differs as drastically from the original as Empedocles thinks our world of experience differs from the ontological account of elements and forces that he describes. We see in Empedocles' fragments how the artist and philosopher both develop complementary approaches to the nature and geometry of light, how it illuminates objects and casts shadows.

According to the Elder Pliny's *Natural History* – admittedly a much later text, written in the 70s CE – it was precisely because of his interest in the contrast between light and dark that Apollodorus initiated the art of *skiagraphia*, literally "shadow-painting".[51] Jeremy Tanner will return to shadow-painting – and indeed to Apollodorus – in the fifth chapter. For now, though, it is enough to note that, in a passage on the nature of colours, Pliny explicitly defines *skiagraphia* as a mode of painting with light and shadow (*lumen et umbrae*):[52]

---

50 DK 31 B23: ὡς δ᾽ ὁπόταν γραφέες ἀναθήματα ποικίλλωσιν | ἀνέρες ἀμφὶ τέχνης ὑπὸ μήτιος εὖ δεδαῶτε, | οἵτ᾽ ἐπεὶ οὖν μάρψωσι πολύχροα φάρμακα χερσίν, | ἁρμονίῃ μείξαντε τὰ μὲν πλέω, ἄλλα δ᾽ ἐλάσσω, | ἐκ τῶν εἴδεα πᾶσιν ἀλίγκια πορσύνουσι, | δένδρεά τε κτίζοντε καὶ ἀνέρας ἠδὲ γυναῖκας | θῆράς τ᾽ οἰωνούς τε καὶ ὑδατοθρέμμονας ἰχθῦς | καί τε θεοὺς δολιχαίωνας τιμῇσι φερίστους· | οὕτω μή σ᾽ ἀπάτη φρένα καινύτω ἄλλοθεν εἶναι | θνητῶν, ὅσσα γε δῆλα γεγάκασιν ἄσπετα, πηγήν, | ἀλλὰ τορῶς ταῦτ᾽ ἴσθι, θεοῦ πάρα μῦθον ἀκούσας. See Lloyd (1966) and Kamtekar (2009) on Empedocles' use of analogy.
51 See Pliny, *Natural History* 35.60 on Apollodorus. Compare Quintillian, *Training of the Orator* 12.10.4 on how Zeuxis (Apollodorus' pupil) laid down a ratio for "light and shadows" (*lumen et umbra*). For a full discussion, see Keuls (1975; 1978b). On the relation between Pliny and Empedocles, see Ierodiakonou (2005).
52 Pliny, *Natural History* 35.29; cf. 33.159–60, where Pliny lists the pigments used for areas of light and shade. For further discussions of *skiagraphia* and Pliny's comments here, see Tanner (this volume).

In time, the art distinguished itself and discovered light and shadow, with the alternation of contrasting colours intensifying the effect of one against the other. After that, luminosity (*splendor*) was finally added, which is different from light (*lumen*). Those qualities that exist between these two and shade (*umbras*) are called "tension" (*tonon*), whereas the conjunctions and transition of colours is called "fitting together" (*harmogēn*).

"Fitting together" (*harmogē*) is here a Greek term that Pliny transliterates. It refers to patches of contrasting colour juxtaposed to form an impressionistic image. The image and the terminology calls to mind Empedocles' own account of colour as the fitting of effluences with their juxtaposed elements of fire and water to the pores of the eye, as well as the painting metaphor we saw above. The "tones" (*tonon* is also a Greek transliteration in the Latin text) of colour on the spectrum between light and dark, too, bear a striking resemblance to Empedocles' account of colours.[53] Just as the juxtaposition of Empedoclean elements create all of the objects of the world, so too the interplay of different colours creates a unified image viewed at a distance.

We need not look for direct influence from one field to the other, instead it is enough to recognize a theoretical conception of light, shade and colour that simultaneously developed across philosophy and art in the fifth century BCE. In particular, *skiagraphia* becomes a powerful metaphor in the Classical period. Plato and Aristotle use shadow-painting to cast doubt upon approaches or definitions with which they disagree. For example Plato uses a *skiagraphēma* ("shadow-painting") to emphasize how what appears clear at a distance, or on first encounter, on closer inspection is puzzling, unclear or an unexpected conjunction of differences.[54] The juxtaposition of colours in *skiagraphia* is also an image of relativity, particularly in relation to notions of virtue. In some instances, the focus of the metaphor is to draw the reader's attention to the way that contrasts are starker when set next to each other.[55] In others, the purpose is to highlight the relative intensities of pleasures and pains.[56]

Vision entails distance, and in art and philosophy we see two complementary attempts to come to terms with how light and colour travel from objects to the eye of the perceiver, and how this relation can be described in geometrical terms. Empedocles represents a radical departure from earlier approaches to vision. He emphasizes the formation of the sensible object and its transmission to the perceiver by means of the proportionally juxtaposed elements of fire and water, which has the advantage of explicitly identifying the object and process of sight. Despite the relative sophistication of this theory, it still fails fully to account for the complexity of vision, the perception of distance and the variety of human visual experience.

---

53 See Ierodiakonou (2005).
54 Plato, *Theaetetus* 208e, *Parmenides* 165c–d. For an analysis of *skiagraphia* and its cognates in these passages (among others), see Keuls (1978b); Bruno (1977); Summers (2007: 16–23). Compare also Aristotle's usage in *Rhetoric* 1414a9.
55 Plato, *Laws* 663b–c.
56 Plato, *Phaedo* 69b6–7, *Republic* 586b. See also *Republic* 583b and *Philebus* 42b.

Sight, images and imprints in Democritus (*ca.* 460–370 BCE)

Democritus of Abdera is the last of the Presocratics. One of the first philosophers to propose an atomic theory, he understands everything to be composed from indivisible bodies and void. Democritus' theory does not rely on teleology to explain the apparent regularity of nature. Instead, everything in nature is achieved by the workings of physical necessity. Democritus appears to take a retrograde approach to sight by suggesting that we see images, not just colours, by means of the visual reflection (*emphasis*) formed in the eye. However, his unique account transforms earlier notions by combining them into a theory of emanations that form a visual reflection through the imprinting of air. For Democritus as for Empedocles, the geometric alignment of an object's component parts is essential to determining its colour. However, unlike his predecessor, Democritus emphasizes the importance of environmental factors in the process of sight. Thus, Democritus, too, explains vision by means of touch.

For Democritus, as for his predecessors, the visual reflection (*emphasis*) is not a garden-variety reflection (*anaklasis*). Unlike Alcmaeon, where the process of image formation is never explicitly described, Democritus sets out an account of the formation of the image:[57]

> ὁρᾶν μὲν οὖν ποιεῖ τῇ ἐμφάσει· ταύτην δὲ ἰδίως λέγει· τὴν γὰρ ἔμφασιν οὐκ εὐθὺς ἐν τῇ κόρῃ γίνεσθαι, ἀλλὰ τὸν ἀέρα τὸν μεταξὺ τῆς ὄψεως καὶ τοῦ ὁρωμένου τυποῦσθαι συστελλόμενον ὑπὸ τοῦ ὁρωμένου καὶ τοῦ ὁρῶντος· ἅπαντος γὰρ ἀεὶ γίνεσθαί τινα ἀπορροήν· ἔπειτα τοῦτον στερεὸν ὄντα καὶ ἀλλόχρων ἐμφαίνεσθαι τοῖς ὄμμασιν ὑγροῖς. καὶ τὸ μὲν πυκνὸν οὐ δέχεσθαι, τὸ δὲ ὑγρὸν διιέναι.

> He makes seeing happen because of the image, and he gives his own peculiar account of this. For the image, he says, does not come into being directly in the pupil, but the air between the organ of sight and the thing seen is impressed because it is compressed by the thing seen and the seeing subject. For all things are always producing some effluence. Then this air, being both solid and of a different colour, becomes imaged in the eyes, which are moist. The dense cannot receive it, whereas the moist lets it pass through.

The most important component in Democritus' account is the eye's capacity to admit, retain and transmit the entering image.[58] For Democritus, everything continually casts off images of itself (called *eidōla*)[59] that shrink as they travel through and imprint upon the air. Finally, the image and the imprint enter the eye together to form the visual reflection (*emphasis*).[60] Democritus postulates that these effluences (*eidōla*), which flow off all things, serve two functions: they are themselves imaged

---

57 Theophrastus, *On the Senses* 50.1–6: the ambiguities of the translation here reflect those of the original Greek.
58 Democritus' ophthalmology reveals close observation of the eye and perhaps some knowledge from dissection: see Theophrastus, *On the Senses* 50.6–11 and Rudolph (2012); for further discussion of image transmission, see Theophrastus, *On the Senses* 53.6–7.
59 Democritus' own technical term is *deikelon*, "representation" (DK 68 B123); cf. DK 68 A78.
60 Cf. C. Taylor (1999); Baldes (1975; 1978).

in the eye and they also have a condensing effect in the process of sight as "visual rays".

Democritus' eye is an active participant in, rather than a passive recipient of, vision. According to Theophrastus (*On the Senses* 50), Democritus understands the "thing seen and the seeing subject" to play a role in the formation of the air imprint.[61] This suggestion of visual rays is beyond irrefutable confirmation, but there is further evidence to suggest that Democritus postulates them.[62] The most important account of the role of rays comes from Vitruvius, an architect of the first century BCE:[63]

> First of all, in Athens, when Aeschylus was producing a tragedy, Agatharchus made the scenery and left a commentary about it. Informed by this, Democritus and Anaxagoras wrote upon the same topic, namely how a fixed centre should be established and the lines should correspond realistically to the sight-line of the eyes and the extension of the rays, so that on unclear evidence, clear images give the appearance of buildings in the murals of the stage, and things that are painted on flat, continuous façades seem to recede in some places and project in others.

Agatharchus' *skēnographia*, according to Vitruvius, influenced visual theories in a particular way, namely, by showing how lines extended from a single point can replicate how all lines of sight converge at the pupil.[64] Although Euclid is our earliest source for the theory of a visual cone, material evidence suggests that many of his principles were well known to artists before his time.[65] An emerging awareness of perspective can be found in a variety of artistic media contemporary with Democritus. We are told that mural- and panel-painters were famed innovators in depicting depth on a flat surface, and vase-paintings and sculptures from the late sixth and early fifth centuries, show a "sustained attempt" to master the art of foreshortening,[66] which may relate to the lost large-scale paintings or stage designs of the period. The surviving artistic representations provide undeniable evidence for the development of basic perspective in art immediately prior to Agatharchus' scene-painting for Aeschylus' tragedy.[67] We can then, with some assurance, assume that Democritus had a theory of visual rays as effluences that flow outward from the eye

---

61 Some scholars, like Nightingale (this volume), do not explain this reference in Theophrastus; in so doing, they deny Democritus a theory of visual rays.
62 DK 68 B155, DK 68 A126a. Cf. Aristotle, *On Sense and the Sensible* 438a25–27. For analysis of the evidence see Rudolph (2011), which I summarize in this section.
63 Vitruvius, *On Architecture* 7 praef. 11.5–13. For further discussion, see Tanner (this volume); our conclusions broadly concur.
64 For a full analysis of this passage, see White (1956: 47–51).
65 Cf. Tybout (1989); Knorr (1991); Lephas (1998).
66 White (1956: 11). See also Pollitt (1974: 242); White (1956: 9–10); Keuls (1978b). The best example is the Siphnian frieze at Delphi, where there is very clear foreshortening in the charioteer's horses. Textual evidence and stylistic elements date the frieze securely to around 525 BCE, which makes it possible that such techniques were also being used in paintings of the same period: see Tanner (this volume) for further evidence and bibliography.
67 On the dating, see Rudolph (2011) and Pollitt (1974: 245).

in a conical pattern that aid in the compression of the image in the direction of the perceiver. After all, the powers of peripheral vision alone suggest that we see not only things at which we glance, but also objects at the margin of our gaze.

In addition to the visual rays, which guide effluences towards the eye, the atomist visual theory also requires air imprints that Democritus himself compares to "pressing something in wax".[68] In daylight, the air infused with light from the sun is dense (*puknos*), and thus ready for imprinting. As the effluences from the visible object press the light-condensed air, visual rays from the eye supply a simultaneous condensing effect. The action of these two effluences moulds the air and results in an impression, differing in colour from the air itself. As an effluence and its newly formed air imprint approach the eye, the shrinking process continues until they are small enough to be "imaged in" (*emphainetai*) the pupil as a visual reflection (*emphasis*). As the imprint and effluence enter the observer, the soft, moist eye lets the image pass through.[69] This is how the air imprint arises.

One of the key features of Democritus' theory of air imprints is that it explicitly emphasizes the effect environmental conditions have on the visual process. The air must be dense and unfragmented, and the sun acts as an ancillary agent of condensation.[70] Light is not a conduit for images moving towards the eye, since that role is performed already by the visual ray. Instead, sunlight is an auxiliary in the formation of the visual reflection: it prepares the air for moulding by the effluences.[71] This suggests that Democritus' air imprints are not, as scholars have generally interpreted them, a source of visual distortion; rather the air imprints are part of the process of vision itself.[72] As von Fritz rightly argues, if air imprints are meant to explain distortions in vision, mentioning the blurring effects of air itself would be enough to suggest such a scenario, making air imprints superfluous.[73] Democritus is certainly challenging the reliability of sight, but he does so by emphasizing that air, by taking an imprint like wax, helps create an image that *appears* to be a precise copy of the thing being imprinted, when in fact it is not.

The imprint theory supplements rather than contradicts the notion of vision by effluences because it explains the miniature size of the reflection in the eye. Moreover, this perspective-via-imprint theory vindicates Vitruvius' testimony. Thus, for Democritus, sight is not merely a case of intromissionist vision; rather, it is a multi-relational process arising from the interaction of four different components: the visual ray from the eye, the effluence from the object, the air imprint formed by these two and the visual reflection that results in the perceiver's eye. More importantly, however, it follows that Democritus, by combining human physiology and mathematical theory in an explanation of perspectival vision, was a much more innovative

---

68 Theophrastus, *On the Senses* 51.1–3.
69 Democritus (in Theophrastus, *On the Senses* 50.6–11) stipulates what makes an eye better for seeing. See Rudolph (2012).
70 Theophrastus, *On the Senses* 51.1–3, 52.1–2, 54.1–4.
71 Cf. Burkert (1977) and C. Taylor (1999).
72 C. C. W. Taylor (1999: 209–10) is the most recent proponent of the interpretation that Democritus' air imprints account for the interference of the environment in the visual process.
73 *Contra* Beare (1906: 26–7). Von Fritz (1953: 94) criticizes air imprints as a mode of visual distortion, suggesting instead that the air imprint makes the image hard, so that it can be imaged in the soft eye.

and sophisticated theoretician than has been previously suggested. This is all the more interesting because an explanation that utilizes air imprints and visual rays has direct connections with and reveals a deep interest in visual representation.

Democritus, like Anaxagoras, is aware of the difficulties that arise from our reliance on the information of the senses.[74] He is ready to admit that colours, flavours and temperatures are "conventional", and there is reason to believe that he extends this "conventional" category to the images that we see.[75] In particular, he seems to embrace the epistemic constraints that the imprint theory imposes. Gem-carvers often engraved images of things – e.g. amphorae, animals and people – onto a stone. When pressed in wax, they produce an image that is not only a replication of the original engraving, but also a miniature mimetic image of a real object,[76] similar to Democritus' visual reflection in the eye. What makes the wax analogy a compelling metaphor for sight is precisely that a wax impression bears a direct relationship to its intaglio: the hollow image engraved on stone appears in relief in the wax, and letters and images are reversed on the wax surface. But, as this description suggests, such impressions are isomorphic copies of the original, never exact replicas.[77] We might then see in Democritus a growing scepticism about the accuracy of vision, since air imprints necessarily constrain and alter sight. First, as Theophrastus suggests, a wax impression is a positive inverse image of the negative depiction on the stone. Second, the impression is mimetic and thus epistemically and ontologically constrained. Democritus seems aware of these difficulties and may have even embraced them.[78] As we will see in the next chapter, although Plato makes sight the preeminent sense, vision of the sensible world lacks the clarity and reliability of intellectual pursuits.[79]

Visualizing Presocratic sight

Throughout this chapter, we have seen how early Greek philosophical theories of vision assume that a goal of perception is to match, or at least to approximate, true properties of a physical world that is assumed to exist independent of any acts of observation. These mimetic assumptions are a universally accepted point of departure for ancient theories of vision.[80] Alcmaeon's and Anaxagoras' reflections, like Empedocles' emanations and Democritus' imprints, are theories of direct perception: they replicate the objective environment because they directly pick up the properties of the objects and the environmental conditions. In these cases, vision is accurate

---

74 See Sextus Empiricus, *Against the Mathematicians* 7.140, who says Democritus praised Anaxagoras for saying that *phainomena* are "the sight of things unseen".
75 DK 68 B9. See Sedley (1988) and Wardy (1988).
76 This method of mechanical reproduction is the only ancient imprinting process that did not require a specialist skill; as such the process would have been familiar to Democritus' readers.
77 On Aristotle's subsequent appropriation of the "seal" analogy, see Nightingale (this volume), along with Platt (2006), on the applicability of such thinking for approaching ancient sealstones and processes of replication.
78 See Sextus Empiricus, *Against the Mathematicians* 7.135–140.
79 An opinion he may share with Anaxagoras (DK 59 B21).
80 The extent to which this is true of the other sense modalities is beyond the scope of this chapter: on the materiality of perception in the Presocratics, however, see Porter (2010: 121–76).

precisely because of the direct interaction between the image and the perceiver: what you see is what you get. When this is true, we have what today is called veridical perception, i.e. perception consistent with the actual state of affairs in the environment. However, all of these early theorists are aware that visual perception is not always accurate or clear, and they go to great lengths to account for variations in how we see.

The growing sophistication that we find in Presocratic theories of sight also coincides with an increasing concern about the accuracy and reliability of seeing. Whereas Alcmaeon challenges the prevailing assumptions about the fire in the eye, Anaxagoras questions vision's capacity to reveal truths about our world. Empedocles attempts to ground the objects of sight in the more theoretically sophisticated realm of mathematical ratios between light and shadow. Democritus brings together these accounts via his imprint theory, by explaining not only how we are in contact with the objects we perceive, but also how environmental factors alter our grasp of them. Thus, we may see the Presocratic interest in vision as exploring the link, broadly speaking, between vision and knowledge.

It is striking that, from its very beginning, Greek visual theories focus on replication via image formation, quite apart from the object itself, as being responsible for vision. In both the art and philosophy of this period, we find an intense concentration on consistent representation of ephemeral experiences.[81] As will become clear in the following chapters, in order to capture the image in all of its dimensions, artists and philosophers develop complex approaches to vision that problematize the extent to which sight is representative of reality. The Presocratic theories of sight focus primarily on the physical side of the perceptual process, aiming first to establish the nature and mechanism of the "information transfer" to the senses and then to explain how this led to knowledge about the world. It is no surprise, then, to find that the relationship between perception, knowledge and understanding becomes a matter of intense scrutiny in the Classical period. For what the Presocratics had made a subject of preliminary intellectual inquiry would emerge as a defining topos of Classical Greek philosophy.

---

[81] The fleeting nature of sensation is a characteristic sight shares with the other senses. I leave it to others to examine the implications of this transience in ancient theories of perception.

2

SIGHT AND THE PHILOSOPHY OF VISION IN CLASSICAL GREECE
Democritus, Plato and Aristotle

Andrea Nightingale

Many early Greek thinkers analysed vision, though (as the previous chapter has suggested) we have rather scanty evidence for their theories.[1] This essay focusses on three Greek philosophers who offered detailed and very different accounts of vision: Democritus (*ca.* 460–370 BCE), Plato (424–348 BCE) and Aristotle (384–322 BCE). I focus in particular on their conceptions of the seeing subject and the object of vision. How does the eye see things? And how does the "mind" or "soul" register this visual event?[2] In order to understand the philosophers' ideas on these topics, I examine theories of "extramission" (in which light emanating from the eyes streams out and grasps an external object) and "intromission" (in which images or effluences of an object hit the eye, arriving from outside). As we will see, these different theories are predicated on specific conceptions of the physical world and of the "mind" or "soul".[3] Finally, I want to consider the difference between passive seeing and active looking. The latter involves attention. One can direct one's attention to some things rather than others (consciously or unconsciously). By deliberately directing one's gaze, one places a given object or scene in the foreground and pushes everything else

---

1 My discussions in this chapter should be read in close conjunction with the contributions of others in this volume – especially Michael Squire (on the "ancient eye" at large), Kelli Rudolph (on Presocratic philosophy), Reviel Netz & Michael Squire (on post-Aristotelian optics) and Jeremy Tanner (on the relations between Greek philosophy and painterly practice). For general discussions of ancient Greek theories of vision, see Beare (1906); G. Simon (1988); Jay (1993); Nightingale (2004); Darrigol (2012): esp. 1–15). In my references to the fragments collected in Diels and Kranz (1951-2), this chapter – like that of Rudolph before it – uses the abbreviation "DK".
2 The philosophers I examine here separated the soul and the mind. In general, they believed that the soul included the mind but also contained other "psychic" elements, such as emotions and passions; they also conceived of the soul as giving life to the body. Still, each philosopher had a different conception of the soul: for Democritus, the soul is bodily and made up of atoms; for Plato, it is immaterial, separable from the body, and immortal; for Aristotle, who believed in hylomorphism ("being" as a compound of matter and form), the soul is not separable from the body and dies with the body (*On the Soul* 2.1, 413a3–5). Note that Aristotle complicates this view by positing an "active intellect" (*nous poiētikos*) that exists separately from the body and is immortal (*On the Soul* 3.5, 430a17–23).
3 It is also worth emphasizing that debates between these intromissionist and extramissionist positions continued not only long into antiquity, but also right up to the seventeenth century: see especially Smith (this volume).

into the background. As I argue, desire and passion are at the root of visual attention.

Democritus

I begin by discussing the philosopher whom we have already encountered in the last chapter: Democritus (*ca.* 460–370 BCE). As Kelli Rudolph has explained, Democritus was a materialist who argued that all things in the universe are made up of atoms and void. But, as will become clear in this chapter, Democritus proves particularly critical in directing the course of Classical theories of sight – albeit more in critical reaction than in affirmation.

Unfortunately, we have relatively few extant fragments of Democritus. To understand his theory of vision, we have to rely almost exclusively on one ancient source: Theophrastus, a member of Aristotle's school. In *On the Senses*, Theophrastus offers a highly critical account of Democritus' views. His account of Democritus' theory of vision is biased and, at times, rather confusing. Still, his discussion sets forth the basic principles of Democritus' views on seeing.[4]

In Democritus' philosophy, the human body and soul are physical entities, through and through. The body and soul (and everything in the universe) are made up of atoms and void. Although atoms come in different shapes and sizes, they are invisible (and indivisible) corpuscles that are in continual motion in the void. Any given body in the phenomenal realm is losing and gaining atoms all the time. This is because bodies are continually being bombarded from the outside by atoms moving around in the void. Some atoms repel each other and, by striking one another, break down one or more bodily thing; other atoms are able (due to their shape and size) to coalesce with each other and build up a given body.

How, then, does a human being see an object in the world? In *On the Senses*, Theophrastus offers the following account of Democritus' views. First, every body in the phenomenal realm continually gives off a series of "effluences".[5] Effluences are thin films of atoms emitted from the surface of an object that retain the object's form and qualities. The effluence flowing from a given body moves through the medium of air and reaches the eye of the perceiver.[6] However, before the effluence hits the eye, the atoms of the air are caught and compressed between the effluence and the eye itself. This causes an "air impression". As Theophrastus puts it: as the effluence

---

4 On Democritus' atomic theory and his conception of vision, see – in addition to Rudolph (this volume) – von Fritz (1953); W. K. C. Guthrie (1965: 2.386–472); Burkert (1977); Baldes (1975; 1978); O'Brien (1984); Rudolph (2011). On Theophrastus' discussion of earlier theories of the senses, including that of Democritus, see Baltussen (2000).

5 "For some kind of effluence (*aporroē*) is always coming from everything" (Theophrastus, *On the Senses* 50). Note that Empedocles also posited effluences (DK B89; Plato, *Meno* 76c–d): these came both from the object and from the eyes of the seer (the latter emitted effluences of light; DK B84).

6 Theophrastus, *On the Senses* 51. There are conflicting accounts of Democritus offered by Theophrastus and Aristotle. Theophrastus claims that the medium that allows for vision is air, whereas Aristotle says that, according to Democritus, people would see the most clearly through the void rather than through air (*On the Soul* 2.7, 419a15–17). Von Fritz (1953), W. K. C. Guthrie (1965: 2.441–6) and Burkert (1977) argue that Democritus had offered two theories of vision; Baldes (1975; 1978) claims that Democritus set forth a single account.

pushes towards the eye, "the air is moulded (*apomattetai*) like wax that is squeezed and pressed (*ōthoumenos kai puknoumenos*)".[7] Like wax that takes on an imprint, the air takes on an "impression" from the effluences that are, themselves, shaped and formed like the original object. The air impression, then, hits the eye, possessing the shape and form of the effluence of the original object.[8]

But what, we must ask, creates the air impression? The atoms in the effluences do not have the density to compress the air atoms. As Theophrastus claims, it is the sun, with its more forceful atoms, that compresses the air and forms the air impression (*On the Senses* 54).[9] Clearly, the light of the sun also allows the effluence and air impression to create a "reflection" (*emphasis*) of the object in the eye. Thus, the sun plays a double role in vision: it compresses the effluences to produce an air impression and it also allows the effluences and imprints to create a reflection in the eye. Note that Rudolph argues against this interpretation in this volume (p. 50). According to her suggestion, Democritus believed that the eyes send forth a visual ray that helps to create the air impression (though she admits that this claim is "beyond irrefutable confirmation" because the sources for it are quite late). I follow Theophrastus' view of Democritus' thinking: in Democritus, vision takes place when a collocation of atoms coming from outside the eye (effluences from the object, the air and the sun) create a reflection in the eye so that it sees an image of the object.

We come, finally, to the human being's perception of an object (and not just the eye's vision of an image). As Theophrastus observes, in Democritus, "visual perception is not simply a function of the eyes but of the rest of the body as well: for he [Democritus] says that the eye must contain void and moisture so that it may be more receptive (*dechētai*) and transmit (*paradidōi*) [the impressions] to the rest of the body" (*On the Senses* 54). We must remember that, for Democritus, the soul is spread throughout the body and does not have a single "seat" within it. Thus, when the eye sees the image of an object, it transmits this image to the soul. Unfortunately, we have no extant sources that tell us exactly how this happens. Nor do we have an account of how the soul or mind retains a given image. We must infer that the atoms of the soul receive the data from the eye and thus enable the human subject (not just the eye) to grasp and understand what he or she sees.

In Democritus, then, we find an example of "intromission": the effluences of the object, the sun and the air impressions hit the eye *from the outside*, thus forming a reflection in the eye. The eye then "sees" an object and transmits this sense to the soul.

---

7 Theophrastus, *On the Senses* 52.
8 See Theophrastus, *On the Senses* 81, where Theophrastus indicates that "the effluence enters" (*tēs eisiousēs aporroēs*) the eye. This would suggest that the effluence, as well as the air impression, hits the eye.
9 Theophrastus (*On the Senses* 54) makes this point as a mode of criticism: "It is possible that the sun creates the reflection (*emphasin*), in sending light in upon the visual sense in the form of rays – as Democritus seems to mean. For the idea that the sun 'drives away (*apōthounta*) the air from itself, forming (*apoplēttomenon*) and condensing (*puknoun*) it', as he [Democritus] says, is indefensible, since the sun by its very nature disperses the air."

Plato

We find a very different theory of vision in Plato. In stark contrast to Democritus' materialistic theory of the universe, Plato posits an ontological dualism of body and soul. The soul and mind are immaterial and ontologically "separate" from the physical realm. How, then, does the mind grasp earthly phenomena through the medium of the eyes? Consider, first, the account of vision in the Timaeus.[10] Here, Plato argues that humans possess "light-bearing eyes" (*phōsphora ... ommata*).[11] The eye contains within it a "pure fire which is akin (*adelphon*) to the light of day" (*Timaeus* 45b). This light, according to Timaeus (45b–d),

> flows through the eyes (*dia tōn ommatōn*) in a smooth and dense stream ... and whenever the stream of vision is surrounded by daylight, it flows out like unto like; by coalescing with this [the daylight], the stream of vision forms a single body (*sōma*) along the eyes' visual path, wherever the fire which streams out from within makes contact with the light which meets it from without.

The human eye, in other words, sends forth its inner light out into the world. The eye's "light" flows forth in a stream and meets with the "light of day", which, as Plato suggests, is "akin" to it.[12] Because of this kinship, the light coming from the eye is able to coalesce with the light of the sun to form a "single body" or, to put it differently, a single "beam" of light. This beam of light comes into contact with bodily objects and "distributes the motions of every object" to the eye. Once the eye sees something in the world via the "beam" of light, the soul of the perceiver "grasps" the object and identifies it.[13]

In Plato, then, seeing does not involve the passive reception of external impressions or effluences; rather, it is a participatory activity in which humans interact with the external world by sending the light from their eyes outwards. The "beam" formed by the "light-bearing eyes" and the sunlight, which coalesce with each other, allows for the perception of the appearance of the object. Here, we have an example of a theory of "extromission", where the eyes send forth rays into the world in order to see.

---

10 There is a vast literature on the *Timaeus*. See e.g. Cornford (1937); Solmsen (1942: 149–74); Vlastos (1975); W. K. C. Guthrie (1978: 241–311); Sedley (2009: 93–132); Broadie (2011).
11 Plato, *Timaeus* 45b. Here, Plato follows Empedocles, who claimed that the eyes were a "lantern" bearing light (DK B84); he conceived of the eyes as sending "effluences" of light into the world. See also Plato, *Meno* 76c–d, where Socrates offers a brief discussion of Empedocles' theory of effluences.
12 It is "similar in its properties because of its similar nature" (45d). On "likeness" and "similarity" in Plato's *Timaeus*, see Bryan (2012: 114–60).
13 Given his dualistic notion of body and soul, Plato has a hard time accounting for the soul's grasp of the physical realm. In a difficult passage in the *Timaeus* (37a–b), Plato claims that the rational part of the soul (which is made of two circles, the "Circle of the Same" and the "Circle of the Different") is a self-moving being that "touches" (*ephaptētai*) the bodily realm through sensation: "when the soul is concerned with that which is sensible, and the Circle of the Other – moving in an upright course – announces [a perception] to the whole of the Soul, opinions and beliefs come into being which are firm and true". We can infer that a vicious soul has a "Circle of the Different" that does not move correctly and thus forms the wrong opinions.

We must emphasize that Plato does not believe that vision is simply designed for seeing, pure and simple. Indeed, he views vision in teleological terms (*Timaeus* 47a–b):

> Vision (*opsis*) is the cause of the greatest benefit to us, since no account of the universe would have ever been given if men had not seen the stars or sun or heaven. The vision of day and night and the months and the revolutions of the years has created the art of number, and it has given us the notion of time as well as the ability to investigate the nature of the universe. From these things we have procured philosophy – and there is no greater good that the gods have given us than this. This, I claim, is the greatest benefit of eyesight.

Plato considered the vision and study of the circular motions in the heavens – motions created by the reason (*nous*) of the divine souls that inhabit each star (40b) – as a helpful path towards philosophy.[14] In particular, seeing the circular motions in the heavens, which traces out the circular motions of divine reason (*nous*), allows one to philosophize about the invisible, immaterial Forms. In Plato, the objects of true knowledge are metaphysical entities called *eidē*, a term which is generally translated as "Forms". More literally, the word *eidos* means the "aspect", "shape" or "look" of something; Plato thus conceives of the Forms as objects of mental "vision". Note that Plato regularly identifies the Forms as true "Being" or "the Really Real": the Forms are not concepts or ideas but rather Beings that enjoy the fullest kind of existence.

Not surprisingly, Plato claims that seeing things on earth (and enjoying this mode of vision) tends to lead us away from philosophy. This is because our senses deceive us. In the *Phaedo* (65b), for example, Socrates says that sight and the other senses do not offer "accurate" (*akribeis*) or "clear" (*sapheis*) perceptions. Indeed, bodily entities in the phenomenal realm – i.e. the objects of our vision – are always in flux (78e–79d). Therefore, when the soul "makes use of the body for inquiry, either by seeing or hearing or by using any other of the senses ... it is dragged by the body to things that never stay the same and it wanders and is confused and dizzy, like a drunken man" (79c). The senses are deceived unless reason comes to the rescue and determines the correct nature of the object.

Plato famously denigrates the earth and the phenomenal realm. To live a happy life, he argues, one must separate one's soul from one's body and use the mind to contemplate immaterial "Realities" (i.e. the "Forms"). And one can only do this by practising philosophy. Plato exemplifies this claim in his "allegory of the cave" (*Republic* 7, 514a–17b).[15] The allegory uses visual images to depict not only the physical world but also the invisible realm of the soul and the Forms. In this myth,

---

14 As Plato explains in the tenth book of the *Laws* (897b–98c), the motion of *nous* is a "revolution" which resembles circular motion, since both "move regularly, uniformly, within the same compass, around the same centre and in the same direction, according to one formula and one ordering plan" (898a–b). On the analogy between *nous* and circular motion, see E. N. Lee (1976); for a discussion of *kuklos*, cf. Bielfeldt (this volume). Aristotle attacks this analogy in *On the Soul* 1.3, 407a2–b11.

15 The literature on the Platonic allegory of the cave (and the fifth to seventh books of the *Republic* in

humans are pictured as chained in one place and constrained to look at the back wall of the cave. There, they see flickering shadows that Plato identifies as the phenomenal world of "appearance". Here, Plato identifies the physical realm with "becoming" or "appearance" and the immaterial Forms with "Being" and "Reality". Indeed, as we see in the *Timaeus*, the physical universe as a whole is a moving and time-bound "image" (*eikōn*; *agalma*) of an immaterial model, which is incorporeal and everlasting (37c–d). Thus, when we see objects in the physical realm, we are beholding images, not real beings. In the allegory of the cave, then, the physical eye sees mere shadows; the philosopher, by contrast, escapes from his chains and uses the "eye of the soul" (the mind) to journey to the luminous realm of the Forms, located outside the cave.[16] But his mind can only make this trip by separating itself from his body through the practice of philosophy.

Plato's theory of vision (physical and mental) is best understood in the context of his conception of the physical and psychic drives of human beings. According to Plato, the soul is not simply rational – it has emotions and desires that are associated with the body (and thus comprise the "irrational" portion of the soul).[17] Strangely, even the rational part of the soul has its own desire – a desire known as *erōs*. In short, the mind has its own motor power, since *erōs* drives the reason forward. In the philosopher, *erōs* has one single object: the Forms. In the irrational parts of the soul, by contrast, we find emotions and desires (*epithumiai*) that drag the soul towards earthly things: physical pleasure (food, sex, drink, etc.) and cultural "goods" such as money, honour or power. The philosopher must use his reason to control the irrational impulses that pull his soul towards the wrong things. Reason, then, must master the irrational appetitive desires and the bodily impulses themselves.

As Plato indicates, even the desire to see and gaze at earthly things can lead the soul astray. Consider, for example, the discussion of "lovers of sights" and "lovers of sounds" (*philēkooi, philotheamones*) in the *Republic* (475d). Out of all the varieties of "lover", the "lovers of sights and sounds" provide the model for the "lover of wisdom" (*philosophos*). Socrates describes the "lovers of sights and sounds" as men who "run around to all the Dionysian festivals, never leaving a single one out, either in the towns or in the cities" (475d). The Dionysian festivals featured exciting spectacles such as civic religious rituals, fancy processions and poetic performances (tragedy, comedy, dithyrambs). Plato uses these "lovers of sights and sounds" as an analogue for the philosopher. Like the "lovers of sights", the philosopher loves seeing. But the philosophers love the right kind of spectacle – "the sight of truth" (*tēs alētheias philotheamonas*; 475e). They "see" this truth with the "eye of

---

general) is substantial. See e.g. W. K. C. Guthrie (1975: 487–520); Annas (1981: 242–71; 1982; 1995); Kraut (1991); Barker & Warner (1992); McCabe (1992); Lear (2006).

16 It is luminous because the Form of the Good – which is higher than all the other Forms – has a sun-like quality that illuminates the entire realm of the Forms.

17 On Plato's conception of the soul in the *Republic* and other middle dialogues, see T. M. Robinson (1970); Annas (1981: 109–52); Bobonich (2002: 216–373); H. Lorenz (2006: 9–53). These texts offer detailed bibliographies on Plato's psychology.

the mind".[18] Seeing bodily spectacles, by contrast, leads the soul away from truth. Thus, Plato sets physical vision in opposition to rational "vision".

We come now to a fascinating part of Plato's account: the beautiful body on earth. In the *Phaedrus*, Socrates claims that the soul is everlasting and transmigrates into bodies again and again; there are also periods where the soul is not incarnate.[19] As he suggests, all human souls have "seen" the Forms when they were not encumbered by a body. However, some souls got a better look at the Forms than others did (247a–e). The incarnation of the soul into a body is, not surprisingly, a traumatic experience. The shock of being embodied makes most souls forget their past visions. Only the philosophers have some memory of the Forms that they once saw in a disincarnate state.

When human souls "saw" the Forms in a disincarnate state, Beauty "shone with light among those visions". For this reason, the Form of Beauty has a special status in the earthly realm: "when we came to earth we found it shining most clearly through the clearest of our senses".[20] Other Forms, such as those of Goodness and Justice, are not easy to see on earth, but the Form of Beauty has a bright sheen in the earthly realm (250c–d). Thus the philosopher can "clearly" behold the Form of Beauty "shining" when he sees beautiful human bodies in the physical realm.[21] In other dialogues, Plato claims that the senses offer unclear and deceptive data – data that needs to be adjusted and corrected by reason. Indeed, as we saw in the *Republic*, all the things that we see in the world are flickering shadows. In the *Phaedrus*, by contrast, Plato makes an exception for the beauty of a human body.[22] This beauty has an immediate effect on the viewer, triggering both psychic and physical reactions.

Plato proceeds to offer an account of a man perceiving the beautiful body of his beloved[23] – a vision that can have two different effects. It can drive a non-philosophical soul to seek and enjoy sex or it can trigger the philosophic soul to "recollect" the Form of Beauty. In this passage, Plato depicts the inner workings of the soul of a philosopher who encounters the beautiful body of his beloved. To portray the soul in action, Plato constructs the image of a charioteer (symbolizing reason) driving two horses, one white and one dark (253c–254e). The dark horse represents the appetitive part of the soul; the white horse is associated with pride and honour. When the man sees his beloved, his appetitive part (the dark horse), desperate for sex, drags him towards the beloved's body. At the same time, the rational part (the charioteer) pulls back on the reins, resisting sex. In the case of a

---

18 See Nightingale (2004: 72–93) on the visual metaphors which Plato used to describe *theōria* or intellectual contemplation, and compare too Squire's introduction to this volume.
19 We find similar accounts of the transmigration of the soul in the Myth of Er in the tenth book of Plato's *Republic*, the *Timaeus* and the tenth book of the *Laws*.
20 For accounts of the myth in the *Phaedrus*, see Nussbaum (1986: 200–33); G. R. F. Ferrari (1987: 113–203); Griswold (1986: 87–155); K. Morgan (2000: 210–40); Nightingale (2004: 139–86); Nichols (2010: 90–151).
21 This is because "there is no light in the earthly copies" of the other Forms, whereas the Form of Beauty radiates its own light (250b).
22 Strangely, Plato does not mention other kinds of beautiful things in the physical realm.
23 This account focusses on male homosexual relationships, but we can infer that a female philosopher would have the same set of impulses.

philosophic person, the sight of the beauty of the beloved's body causes his reason to recollect the Form of Beauty; his *erōs* for the Forms drives him upwards, away from the physical realm. The philosopher's soul thus "recollects those things which it once saw [in a disincarnate state] ... lifting up its vision to the things which are really real [i.e. the Forms] and disregarding those things which we now say are real" (249c). These moments of recollection mark the beginning of the development of the philosopher; once a philosopher has matured, he can grasp the Forms without having to see beauties on earth (instead, he uses philosophical arguments, which Plato calls "dialectic"). The mature philosopher, then, denies himself physical pleasure and opts for the more thrilling experience of "seeing" the Form of Beauty and other Forms.[24]

We come, finally, to the notion of attention. Clearly, in Plato, the goal of the philosopher is to see some things (the Forms) and blind himself to others (things on earth). In the *Republic*, Plato suggests that souls must be "turned" towards the Forms through philosophic education (518c, 521c). As he claims, all human minds have the capacity to "see" the Forms but are not turned in the right direction (518c). One does not need to put ideas into another person's mind but rather to "turn" him away from earthly things to the higher realm of the Forms. This involves teaching him to control his physical desires and to engage in a philosophical pursuit of the Forms, a discipline that will offer him "happiness" (*eudaimonia*) in an ongoing way. Since earthly things are always in flux, they simply cannot offer a person the continuous sense of happiness and wellbeing. They fill or fulfil our bodies and then pass away, creating unfulfilment. Note that Plato uses powerful rhetoric that is designed to "turn" the readers to look down on earthly things and affairs and to turn their minds upward to the Forms. Plato was well aware that he was countering powerful ideologies in his society: the desire for wealth, status, power and physical pleasure. Plato asks his readers to look away from these things. He offers an education in the "right" and "wrong" ways of seeing the world.

Plato uses rhetoric and imagistic discourse to "turn" his readers towards philosophy. By depicting the people in the physical realm as benighted cave-dwellers, and by portraying luminous incorporeal Beings that exist above and outside our own world, Plato aims to unsettle his readers and to make unfamiliar all that is familiar. He thus uses a rhetoric that says to the reader: "you do not know who or where you are". I have called this the "rhetoric of estrangement", since it aims to uproot and disorient the reader by depicting the ordinary world as strange and the seemingly alien realm of the Forms as "kindred" to the human soul.[25] By using this mode of rhetoric, Plato invites the reader to adopt the practice of philosophy.

In Plato, controlling bodily desires and impulses – including the desire to gaze at physical spectacles – involves a major psychic struggle. Reason must resist the desire to attend to things in the physical realm. To take one example, Plato relates the story

---

24 According to Plato, it is more thrilling because the Forms "feed" and "nourish" the soul, whereas bodily pleasures are temporary and leave one wanting more and more. Note that Plato depicts this interaction of the soul and forms in sexual terms: at *Republic* 490a–b, the mind of the philosopher, driven by *erōs*, "has intercourse" with the Forms, gets pregnant and "gives birth to truth and wisdom, at which point it is released from its birth-pangs".

25 See Nightingale (2004: 36–7, 96).

of a man named Leontius coming across corpses of people who had recently been killed at a public execution (*Republic* 439e–40a):

> At the same time Leontius desired (*epithumoi*) to see them and, simultaneously, was disgusted and turned himself away. For a time he struggled and covered his face, but he was conquered by his desire (*kratoumenos ... hupo tēs epithumias*): opening his eyes, he ran towards the corpses.

Clearly, Leontius felt a desire to see a spectacle that was repellent but also titillating. He realized that he should avert his gaze, but he could not overcome his appetites. We have already seen the "lovers of sights and sounds" rushing to every Dionysian festival to see poetic performances. As Plato says in the tenth book of the *Republic*, "when the best of us listen to Homer or some other tragic poet, representing one of the heroes in grief ... or men chanting and beating their breasts – we take pleasure (*chairomen*) and, surrendering ourselves, we follow sympathetically (*sumpaschontes*) and earnestly praise as a good poet whoever disposes us this way in the highest degree" (605c–d). Plato explains why the irrational part of the soul of a person who watches tragic spectacles enjoys feeling grief: "that part of the soul which, in the case of a man's personal misfortunes, was forcefully restrained, being hungry to cry and lament and to have its fill of this – because it desires these things by nature – is fed and gratified by the poets" (606a–b). In short, non-philosophical people are eager to see things that are shocking and pitiable because they want to experience emotions that they attempt to restrain in their private lives. They thus direct their energy and attention towards such spectacles. Certain physical spectacles – be they beautiful or ugly – generate an emotional response that overcomes reason and leads one to live a bad and unhappy life.

As a cultural critic and as a philosopher advocating a specific mode of life, Plato offered a detailed meditation on the desires and impulses that make a person pay attention to one thing and not another. He wrote his dialogues, in part, to get his readers to learn how to attend to higher realities – to "see Being" and look away from the realm of becoming. He praises specific desires and condemns others. He asks us to pay attention to the "truth" and to turn away from illusions.

Aristotle

In his account of vision, Aristotle rejects the theories of extramission and intromission. In *On the Soul*, he offers a very different model. First, he argues that vision takes place through the transparent medium of light – a medium that stretches from the external object to the interior of the eye. As he suggests, the eye itself must not touch the object; for if one puts an object right up against a person's eye, he or she will not be able to see. One needs the medium of light for the eye to see an object. But how does this happen?

According to Aristotle, sensation occurs when "that which perceives" is "moved (*kineisthai*) or acted upon (*paschein*) ... and this seems to be some kind of alteration (*alloiōsis*)" (*On the Soul* 2.5, 416b). In short, some sort of change takes place in the sense organ when an object is seen. In explaining how the eye sees objects, Aristotle introduces the notion of actuality and potentiality: "that which perceives" (the sense organ) exists only in potentiality and not in actuality. The sense organ is only actualized when it is in fact perceiving an object. As Aristotle puts it, "that which perceives (*to aisthētikon*) is in potentiality what the sense-object (*to aisthēton*) is in actuality" (*On the Soul* 2.5, 418a3–4). Once the eye is acted upon by an object, it becomes what that object is "in actuality".[26]

Aristotle clarifies this claim by saying that the eye "becomes *like*" the object in actuality. As he suggests (2.5, 417a17–20):

> All things are acted upon or moved by something that acts and exists in actuality. For this reason, the thing acted upon is in one sense acted upon by that which is like it (*homoion*), but in another sense by that which is unlike it (*anomoion*).[27] For, during the process of being acted upon, it is unlike [the object], but when it has been acted upon it is like [the object].[28]

Here, we must understand "the thing acted upon" as the eye. Of course the eye becomes "like" its object in a certain way: it becomes like the *form* of the object, not the object itself. For the eye receives sensible forms without their matter.[29] Vision, then, takes place when the eye receives the form of an object through the medium of light and thus becomes "like" that form.

Thus far, Aristotle has offered a coherent account. But, in *On the Soul* 2.5 (417b2–4), he creates confusion by claiming that there are different ways of being "acted upon". Earlier, he had spoken of the eye as being "acted upon" and "altered". Here, he says that (1) something that "acts upon" a sense organ can "alter" and "destroy" it by being unlike it; or, alternatively, (2) something that "acts upon" the sense organ can "actualize" the potentiality of the organ and "preserve" it by virtue of its own actuality and its similarity to the organ. In the case of vision, does an object "alter" and "destroy" the organ, or "preserve" and "actualize" it? Clearly, Aristotle was dealing with the second scenario in his discussion of perception: the object acting on the eye "actualizes" it (because the eye sees by becoming "like" the form of the object). However, he had said that seeing involved the eye being "altered" (which is mentioned in the first scenario). To elucidate his earlier point about alteration, Aristotle uses the analogy of the mental "knowledge" of

---

26 *On the Soul* 2.5, 416b33–5, 417a6–20, 418a3–4.
27 In discussing this "likeness", Aristotle says that the sense organs can receive the object "just as wax receives the sign (*sēmeion*) of a signet ring without its iron or gold; it receives the gold or bronze sign but not because the ring is gold or bronze. Likewise the sensation of each thing is acted upon (*paschei*) by that which has colour or flavour or sound, but not because it is said to be each of these but because it is this sort of thing (*toion*) in accordance with its logos" (*On the Soul* 2.12, 424a17–24): for discussion (from a visual cultural perspective), see Platt (2006).
28 For interpretations of Aristotle's theory of sight, see Sorabji (1974; 1992); Lear (1988); Nussbaum & Putnam (1992); Caston (2004); Gregoric (2007: 19–63).
29 Aristotle, *On Sense and the Sensible* 2, 438a–b; *On the Soul* 2.5 418a–419a, 2.11–12 424a–425b, 3.8 432a, 3.12 435a. In the *Metaphysics*, Aristotle offers a different account of vision, where he uses the theory of the extramission of visual rays (*Metaphysics* 2.9, 370a–3.4, 374b). On Aristotle's accounts of vision, see Sorabji (1974; 1992); Lear (1988: 101–16); A. Silverman (1989); Burnyeat (1992); Nussbaum & Putnam (1992); Everson (1997: esp. 24–5, 115–16).

things. Here, he claims (surprisingly) that "alteration" is not in fact the right term – or "alteration" should be used in a special sense (2.5, 417b5–9):

> For the thing possessing knowledge [the mind] achieves knowledge, which is either not an alteration (*alloiousthai*) at all – for it develops into its own self and actuality – or is a completely different kind of alteration. For this reason it is wrong to speak of that thing which is thinking, when it is thinking, as being "altered" (*alloiousthai*).

Like the mind of the knower that is actualized when it knows something, the eye, which has the potentiality to see, is actualized when it sees an object. This "actualization" of an eye that has the potential to see is not, as it seems, an "alteration" after all.

This leads to a serious problem. For earlier, Aristotle had said that perception involves an "alteration". Here, though, he appears to reject the notion of alteration. Aristotle himself admits that he cannot find the right terminology to express his point: "the difference between these cases [i.e. that which acts to destroy a sense organ and that which acts to preserve it] has no terminology"; therefore, "it is necessary to use the terms 'to be acted upon' (*paschein*) and 'to be altered' (*alloiousthai*) as though they are appropriate terms" (2.5 417a–b). He thus manages to keep the discourse of "alteration" while claiming that this is not really what he means.

This complex and seemingly contradictory account raises a key question: is it the eye that is "acted upon" by an object (a physiological change involving alteration) or is it the mind (a mental event involving actualization)? We may assume, based on Aristotle's initial account, that the eye is being acted upon and is "altered" when it receives the form of the object. But, as we have seen, Aristotle qualifies these claims in his discussion of alteration. It is impossible to resolve this question because Aristotle never fully explains how the human mind or the central sense organ (the heart) becomes aware of a given perception. Indeed, Aristotle's account of vision has led to major scholarly differences. Burnyeat famously offers a nonmaterial account of vision, arguing that perception does not require any concomitant material change in the eye.[30] In his view, the eye takes on the sensible form of the object only insofar as the mind becomes aware of the object. By contrast, scholars such as Sorabji offer a purely physiological account, claiming that the eye itself receives the form of the object and is altered by virtue of becoming like the form of the object.[31] Against the purely mental account, one can emphasize Aristotle's claims that perception always involves the body and that, in vision, the eye is "altered".[32] Against the purely physiological account, one can point to the fact that Aristotle explicitly says that the reception of the form of the object is an "actualization" and not an "alteration" (which is a movement [*kinēsis*], not an actualization [*energeia*]). As many scholars

---

30 See Burnyeat (1992); cf. Broadie (1993). Note that Aristotle criticizes the materialist accounts of Empedocles and Democritus (*Physics* 2.8; *On the Generation of Animals* 5.8).
31 Sorabji (1974; 1992).
32 Aristotle says (*On the Soul* 1.1, 403a3–8, a16–19, b17–19) that the soul does not undergo or create anything without the body; on the eye being "altered", see *On the Soul* 2.5, 416b32, 423b29; 3.2, 425b22–25.

have suggested, Aristotle is struggling to offer an account that is both physiological and mental.[33]

Although I cannot offer a satisfactory account of Aristotle's puzzling discussion of visual perception, it is clear that his theory does not fall squarely into the category of either "intromission" or "extramission". Rather, it focusses on the sense organ becoming like the form of an object through the medium of light and the eye and/or mind "seeing" the object.

Let us turn, finally, to Aristotle's notion of visual attention. In the *Parts of Animals*, Aristotle discusses viewing things that are beautiful and ugly. Here we find a very un-Platonic conception of attention. For Aristotle focusses on animals and their inner parts. As he suggests, some things in the world are visibly ugly but beautiful to the eye of the philosophical investigator. Aristotle uses the beautiful artwork as an analogy for the physical investigation of animals (*Parts of Animals* 645a):

> It would be absurd and strange if we rejoice when viewing artistic representations [of animals] – because then we are contemplating the art which fashioned them (*tēn dēmiourgēsasan technēn*), such as we find in painting or sculpture – but do not rejoice all the more in contemplating those things constructed by nature, when we are able to see the causes (*tas aitias kathoran*).

In this passage, Aristotle uses the example of viewing artistic representations to illustrate the philosophic investigation of the animal world. Even if an animal appears ugly or disgusting to the naked eye, the "eye" of the natural philosopher (who seeks to find out how the animal is put together) can see it as beautiful. Here, Aristotle draws a direct parallel between nature and art, thus encouraging us to view the animal body as a kind of design. In this case, nature is the designer, though it does not operate intentionally or deliberately (as human artists do). In drawing this analogy, Aristotle suggests that the investigation of animals gives the philosopher the same pleasure that people get when they look at beautiful artistic representations. Amazingly, ugly and repellent animals produce a visual and intellectual pleasure when viewed through the lens of natural philosophy.

Note that Aristotle has to turn to rhetoric and analogies to make this case to his readers. He clearly feels that the reader needs to be persuaded: "we should not behave like children and recoil from the investigation of even the lowliest animals, for there is something wondrous (*thaumaston*) in all natural things". As he goes on to say (645a):

> Heraclitus (it is reported) responded to some strangers who, though eager to meet him, stopped when they saw him warming himself at the stove. He told them to take heart and come in for, as he said, "there are gods even here". In like manner, we ought not be ashamed to enter into the investigation of animals, since in all of them there is something natural and beautiful (*phusikou kai kalou*).

---

33 See Nussbaum & Putnam (1992); Caston (2004); Gregoric (2007: 19–63): all three argue that Aristotle offers an account that is both physical and mental (with varying success).

Aristotle, like Plato, uses rhetoric to introduce a mode of vision that is fuelled by a desire to see certain things in a very specific way. He uses this rhetoric to instil desire in his readers. He understands that people who seek out statues and paintings want to enjoy a great work of art. It is this same desire, he suggests, that makes the philosopher want to discover the way that animal bodies work: indeed, given the ugliness of the innards, this desire must be a serious passion.

In contrast to Plato, Aristotle encourages the philosopher to pay attention to animals and to the natural world. For Plato, this would mean attending to (and enjoying) the deceptive flux of phenomena rather than to "true" higher realities. Indeed, Plato rejected the vision of seeming beauty in artworks as well as in natural things (making an exception for beautiful young male bodies). Still, Aristotle makes a similar move to Plato by using rhetoric to encourage the philosophical (or proto-philosophical) readers to direct their gaze towards specific things and to ignore other things. It is not enough to see things passively: one has to pay attention to the right objects. In short, the philosophers invite us to focus on some things at the expense of others. To do this, they must generate desire in the reader – the desire to look at a specific set of objects. Plato and Aristotle use powerful discourses to fuel the reader's desire to see the world in a "true" and "proper" way. That is, to see things as a philosopher (Platonic or Aristotelian).

Conclusion: vision in the bodily and mental realm

Each of my three philosophers offers a conception of vision that is embedded in a specific theory of the mind and of the physical cosmos. For Democritus, both mind and world are made of atoms: vision thus takes place by atomic motion. Plato, by contrast, creates a dualistic scheme that separates the immortal mind from the body. This mind is able to "see" the physical world through the eyes. And, if the person practises philosophy, he also "sees" the incorporeal and everlasting Forms (through the "eye of the mind"). In Plato's view, one should not trust the senses or seek for truth in the natural world: the mind must endeavour to escape from the body and to contemplate the Forms. Aristotle offers a different philosophical paradigm: in contrast to Plato, he places great value on the physical world.[34] He views the natural world teleologically and views things in terms of potentiality and actuality. In the case of vision, the eye has the potentiality to see objects; it becomes actualized (or, alternatively, altered) when it perceives an object through the medium of light. Although Aristotle offers a much more detailed account of vision than Democritus and Plato, his theory should not be seen as an improvement over his predecessors. Each thinker offers a theory that works within a specific philosophical paradigm.

It is worth noting that, in our present moment, many scientists and intellectuals would reject the philosophy of Plato and Aristotle and champion that of Democritus. As they argue, the universe is purely material and does not operate teleologically. This applies to humans as well: our minds are made of matter and are not

---

34 As one can see in his *Physics*, *History of Animals*, *On the Parts of Animals*, *On the Motion of Animals* and *On the Generation of Animals*. Needless to say, Aristotle sees theoretical contemplation (via *nous*) as the highest activity possible for man. Ultimately, he champions the mind over the body.

separable from the body (or immortal). This is a view that, of course, continues to be challenged: many religious believers believe in a separable and everlasting soul. And, even among philosophers, we continue to debate the relation between the brain and the mind. Of course, we now better understand the physiology of the eye and the way that it operates as a sensory organ. But our very consciousness – and the way that it operates – continues to confound us.

3

SIGHT AND THE PERSPECTIVES OF MATHEMATICS

The limits of ancient optics

Reviel Netz & Michael Squire

Within a book on *Sight and the Ancient Senses*, all manner of Graeco-Roman materials can be called upon as evidence – among them, philosophical discourses about seeing and knowing, visible objects which play out the dynamics of spectatorship and literary texts exploring sight in relation to (for example) hearing or reading. When approached from a global comparative perspective, however, one of classical antiquity's most original contributions was to conceive of sight *mathematically*. "Optics" is the word usually associated with this tradition, derived from the Greek term for "appearances" or "looks" (*ta optika*). Fundamental to ancient optics were ideas about reflection and refraction. Yet what ultimately defines this optical tradition, and what differentiates it from more philosophical modes (as introduced in the previous two chapters), is its "geometrical" approach: sight could be theorized in terms of mathematical relationships – that is, by determining the angles at which rays of light were emitted from either the eye or the perceived object.[1]

This chapter offers a preliminary survey of ancient optics, introducing some of the key writers while also showcasing their most important (albeit highly complex) mathematical theories. In one sense, our survey is designed to foreshadow A. Mark Smith's comments in the volume's final contribution. As Smith argues, ancient mathematical approaches to vision would have a substantial posthumous impact: on the one hand, they contributed to the rise of Islamic contributions in places like Baghdad and Cairo, especially between the ninth and eleventh centuries; on the other hand, those ancient Greek texts (heavily mediated through Arabic sources) would make their way back to the mediaeval western world, profoundly influencing ideas about

---

[1] There is no comprehensive book-length survey of ancient mathematical optics in English. Indeed, it says much about *ancient* optics – as we suggest in this chapter – that the best introductions come in the context of mediaeval traditions: the classic introductory analysis here is Lindberg (1976: 1–17); cf. Lindberg (1978) (a magisterial overview of mediaeval optics), along most recently with Darrigol (2012: esp. 1–15) and above all A. M. Smith (2015: esp. 23–129) (which appeared while this book was being copy-edited); for a hugely scintillating French introduction, centred around the contributions of Euclid and Ptolemy, see also G. Simon (1988). Important articles studying particular problems (largely concerned with questions of authorship and authenticity – which are central to this problematic field) include Knorr (1985; 1994) and Jones (1994); on the etymology of "optics", see also A. M. Smith (2015: 25–6). All translations in this chapter are our own.

both the sense of seeing and the science of geometry all the way up to the seventeenth century (and indeed beyond).

But where Smith's chapter is interested in issues of *legacy*, our contribution instead probes the *antiquity* of "ancient optics". Any such distinction between "antiquity" and its "legacy" is of course problematic, for reasons that will quickly become clear: our knowledge of ancient texts about sight and mathematics is necessarily filtered through the lens of subsequent engagements. Yet it is precisely that difficulty that our chapter sets out to explore: the very afterlife of ancient treatises, we suggest, risks blinding us to the *ancient* (pre-)history of "optics" in classical antiquity.

Our argument here therefore relates not just to "ancient optics", but to the "limits" of any such delineation. From a historical perspective, focussed around the ancient Greek and Roman world, ancient optics provides a far less coherent take on "sight and the ancient senses" than scholarly shorthand tends to assume. Although some scholars have argued that ancient mathematical approaches to vision actively directed the history of ancient image-making,[2] our preliminary aim is to ask just how influential ancient "optics" proved in antiquity – indeed, to question whether we can talk about optics as a straightforward category of ancient writing in the first place. This is not to deny that mathematical approaches to vision have a role in understanding ancient ideas about sight; as we explain, the chief importance of these texts lies in "geometricizing" vision, ambitiously framing issues of visual sensory perception around mathematical proportions, calculations and measurements. Crucially, though, the evidence available to us suggests that "optics" – at least as understood as a sort of delineated literary or scientific "genre" – was not a clearly defined field in antiquity: it had much less of a cultural presence than the later reception of ancient optical texts might have us think.

With these themes in mind, our chapter proceeds in three distinct but interconnected stages. We begin by surveying the extant sources, introducing the ten most important treatises (which most often survive in highly fragmentary, translated or otherwise refracted form). In the second section, we then evaluate this evidence in relation to the larger field of ancient optics, commenting on the specific contributions of Archytas in the fourth century BCE, Archimedes in the third century BCE and Ptolemy in the second century CE: in each case, what strikes us as significant about ancient "optical" texts is their sheer paucity – something which speaks volumes about historical understandings of the field. Third and finally, a brief conclusion returns to the cultural workings of ancient mathematical approaches to sight, and in broader comparative perspective. Once again, our aim here is to challenge and complicate conventional accounts: it is the combined ambition *and* failure to make a lasting contribution to the philosophy of vision that we find most remarkable about ancient "sight and the perspectives of mathematics".

---

2 See in particular Jeremy Tanner's chapter in the present volume. Among recent contributions, cf. especially Camerota (2002); Gros (2008); Stinson (2011); Sinisgalli (2012); specifically on Graeco-Roman "perspective" and the contributions of Euclid, see also Tobin (1990).

Gathering the sources

Let us begin, then, by surveying the different sources for Greek optics that are available to us. In what follows, we review the ten most substantial texts that survive (in some form or other) from antiquity. At the same time, we use those texts to sketch the broader parameters of the field.

It is worth prefacing our survey with two broader caveats. First, as we have already noted, the evidence available to us is highly fragmentary. Most of the extant sources have been mediated by later "translations" and "adaptations", above all those written in the mediaeval Arabic world. Even to call these sources "extant" is therefore somewhat misleading: while we know about numerous texts, we have very little information about their contexts; indeed, we are most often faced with treatises that have only a loose connection with their "original" forms – with Greek texts that have themselves been refracted through the prism of later Arabic engagements.

Our second qualification concerns the divergent remits of the ten works surveyed. All the texts that we introduce in this section were written at different times and places within the Graeco-Roman world (or else composed as much later Arabic or Latin translations after Greek treatises). But they were also written in connection with divergent themes and problems: they have less to do with a defined field of "optics", in other words, than with more specific mathematical dilemmas, hypotheses or theorems.[3]

Such caveats serve as a useful introduction to our first cluster of four texts, concerned as they are with "burning mirrors". The subject makes for a useful starting point: as we shall see, the delineation of "burning mirrors" throws into relief the diffuse nature of ancient optics at large; indeed, the field of "burning mirrors" has a (literal and metaphorical) focal point which optics as a whole lacks.

What did ancient thinkers mean by "burning mirrors"? At work was a key geometrical observation. If we assume that rays of light are reflected by certain mirror-like surfaces at predictable angles, or so the logic went, those reflecting surfaces have a common defining property: they cause the rays reflected onto them to converge around a single focal point. Ancient writers approach the issues theoretically (and above all, as we shall see, within the pictorial space of two-dimensional, mathematical diagrams). In more concrete terms, though, the geometrical "focal point" might also be interpreted as the point at which rays of light bring about a fire: the name "burning mirrors" thus relates to a geometrical explanation of a phenomenological trait – the capacity of a reflective surface to set something ablaze.

Ancient authors were generally less interested in the effects or physical qualities of mirrors than in their mathematical reflections of rays. One question concerned precisely which surfaces were able to produce such effects. More pressing, though, was the phenomenon's relationship to the larger field of advanced Greek geometry. This is where things become more technical. During the fourth century BCE, Greek geometers came to think about curved surfaces, and above all how special sorts of curves have

---

3 On the problems here, see A. M. Smith (2015: esp. 23–5): "Forming a coherent historical narrative from such a hodgepodge of textual snippets is therefore much like piecing a few scattered pottery shards together into some recognizable shape, with most of them missing or known only through description" (24).

remarkable mathematical properties: because these curves have certain proportions – containing within them particular areas and lines that are equal to one other – they proved helpful for theorizing and solving all manner of geometrical problems. The curves themselves were discussed as "conic sections" (obtained from the intersection of a conical surface with a plane), and further catalogued under the subheadings of parabola, hyperbola and ellipse (each relating at once to graphic forms and mathematical proportions). Without getting overly bogged down in the important technicalities, the crucial point is that the properties of such curves intersected with the development of advanced Greek geometry: on the one hand, the study of "burning mirrors" belongs within a theoretical tradition that relates "focal points" to conic sections (especially the parabola); on the other hand, such studies emerged not so much as an exercise in physics, but as a result of advances in pure geometry.

This brief introduction takes us to our first four texts, which all deal in some way or other with "burning mirrors", and which we present here in their most likely chronological order:[4]

1   Our first text is the opening section of a treatise by Diocles *On Burning Mirrors*, known only in later Arabic translation. The Greek original can most plausibly be dated to around 200 BCE: it studies the reflection of rays of light from not only "parabolic" but also "circular" surfaces. Diocles was evidently concerned with concrete problems related to the mechanical construction of a parabolic surface: as a result, his treatise was perhaps intended not as a pure exercise in geometrical ingenuity, but as an answer to more practical concerns within a more mechanical context.[5]

2   "Dtrūms" is the name attached to a second Arabic treatise, albeit this time preserved anonymously.[6] The theme, context and sophistication of this text are roughly analogous to those of Diocles'. Although the author of the original Greek treatise is unknown, he is most likely datable to the Hellenistic age.

3   The *Mechanical Paradoxes* by Anthemius of Tralles (a sixth-century CE Greek author) was also known and translated by Arabic authors: in this case, Anthemius' Greek text also survives in a fragment that discusses the construction of "burning mirrors" based on not only the parabola but also the ellipse.[7]

---

4   Needless to say, the number and nature of these "burning mirror" treatises has been debated: for the sake of this introductory survey, we nonetheless pass over controversies that are not directly relevant to our general argument. Rashed (2000: 325–42), for example, would wish to include an additional Arabic text attributed to a certain "Didymus"; as argued by Toomer (1976: 28), however, this is almost certainly a later Arabic forgery. Several scholars – most recently Knorr (1983) – have likewise suggested that the author of the "Bobbio fragment" (our fourth source) was the "Anthemius" responsible for the *Mechanical Paradoxes* (our third source): while Knorr's argument has been countered by e.g. Rashed (2000: 264–71), we do not mean to rule out the possibility.

5   We will see this duality recur again and again throughout the course of this chapter (on which, see Toomer 1976): a problem which emerges as a pure discussion in advanced geometry is *also* discussed in terms of its physical implementation; in the case of Diocles specifically (as indeed of numerous other writers), that potential for physical implementation was most likely introduced as a thought experiment.

6   See Rashed (2000: 194–213). There is an interesting question here about how to explain the title: there are several Greek names whose root consonants could have been garbled into the Arabic word ("Dtrūms"), but "Demetrius" suggests itself as the most plausible.

7   See Rashed (2000: 349–59).

4   Finally, there is a small fragment surviving within a palimpsest manuscript – known as the "Bobbio fragment" – whose script dates from around the sixth to seventh centuries CE.[8] The "Bobbio fragment" mentions a property of the parabola relevant for its use in burning mirrors, and then proceeds to discuss a spherical "burning mirror".

Before proceeding to other extant works, it is worth pausing to note how this corpus of treatises on "burning mirrors" form a compact cluster. Because these texts address a specific geometrical problem, their structural concern is best understood in relation to other specialized types of pure geometry.[9] In that sense, at least, these four texts are easy to categorize, concerned as they are with a particular geometrical objective ("find a curve such that an arbitrary line, falling upon the curve and reflected on it, will be reflected to a given point"). The situation with our remaining texts is quite different: while we all too often subsume them under the category of "Greek optics", there is in fact no single theme that all of them have in common.

So what allows us to classify our remaining "optical" texts together? Despite the lack of any single umbrella conceptual category, these six other treatises cluster around three main (and sometimes intersecting) thematic approaches. The first relates to the mathematical study of visual appearances, based on direct lines of sight (although the term implies some rather anachronistic connotations, we refer to it below under the category of "perspective").[10] Second is the study of images on mirrors, whether plane, convex or concave: this is referred to as "catoptrics", from the Greek word *katoptron* or "mirror" (but to be distinguished from the treatises dedicated to "burning mirrors" already discussed).[11] A third approach pertains to the study of instruments of measuring or "sighting" based on optical relations: we refer to this as "dioptrics", from *dioptra*, a Greek instrument of land measurement.

Defining "optics" in these three interrelated ways allows us to introduce six more extant texts – which we present, once again, in tentative chronological order, while this time grouping together multiple works by the same supposed author:

5–6 First come two Greek texts attributed to the Euclid, written (if genuinely Euclidean) at the turn of the fourth and third centuries BCE: on the one hand, a

---

8   Cf. Huxley (1959: 53–8). In this case, the treatise is known in Greek. Significantly, though, the text was not directly preserved or copied but survives through a series of fortuitous accidents: this fragmentary "palimpsest" relates to a manuscript whose text was later "deleted", with its material then recycled for use in a different context. Because the text is so fragmentary, we cannot be sure of its relation to other preserved works.
9   Some examples might include "squaring the circle" (i.e. finding a square equal to a given circle), "trisecting the angle" (dividing an angle into three equal parts) and "doubling the cube" (finding two lines in continuous proportion between two given lines – equivalent to the problem of finding a cubic root).
10 For more on "perspective" in the strict sense – and above all, the relationship between ancient mathematical theories pertaining to lines of sight and ancient painting – see Tanner's chapter in this volume.
11 The distinction is important: texts on "burning mirrors" were concerned with the geometry of focal points within conic sections; these "catoptric" texts were interested in the production of mirror-images.

treatise on *Optics*; on the other, a treatise on *Catoptrics*.[12] The Euclidean *Optics* is the only text introduced in this section to have received anything like a "commentary" in antiquity: it was discussed in the sixth book of Pappus of Alexandria's mathematically oriented *Collection* (composed in the fourth century CE).[13] The Euclidean attribution of the *Catoptrics* in particular has been almost universally contested. In our view, the Euclidean authorship of both texts can be persuasively defended;[14] if one accepts the Euclidean attribution of these two treatises, moreover, they provide our earliest extant examples – both preserved in original Greek form – of ancient mathematical approaches to sight.

7–8 Next come two more works, this time attributed to Hero (likely active in the early Imperial era).[15] On the one hand, there survives an original Greek treatise on *Dioptra* (covering, among other things, dioptrics), which is almost universally accepted as Hero's work.[16] On the other hand is a treatise – this one surviving in a Latin translation – on *Catoptrics*.[17] The Heronic attribution of the *Catoptrics* remains hypothetical, since the transmitted Latin translation in fact ascribes the work to Ptolemy (active in the second century CE).

9 Whatever we make of the "Heronic" *Catoptrics*' attribution to Ptolemy, we can be sure that Ptolemy himself wrote an independent treatise on optics in the second century CE.[18] Ptolemy's text is by far the most important ancient survival within the field. But it is available to us today only in truncated and translated form. In its extant state, the treatise consists of four books (books two to five) of a treatise that could originally have been substantially longer (the fifth book itself survives in an incomplete form, so that we do not know whether, or for how long, the text continued); the loss of the opening book is especially unfortunate since we cannot be sure how Ptolemy originally framed his project. More importantly still, the text is once again known only via a later translation – in this case, one that is doubly removed from Ptolemy's original: we are dealing with a twelfth-century *Latin* translation of an *Arabic* translation of Ptolemy's *Greek* text…

Regardless of its original form, Ptolemy's text was certainly a wide-ranging treatise. The core of the extant Latin translation consists of an extensive study of

---

12 The "Euclidean" *Optics* and *Catoptrics* are edited in Heiberg (1895: 2–246, 286–342) respectively. In the case of the *Optics*, we in fact have two quite distinct versions of the Greek text: Heiberg thought that one was early, the other a late antique revision, but his judgement has been reversed by e.g. Knorr (1994) and Jones (1994). Whatever we decide here, the very instability of the text – and the lack of an agreed "canonical" version – is worth emphasizing.
13 On Pappus, *Collection* 6.80–103, see below, n.26.
14 For the strongest arguments in favour of authenticity, see above all Knorr (1985) (with reference to the major controversies).
15 The precise date remains unknown: the argument advanced by Neugebauer (1938) – namely, that Hero was active in 62 CE – is shown by Sidoli (2005) to have been based on a misunderstanding.
16 See Schöne (1903: 188–314).
17 Jones (2001: 153–66). Jones provides an English translation of the *Catoptrics*; also helpful, however, is the earlier German translation by Schmidt (1900: 317–65) (who translates and discusses both of Hero's surviving works).
18 Even this statement should be qualified, however: we mean that *we* feel sure of the attribution – even though others (notably Knorr 1985) have questioned the attribution (cf. below, p. 79). For the text, see Lejeune (1989) and A. M. Smith (1996), along with the detailed discussion of A. M. Smith (2015: 76–129).

catoptrics (in the third and fourth books), and the original work seems also to have included a physical discussion of light and vision (in the now lost first book).[19] The extant second book contains an array of psychological and physical solutions to optical illusions, with only occasional geometrical considerations. Although incomplete, the fifth book is likewise a remarkable treatment of the problem of refraction.

10. Finally, we have a short, additional elementary treatise on optics (covering both perspective and catoptrics) by a late antique author named Damianus of Larissa. Damianus makes a number of references to previous writers and traditions; the resulting text also testifies to the ways in which mathematical optics came to be absorbed into a late antique educational curriculum.[20]

Our survey of ancient "mathematical" approaches to sight has introduced ten extant texts – four of them dedicated to "burning mirrors" and six to issues of perspective, catoptrics and dioptrics. As is already clear, what we label "optics" was understood to encompass a variety of intellectual questions and approaches. Indeed, when we put aside the special problem of "burning mirrors" and consider the six extant works in optics more generally, we find – even within one and the same treatise – a similar heterogeneity at work.[21]

The point is worth emphasizing because it introduces something fundamental about ancient traditions. In all of these extant texts, we are dealing with related discussions of different optical phenomena, sometimes set sequentially side-by-side in one and the same treatise. Crucially, though, these texts display little overarching deductive structure: what unifies them is less their specific questions or subjects than their mathematical technique of answering them. Wherever we look among extant works, we find sight being approached in relation to a set of geometrical calculations – as something that can be reduced to a series of lines and angles. What facilitates this geometrical reduction, moreover, is the integration of two-dimensional, linear diagrams: as so often in antiquity, these works testify to the mastery of abstract pictorial schemata over the exact sciences.[22]

To demonstrate both the principles and working practices that inform extant

---

19 Cf. A. M. Smith (2015: 76–129, esp. 77–8). Our interpretation here is based on the extant summary at the beginning of the *Optics*' second book ("we have explained everything that one can gather about what enables light and visual flux to interact"). The handful of ancient testimonies to Ptolemy's *Optics* (cf. Lejeune 1989: 271) all relate to physical questions concerning light – colours, the ether, etc.: it therefore seems likely that these kinds of generalized references allude to the earlier (and more introductory) passages of the work. But did the missing first book also treat issues of "perspective" specifically? Scholarship (especially scholarship on sight-lines in ancient painting) often assumes this to have been the case. Were this to have been so, however, we would expect the basic underlying assumptions – arguments about vision and its linear operation – to have been mentioned in the opening of the second book. Whatever we decide here, the absence of any Ptolemaic commentary on "perspective" is revealing.

20 See Schöne (1897: 2–22). The later absorption of such texts into a much later curriculum probably also explains the two distinct versions of Euclid's earlier treatise on *Optics*: see above, n.12.

21 C. Webster (2014) draws out that heterogeneity very persuasively – with particular reference to the Euclidean *Optics*. We would only add that the same heterogeneity is even more evident in the Euclidean *Catoptrics*.

22 On the place and role of such diagrams in ancient technical texts, see especially Stückelberger (1994),

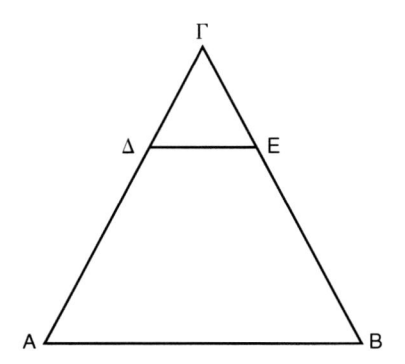

Figure 3.1 Modern reconstruction diagram based on chapter 21 of Euclid's *Optics* (image reproduced by kind permission of Eunsoo Lee).

works, consider just one specific passage: a translated excerpt from the Euclidean *Optics* (our fifth text above), which we pair here with a reconstructed diagram (Figure 3.1). Although the Euclidean authenticity of this text has been questioned – and by no means all scholars agree about its supposed date between the fourth and the third centuries BCE – the passage is typical for its geometrical formulation and reliance on a real or imagined picture (*Optics* 21):

> To tell, how much is the given length:
> Let there be the given length, AB, and let Γ be the eye, and let the requirement be to know how much is the length AB. (a) Let rays fall: ΓA, ΓB; (b) let a chance point Δ be taken on a ray, close to the eye; (c) and let a line parallel to AB, <namely> ΔE, be drawn through the point Δ.
> (1) Now, since ΔE has been drawn parallel to one of the sides of the triangle ABΓ, <namely, parallel to> BA, (2) ΓΔ to ΔE is as ΓA to AB. (3) But since the ratio of ΓΔ to ΔE is known, (4) the ratio of AΓ to AB is therefore known as well. (5) Since AΓ is also known, therefore AB is known as well.

Rather than be drawn into the mathematical principles at work here, we introduce the passage to demonstrate two broader points. The first concerns the Euclidean dependence on the medium of the diagram: to understand the underlying mathematics, readers are required to visualize the various lines described. In this sense, diagrams serve as graphic proof for a mathematical approach to visual perception, developing the sorts of formulations found in pure geometry. At the same time, the technique also draws on the tools of plane geometry, using the similarity between geometrical figures, produced by angles, to derive claims about proportions (which in turn determine the size of the perceived object).

The second point to note about the passage concerns its very language of analysis. There can be no denying Euclid's "abstraction" of sight: the seeing subject, no less

---

along with Roby (forthcoming); for discussions of ancient manuscript "illustrations" more generally, see Squire (2009: 122–39; 2011a: 129–39), with more detailed bibliography.

than the object seen, is conceptualized according to a series of conjectural formulae; so it is, moreover, that within the geometrical shapes that Euclid imagines, each line is labelled according to a series of schematizing Greek letters (ΑΒΓ, ΑΒ, ΓΑ, etc.). But our "Euclidean" passage does not overlook more physical modes of interpretation altogether: note, for example, how Γ is not delineated as something immaterial ("the point of vision"), but rather labelled as a physical, embodied, seeing "eye" (*omma* in Greek).[23] The formulation is typical of other works, which often specify their referents in concrete terms: for all their geometrical rationale, the workings of sight are simultaneously understood in real, tangible ways. We shall return to this observation in the chapter's conclusion, discussing " 'ancient' optics in comparative perspective". For now, though, it is simply worth noting the materialist point: again and again, and from Euclid onwards, we find authors referring their geometrical lines and angles back to tangible entities – whether the substance of mirrors, the refracted forms of objects, the burned flax set ablaze by a "burning mirror" (Euclid, *Catoptrics* 30) or an obliquely perceived chariot-wheel (Euclid, *Optics* 36).

Evaluating the evidence

So much for the extant texts available to us – whether in their original Greek, or in later Latin or Arabic translations. But is there any additional, *indirect* evidence for the development of ancient mathematical approaches to sight? The number of testimonia available here is in fact remarkably small. As a collective, moreover, these texts suggest an understanding of "optics" that is much more restricted – at least in terms of cultural presence – than that of later Arabic (and by extension western mediaeval) intellectual traditions.

This is not to deny that there were at least some additional ancient texts that are now lost. Sometimes we hear of treatises that – though no longer extant – were deemed of sufficient value to attract reference in surviving works. In his extant mechanical works, for example, Biton – a Hellenistic author interested in mechanics – refers to his own (today non-extant) contribution to dioptrics.[24] Likewise, there survives a brief inset on dioptrics within Julius Africanus' *Cesti* or "Quilts" (a late antique miscellany "stitched" together from all manner of different fields).[25] Within the field of astronomic texts too, we occasionally find short sections dedicated to dioptrics (as in Archimedes' *Sand-Reckoner* from the third century BCE).[26] When it

---

23 For antiquity's understanding of the "embodied eye", see Squire's introduction to this volume.
24 See Biton, *Construction of War Engines and Artillery* 52–3, with Marsden (1971: 70).
25 See Julius Africanus, *Cesti* 7.15. Several treatises with seemingly "optical" titles are likewise reported for a number of early philosophers, among them Democritus (cf. Diogenes Laertius 9.48) and Philip of Opus (*Suda, s.v.* "φιλόσοφος": cf. Adler 1928–38: 4.733). Since Philip of Opus was a follower of Plato – and thought to have written fairly extensively on astronomical treatises – discussions of mathematical approaches to vision would certainly seem plausible. As so often (cf. Rudolph and Nightingale's chapters in this volume), we are reduced to little more than guesswork when it comes to Democritus.
26 There are a couple of additional "optical" insets in other astronomical treatises besides: it appears likely, for example, that a tiny excerpt on the science of optics (cf. Schöne 1897: 22–31) could have been lifted from Geminus' astronomy. Dedicated optical passages pop up in astronomical commentaries too – for instance, in Theon of Alexandria's commentary on Ptolemy's *Syntaxis* (cf. Rome 1931–43:

comes to the specific field of catoptrics, there again sometimes survive short passages incorporated within diverse generic contexts: so it is, for example, that Aristotle's *On Meteorology* contains a couple of extended catoptric-like arguments concerning the bending of light (even though these are most likely later interpolations, as has recently been suggested).[27]

In all of these passages, optical discussions of dioptrics and catoptrics are introduced as a digression – and as a rare aside. To be sure, optical considerations are brought to bear on specific issues and problems. The crucial point, though, is that they are introduced in the context of doing *something else*. What makes this scenario all the more striking is that it contrasts with that of other mathematical fields. When it comes to geometry, astronomy and even music, we have not only a larger group of extant texts, but also a greater number of ancient commentaries and references. Comparatively speaking, optical themes seem to have attracted much less attention: most ancient writers only rarely discussed optical themes; indeed, as our previous paragraph confirms, to find *any* evidence we have to rely on wholly obscure (and often much later) texts.

How should we make sense of this situation? Before tackling that question, it is worth pausing to say something about three particular Greek thinkers championed for their innovative "optical" approaches: Archytas (in the fourth century BCE), Archimedes (in the third century BCE) and Ptolemy (in the second century CE). There can be no doubting the intellectual advances of these writers. But what interests us about their respective contributions is once again the difficulties we face in assessing them. Whatever their originality and ambition, these writers seem in fact to have had only a tangential impact on ancient intellectual thought: historically speaking, the importance of Archytas, Archimedes and Ptolemy lies less in their contributions to ancient intellectual history than in their *lack* of immediate influence.

The argument that Archytas, Archimedes and Ptolemy were responsible for evolutionary development of ancient optics is both difficult and controversial.[28] To deal first with Archytas in the fourth century BCE, we can be sure that this figure played a major role in rendering earlier Pythagorean speculations into a more scientific, mathematical approach: Archytas made substantial contributions in the study of music (effectively rendering it into a scientific, mathematical field); he also tackled all manner of other problems concerning three-dimensional geometry and mechanics. As a result of these innovations, or indeed in connection with them, it is tantalizing

---

2.334–80, esp. 349–50). Likewise, the source that comes closest to an ancient commentary on a work in mathematical optics (Pappus, *Collection* 6.80–103 – a brief series of observations on the Euclidean *Optics*, penned in the fourth century CE) is included among Pappus' other commentaries on astronomical works. It was perhaps because of this arrangement (original to Pappus himself?) that the Euclidean *Optics* came to be transmitted within an astronomical context: cf. Heiberg (1882: 152).

27 On the likely elaborations of Aristotle's *On Meteorology* by later mathematically inclined readers, see Vitrac (2002). If we accept these passages as later interpolations, that situation can be compared with other later commentaries on Aristotle's work: note, for example, the inclusion of mathematical optics in late Aristotelian commentary on *On Meteorology* (e.g. Olympiodorus, *On Aristotle's Meteorology* 209–14). In their original Aristotelian form, such passages probably had the character of an ordinary philosophical text in physics, albeit accompanied by diagrams.

28 With this in mind, we therefore sketch only the basics here: Netz intends to develop the argument at greater length elsewhere.

to think that Archytas' seminal contributions also stretched to mathematical optics.[29] But the evidence here is indirect and fragmentary: the most important source is a brief aside within a Latin forensic speech by Apuleius in the second century CE (which in fact only cites Archytas' intromissionist theory of visual perception).[30]

The same Apuleian passage (*Apology* 15–16) also constitutes our most important source for the contributions of Archimedes in the third century BCE. Still discussing mirror-images and their contribution to philosophy, Apuleius goes on to note how Archimedes wrote on such issues in a "huge volume" (*uolumine ingenti*):

> [These and many other phenomena of the same sort] Archimedes of Syracuse treated in a massive volume – a man greatly admirable above all others for his subtlety in all branches of geometry, but who was perhaps particularly remarkable for his frequent and attentive inspection of the mirror (*quod inspexerat speculum saepe ac diligenter*).

What is striking about this statement is not just that Archimedes' work on catoptrics has not survived, but that it is barely attested among other writers. We do have a very late antique source that refers to a possible contribution that Archimedes made to the study of refraction.[31] If we take the reference at face value, we might likewise think that Archimedes himself pioneered this particular branch of optics; indeed, it becomes likely that the more complicated and advanced developments in the study of reflection and refraction, found in Ptolemy's Imperial Roman *Optics*, are ultimately descended (at least in some form) from Archimedes' earlier Hellenistic work.[32] But this is mere speculation. Whatever Archimedes' contribution – and his later Ptolemaic influence – the overriding response of ancient authors to Archimedes' mathematical works on vision is silence.

Ptolemy's own contribution to optics is not quite lost. But as we have already noted (with reference to the ninth source discussed in the previous section), the only available version of his treatise comes down to us in highly refracted form: a Latin translation descended from an Arabic translation of a second-century CE Greek text (and even then we have access only to the work's second to fifth books). Now, whether we interpret this as a "loss" or a "gain" will depend on personal

---

29 This interpretation was made most forcefully by Burnyeat (2005). For the figure (and contributions) of Archytas, see especially Huffman (2005).
30 Apuleius, *Apology* 15–16: see Butler & Owen (1914: 42) on *Apology* 15; more generally on Apuleius' intellectual context, see Fletcher (2014).
31 The main piece of evidence comes in Olympiodorus' commentary on Aristotle's *On Meteorology* (chapters 209–14): cf. above, n.27. Olympiodorus was active in the sixth century CE: he already belonged, in other words, to a world more characteristically "Byzantine" than "ancient" in intellectual outlook.
32 It should perhaps be emphasized here that, somewhat perversely, we generally know less about Ptolemy than we do about Archytas and Archimedes: on the one hand, we have numerous (and often substantial) mathematical testimonies for other branches of Archytas' mathematical contributions; on the other, we have still more scraps of evidence concerning Archimedes (not least via extant Greek parts of some ten treatises – perhaps the bulk of his work; after all Archimedes is among the best-preserved of all authors of his time, and indeed across all genres). It is clear that Archimedes' *Optics* is his most important work to have been lost.

perspective. But it is nonetheless worth emphasizing that, of all the various mathematical branches to which Ptolemy made a contribution, this is least well attested. As so often with optical subjects, ancient writers in fact seem to have paid only marginal attention to Ptolemy's contribution. So little interest did Ptolemy's *Optics* spark in antiquity, indeed, that some scholars have gone so far as to doubt its Ptolemaic authorship (and authenticity) altogether.[33] Now, our own opinion here is that such doubts are unfounded: despite the lack of corroboratory attestations, we are dealing, in our view, with an authentically "Ptolemaic" work. But that there should be room for doubt is revealing: the very absence of ancient attestations – the very lack of ancient writers discussing, commenting upon or responding to the *Optics* – has led to a situation where scholars have even questioned its Ptolemaic authorship.

Such issues of evidence return us squarely to the field of optics in antiquity. Even when it comes to the most important thinkers – to figures like Archytas, Archimedes and Ptolemy – we have remarkably little to go on. As we have already noted, moreover, this situation is further corroborated by the small number of extant ancient texts available to us.

So how should that situation be explained? At work, in our view, is an essential fact about how optics operated in antiquity. Wherever we look among extant ancient authors, we find optical modes of conceptualizing sight being introduced in a manner that is strikingly divergent from other fields. Even among later commentators on Aristotle, talk of optical lines and angles is applied in a different way from (for example) astronomical or musical parallels. For all the long-standing Greek philosophical critique on vision, optical considerations were never commonplace in broader critical discussions of the workings of the eye: while thinkers talk at length about different visual media (or for that matter about the physical nature of light and the psychology of illusion), mathematical approaches were only rarely brought to bear on such philosophical dilemmas.

Of course, not all ancient writers shied away from mathematical approaches to vision. But they do seem to have conceptualized such approaches quite differently from later Arabic and mediaeval authors: for all their advances, ancient optical models of theorizing sight were not generally seen to lend themselves to the same sorts of working questions. Aristotle's own mathematical take on vision, for example, draws parallels between visual phenomena and music (so that colours are understood as different ratios or perhaps harmonies between the poles of black and white).[34] Likewise, in his second-century CE treatise on *The Usefulness of the Parts*, Galen introduces mathematical parallels to explore the anatomy of eyes (albeit less to develop an optical argument about sight than to further a stereometrical hypothesis about brain anatomy).[35] While both authors turn to mathematics to discuss visual radiation (Aristotle) or the workings of the visual organ (Galen), they rely on

---

33 See Knorr (1985). For "Ptolemy's little or no discernible effect on visual theory in late antiquity" – despite its "relative comprehensiveness, coherence, and methodological sophistication" – see A. M. Smith (2015: 130–1; quotation from 130).
34 See Aristotle, *On Sense and the Sensible* 3, 439a–40b, with Sorabji (1972).
35 Galen, *The Usefulness of the Parts* 821.4–822.13. Even here, it is worth noting the simplicity of Galen's concern: rather than develop a fully fledged optical approach, the author points out that the anatomy of the visual nerves corresponds to a plane intersected by two lines; crucially, though, he

broader mathematical theories rather than a specific branch of mathematical optics. Aristotle and Galen turn to the mathematics of music and geometry, we might conclude, because these spheres – unlike mathematical optics – were domains of wider cultural familiarity.

What we are faced with here is the very *weakness* of ancient mathematical optics, at least as an intellectual discourse with any widespread cultural familiarity. So much so, in fact, that we may begin to wonder if mathematical optics ever became a settled mathematical genre to teach or collect in antiquity. There seems to have been no readily identifiable idea of "an author in optics"; generically, too, "optics" seems never to have been understood as an independent field or even subfield of mathematics (in the same way that it was among later thinkers). In astronomy, harmonics or mechanics – the other "applied" fields of the ancient exact sciences – it is easy to find authors whose primary identity was defined by those fields. In the case of optics, by contrast, nearly all authors known to have contributed to the field are renowned for just one or two works (and always within the context of a larger mathematical corpus): while there was a distinct ancient *technique* of mathematical optics, this did not define – at least within antiquity itself – a distinct authorial identity.

What does all this mean for approaching ancient mathematical optics? We can perhaps marshal our findings into three interrelated hypotheses. Our first argument is a qualitative one: that there was no straightforward authorial category of the "optical" author in antiquity. This qualitative argument relies on two preliminary premises. (i) There were no authors producing an entire series of works on optics in antiquity (in the manner, for example, of Ptolemy's series of astronomical works): to put the point more forcefully, and to prefigure A. Mark Smith's comments in the book's final chapter, we might say that there was no ancient equivalent to Alhacen in the tenth to eleventh centuries.[36] (ii) We have also suggested that the ancient authors who did write on optical themes treated it as a "minor" (and loosely demarcated) subfield: in antiquity, those writers who turned to optics (or at least those known to have done so) typically wrote on subjects like geometry, astronomy, mechanics or music. Take premises (i) and (ii) together, and two more general deductions follow: (a) that the number of ancient *authors* in mathematical optics is a useful index for the total number of ancient *works* in the field; (b) that the field was top-heavy – produced primarily by the main authors whose corpus extended across the various mathematical subdisciplines.

Our second – and inherently more hypothetical – hypothesis corroborates this qualitative point by quantitative means, relating to the total number of broadly

---

does not make any substantive reference to the sorts of angles and proportions used in mathematical optics.

36 On Alhacen and his creative "resynthesizing" of earlier Graeco-Roman texts, see Smith's chapter in this volume (with further references to bibliography). Put simply, our argument here is based on the fact that Alhacen wrote several works in optics and might be said to have seen this field as constitutive to his identity as an author. In this strong sense, it is therefore possible to delineate him as the first "author on optics". Of course, from the standpoint of the history of ideas, we do not mean to minimize the continuity between ancient and mediaeval optics (nor indeed to deny the heterogeneity of mediaeval traditions). In terms of genre and authorship, however, the Middle Ages signal a transition – one that would ultimately give mathematical approaches to seeing a more central role in the constitution of overall cultural understandings of sight.

"optical" treatises composed in antiquity. When it comes to the field of ancient sciences as a whole, there is an argument for determining an approximate ratio between authors known to us from ancient testimonia and the total number of authors within a field; this ratio is of course beyond empirical proof, but there are good reasons for considering it to be somewhere in the region of 1:5.[37] In terms of authors whose works have been entirely lost, it is likewise fair to assume that, at least in most cases, these writers were minor figures in the field (since this is how academic fields structure themselves).[38] Taking as our starting point some 20 attested works in total (of which, as we have surveyed, ten survive in some more or less preserved form), and using an approximate ratio of 1:5 as an upper guide for the total number of works (and indeed something broadly similar for the total number of authors), we might conclude that, between the fifth century and late antiquity, there were perhaps fewer than 100 works related to mathematical optical fields. Such figures are necessarily provocative. Still, the general point is illuminating: even with a broad definition of "optics", and with fairly generous set of criteria and figures, we would be looking at an average of less than one "optical" work per decade.[39]

Allow us to add a third argument, this time pertaining to the "contents" of ancient optical treatises. As we have said, there survives but a single work touching significantly on perspective (namely the Euclidean *Optics*), but three works that are mostly dedicated to catoptrics (if we include not just the Euclidean and "Heronian" *Catoptrics*, but also Pappus' brief fourth-century CE commentary on the Euclidean *Optics*).[40] This spread seems significant – not this time as a matter of statistics, but rather as an indicator of interpretative leaning. Needless to say, there were perhaps some additional works on scenography lost to us today – a number of more or less mechanical treatises that applied some aspect of "perspective" theory to stagecraft.[41] That qualification notwithstanding, ancient optics seems to have been approached in a specific way: most contributions emphasized the more technically challenging field of catoptrics over and above the more strictly perspectival optics of later (Arabic and

---

[37] See Netz (forthcoming), developing the argument of Netz (1999: 283–4; 2002: 201–8). It is of course possible that some prolific authors did write on optical subjects. Still, in the case of optics, this situation seems unlikely: given what we have said above about the "top-heavy field", it is possible that the ratio of attested to lost authors was even lower than 1:5.

[38] Cf. Collins (1998: 33): of course, being a major author to some extent correlates with being a prolific author.

[39] Since this sort of approach can all too easily provoke outrage, it is perhaps worth saying that we use it merely to articulate, in quantitative terms, a series of qualitative assumptions. But this is emphatically not a case of circular argumentation, since our assumptions are derived from the historical evidence available to us (as surveyed in this chapter). Needless to say, a plausible counter-argument can be advanced: assuming there was so little interest in antiquity in mathematical optics, after all, one might think that a work in this field would have, per se, a smaller likelihood of survival. But this riposte would clearly be wrong-headed. After all, so much of what we know about ancient optical works comes to us via the corpora of more central and prolific authors (which themselves have a higher likelihood of survival). All this corroborates the pattern that we have observed: works in ancient mathematical optics are *less* transmitted among the corpora of the *more* transmitted authors.

[40] On Pappus' *Collection*, see above n.26.

[41] Vitruvius attests to the existence of such a tradition and claims that it goes back to the early days of Classical theatre itself: see Tanner (this volume) on Vitruvius, *On Architecture* 1.2 (with further bibliography and parallels).

western mediaeval) intellectual tradition. Insofar as optics existed as a field in antiquity, it served as a forum to test and display an author's geometrical ingenuity. We only need consider the case of "burning mirror" treatises to appreciate the point – in fact the most abstract and mathematical branch of optics in antiquity.

Conclusion: "ancient" optics in comparative perspective

We began this chapter by promising a survey of what ancient optics *was*. We have ended up – whether as a result of chance survivals, or (as we maintain) on the basis of the evidence available to us – with some important conclusions about what ancient optics was *not*. Within a book on *Sight and the Ancient Senses*, our survey allows us to tender two broader arguments by way of conclusion.

First, we have suggested that, at least during Graeco-Roman antiquity, the field of optics had a markedly smaller cultural presence than that of other mathematical fields. The conclusion is important, since as we have already hinted (and as A. Mark Smith argues in much greater detail in the final chapter), that scenario no longer holds true for the Arabic-Latin reception of the ancient tradition – or, indeed, for the more modern reception of ancient science.[42] To express the point more strongly, it seems that mathematical approaches to sight played a quite different role in antiquity from the ones they would subsequently come to play. It is not as if the field of mathematical optics was some kind of a scientific dead-end in antiquity, nor that ancient geometrical approaches to vision were somehow intellectually unambitious: to avoid optics, we have suggested, was instead a cultural rather than a scientific decision. That this situation should *change* between Graeco-Roman antiquity and the later landscapes of the Arabic-speaking East (and even more so in those of mediaeval Europe) is likewise hugely significant: despite its important intellectual prehistory, ancient optics only emerges as a cultural field in a *post*-antique world.[43]

Our second conclusion is more complex, but relates this time to the place of optics within the broader pursuits of ancient philosophy. For if optics never gained significant cultural or intellectual traction, how should this situation be explained? To phrase the question more provocatively: was there something *about* ancient mathematical approaches to vision that rendered such approaches unsuitable (or at least unattractive) within the broader pursuits of ancient philosophy?

Before tackling that question head-on, it is worth first returning to some of Kelli Rudolph's and Andrea Nightingale's observations in the preceding two chapters. Right from the very beginnings of Greek philosophy, Rudolph and Nightingale remind us, ancient thinkers probed the nature of light and sight, developing complex models of theorizing the processes of someone seeing and something being seen. In theory, at least, ancient mathematical approaches to vision *could* have comfortably fitted into this tradition; indeed, that confluence would define the subsequent fate of optics in mediaeval and Renaissance Europe. Likewise, it seems that Greek

---

42 See Smith (this volume).
43 The question of *how* to explain that change is the one we find most exciting – even if beyond the remit of the present chapter (and the capabilities of its authors): although we would take issue with many of his conclusions, fundamental, it seems to us, is the argument about an eastern/western "exchange of glances" ("Blickwechsel") developed by Belting (2011a: esp. 4).

philosophy itself proved decisive in shaping the projects of mathematical writers. Ptolemy's discussion of optical illusion – and how mathematics can account for it – should probably be understood in this way: as an active attempt to insert mathematical approaches to sight within a larger philosophical tradition. Although we have much less to go on in the case of Archytas (in the fourth century BCE), something similar might plausibly be claimed: if we can take his contribution to music as an indicative guide to his work on more optical themes, it is likely that Archytas provided an early account of light and sight that was conceived in geometrical terms – that is, as an account that again framed its mathematical approach to vision in response to a specific set of philosophical issues.

Whatever ancient philosophy's contribution to optics, mathematical approaches to vision made only the most tangential contributions to ancient philosophy. Consider here the case of Plato, as discussed in greater detail by Andrea Nightingale in this volume. When Plato set out the mathematical disciplines in the seventh book of his *Republic* – discussing the "ideal" curriculum for his ideal citizens to learn in his ideal state – he includes several mathematical subjects, including astronomy and music.[44] Yet Plato scrupulously avoids any mention of mechanics and optics. It is obvious why mechanics should have no place in a Platonic education: by turning students back from immaterial truths to concrete applications – from ideals to earthly forms – mechanics risked sullying the minds of the young. But why should this hold true of optics? It is not that Plato had no precedents to turn to here: remember, for example, the possible case of Archytas. Plato appears instead to have ignored such mathematical approaches to sight because sensory visual perception was itself something to be transcended by philosophy. Yes, mathematics could conceive of vision in geometrical terms. But – at least for Plato – geometry was perhaps deemed an insufficient means of overcoming the sensory force of seeing: the intellectual stakes of sight were too important to be left to those philosophically suspect mathematicians.[45]

All this helps to explain why mathematical approaches to sight never quite made it onto the ancient philosophical and cultural radar. The limited place of optics within ancient intellectual landscapes, we suggest, has to do with the very frameworks of ancient philosophy. We have already seen (at the end of our first section) how ancient mathematical discussions of sight are premised on a curious sort of "ontological" duality. On the one hand, mathematical optics was marked by a technique of radical idealization so that the subjects and objects of sight could be schematized according to a simple system of lines and angles.[46] On the other hand, we saw how that idealized abstraction was always underpinned by a sense of material

---

44 The following argument about Plato largely follows Burnyeat (2005: esp. 35–6); cf. Lloyd (1990).
45 On such debates in Presocratic and Classical philosophy – and the role of Plato and Aristotle in directing more materially and sensorially attuned branches of aesthetics along an abstractified "idealist" path – the most important recent analysis is Porter (2010: esp. 1–21). Porter has frequent recourse to "optics". Throughout his book, though, Porter exploits the term to collapse a plurality of different cultural definitions: as a result, Porter never quite defines this cultural, intellectual and above all mathematical field within (or indeed across) antiquity.
46 Indeed, it seems that the more abstract its set-up, the more actively it was in fact pursued by mathematicians: so it is, for example, that the most sustained open research question – that of "burning mirrors" – effectively turned optics into a branch of studying conic sections.

substantiation. More than in any other mathematical field save mechanics, concrete physical references pervade the field of optics. The earliest Euclidean texts demonstrate – in what are, mathematically speaking, gratuitous asides – such physical instantiations: they deal not just with circles seen obliquely, but with *wheels* specifically (*Optics* 36), or indeed with the material *flax* set ablaze by the rays of a "burning mirror" (*Catoptrics* 30). Even while maintaining an idealized sort of conceptual abstraction, then, ancient mathematicians recurrently assert a physical significance: such approaches to sight are grounded in the *material* world.

In our view, this tension between the abstract and the material reveals something fundamental about optics – or at least the Greek prehistory of optics – within broader ancient ideas about sight. To study the surface and volume of a sphere was something mathematicians could understand within a self-defined intellectual remit: because they were not intruding on anyone else's territory, they could proceed in their own independent way, relying on mathematical techniques which they had themselves forged and developed. To account for light and sight, by contrast, was a central problem of Greek philosophy, and one that was firmly established as a problem of physics. This put ancient mathematical approaches to sight in a metaphorical "catch-22". If they were to emphasize the field's unique philosophical strength – that is, its radical idealization – ancient mathematical writers risked indulging in a mere *jeu d'esprit*: their calculations were in danger of seeming divorced from the serious concerns which made questions of light and sight so philosophically important in the first place.[47] Conversely, if such interventions were to claim any sort of philosophical authority, they could be exposed for their conceptual weakness – as a theory of light and sight without either epistemology or metaphysics to support it.

That "catch-22" was the ultimate fate of optics in antiquity. Oscillating uneasily between the material and the immaterial, ancient optics subsisted as a field where a few masters could display their technical virtuosity, but only rarely receive more mainstream philosophical attention. For optics to emerge as a more substantial intellectual field – for it to be capable of any more mainstream philosophical impact – would require a wholesale intellectual revolution: mathematics would itself have to emerge as a way of doing philosophy.

We leave that revolution – facilitated by the innovations of Islamic mathematicians at the end of the first millennium, who transformed an ancient impetus for mathematizing rays of light into an effective science of seeing – for A. Mark Smith to take up in the book's final chapter. Suffice it to say here that this change was premised on a transformed way of thinking about not only sight, but also knowledge, philosophy and empirical experience. It was only in that intellectually removed context that optics could emerge in any meaningful sense. And it was only via the distinctive contributions of Arabic mathematics that ancient mathematical approaches to sight would give rise to a modern theory of matter.[48]

---

47 It is perhaps for this reason that the most radically idealizing works (those in the "burning mirrors" tradition, and likely also the contributions of Archimedes) emphasized the physical *meaning* of the optical argument.

48 The authors are grateful to Jeremy Tanner and A. Mark Smith for their comments on an earlier draft of this chapter.

4

SIGHT AND REFLEXIVITY
Theorizing vision in Greek vase-painting

Jonas Grethlein

The link between sight and pictures needs no arguing: we see pictures. In the nineteenth century, Konrad Fielder even claimed that pictorial representation seamlessly continued the activity of vision. Creating an "expression that is independent of other sensual perception",[1] pictures are pure "visual objects" (*Sichtbarkeitsgebilde*). Such a view contrasts with more recent approaches by phenomenologists and neuroscientists who instead emphasize that our response to pictures is bodily.[2] Seeing pictures, they try to show, involves our entire sensorimotor system. These qualifications notwithstanding, the eye remains the organ through which we access pictures.

Sight can also be represented *in* pictures.[3] Many figurative paintings feature characters that look at each other. Those who are not fully integrated into the pictorial action have been aptly labelled spectator figures. Figures may even look out of the picture and fix their gaze onto the external beholder. Given that sight is also the sense by which we perceive pictures, its pictorial representation always has the potential to be reflexive: the gaze of figures in a picture can reflect or refract the act of vision by which the beholder takes in the representation. In his investigation of *Absorption and Theatricality* in eighteenth-century painting, Michael Fried argues that the French painter Jean-Baptiste-Siméon Chardin "found in the absorption of his figures both a natural correlative for his own engrossment in the act of painting and a proleptic mirroring of what he trusted would be the absorption of the beholder before the finished work".[4] The absorption, for example, of the young man regarding the bubble of the blowpipe and the boy watching him mirrors the response of the imagined "ideal" beholder to the painting (Figure 4.1).

In this chapter, I set out to explore how Archaic and Classical vase-painting engaged with the reflexivity encapsulated in representations of sight. By doing so, my inquiry aims to complement the analysis of vision in ancient philosophy and

---

1 Fiedler (1991: 1.161).
2 E.g. Sobchack (1992); O'Regan & Noë (2001).
3 On the representation of vision in ancient vase-painting, see Vernant (1990b); Frontisi-Ducroux (1995); Mack (2002); Stansbury-O'Donnell (2006); Haug (2015). On represented eyes, see (in addition to Squire's introduction) Martens (1992: 284–363); Steinhart (1995); Moser von Filseck (1996); Rivière-Adonon (2011). On the trope of "pictorial reflexivity", cf. Lissarrague (1987); Martens (1992). More generally on vision and ancient art, see especially Bérard (1984); Elsner (1995; 2007b); Fredrick (2002).
4 Fried (1980: 51).

Figure 4.1 Jean-Baptiste-Siméon Chardin, *Soap Bubbles*, 1733–4. New York, Metropolitan Museum of Art: inv. 49.24 (© bpk – Bildarchiv preussischer Kulturbesitz, Berlin: Bildagentur für Kunst, Kultur und Geschichte).

science tackled in the preceding chapters. And yet my chapter also introduces a self-consciously visual dimension: to show how not only ancient texts, but also ancient *pictures* offer meditations on the act of viewing. These reflections are by no means strictly separated from each other. As we shall see, the symposium (or Greek "drinking-party") was just one place where verbal and visual reflections on sight could intersect with one another. Indeed, the painted reflections that we shall explore may themselves have instigated and influenced discussions about sight and optics which would then have fed into professional treatises.

Painted pottery provides rich fodder for such an investigation. Wherever we look, we find Greek vase-painters showcasing an extraordinary sensitivity to the act of seeing. One need only think about the prominence of eye motifs on Greek vases.

Figure 4.2 Attic black-figure *olpē* by the Amasis Painter, *ca.* 550–500 BCE. New York, Metropolitan Museum of Art: inv. 59.11.17 (© bpk – Bildarchiv preussischer Kulturbesitz, Berlin: Bildagentur für Kunst, Kultur und Geschichte).

Eyes that are free-floating and unattached to a represented body, thereby oscillating between the realms of figure and ornament, can be traced back to the Bronze Age, but they become particularly pervasive in Attic black-figure pottery.[5] We find eyes emblazoned in the space that is encircled by the handles of various vessels. A good number of black-figure *olpai* also showcase two triangles on the reverse: the round black space in the centre of these triangles is now commonly identified as an eye (Figure 4.2).[6] Many black-figure cups from Athens and Chalcis surviving from the last third of the sixth century BCE likewise feature two large eyes on the exterior between their two handles, sometimes also on both sides (Figure 4.3). There are numerous other vessels with eyes, including Rhodian jugs, Ionian bowls and Attic *skyphoi*.

The motif of the eye has been interpreted in various ways. Some scholars ascribe to it an apotropaic function,[7] while others are inclined to see (above all in eye-cups) depictions of masks.[8] The effect of animation – turning the vessel into a visage – is

---

5 Cf. Martens (1992: 295–328), along with Squire's introduction and Bielfeldt's chapter (this volume).
6 Jacobsthal (1927: 16) was the first to develop this argument.
7 This interpretation seems to go back to Jahn (1885).
8 E.g. G. Ferrari (1986); Kunisch (1990).

Figure 4.3 Attic red-figure "eye-cup" (Type A) by the Hischylus Potter, *ca.* 525 BCE. Cambridge, Fitzwilliam Museum: inv. 37.14 (© The Fitzwilliams Museum, Cambridge).

the subject of an important study by Didier Martens.[9] The result is particularly striking in the case of eye-cups which become a mask in the context of their sympotic use: the cup covers the face of the drinker and shows the face painted on the exterior to fellow symposiasts. What has received considerably less attention is the fact that eyes represent the very organ by which the beholder perceives the picture. Besides their capacity to anthropomorphize the vessel, eyes are also always charged with the potential for reflexivity. When the beholder regards an eye regarding him, he is alerted to his own act of seeing. The motif of the eye itself visualizes – and reflects upon – the beholder's act of viewing.

Instead of focussing solely on the painted motif of the eye, this chapter sets out to explore the representation of vision in the narrative scenes of Greek painted pottery. Spectator figures have already attracted a fair amount of attention here. Mark Stansbury-O'Donnell, for example, has proposed a system of classification that is predicated on the degree of involvement of spectators in the represented action.[10] Perhaps more importantly, he has also explored how spectator figures guide the onlooker's eye: serving as models for social and gender identification, they help the

---

9 Martens (1992: 284–363).
10 Stansbury-O'Donnell (2006).

viewer relate to the representation, mediating the viewer's own act of visual response in a given context. My approach in this chapter will differ from Stansbury-O'Donnell's in two important aspects. First, it is not spectator figures per se but rather figures fully involved in the action that will be the object of my inquiry. Second, I will touch on the socio-cultural contexts of viewing only in my conclusion. While one aspect of this chapter concerns the cultural particularities of Greek "visuality" (above all within the symposium), my main point is concerned with the workings of pictorial seeing across different visual cultures.

It is crucial to note that the gaze of the person beholding a picture, while potentially mirroring the gaze of figures depicted on it, ultimately works in a different sort of way. Pictorial seeing is distinct from ordinary seeing. To explain its peculiar nature, Richard Wollheim coined the concept of "seeing-in".[11] When we see pictures, we simultaneously see the represented object and the representation. While regarding, say, the shoes painted by van Gogh, we are aware not only of that represented object, but also of the canvas and the brush-strokes that let us see the shoes. We may either concentrate on the represented object as when we muse on the worn look of the shoes, or else, attending to the blots of colour on the canvas, focus on the means of its representation. Crucially, however, seeing something in a picture necessarily implies both aspects: this "twofoldedness" distinguishes the act of "seeing-in" from the everyday act of "seeing-as".

Wollheim's distinction provides a key conceptual backdrop to the present chapter. I will focus on two narrative scenes in which the presentation of sight throws into relief the detachment of "seeing-in": first the blinding of Polyphemus and second the beheading of the Gorgon Medusa. My discussion of these motifs on vases from different epochs, regions and contexts may perhaps be disconcerting to specialists in ancient iconography who, for good reasons, are used to paying close attention to such distinctions. And yet, such panoramic roaming across firmly established boundaries (perhaps the privilege of somebody approaching the field from outside its specific disciplinary remit...) is, I hope, justified: it showcases something that is as intriguing as it is pervasive in ancient vase-painting. While many of the chapters in this book home in on verbal theories of vision, this chapter explores a theory in the literal as well as the metaphorical sense: a visually mediated reflection on vision.

Combining the motif of Polyphemus with that of Medusa, the Eleusis amphora provides an apt starting point for my argument. The chapter then examines further depictions of Polyphemus and Medusa. In both subjects, as we shall see, the representation of vision revealingly interacts with the beholder's own act of seeing. While "seeing-in" seems to be a transhistorical phenomenon, the reflexivity of the vases discussed gains a specific connotation from their contexts. This will be spelt out for *gorgoneion* motifs painted in the inside space ("tondo") of Attic drinking-cups, which nicely demonstrate how such visual reflexivity can feed into the negotiation of identities at the symposium.

---

11 Wollheim (1980: 205–26; 1987: 43–79).

The Eleusis amphora: seeing beyond death

The Eleusis amphora from the first half of the seventh century BCE (Figures 4.4 and 4.5) was used as a vessel for the corpse of a young boy. Because the body was too big to fit through the amphora's mouth, the amphora evidently had to be cut into two halves before being put back together with the corpse inside. The three scenes painted on the pot are remarkable. The neck features the blinding of Polyphemus, the shoulder shows a boar fighting with a lion and the body depicts two Gorgons chasing Perseus, who is protected by Athena while the headless Medusa is floating horizontally through the picture. The reverse of the amphora is ornamental, but it ought to be noted that the lower part of Medusa extends into it and that ornaments also permeate the pictorial space on the front. Figuration and ornament are thus interlaced with one other.[12]

The use of white and black colour sparks an intense and complex interconnection between the three images on the front: the white of Odysseus on the neck[13] is continued by the white head of the lion and, a little further to the right, by the white figure of Athena, the protector of Odysseus. The black colour aligns Polyphemus with the body of the lion and Perseus just as, on the left side, Odysseus' comrades correspond with the boar and the two Gorgons. The links established through colour are reinforced through the repetition of forms:[14] the legs of the four figures on the belly form four triangles that, besides echoing the form of an ornamental band at the bottom of the vessel, are taken up by the legs of the animals on the shoulder and the legs of the men on the neck. The three pictures on the Eleusis amphora are thus formally related to each other in manifold ways that forgo a neat structuralist scheme and open up the space for various interpretations.

For the purposes of my argument, it is the dialogue between the assault against Polyphemus and the chase of Perseus that is most important. Both scenes feature an encounter of man with monster, albeit inversely: while three men attack Polyphemus, Perseus is pursued by two Gorgons (a third depicted Gorgon is already dead). Strikingly, both motifs revolve around vision: where Odysseus and his comrades ram the spear into the open eye of Polyphemus, the Gorgons threaten to petrify their viewers with their gaze. As on most other ancient vases, the Gorgons are here represented *en face*; they direct their gaze at the beholder of the amphora. The petrifying look of the Gorgons therefore at once corresponds and contrasts with the blinding of Polyphemus. While the one scene exacerbates the power of the eye, the other reveals its vulnerability.

Robin Osborne, who was the first to champion the vase's prominent reflections on ideas about vision, relates this imagery to the use of the amphora as a burial-container:[15]

> The whole vase is a construal of death, a discussion of the nature of death as sensory deprivation. Death comes when the visual world closes in on you when you yourself are to be seen in a pot. To die is to enter Hades, and to enter Hades is, by the very name, to become unseeing and unseen.

---

12 On the ornaments decorating the vase, see Martens (1992: 258–64). On the blurred borderline between figuration and ornament in Archaic vase-painting, Himmelmann (1968) is still essential.
13 Cf. R. Osborne (1988: 2); Martens (1992: 261–2).
14 Cf. Martens (1992: 261–2).
15 R. Osborne (1988: 4). The author's argument is reprised and developed in R. Osborne (1998: 57–61).

Figure 4.4 Detail of a Protoattic black-figure amphora by the Polyphemus Painter, *ca.* 670–660 BCE. Eleusis, Archaeological Museum: inv. 2630 (© DAI Athen, DAI-Neg. D-DAI-ATH-Eleusis 544 (Eva-Maria Czakó)).

The visual metaphor for dying permits us to connect the representation of vision to the vessel and its function. One of the objections raised against this interpretation is that the use of the Eleusis amphora as a coffin was only secondary.[16] While I do not reckon that this detracts from the interaction between the representation of the vase

---

16 For critiques of R. Osborne's interpretation of the Eleusis amphora and its use for reconstructing social history, see I. Morris (1993: 28–32); Whitley (1994: 63–5).

Figure 4.5 Protoattic black-figure amphora by the Polyphemus Painter, *ca.* 670–660 BCE. Eleusis, Archaeological Museum: inv. 2630 (© DAI Athen, DAI-Neg. D-DAI-ATH-Eleusis 546 (Eva-Maria Czakó)).

and its (secondary) use, I think that, more profoundly, the Eleusis amphora also furnishes an iconographic meditation on pictorial seeing. The eyes of the Gorgons meet the eyes of the viewer and invite him to relate the gaze depicted *on* the vase to his gaze *at* the vase. More specifically, the *en face* depiction of the Gorgons underscores that the beholder is immune to their visual threat. The petrification is even reversed: it is not the viewers of the vase, but rather the Gorgons who are petrified as figures on clay.[17] This inversion is highlighted by much later poets who refer to the victims of Medusa as pictures or statues (e.g. Ovid, *Metamorphoses* 5.198–9, 206, 226–9). The pictorial metaphor for petrification chiastically intersects with the metaphorical petrification effected by painting. Being petrified on a vase, Medusa cannot transform her onlookers into images anymore.

The pictorial discharging of Medusa's gaze here makes the peculiar quality of "seeing-in" palpable. We see not simply the represented object, but simultaneously

17 For more on the visual cultural stakes of viewing the Gorgon, see also Turner (this volume).

the represented object and its representation. Something which would be lethal to see is here instead transformed into a harmless object to "see in" the picture.[18] As Hans Jonas aptly puts it in an essay on *homo pictor*, pictorial mimesis "can represent the dangerous without endangering, the harmful without harming, the desirable without satiating".[19] The *en face* depiction of the Gorgons thus drives home that pictures let the beholder engage in an act of viewing that is bracketed by the frame of "as-if". We see the Gorgon and at the same time know that what we see is only a representation, not the real Gorgon which would petrify us.

In this sense, the viewer's gaze makes for a striking contrast with the scene depicted on the vase's neck. While the viewer looks undisturbedly at the vase, Polyphemus is shown losing his eyesight. More pointedly, we might say that the beholder's eyes here look upon the very loss of seeing. The subject of representation thus throws into relief its own act of mediation. Better, perhaps, the depiction of the loss of the organ by which the beholder perceives the representation serves to highlight this act of perception. In viewing the blinding of Polyphemus, the beholder simultaneously experiences that safe distance which characterizes "seeing-in": the annihilation of eyesight illuminates the detachment of pictorial seeing.

This sort of self-referential interpretation is further supported by the play with the framing of the images, blurring the boundaries between representation and represented object. Strikingly, all figures with the exception of the Medusa exceed the height of their framing friezes (stretching beyond both its lower and upper borders). Likewise, the spear rammed into Polyphemus' eye is identical to the upper parameter of the framed image. It is only between Odysseus and Polyphemus, where it has been lowered to reach its target, that the spear within the picture distinguishes itself from its outer frame.[20] As Robin Osborne notes: "the stake which blinds the Cyclops is also the frame of the picture ... As the beam is thrust into his eye the Cyclops' whole visual world collapses in on itself; as Polyphemus' sight is destroyed so also is the picture, and with it Polyphemus and his attackers."[21]

But is the picture actually destroyed? For external viewers, the depiction is not in fact impaired, as Osborne seems to propose; instead, it is fixed on the vase – as visible now as it was in the seventh century BCE. We might say that the partial convergence of external frame with figurative stake consequently emphasizes the distinction between represented subject and its representation. The instrument that extinguishes Polyphemus' eyesight simultaneously provides the frame that renders the picture stable as object of the beholder's gaze. Polyphemus' loss of vision does not so much question as throw into relief the gaze of the viewer, whom not even the frontal stare of the Gorgons can petrify. The Eleusis amphora presents the viewer with a visual reflection on the force and vulnerability of all seeing at one and the same time.

In combining two motifs centring on vision, the Eleusis amphora reinforces their reflexivity. Both the blinding of Polyphemus and the stare of the Gorgons relate to

---

18 From alternative angles and with different nuances, Frontisi-Ducroux (1995: 73) and Mack (2002: 589) argue that the depiction of the Gorgon heralds the "naissance de l'image" – and hence the "aetiology of the gaze".
19 Jonas (1994: 111).
20 Cf. Hurwit (1977: 24–5) and S. P. Morris (1984: 44–5), who both also adduce parallels.
21 R. Osborne (1988: 4).

the beholder's act of viewing. While Polyphemus' loss of eyesight contrasts with the detachment of pictorial seeing, the frontal depiction of the Gorgon iconographically highlights the twofoldedness of all pictorial perception. The Eleusis amphora homes in on the topic of viewing to reflect not only on death, but also on pictorial representation and its reception.

Seeing (and not seeing) the blinding of Polyphemus

Before proceeding, it is perhaps worth saying something here about my assumption that the Eleusis amphora and other vases actually depict the "Homeric" Polyphemus.[22] The scepticism of so much recent scholarship about interpreting such Geometric and early Archaic scenes in relation to Homeric epic is of course legitimate.[23] But just as generations of earlier scholars had been rather uncritical of their "Homericizing" assumptions, so too is there now a danger of raising the bar too high. Michael Squire has argued compellingly that ancient narrative vase-painting ought not to be approached as illustrations of texts.[24] Picture and text instead offer two distinct working media. Differences between poetic and visual scenes may be due to the conventions of the medium and the liberty of the artist, who was of course not bound to reproduce every detail of the Homeric account. If, for example, the object rammed into the eye of the giant does not exactly conform to the stake of "burning" olive wood described by Homer, or if the number of protagonists deviates from that of the comrades said to accompany Odysseus, this does not necessarily mean that another story is depicted. Indeed, the drinking vessel held by the giant on the Eleusis amphora and other vases might suggest a specific connection with the Homeric Polyphemus: there is a rich tradition of stories narrating encounters with a one-eyed monster, but the narrative prerequisite of the Cyclops' drunkenness seems a distinctive feature of the *Odyssey*.[25] I will thus continue to speak of "Polyphemus" in what follows, although my overriding argument about sight and reflexivity does not hinge on the identification.

The reflexivity inherent in the blinding of Polyphemus on the Eleusis amphora is paralleled and further developed in other depictions of the same motif, as two examples may illustrate. Paintings that show Polyphemus not in profile, but rather looking out of the image, underscore the correspondence between subject and medium of representation.[26] A *skyphos* from around 500 BCE shows three men driving a long stick into the right eye of Polyphemus, who is lying with part of his upper body propped up to what seems to be the rock of his cave (Figure 4.6). Polyphemus' right hand touches the back of his head, while the left hand lies next to his body. The posture expresses the relaxed state of Polyphemus who is caught off-guard. The

---

22 For catalogue-collections of such images, see Touchefeu-Meynier (1968: 10–41; 1992: 956–7) and Burgess (2001: 118–19). For discussion, see especially Schefold (1993: 158–61); Andreae (1996); Giuliani (2003: 96–105, 159–67); von den Hoff (2009).
23 E.g. Snodgrass (1998); Burgess (2001). See also Lowenstam (1992).
24 See Squire (2009: 122–39, esp. 126), discussing "Polyphemus" scenes explicitly.
25 Cf. Giuliani (2003: 111).
26 On the effect of an *en-face* presentation of eyes, see Frontisi-Ducroux (1995: 90–3); Moser von Filseck (1996: 259); Neer (2002b: 79–81).

SIGHT AND REFLEXIVITY

Figure 4.6 Attic black-figure *skyphos* by the Theseus Painter, *ca.* 525–475 BCE. Berlin, Staatliche Museen (Antikensammlung): inv. 3283 (© bpk – Bildarchiv preussischer Kulturbesitz, Berlin: Bildagentur für Kunst, Kultur und Geschichte).

turning of the Cyclops' head away from the attackers emphasizes the surprise by which he is taken. The depiction of the Cyclops with two eyes may be owed not so much to a non-Homeric tradition of the saga as to the *schema* of the frontal face (as already witnessed in the context of the Eleusis amphora's Gorgons).[27] For my interpretation, it is worth noting that the gaze of Polyphemus responds to the gaze of the viewer: our eyes meet the eyes of the Cyclops, the one blinded, the other seeing. The parallel between Polyphemus and external viewer is further highlighted by the *kantharos* next to Polyphemus, mirroring as it does the *skyphos* that we are viewing.[28]

A black-figure pseudo-Chalcidian amphora dating from the last third of the sixth century BCE stresses the thematic of eyesight by a slightly different means (Figure 4.7). Here, we do not in fact see the eye of Polyphemus, occluded as it is by the stake that the Greeks ram into it. The invisibility of the eye makes Polyphemus' blinding tangible for the viewers: the Cyclops' loss of (active) sight is iconographically expressed through the viewers' loss of (passive) sight; the represented act of blinding is at once paralleled by and mediated through the representational occlusion of the organ for seeing. As if to underscore the point, the neck of the amphora features a

---

27 Cf. Giuliani (2003: 164–5). Andreae (1962: 193–4) argues that Polyphemus here is modelled on earlier representations of Alcyoneus.
28 On the self-referential effect of vases depicted on vases, see Frontisi-Ducroux (1995: 97–9).

Figure 4.7 Pseudo-Chalcidian black-figure amphora, *ca.* 520 BCE. London, British Museum: inv. 1866.0805.3 (© Trustees of the British Museum).

Silen's mask with two large eyes staring frontally out at the viewer. Such masks recur on Chalcidian vases, adding a Dionysian theme.[29] On the vase under discussion, however, the Silen's mask takes on an additional significance: the prominent eyes lend emphasis to the sense of seeing and underscore that the organ which Polyphemus is about to lose on the amphora's body is the one by which we perceive this scene. The negative representation of viewing *on* the vase throws into relief the safety of our gaze *at* the vase; it drives home the special mediations of pictorial seeing.

Reflecting (on) Medusa's petrified stare

We have seen that the Eleusis amphora pairs the blinding of Polyphemus with the frontal stare of the Gorgons. The annihilation of sight contrasts effectively with a gaze that has the power to annihilate. The gaze of Medusa has invited a wide range of critical responses, among them prominent psychoanalytical and gender readings.[30] Rainer Mack, in particular, has shown that the *en face* depiction of Medusa also

---

29 Cf. Steinhart (1995: 62–3). Note also G. Ferrari (1986: 11–20) and Frontisi-Ducroux (1995: 100–3) on masks on vases.
30 For a collection of texts on Medusa from Homer to Cixous, see Garber & Vickers (2003); for various artistic responses, see Conticelli (2008).

features an aetiology of the gaze.[31] In this section, I shall approach the motif of Medusa from a slightly different angle, arguing that it provides a visual meditation on pictorial seeing.

In the form of the *gorgoneion*, the head of Medusa is ubiquitous in ancient Greek art. First monstrous, later also the face of a beautiful maiden, the *gorgoneion* serves as decoration on gems, roof tiles and shields, as well as on vases and burial monuments. The fearsome mask or face may have preceded the myth of Medea and Perseus, but already in the Archaic age it was generally identified with the decapitated Medusa. Needless to say, it would make no sense to attribute to all occurrences of the *gorgoneion* the reflexivity to be detected in the loaded depiction of the Eleusis amphora. And yet, a reflection on pictorial seeing is encapsulated, if lying dormant, in any *gorgoneion*:[32] the beholder can face the depiction of something that would petrify her in nature. To complement my discussion of the Eleusis amphora, I shall focus here on a group of vases that make the reflection on seeing explicit by presenting the head of Medusa together with its reflection. Besides coming from the south of Italy, these "Apulian" vases are much later, mostly from the first third of the fourth century BCE, and yet they continue and develop further the visual meditation on sight that we have found in the Eleusis amphora. The pictorial reflexivity for which I argue here was not bound to a specific period or context, but pervades Greek vase-painting at large, if in different ways.

The Apulian vases I wish to discuss show Perseus regarding the reflection of Medusa's head in the presence of Athena.[33] There is significant variation among the surviving depictions: on some vases, the head is reflected in water, on others it is to be seen on Perseus' shield. Athena is shown holding the head on most but not all vases. The number of additional figures, such as Hermes and Silens, likewise varies. These differences notwithstanding, all of these pictures can be interpreted as *mise-en-abîme*: in each case, the reflection *in* the painting illustrates the power *of* the painting. The water or shield permits Perseus to regard Medusa just as the beholder can gaze at her on the vase. The represented object thus mirrors the very act of representation.

Those vases that use Perseus' shield as mirroring device merit special attention here. Take a bell-krater by the so-called Tarporley Painter in the Boston Museum of Fine Arts, which shows the reflection of Medusa's head right at the centre of the shield (Figure 4.8). Such depictions have been interpreted aetiologically, justifying "a posteriori the custom that is attested from the earliest period of representing Gorgo on warriors' shields in order to heighten their prestige, provoke terror in the foe, and consign them in advance to flight and death".[34] The link between reflection and

---

31 Besides Mack (2002), see especially Howe (1954); Vernant (1990b: 115–17); Frontisi-Ducroux (1995: 71–4). Cf. Turner (this volume) on the deadly gaze of the Gorgon Medusa in a variety of contexts. Further literature can be found in Neer (2002b: 43 n.56).
32 See Mack (2002) for the argument that the *gorgoneion* evokes the story of Medusa's decapitation.
33 For a list and brief discussion of seven Apulian vases, see Schauenburg (1960: 77–9) and Balensiefen (1990: 32–4). More broadly on mirrors and their semantics in ancient thinking, see especially R. Taylor (2008).
34 Vernant (1991: 148–9). Cf. Frontisi-Ducroux (1995: 71–3); Mack (2002: 592). For shield-devices on ancient vases, Chase (1902) remains fundamental; for further bibliography, see Squire (2013b: 189, n.92).

Figure 4.8 South Italian bell-krater by the Tarporley Painter, *ca.* 400–385 BCE. Boston, Museum of Fine Arts: inv. 1970.237 (© 2015 Museum of Fine Arts, Boston).

shield device (*episēma*) is compelling, but the situation is, I think, rather more complex than Vernant, Frontisi-Ducroux and Mack would have it. The reflection is centred and placed where we expect the *gorgoneion*, and yet the motif is simultaneously rendered upside-down; it is therefore markedly different from a *gorgoneion* shield device. Instead of merging into one and the same image (as seems to be the case with Caravaggio's Medusa),[35] reflection and *gorgoneion* each throw the other into relief: while the shield device uses the terror of Medusa's head for apotropaic purposes, the reflection inverts its lethal force. The upside-down representation of this reflection exploits a customary *episēma* to highlight the "as-if" of pictorial seeing.

The idea of a shield in which Perseus can safely regard Medusa also resurfaces in the later literary tradition. Here, though, the shield is fully integrated into the course of the action: Ovid and Lucan have Perseus hold a shield while engaged in beheading Medusa (while in Lucian it is Athena herself who helps him).[36] The shield is hence a device to guide Perseus' blow. There is an extensive debate in scholarship on the priority of either pictorial or textual tradition as well as on the relationship

---

35 Cf. Marin (1977: 161).
36 Ovid, *Metamorphoses* 4.782–3; Lucan 9.669–70; Lucian, *The Hall* 25; *Dialogues of the Sea-Gods* 14.2.323. Apollodorus, *Library of Greek Mythology* 2.4.2 refers to the shield without mentioning who holds it. The motif of Perseus looking at Medusa while in the act of beheading her is rare in ancient visual art: for the scant evidence, see Balensiefen (1990: 120–4).

Figure 4.9 Apulian red-figure *pelikē* by the Tarporley Painter, *ca.* 380–370 BCE. Private collection (photograph supplied by the author).

between the two versions.[37] No matter which position we opt for, the comparison with the literary tradition underscores the particular concerns of our Apulian vases: here the viewing of Medusa does not serve a narratological purpose taking place after the beheading; it is a purely contemplative motif.

The contemplative character of the gaze at Medusa comes to the fore on a second Apulian *pelikē*, also attributed to the Tarporley Painter (Figure 4.9). Perseus stands fully at ease: his left leg is slightly bent, the right straight, while the upper body leans on the left arm resting on a column, over which Perseus' clothes are draped. Perseus' pose is echoed and partly inverted by that of Hermes, the one holding a sickle, the other a sceptre. Hermes bends his left leg and leans on a column which is not in front but behind him. Like Perseus, Hermes looks downwards and directs his gaze at the shield, but given the perspective he is unable to see the reflection on it. The tranquillity of the scene is formally supported by the composition of the image: Perseus and Hermes frame the scene on the left and right; the shield in the lower left of the centre is balanced by Athena in its upper right. While their heads form a horizontal line above which Medusa's head appears, Medusa and her reflection on the shield establish a vertical axis, made explicit through the tree in the background.

Hermes' and Perseus' relaxed poses and their concentrated gazes are reminiscent, with all due qualifications, of the absorption that Fried detects in the paintings of

---

37 For a survey, see Balensiefen (1990: 113–30).

Chardin and other classical French painters (Figure 4.1).[38] The absorption of the figures within the vase-painting in one sense prefigures the immersion experienced by the ideal external beholder of the vase. Likewise, the detachment of Perseus reinforces the self-referentiality of the depiction. Perseus' disinterested gaze aptly expresses the "as-if" of "seeing-in".

In addition to Medusa's head and its reflection on the shield, the Apulian *pelikē* shows a *gorgoneion* on Athena's tasselled cloak. The vase thus provokes us to ponder the different status of different sorts of images within the visual field. It might be said to juxtapose at least two different modes of mimesis, reflection and representation. While the former is a natural form of mimesis, the latter is man-made and artificial. The shield-framed reflection of the Medusa's head is an inverted mirror-image, but otherwise appears an exact copy of its source. The *gorgoneion* on the cloak, on the other hand, is smaller than Medusa's "actual" head and highly stylized in appearance, lacking, for example, the neck that is still visible on the head. The depiction is all the more intriguing when seen against the backdrop of the tradition that Medusa's head itself forms the sign on Athena's aegis.[39] The fact that Athena is brandishing Medusa's head ostentatiously excludes the possibility that the sign on the aegis is the "original".[40]

While somewhat earlier in date, a calyx-krater by Euphronios corroborates the idea that the motif of the *gorgoneion* on the aegis could lend itself to reflection about originals and copies (Figure 4.10).[41] Heracles and Athena on the left are shown fighting Cycnus and Ares on the right. The real lionskin around Heracles' shoulder contrasts with the depiction of lions on Cycnus' armour and Ares' shield; likewise the head of Medusa on Athena's aegis is juxtaposed with the emblem of the Medusa's head as a sign on Ares' shield. Whereas Euphronios thus seems to play subtly with the tradition that Athena's aegis features the very head of Medusa, the Apulian krater discussed above abandons this tradition and casts the *gorgoneion* as pictorial representation: the juxtaposition with the reflection on the shield draws attention to the representational status of the present picture. The exact copy furnished by the reflection throws into relief the distance that separates pictorial representation from the original. If even a reflection deprives Medusa of her lethal power, pictorial representations, not limited to but certainly including the depiction on our vase, *a fortiori* grant the beholder a safe mode of "seeing-in".

Toasts to reflexivity: the *gorgoneion* at the symposium

This brief chapter has examined just some of the reflexive ways in which Greek vase-paintings explored the nature of vision. While the represented excision of Polyphemus' eye contrasts with the beholder's gaze at the vase and throws into relief the detachment of pictorial seeing, the frontal depiction of the Gorgon Medusa

---

38 Fried (1980).
39 In Lucan 9.669, Athena's support of Perseus is even contingent on her receiving the head of Medusa.
40 See also an Apulian bell-krater in St. Petersburg (Hermitage inv. 637 (1723)), which shows Perseus putting on his winged shoes, that means before killing Medusa, opposite of Athena whose shield features a *gorgoneion*.
41 Cf. Neer (2002b: 61–2).

Figure 4.10 Attic red-figure calyx-krater by Euphronios, *ca.* 525–475 BCE. New York, Shelby White & Leon Levy Collection (© bpk – Bildarchiv preussischer Kulturbesitz, Berlin: Bildagentur für Kunst, Kultur und Geschichte).

highlights that we are facing only a representation, thereby flagging the process of "seeing-in": we attend not only to the represented subject, but also to the act of representation. As conceptualized by Wollheim, the phenomenon of "seeing-in" is transhistorical and applies to all kinds of pictures in a wide range of visual cultures. Whether or not we accept this claim (which, I am sure, will make many scholars feel uncomfortable), it is illuminating to contextualize the pictorial reflections that I have discussed within their specific historical contexts.[42] Unlike modern paintings, ancient vases were not aesthetic objects, but commodity goods. We have already seen that the use of the Eleusis amphora as a coffin urn gives its represented themes a special twist: the meditation on the detachment of pictorial seeing contrasts starkly with the idea of death as the ultimate loss of sight. In this final section, I shall turn to another prominent context of vase-painting – that is, the symposium. I will address the

---

42 See Grethlein (2015a) for some thoughts about the tension between transhistorical and historicizing approaches in aesthetics.

relation between this sympotic context and the vases' interest in visual reflexivity by focussing on one common motif: the *gorgoneion* in the tondo of Attic cups.

First, however, a word on the symposium. The symposium was a ritualized drinking party attended only by male guests.[43] A *symposiarch* controlled the consumption of wine which was mixed with water. The entertainment at symposia embraced a wide range of activities: the participants would recite poetry and challenge each other in speech duels and through riddles. In a game called *kottabos*, often represented on vases, the guests shot wine-dregs from their cups, aiming at a metal-disk, which would fall from a lamp-like construction on a soundboard. Female and male slaves would play music and potentially provide sexual gratification, which could of course also be sought from other guests. The symposium has been aptly described as: "a social activity of a ludic nature ... a clearly demarcated cultural occasion, in which the social norms which regulate the public life of the wider civic community can even be ignored or disobeyed, but in which the members commit themselves to accepting and following the laws which the gathering itself imposes".[44] Through its ludic nature, the symposium was crucial for the formation and calibration of identities, especially of elite citizens.[45] Experimenting with alternative personae through masquerade and the recitation of poems in the first person (not to mention the practice of indulging in flights of fantasy and challenging one's peers over riddlesome questions) all contributed to defining what it meant to be a member of a particular social group.

The self-referentiality that I have traced in Greek vase-painting obviously chimes with the playfulness pervading the symposium *tout court*. Eye-cups, in particular, lent themselves to the sympotic negotiation of identities, furnishing the visual equivalent to poems in which the speaker exploits the first-person voice to adopt a new persona. It has been argued that the eye-cup not only masked and transformed the person drinking from it, but also invited viewers to experiment with other personae linked to the one represented by the mask.[46] The eye-cups' play with identity has a further aspect that harks back to one of the motifs discussed earlier. For one of the most common interior motifs is that of the *gorgoneion*, placed right at the centre (Figure 4.11).[47] Whoever drinks from a cup not only holds up a mask to his fellows, but also faces a representation that uncannily interacts with his own. At the very moment of imbibing the cup's intoxicating liquor, the drinker encounters the face of Medusa – at first lurking underneath his own reflection in the wine, but then emerging in its own pictorial right. The process imposes an extreme form of the "other" onto the drinking "self"; it does so, however, through the layering of two representational media, namely reflection and mimetic painting. The beholder is made to see himself in the face of the otherly Gorgon – in the eyes of the mythical monster

---

[43] The literature on the symposium is vast: see especially Lissarrague (1987); Schmitt-Pantel (1992); Murray (1990); Slater (1991); Vetta (1995); Catoni (2010).
[44] Pellitzer (1990: 178).
[45] Cf. Neer (2002b: 9–26).
[46] Cf. Hedreen (2007b).
[47] The *gorgoneion* in the tondo of black-figure cups is so widespread that it tends to be bypassed both in studies of the *gorgoneion* (e.g. Besig 1937; Floren 1977) and in investigations of the pictures in tondi (e.g. T. B. L. Webster 1939; van der Grinten 1966).

Figure 4.11 Attic black-figure "eye-cup" (Type A) by the Lysippides Painter, *ca.* 525 BCE. Cambridge, Fitzwilliam Museum: inv. GR.12.1937 (© The Fitzwilliam Museum, Cambridge).

directing her lethal gaze at him. As I have argued above, the frontal representation of the Gorgon drives home the detachment of pictorial seeing: the *gorgoneion*'s positioning in the tondo enmeshes this reflection on "seeing-in" with the identity of the beholder.

Such confrontation of the self with the other is given particular force in numerous cups where the *gorgoneion* is shown not perpendicular to the axis of the two handles, but instead shifted slightly clockwise.[48] Propped up on the *klinē* with his left arm, the symposiast would hold the cup with the left handle closer to his face. The asymmetry of the Medusa-esque medallion would compensate for the anticlockwise rotation of the cup so that the user would face the *gorgoneion* face-on. But even the less numerous vases where the inner medallion is perpendicular to the axis of the

---

[48] The asymmetry of the medallions in Greek cups has been explained along the lines of production, reception and aesthetics: while some have argued that it is due to the way in which the painters held the cups (e.g. Houssay 1912), others (like Hampe & Gropengiesser 1967) see it in light of the position in which cups were held. Compositional reasons have likewise been adduced by e.g. Neutsch (1949) and E. Simon (1976). For a survey of different approaches, see Martens (1992: 179–234): Martens sees the asymmetry as a device of animation that goes against the strict symmetry that otherwise defines Greek vase-painting.

handles (or else shifted anticlockwise) would allow for a face-to-face encounter with the *gorgoneion*, which, due to its round form, is less affected by the angle of the perspective than other tondo motifs.

A *kylix* in Cambridge's Fitzwilliam Museum offers a particularly sophisticated meditation on the "visual pragmatics" of the interior *gorgoneion* (Figure 4.12).[49] The two pairs of eyes on the exterior of this cup are filled with *gorgoneia* very similar to the *gorgoneion* emblazoned in its interior tondo. Scholars have not failed to comment on the vase's underlying visual-verbal pun. The Greek word for "pupil", *korē*, simultaneously signifies "maiden", and not least the ultimate "maiden" figure of Persephone – Hades' female consort in the underworld, "with whom Gorgo has certain affinities".[50] The vase has thus been interpreted in light of Socrates' observation in Plato's *Alcibiades* (132e–133a): "And have you observed that the face of the person who looks into another's eye is shown in his pupil as in a mirror, and we call this the pupil/maiden (*korēn*), for in a sort it is an image of the person looking?" The visual pun is reinforced by the figure of a young maiden painted between the two pairs of external eyes. Instead of seeing himself, the beholder faces Medusa in the eye of the other.[51] What I find most remarkable of all here is that the projection of the *gorgoneia* into the eye represents what the symposiast himself sees upon drinking from the cup: it shows Medusa in the reflection of an eye – just as in the act of drinking, the symposiast sees her in the reflection of his *own* eye. The exterior of the cup thus playfully relates to the uncanny visual experiencing of its interior: where the act of seeing the tondo lasts only for the duration of drinking, the exterior images emblazons that internal, subjective and ephemeral moment for all to see.

Although the motif of two eyes on the exterior of the cup cannot be derived from the *gorgoneion* per se, it has been noted that "the two visual motifs or decorative schemes, eye-cup and *gorgoneion*, were understood to be intrinsically related in some important way".[52] If we again consider the use of the cup, the connection becomes more precise: the external mask shown to the drinking companions can be seen as the petrification effected by the internal *gorgoneion* when faced by the user of the cup. The petrification lasts only as long as he is drinking and facing the Gorgon. As soon as the vase is put down, the *gorgoneion* is covered by wine once more, so that the symposiast reverts to wearing his own face.[53]

What should we make of such visual reflexive games? My argument here is not of course that every time a symposiast took a sip he would meditate on the "as-if" of pictorial seeing, racking his brain over the relation between self and other. As we have said, the *gorgoneion* is a very common tondo-motif; it might also have provoked all manner of jesting remarks – that the *oinarches* ought to hurry up with the refill before Medusa sends out her lethal rays, for example. That said, it is worth noting that such reflections about sight and seeing feature on objects intended as everyday commodities. In this sense, the case of vase-painting drives home the fact that reflexivity is not confined to "Art" in the modern sense: far from being aesthetic

---

49 See Beazley (1956: 202: "Painter of Cambridge 61", no. 2).
50 Frontisi-Ducroux (1995: 102); cf. Lissarrague (1987: 136).
51 Cf. Frontisi-Ducroux (1995: 102).
52 Hedreen (2007b: 222).
53 Cf. Neer (2002b: 43).

SIGHT AND REFLEXIVITY

Figure 4.12 Attic black-figure "eye-cup" (Type A) by the Cambridge Painter, *ca.* 520 BCE. Cambridge, Fitzwilliam Museum: inv. GR.39.1864 (© The Fitzwilliam Museum, Cambridge).

objects in their own right, the vases discussed here had a very practical purpose as drinking vessels. Part of their reflexivity even hinges on their practical use: the cup needs to be lifted to one's lips in order to be transformed into a mask; indeed, it is only the person who drinks from the cup who will see the face of the Gorgon in his own reflection.

Conclusion: meta-seeing

I am aware that my argument in this short chapter risks going against the grain of some deeply entrenched assumptions about Greek vase-painting. Art historians will wonder whether the reflexivity for which I have argued is compatible with the horizon of expectations, not least in the Archaic Greek world, from which, for example, my touching point, the Eleusis amphora, stems.[54] Does my approach not project a later Hellenistic Greek or indeed Imperial framework back onto a time that was less invested in plays with medium and self-reference? The prominence of the eye motif mentioned at the beginning of this essay should perhaps help to allay such

---

54 Cf. Grethlein (2015b) on reflexivity in Archaic Greek visual and verbal art.

qualms, I think; likewise, those vases that combine different scenes centred around the thematics of vision in one and the same field (or indeed complement such scenes with ornamental eyes: e.g. Figure 4.7) underscore the fact that sight was a salient subject of vase-painting in and of itself.

No less important is the high degree of self-reference found in poetry, corroborating as it does an interest in reflexivity across media in the Archaic age. One thinks here, for example, of the Homeric description of the shield of Achilles, with its playful collapsing – right at the beginning of the Greek literary tradition – of relations between representation and represented objects.[55] While the Homeric shield of Achilles testifies to a keen eye for issues of representational medium, the meta-poetic significance of bards in Homer provides a close parallel for my argument about the reflexivity of vase-painting: it is widely acknowledged that the singing embedded in epic mirrors the recital of the epic itself.[56] Just as in book eight of the *Odyssey* the Homeric audience is invited to compare their response to the reactions elicited by Demodocus' song (as recounted *in* the poem), the vase-paintings explored in this chapter prompt the beholder to relate his vision to that of the represented figures. As the sense by which we perceive pictures, sight was an object of pictorial representation that appealed to a broader fascination with reflexivity – as both the object and subject of visual inquiry.[57]

---

55 See especially Becker (1990; 1995) and, most recently, Squire (2013b).
56 E.g. Macleod (1983); Ford (1992); Segal (1994).
57 I wish to thank Nikolaus Dietrich, Tonio Hölscher and Matthias Steinhart for thought-provoking comments. Most of all, I am indebted to Michael Squire for his incisive suggestions as well as for long discussions about visual art in antiquity and beyond.

5

SIGHT AND PAINTING

Optical theory and pictorial poetics in Classical Greek art

Jeremy Tanner

For the ancient Greeks "sight" was central to the experience of painting, as was the cultural character of seeing as sensory mode. On one level, this might seem a truism: what tradition of visual art does not address issues of sight and visuality? Classical Greek painting, however, seems to have been especially concerned not just with the appropriation of sight to encode social and cultural values, but also with the exploration of the character and meaning of seeing itself, and above all with the relation between seeing, the rational intellect and sensory experience more generally. In a dialogue between Socrates and the painter Parrhasius, staged by Xenophon in his fourth-century BCE *Memorabilia*, Socrates gains Parrhasius' assent to the assertion that painting (*graphikē*) is the "making of likenesses of things seen" (*eikasia tōn horōmenōn*): "by making likenesses with colours", Socrates continues, "you imitate things that are deep and high, shadowy and light, hard and soft, rough and smooth, young and old". In short, painting should be able faithfully to imitate, even replicate, the whole of human sensory experience, as mediated through sight, to the extent that it could stand in for it. Even the character of the soul (*to tēs psuchēs ēthos*), lacking form and colour and thus not wholly accessible to sight (*mēde holōs horaton*), could be rendered by the depiction of facial expression and the attitudes of the body (whether standing still or in motion): all of these aspects were proper objects of the painter's mimetic skills.[1]

Seeing the truth in painting

This concept of painting is most famously expressed in the story of the competition between Zeuxis and Parrhasius, set (not without significance, as we shall see) *in scaenam*, or on the stage-buildings of a theatre. According to the Elder Pliny's famous story, Zeuxis:[2]

> produced a picture of grapes so successfully painted, that birds flew up to the stage buildings (*in scaenam*). In response, Parrhasius produced a painting

---

1 Xenophon, *Memorabilia* 3.10.1–5 – adjusted from the translation of Pollitt (1993: 155); cf. Goldhill (1998); Steiner (2001: 33–5).
2 Pliny, *Natural History* 35.68.

of a curtain, represented with such verisimilitude (*ita ueritate repraesentata*), that Zeuxis, proud of the judgement of the birds, demanded that the curtain be removed and his painting displayed; and when he had realized his mistake, with a modesty that did him honour he yielded up the prize, saying that whereas he had deceived (*fefellisset*) birds, Parrhasius had deceived him, an artist.

These texts encapsulate the way in which Greek painting, and reflections on painting, during the course of the fifth and fourth centuries BCE became intimately tied up with painters' efforts to imitate the experiences afforded by natural sight, and specifically the capacity of painting to be so true to optical experience that it could deceive viewers into taking representation for reality. According to one sophistic author, "in the writing of tragedies and in painting, the best person is the one who deceives the most in creating things that are like the real thing (πλεῖστα ἐξαπατῇ ὅμοια τοῖς ἀληθινοῖς ποιέων)".[3] Rhetoricians, like Gorgias, lauded this *psychagogic* or "soul-transporting" capacity – the potential of the visual arts to create a second reality parallel to that of everyday experience, and thereby to transport viewers, both cognitively and emotionally, into new fictional worlds. "Pleasuring the eyes" (*terpein tēn opsin*), it was suggested, was the most direct means to persuade the soul. Painting, with its capacity to manipulate forms and colours, was the most powerful technology for achieving these effects.[4] Plato, famously and decisively for the history of western aesthetics, set himself against this vision of painting, though sharing many of the assumptions which informed it. On the basis of optical illusions, such as the straight stick which appears bent when placed in water due to the refractive character of that medium, he argued that sight was a defective organ, and a poor basis for the construction of reliable knowledge. Illusionistic painting exploited this "disability in our nature"; it was a form of witchcraft (*goēteia*) which undermined the rational element within our soul.[5] The worlds produced by painting were worlds of phantoms, *eidōla*, "not the real but something which is like the real, but not real itself".[6] At two removes from the true reality of the Forms, painted images can give at best only a very dim or indistinct (*amudron*) impression of the truth.[7]

Against the background of ancient debates, it is perhaps unsurprising that the question of the truth in Greek painting has exercised an inescapable attraction in the historiographic tradition right up to the present.[8] Erwin Panofsky's classic study of

---

3 *Dissoi Logoi* 3.10.
4 For the vocabulary of *psychagōgia* in relation to visual art, see Xenophon *Memorabilia* 3.10.6; Gorgias, *Helen* 13–14, 18; for discussion, see Brancacci (1995); R. Robert (1992: 402–10); Halliwell (2011: 274–81).
5 *Republic* 602d.
6 *Republic* 597a.
7 *Republic* 598b. For some analyses of the Platonic position, cf. Squire's introduction and Nightingale's chapter in this volume.
8 Much of Hans Belting's argument in *Florence and Baghdad: Renaissance Art and Arab Science* (Belting 2011a) hinges on the assertion that "if we exclude stage craft, a true concept of perspective did not exist in ancient times" (161). This procrustean exclusion allows Belting simply to ignore the Greek traditions which informed both Arab science and Renaissance art, and create the rather specious "shock" of his title. Within classical art history, Stinson's (2011) interesting account of the craft

Perspective as Symbolic Form is at least in part a subtle exploration of the differing truth claims of ancient Greek central vanishing axis perspective and Italian Renaissance central vanishing point perspective. Panofsky argues that vanishing axis perspective – found in some Greek vase-paintings and Roman wall-paintings – is the result of ancient attempts to project the curvilinear retinal image onto the flat surface of a wall- or panel-painting. By virtue of its close dependence on the retinal image, such a perspectival schema has, according to Panofsky, a certain, subjective, claim to be a true representation of our visual experience. Renaissance central vanishing point perspective, by contrast, abstracts from the embodied eye which characterizes its ancient counterpart, positing the eye instead as a single fixed point. This provides the basis for constructing the relationship between an ideal viewer and the corresponding single, infinitely distant, vanishing point projected in pictorial space. From God's point of view (the perspective of the infinite), it undergirds the objectivist disembodied truths of Cartesian philosophy and modern science.[9] Ernst Gombrich's still influential account of the "Greek Revolution" and the development of naturalism (of which perspective is understood as just one important element) emphasized the veridical character of Greek mimesis of optical experience, seeing the progress of Greek art as one of making and matching, correcting artistic schemata to conform to the truth of visual perception, following Karl Popper's positivistic model of the logic of scientific inquiry.[10] Conversely, Norman Bryson, informed by structuralist semiotics, has made a case for the purely conventional character of both ancient and modern "naturalism", arguing that optical perspective and chiaroscuro are merely techniques for the creation of culturally specific "reality effects", which have no privileged claim to truth outside the tradition of their creation.[11]

In this chapter, I wish to shift the discussion away from the issues of the relative truth of Classical Greek painting to universal visual experience, focussing instead on the role played by the intersections between Greek optical theory and Greek painting in the cultural appropriation and construction of sight. In particular, I explore the institutional settings and social frameworks which afforded the reconstruction of sight and seeing within the context of the practices of painting, and the ways in which that pictorial exploration of the character of seeing resonated with the character of those institutional settings. The first half of my chapter looks at scene-painting in the Athenian theatre as the context for the elaboration of a specific style of perspective painting, *skēnographia*. The second half explores the character of *skiagraphia*, or shadow-painting, with a particular focus on the paintings of the monumental Macedonian tomb at Lefkadia in northern Greece.

---

practices of the painters of perspective schemes in Roman "Second Style" wall-painting also draws a contrast between the true perspective of the Renaissance, and the various approximations to it in Roman wall-painting.

9 Panofsky (1991) (with Christopher Wood's excellent introduction) – translating the German essay first published in 1927. The literature on perspective is vast. Important for comparison of ancient and modern perspective representation is White (1987). The most insightful of recent contributions, with ample discussion of earlier bibliography, is Elkins (1994).
10 Gombrich (1960); Elsner (2006c).
11 Bryson (1983). Mediating between the objectivism of Gombrich and the relativism of Bryson is Layton (1977).

Painting, perspective and the rationalization of sight

Foreshortening in representations of the body and objects such as chariot wheels appears in Attic vase-painting as early as the late sixth century BCE.[12] Textual evidence suggests that these tentative beginnings in the opening up of depth in pictorial space began to be developed into more systematic perspectival schemes only in the middle of the fifth century, and in the specific context of the theatre. The Roman architect Vitruvius, writing in the late first century BCE, relates that the painter Agatharchus painted a stage-set for a play by Aeschylus, and wrote a commentary on it (*On Architecture* 7 praef. 11):

> Following his suggestions, Democritus and Anaxagoras wrote upon the same topic, in order to show how, if a fixed centre is taken for the outward glance of the eyes and the projection of the rays (*ad aciem oculorum radiorumque extentionem certo loco centro constituto*), we must follow these lines in accordance with a natural law (*ad lineas ratione naturali respondere*), such that from an uncertain object, certain images (*uti de incerta re certae imagines*) may give the appearance of buildings in the scenery of the stage, and how what is figured on vertical and plane surfaces can seem to recede in one part and project in another.

In another passage in Vitruvius, scene-painting, *scaenographia*, is further defined as "the shading of the front and the retreating sides, and the correspondence of all lines to the point of the compasses (i.e. the centre of a circle: *frontis et laterum abscedentium adumbratio ad circinique centrum omnium linearum responsus*)".[13]

The critical evaluation of these texts presents numerous problems. First, it is not clear whether the "fixed centre" of the first text and the "centre of a circle" in the second refer to the same centre, or whether either text is describing a central vanishing point. On the contrary, it seems likely that in the first case the centre in question is the viewer/painter's eyes, from which lines of vision radiate (in a cone) to construct the objects of vision at the base of the cone. In the case of scene-painting the point in question would be the privileged position within the space of the seating in a theatre, from which the appearance of the three-dimensionality of the painted scenery would appear most convincing.[14] Second, it seems likely that Vitruvius' ideas about scenography are in some degree informed by later developments in optics and painting, in particular the work of the third-century BCE mathematician Euclid (*ca.* 325–250 BCE). In his *Optics*, Euclid operates with a ray theory of vision which he uses to explain the character of sight in a series of geometrically demonstrable theorems. The surfaces of phenomena in the visual field above eye level descend, Euclid explains, whilst those below ascend; comparably, surfaces to the left and right seem to converge towards each other in the distance. The true size of objects in the visual field could be calculated on the basis of the distance of the object from the eye, as

---

12 Cf. White (1987: 236–42).
13 Vitruvius 1.2.2. My translations of Vitruvius are adapted from those of Granger (1931–4), with the important modifications of White (1987: 250–4).
14 Cf. Rouveret (1984: 155); Gros (2008: 12).

well as by means of the angle formed by the visual rays with their apex at the eye and their base at the object in question.[15] In a fragment from a treatise on optics, Geminus, writing in the first century BCE, defines *skēnographia* as a field within optics concerned with the drawing of images of buildings in such a way that they appear with the requisite symmetry and eurhythmy. This requires optical corrections (*alexēmata*) in the drawing – for example, representing circles as ellipses and foreshortening rectangular elements.[16]

Concern with whether or not Agatharchus' stage-paintings involved "true perspective" may, however, be missing the larger point, namely that Greek artists of the fifth century BCE drew on mathematics and geometry in order to try to construct visual representations which corresponded to the logic of what were taken to be laws of vision given in nature (*naturali ratione*).[17] The conceptualization of light in terms of rays travelling in straight lines, and an interest in the geometry of the figures projected by the shadows cast by light, can be traced back to the sixth century, when Thales of Miletus used the shadow cast by a sunlit rod of known height to calculate the height of a pyramid on the basis of its cast shadow. Euclid's theorems build on interests and systematize ideas which already had some history in Greek thought, and more importantly in Greek artistic practice.[18] As Vitruvius relates, Agatharchus' commentary on his scene-painting was sufficient to stimulate further optical researches by Anaxagoras (500–428 BCE) and Democritus (b. *ca.* 460 BCE). The latter wrote a treatise on *aktinographiē* ("drawing with rays") and also seems to have been particularly interested in the geometrical properties of cones.[19] An awareness of some of the optical principles which inform perspective representation is also implied by the use of optical refinements in Greek architecture, which find their most systematic use in the architecture of the Parthenon, and also in the design of the Propylaea, broadly contemporary with Agatharchus' scene-painting, and with the presence of Anaxagoras and (possibly) Democritus in Athens.[20] The realization of such refinements involved the use of an elaborate applied geometry, using rulers, protractors, setsquares, compasses and plumb lines to plan the design for the fluting and the *entasis* (literally "distension" or "swelling") of columns in reduced diagrams, from which the measurements could then be scaled up for the accurate realization of the properly proportioned final columns.[21] The high level of mathematics and geometry involved in architecture won Plato's approval: he ranked it above other *technai* such as medicine or agriculture, since its procedures and practices entailed a high level of precision (*akribeia*), and thus a more scientific (*technikōteran*) approach.[22]

The esteem in which mathematics was held motivated other artists to transform their artistic practices along parallel lines. Polyclitus, a sculptor from Argos and the

---

15 Cf. Camerota (2002: 122–3). On Euclid and his place within ancient "optical" traditions, see the chapter by Netz & Squire in this volume.
16 Cf. Schöne (1897: 29–30); Camerota (2002: 127).
17 Cf. Andersen (1987: 86); Camerota (2002: 137).
18 For discussions, see Camerota (2002: 123); Summers (2007: 20); cf. Rudolph (this volume).
19 Diogenes Laertius 9.48: cf. Rudolph (2011: 71).
20 Cf. Senseney (2011).
21 Cf. Senseney (2011: 104–32).
22 Plato, *Philebus* 56bc: cf. Camerota (2002: 128); Senseney (2011: 56).

more or less exact contemporary of Agatharchus, formulated a canon for the representation of the human figure in sculpture, based on a complex system of symmetries – measured correspondent proportions – and "many numbers" (*polloi arithmoi*). He was followed by other painters and sculptors who sought to transform their own and their crafts' status by emulating the practices of other intellectuals, like sophists and doctors, establishing their arts on rational foundations systematically explicated in written treatises.[23] In the case of painting, this process of artistic rationalization culminated in the figure of Pamphilus, a painter from Sicyon, celebrated for his learning in arithmetic and geometry. These subjects formed the core of the systematic education in painting offered – at a price, on the model of the sophists – by Pamphilus at his workshop in Sicyon.[24] The preoccupation with elaborating mathematical principles for artistic design seems to have been so widespread, and so widely known, that it could be exploited by comic poets like Aristophanes for comic effect. In his *Birds* (414 BCE), Aristophanes presents on stage the astronomer Meton, designing a city in the sky for the creatures that gave the comedy its name. Manipulating a compass, a straight ruler and a curved protractor, Meton plots out before the audience's eyes an ideal city, complete with circular agora and streets radiating out from the compass-defined centre point of the city, all echoing – as part of the joke, according to John Senseney's attractive argument – the radiating lines of the scene-painting in front of which Meton would have been standing.[25]

No direct evidence of the character of the scene-paintings of Classical Athens survives. Consequently much of the debate about the character of ancient perspective, and whether or not it might count as "true perspective", has focussed on Roman wall-paintings with representations of stage-sets, which may have developed out of Alexandrian traditions of scenography, possibly shaped in part by the optics of Euclid.[26] Concentration on the later material – with the tacit assumption that, if perspective cannot be demonstrated here, there is little reason to believe that it could have existed earlier, before Euclid – seems to have entailed an undue neglect, and perhaps a slightly tendentious interpretation, of the closest available material evidence for the character of Athenian stage-painting, namely monumental vase-paintings from the Greek cities of southern Italy. Some of these depict scenes from and even stagings of plays from the repertoire of Attic drama, which became extraordinarily popular in south Italy and Sicily in the late fifth century and the fourth century. Panofsky used these vases – the larger ones of which were tomb monuments – to exemplify the central vanishing axis perspective, which, he argued, was the practical entailment of attempts to project the curved retinal image on a flat surface. Often a device like a shield is used to cover the awkward join between partially

---

23 For an introduction here, see Tanner (2006: 161–73).
24 Pliny, *Natural History* 35.76.
25 Aristophanes, *Birds* 992–1020: cf. Senseney (2011: 88–92).
26 On Roman wall-painting and theatre painting, see Beyen (1957); Leach (2004: 93–114); Gros (2008); Sinisgalli (2012). McKenzie (2007: 80–112) discusses the role played by teams of Alexandrian painters in the creation of "Second Style" wall-paintings in the area of Pompeii. On Euclid and Graeco-Roman perspective painting, see Tobin (1990) (arguing in favour of a Euclidian basis for central vanishing point perspective) and Knorr (1991) (arguing against). Rouveret (1989: 87–90) is also relevant here, demonstrating an ancient concept of central vanishing point perspective grounded in atomist theory.

converging orthogonals, as exemplified in a vase depicting a shrine, or *naiskos* (Plate 3), where the depth in which the figures are set is intimated by ceiling-beams seen from below. These converge towards each other so sharply that they would actually meet and form a visible vanishing axis within the shrine itself, were it not for the covering shield.[27] Other vases, however, are much less ad hoc in their construction of perspectival space, and betray a more systematic organization of the convergence of orthogonals.[28] A fragment of another fourth-century south Italian vase depicts a theatrical scene. It takes place in front of the façade of a palace – exactly the kind of building that would have typically been the subject matter of scene-painting (Plates 1 and 2). The centre seems to show a libation taking place at an altar. The figures are framed on their left-hand side by a strong projecting wing, with Ionic columns supporting a Doric triglyph and metope frieze, and a pediment with floral decoration and *acroteria*. The artist has struggled to reconcile two aims, namely maintaining the parallelism of the entablature across the surface of the vase, and representing the projecting portico itself (and the coffering of the ceiling) in perspective. The alignment of ceiling and architrave on the left, and of the back lintel with the coffers, is achieved at the expense of a slightly divergent perspective of the receding architrave. More remarkable than this slight awkwardness is the convergence of more than a dozen orthogonals of the wing and the coffered ceiling on a single vanishing point; other examples have as many as twenty orthogonals converging on a single point, and this cannot be the result of mere chance.[29]

To be sure, these vases are exceptional, but that does nothing to lessen their importance as significant indicators of the development of perspectival representation in Greek scene-painting. There is no good reason to suppose that this remarkably high level in the systematization of perspective projection developed autonomously in the context of the relatively low-status medium of vase-painting, which in certain respects – due to the curvature of the surface of the vase – was less well adapted to it than wall or panel-painting. Furthermore, if this degree of integration could be achieved in the depiction of scenographies on vase-painting, there is every reason to believe that an equivalent or higher level of perspective systematization is the likely model for such paintings, namely the scenographies of the theatre.[30] Indeed, it may not be entirely coincidental that the best evidence for this interest in the systematization of perspective is found on south Italian vases. Not only was south Italy the focus of a considerable enthusiasm for Athenian drama in the fourth century BCE, it may also have been the site for the further elaboration of the optical studies of Democritus and Anaxagoras, based on Agatharchus' scene-paintings, from the fifth century. As Reviel Netz & Michael Squire have argued, the Pythagorean philosopher Archytas of Tarentum (*fl.* 400–350 BCE) seems to have played a particularly important role in the mathematization of optics, according to a geometrical model based on lines conceptualized as physical rays.[31] Here, the rather Athenocentric character of our sources, and the simple but massively influential survival of

---

27 For an illustration, see Panofsky (1991: 38–40, plate 3).
28 For analysis, see Christensen (1999: 162–5).
29 Cf. Christensen (1999: 162).
30 Christensen (1999) offers an excellent discussion of the key issues and materials.
31 Cf. Netz & Squire (this volume) with Burnyeat (2005) (reconstructing Archytas' optics: particularly

Plato, may occlude our vision of the development of perspective in Greek art. Areas beyond Athens – and far from Plato – may have offered particularly favourable intellectual and institutional environments for its development.[32]

But why does the theatre play such a central role in the development of perspective in the ancient Greek world? Although the development of naturalism in Greek art, in particular the use of foreshortened and three-quarter representations of bodies and objects, entailed an initial opening up of the pictorial surface of both vases and wall-paintings to the depiction of spatial depth, there does not seem to have been any straightforward relationship between narrative painting and the development of perspective. Indeed, the political functions of paintings of myth and history, and the symbolic values they communicated, may, at least initially, have militated against perspective. The early-Classical painter Micon, in what seems to have been an early attempt at perspective painting, was fined for depicting the Greeks (presumably in the background) as smaller than Persians (presumably in the foreground), infringing long-established symbolic conventions where smaller size was associated with lower status (as clearly seen in depictions of slaves).[33] Stage-painting provided a context in which such problems did not occur. Since it involved the depiction only of buildings, not people, it offered a relatively open field for experiments with perspectival representation. Furthermore, as Ruth Padel has argued, there were certain cognitive affinities between theatrical representation and scene-painting which might have further encouraged experiments with perspective.[34] The *skēnē* – that is, the "tent" or "hut" on which scene-paintings were made – played a central role in the illusionary poetics of tragedy. It was the place in which actors changed their masks in order to be able to return to the stage as a different character. With the assistance of scene-painting, the *skēnē* was often made to represent the entrance to the royal palace at the heart of so many Greek tragedies. The interior space of the *skēnē*-palace necessarily remains unseen, but the audience is constantly making inferences, on the basis of speeches by actors on the stage, about what has gone on or what is going on there, like Oedipus' liaison with his wife/mother, or her suicide and his self-blinding, none of which is represented on stage. Tragedy and painting – both in perspective and in the representation of character, another central innovation of fifth-century art and one in which pictorial art and dramatic art run along parallel lines – play with the boundary between surfaces and depth, illusion and reality.

---

relevant is Burnyeat (2005: 51), where the author tenders a link with south Italian vase-painting and the Würzburg vase, a product of Apulia and possibly even of Tarentum).

32 Zeuxis, who played a key role in the development of light and shade in Greek painting (see below), was from Heraclea, also in south Italy.
33 Cf. Tanner (2006: 151).
34 Padel (1990); cf. Goldhill (2000b) and Coo (this volume), on the ways in which "seeing" is thematized in Greek tragedy (the *theatron* is, after all, a place for seeing or spectating, *theasthai*).

Plate 1 Fragment of an Apulian krater from Tarentum, *ca.* 360–350 BCE. Würzburg, Martin von Wagner Museum: inv. H 4696/H 4701 (© Martin von Wagner Museum der Universität Würzburg; photograph by P. Neckerman).

Plate 2 Reconstruction drawing of the same fragment (© Martin von Wagner Museum der Universität Würzburg; drawing by B. Otto, photograph by E. Öhrlein).

Plate 3 Detail of a funerary shrine on an Apulian volute-krater by the Helm Painter, last quarter of the fourth century BCE. Hamburg, Museum für Kunst und Gewerbe: inv. 1917.1092 (© Museum für Kunst und Gewerbe, Hamburg; photograph by Maria Thrun).

Plate 4 Painted wooden votive tablet from Pitsa, sixth century BCE. Athens, National Archaeological Museum: inv. 16464 (© Hellenic Ministry of Culture, Education and Religious Affairs – Archaeological Receipts Fund; photograph by Giannis Patrikianos).

Plate 5 Watercolour reconstruction of the Great Tomb at Lefkadia, late fourth century BCE. After P. M. Petsas (1966: plate A) (photograph reproduced by kind permission of the Archaeological Society at Athens).

Plate 6 Painted metopes depicting a centauromachy from the Great Tomb at Lefkadia. After P. M. Petsas (1966: plate I) (photograph reproduced by kind permission of the Archaeological Society at Athens).

Plate 7 Centauromachy metope from the Great Tomb at Lefkadia. Water-colour sketch by Vincent J. Bruno, after V. J. Bruno (1981) "The Painted Metopes at Lefkadia and the Problem of Color in Doric Sculpted Metopes", *American Journal of Archaeology* 85: 3–11, figure 2. Courtesy of the Archaeological Institute of America and the *American Journal of Archaeology*.

Plate 8 Warrior: detail of the fresco paintings from the Great Tomb at Lefkadia. After P. M. Petsas (1966: plate S) (photograph reproduced by kind permission of the Archaeological Society at Athens).

Plate 9 Hermes: detail of the fresco paintings from the Great Tomb at Lefkadia. After P. M. Petsas (1966: plate Z) (photograph reproduced by kind permission of the Archaeological Society at Athens).

Plate 10 Aeacus: detail of the fresco paintings from the Great Tomb at Lefkadia. After P. M. Petsas (1966: plate H) (photograph reproduced by kind permission of the Archaeological Society at Athens).

Plate 11 Rhadamanthus: detail of the fresco paintings from the Great Tomb at Lefkadia. After P. M. Petsas (1966: plate Θ) (photograph reproduced by kind permission of the Archaeological Society at Athens).

Shadow-painting and the limits of sight

In a passage somewhat reminiscent of Meton's drawing of the plan of a city in the sky in Aristophanes' *Birds*, Adeimantus, a speaker in Plato's *Republic*, describes how one might make a pretence of virtue: "I must draw a *prothura* [a façade or portal, like a stage-painting] and a mathematical figure (*schēma*) in a circle (*kuklos*) around myself, which will be like a *skiagraphia* of virtue".[35] The passage is a slightly odd one, since it seems to describe perspective painting, but the term used by Plato is not *skēnographia* but *skiagraphia*, or "shadow-painting". Whereas *skēnographia* relied on a geometry of lines to depict on a two-dimensional surface the recession and projection of objects and buildings in a virtual three-dimensional space, *skiagraphia* used light and shadow to model painted figures in relief. But both were associated in Greek thought with the theatre,[36] and the distinction between the two is regularly blurred in the writings of Plato, according to the precise character of the analogy between painting and dramatic art or poetry which he wished to develop in the context of any specific polemic against mimetic art. Just as the concept of "perspective" acquired extraordinary metaphorical range in western culture after the Renaissance as a way of thinking about knowledge and world views more generally – "a fresh perspective", "an illuminating perspective", "a conservative point of view", etc. – so, in the classical world, *skiagraphia* seems to have acquired a comparable metaphorical resonance, largely as a function of Plato's elaborate development of the shadow-painting metaphor as a way of describing every kind of sloppy thinking and dangerous deception which might be antithetical to the truth.[37]

Panel-paintings from Archaic Greece, like those from Pitsa (Plate 4), depict figures by means of flat uniform fields of bright colour, and their aesthetic appeal derives largely from the rhythmic contrast of those fields of colour. Athenian white-ground vessels, perhaps the best proxy for contemporary panel- and wall-painting, display a similar practice, with the occasional introduction of lines of darker tone to indicate drapery folds in the middle of the fifth century BCE. The introduction of more systematic exploration of light and shade only seems to have begun in the late fifth century. The material evidence for it is extremely scrappy – the use of hatching in some giant white-ground *lekythoi* and added highlights in some south Italian vase-painting. But by the time of the Macedonian tomb paintings (all from the latter part of the fourth century), the full range of possibilities of modelling light and shade – reflected light, highlights, cast shadow and so on – had clearly been mastered by Greek painters.[38] The discovery of shadow-painting, and the exploration of virtual light and shadow, represented an important transformation in the character of painting, and in particular in the relationship between paintings and their viewers. The representation of "virtual light" entailed by highlighting and shading implies a specific physical relation in space between the object being depicted and the viewing subject:

---

35 Plato, *Republic* 365c: cf. Beyen (1957: 148); Rouveret (1989: 56).
36 See especially Rouveret (1989: 25); Trimpi (1978: 405).
37 See Elkins (1994: 12–22) on metaphorical resonances of "perspective" in post-Renaissance thought. For the *skiagraphia* metaphor from Plato through to late antiquity, see Trimpi (1978).
38 Cf. Walter-Karydi (2002) on the development of shading techniques; Brécoulaki (2006) for a comprehensive analytical survey of colour use in the Macedonian tombs.

in real life, the positioning of highlights and reflected light – for example, on the rim of a shield or fine silk garments – shifts with the movement of the viewer.[39] Variations in the reflectivity of different surfaces – metals, human skin, different kinds of textile – is also indicative of the textural and tactile qualities of those materials, appealing to our sense of touch, as suggested in the passage from Xenophon's *Memorabilia* quoted at the beginning of this chapter.[40]

The development of mastery of light and shade plays a central role in the Hellenistic and Roman histories of Greek painting, ultimately indebted to Xenocrates, writing in the third century BCE.[41] The Elder Pliny describes the process by which painting emerged as an art form in terms of the discovery of light and shade, and the development of specific techniques for their representation (*Natural History* 35.29):[42]

> Eventually art differentiated itself, and discovered light and shade, contrast of colours heightening their effect reciprocally. Then came the final addition of highlight (*splendor*), quite a different thing from light (*lumen*). That which mediates between *splendor* and *lumen* on the one side and shades (*umbras*) on the other was called *tonos*, while the juxtaposition of colours (*commissuras*) and their passage into one another (*transitus*) was termed attunement (*harmogē*).

Apollodorus, active in the late fifth century and also known as "the shadow-painter" (*ho skiagraphos*), is celebrated by Pliny as the "first to shine forth" (*primus refulsit*) amongst the luminaries of painting, and the earliest painter whose work could still "hold the eyes" of spectators even in Pliny's own day.[43] He was followed by Zeuxis, who "entered the gates thrown open by Apollodorus", and, in the words of the Roman orator Quintilian, discovered *luminum umbrarumque rationem*.[44] Exactly what this "logic of light and shade" comprised is not perfectly clear, but seems likely to have involved some kind of systematization of the schemes of shading and highlighting bodies in order to ensure that they stood out in relief in the picture, without the *trompe l'œil* effect being undermined by contradictory perceptual cues.[45]

As with *skēnographia*, so also with shadow-painting, there seem to have been intersections between developments in the field of painting, and scientific reflections on optical phenomena. Democritus, whom we encountered in the first section of this chapter writing about scenography and drawing with rays, also wrote a treatise "On Colours" (*peri chroōn*), in which he seems to have conceptualized the colour of objects as an epiphenomenon of the interaction within them of atoms and void, according to the specific rhythm, dynamics and ordering of their mutual impacts.[46]

---

39 Cf. Summers (2003: 469, 544–6).
40 Cf. Summers (2003: 483).
41 For discussion, see Rouveret (1989: 42–8).
42 I adjust my translation here after that of Rackham (1949–52: 9.281–3).
43 Pliny, *Natural History* 35.60: the key texts are collected by Reinach (1981: nos. 193–8).
44 Pliny, *Natural History* 35.61; Quintilian, *Training of the Orator* 12.10.4.
45 The developments in systematic depictions of light and shade, and the elimination of contradictory perceptual cues, are discussed by Bruno (1977: 37–8) in relation to the stelai from Volos.
46 Cf. Rouveret (1984: 159), discussing the passage collected in Diels (1922: 2.125, no. 112).

In his *On Sense and the Sensible*, Aristotle describes a method of colour mixture for painting in terms of a system of mathematical proportions. He categorizes colours by assessing whether they can be mixed out of his primary colours (black, white, yellow and grey) according to proportions expressible in rational numbers, or only in terms of incommensurable relations of super- and subordination, which he compares to consonant (or rational) and inconsonant tonal combinations in music.[47] Some of the technical terms used to describe *skiagraphia* in Pliny's art history – notably *tonos* and *harmogē*, both Greek terms used by Pliny – are also found in the musical theory of Aristoxenus of Tarentum (*ca.* 370–320 BCE), where the concept of colours (*chroai*) describes permissible free variation on the interior notes of tetrachords.[48] In both painting and music, this "attunement" and "harmonization" of tones seems likely to have been conceptualized in mathematical terms.[49]

Classical art historians have expended much effort in trying to identify the exact pictorial technique which corresponded to the term *skiagaphia*. Eva Keuls, for example, suggested that it might involve pointillist techniques whereby tiny flecks of different colours were juxtaposed on the painting surface, and integrated only on the retina of the eye into coherent patterns of light, shade and colour representing specific objects.[50] This is in certain respects an attractive argument, since it corresponds well with the Democritean account of vision, and techniques of juxtaposition or colour patching can also even be found in examples of Classical Greek wall-painting, like the figure of Rhadamanthus from the Great Tomb at Lefkadia. In the last generation, however, the range of evidence we have for Classical Greek wall and panel-painting has been vastly expanded by the discoveries from the tombs of Macedonia, above all the royal tombs at Vergina. These demonstrate a wide range of different techniques for modelling light and shade, including colour-mixing, hatching, superposition (the building up of layers of variably transparent pigments) and the adding of impasto to suggest highlights, as well as colour-patching. In any particular painting a number of these techniques may be used in combination, the paintings from Lefkadia being a case in point.[51] It is probably a mistake to think of scientific theories of optical perception as determining in any straightforward way painterly practice; rather, both fields offered each other stimulation and possible directions for exploration, elaborated or not according to each field's own specific logic and practical constraints.

Plato's objections to *skiagraphia* seem to have been heavily determined by his metaphysical commitments. The only knowledge that was worthy of the name was knowledge of the world of Forms, the one true reality, pure intelligibles which were the proper object of philosophical contemplation and intellectual nourishment for

---

47 Aristotle, *On Sense and the Sensible* 439–48, discussed by Sorabji (1972: 295–8) and Rouveret (2006: 21–2).
48 Cf. Rouveret (2006: 21–2; 2007: 73). Pollitt (2002: 5) also comments on the musical parallel of *tonos*; cf. Pollitt (1974: 270–1).
49 Cf. Netz & Squire (this volume) on Archytas and theorems concerning attunement (*harmonia*) realized through numbers, and for Archytas' interest in musical as well as optical theory.
50 Keuls (1978b: 78–87).
51 See Brécoulaki (2006); cf. Rouveret (2007) for the best discussion of the relation between the textual evidence for colour and modelling in Greek painting and the new discoveries in Macedonia, revising her 1989 study in their light.

the higher rational element in our souls, *to logistikon*. In Book 10 of the *Republic*, when Plato discusses painting in its own right, alongside other mimetic arts, *skiagraphia* is described as the antithesis of truth, and as far removed as it is possible to be from the world of the Forms, imitations of imitations. A *skiagraphic* painting is a mere simulacrum (*eidōlon*) or apparition (*phantasma*), like the real (*to on*), but not the real, a faint or indistinct (*amudron*) impression of the truth.[52] *Skiagraphia*, like such naturally occurring illusions as a straight stick appearing bent because of the refractive powers of water, exploits by a kind of witchcraft (*goēteia*) a deficiency rooted in our embodiment. The intellectual confusion created by such illusions, creating a contradiction between what we seem to see and what we know to be the case, has the potential to undermine and destabilize the rational element in our soul.[53] The victim of such an illusion – "at odds with himself as regards his vision" (*kata tēn opsin estasiazen*) and "at war with himself" (*machetai autos hautōi*) – is unable "to keep a steady frame of mind" (*homonoētikōs anthrōpos diakeitai*).[54] In other books of the *Republic*, and in other Platonic dialogues, this theoretically grounded account of visual *skiagraphia* forms the basis of a series of metaphors used to describe everything that is false, sham and insubstantial, every kind of deception and untruth.[55] Sketchy arguments (*eskiagraphēmena*) which blur the issues – in contrast to the apodictic clarity of mathematical or dialectical reasoning – are persuasive at first sight, but dissolve on closer inspection.[56] The specious appearance of virtue, as opposed to true virtue, is a *skiagraphia aretēs*, a shadow-painting of virtue.[57] The constantly shifting character of skiagraphic representation – constructed out of contrasting patches of colour which coalesce into an object at a distance but dissolve into chaos close up – offers an analogy to the relative character of false goods such as sensory pleasures, deriving their character from the contrast with pain, mere "phantoms" (*eidōla*) of the true intellectual pleasures of the philosopher.[58]

How then did *skiagraphia* put vision to work in relation to the task of painting – that is, the representation of seen things (*eikasia tōn horōmenōn*)? Much recent work has explored the range of depictive techniques employed in the spectacular paintings of the royal tombs of Macedon: the different media used, the techniques of application, and the differing visual effects to which they give rise.[59] However, in order to analyse further the interactions between these cultural themes and the appropriation of visual perception which *skiagraphia* entailed in practice, I want to return to a painted tomb which has been known for a much longer time (and is now in a sadly degraded state of preservation), but which has not perhaps received the close analysis

---

52 Plato, *Republic* 597a–598c.
53 Plato, *Republic* 602c–d.
54 Plato, *Republic* 603c–d.
55 Keuls (1978b: 78–9) and Rouveret (1989: 26) both have excellent summaries and comprehensive lists of references for these metaphorical uses.
56 See e.g. Plato, *Republic* 523a–526a, *Critias* 107c–d (with Trimpi 1978: 406). On *skiagraphēma* in *Theaetetus* 208e, see Keuls (1978b: 81–1).
57 Plato, *Republic* 365c.
58 Plato, *Republic* 586b: cf. Keuls (1978b: 82–3); Rouveret (1989: 26). As Trimpi (1978: 406) summarizes, to inhabit the world of *skiagraphia* is to find oneself in a "constantly fluctuating hallucinatory state".
59 Cf. Brécoulaki (2006); Descamps-Lequime (2007).

it deserves – namely the Great Tomb at Lefkadia. The paintings of this tomb highlight in a particularly striking way the very self-conscious, even reflexive, way in which late Classical artists explored the relationship between sight and painting.[60]

The Great Tomb at Lefkadia dates to the early third century BCE (Plate 5);[61] 28-feet wide, by 28-feet high, it is one of the largest tombs from Macedonia, and must have been built for an individual of exceptional wealth and social standing. The façade seems to be modelled on a palace or possibly even on a stage representation of a palace: it is not easy to tell the difference, since the depictions of palaces in theatres became the model for royal palaces, and were eventually realized in stone as stage buildings.[62] A pediment, originally painted but now almost entirely lost, is supported by a series of Ionic half-columns flanking false doors or possibly shuttered windows, all in relief stucco. Beneath them is a continuous Ionic frieze, with representations of Greeks battling Persians, in relief stucco painted in full polychrome. Beneath that is a Doric triglyph and metope frieze, representing a centauromachy. The architrave is supported by four Doric half columns and pilasters. Between the central columns is the doorway into the tomb. On either side of the doorway, a dado of stucco masonry in five courses supports a ledge on which stand four painted figures, about four-feet high, one between each of the columns. On the left-hand side, Hermes leads the deceased, dressed as a military man, with cuirass, spear, boots and *himation*. On the right-hand side, two judges from the underworld, Aeacus seated and Rhadamanthus standing, are both named in inscriptions.

The paintings of the façade seem deliberately designed to explore a series of differential claims about the ontology of images, each grounded in distinctive ways of playing with colour, light, shade and sight. The frieze showing Greeks battling Persians is modelled in relief and evokes reality not only through the polychromy of the figures, but also by the real shadows cast by their relief forms. At first sight the centauromachy metopes, painted as if seen from below, look like carvings in marble (Plate 6): the flesh of the figures is painted in a restricted palette of pale tones – yellows, browns and greys – effectively modelled with darker and lighter passages to suggest relief. A *trompe l'œil* effect is created by the shadows apparently cast by the painted figures, consistently lit from above and to the left. The cast shadows themselves are even modulated according to the *ratio* of light and shade: dark at the edge of the body, they then lighten in the middle zone with the (virtual) reflected light from the bodies, before darkening again, and lightening to the point of being fully bleached out by the sunlight (Plate 7).[63] The figures of the warrior and Hermes are painted in bright colours, carefully modelled in light and shade, to give them a living presence. The warrior (Plate 8) wears a bright red tunic

---

60 On the underlying themes of sight and reflexivity here (albeit in the field of Greek vase-painting), cf. Grethlein's chapter in this volume.
61 Key earlier discussions include Robertson (1976: 568–71) and Rouveret (1989: 174–7). The tomb and its paintings were published by Petsas (1966), which includes the best plates (now in a better state than the originals).
62 See R. Robert (1996: 30–3) for a good discussion, pointing out that Zeuxis was employed by Archelaus to decorate the royal palace at Pella, and discussing the self-consciously theatrical character of the self-presentation of Hellenistic kings like Demetrius Poliorcetes; cf. R. Martin (1968) for discussion of architectural parallels for the façade.
63 Cf. Bruno (1981: 4–7).

underneath a glistening white cuirass, decorated with a purple belt and shoulder straps, detailed in fine white lines perhaps evoking the glinting of metallic ornament. With well-muscled legs, he stands in a *contrapposto* pose, a spear in his raised right hand, evoking a strong real presence reminiscent of statues of Alexander the Great as a *Doryphoros* or "Lance-bearer". Hermes (Plate 9) turns towards the warrior, beckoning him. He also is a substantial figure, dressed in a red tunic and a two-tone cloak (part blue, part purple): these are modelled with systematic treatment of light and shade so as to suggest the folds of the cloth wrapping the body on the one hand, and its real substance fluttering in space where the fabric hangs over his left arm on the other.

The figures on the other side of the door have a radically different character. Here the only hint of the light and bright colour which characterizes the world of the warrior and Hermes are the shoes of the figures, striking in purple and blue and dramatizing by contrast the otherwise dark and dismal character of this underworld scene. The creamy-pink flesh and clear outlines of the figures of Hermes and (perhaps less clearly – already becoming a shadow of himself?) the warrior, are replaced by blurred outlines and grey-white flesh tones, barely discriminable from the white of the wall. Rhadamanthus and Aeacus are wraithlike shadows of real beings, who would seem to merge into the wall itself, were it not for their sombre brown *himatia*, endowed with a certain substance through the modelling of their folds in subtly contrasted darker and lighter tones of brown (Plates 10 and 11).

For a viewer like Plato, potentially disturbed by a straight stick apparently bent by the refractive properties of water, contemplating the paintings at Lefkadia would have been a truly dizzying experience, drawn this way and that by the various levels of imaging – by the shadow-paintings of shady entities of indeterminate status. But this display of skiagraphic virtuosity was not simply a technical display: it was integrated with the thematics and function of the tomb-paintings, framing the ritual processes of burial, and exploring the liminal character of death. Painted façades like that at Lefkadia were designed specifically as a setting for the performance of the funeral ceremony and the burial of the deceased, a ritual process in which both the deceased and the mourners entered a liminal space, neither the "here" of the world of the living nor the "there" of the other side, the world of the dead.[64] The manipulation of the viewers' sense of sight – through the techniques of *skiagraphia* deploying colour, light and shade – frames and dramatizes that ritual process, and affords viewers a virtual experience of that destabilization and dissolution of the self which is death. The painting is "psychagogic" – in the terms of fourth-century rhetorical and art theory – on multiple levels.[65] It entrances and bewitches the viewer with its skiagraphic play. Setting, as Plato suggests, the different parts of the soul at war with themselves, it affords a premonitory experience of the dissolution of the self in death. It is also more literally psychagogic, framing the entry of the deceased into his tomb, led by Hermes Psychopompos, the escort of souls. The vocabulary used to describe

---

64 See R. Robert (1996: 30–1) on the function of painted façades, suggesting that they may have been covered over by the tumulus relatively soon after the funeral.
65 For the vocabulary of *psychagōgia* in relation to visual art, see Xenophon, *Memorabilia* 3.10.6 and Gorgias, *Helen* 13–14, 18 (with Brancacci 1995 and R. Robert 1992: 402–10). The same language is used negatively – of mimetic art and the power of images – by Plato, *Timaeus* 71a.

the dead, from Homer onwards, has considerable overlap with that used by Plato to describe skiagraphic painting. In the eleventh book of Homer's *Odyssey*, for example, the hero travels to the very boundaries of the Ocean, and to the threshold of Hades where he summons souls of the dead with an offering of blood. Among those he encounters are his mother, Anticlea, and before she leaves he seeks to grasp her, only to have her slip through his hands "like a shadow or a dream" (*skiēi eikelon ē oneirōi*), evanescent like an *eidōlon* or phantom.[66] It is their very shadowiness, their dim and indistinct character (*amudron*, as Plato characterizes *skiagraphia*) that underscores the "truth effect" of these paintings of the judges of the underworld.[67] Playing with the viewers' sense of reality, deliberately unsettling it in exactly the ways that Plato condemned, these skiagraphic images visually destabilize the viewer's sense of self, undermine the taken-for-granted ontological stability of everyday life, conjuring up instead the flickering shadows of the world of the dead, which the mourners and the deceased approach together, in the funeral. The mourners return to the world of light and colour,[68] the dead warrior enters through the door of the tomb into the darkness of the halls of Hades, Ἅιδης, a world without sight (ἀϊδής).[69]

Conclusion: sensing sight through painting

Both *skēnographia* and *skiagraphia* are ancestral to traditions of western painting in post-Renaissance art, as "perspective" and "chiaroscuro", and it is all too easy to take them for granted as simply passive registrations of human visual experience, the natural way of representing the world, as implied in the concept of "naturalism".[70] The development of these pictorial practices in Classical Greece, however, involved an active cultural appropriation of vision and a deep exploration of the cultural meanings and the cognitive value of sight as a mode of sensory experience. Both *skēnographia* and *skiagraphia* were developed in the context of a complex interplay with contemporary optical theory and philosophy, which variably bolstered and undermined the claims of both vision and painting as media for veridical experience. The specific ways in which the claims, and the limits, of sight as a mode of sensory experience were articulated in painting owed much to the institutional contexts in which the relationship between sight and painting were explored. Scene-painting in

---

66 Homer, *Odyssey* 11.206–13; cf. Turner (this volume); Bardel (2000: 145–53).
67 Cf. Plato, *Republic* 597b: painted images are said at best to be able to give a very dim or indistinct (*amudron*) impression of the truth.
68 "Seeing the light" was a periphrasis for being alive (cf. Squire's introduction to this volume). When Odysseus, like the mourners at Lefkadia, approaches the threshold of death in the *Nekuia* of the *Odyssey*'s eleventh book, the soul of Tiresias asks him why he has "left the light of the sun, in order to see corpses and a land without pleasure". His mother, Anticlea, also questions him: "My son, how did you come to this place of murky darkness, still being alive; for these realms are hard to see for living beings" (*Odyssey* 11.155–6). The colourful figures of Hermes and the warrior doubtless "pleasured the eyes", to use Gorgias' terms, whilst the gloomy Aeacus and Rhadamanthus evoke the shadowy existence of beings in a land without pleasures, far from the light of the sun.
69 For the etymology of Hades in terms of privation of sight (*idein* means to see), see Plato, *Phaedo* 80d, *Cratylus* 403a – along with the discussion by Coo in this volume.
70 Cf. Gombrich (1960); Bryson (1983); W. J. T. Mitchell (1986: 75–94).

the theatre staged the power of painting to rationalize sight, to coordinate and focus vision as collective experience, the *demos* putting itself and its values on show in the theatre. The shadow-paintings of the Great Tomb at Lefkadia explore the limits of sight as individual experience, defining both the limits of painting and the limits of individual life in terms of seeing and its deprivation.

6

SIGHT AND LIGHT

Reified gazes and looking artefacts in the Greek cultural imagination

Ruth Bielfeldt

In his ninth *Paean Ode* (frg. 52k), Pindar addresses the sun's ray as the mother of all eyes. Like many other such phrases, Pindar's label attests to the powerful idea, pervasive in early Greek poetry, that there is a natural kinship between the eye and the sun. The image of the sun as "seeing" goes back to the Homeric epics, which adopted concepts of the all-seeing sun-god from Egypt and the ancient Near East. But it is only with the emergence of Greek philosophy and science (above all from the fifth century BCE onwards) that this poetic notion is converted into a systematic model of perception, based on paradigms of organic equality or even connaturality. Sun and eye are thought to share physical and operational similarities: the very emission of fire is associated with the ability to see. The fact that seeing is a capacity inherent in light and fire implies, however, that sight does not necessarily need a living body or mind to be exercised. Sight is an activity that can be unconnected, even detached, from subjectivity: it can be understood in relation to anything that is endowed with fire or reflective of light.[1]

In this chapter, I want to suggest that the materiality and exteriority of sight explain why vision is a faculty that may be enacted even by objects otherwise considered inanimate. As a quality of an object, vision can also be a product of manufacture. To explain what I mean here, I will turn to one particular group of objects that were understood to be endowed with eyesight, even material intelligence: manmade lamps. Although I will focus on a number of material case studies, I centre my argument around a close reading of the opening lines of Aristophanes' *Assemblywomen* (performed in the early fourth century BCE). This passage, as we shall see, sheds light on the manifold cultural lives of ancient lighting devices – as microcosmic organs that simultaneously materialize the sun's macrocosmic gaze, and thus serve as a primary tool within the world.

---

1 In *Iliad* 14.16–17, for example, *ossesthai* is used even for the sea (*pelagos*), watching out for the winds. On the whole question of "l'œil et la lumière" – tackled from a broad anthropological perspective, but with special reference to Greek and Roman materials – see Deonna (1965: 251–300, esp. 251–8). Throughout this chapter, I use the abbreviation "DK" to refer to the fragments collected in Diels & Kranz (1951–2).

To see is to shine

First let me return to Greek languages of "sight" and "light" more generally, surveying some of the philosophical themes explored earlier in this book by Kelli Rudolph and Andrea Nightingale. The basic axioms of sense perception through visual fire are already present in Homer. In both the *Iliad* and the *Odyssey*, we find the idea that fire, light and vision form an inseparable unity: not only is fire endowed with sight, but the eyes are in turn also conceived as fire-like, their glance figured as spraying sparks. Homer considers eyes and glances as themselves emissive of fire. In the *Iliad*, for example, the eyes of Achilles are said to sparkle like flames while he arms himself with Hephaestus' new armour (*Iliad* 19.365). Likewise, Hector assaults the Greek camp with a "fire-glance" that serves as his main weapon (*puri d'osse dedēei*, *Iliad* 12.466); so too, in *Odyssey* 19.446, a boar is said to flash fire from his eyes, once again as a means of attack.[2]

Homer's view of perception lays the ground for the first scientific explanations of vision in Presocratic philosophy. According to early "extramissionist" theories of seeing, eyesight is explained as an event of a physical and material nature: the eye itself contains fire and emits fiery rays of light that touch the surface of the perceived objects.[3] According to Plato's later reworking in the *Timaeus*, those emitted fiery rays meet the physical images emanated by the objects in the air before transporting an imprint of that "clash" back to the eye. While critical of Empedocles, Aristotle and Theophrastus both credit him with developing the extramission theory and quote his famous lantern simile, in which the eye is compared with a lantern carried outside into the winter night. Like the light in the lantern, the fire in the eye has to pervade a humid membrane (the conjunctiva) in order to effuse into plain air.[4]

Since, according to such extramissionist theories, seeing is understood as a physical process that involves matter in motion, it is also an activity to be seen. Bruno Snell has argued that Homeric words for seeing – *derkesthai*, *paptainein*, *ossesthai*, *leussein*, etc. – conceptualize vision not as an intentional cognitive act entertained by a conscious subject, but as an affective gesture, and hence an expressive manifestation of an individual's outward character.[5] The question such epic language consequently raises about the viewing subject is not *what* he sees, but rather *how* he looks (and, by extension, what he *looks like*). According to this model, to look is to shine, and thereby also to appear. It is the moment of casting a look that lends the human eye an epiphanic character, turning it into an affective object that also begs to be beheld. Consequently, Homeric viewing is embedded in a web of relations between the looker, the looked-upon (that is, the person or object that in being touched itself tinges the looker's gaze) and third parties – often external

---

2 Cf. Malten (1961: 56).
3 On ancient theories of "extramission", see the earlier discussion in this volume by Squire (in his introduction), as well as the chapters by Rudolph and Nightingale.
4 For ancient theories of perception, Beare (1906: 9–92) still offers an excellent text-oriented discussion. For Theophrastus' reading of Empedocles, see the study by Baltussen (2000), along with Schirren (1998: 221–9). On Plato, *Timaeus* 45b–d, see Brisson (1998: 147–74).
5 Snell (1975: 13–16). For a phenomenological reading of Homeric *aisthēsis* and a discussion of Snell's own interpretations, see Prier (1989: 25–42, 68–108).

onlookers, human or divine, who are manifestly impacted by the expressive gaze of the looker.[6]

The notion of vision's visibility also inheres in post-Homeric terms for seeing. In line with earlier Homeric terminologies, Archaic and Classical Greek languages of sight combine both aspects: on the one hand, the idea of looking, and on the other the "looks" (which are understood as the subject's appearance or aspect). Gérard Simon has pointed out that terms for the eye and for seeing, such as *opsis*, *omma* and *ophthalmos*, have both an active and a passive meaning in Classical Greek: *omma* stands not only for the eye and for light, for example, but also for the face and (as *pars pro toto*) for a person.[7] The same holds true for *opsis* and *ophthalmos*. The notion of vision as coincidence of passive and active, subject and object, likewise lives on in Roman thinking. Latin terminology does not offer the same linguistic options to express sight's physical embeddedness by means of a single word. But the Latin words *species* and *uisus* both cover a wide semantic spectrum, ranging between the act of seeing/looking, the thing seen and outward appearances.[8] Cicero found a compelling way to bring together those different aspects in labelling the eye the discloser of the inner spirit (*imago animi uultus, indices oculi*: Cicero, On the Orator 3.221.4).[9]

As something endowed with fire, the eye is a manifestation of the sun. Yet, as Ilaria Rizzini has argued, the relation between the two makes for more than a metaphorical analogy: eye and sun are congruent in the ways that they work.[10] The bodily organ is understood as a luminary, just as the celestial body is believed to operate as a cosmic sensory organ. Already in Homeric poetry, the sun (Helios) could be addressed as a universal organ whose gaze nothing escapes. Other *luminifera*, such as the moon (Selene) and the stars, are likewise thought to be endowed with perception due to their emission of rays (*aktines*). The Homeric concept of the sun-eye and the eye-sun lived on in the language of Greek and Roman poetry too, as well as in Greek philosophy and science (from the Ionian scientists and Plato to the optic treatises of Hellenistic and Imperial times). The best testimony to this tradition in Latin poetic language can be found in the fact that *lumen*, a term that in itself carries the notions of the fiery and solar eye, is used interchangeably with *oculus*.[11]

---

6 The function of the external onlookers is to exteriorize the effect of the looker's gaze on the one hand, and to mediate their responsiveness to the epic's audience on the other. The role of the third party can also be taken by the narrator himself. More generally on how such "focalization" of looking relates to Homeric narratology at large, cf. de Jong (2004).
7 G. Simon (1992: 35–40), with reference to Mugler (1964: 290–6, *s.v.* "opsis"); see also Cairns (2005).
8 Cf. Bettini (2000: 3–4).
9 On the expressive eye in texts discussing the efficacy of art theory cf. Rizzini (1998: 165–7), especially on Xenophon, *Memorabilia* 3.10 and the Elder Philostratus' *Imagines*.
10 Rizzini (1998: 127–43).
11 Cf. *Oxford Latin Dictionary*, *s.v.* "lumen". While *lumen* for the most part designates an active source of light, it can also describe an opening through which external light enters, i.e. an aperture, window or airhole; cf. Vitruvius 4.6. For the interchangeable use of *oculus* and *lumen* see, for example, Lucretius 3.359–68. Why Lucretius makes use of the term *lumen* is an open question, given that Lucretius is an "intromissionist" in the tradition of the Atomists, and overtly does not believe in fiery sight rays. In some passages, however, Lucretius nonetheless plays with the idea that the eye might be in possession of its own light. So it is, for example, that in 3.408–16 Lucretius states that the light dies (*occidit extemplo lumen*) if the eye is seriously hurt. Similarly Lucretius' comments at 3.289 – discussing the

As the celestial eye par excellence, *oculus* is a well-attested poetic term for the sun, paying tribute to a long-standing conceptual equation between the cosmic and human organs of sight.[12]

Looking light: the lamp as a man-made eye in Aristophanes' *Assemblywomen*

As we have seen, extramissionist theorists conceptualize sight as a process that needs fire and light to be enacted: "looking" is understood as an activity as much about being seen as it is about seeing. But this extramissionist model has important implications for understanding the role of the person viewing – not simply as cognizant subject, but also as something to be perceived. The strong sense of objecthood associated with the Greek eye – and by extension, the visibility and tangibility of the viewer's gaze – may offer one explanation as to why, in Greek art and especially Attic vase-painting, the motif of the eye could be prominently marked on inanimate objects like vases, coins, shields and ships (Figure 6.1; cf. Figures I.4, I.7).[13] As Jonas Grethlein has already discussed in this volume, eyes are painted on the underside of sixth- and fifth-century Attic drinking-cups (*kylikes*) to bestow the vessels, once lifted, with an affective stare: the cup's own gaze imprints itself upon the group of symposiastic banqueters (cf. Figures 4.3, 4.12).[14] Such painted eyes do not necessarily turn the object into a person that sees in and of itself; rather, they render the vase a counterpart that manifests itself through its gaze.[15] As such, the appeal of such devices lies in their non-naturalistic, artificial appearance. On numerous cups, the illusion of the humanoid or animal face is intentionally broken by means of inserted figures or entire narrative scenes separating the eyes. On amphorae, moreover, the eyes can be positioned below the handles on each side of the vessel so that they can never be seen simultaneously; alternatively, they can be shown in mirror-image, with the tear duct pointing outward, thus deviating from any "realistic" facial model.[16]

---

eye of an irate person (*ex oculis micat acrius ardor*), and qualifying it with the comparative acrius ("sharper") that is given by the manuscripts – have also caused confusion among scholars: after all, the passage would suggest that Lucretius' overall concept of vision assumes a flow of fire emanating from the eye, which would only be intensified by anger; it is for this reason that Laminus emended *acrius* to *acribus* (cf. Kenney 2014: 115).

12 For *mundi oculus*, see Ovid, *Metamorphoses* 4.228; Pliny the Elder, *Natural History* 2.5.
13 On eyes on artefacts, see Steinhart (1995), as well as Squire's introduction to this volume.
14 Among numerous recent publications, see Rivière-Adonon (2011) (with survey of earlier bibliography – and noting some 2,225 examples between 540 and 485 BCE); I have been unable to consult Moser von Filseck (1996). On literal masks – and their rendering of the eyes – in the Greek theatre, see Coo (this volume).
15 Eye-cups often present entire faces, including nose, sometimes ears, and mouth in the form of the stem. They have therefore been interpreted as Dionysian masks shielding the drinker's head when raised to the mouth: see e.g. Vernant & Frontisi (1983); Kunisch (1990); Frontisi-Ducroux (1991: 178–88); Steinhart (1995) and Grethlein (this volume). Steinhart (1995: 55–61) interprets cups with eyes and nose as panther masks.
16 For eyes inverted in the mirror, see Steinhart (1995: pl. 29.3–4); for single eyes, see Steinhart (1995: pl. 29.2, 30.1, 3–4; 31.1); for carried eyes, see Steinhart (1995: pl. 20–1). More generally on Greek and Roman ideas of the "embodied eye", see Squire's introduction to this volume.

Figure 6.1 Attic red-figure eye-cup attributed to the Nikosthenes Painter, *ca.* 520–510 BCE. Cambridge, Fitzwilliam Museum: inv. GR.1.1927 (© The Fitzwilliam Museum, Cambridge).

The materiality of the gaze may also lie behind the attribution of eyesight to other sorts of inanimate objects. In literary texts we find a variety of objects, both natural and manufactured, labelled as *martures*, or "witnesses" of human life.[17] But one class of humble household items is consistently singled out in both Greek and Roman texts as being capable of eyesight: lamps. As the following discussion will show, lamps (in both their operation and their form) offer the ultimate illustration of the coincidence of sight and light in an object.

The earliest extant instance in which a lamp is addressed as an eye comes in the prologue to Aristophanes' *Assemblywomen*, performed in Athens after 392 BCE. While sneaking out of her house at dawn in order to plan a female *coup d'état*, the protagonist, Praxagora (here dressed as a man), takes a lamp in her hand and addresses it as though it were a god. It is a powerful apostrophe, albeit simultaneously also an ironic one, with multiple linguistic echoes to Greek tragic language (vv. 1–18):[18]

---

17 Anything endowed with light can act as a *martus*: the gods, the bolt of Zeus, the days (cf. Pindar, *Olympian Odes* 1.34) or for that matter eyes themselves (cf. Heraclitus, DK 22 B 101a). Pindar (*Pythian Odes* 12.27) calls reeds – as future flutes – witnesses to the dancing Charites. Aristophanes (*Wasps* 937ff.) has even household items serve as witnesses in court. For the lamp as witness cf. Kost (1971: 125, 131–2).
18 Cf. Ussher (1973: 70–6); Sommerstein (1998: 137–40).

ὦ λαμπρὸν ὄμμα τοῦ τροχηλάτου λύχνου,
κάλλιστ᾽ ἐν εὐστόχοισιν ἐξηυρημένον—
γονάς τε γὰρ σὰς καὶ τύχας δηλώσομεν·
τροχῷ γὰρ ἐλαθεὶς κεραμικῆς ῥύμης ὕπο
μυκτῆρσι λαμπρὰς ἡλίου τιμὰς ἔχεις—
ὅρμα φλογὸς σημεῖα τὰ ξυγκείμενα.
σοὶ γὰρ μόνῳ δηλοῦμεν εἰκότως, ἐπεὶ
κἀν τοῖσι δωματίοισιν Ἀφροδίτης τρόπων
πειρωμέναισι πλησίος παραστατεῖς,
λορδουμένων τε σωμάτων ἐπιστάτην
ὀφθαλμὸν οὐδεὶς τὸν σὸν ἐξείργει δόμων.
μόνος δὲ μηρῶν εἰς ἀπορρήτους μυχοὺς
λάμπεις ἀφεύων τὴν ἐπανθοῦσαν τρίχα·
στοὰς δὲ καρποῦ Βακχίου τε νάματος
πλήρεις ὑποιγνύσαισι συμπαραστατεῖς·
καὶ ταῦτα συνδρῶν οὐ λαλεῖς τοῖς πλησίον.
ἀνθ᾽ ὧν συνείσει καὶ τὰ νῦν βουλεύματα
ὅσα Σκίροις ἔδοξε ταῖς ἐμαῖς φίλαις.

O radiant eye of the wheel-whirled lamp, fairest invention of skilled artisans. I shall reveal your birth and fortunes, for whirled on the wheel by the potter's impetus, you bear the sun's radiant offices in your nostrils. Broadcast now the fiery signal as arranged. In you alone we confide, and rightly, for also in our bedrooms as we essay Aphrodite's manoeuvres you stand close by; your eye supervising our flexed bodies will no one banish from the house. You alone illuminate the ineffable nooks between our thighs, when you singe away the hair that sprouts there; and when stealthily we open pantries stocked with bread and the liquor of Bacchus you stand by and with us; and doing this together with us you never blab to those around us. So you'll be in our present plans too, all that my friends agreed on at the Scira.[19]

While we can be certain that the humorous verses on the lamp – characterized as a sort of "bodyguard" of women (vv. 7–13) – will have produced laughter, we cannot be sure how ludicrous or amusing this opening prologue was meant to be. What lends the passage its sense of irony? Is it what Praxagora says that is funny? Or did the humour lie in how she said it, or indeed the fact that she speaks these words at this particular moment and in this context? Such apostrophic address of inanimate objects was frequent in tragedy, and ancient scholia on the *Assemblywomen* suggest that our opening verse quoted a famous tragic line (perhaps one that likewise invoked a lamp). It was probably not Praxagora's hymnic tone and elevation of a humble object to semi-divine status that was inappropriate or eccentric, but rather the pomposity of her paratragic entrance, aping specific passages of recently performed tragedies in style, language and content.[20] I thus propose to read the hymn to

---

19 Translation adapted from J. Henderson (2002: 247).
20 The scholia (*sch. Eccl.* 1.1) see in the first iambic verse (ὦ λαμπρὸν ὄμμα τοῦ τροχηλάτου λύχνου) a direct adaption of either Agathon or Dicaeogenes, both Athenian dramatists of the late fifth century BCE. It is

the lamp from Praxagora's own vantage point, and to take it for what it is: the biography of an object that has multiple lives – physical, mythical and social.

So what, then, to make of Praxagora's lamp? The lamp itself appears on the scene as silent co-protagonist, and Praxagora converses with "him" (*luchnos*, after all, is grammatically gendered male) on an equal footing. Yet already in the prologue's first line, Praxagora draws out the lamp's paradoxical nature. The object is addressed as a radiant eye, one that operates simultaneously as a light-emitting entity and sensory organ. At the same time, the lamp is said to be "wheel-whirled" (*trochēlatou*, v. 1, and *trochōi gar elatheis*, v. 4), and hence a man-made device. The organic nature of the lamp stands in contradiction to its artificial manufacture.

The following lines develop that ambivalent half-creature, half-thing status. They also comment on the lamp's conflicting materiality that encompasses both fire (and hence bodily life), and also earthenware (as something brought into shape by the turnings of the potter's wheel). While rendered an "organic" entity, the lamp is characterized in eclectic terms. If the presence of solar fire makes the lamp itself an eye, the brilliance that "Luchnos" emits is said to exude not directly from the eye, but rather from the nostrils (*muktērsi*). *Muktēr* (later rendered in Latin as *myxa* or *rostrum* – a "beak" or "muzzle") is a zoographic term: it describes the lamp's wick-holding "nozzle" in relation to an animal's nose and mouth.[21] Vision is thus concurrently imagined in terms of the lamp's emitted light, as well as via the fumes exhaled from its nozzle. Described in both technical and zoographic terms, the lamp emerges before our eyes as both passive object (*exēurēmenon*) and active living being (*echeis*).

The lamp's ambivalent nature also extends to its ancestry, and above all to Praxagora's myth-making about its "birth". While the lamp is the invention of a skilled artisan, the fact that it holds and protects resplendent solar fire makes it representative of Helios ("Sun") himself. The lamp, once again, is more than mere object: it is a microcosm crafted after macrocosmic principle. By extension, the fire that sits in the nozzle as something to be exhaled is poetically deemed "the bright honours of the sun" (*lampras hēliou timas echeis*).[22] The use of the term *timē* is important here, characterizing the lamp's "glory" and "public honour" in at least two interconnected ways. On the one hand, the lamp has the "honour" of bearing the sun's divine fire. On the other, the lamp has been bestowed with a specific public duty – which is why Praxagora can summon it to take political action and cast a fiery signal (*horma phlogos sēmeia*).[23] In the lamp, shining, looking and interacting coincide.

---

debatable whether the iambic opening of the tragedy was exactly copied and hence contained itself an apostrophe of a lamp, or rather a salutation of the sun. In the latter case, the last word of the first verse would have been either *kuklou* or *theou*, cf. Snell (1986: 168) for Agathon F 32.

21 For ancient zoomorphic terms for the lamp's nozzle, see Hug (1927: 1570–1).

22 The sun could also be imagined as an exhaling luminary. According to Anaximander (DK A 21), the sun – similar in shape to a chariot's wheel – is thought to be blowing out fire from its interior through a pair of bellows (*presterōn aulos*: literally: "through a double-pipe of burning winds").

23 *Timē* can, however, have an even more concrete meaning. The rays of the sun were seen to form a crown all around, as if the sun wore a wreath: a similar crown of rays could be worn by the lamp.

Vision from a wheel? The making of sight

The two sides of Praxagora's lamp – fire and clay, life and manufacture – are not as irreconcilably opposed as they might first seem. One conceptual connection is provided by the notion of *omma*. We have already noted how Praxagora's address of the *lampron* as *omma* recalls extramissionist theories of the light-emitting, sensory organ of sight. But it also brings a material dimension to the fore: the word emphasizes the outwardness of a looking eye as something simultaneously to be looked at. As was said earlier, *omma* could refer to the face or appearance of a beheld person, and was even sometimes used as a term of endearment (like our expression, "apple of one's eye"). When Aristophanes' Praxagora calls her lamp *omma*, then, she evokes a triad of inter-associated meanings: the lamp is understood first as a source of light, second as a sensory organ and third as a looking artefact that doubles up as an expressive, visible entity. As *omma*, the lamp performs an act of perception that is doubly manifest – physically, in the light it produces, and corporeally, in the shape of the artificially forged terracotta body. *Luchnos* is an eye that shines for "us".

Another figure that challenges the assumed dichotomy of fire and matter, sun and potter, is that of the wheel (*trochos*). The wheel is the instrument on which the lamp is made (vv. 1 and 4). For Anaximander in the sixth century, however, *trochos* also became a metaphor for the sun's disk and its incessant motion.[24] Aristophanes himself makes prominent use of the term when talking about the artefactual nature of the human eye. In v. 17 of the *Women of the Thesmophoria* he has "Euripides" state that the Aither fabricated (*emēchanēsato*) the eye in imitation of the solar wheel, implicitly mocking Euripides for his pseudo-philosophical language (with all their distortion of Empedoclean cosmological and biological motifs).[25] Yet, parody aside, what ideas stand behind the association? One aspect of the description concerns movement, as the principle of rotation unites both lamp and luminary. Although implicit, the reference to the sun's *trochos* is meant to ennoble the lamp's elementary form. Its manufacture, emphasized twice in the first four lines, assimilates the ceramic object to the solar disk of the sun: it is the centrifugal force – the momentum of the turning apparatus (*keramikēs rhumēs*) – that guarantees the lamp's perfect (*kallist'*) circular shape.

Praxagora's opening lines seem to mimic the wheel's rotation in their cyclical, spiralling lexical structure, praising the lamp for being a wondrous invention (*exeurēmenon*)[26] by someone who aimed well (*en eustochoisin*), an almost tautological

---

[24] Anaximander, DK 12 A 21, l.2 and 1.8 (*harmatiaiōi trochōi paraplēsion*); Aristophanes, frg. 188.1–2; see also Sophocles, *Antigone* 1066 and 1076, where *trochos* stands for the daily race of the sun. To the Athenian audience the reference would have been unmistakable if Aristophanes indeed mimicked an opening line by Agathon that ended with *trochēlatou kuklou*, "of the wheeldriving disk".

[25] [Αἰθὴρ...] πρῶτ' ἐμηχανήσατο ὀφθαλμὸν ἀντίμιμον ἡλίου τροχῷ: cf. the commentary in Austin & Olson (2004: 57–8). For the distortion of Empedoclean principles by the character named "Euripides" in the *Women of the Thesmophoria*, see the excellent analysis of Clements (2014: 23–6).

[26] The exact wording is unclear; cf. Ussher (1973: 71) on the possible emendations of EXĒTĒMENON (*exeitēmenon*: "demanded", "begged for") transmitted by the manuscripts; most plausible is *exeurēmenon* ("invented") or *ezētēmenon* ("sought after"). The only option that is to be excluded is *exertēmenon* ("suspended"), as Praxagora is definitely not talking about a suspended street lantern when highlighting the lamp's role for female cosmetics and night-time visits to the pantry.

phrasing. In fact, the passage is meant as a eulogy of the artefact's creator: it honours the potter who, by mere artisanal craft and technology, strove to echo the revolving motion of the celestial body. As it stands, the point about the correspondence between ceramics and luminaries applies to virtually any other Athenian ceramic object, which were standardly "wheel-made" on the potter's wheel. But only in the lamp does the spinning movement connect the device's sun-like manufacture with its solar appearance. It is for that reason that Aristophanes singles it out.

As we saw from the "Euripidean" statement in the *Women of the Thesmophoria* quoted above, the figure of the wheel also links sun and eye, both physically and conceptually. *Trochos*, itself a man-made instrument, stands here as synonym for *kuklos*, or "circle". The fact that Presocratic philosophers invested circularity with a sense of perfection is well known.[27] The sun's very shape – its movement along a circuit, its spiralling emission of fire,[28] its cyclic temporality and spatial environment, the spherical and revolving body of the universe – were all thought to be intrinsically related and connoted in this "cyclical" term. *Kuklos*, like *trochos*, is a designation of a round form. With Aristophanes, though, the word connects sun and eye in a corporeal manner that can be mapped onto the lamp. Greek authors (and in particular Attic dramatists) frequently speak of the sun as a *kuklos* – that is, as a disk or orb – just as they do of the eye, iris and pupil; by extension, the plural form of the word (*kukla*) could denote a pair of eyes.[29] Latin authors likewise use the term *orbis* to describe the globular forms of both sun and eye. When addressing the very *luchnos*, Praxagora does not comment on its roundness, as the device would have been familiar to everyone and visible on stage. But what kind of object did the Athenians see in Praxagora's hand in 392 BCE, when the comedy was first performed?

Considering Athenian oil lamps will help to corroborate my argument that the lamp's design referenced the disk of the sun in its geometric form and simulated, quite closely, the diagrammatic image of an eye in frontal view. Greek lamps have a disk-shaped body with a protruding snout; from the late sixth century onwards, Attic lamps were generally black-glazed apart from an incised, clay-coloured or white band around the flat rim of the circular oil chamber,[30] pierced by a vertical tube in the centre (e.g. Figure 6.2). From that perspective, we might venture the hypothesis that, when seen from above, lamps invite a comparison with the frontal, staring eyes that decorate late Archaic pots. Encircled with a bright ring, and filled with shining oil within, the lamp's large circular opening could recall the iris and

---

27 DK 58 C 3 l. 25.
28 Cf. Anaximander, DK A 21; Euripides, *Phoenician Women* 3: Ἥλιε, θοαῖς ἵπποισιν εἰλίσσων φλόγα ("Sun, who on swift steeds whirl your blaze in an arc"). Here the idea of the sun as a wheel is framed mythologically, thereby referring to Helios' chariot. For a comprehensive view of *kuklos* as fundamental governing principle of the entire cosmos, see Aristotle's treatise *On the Heavens*.
29 *Kuklos* for the shape of the sun or the moon, rather than the circuit, occurs in the above-quoted passage in Anaximander, and in Empedocles DK B 47 (*hagea kuklon*), as well as in Athenian tragedy (Aeschylus, *Prometheus Bound* 91; *Persians* 504; Sophocles, *Antigone* 416; Euripides, frg. 82 l.49). *Kukla* (mostly in the plural) for the eyes is frequent in Sophocles (e.g. *Oedipus Tyrannus* 1270; *Philoctetes* 1352; *Antigone* 974).
30 The clay-coloured band around the rim is found especially in lamp types that were produced from the late sixth century BCE onwards – classified by Howland (1958) in his publication of the lamps from the Athenian agora as types 17a–b, 18, 20 and 22.

Figure 6.2 Attic wheel-made clay lamp, *ca.* 475–425 BCE. Munich, Staatliche Antikensammlungen und Glyptothek: inv. NI 5310 (© Staatliche Antikensammlungen und Glyptothek, Munich).

pupil of stylized black-figure (and still more so red-figure) eye-cups, complete with oversize dark pupil and red- and/or white-rimmed iris drawn with a compass (Figure 6.1). Admittedly, a direct comparison between lamps and painted eyes – those of eye-cups as well as other frontally shown faces such as Gorgons or Satyrs – could have worked only until the eye-pots fell out of use in the early fifth century BCE; after that, the emphatically round and protruding pupils of animal statues and animal-shaped vessels might have been a closer point of reference for the lamps.[31] As the plural *muktēres* indicates, Praxagora's lamp (probably of the black-glazed type that Howland classified as no. 23), was most likely conceived as one with two snouts, one on each end (Figure 6.3).[32] This rare, yet well-attested form looked even more like a fully fledged eye with the nozzles standing for the two corners of the eye and the circular body for the eye's orb. I would thus like to suggest that the association between sun, eye and lamp – all instances of *kuklos* – is grounded in a fundamental sameness in form and operation. The formal correlation is the accomplishment of the potter who crafted the lamp, just as Aither in the *Women of the Thesmophoria* fabricated the human eye after the likeness and the operating principles of the sun. The potter himself is likened to a creator of Promethean or

---

31 If Praxagora's lamp did indeed have two nozzles, as the plural *muktērsi* suggests, its similarity to the eye would even be more emphatic: the round core could stand for the iris and pupil, and the two nozzles on opposite ends represent the corners of the eye.
32 Howland (1958: 56) mentions two-nozzled specimens in connection with his type 23; the Tübingen example (Figure 6.3) shows a slightly later variant of this type, complete with elongated nozzles.

Figure 6.3 Attic wheel-made clay lamp with two nozzles, *ca.* 400–375 BCE. Tübingen, Institut für Klassische Archäologie: inv. 7414 (© Institut für Klassische Archäologie, Tübingen).

even divine calibre. The praise is not unwarranted because the tool he invented rivals the sun in the way it enables the experience and intelligibility of the world – at night. Making the lamp is, in fact, a re-creation of sight, not only within the object, but also within the subjects for whom the light device performs its service.

Excursus: micro-cycles in terracotta

Such embodied ways of thinking about material form are not, however, confined to lamps. Any clay vessel – with its round foot, body, shoulder and neck – could appear to blend its terracotta surface with anything whose formal and kinetic principle was considered circular.[33] Several examples explore the slippage of microcosm to macrocosm. Consider a black-figure Athenian neck-amphora in Munich (Figure 6.4), which seems to feature Atlas as a stiff frontal figure supported by two maidens.[34]

---

33 *Kuklos* has a wide semantic range and can describe anything round-shaped or rotating, such as dance, race or *agora*, or indeed the round shield. From the sixth century BCE onwards, Athenian pots engaged visually with various notions of *kuklos* – a topic too vast to be explored here. For thoughts on circular and spherical decorations in Attic vases, see Lissarrague (2009b), who discusses, among others, the circularity of dance (2009b: 16–18) and the shield (2009b: 28–31), yet without discussing the underlying notion of *kuklos*.
34 Munich, Staatliche Antikensammlungen 1540 WAF, from Vulci, around 510–500 BCE. Kunze-Götte (1973: 86–90 pl. 428, 2; 429) suggests that the figure is Prometheus; De Griño & Olmos (1986: 8 no. 22) convincingly point towards Atlas.

Figure 6.4 Attic black-figure neck-amphora, showing Atlas (?) carrying the universe, *ca.* 510–500 BCE. Munich, Staatliche Antikensammlungen und Glyptothek: inv. 1540 WAF (© Staatliche Antikensammlungen und Glyptothek; photograph by Renate Kühling).

The universe that he carries on his head is indicated by nothing but the circular tongue-pattern on the pot's shoulder. In this case, the pot's framing ornamentation serves as a visual figuration whose circular structure articulates the vessel's three-dimensional form as well as the spatial quality of the celestial firmament. An even more dynamic strategy can be found on a red-figure clay spindle ("bobbin") from the Athenian *agora* (Figure 6.5).[35] The round object shows Helios pulled by a band of winged horses that arise from the sea. Helios carries the red solar disk on his head, which itself echoes the bobbin's outer circular shape. In use, the object, whether a yo-yo or love-charm, would turn with a thread: in its spinnings, the object recreates the macrocosmic circlings of the sun, as well as the spinning motion of the potter's wheel. Such congruencies between form and motion are similarly played out

---

35 Athens, Agora Museum P5113: Moore (1997: 351, no. 1640, pl. 153) (the material from the well-deposit seems to be public dining equipment); Yalouris (1990: 1009, no. 11); Ehrhardt (2004: 21, figure 15). For the uses of the so-called bobbins, see the debate between Shapiro (1985: 115–20) and Böhr (1997: 118–20).

Figure 6.5 Attic white-ground bobbin from the Athenian Agora showing Helios with chariot, ca. 480–470 BCE. Athens, Agora Museum: inv. P5113 (© American School of Classical Studies at Athens: Agora Excavations).

in Athenian *pyxides* of the mid-fifth century (not least on their round and convex lids, which likewise map onto the spherical body of the universe). A lid of a "bobbin"-shaped *pyxis* in Berlin (Figures 6.6–6.8) shows the half-seen figures of Helios, Selene and Eos racing along its circular rim.[36] The handle on top of the lid has been made part of the image, framed by a black-glazed crown of rays. The circle of rays is shown resting on a painted vertical column (rendered as if supporting the

---

36 Berlin, Staatliche Museen, Antikensammlung F2519. Schauenburg (1955: 59 with n. 173, figure 16); Greifenhagen (1962: 23, no. 138, pl. 138. 2–4); Ehrhardt (2004: 15–16, figure 9). The series of similar *pyxides* is discussed in Ehrhardt (2004). Several specimens show a wedding procession on the body and add yet another meaningful layer to the overall theme of motion. The passage of the bride, remarkably, is visualized in a design that emphasizes cyclicity rather than uni-directionality.

Figure 6.6 Attic red-figure *pyxis* ("lid"), showing either Helios, Selene (or Nyx?) and Eos, *ca*. 430 BCE. Berlin, Staatliche Museen (Antikensammlung): inv. F2519 (© Staatliche Museen zu Berlin, Antikensammlung; photograph by Johannes Laurentius).

firmament), which functions concurrently as the turning point (both *polos* and *terma*) of their infinite circling race (*kuklos*).[37] As such, the handle invites the hand to spin the lid around, thereby actualizing the movement implied within the image. The outer edge of the convex lid echoes the handle's crown of rays, converting the entire universe to a radiant circle of light (*kuklos*). A terracotta container, in other words, maps out the revolution at work within the celestial orbit.[38]

One further case study, however, deploys the concentric decoration to evoke the eye as *kuklos*. An Attic eye-cup in Virginia features unconventional, artificial eyes that consist of a series of narrow concentric bands (Figures 6.9–6.10), perfectly painted with the aid of multiple brushes fixed to a compass.[39] The very same design is repeated on the underside of the cup's foot where it resonates the vessel's "cyclic"

---

37 On the column, see C. Robert (1919: 47, figure 32), with reference to Homer, *Odyssey* 1.52–4. On the astral race, see Kratzmüller (2009).
38 The structural link between the ceramic and the universe is visualized on the underside of the Berlin *pyxis* (Figure 6.8): its bottom consists of a plain ornament of dark concentric bands enclosing a clay-coloured disk at the centre. As such, this pattern illustrates the *kuklos* to be the formal and kinetic principle that is shared by entities as distinct as the terracotta container and the universe.
39 Figure 6.9 = Virginia Museum of Fine Arts, Richmond, VA, inv. no. 62.1.11; *Paralipomena* 109/15 bis; cf. Lissarrague (2009b: 25) emphasizing the hypnotizing effect of the decoration.

SIGHT AND LIGHT

Figure 6.7 The same Attic red-figure *pyxis*, *ca.* 430 BCE (as seen from the side). Berlin, Staatliche Museen (Antikensammlung): inv. F2519 (© Staatliche Museen zu Berlin, Antikensammlung; photograph by Jutta Tietz-Glagow).

Figure 6.8 The same Attic red-figure *pyxis*, *ca.* 430 BCE (bottom). Berlin, Staatliche Museen (Antikensammlung): inv. F2519 (© Staatliche Museen zu Berlin, Antikensammlung; photograph by Jutta Tietz-Glagow).

Figure 6.9 Attic black-figure eye-cup attributed to the Nikosthenes Painter, *ca.* 520 BCE. Richmond, VA, Virginia Museum of Fine Arts: Adolph D. and Wilkins C. Williams Fund, inv. 62.1.11 (© Virginia Museum of Fine Arts; photograph by Katherine Wetzel).

Figure 6.10 Interior tondo of the same Attic black-figure eye-cup attributed to the Nikosthenes Painter, *ca.* 520 BCE. Richmond, VA, Virginia Museum of Fine Arts: Adolph D. and Wilkins C. Williams Fund, inv. 62.1.11 (© Virginia Museum of Fine Arts; photograph by Katherine Wetzel).

production history. The inside of the cup consists of a small Gorgon-emblazoned tondo encircled, again, by the pattern of concentric bands. The visually trained user of the cup will have realized that the vessel's interior confronts him with an oversize eye whose small pupil appears to reflect not his face, but that of the Gorgon Medusa (Figure 6.9).

Objects with social intelligence

Let me return to Praxagora and her lamp one final time. The second part of Praxagora's address to the lamp (vv. 7ff.), expanding on its fortunes (*tuchai*), differs substantially from the first. Contemplating how the instrument has become a co-conspirator, Praxagora switches abruptly to talk about the social life of the lamp as a connoisseur of women's bodies and activities. Now, one might think that the unabashed description of the lamp's role in female everyday life would ironically undercut Praxagora's earlier mythologizing about its noble creation. Yet strangely enough, Praxagora's bawdy talk does not render the lamp a banality. Instead, Praxagora's portrait of the private activities of women (in all their trivial aspects) serves to single out the artefact as a unique companion in human life. Again in v. 11, the lamp is called an eye (now with the prose term, *ophthalmos*), characterizing the device as a controller and protector of the female body – and, in short, of sex.

The joke, though, is that the nomenclature evokes public Athenian offices and titles. The expression in v. 10 that characterizes the lamp as a "supervisor of women's flexed bodies" (*lordoumenōn somatōn epistates*) probably adapts an official title of a magistrate supervising athletic training and competitions. By claiming the role of someone who oversees the erotic *agōn*, the lamp is humorously portrayed in terms of an official, publically sanctioned role.[40] I am inclined to think that this passage is meant to elaborate the motif of the lamp's offices (*timai*) introduced in v. 5. The word *ophthalmos* itself, when used for lamps, could bring to mind their role in public surveillance. In fourth-century BCE Athens, according at least to Athenaeus' *The Deipnosophists*, the overseers of wine consumption at public feasts gave out lamps and wicks to the guests to make sure that each participant received an equal share of wine; the unofficial term used to designate these control lights was *ophthalmoi*.[41] Yet, as quickly becomes clear, the master of indoor love-making is no arbiter of order and control. Rather, the lamp is a biased companion whose purpose is to become co-involved. It stands by (*plēsios parastateis*, v. 9), and stands by to assist (*sumparastateis*, v. 15): in this sense, the cyclic iteration of the term *parastateō*[42] suggests that rotation is still a structural principle guiding the word choice and semantics of Praxagora's speech.

---

40 *epistatai athlōn*, "stewards of games": Plato, *Laws* 949a; cf. also Xenophon, *On the Constitution of the Lacedaemonians* 8.4; Xenophon, *Memorabilia* 3.5.18 (referee); "supervisor of training": Plato, *Republic* 412a. For the *palaistra* in the Academy and for the Lykeion an *epistatēs* is attested; cf. Hyperides, *Against Demosthenes* frg. 7. col. 26; Hesychios, *s.v.* "*archelas*".
41 Athenaeus, *The Deipnosophists* 10.25.
42 Sommerstein (1998) argues against Ussher (1973: 72) that *parastatein* implies divine protection and presents analogies. Yet it remains to be asked why Aristophanes used *parastatein* rather than *pareistanai*, which is a much more common term for gods assisting their protégés.

As a supporter and attendant, physically close and emotionally attached to the female members of the *oikos*, the lamp takes on the social role of a slave. What fundamentally distinguishes the object from slaves, however, is its discretion. This helps to explain why Praxagora takes the humble luminary out of the house to become a co-actor within the public sphere. For all its public role, the little lamp is also an intimate object, not least when it comes to depilation. In exploring the unnameable and unknowable corners of the body, it comes close to rivalling the husband: touching the skin, the flame protruding from the lamp's phallic nozzle partakes in an almost sexualized act. An Athenian bell-krater of the early fourth century (currently on loan at the Harvard Art Museums) draws out the point. It shows Eros himself about to depilate the pubic area of a naked woman; the lamp held in his hand is both a tool and an embodiment of erotic prowess (Figure 6.11).[43] Sexual appetite gives way to culinary appetite in Praxagora's last scenario, as lamp and woman are made to explore the pantry and become inebriated together (a clear rejection of Athenaeus' *ophthalmoi* introduced to stop excessive public drinking).[44]

Twice the lamp is singled out (*monos*, vv. 7 and 12) and three times we find the prefix *sun-* attached to verbs describing the lamp's actions (*sumparastateis* in v. 15; *sundrōn* in v. 16; *suneisei* in v. 17). The lamp is unique and exclusive in the way it grants the experience of co-presence to its human users. The same idea is powerfully articulated in Aristophanes' *Birds*: in v. 1484, the underworld is said to lie in darkness and to be bereft of lamps (*en tēi luchnōn erēmiai*). This "lamp-loneliness" is presented in opposition to the reality of shared life and worldly light.

What may surprise us about the second part of Praxagora's speech is that it does not dwell further on the theme of sight, neither with regard to the lamp nor with reference to people who see thanks to its illuminations. Vision, however, never slips from the frame. The focus has merely shifted from communal viewing to its consequences – the experience of shared activities. By insisting on the prefix *sun-*, the nexus between women and their lighting devices, Praxagora honours the lamp as a primary key to social life. Her scenarios of intimacy may have provoked laughter (above all, by rendering the most private public), but they do not make banal the grand story of the lamp's creation; it is together with people that the object's abilities come to light. In bringing together fire and earth, sun and potter, cosmos and craft, and not least vision and visibility, the object emerges as a powerful instrument capable of synthesizing nothing less than human life itself.

---

43 Figure 6.11 = an Attic red-figure bell-krater attributed to the Dinos Painter, Harvard Art Museums, inv. 9.1988; cf. Paul (1994–5: 60–7); Kreilinger (2007: 70–1. 149, figure 14 a–c). In Aristophanes, *Lysistrata* 828 an old chorus woman brags about her pubic cosmetics performed with the help of a lamp.

44 Lamps' thirst for oil in antiquity was legendary: in *Clouds* 57, Aristophanes even calls a lamp a "tippler", a motif that had many reverberations in later Greek and Roman texts. For the *stilbē potis*, see Plato Comicus, frg. 190 K.-A. We may remember that even Trimalchio fed his lamps with pure wine (Petronius 74.1).

Figure 6.11 Attic red-figure bell-krater attributed to the Dinos Painter, showing Eros depilating a woman with a lamp, *ca.* 430–420 BCE. Cambridge, MA: Harvard Art Museums (Arthur M. Sackler Museum): inv. 9.1988 (anonymous loan). Imaging department (© President and Fellows of Harvard College).

Conclusion: sight and co-presence

How does all this relate back to my opening comments about "sight and light"? Lamps, I have argued, not only illuminate but also themselves embody a number of critical ideas about *Sight and the Ancient Senses*. As stated in the beginning of this chapter, the very language used to make sense of Greek sight framed it as a mode of appearing, whereby to cast one's gaze was also to express oneself to the faces of others. By creating a nexus of social relations, the act of looking lies at the root of intersubjectivity. The same thinking holds true of lamps, which were likewise endowed with a visual glow, and one that was understood to resemble that of the eye itself. As looking, light-giving instruments, lamps were imagined as materializing vision in a very concrete sense.

But in this capacity, we have also seen how lamps did something else besides, bringing together a community and bringing about a sense of togetherness. The powerful idea of the watchful lamp as social mediator – first attested, even if not in fact invented by Aristophanes – was to have a long and successful afterlife in the

Graeco-Roman cultural imagination. In a variety of Hellenistic and Roman texts, not least in love poetry, lamps are addressed as witnesses to human life, actively observing what they shed light on.[45]

Allow me to end on a slightly different note. For one of the things lamps help us to understand, I think, is why the sense of sight came to be so privileged in antiquity. Approached phenomenologically, sight is of course not the only sense that can be shared between subjects. Yet the very nature of seeing nonetheless lends vision a particular sort of socially cohesive role. We cannot ever know whether somebody hears, touches or tastes as we do. When it comes to vision, though, we have an enduring sense that sight operates across our sensual subjectivities and objectivities – that we can see somebody seeing something as we too see it. Ancient Greek thinkers championed the point: again and again, we find eyes being used to reflect upon the relationship between self and others; to see, the thinking ran, was also to look upon others looking at us, even seeing themselves in the mirror of our eye.[46] Today we may rationalize things rather differently, having debunked Greek extramissionist beliefs in the gaze as something outwardly directed – as a visible and expressive emanation from the eye. Crucially, however, we too understand that seeing is key to the experience of being with others.

---

45 On the witnessing lamp, especially in the epigrams of the *Palatine Anthology* and in Roman love poems, see Kost (1971); Zografou (2010); Kanellou (2013); Bielfeldt (2014).

46 Cf. Plato, *Alcibiades* 133b for the famous discussion of the eye of a beheld person serving as a mirror for the self, with discussion in Bartsch (2006: 41–56).

7

SIGHT AND DEATH

Seeing the dead through ancient eyes

Susanne Turner

Ashes to ashes, dust to dust: the living have a strange habit of disappearing from sight when they die. Committing the dead to the ground or to fire is a process forged of both necessity and disavowal. Bodies are, alas, fragile things: death softens the contours of the body, changing loved ones from the comforting and familiar to the unrecognizable and even threatening. And yet, at the same time, the dead also take on new forms of visibility in the days and months following their demise. Tombs and gravestones, funeral processions and burial rituals, mementos and keepsakes – all ensure that the dearly departed maintain a perceptual presence in the world of the living.

Death comes to us all but, as this chapter argues, viewers in antiquity seem to have been particularly attuned to the specular – and, more often, the spectacular – power of the visual in the face of death.[1] Funerary rituals and tombs, whether elaborate or modest, put the dead on show to what often seems a surprisingly wide viewership: unlike their modern counterparts, the ancient dead are located in plain sight, often on roadsides. Vision was "good to think with" when it came to myth, too, where sight proves to be fertile ground for the negotiation of the loss of selfhood that dying entails. In what follows, I therefore want to explore the role that seeing plays in mediating death and dying in the ancient world. How, where and

---

1 Spectacles of death have been most fully studied in relation to ancient Rome (e.g. Kyle 1998; Bodel 1999; Dodge 2011), and particularly in the context of the Roman arena (e.g. Gunderson 1996; Futrell 1997; Kyle 1998; 2007: 269–74, 312–23; C. Edwards 2007), with special emphasis on witnessing death in Rome. In the case of Greece – and especially Athens – viewing and death have most often been explored in terms of visual culture: e.g. R. Osborne (1988); Shapiro (1991); Neer (2002a; 2010: 182–214); Younger (2002); Turner (2009; 2012). In several important articles, moreover, Jean-Paul Vernant has explored the discursive concatenation of death and viewing in Greek culture more generally (most influential are Vernant (1991: 50–74 [= Vernant 1982], 95–110 [= Vernant 1985a], 111–38 [= Vernant 1985b], 141–50 [= Vernant 1987], 186–92). Since the funeral is so rarely represented in Roman art (Bodel 1999), studies of the ways in which vision negotiates death in Rome have explored the high visibility of Roman tombs (e.g. Koortbojian 1996; P. Davies 2000; Hope 2003; Wallace-Hadrill 2008: 77–109; Scott 2013), as well as the metaphorical role of mythology on sarcophagi (e.g. Koortbojian 1995; Ewald 2004; Platt 2012; Zanker & Ewald 2012, translating Zanker & Ewald 2004).

This chapter uses the following abbreviations: *CAT* (= Clairmont 1993); *CEG* (= Hansen 1989); *IG* (= *Inscriptiones Graecae*, 1873–, Berlin: De Gruyter); *LIMC* (= *Lexicon Iconographicum Mythologiae Classicae*, 1981–97, Zurich: Artemis).

when did the dead become visible to the living? What did it mean to see them? And, in the face of death, what sort of sense did "seeing" entail?

To answer these questions, I situate death and dying in the ancient world by looking in turn at how funerals, tomb and myths envision, embody and negotiate the continuing presence of the dead for the eyes of the living. But of course, that "ancient world" was geographically and culturally diverse and the funerary – ritual, commemoration, discourse – has often been deemed more static and traditional than other aspects of culture.[2] Although it would be impossible to do justice to the full breadth of Greek and Roman views on death in the present chapter, the sheer variety of introduced examples here should go some way in demonstrating the short-sightedness of such assumptions.

Another warning note is in order before we start. Ancient Greek and Roman viewers were well aware that representation offered a thorny world not only of possibility but also of limitation: it would be a risk too far to take the dead at face value. The question of what the dead look like, no doubt, always carries an unearthly fascination for the living; the roll-call of Odysseus' *Nekuia* (that is, his visit to the "underworld" in the eleventh book of Homer's *Odyssey*) was visualized in paint by Polygnotus on the walls of a building in fifth-century Delphi.[3] But already in Homer the theme of seeing the dead is thematized as problematic when Odysseus sees his dead mother, Anticlea, for the first time (*Odyssey* 11.206–8):

τρὶς μὲν ἐφωρμήθην, ἑλέειν τέ με θυμὸς ἀνώγει,
τρὶς δέ μοι ἐκ χειρῶν σκιῇ εἴκελον ἢ καὶ ὀνείρῳ
ἔπτατ'. ἐμοὶ δ' ἄχος ὀξὺ γενέσκετο κηρόθι μᾶλλον.

Three times I moved toward her, and my heart desired to take hold of her,
and three times she drifted out of my hands like a shadow or a dream,
and a pain pierced right through the heart within me.

Anticlea is now a *psuchē*, a spirit or shade; she is no longer flesh and blood, even though she is apparently still furnished with her former appearance.[4] As Odysseus discovers when he tries to get closer, however, appearances can prove deceptive. It is no accident that Anticlea is described as sliding from her son's grasp like a "shadow" (*skia*) or a "dream" (*oneiron*); her ontological status is now so slippery that it can only be described through things it is not. A few verses later (11.213), Odysseus asks if she is an *eidōlon*, an ancient Greek word which denotes a whole range of such mutable, deceptive images, including reflections, doubles and other insubstantial surface-based apparitions.[5] As Odysseus discovers here to his dismay,

---

2 E.g. Vermeule (1979: 2).
3 On the Knidian Lesche at Delphi (Pausanias 10.25–31), see Stansbury-O'Donnell (1990); Castriota (1992: 89–95); Neer (2012: 289–90). On its underworld imagery, see Sourvinou-Inwood (1981). It is worth noting here how rarely underworld scenes are depicted in Roman sarcophagus contexts; cf. Toynbee (1977: 377–412).
4 More generally on the relationship between *psuchē* and the body here, see Vernant (1991: 186–92).
5 On the language of *eidōlon*, see Vernant (1990a; 1991: 164–85 [= Vernant 1975]) and Steiner (2001: 23–4, 193–4). On representations of *eidōla*, see Bardel (2000).

death transforms the dead into images, reducing them to representation.[6] In a very basic way, memorialization rests upon the substitution of the body with an image – a theme already analysed by Jeremy Tanner in his discussion of *skiagraphia* ("shadow-painting") in the monumental Macedonian tomb at Lefkadia.[7]

But if death goes hand-in-hand with representation, it facilitates a mode of viewing which is predicated upon the physicality, the feelings and emotions, of a body. Odysseus feels the illusoriness of his dead mother's *psuchē* in his very body: anxiety in his abdomen (*phrenes*: *Odyssey* 11.204) and both boldness and pain in his heart (*thumos*: *Odyssey* 11.206; *kerothi*: *Odyssey* 11.208). Unlike the epiphanic discourses explored by Platt in this volume, the visual does not displace the haptic in the context of death. Death may demand a viewing, but it is not ocularcentric as such: no one makes sense of death through sight alone.

Seeing the funeral

A funeral will nearly always necessitate a trip outside the home: few societies endorse burying the dead in one's back garden, especially in cities where large numbers of people live in close quarters. But since no funeral can take place solely behind closed doors, households laying their dead to rest always have the potential to see and be seen. Ancient burial rituals often fell into the category of the spectacle, designed to draw the gaze and incite the viewing "pleasure" of observers. Funerals are not restricted to the visual: loud lamentation, for instance, not to mention strongly scented incense, might draw attention and underwrite memory-making in multi-sensory ways. Still, as will become clear, vision often seems to take centre stage.

Reconstructing the Athenian funeral relies on broad strokes and a synchronic picture drawn from visual and literary evidence ranging across time periods; for the most part, tracing out change over time is tricky at best. The laying out of the corpse (*prothesis*) happened in the home, while the procession to the grave (*ekphora*) drew the mourners out onto the streets where they might be seen – yet by around 530 BCE, this procession, by decree of the lawgiver Solon, could only take place under cover of night.[8] At the same time, participation in the *ekphora* was limited to close kin of the deceased and women were relegated to the bringing up the rear. One of the most plausible explanations for this restriction in ritual behaviour is that aristocratic funerals had simply become *too* attention-seeking: a large and unruly group of mourners, complete with lamenting women and additional hired wailers, could too easily become a social nuisance – and might even, if the emotionally charged lamentation were hijacked to stir up rivalries and revenge between families vying for

---

6 On death and representation here, see Bronfen (1992) and Bronfen & Goodwin (1993); cf. also Tanner (this volume).
7 More generally on statues as substitutions, see K. Gross (1992); Bettini (1999); Steiner (2001: 5–19). On the relationship between image and model in Greek culture, see Platt (2014).
8 On the practical aspects of the Greek funeral, see Kurtz & Boardman (1971: 142–61); Garland (2001: 21–37); Alexiou (2002: 4–7). For ancient testimonia on Solon's decree, see Demosthenes 43.62; Plutarch, *Solon* 21.4–5; Cicero, *On the Laws* 2.59; discussions include Garland (2001: 3–5) and I. Morris (1992–3: 36–8).

leverage, incite violence.⁹ In short, Solon limited the disruption caused by the aristocratic funeral by limiting its visibility.

But the Athenian funeral was not exactly invisible, even after it was restricted to non-daylight hours. Bereaved Athenians had long ensured a longevity for their funerals which extended far beyond the performative ephemerality of the ritual itself by representing their burial rituals on their tombs. Around the same time that Solon restricted the ritual, Athenians were representing their funerals on terracotta plaques which they hung on roadside tombs – and although the *ekphora* was the part of the ceremony which might most obviously bring the mourners into sight, it was the *prothesis* which they chose to represent most frequently. An example from Cape Kolias (Figure 7.1) focusses on the relationships between the family members by foregrounding the physical contact between them – and labelling each according to his or her relationship to the deceased.¹⁰ Such a practice had begun centuries earlier, when some of the earliest instances of figural representation in Greece were *prothesis* scenes born on monumental vases marking graves, like the famous Dipylon amphora.¹¹ Indeed, death was no less than the impetus behind the figural turn in the late Geometric period.

The effect is to make a private ritual public. That this is a powerful – and complex – strategy of memorialization should not be overlooked. Private, familial mourning is displaced into a public arena in which it becomes part of a memory-making process not restricted to those who were present at the rite itself. That memory-making process, moreover, did not depend solely on sight – the overwhelming impact of the Cape Kolias scene is of a tightly packed group of mourners writing their memories *into* their bodies as they touch each other, themselves and the corpse. Viewers of the monument are, in a sense, invited to touch with their eyes as they take in the ritual scene.

Memorialization took place not just through the erection of the monument, but in the relationships built between the tomb, the viewer and the absent deceased, pointed up by words like *sēma* ("sign") and *mnēma* ("memory", "reminder") in commemorative inscriptions.¹² "[I am/This is] the *sēma* of Phrasikleia", says one well-known example, "*Korē* will I be called forever, since in place of marriage I have been allotted this name by the gods".¹³ Phrasikleia may be re-presented in death by the accompanying statue of a young woman – and trapped in stone, as in text, as an unmarried maid – but the distance between monument and dead girl is slyly written into the word *sēma*. Commemoration consists of markers and signs which must be "read" by a third party and the ancient viewer who reads those words aloud animates them, continuing

---

9 See Alexiou (2002: 18–23), followed by Foley (1993); Simms (1998); Foley (2001); Suter (2003); McHardy (2004). Cf. Blok (2006) on the topos of pollution. On the noisiness of Roman mourning, note also Hope (2010: 39–42).
10 Paris, Louvre MNB 905 (attributed to the Sappho Painter, *ca.* 500 BCE): cf. Boardman (1955: no.28).
11 Athens, National Museum 804: cf. Arias (1962: 267, no. 4). On representing death in Greek art, see R. Osborne (1988) and Shapiro (1991).
12 On *sēma* and *mnēma*, see Nagy (1990: 202–22); Svenbro (1993: 15–18); Stears (1993: 175–85); Sourvinou-Inwood (1995: 109–20).
13 See *IG* I3 1261; *CEG* 24. On the Phrasikleia statue (Athens, National Museum 4889, *ca.* 550–540 BCE), see Stieber (2004: 141–77), with further discussion and bibliography on the "speaking" games in Squire (2009: 151–3).

Figure 7.1 Black-figure Attic funerary *pinax* from Cape Kolias, attributed to the Sappho Painter, *ca.* 500 BCE. Paris, Louvre: inv. MNB 905 (© RMN-Grand Palais (Musée du Louvre)/Hervé Lewandowski).

the visual rituals begun in the funeral by performing his or her own oral (and aural) lamentation for the dead.[14]

If Athenian commemorative practices had their eye on an audience for the funeral beyond the immediate circle of the bereaved, so too did their counterparts amongst the elites of Republican Rome. Representation of the Roman funeral, however, was rare – the spectacle was the ritual itself.[15] The Greek historian Polybius, an outside viewer, details the ways in which the Roman aristocratic funeral was played out not in private but in front of large crowds who gathered in the Forum, the civic centre of the city: it was an essential feature of the ritual that it was witnessed by as many people as possible.[16] One of the functions of funerary ritual is to help those left behind re-cohere when the group loses one of its members, and the Roman funeral certainly encouraged group bonding on a large scale.[17] Those gathered together saw the dead man carried to the rostra on his bier, gazed upon the funeral cortege as it wove through the streets from his home and watched as a relative, usually a son, took the stage in front of the assembled populace to perform a eulogy. The experience of seeing these sights must surely have been shaped as much by the jostling of

---

14 On inscriptions animating funerary ritual, see Svenbro (1993); Sourvinou-Inwood (1995: 140–297). On related Archaic inscriptions, see Day (1989).
15 Cf. Bodel (1999); Hope (2009: 65–96). On the rituals of Roman funerals, see recently Lennon (2014: 136–66).
16 Polybius 6.53–4.
17 Cf. Mandelbaum (1965); Bloch & Parry (1982); Metcalf & Huntingdon (1991).

the throng as by the sight of the participants on the stage. And the sea of people themselves, crammed in between the public buildings, also became part of the spectacle.

Still, to dwell too long on the spectators would be a diversion, for it is the dead body which lies at the heart of the funeral.[18] Every funeral is always a confrontation with death, refracted through the inanimate and unfeeling corpse – and the Roman and Athenian funerals explored here exploit that confrontation to great (and deliberate) effect by bringing it into view. The Athenian commemorative fascination with the *prothesis* ensured that the corpse was placed at centre stage and its representation was a poignant reminder of the presence of the remains, out of sight beneath the ground. In the Republican funeral, no such substitution was required; with the body on view on the rostra, there was no escaping seeing the corpse.

It is worth looking a little harder at those Roman customs, for a carefully calibrated visibility of the dead is especially apparent in the Republican funerary procession. A closer look reveals that the Roman procession not only showcased the dead – in the plural – in extraordinary ways, but also troubled the dividing line separating them from the living, for participating in the procession were not only the surviving family members but also the household's ancestors from generations past.[19] This uncanny parade of revenants, however, was not achieved through necromancy or voodoo, but through the use of masks and actors – individuals chosen for their physical likeness to the dead and furnished with appropriate clothing and wax masks, carefully coloured to replicate lifelike incarnations of the family's forebears, both embodying and re-presenting the dead at the same time.[20] Imagine the scene: a parade of dead men (and women), stepping out to welcome a newly deceased relative to their number.[21] There is something especially Roman in this visual "presentification" (and active construction) of the trans-generational family, the *gens*, its living members bound to their illustrious forebears. No aristocratic man (or woman) could avoid the past; indeed, he might be expected in one sense to re-embody it. Walking in the procession – with one's identity blacked out by a warm wax mask, so as to see through another's eyes – must have been something of an out-of-body experience.

The masks themselves, however, are something of a mystery. Wax is delicate and no example survives, although plaster-cast masks are sometimes found in much later tombs – like the tomb of Valerius Herma, beneath the Vatican in Rome, which contained two stucco masks of children and the mould for a mask of a bearded gentleman (probably Herma himself).[22] None were masks designed to be worn; they have

---

18 Hope (2010: 34–8) puts the centrality of the corpse in the elite Republican funeral in its wider context.
19 On such processions, see Polybius 6.53.5–9; Cicero, *On the Orator* 2.225; Horace, *Satires* 1.6.42–4. Flower (1996: 97–106) offers the best discussion.
20 Polybius 3.53.6 emphasizes physical likeness (κατά τε τὸ μέγεθος καὶ τὴν ἄλλην περικοπήν, "according to their build and their bearing"). The Elder Pliny (*Natural History* 6.35) speaks of the material (*expressi cera uultus*, "faces pressed out of wax"). On the realism of such masks, see Pollini (2007); on the studied mimicry of mask-wearers, cf. Bettini (2005: 195–8) on Diodorus Siculus 31.25.2.
21 On the question of "women" here, see especially Flower (2002).
22 On the Tomb of Valerius Herma, see Gee (2003: 144–5); Wallace-Hadrill (2008: 74–5, pl. 2.13–15); Noy (2011: 9–11). On plaster masks found in tombs, see Drerup (1980).

no eye-holes. Their deposition in a tomb contradicts the account of Polybius (and others) that ancestral masks were displayed in special wooden cupboards in the *atria* of houses when they were not in use in funerals.[23] These later plaster casts are probably not reliable evidence for earlier Republican practice. The truth is, we just do not know what the Republican masks looked like, nor how they were made. Just how *lifelike* were they? Were they cast from life – or from death...?[24]

Whether or not they were direct imprints of their subjects, ancestral masks certainly seem to have impressed upon their viewers the belief that they were faithful imitations of the dead person's appearance. For both the Elder Pliny and Polybius, the masks were, quite literally, faces – *uultus* and *prosōpa*, respectively.[25] The Latin word *imago* (pl. *imagines*), used to denote the masks, is – like the Greek *eidōlon* – one which ties the practice of re-presenting the dead into the precarious world of the visual. *Imago* is not just used of ancestor masks, but of shadows and apparitions, likenesses and copies, semblances and echoes, even images in the mind's eye.[26] It is, unsurprisingly, the origin of the English word "image". There is a tacit semantic acknowledgement here that however "lifelike" the ancestral dead look, theirs is an appearance which rests on the surface and is not even skin-deep.[27]

In short, the term *imago* suggests that the masks (and their wearers) occupy the same uncanny ground as Anticlea in the *Odyssey*, troubling the boundary between life and death. Roman audiences, however, do not seem to have been as conflicted by this "troubling" as was Odysseus. "For who", says Polybius, "would not feel inspired on seeing the likenesses of men held in honour for their excellence, all together as if living and breathing? What vision could be more noble than that?"[28] The Romans, Polybius seems to be saying, harness the latent potentiality of the representational realm to channel reactions in a positive way.

Viewing the dead

Funerary rituals may commit the dead to the eradicating forces of earth or flame, but commemorative practices are usually designed to do the opposite – tombs, monuments and cemetery spaces all carve out a visible and (hopefully) enduring space for the dead in the world of the living. Burial and commemoration serve to *place* the dead, and in a most literal way; likewise, grave markers make sure the

---

23 On ancestor masks in *atria*, see the ancient *testimonia* of Juvenal 8.19–20; Martial 2.90.5–8; Ovid, *Fasti* 1.591; Pliny, *Natural History* 35.6, 8; Polybius 6.53.4; Seneca, *On Benefits* 3.28.2, *Moral Letters* 44.5; Valerius Maximus 5.8.3. For discussion, see Flower (1996: 185–222). The discrepancy between the texts and the finds of plaster masks is noted by Wallace-Hadrill (2008: 75–6).
24 On death masks, see Bethe (1935); Rowell (1940); Jackson (1987). On "life masks", see Flower (1996: 2, 36, 340); Pollini (2007: 238). Noy (2011: 8–9) notes the silence of ancient sources. For an appropriately grisly description of what masks taken from death look like, see Zadoks-Josephus Jitta (1932: 47–8).
25 Pliny, *Natural History* 35.6; Polybius 6.53.5. Polybius' use of *prosopōn* ("face") over *prosopeion* ("mask") is discussed by Zadoks-Josephus Jitta (1932).
26 On *imago* here, see especially Bartsch (2006: 125–30). The subject returns us to some of the themes explored in Tanner's chapter (this volume).
27 *Contra* Bettini (2005: 191–2).
28 Polybius 6.53.10.

location of the remains can be seen, so that lost loved ones can be visited and remembered.[29] Yet some monuments – and some dead – are easier to see than others. In no small part, this is because not all men (or women) are born equal. Large swathes of the ancient dead, buried in modest ways which have not stood the test of time or acidic soil, remain invisible to us today.[30] At the same time, the families with the largest tombs are not always the ones with the greatest influence or wealth (although they may wish to be seen that way). Tombs can manipulate those who see them, massaging their messages.[31]

How, then, did ancient memorials keep the dead in view and guide the eyes of their viewers? Their most striking strategy, in both Greece and Rome, was to bury the dead on roadsides, often busy ones where high visibility could be guaranteed.[32] The most important burial space in Athens was the Kerameikos, which was sited (or better, sighted) where two important roads, the Sacred Way and the Dromos, entered the city.[33] This was where the Panathenaic procession began and it was also where the state tombs to the war dead were located.[34] The use of this area for burials dates back to Mycenaean times and beyond. As time passed, the funerary landscape on either side of the two roads ebbed and flowed with the changing Athenian commemorative customs. The large *tumuli* and smaller mud-brick tombs of the Archaic period, for instance, gave way to the high stone-built walls of Classical *peribolos* tombs, hemming in the road on either side.[35] By the middle of the fourth century BCE, these *peribolos* precincts had cropped up at all the major entrance-ways to the city and along the Long Walls which protected the route to the Piraeus, the harbour.[36] No traveller, in other words, could fail to notice the Athenian dead. But although it seems likely that more Athenians in democratic Athens found their graves marked by monuments than the generations before them, few could probably afford a *peribolos* tomb.[37] Those households which could were making a conscious decision to appear well-to-do.

A similar story could be told of the city of Rome. The Via Appia was lined with tombs for miles as it extended beyond the city into the outlying suburbs.[38] But where, for instance, the *peribolos* tombs of Classical Athens were rather uniform in

---

29 On the functions of Greek funerary monuments, see especially Sourvinou-Inwood (1995: 109–20).
30 Analysed most memorably by I. Morris (1987); cf. I. Morris (1998) on other forms of invisibility in the archaeological record.
31 Although archaeologists in the 1960s assumed that mortuary archaeology *reflects* social structure (e.g. Binford 1971), studies in the 1980s showed how burial evidence might be better said to *construct* it (e.g. Parker Pearson 1982). For discussion, see I. Morris (1992: 1–30).
32 On roadside burials in Athens, see Kurtz & Boardman (1971: 91–6); Wycherley (1978: 253–60); Leader (1997: 684–5). On viewing the Archaic roadside landscape, see Neer (2010: 20–69). For comparable situations in Rome, cf. Purcell (1987); Koortbojian (1996); Patterson (2000: 265).
33 Cf. Knigge (1988).
34 On *polis* war tombs and their contexts, see especially Arrington (2010), now developed in Arrington (2015) – which appeared while this chapter was in proofs.
35 On Archaic tumuli and mud-brick tombs, cf. Knigge (1988: 24–32, 85–110); Houby-Nielsen (1995). On Classical tombs, cf. Garland (1982: 134–52); Knigge (1988: 40–2, 110–50); Clostermann (1999: 323–57).
36 Garland (1982: 152–60); Clostermann (1999: 299–323, 357–60).
37 I. Morris (1992: 135–8).
38 Coarelli (2007: 364–400) offers a good discussion of monuments on the Via Appia.

their construction, competition between wealthy Roman families is visible in the highly varied and innovative design of their tombs. Marcus Vergilius Eurysaces, a freedman baker, for instance, built his tomb in the shape of a bread oven; Gaius Cestius, a magistrate, built his in the shape of a pyramid.[39] Even the emperors were not above showing off their status through grand dynastic tombs: both Augustus and Hadrian built their respective mausolea on the banks of the Tiber, the former right at the start of his imperial career some 40 years before his own death.[40]

Roadside tombs are always designed to be seen – not just by mourners, but also by passers-by.[41] In the case of the Attic *peribolos* tombs, monuments were aligned not with individual burials but with the high front walls of the precinct – all the better to be seen from the road.[42] These are memorials which stand on the cusp between public and private, commissioned and erected by individual families but displayed to the eyes of anyone strolling by.[43] It is a point worth labouring that mourners and passers-by are very different types of viewer. The bereaved families visiting *periboloi* interacted directly with the tombstones, their tender care made visible by the wreaths, ribbons and small oil vessels they left behind.[44] But beyond the practical, mourners, unlike passers-by, view with eyes shadowed by bereavement.[45] Commemorative monuments anchor the memory-making process, negotiating loss and constructing continuing bonds with the dead. Mourners and passers-by quite literally *see* differently. Mourners, more importantly, did not just look. Their ministrations ritualized their viewing. They touched, smelled, listened as they continued the memory-making process begun during the funeral, which may have been months or years before.

The monuments lined up on *peribolos* walls actively exploit the divide between different types of viewer, most particularly in the eye-catching figural reliefs (stelai) with which most families chose to adorn their tomb façades.[46] These multi-figure stelai, with their scenes generally oriented towards the private home (*oikos*), often stood out against the non-figural and inscribed memorials which stood alongside them.[47] By representing figures who looked at one another in complex configurations, the monuments put viewing on show in self-conscious ways.[48]

The vast majority of stelai use intimate scenes to put the family on view for public

---

39 On the Tomb of Eurysaces, see Petersen Hackworth (2003; 2006); for the Tomb of Cestius, see e.g. Vout (2003).
40 P. Davies (2000).
41 Cf. Wallace-Hadrill (2008).
42 Cf. Garland (1982: 128); Clostermann (1999: 2–3). I explore the following points at greater length in Turner (2009).
43 Cf. Leader (1997: 684–5); Burton (2003).
44 On the visibility of repeated visits to tombs, see Clostermann (1999: 73–84).
45 On burial archaeology and emotion, cf. Tarlow (1999; 2000).
46 On family tombs, cf. Clostermann (2006; 2007).
47 The Classical Attic grave stelai are catalogued in Clairmont (1993); useful discussions include K. F. Johansen (1951); Schmaltz (1983); Bergemann (1997). On the high visibility of women, see R. Osborne (1997); Stears (1995); Younger (2002); Burton (2003).
48 On the reflexivity of such represented viewing, see Grethlein (this volume). For broader studies of the representation of viewers in ancient art, see e.g. Stansbury-O'Donnell (2006); K. Lorenz (2007). Specifically on the ontological games of Attic stelai – and their culmination in the monumental complex of the so-called "Kallithea Monument" – see Squire (forthcoming).

Figure 7.2 Marble funerary stele from Attica, *ca.* 375–350 BCE. London, British Museum: inv. 1910.0712.1 (© Trustees of the British Museum).

consumption. A stele in the British Museum (Figure 7.2), for instance, represents its three family members as upstanding members of society: two well-dressed women shake hands in a gesture known as *dexiōsis* in the foreground, while a bearded *himation*-clad man stands looking on in the background.[49] Even in the face of death, the household's cohesion and resilience are on display, since the short name inscriptions emphasize that it is family ties which bind them to one another: a daughter

---

49 London, British Museum 1910.7–12.1: cf. *CAT* 3.415a.

Figure 7.3 Marble "Ilissos stele" from Athens, *ca.* 350–330 BCE. Athens, National Archeological Museum: inv. 869 (© DAI Athen, DAI-Neg. D-DAI-ATH-NM 467 (Eva-Maria Czakó)).

(*thugatēr*) and wife (*gunē*) of one Epikhares, presumably the man in the background.[50] Representing the family here is an emotionally charged choice. It is bereaved family members who will visit the tomb to mourn the dead, their own group gathering mirrored in the figures carved into the stone.

In contrast, the famous "Ilissos stele" in Athens offers up a viewing dynamic which is not (necessarily) so family-focussed (Figure 7.3).[51] The impressively naked young man and hunched elderly gentleman might be read as father and son, but any

50 *IG* II2 107582: ΑΡΙΣΤΕΙΣ ΕΠΙΧΑΡΟΥΣ ΘΥΓΑΤΗΡ [--]Η ΕΠΙΧΑΡΟΥΣ ΓΥΝΗ.
51 Athens, National Museum 869: cf. *CAT* 2.950.

reading of their relationship depends as heavily on the signs of distance between them as it does on assumptions about paternity. Not only do they look *different* – the clothed old man in profile contrasted with his young counterpart's full-frontal nudity – but they look *differently* too, especially when these figures are compared with those on the British Museum relief. While the subtle interplay of mutual gazes on the latter reinforces the strong sense of familial harmony, the Ilissos youth's frontal gaze has him entirely ignore the figures around him; he instead privileges a direct engagement with the external viewer. Where the composition of the Ilissos stele makes it easy to identify the naked young man as deceased, moreover, the habit of inscribing everyone's names on family scenes makes it remarkably difficult to identify a single person as the "primary" deceased recipient of the monument, disavowing the way in which death fractures relationships between living and dead. Family groups, in other words, mirror and mimic the multi-generational dynamic of mourning, but scenes which single out individual figures as defiantly dead seem to speak to (and of) the passer-by through the representation of estrangement.[52]

In both cases, however, only mourners visiting the tomb could have fleshed out such scenes by filling in the backstory of deaths and losses. The relationships on view on the stelai are always as personal as they are public. The advantage of figural representation in this context is that it is so very tactile, so very physical; it hardens the boundaries of bodies loosened by death. The Ilissos youth's insistent corporeal presence belies (defies?) his apparent status as deceased. *Dexiōsis*, too, is a gesture which grounds relationships in physical encounters.[53] The mutuality of shared gazes on the relief in the British Museum may work to enclose the members of the group, but seeing on its own is simply not enough: the figures must also *touch* (or at least be seen to). Something similar might be observed of the sarcophagi – literally "flesh-" (*sarx*) "eaters" (*phagein*) – which came into fashion across the Roman world in the second to fourth centuries CE.[54] The tight press of bodies on the mid-third-century "Badminton sarcophagus" in New York's Metropolitan Museum (Figure 7.4), for instance, not only figures death as transition through the representation of a Dionysian triumph combined with the passing Seasons, but also mobilizes its own sense-filled discourse of life and death, sight and touch.[55] The very embodiment of death – in both funerary ritual and commemoration, and the responses of the living to (or during) both – set in motion a powerful means of negotiating loss which was not dependent on vision alone. Cold hard stone could hardly replicate the feeling of soft warm flesh, but the very dissonance itself provoked opportunities for remembering and mourning.

Perhaps as a result, the frontal gaze of the Ilissos youth also indicates the ways in which looking offers a particularly powerful mode of engaging living and dead. A frontal gaze creates a connection between viewer and viewed;[56] in this case, the

---

52 On the youth's identification with the deceased, see Himmelmann (1956).
53 Discussions of *dexiōsis* – e.g. G. Davies (1985) and Pemberton (1989) – have not tended to acknowledge the tactility of the gesture, focussing instead on the connotations of unity.
54 For the "flesh-eating" terminology, see Pliny, *Natural History* 2.98, 36.131.
55 New York, Metropolitan Museum of Art: inv. 55.11.5: Alexander (1955); Zanker & Ewald (2012: 165). On figural absence and presence, see Ewald (2004); Platt (2012).
56 On the dynamics of the frontal gaze, see Korshak (1987); Frontisi-Ducroux (1995); Elsner (2006c); Hedreen (2007a).

Figure 7.4 "Badminton sarcophagus" with scene of Dionysus and the Seasons, *ca*. 260–270 CE. New York, Metropolitan Museum of Art: inv. 55.11.5 (© The Metropolitan Museum of Art (Joseph Pulitzer Bequest, 1955.11.5); photograph by Schecter Lee).

young man favours the external viewer over his companion, who, on closer inspection, seems not really to see him at all but rather to stare right through him.[57] Through a complex dynamic of seeing and not-seeing, mapped across the worlds of stone and flesh as well as those of living and dead, the Ilissos stele gets to the very heart of what is at stake in representing the dead. Has the dead young man really been pinned down in representation at all? Neither insubstantial nor flighty like Anticlea yet equally illusory in his own way, he turns on its head the paradigm of the *eidōlon* we encountered in the *Odyssey*: he appears least visible to those dearest to him. Vision, in the face of death, has its limits.

Death resides in the eyes

Perhaps unsurprisingly, the particular challenges which death and the dead posed to viewing were not only negotiated in the concrete rituals and commemorations which followed a death. Ancient myth also often thematizes the role of vision, underscoring especially the ways in which death can play tricks on what we see. The story of

---

57 R. Osborne (1998: 200).

Orpheus and Eurydice, for instance, as told by Roman poets and prose writers, is almost the opposite of Odysseus and Anticlea: Orpheus finds himself able to touch but not to look upon his dead beloved.[58] If he wants to restore his dearly departed wife, he must lead her out of the underworld by the hand, never once turning around to see her. Orpheus, however, cannot resist a stolen glance (Ovid, *Metamorphoses* 10.56–9):

> Afraid and desiring to see her, lest she give him the slip,
> The lover turned his eyes; and in that instant she slid back
> And, stretching out his arms, struggling to hold her and be held,
> He seized at nothing, unhappy man, except yielding air.

Eurydice slides out of Orpheus' line of vision, as Anticlea slid out of Odysseus' hands. Instead of his promised happy ending, he finds that the dead are, ultimately, both untouchable and unviewable – and it is his own desire to view which trips him up. The dead, it seems, resist being seen.

Eurydice resides on the margins of Orpheus' eyesight: she lies in his peripheral field of vision. But what would it mean for Orpheus to meet his dead wife's gaze? Commemoration tends to sidestep such questions: the Illissos youth does not really stare back, for his sculpted eyes are, after all, unseeing; he is just an image.[59] No viewer really suspends his or her disbelief, always, to borrow a term from Wollheim, "seeing-in" as well as "seeing-as".[60] And yet, is it not unsettling – threatening, even – to see and be seen by a dead man? The motif of the frontal gaze certainly creates a dynamic visual exchange which extends beyond the image's own frame to draw the external viewer into a direct relationship with the deceased youth. Theories of "extramission" and "intromission" also suggest that ancient viewers had a tendency to think of the meeting of eyes as far more loaded and far less passive than we do today; if we thought of our eyes as constantly giving out or receiving streams of tiny particles through which emotions like love or hate could travel, we might well feel anxious when caught by the gaze of a dead young man, sculpted or not. In ancient thinking, sight proves surprisingly tactile. It always involves a direct exchange.[61]

Death, as Orpheus discovered, can also cloud vision. As early as Homer, death itself was conceptualized as a form of blindness.[62] Death is a darkness that settles over the eyes themselves, as the *psuchē* departs from the body. Indeed, dying in Homeric verse is highly formulaic: time and again, darkness or night enfolds the eyes of the unfortunate souls who die on the battlefield.[63] And yet, death in Homer is

---

58 E.g. Virgil, *Georgics* 4.454–503; Ovid, *Metamorphoses* 10.1–73; Seneca, *Hercules Furens* 569–91, *Hercules Oetaeus* 1061–89; Apollodorus, *Library of Greek Mythology* 1.3.3.
59 Cf. Neer (2010: 52).
60 See Wollheim (1980: 205–26) – with further discussions by Grethlein in this volume.
61 On the "embodied eye", see Squire's introduction to this volume; on "intromission" and "extramission", see also the chapters by Rudolph, Nightingale and Bielfeldt. For some broader introductions to ancient theories of viewing, see Lindberg (1976); G. Simon (1988); Goldhill (2001); Hubbard (2002); Darrigol (2012).
62 Morrison (1999). On the Greek cultural poetics of "blindness", see Coo (this volume). Grethlein (this volume) likewise explores blindness as a meditation on viewing.
63 E.g. Homer, *Iliad* 4.525–6 or 5.657–9.

never only visionary; it is also a moment in which (or process through which) the body is both felt and numbed, its boundaries threatened as its organs are pierced and displaced.[64] Similarly, Ovid's narrative of Eurydice's attempted rescue moves pointedly from darkness to light, but it is Orpheus' haptic frustration which carries the greater poignancy.[65] By capturing the loss of selfhood which death entails, such notions of the snatching away of sight are not just metaphysical – but they are always written on a more holistic (or even synaesthetic) understanding of the experience.[66]

It is in the mythical figure of Medusa that sight and death – as well as representation and blindness – coalesce most forcefully. Medusa's power lay in her eyes: those unlucky enough to fall prey to her gaze found themselves turned to stone. The violence of her gaze, however, was always destined to be curtailed and controlled – the hero Perseus not only bypassed her terrifying vision using a shield as a mirror, but also repurposed her petrifying look by gifting her snaky-haired head to his patron goddess Athena for use on the battlefield.[67]

But if Medusa's power lay in her glassy stare, then coming upon her image was always a troubling encounter – even if, as with the Ilissos youth, viewers were likely to "see-in" her imaged status. Early temples exploited her ability to discombobulate, placing the gorgoneion in prominent positions.[68] On the sculpted pediment of the Archaic Temple of Artemis at Corfu (Figure 7.5) a full-figured Medusa displaces the goddess herself, taking pride of place in the centre above the entrance.[69] As Platt shows in this volume, viewing and representing the gods was always fraught with difficulty; here at Corfu, Medusa embodies and turns outwards the threatening Otherness of the divine while simultaneously deferring Artemis' own epiphany.[70]

Medusa's Otherness, moreover, is underlined by her monstrous femininity, for she hardly has much in common with the bashful maiden who looked away when stared at.[71] Like other female figures of death (the siren, the sphinx, the *kēr*), her violence is indelibly linked to her femininity and sexuality.[72] Rather than look away when stared at, she inverts social norms and stares right back; she takes control of

---

64 Holmes (2010: 41–83) usefully, for our purposes, distinguishes between the "felt" and the "seen" (rather than the "body" and the "mind") in her discussion of Homeric selfhood.
65 On darkness to light, cf. Ovid, *Metamorphoses* 50–4. On the converse association of light with the gods, see Platt (this volume).
66 On death and synaesthesia, see Walters (2013).
67 Cf. Hesiod, *Shield of Hercules* 220–37, *Theogony* 270–83; Apollodorus, *Library of Greek Mythology* 2.4.2–3; Ovid, *Metamorphoses* 4.606–893, 5.1.236. For the visual materials, see (in addition to Grethlein's chapter in this volume) *LIMC*, s.v. "Perseus"; Frontisi-Ducroux (1989; 1995); Mack (2002).
68 On the *gorgoneion*, see *LIMC*, s.v. "Gorgo/Gorgones", along with Marconi (2007: 214–22) on its appropriation in temple contexts.
69 On the temple of Artemis at Corfu specifically, see Rodenwaldt (1939: 11–4); Benson (1987); Marconi (2007).
70 On the visual stakes of epiphany, the classic analysis is now Platt (2011).
71 A downturned gaze is a sign of *sophrosunē* ("modesty", "self-awareness"): see e.g. Cairns (1993: 98 n.151, 158, 217–8, 292–3, 312; 2005); G. Ferrari (2002: 54–6); Llewellyn-Jones (2003: 262–3).
72 On female death demons, see Vermeule (1979: 145–78); Vernant (1991: 95–110 [= Vernant 1985b]); Tsiafakis (2003); Burton (2005). Medusa's visage was generally represented as grotesque (see Vernant 1991: 111–38 [= Vernant 1985a]); "beautiful" Medusas emerge in the late fifth century BCE (cf. Topper 2007).

Figure 7.5 Plaster cast of the limestone pediment with Medusa, Pegasus and Chrysaor from the Temple of Artemis on Corfu, *ca.* 580 BCE. Cambridge, University of Cambridge Museum of Classical Archaeology: inv. 12 (© University of Cambridge Museum of Classical Archaeology).

vision in a context where women were more likely to be objects than subjects of the gaze. There is a sense in which her death at the hands of Perseus might be read on a narrative level as a punishment to put her back in her place.[73] Perhaps unsurprisingly, Medusa has functioned as a foil for modern thinkers from Freud to Cixous, embodying an apparent autonomy upon which feminine subjectivity could be theorized and recuperated: the ancient figure herself – and her powerful implication within the cultural poetics of sight – has tended to recede into the distance under such a heavy burden.[74]

The story of Medusa's own death was essential to her essential apotropaic function, since her very power to protect lay in how Perseus took possession of her petrifying gaze. The pediment at Corfu, with its clever narrative telescoping, ensured that, through the inclusion of her offspring Chrysaor and Pegasus who should rightly

---

[73] Feminist work on narrative in cinema has long theorized (not unproblematically) that women are punished for their "Otherness" on the big screen, beginning with Mulvey (1975).

[74] A selection of modern entanglements with Medusa are collected and translated in Garber & Vickers (2003); cf. Zajko & Leonard (2006).

SIGHT AND DEATH

Figure 7.6 Wall-painting showing Perseus and Andromeda with the head of Medusa, from the Casa del Vaticinio di Cassandra (Pompeii, VI.10.2), late first century BCE. Naples, Museo Nazionale Archeologico: inv. 8995. Su concessione del Ministero dei Beni e delle Atiività Culturali e del Turismo (Soprintendenza per i Beni Archeologici di Napoli).

be borne from her blood, her death took centre stage. But her backstory was more subtly and self-consciously footnoted when she was represented as a disembodied head.[75] On the tondo of a black-figure drinking-cup, her grinning visage might rush up to meet the symposiastic drinker as he drained the dregs, blacking out his own vision as he tipped up the vessel (cf. Figures 4.11, 6.10).[76] The effect was to play out the type of sensory deprivation noted in the concatenation of death and blindness, allowing the viewer to imagine (if now perhaps even fantasize about) his own death. In several later wall-paintings from Pompeii, Medusa's disembodied head is transformed into a lover's plaything, her power neutralized: in one image, for example, Perseus and Andromeda are visualized as staring – safely – at its mirrored reflection (Figure 7.6).[77]

---

75 Cf. Mack (2002).
76 On eye-cups, see Boardman (1976) and Hedreen (2007a) – along with Squire's introduction and the chapters by Grethlein and Bielfeldt in this volume.
77 Cf. Balensiefen (1990: 54–6, 234–6, K 35.1–14); *LIMC, s.v.* "Perseus", nos. 224–8. See also Grethlein

There was thus an important ambivalence at the heart of viewing Medusa's image. Medusa was the image-maker *par excellence*,[78] but she is also a paradigmatic image in her own right. As Jonas Grethlein demonstrates in this volume, when Medusa is represented she opens up a self-reflexive discourse on viewing – but she also destabilizes the relationship between death and viewing with which I began this chapter. In essence, Medusa rendered the power of commemoration itself into a weapon, transforming her victims into their own macabre funerary monuments – and doing so in a particularly efficient way, collapsing the gap between the image and its prototype. The ambivalence in Medusa's imagery, we might say, turns upon the concept of the *eidōlon* itself. If the *eidōlon* depends upon the gap between representation and its subject, then Medusa's "statue-ified" victims – bodies aestheticized beyond the limits of flesh and blood – hardly qualify. Rather, it is Medusa herself who is the archetypal *eidōlon*: every time Medusa is represented, she personifies and embodies (the effects of) her own power.

Dying to see?

The figure of the Medusa consequently stands as the supreme example of the complex interconnections between death and visual representation that this chapter has explored. As I hope to have shown, ancient attitudes to death are inexorably bound up with ideas about the sensory experience of seeing. Since the visual representation of the dead makes re-visible that which had been lost, sight structures a confrontation with death in both funerary practice and funerary commemoration. In both Athens and Rome, death was bound up with visual spectacle, whether through the display of the corpse during a eulogy, the presence of an impressively large tomb on a roadside or the comely commemorative figure of a dead young man.

But it is also the limits of visibility which frame the ways in which the living build continuing relationships with the dead. Death may demand viewing, but it also destabilizes sight: it is the very ontology of the dead (and death) which is at stake when commemoration mobilizes representation to disavow physical absence. In this context, the prominence of viewing is simultaneously predicated upon the power and failure of the other human senses: consider the power of the haptic, for instance, which figures loss as an issue of touch and frustrated reciprocity. It is not so much that there is a tension between an occularcentric discourse of death and a more holistically sensory performativity of ritual, in other words. My point, rather, is that seeing, envisioning and reflecting on death only makes sense within a context of heightened sensitivity – and vice versa.

(this volume), for the motif on Apulian vases.
78 For Medusa as image-maker, see especially Frontisi-Ducroux (1993).

8

SIGHT AND THE GODS

On the desire to see naked nymphs

Verity Platt

optaui Dacos tenere caesos: tenui.
[opt]aui in sella pacis residere: sedi.
optaui claros sequi triumphos: factum.
optaui primi commoda plena pili: hab[ui].
optaui nudas uidere nymphas: uidi.

I wished to carry out Dacian slaughters: I did so.
I wished to sit in the chair of peace: I sat in it.
I wished to march along in glorious triumphs: I did.
I wished for the full rewards of the *primus pilus*: I had them.
I wished to see naked nymphs: I saw them.

Discovered in the thermal baths at Aquae Flavianae in Roman Algeria, the inscription above lists the *cursus honorum* of a Roman centurion who has fulfilled his every heart's desire (*optaui*) (Figure 8.1).[1] Having fought under Trajan in his Dacian campaigns (101–2 and 105–6 CE), marched in triumphal processions and reached "the pinnacle of the legionary hierarchy" as a *primus pilus*, the author presents his ultimate achievement as an act of viewing (*uidere ... uidi*).[2] In the inscription's final line, the focus shifts from the daring deeds of military service to a vision of those most tantalizing of supernatural beings: the nymphs. In a reversal of Caesar's famous claim at Zela (*ueni, uidi, uici!* "I came, I saw, I conquered!"), presence and surveillance do not in this case lead straightforwardly to military victory. Rather, the performance of Roman authority is presented as a sequence of superhuman feats that leads to the rewards of visionary experience. The poem's structure, a "priamel" building to a striking and unexpected final statement, affords a climactic role to the act of autopsy (seeing for oneself). But in light of both conquest and spectacle, what kind of encounter does the centurion's vision ultimately imply?

---

1 *L'Année épigraphique* (1928: no. 37): the stele is 62cm high and 30cm wide, and comes from Aquae Flavianae (Hammam Essalihine) in the Kenchela province of Algeria. For discussions, see Balland (1976); Diez De Velasco (1998: 85–6, no. 14.5); and Adams (1999: 127–8). More generally on the site's thermal baths, cf. Thébert (2003: 189–200). All translations in this chapter are my own unless otherwise indicated.
2 See Speidel (2012: 183), who interprets the "Chair of Peace" as an administrative position within the military, like the *centurio regionarius* (a centurion appointed to the military and administrative supervision of a particular locality).

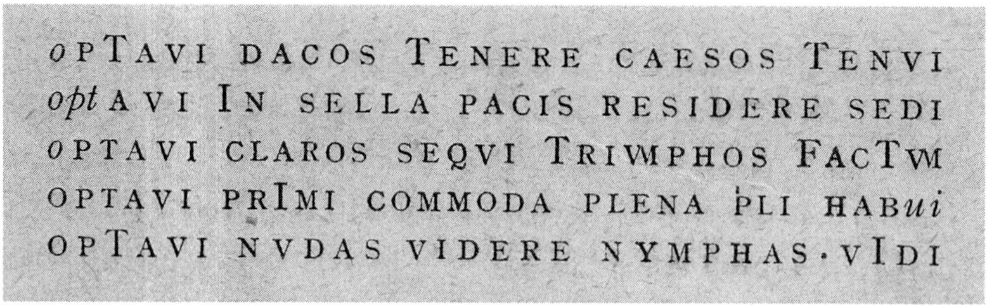

oPTAVI DACOS TENERE CAESOS TENVI
optAVI IN SELLA PACIS RESIDERE SEDI
OPTAVI CLAROS SEQVI TRIVMPHOS FACTVM
OPTAVI PRIMI COMMODA PLENA PLI HABui
OPTAVI NVDAS VIDERE NYMPHAS·VIDI

Figure 8.1 Inscription from Aquae Flavianae, Algeria, second century CE. After R. Cagnat & M. Besnier, "Périodiques", *L'Année épigraphique* 1928: 10, no. 37.

Any investigation of sight in antiquity must contend with the fact that "seeing the gods" played a vital role in Graeco-Roman practices and discourses of vision. Classical literature was profoundly concerned with the question of how, when and in what form the gods might appear to their mortal worshippers. Likewise the rhythms of social, political and domestic life were punctuated by ritual engagements with the gods, predicated on the memory or expectation of divine presence, often in the form of direct visions or visual representations. Sensory perception of the divine was primarily formulated through the concept of "epiphany", whereby the gods were understood to make themselves temporarily perceptible to mortals in "manifest form", under certain special conditions.[3] Given antiquity's highly developed system of anthropomorphism, the ancient gods were regarded as especially *visual* and *visualizable* beings. However, as the jubilance of our centurion's claim to have seen the nymphs at Aquae Flavianae implies, they were not always easily *visible*.

---

3 For an introduction to this phenomenon, cf. Platt (2015). For more detailed analysis, see Koch Piettre (1996), on the semiotics of epiphany in Archaic and Classical Greek thought; cf. the 2004 issue of *Illinois Classical Studies* (vol. 29) – the proceedings of a conference on epiphany in Greek religion; Platt (2011), a study of the relationship between epiphany and visual representation, with further bibliography; Kindt (2012: 36–54), on cognitive approaches to epiphany; Petridou (2013), on vision and ritual; Petridou (forthcoming a), a comprehensive study of epiphany's role in Greek religion; and Petridou et al. (forthcoming), an edited volume on divine presence in Graeco-Roman cult and culture. Those looking to earlier literature should start with Friedrich Pfister's foundational 1924 article; see also Pax (1955), on the relationship between Greek, Indo-European, Babylonian, Egyptian and Christian models of epiphany. Versnel (1987) asks what ancient viewers actually saw when they encountered the gods, exploring important questions about the cognitive and theological dilemmas raised by sacred vision (also addressed in Versnel 2011), while Lane Fox (1986: 102–67) traces the history of Greek epiphany against the background of religious change in late antiquity. On sacred modes of viewing and representation in antiquity, see especially Gordon (1979); Gladigow (1990); Elsner (1995: 88–124; 1996; 2007b: 1–26); Steiner (2001: 95–104); Platt (2010; 2011); Squire (2011b: 154–201); Gaifman (2012); cf. Elsner & Rutherford (2005) on viewing the divine in the context of pilgrimage. Much scholarship on the conception, perception and representation of the divine in antiquity is indebted to the structuralist anthropological approach of the so-called "French School" of classical studies: see especially Frontisi-Ducroux (1986b; 1988; 1991); Malamoud & Vernant (1986); and Vernant (1990b; 1991). On dream visions of the gods (an important category of visionary encounter), see below.

This tension raises difficult questions. What does it mean to "see" beings whose very nature gives them the capacity to elude mortal perception?[4] Should we take such claims seriously, given the subjective nature of sensory experience and the unverifiable, elusive and even playful character of much epiphanic narrative? As modern scholars rather than religious insiders, we approach such material beset by a particularly challenging set of cognitive and methodological limitations. On one hand, we might read ancient assertions of epiphanic autopsy as exemplary demonstrations of the "constructed" nature of vision. According to such a view, seeing the gods was a historical and psychological phenomenon informed by a range of cultural and religious influences (with their concomitant models of "visuality") that are now lost to us: the centurion sees the nymphs, in effect, because he desires and expects to do so.[5] On the other hand, the seriousness with which claims to epiphanic autopsy tended to be treated within antiquity – not to mention the sheer volume of evidence for such claims – means that visionary encounters with the gods cannot be easily dismissed as mere fantasy, delusion or cultural trope.[6] For many ancient witnesses, epiphanic vision was a very real phenomenon that had significant implications for and demanded specific responses from mortal viewers and their communities.

That notwithstanding, determining how sacred forms of "visionary" experience related to everyday modes of "vision" is a delicate interpretative exercise. To see the gods was to undergo a form of perception that challenged the capabilities of the human sensorium, putting mortals into ocular contact with beings who tested and defied the physical limitations of the human body. Despite the intensely visual nature of Graeco-Roman religion, which depended on a rich and complex system of image-making and viewing, seeing the gods themselves was a particularly elusive – even dangerous – phenomenon. As we shall see, claims to epiphanic vision in antiquity are beset by perceptual and epistemological ambiguity to the extent that ambiguity might itself be described as integral both to epiphanic vision and to its cultural expression.

Taking our centurion's vision of the Aquae Flavianae nymphs as a paradigmatic example, this chapter explores the particular problems that arise for historians of the senses when we attempt to grapple with perceptions of the sacred. What is possible, or permissible, in such exchanges? How do the asymmetries of the human–divine relationship engage the complex dynamics of seeing and being seen in Graeco-Roman culture? Why is ancient perception of the gods so seemingly ocularcentric? And how does the tradition of anthropomorphism – in which humans encounter beings with parallel (if not equivalent) sensory capacities to themselves – influence cultural formulations of sacred sight? First, I address the playful ambiguity of our soldier's claim, contextualizing his encounter within both a broader Graeco-Roman discourse about the viewing of elusive divine bodies and specific cultic traditions of

---

4 Note that Strabo, commenting on the secret rites of mystery cults, claims that such concealment "induces reverence for the divine, since it imitates the nature of the divine, which is to avoid being perceived by our human senses" (10.3.9): see Bremmer (1995).
5 On socially constructed modes of "visuality" (as opposed to biological "vision"), see Squire's introduction to this volume.
6 For an example of this approach, see Chaniotis (2005: 145), on epigraphic evidence for Hellenistic battle epiphanies.

invoking divine presence. Concentrating on the relationship between divine and human agency that coalesces around the act of seeing, I investigate the highly visual language that clusters around the Greek concept of *epiphaneia*, or "manifest appearance", as well as the limitations of sight as a sensory means of experiencing the gods. Second, I turn from the *act* of seeing to the question of what, in fact, is seen in such encounters. Here, I examine the relatively laconic character of claims to epiphanic autopsy, relating the centurion's *uidi* ("I have seen") to the proliferation of inscriptions across the ancient world which attest to religious vows made "according to a vision" (*kata opsin* in Greek, or *ex uisu* in Latin). In such cases, private, ephemeral experiences of seeing the gods are not described in detail, but are reified, perpetuated and made public through material acts of inscription, which – like other artefacts such as votive reliefs and cult statues – themselves become visible loci of divine presence. Figural representation, however, both requires and transmits more information about divine appearance, raising difficult questions about the slippery relationship between gods and their images: how do we know that the gods look the way they do? And how far can representations of the divine capture or convey the polymorphic, hidden or inscrutable aspects of godhead that defy human modes of perception and depiction?

Acts of seeing

At first glance, our centurion's claim to have seen "naked nymphs" might be read as a crude metaphor for sexual conquest – the final victory of a lusty *miles gloriosus* (a "swaggering soldier") who has performed Caesar's triple triumph in reverse. After all, as the dynamics of the erotic gaze in antiquity imply, to see is to possess – and it is tempting to extend the soldier's claim to have "seen" to an altogether more *tactile* form of sensory engagement.[7] Here, the mastery demonstrated by Roman expansion in North Africa (and the army's enjoyment of the sensory pleasures of peace) is implicitly extended to nubile female bodies visible – and, implicitly, available – at the local baths. When perceived through the lens of the centurion's self-aggrandizing fantasies, such bodies are raised to divine status, generating a visionary encounter that serves as a fitting reward for his own Herculean labours.

This reading, however, depends upon the ambiguity of the term *nymphae*, which can refer both to divine nymphs and mortal women – most often girls of marriageable age.[8] While the inscription's verbal play adds to its humorous appeal, it simultaneously echoes a deep and abiding uncertainty in Graeco-Roman culture about the nature and perceptibility of divine bodies. We might read the centurion's claim to have "seen" as a synecdoche for a more multi-sensory encounter, yet it is striking that, here, "to see" the nymphs is presented as a triumphal, even transgressive, act *in itself*. *Nymphae* may refer to young women on the brink of marriage, but only insofar as their beauty and virginal promise emulates the desirability and elusive nature of divine nymphs, spirits who both inhabited and embodied the generative power of natural, and especially watery, locations.[9]

---

7 See Squire (introduction to this volume). On the sight of the naked female body as a form of possession in Roman Imperial culture, see e.g. Fredrick (1995); Goldhill (2001); Morales (2004: 8–34).
8 On this ambiguity, see Andò (1996) and Larson (2001: 3–6).
9 On the watery associations of nymphs (or Naiads), see Larson (2001: 8–11).

In Catullus' 64th poem (to which this inscription may allude), the narrator looks back to the age of heroes, when Jason and his Argonauts "saw the nymphs with their eyes", their naked bodies rising above the waves "as far as their breasts".[10] Such privileged modes of vision, it is implied, are located in the heroic past, when they were only accessible to a fortunate few, and even then were only partial or fleeting.[11] The elusive, fragmented and even hazardous nature of epiphanic encounter has a deep literary heritage: as the goddess Hera comments in Homer's *Iliad*, "the gods are dangerous when they appear in manifest form (*enargeis*)".[12] Greek myth abounds with examples of humans whose sight of godhead results in injury, mishap or even death (such as Semele's vision of Zeus or Actaeon's accidental sight of the naked Artemis bathing with her nymph companions).[13] Moreover, as polymorphous beings who shift between multiple forms and identities at whim, the gods have a habit of appearing to their mortal viewers in disguise, and are seldom easily identified: as Odysseus remarks to Athena in Homer's *Odyssey*, "it is difficult, goddess, for a mortal man to know you when he meets you, however wise he may be, for you take what shape you will" (*Odyssey* 13.312–13).[14] When Aeneas encounters his mother Venus in the first book of Virgil's *Aeneid*, for example, she appears in the guise of a huntress, prompting him to ask if she is in fact Diana or one of her nymphs (328–9): famously, he realizes her true identity only in the fleeting moment of her shimmeringly elegant departure.[15]

How, then, might we interpret our centurion's confident claim to have seen *nudas ... nymphas* at Aquae Flavianae? Insofar as the inscription implies an especially privileged view of divine bodies (as the climax of or reward for heroic labours), it also implies a form of apotheosis, in which visionary encounter symbolizes the subject's entry to the realm of the gods. Might we, then, be encouraged to read the inscription

---

10 Catullus 64.16–18: *illa, atque alia, uiderunt luce marinas | mortales oculis nudato corpore Nymphas | nutricum tenus exstantes e gurgite cano* ("On that day, if on any other, mortals saw with their eyes the sea nymphs standing forth from the foaming waters, their bodies naked as far as their breasts"). The allusion is suggested by Balland (1976), and followed by Adams (1999: 127).

11 On the nostalgic, "postlapsarian" qualities of epiphanic vision, see Platt (2011: 215–52), concentrating on Imperial period Greek texts such as Pausanias' *Description of Greece*, with Fitzgerald (1996: 140–69), on belatedness in Catullus 64. Note that Thetis, who submits to partnership with a mortal in Catullus' poem, was a famously slippery, metamorphic and intangible being – with a quintessentially elusive kind of body.

12 *Iliad* 20.131: χαλεποὶ δὲ θεοὶ φαίνεσθαι ἐναργεῖς. On Homeric scenes of epiphanic vision, see (from a vast bibliography) Pucci (1998); Stevens (2002); Turkeltaub (2003; 2007); and Bierl (2004). On *enargeia* as a key term in the language of visionary encounter, see Koch Piettre (1999) and Platt (2011: 54–7, 173–8, 215–52).

13 On Semele, see Buxton (1980: 34–5) and Vernant (1991: 41–6). On Actaeon, see Lacy (1990); John Heath (1992: 25–52); Platt (2002); and Squire (2011b: 102–14). On surprise and terror as a classic response to epiphany, see Richardson (1974: 208–11, 306–7).

14 ἀργαλέον σε, θεά, γνῶναι βροτῷ ἀντιάσαντι, | καὶ μάλ᾽ ἐπισταμένῳ· σὲ γὰρ αὐτὴν παντὶ ἐΐσκεις. On divine metamorphosis and disguise, see Buxton (2009).

15 *Aeneid* 1.405: *uera incessu patuit dea* ("the goddess' true nature was revealed in her [departing] step"). On visions of the divine in Virgil, see Kühn (1971); Block (1981); Feeney (1991: 129–87; 1998: 104–7); Alden Smith (2005: 24–59); and Cioffi (2014), with Lovatt (2013: 78–121), on epiphany in Latin epic more broadly. Aeneas' encounter with Venus in the first book of the *Aeneid* is closely based on the encounter between Anchises and Aphrodite in the *Homeric Hymn to Aphrodite*, on which see Turkeltaub (2003) and Platt (2011: 60–76).

Figure 8.2 Front of a marble sarcophagus depicting Hylas and the Nymphs, installed in Rome's Palazzo Mattei, early third century CE (© DAI Rom, DAI-Neg. D-DAI-ROM 65-1345 (Koppermann)).

as a form of epitaph – a *Res Gestae*, as it were, intended for the speaker's tomb? In Imperial Roman culture, eroticized encounters with the gods offered a popular metaphor for death.[16] Indeed, the myth of Hylas, who was fatally pulled into a Bithynian spring by desirous nymphs, is depicted on a second-century CE sarcophagus. Here, the doomed youth (complete with the portrait features of the deceased) is suspended forever in an exchange of gazes with a nubile sprite who lures him to his watery end (Figure 8.2).[17] In such cases, the act of seeing – and being seen by – supernatural beings attests to the status and desirability of the dead, marking their entry into an exalted, altered state of hyper-vision. At the same time, this moment of ocular exchange draws its power from the very real dangers that were associated with sensory perception of the divine: to see the deathless gods (the *im-mortales* or *a-thanatoi*) is to enter a dimension of experience that is not only barred to ordinary mortals, but also threatens the integrity of the mortal body itself.[18]

Nymphs, however, could be said to occupy an interstitial category between the human and divine, being closely tied to the landscape and thus more immediately accessible – and visible – to mortal eyes. In this sense, they are closer to heroes (or

---

16 See (from a vast bibliography) G. Davies (1986); Koortbojian (1995); Wood (2000); Platt (2011: 335–93, with further bibliography); and Zanker & Ewald (2012: 84–103).
17 For literary treatments of Hylas' abduction, see Apollonius, *Argonautica* 1.1207–39; Theocritus, *Idyll* 13; Apollodorus, *Library of Greek Mythology* 1.117; Strabo, *Geography* 12.4.3; Propertius, *Elegies* 1.20; and Valerius Flaccus, *Argonautica* 3.474–4.57. On abduction narratives concerning Greek nymphs, see Larson (2001: 66–73) and Sourvinou-Inwood (2005: 67–116). Wypustek (2013: 158–75) explores references to abduction by nymphs in funerary epigraphy and iconography of the first to third centuries CE. On the Hylas sarcophagus (displayed in the Palazzo Mattei, Rome), see Zanker & Ewald (2012: 90–1), who interpret the scene as a family group portrait, with Ling (1979), a comprehensive treatment of Hylas in Roman art.
18 More generally on "sight and death", see Turner (this volume). On the conceptual relationship between mortal and immortal bodies, the classic analysis is Vernant (1991).

SIGHT AND THE GODS

daimones) – semi-divine beings whose former mortality and association with specific locales (such as tombs) affords a greater degree of bodily presence and perceptibility.[19] Likewise, the nymphs' relative accessibility parallels that of collective female deities such as the Muses, whose role as a conduit of inspiration between mortal poets and the god Apollo gave them a particularly epiphanic quality, celebrated through the poetic trope of the *Dichterweihe* (or "poetic initiation"), in which the poet enters into his or her life's vocation as a result of visionary encounter.[20] Significantly, the cult of the nymphs was widespread in Roman North Africa, and the thermal springs at Aquae Flavianae, in particular, have yielded numerous dedicatory inscriptions which suggest that nymphs were worshipped as local tutelary deities (and, potentially, goddesses of healing).[21] Amongst these, an inscribed altar incorporates the phrase *ex uisu*, a widespread Latin formula which, like the Greek *kata opsin*, can be translated as "according to a vision".[22] While our centurion's claim to have seen "naked nymphs" may titillate and amuse, then, his inscription also constitutes part of a more extensive material assemblage and its attendant religious discourse, both of which are grounded in local cult, whilst also representing a broader set of visionary sacred practices attested across the Roman empire.

I will discuss the implications of this visually engaged epigraphic (and epiphanic) habit in greater detail later in this chapter.[23] For now, let us observe that the playful ambiguity of the centurion's claim and the erotic dynamics of his visionary desire are displayed within a context where epiphanic encounter seems to have been both ritually expected and dutifully recorded. While the desire to see naked nymphs might suggest a transgressive voyeurism (casting our centurion in the role of a "Peeping Tom"), his final *optaui* crowns a series of desires that are nevertheless requited within the conventional institutional structures of the Roman military.[24] In contrast to mythical figures such as Actaeon or Hylas, whose epiphanic encounters occur by chance (with fatal results), his final declaration "I have seen!" is presented, like his other achievements, as a self-generated *act* of seeing, rather than a passive experience of vision.

In this sense, the centurion's vision falls into the category of sacred sights that are invoked and prepared for within the context of cult, such as rites of *theoxenia* (in which gods are invited to "dine" with their mortal worshippers), incubation in

---

19 On the nymph as a mediating figure between gods and humans, see Larson (2001: 65). On the interstitial role of *daimones* (and their relative accessibility), see J. Z. Smith (1978) and Platt (2011: 235–8). On epiphany and hero cult, see Bravo (2004).
20 The foundational text for poetic initiation by the Muses is the opening of Hesiod's *Theogony* (vv. 22–34): see Kambylis (1965) and Latte (2010), with Clay (2004) on a parallel episode in the life of Archilochus.
21 On the relationship between shrines to the nymphs and thermal springs, see Larson (2001) on Greece, and Diez De Velasco (1998) on Spain and North Africa.
22 *L'Année épigraphique* (1960: no.96), discovered near the thermal baths at Aquae Flavianae, and associated with the nymphs by Diez De Velasco (1998: no. 14/2), who compares it to *Corpus Inscriptionum Latinarum* (CIL) 2.2527, an altar dedicated to the nymphs *ex uisu* at the thermal baths at Orense, Spain (no. 14/28). For a catalogue and discussion of *ex uisu* inscriptions (which are often related to dream visions, discussed below), see Renberg (2003).
23 On the notion of the "epigraphic habit", see MacMullen (1982), with Platt (2011: 147–69) on epiphanic epigraphy.
24 See Speidel (2012: 182–4).

healing sanctuaries (in which deities are encountered in the form of dream visions) or climactic moments in mystery cult (such as the *epopteia*, the dramatically staged moment of "seeing" which featured in the initiation rites of the Eleusinian Mysteries).[25] Sacred modes of visuality, then, could prompt particular kinds of visionary encounters. To yearn for sensorial contact with the nymphs, as our centurion does, is itself a characteristic of their cult, demonstrated most strikingly by the phenomenon of "nympholepsy" (attested in fifth and fourth-century BCE Greece), in which devotees would frequent shrines of the nymphs in natural locations such as caves.[26] Possessing an acute awareness of divine presence and claiming to commune directly with the nymphs, *nympholeptoi* (literally "those seized by the nymphs") testify to heightened powers of perception and expression. These are not demonstrated by direct sensory encounters with the nymphs' *bodies*, however, but through an intensive material engagement with their *cult* (through the cultivation of cave shrines and the production of inscriptions) and, in some cases, prophetic inspiration. While the inscription from Aquae Flavianae suggests a somewhat less intimate relationship with the nymphs than that of famous *nympholeptoi* such as Archedamus of Thera, its self-consciously poetic form and diction nevertheless suggest an "inspired" response to epiphanic vision, in which the appropriate response to sacred sight is an elevated form of utterance, made permanent in the form of a dedicatory inscription.[27]

In contrast to the formal context of the sanctuary, epiphanies that take place outside the framework of ritual tend to occur unexpectedly, often in extreme situations (such as the tumult of battle or dramatic natural phenomena such as storms and earthquakes) or remote and liminal locations (such as mountains, woodland glades and the seashore).[28] In such cases, revelatory agency is wholly ascribed to the gods, whose appearance may be dangerous or salvific, depending on their relationships to the mortal witnesses in question. The divinity's identity is often unknown: in such cases, accurate identification and an appropriately reverent response are crucial to the successful management of its disruptive presence within the human realm. As literary scenes of epiphany repeatedly attest, those who encounter the gods must acknowledge, recognize and process their experiences in active terms – most often through pious traditions of ritualized response, such as the performance

---

[25] On *theoxenia*, see Bruit (1989; 2004) and Jameson (1994); on incubation, see below. On ritual viewing and the *epopteia*, see Clinton (2004); cf. Petridou (2013), who concentrates not on "things seen" in the mysteries (so inaccessible to non-initiates and modern scholars alike), but on "the possible ways they were perceived by the initiates and the culturally defined scopic regimes that informed that perception" (310).

[26] On "nympholepsy", see Connor (1988); Larson (2001: 11–20); Pache (2011). For a parallel episode in Roman culture, consider the legend of Numa's (often eroticized) relationship with the nymph Egeria, a source of inspiration for the foundation of Roman law and ritual (Livy 1.19; Plutarch, *Life of Numa Pompilius* 8), with Wiseman (2004: 51).

[27] On the inscription's literary qualities, see Adams (1999: 127). On Archedamus, who tended the cave shrine of the nymphs at Vari in Attica, see Larson (2001: 14–19); Schoerner & Goette (2004); and Pache (2011: 44–52).

[28] On such contexts, see Platt (2011: 55–6, 124–69, 218–20; 2015; forthcoming) and Petridou (forthcoming b), with Pritchett (1979: vol. 3, 11–46); Speyer (1980); and Chaniotis (2005: 143–65), on battle epiphanies.

of sacrifices, the foundation of cults and festivals, or the creation of temples, images and inscriptions.[29] Experiences of sacred sight thus have an important aetiological function, providing "origin myths" for religious and cultural institutions: in this way, a mode of perception normally inaccessible to the human sensorium is held to act as a vital catalyst for change. When divine bodies become perceptible, they invariably have a metamorphic effect, whether by instigating shifts in the social, political or religious order or by quite literally transforming the bodies of those who witness them.[30]

It is important to note that while vision tends to dominate epiphanic discourse (both in antiquity itself and in later scholarship on ancient religion), sensory encounters with the gods are not always purely visual. While inscriptions from Greek shrines to the nymphs attest to a powerful sense of presence, they tend to couch this in the language of companionship and voice, rather than sight – a tendency that is echoed in the Greek notion of divine *parousia* ("presence") or the Latin *deus praesens* ("god at hand").[31] Likewise, ritual invocations of divine presence frame climactic moments of visual revelation synaesthetically, combining the aromas produced by incense and burning offerings with the sonic effects of vocal or musical performance and tactile engagement with the paraphernalia of cult (not to mention the gustatory aspects of sacrificial feasting).[32] Divine presence in such contexts is often couched in the language of motion and arrival, rather than visual spectacle – the act of seasonal return (*epidēmia*) to a cultic shrine, such as Apollo's return to Delphi from the Hyperboreans, or the "ascent" (*anodos*) of Kore and Semele from the underworld.[33] Hellenistic evidence for *epiphaneiai* of the gods refers to both visual and sonic manifestations, such as the howling of Hecate's hounds heard

---

29 A classic case of epiphany in a remote location is that of Pan to the Athenian runner Philippides in the Arcadian hills before the battle of Marathon, which led to the foundation of his cult in a cave-sanctuary at the base of the Athenian Acropolis: see Herodotus 6.105, with Borgeaud (1988: 133–62); Garland (1992: 47–63); and Harrison (2000: 82–92).

30 One thinks of the case of Actaeon (transfigured into a deer), or of the Greek priestess Iodama, who was supposedly turned to stone by the sight of Athena in her temple (Pausanias, *Description of Greece* 9.34.1). On metamorphosis as a response to epiphany, see Buxton (2009).

31 The fifth-century BCE *nympholeptos* Archedemus of Thera, for example, claims to have worked out the grotto of the nymphs at Vari "at their instructions" (*phradaisi*, from *phrazō*, "to tell" or "advise"): *Inscriptiones Graecae* I² 788, discussed by Pache (2011: 44–52). On *parousia* and the use of *pareimi* ("be present") as a technical term for divine appearance, see Koch Piettre (1996: 384–7) and Versnel (2011: 447). On the Roman notion of *praesentes diui* or *praesentia numina* – applied to the Muses (Ovid, *Metamorphoses* 15.622), Fauns and Dryads (Virgil, *Georgics* 1.10), Asclepius (Ovid, *Metamorphoses* 15.677), Hercules (Cicero, *Tusculan Disputations* 1.28) and Augustus (Horace, *Epistles*. 2.1.15–17; Ovid, *Tristia* 2.54) – see Brink (1982: 50–5), Hardie (2002: 4–5) and McGowan (2009: 84–8). On the language of *praesens* in relation to ruler cult, see Clauss (1996), Platt (2011: 143–7) and Versnel (2011: 449–50). It is notable that the language of presence is most often applied to mediatory divine figures such as nymphs, Muses, healing deities, apotheosized heroes and deified rulers.

32 Tanner (2006: 45–8). On the scent of the divine in antiquity, see Clements (2015). On synaesthesia and the ancient senses, see Butler & Purves (2013b).

33 On "divine commuting", see Versnel (2011: 88–102), who claims that *epidēmia* is particularly associated with oracular cults. On the *anodos* or *katagōgē* of Kore/Persephone in the Eleusinian Mysteries, see Mylonas (1961: 148–53) and Clinton (1992: 85–90); on the *anodos* of Semele, see Larson (1995: 95–6). For these and other examples of epiphanic return and arrival in the context of cult, see Bérard (1974) and Petridou (2006: 10–12).

during a battle in Carian Stratonikeia, or multi-sensory phenomena such as the earthquakes and avalanches that impeded the Gauls' invasion of Delphi in 279 BCE.[34] Rather than "visions", such events are better understood as *aretai* ("miracles") or acts of *sōteria* ("salvation") – divinely ordained phenomena that generate a range of bodily sensations and responses.[35]

Despite these diverse modes of epiphanic sense-perception, sight is nevertheless paramount within the vocabulary of divine presence. We have already seen how the language of "vision" (the Greek *opsis* and the Latin *uisus*) is central to epigraphic formulae; likewise, poetic accounts of epiphany return repeatedly to the notion of *enargeia*, exploring human longing for access to a "clarity" of divine form that is both vivid and unmediated.[36] In such cases, sacred sight is focalized explicitly through the subjective experience of mortal witnesses, suggesting a process of active visual attention.[37] The language of *epiphaneia*, on the other hand, which has been so influential on modern formulations of divine encounter, stresses the *external* agency of the divine.[38] Derived from the verb *epiphainein* ("to show" or "cause to appear") and closely related to *phaō* ("to shine" or "give light"), *epiphaneia* is used from the Hellenistic period onwards to refer to "divine manifestation" as a form of active presence, a "coming into appearance" upon, near or by a beholder, that, crucially, occurs at the god's initiative, and can be experienced as either a private or a collective phenomenon.[39] Its origins lie in the earlier use of *epiphaneia* to refer to a "surface" or "plane", the *external* aspects of objects that are the most striking and immediately perceptible (*enargēs*).[40]

This emphasis on "appearing" and "bringing to light" (*phainein*) in the language of epiphany firmly associates sense-perception of the divine with sight, as befits its

---

34 See Şahin (1981: 10–12, no. 10), discussed by Belayche (2009). On the storm, earthquake and avalanche that helped local heroes drive invading Gauls away from Delphi in 279 BCE, see Pausanias, *Description of Greece* 1.4.4 and 10.23.1–2. For examples of epiphanic fragrance, see Philostratus, *Heroicus* 9.6 (where the hero Protesilaus is described as "smell[ing] sweeter than autumn myrtles") and Aelius Aristides, *Sacred Tales* 1.3 (where Athena appears in a dream, her aegis smelling of wax), with discussion by Platt (2011: 246, 262).

35 On epiphanies as *aretai*, see Lührmann (1975), who rather overstates their soteriological function; cf. Versnel (1987: 42–3); Kearns (1990).

36 See e.g. Homer, *Iliad* 20.131 and *Odyssey* 7.201; Hesiod, *Catalogue of Women*, frg. 165.5 M-W; on the epiphanic dimensions of *enargeia* more generally, cf. Koch Piettre (1996) and Platt (2011: 215–52).

37 On active "looking" as opposed to passive "seeing", see Nightingale (this volume).

38 On James Joyce's adaptation of divine epiphany (most notably in *Stephen Hero* and *A Portrait of the Artist as Young Man*), to refer to a "a sudden ... manifestation, whether in the vulgarity of speech or of gesture or in a memorable phrase of the mind itself" (1963: 216), which enables the thinker to access a kind of *inner* vision, or mental clarity, see Hendry (1963); Beja (1971); Bowen (1979); cf. Maltby (2002) on moments of vision in the postmodern novel.

39 On *epiphaneia*, see Koch Piettre (1996: 397 n. 9); Platt (2011, esp. 148–51, with further bibliography); Petridou (forthcoming a). On the relationship between individual and collective epiphanies, see Graf (2004); Platt (2015).

40 On e.g. Democritus, frg. B155 (where *epiphaneia* refers to a "surface plane"), see Vlastos (1995: 293 n. 39) and Koch Piettre (1996: 396–8). The first-century BCE author Strabo uses *epiphaneia* to refer to the "visible presence" of the god Asclepius at Epidaurus (8.6.15), an underground river rising to the "surface" in Sicily (6.2.9), the "fame" of Olympia (8.3.30) and the striking "appearance" of elephants (15.2.13).

SIGHT AND THE GODS

status as the highest of the senses.[41] Ancient models of vision attend closely to the relationship between sight and light: as the medium that enables vision, light is also characteristic of divine epiphany, whether gods are perceived in the form of the "heavenly bodies" of the cosmos or in narrative accounts of corporeal manifestation, such as the "beautiful light" (*phaos perikalles*) that Athena projects before Telemachus in the *Odyssey*.[42] As the more esteemed and developed of the so-called "distance senses" (sight and hearing), vision is also less tactile: it is held to be closer to rational thought (*dianoia*), and thus to the knowledge that comes through insight, the "eye of the mind".[43] It is partly for this reason that *theōria*, the act of "going to see" a god in the context of pilgrimage and religious festivals, is adopted by Plato and his successors in order to express the visionary, enlightened knowledge of the immaterial Forms that comes with sustained philosophical enquiry.[44]

Likewise, as the most "disembodied" (and thus most refined) of the sensory faculties, vision particularly lends itself to the apprehension of elusive *divine* forms: able to receive and mentally process phenomena remotely and with great speed, vision provides "cognitive reliability" that the gods exist, whilst simultaneously eschewing the demands of tactile verification.[45] Though they might invite and even promise tactile engagement, divine bodies tend to evade the physical verification that is afforded by human touch – a sensory mode that is curiously absent from Graeco-Roman epiphanic discourse (in contrast to its critical examination in the context of the Christian incarnation, as exemplified by the figure of "Doubting Thomas").[46] In this way, pagan models of sacred sight convey the striking immediacy and dramatic spectacle of divine manifestation, whilst preserving the gods' distance and corporeal alterity. Despite the predominance of materialist, haptic models of vision in antiquity

---

41 Note that although in rare cases *phainein* can be used of sonic phenomena (as in "to make clear to the ear" or "make ring clearly"), it is predominantly used of visible appearances.
42 *Odyssey* 19.34: on epiphany in this episode, see Bierl (2004). On the role of light in Greek religion, see Parisinou (2000). More generally on the role of light in ancient models of sight, see the chapters by Rudolph, Nightingale and Bielfeldt (this volume).
43 On the privileging of vision within philosophical hierarchies of the senses in antiquity, such as Aristotle, *On the Soul* 2.6–12 (418a–424b), see Sorabji (1971); Jay (1993: 21–33); T. K. Johansen (1997); Korsmeyer (1999: 11–37); and Jütte (2004: 54–71), along with Squire's introduction to this volume. On the distinction between the "distal" and "proximal" senses, see e.g. Aristotle, *On the Soul* 2.11 (432b12–20) and *On Sense and the Sensible* 445a5–8.
44 On the religious origins of *theōria*, see Rutherford (1995; 2000) and Montiglio (2005: 118–79), with Elsner & Rutherford (2005) on the importance of "seeing the gods" in ancient traditions of pilgrimage. On the appropriation of the language of *theōria* in Greek philosophy, see Rausch (1982); Nightingale (2001; 2004; 2005); Squire (2009: 114–15, 119).
45 On the idea of "cognitive reliability" in relation to epiphany, see Platt (2011). As cognitive approaches to religion – such as Boyer (1994), S. Guthrie (2001) and Tremlin (2006) – become increasingly of interest to historians of ancient religion (e.g. Kindt 2012: 36–54; Mackey forthcoming), epiphany offers an interesting test-case. Gabriel Herman has recently put ideological factors and theories of social manipulation aside in order to tackle head-on the tricky issue of what might have "caused" divine visions, relating crisis epiphanies, in particular, to the transhistorical psychological phenomenon known as the "Third Man Factor" or "Sensed Presence" – Herman (2011); see also Geiger (2009).
46 For an exploration of theological and visual approaches to the "Doubting Thomas" episode, see Most (2005), along with Heath (this volume), who also discusses the role of vision in Christian theology more generally.

(in the context of both "intromissionist" and "extramissionist" theories), sight is paradigmatic amongst the senses in its capacity to mediate *between* body and mind. As such, it also mediates between the physical and the *meta*physical, lending itself to a dualism that chimes closely with the ambiguous, ever-shifting corporeality and perceptibility of divine bodies themselves.[47]

Sacred sights

So far, we have observed that Graeco-Roman formulations of divine epiphany draw attention to epistemological and cognitive dilemmas that are fundamental to the faculty of vision. The difficulty of seeing the gods "clearly" (*enargēs*) is paradigmatic of a tension between the seemingly direct, unmediated quality of our visual experiences and their capacity to confuse and deceive.[48] At the same time, sacred sight is held to lead to (or spring from) privileged "insight", suggesting special access to truth and knowledge.[49] Likewise, visionary encounters with the gods provide access to divine bodies that may be corporeal in form, but are ambiguous in substance, capable of intense physical effects upon and within their mortal beholders, yet simultaneously resistant to sensory contact and cognitive processing. So it is that although diverse attestations of epiphanic vision in antiquity assert the *fact* of seeing divine bodies, they rarely tell us much about them. In this section, I turn from the act of seeing to the specifics of sacred sight, exploring the difficulties involved in determining the status and character of divine appearance, alongside the role of visual representation in shaping and communicating epiphanic experience.

Let us return, then, to Aquae Flavianae, where we might note that in celebrating his vision, our centurion leaves the details to his readers' imaginations. While the stele itself displayed a figure of a "quadruped" (perhaps an allusion to the equestrian status of those who held the position of *primus pilus*), the text tells only us that the nymphs were *nudae* – a detail that suggests a particularly sensuous form of anthropomorphic embodiment, but tells us little about the nature of his experience.[50] In asking what the centurion actually *saw*, we might first tackle the question from an ontological angle, examining the degree of "reality" afforded to his vision. First, did he encounter "actual" naked nymphs, or nymph-like maidens? As the ambiguous term *nympha* suggests, Graeco-Roman anthropomorphism could lend itself to considerable confusion and even manipulation in this regard.[51] While deities frequently appeared in the form or guise of humans (as in many scenes of Homeric epiphany), mortals could also be experienced as gods, whether in the context of ruler cult (in which kings and emperors were often hailed as divine, even taking the title *Epiphanēs*, "Manifest

---

47 On materialist models of vision, see Squire's introduction along with the chapters by Rudolph and Nightingale (this volume); cf. Webb (this volume) on the relationship between "sight and insight". On the ontological instability of divine bodies, see Vernant (1991) and Clements (2015).
48 *Iliad* 20.131, discussed above.
49 On the linguistic connection between the Greek *eidon* ("I saw") and *oida* ("I know"/"I have seen"), see Squire's introduction along with Coo (this volume).
50 See *Bulletin archéologique du comité des travaux historiques et scientifiques* (1929: 93–4, no. 2): a photograph of the inscription is sadly unavailable.
51 See above, n.8.

One"), at especially highly charged moments (such as a warrior's heroic endeavours on the battlefield), or in the context of ritual performance (such as the frequent assimilation of priests and priestesses to the deities they served).[52] In certain cases, this slippage between mortal and immortal is strategically exploited. Herodotus, for example, tells us of a staged epiphany of "Athena" by the Athenian tyrant Peisistratus, when he processed into the city accompanied by a statuesque maiden called Phye in order to legitimize his return to Athens as ruler in 556/5 BCE.[53] Although the historian is shocked that "clever" Athenians were so easily duped, the event's political success suggests that it took place within a ritual framework that encouraged and celebrated such ambiguity of status: Phye may have been a "mere" woman, but she was willingly experienced as a goddess by the community that beheld her. Sacred modes of vision in this sense raise particularly challenging questions about the relationship between physical sight and mental processes of cognition and interpretation.

Second, rather than forcing a distinction between deities and their mortal embodiments, we might examine our centurion's mental state. Could it be that the nymphs of Aquae Flavianae appeared to him in the context of a dream? In antiquity, dreaming is primarily described as the passive reception of a visitation in the form of a specific individual (often described in epiphanic terms).[54] Greek authors write of "seeing" rather than "having" a dream (*onar idein, enupnion idein*), while divinities often appear "standing over" the dreamer (*epistas*).[55] Significantly, the majority of *ex uisu* and *kata opsin* inscriptions come from religious sanctuaries where visitors practised incubation, a ritual in which they would sleep in the temple precinct overnight in the hope of meeting the deity in the dream-world in order to receive advice or healing.[56] Thermal baths associated with nymphs are prime sites for healing cults.[57]

---

52 On the epiphanic aspects of ruler cult and the title *Epiphanēs*, see Nock (1972: 720–35); Mittag (2006: 128–39); Platt (2011: 142–6, with further bibliography); Versnel (2011: 439–55). On the comparison of heroes to gods, see e.g. the dead Hector admired by the Trojans (*Iliad* 22.370) or Menelaus and Odysseus seen from the walls of Troy (*Iliad* 3.208). On priestly impersonation of or assimilation to the divine, see Back (1883); Lyons (1996: 134–70); Petridou (2006: 31–9; 2013: 328–30); Tanner (2006: 57–60); Connelly (2007: 104–15); Platt (2011: 13–17).
53 Herodotus, *Histories* 1.60. The bibliography on this complex episode is vast, but on the issue of epiphany and performance in particular, see Connor (1987: 42–7); Sinos (1993); Kavoulaki (1999); Harrison (2000: 90–2). On parallel cases of the staging of epiphany in the context of war, see Petridou (2006: 135–45) and Platt (forthcoming), on Polyaenus' *Strategems*.
54 On the epiphanic quality of ancient dream narrative, see Dodds (1951); Hanson (1980); Cox Miller (1994); Weber (2000); Walde (2001; 2004); W. V. Harris (2009: 23–90); Platt (2011: 253–92).
55 On Greek terminology for the perception of dreams, see Björck (1946); Kessels (1978: 156–7); Hanson (1980: 1407–8). On the parallel phenomenon of audio dreams (which tellingly employ the terminology of dream *vision*, e.g. Plutarch, *Agesilaus* 6.5, *Acts* 18.9), see Hanson (1980: 1411–12); cf. van Lieshout (1980: 20–4), who interestingly claims not to know of a single sonic dream experience unaccompanied by visual images. On the use of *epistas*, see Petridou (2006: 157–8, 292–3) and Platt (2011: 168).
56 On epigraphic evidence for dream visions during incubation, see Edelstein & Edelstein (1945); van Straten (1976); Renberg (2003; 2010). On the use of epiphany as a diagnostic and therapeutic tool in healing cult, see Oberhelman (1987) and Petridou (2014). For a visual example of such an encounter, see Figure I.7 in the Introduction, discussed by Petsalis-Diomidis (2006) and in Squire's introduction to this volume.
57 See Diez de Valasco (1998: 82–100).

Figure 8.3 Votive altar from the sanctuary of Asclepius at Pergamon, second century CE (*in situ*). The translated inscription reads "To Taras: G[aius] Julius Nabus, Senator, dedicated this altar according to a vision seen in a dream" (photograph supplied by the author).

In this context, it is striking to compare the Aquae Flavianae inscription with a contemporary votive altar from the sanctuary of the healing god Asclepius at Pergamon in Asia Minor (Figure 8.3). Dedicated by the Roman senator Gaius Julius Nabus to "Taras" (possibly a hero of the Sicilian city of Tarentum), it records a vow made "according to a dream vision" (*kata enupniou opsin*).[58] Like the inscription at Aquae Flavianae, it gives striking linguistic and visual prominence to the term for vision itself (*opsin*), celebrating the primacy of autopsy in the experience of divine

---

58 Habicht (1969: no. 132: *kata enupniou opsin*). Habicht suggests that the altar was dedicated in thanks for safe passage past the dangerous Sicilian straits on Nabus' way to or from Rome. On the role of epiphanic vision at the Pergamene Asclepieion, see Petsalis-Diomidis (2010); Platt (2011: 260–66); and Downie (2013), all focussing on the experiences of incubation recounted by the second-century CE orator Aelius Aristides in his *Sacred Tales*.

presence.[59] In this way, the altar also generates a visual experience in its own right, transforming the private, ephemeral experience of dream vision into a visible, material monument. It thus contributes to and affirms the sanctity of the Pergamene Asclepieion, inviting the viewer-reader to pursue his or her own visionary perception of the divine.

When the ancients beheld deities in their sleep, what did they actually see? When local nymphs pay a dreamtime visit to the shepherd Daphnis in Longus' second-century CE novel *Daphnis and Chloe*, they are described as "looking in every respect like their statues".[60] Given the close relationship between dreams and images in antiquity, it is not surprising to find that oneiric visitations from the gods often take the same form as their physical representations, not only borrowing the same iconography, but also appearing in the form of animated cult images.[61] The second-century CE dream interpreter Artemidorus claims that when it comes to drawing prophecies from dreams, "statues of the gods have the same meaning as the gods themselves".[62] This parallel between dream visions and statues is telling: images, like dreams, exist in an ambiguous zone of being, whereby they can be viewed as *representations*, or experienced as instantiations of divine *presence*. We thus find a mutually reinforcing relationship between visions and representations in antiquity, whereby gods appear to humans in the likeness of their images while images themselves are often said to be based on divine epiphanies.[63] In this way, the "cognitive reliability" of epiphany is validated by the god's appearance in recognizable form, while the authority of sacred images is authenticated by their adherence to the details of unmediated divine appearance.

We should not rule out a third possibility, then – that our centurion actually beheld *images* of local nymphs at Aquae Flavianae, perhaps in the form of statues, paintings or mosaics. After all, the iconography of nymphs was widespread across the ancient Mediterranean, including Roman North Africa, where the Hylas and Actaeon myths both seem to have been especially popular (Figure 8.4).[64] If so, the inscription's refusal to distinguish between the nymphs and their images is typical of

---

59 Habicht (1969: no. 132) notes that although the inscription's average letter height is 4.2cm, the stem of the *psi* in *opsin* is 12.6cm high.
60 Longus, 2.22–3: *tois agalmasin homoiai*. On epiphanic encounters in the Greek novel, see Hägg (2002) and Cioffi (2013).
61 In his *Sacred Tales*, for example, Aelius Aristides tells us that during incubation at Pergamon, Asclepius appeared to him "in the posture in which he is represented in his statues" (ἔχων ἤδη τὸ ἑαυτοῦ σχῆμα ἐν ᾧπερ ἕστηκεν, 50.50), and that he received surgical treatment from Serapis "in the form of his seated statues" (ὥσπερ κάθηται τῷ σχήματι, 49.47): see Petsalis-Diomidis (2005; 2008) and Platt (2011: 260–6).
62 Artemidorus, *Interpretation of Dreams* 2.39 (κοινὸν δὲ λόγον ἔχουσιν οἱ θεοὶ καὶ τὰ ἀγάλματα αὐτῶν). On the implications of this statement for models of sacred sight, see Platt (2011: 259, 275–92).
63 On this phenomenon, see Platt (2011).
64 Figure 8.4, from the House of Venus in Volubilis, Morocco, is one of five Imperial period North African mosaics depicting Diana and her nymphs bathing: see Rebuffat (1965); Dunbabin (1978: 277); and Schlam (1984: 102–4), who notes that Actaeon's head may have appeared in the damaged top right corner. On Hylas (whose abduction is also depicted in the House of Venus at Volubilis), see Ling (1979: 804–6), who also notes examples in the Algerian cities of Constantine (a second/third-century CE mosaic and ash-chest) and Cuicul (a fourth-century CE mosaic in the so-called "House of Hylas").

Figure 8.4 Mosaic depicting Diana bathing with her nymphs, from the House of Venus at Volubilis in Morocco (*in situ*), early third century CE (photograph supplied by the author).

a strong tendency in antiquity, whereby statues of the gods are referred to as embodiments of the deities they represent.[65] Just as Herodotus' Phye was experienced as "Athena", for example, so the great chryselephantine statue of Athena in the Athenian Parthenon was referred to as "the Parthenos", or "the goddess".[66] Indeed, the architectural and ritual framing of cult statues in Greek and Roman religion was often designed and carefully controlled so that viewing such sacred objects was understood to be akin to viewing the deity. The gleaming gold, flesh-like ivory and magnificent size of colossal statues like the Parthenos emulated the *kalos kai megethos* – the "beauty and magnitude" – of the gods' appearances in Homeric epiphanic narrative.[67] Meanwhile, the subtle naturalism of Classical Greek sculptures such as Praxiteles' infamous marble statue of Aphrodite at Knidos, in Asia Minor, celebrated the seductive power of anthropomorphism.[68] A series of ecphrastic epigrams

---

65 This phenomenon has been much commented upon since its identification by Richard Gordon (1979: 8–11): see e.g. Gladigow (1985–6); Versnel (1987: 46–7); Vernant (1991: 27–49); Donohue (1997: 44–5); Steiner (2001: 99–104); Elsner (2007b: 30–2, 43–5); Squire (2009: 111–16); Platt (2011: 77–123); for a cross-cultural approach, cf. Freedberg (1989: 27–40).
66 E.g. Aristophanes, *Birds* 667–70, *Knights* 1168–70; cf. e.g. Thucydides 2.13.5.
67 E.g. *Homeric Hymn* 2.275–9 and 5.171–5: see Lapatin (2001: 5–6); Steiner (2001: 95–7); Platt (2011: 63–8, 105–14).
68 On the Knidian Aphrodite, see (from a vast bibliography) C. M. Havelock (1995), Ridgway (2004: 713–25) and Squire (2011b: 69–114).

SIGHT AND THE GODS

from the *Greek Anthology* repeatedly plays with the Knidia's ability to blur the categories of image and prototype for her viewers to the extent that the goddess herself wonders, "Where did Praxiteles see me naked (*gumnēn*)?"[69]

The degree of correspondence between – and willing confusion of – statue and deity in antiquity was by no means straightforward, however. While ritual visualities may have encouraged epiphanic modes of viewing such objects, other cultural discourses explicitly problematized them (whether through philosophical critiques of representation or by reference to learned practices of connoisseurship). Moreover, within the context of religious practice, anthropomorphic means of envisioning and representing the gods existed alongside a host of other strategies in a "spectrum of iconicity" that stretched from the naturalistic corporeality of the Knidia to symbolic and even purely aniconic forms.[70] While votive reliefs to the nymphs from Classical Attica often depict them as decorous young women, for example (Figure 8.5), a stele from Arcadia inscribed with the genitive plural *Numphān* ("Of the nymphs") presents us with a rectangular block topped with three triangles (Figure 8.6).[71] The tripartite division of the stele conveys a sense of the nymphs' number and presence, associating them closely with the landscape they were held to inhabit, but leaves the details of their form to the imagination of the viewer.[72] The relief, however, presents us with a figural scene in which the nymphs are encountered as supra-life-size, sensuously draped female bodies. While the model of vision it presents is fleshed out in greater detail, it is focalized – and therefore more explicitly mediated – through the vision of a mortal worshipper, named as "Archandros" in the inscription. The artefacts thus invite very different forms of engagement from their beholders, occupying divergent positions on the spectrum between mediation and immediacy, on the one hand, and figuration and abstraction on the other. Despite their differences, however, it is striking to observe that neither object presents us with *naked* nymphs: whether through the veiling strategies of elaborate drapery or the total rejection of figuration, each preserves a sense of the limits enforced by pious strategies of presentation. As the myth of Actaeon reminds us, it should be the preserve of the gods themselves to choose the timing and conditions of their self-revelation.

---

[69] *Planudean Anthology* 160.4 (Ποῦ γυμνὴν εἶδέ με Πραξιτέλης;): on the ecphrastic tradition associated with the Knidia (and its uneasy exploration of the statue's epiphanic status), see Platt (2011: 180–211) and Haynes (2013). On these tendencies in Hellenistic epigram more broadly, see Prioux (2007) and Squire (2010b), with further discussion of ecphrastic literature in Squire's introduction and Webb's chapter (this volume).

[70] On the notion of a "spectrum of iconicity" for the representation or denotation of the divine, see Gaifman (2012: esp. 13), who explores the function and appearance of aniconic objects in Greek religion. On semi-iconic forms such as Archaicizing cult statues and herms, see Frontisi-Ducroux (1986b); Donohue (1988); Rückert (1998); Platt (2011: 34–7, 92–100).

[71] Figure 8.5 is a votive relief from the Asclepieion in Athens, dated 425–400 BCE and inscribed *Archandros Nunphais* ("Archandros to the nymphs"), now in the Athens Archaeological Museum (NM 1392): see Kaltsas (2002: 135, no. 260) and, for a full discussion, Gaifman (2008: 90–4), who explores votive reliefs to the nymphs more generally. Figure 8.6 is a stele with three pyramidal tops from Alea in Arcadia, inscribed *Nymphān* ("Of the nymphs"), in Arcadian dialect: Tegea, Archaeological Museum, *IG* 5.2.65; see Rhomaios (1911: 154, no. Ark.14) and Gaifman (2012: 218–22), with Larson (2001: 97–8, 152–7), on nymphs in Arcadia more generally.

[72] As discussed by Gaifman, who notes that like the Graces, the nymphs are most often represented in groups of three (2012: 220).

Figure 8.5 Votive relief dedicated by "Archandros to the nymphs [and Pan]": from the sanctuary of Asclepius at Athens, *ca.* 425–400 BCE. Athens, National Archaeological Museum: inv.1392 (© DAI Athen, DAI-Neg. D-DAI-ATH-NM-6233 (Gösta Hellner)).

Figure 8.6 Votive stele of the nymphs from Arcadia, inscribed *Nymphān* ("Of the Nymphs"), *ca.* 300 BCE. Tegea, Archaeological Museum, Tegea (no inventory) (© DAI Athen, DAI-Neg. D-DAI-ATH-Arkadien-6).

Fluid visions

Nymphs, then, are the most sensually embodied and yet the most slippery and elusive of beings. As fluid as the waters they inhabit, they are highly visualizable, yet visible only to a privileged few – both dangerous and delectable to encounter. As we have seen, sacred sights both drew upon and inspired the richly imagined anthropomorphism of epic poetry and the naturalistically rendered deities of the visual arts. At the same time, such visionary plenitude existed in tension with a sense of the limitations of mortal perception and the incomprehensibility of divine revelation. Strikingly, the centurion's laconic "I saw" at Aquae Flavianae and the aniconic stele of the nymphs from Arcadia both refrain from a full description or presentation of nymphly form: each artefact intimates a sense of the inadequacy of language and representation in the face of the divine, whilst conveying a powerful sense of divine presence that stimulates the beholder's own sensory and imaginative faculties. Such invitations to envision the nymphs are also, of course, an invitation to the *tactile* imagination, prompting a series of fantasies that elude the grasp of the senses by virtue of their very lack of corporeality. The ontological instability and physical ambiguity of divine body is thus revealed by – and even constituted in – its resistance to the mortal sensing body. At the same time, for the mortal body to recognize the limits of its sensory capacities is also, by extension, to attain a valuable form of knowledge, or insight.[73]

In literature of the Greek Imperial period, the fraught relationship between sight and insight, the sensible and the ideal, is expressed through the language of *phantasia*. As a term that has a specific meaning in the philosophy of sense-perception (referring to mental "presentations" or "impressions" derived from sensible phenomena), *phantasia* eventually acquires a meaning closer to our concept of "imagination" or "fantasy".[74] As such, it mediates between the external world of appearances and the inner life of the mind, giving expression to the interstitial space between vision and the visionary that is inhabited by sacred modes of seeing. As the centurion's inscription reminds us (*optaui*), this fluid relationship between externally perceived bodies and inner sensation is also a key domain for the operation of desire. "All men", claimed the Greek orator Dio Chrysostom, "have a strong desire (*erōs*) to honour and worship the deity from close at hand".[75] This tension between a yearning to perceive the divine and the gods' resistance to perceptibility, between the sensory allure of divine bodies and the risk to the mortal bodies that sense them, between the act of seeing and the inevitable deferral of the experience of sight, typifies a fundamental asymmetry in mortal–immortal relations. The desire to see the gods is, fundamentally, a desire that knows its own limits. Understood as the most corporeally ambiguous yet conceptually acute of the sensory faculties, sight therefore offered the ideal medium by which desire for proximity to the divine could convey both the frustration and the possibility of its own fulfilment.

---

73 In this sense, my conclusions here about "sight and the gods" richly intersect with those of Turner (this volume) on "sight and death".

74 See Webb (this volume). On the complex history and shifting meaning of *phantasia*, see Watson (1988; 1994); Fattori & Bianchi (1988); Labarrière (2004); Serra (2007); Webb (2009a: 107–30); Squire (2013a: 101–4). On the use of *phantasia* in Stoic theory of sense-perception, see Sandbach (1971); Imbert (1980); Ioppolo (1990); Barnouw (2002). On the role of *phantasia* in epiphanic modes of vision, see Platt (2011, esp. 293–329).

75 Dio, *Oration* 12.61 (ἔρως πᾶσιν ἀνθρώποις ἐγγύθεν τιμᾶν καὶ θεραπεύειν τὸ θεῖον); cf. Squire (2011b: 167–8).

9

SIGHT AND MEMORY
The visual art of Roman mnemonics

Jaś Elsner & Michael Squire

In the ninth book of his *Description of Greece* (written in the second century CE), the Greek travel-writer Pausanias makes an extraordinary art-historical connection. The passage comes amid a commentary on a statue encountered in the Temple of Ismenian Apollo at Thebes. But what catches the author's eye is the Theban statue's visual relationship to another image, one seen elsewhere on Pausanias' travels – displayed at the Branchidian sanctuary at Didyma in Asia Minor (9.10.2):[1]

> τὸ δὲ ἄγαλμα μεγέθει τε ἴσον τῷ ἐν Βραγχίδαις ἐστὶ καὶ τὸ εἶδος οὐδὲν διαφόρως ἔχον· ὅστις δὲ τῶν ἀγαλμάτων τούτων τὸ ἕτερον εἶδε καὶ τὸν εἰργασμένον ἐπύθετο, οὐ μεγάλη οἱ σοφία καὶ τὸ ἕτερον θεασαμένῳ Κανάχου ποίημα ὂν ἐπίστασθαι. διαφέρουσι δὲ τοσόνδε· ὁ μὲν γὰρ ἐν Βραγχίδαις χαλκοῦ, ὁ δὲ Ἰσμήνιός ἐστι κέδρου.

> The statue is equal in size to that at Branchidae (Didyma) and does not differ from it at all in shape. Whoever has seen one of these two statues and learnt who the artist was does not need much wisdom to work out, when he looks at the other one, that it is the work of Canachus. The only difference is that the image at Branchidae is made of bronze, while the Ismenian one is made of cedar-wood.

It is a remarkable observation on a number of levels. For one thing, it shows Pausanias' expert visual skills in action: in responding to the statue's formal qualities (*to eidos*), Pausanias makes a judgement based on the object's size, shape and material. No less importantly, the wandering Greek traveller might be said to prefigure the more modern connoisseurs of post-Enlightenment art history. Just as, in the twentieth century, Sir John Beazley famously trotted the globe's museums to pair fragments of Attic vase-painting with their respective attributed "artists", so too, in the second century, Pausanias here forges an artistic connection between statues displayed across the Greek-speaking world: both are the work of Canachus.[2]

---

1 For the passage, see Kansteiner *et al.* (2014: 1.391–2, no. 476): the Didyma statue is also mentioned by the Elder Pliny, *Natural History* 34.75 – where it is likewise attributed to "Canachus of Sicyon".
2 On Pausanias and connoisseurship, see Elsner (2007b: 51–8); on Beazley's own connoisseurial method, see e.g. Elsner (1990); Neer (1997). For ancient ideas about "artists" more generally, cf. e.g. R. Osborne (2010) and Squire (2013c; 2015b), with further bibliography.

Within a chapter on "sight and memory", Pausanias' observation has a still more pressing significance. Of course, we have no way of knowing whether Pausanias' attribution of the sculpture to "Canachus" was correct (both the statues at Thebes and Didyma are long-since lost). Yet what interests us about this passage is the very gesture of relating one visual stimulus back to another. In an age before the paraphernalia of modern art-historical attribution (prints, illustrations, photographs, etc.), Pausanias had to rely solely on the subjective recall of what he saw. Despite the distances in both time and space between Pausanias' viewing of the statue in Didyma and his visit to Thebes, the author is able to observe the similarity in both size and form between the two objects; although the medium has changed from bronze to cedar-wood, moreover, the person who has "seen" (*eide*) one of the two statues is said, upon visual inspection of the other (*theasamenoi*), to understand (*epistasthai*) the connection. For Pausanias, "visual memory" was a reality on which a significant argument about attribution – and hence value (or as Pausanias puts it, the cultural value of "wisdom", *sophia*) – could respectably be based.

Our aim in this chapter is to explore the workings of such "visual memory" in ancient thought and practice, focussing primarily on the Roman Imperial world. The connoisseurial connections that Pausanias draws at Thebes may be exceptional, at least in the field of Greek and Roman visual criticism. As we hope to demonstrate, however, other authors laid out the visual underpinnings that could structure the mechanics of memory: within a Roman cultural imaginary (and not least, within the educational structures of a Roman rhetorical education), the very act of remembering was deemed inseparable from that of seeing. To explain what we mean here, this chapter proceeds in two interconnected stages. First, we examine Roman rhetorical theories of memory, showcasing their close-knit interassociations between the acts of seeing and remembering. In the second part, we then explore what such rhetorical training, with all its intertwined theorizing of sight and memory, might mean for the workings of Roman art more generally, above all in the medium of Roman wall-painting. Throughout, our aim is to showcase just one aspect of "sight and the ancient senses", albeit one (or so we suggest) with broader repercussions for approaching Roman texts and images alike.

Theorizing visual memory in Roman rhetoric

"Memory" has become a major field in both the sciences and humanities over the last few decades. Scholars have learned to discuss the topos of "remembering" from a variety of perspectives: they have examined questions of "collective memory" in a given culture;[3] they have explored "social memory" as a fundamental engine of collective identity and a vehicle of social cohesion;[4] likewise, they have explained how "cultural memory" might serve to generate a sense of shared values,[5] defining ideas

---

3 See especially Halbwachs (1950), translated as Halbwachs (1992).
4 Key discussions of "social memory" include Halbwachs (1936; 1941); Nora (1984–92), reprinted as Nora (2001); Connerton (1989); Fentress & Wickham (1992). Within the disciplinary frame of classics, see especially Alcock (2002) and van Dyke & Alcock (2003).
5 On "cultural memory", the works of the Assmanns are fundamental: A. Assmann (2006; 2011); J. Assmann (2011); cf. also Erll (2011) and Erll & Nünning (2010). Within classics, see Galinsky (2014),

about the historical past and its relationship to the present.[6] No less rich have been studies of targeted "forgetting" – of attempts to erase memories for particular political, social or cultural ends.[7] In each case, the very definitions of "memory" (and the processes with which memory is associated) are far from simple: if memory can be used to enhance what may be the fictitious cohesiveness of collective communities and groups, it can also determine the specific differences between social sub-groups (whether religious sects or ethnic communities). Memory, in other words, plays an important – and often very subtle – role in engineering social control and political resistance.

But what about *sight* and memory? Needless to say, some scholars have examined how topography, material culture and monuments prove central to the constructions of memory.[8] In classicist circles too, there have been numerous recent studies of how memory might shape the material environment of an ancient urban landscape (especially when it comes to Rome).[9] Despite these interests, considerably less attention has been paid to the significance of sight within the processes of remembering, as indeed to the ways in which memory can shape cultural ideologies about how "seeing" works. That emphasis on "cultural" determination is hugely important. While "sight and memory" is of course a transcultural theme, the connections between seeing and remembering are dependent on particular cultural perspectives – on what has been labelled "visuality" as much as on "vision".[10]

When it comes to Greek and Roman cultures specifically, we have a rich array of texts that draw out the visual parameters of memory, testifying to particular cultural assumptions about the interconnected thematics of seeing and remembering. Already by the late fifth century BCE, we find Greek writers conceptualizing visual schemata as a means of remembering proper names. The anonymous author of the *Dialexis* (also called *Dissoi Logoi*) emphasizes the point, advising that, in order to bring to mind words and ideas, speakers should associate them with imagined visual forms. So it is, for example, that the name "Chrysippus" could be remembered by imagining "gold" (*chrusos*) on a "horse" (*hippos*), just as more abstract ideas could be summoned up in association with visualized mythological or divine figures ("courage" in relation to Achilles or Ares, "metal-working" through that of Hephaestus, and "cowardice" by imagining Epeius).[11] The *Dialexis* discussion has important ramifications for understanding the symbolic and allegorical workings of Classical Greek art, whereby images could be infused with an emblematic potential

---

with detailed bibliographic survey in the editor's introduction; Galinsky (forthcoming); Galinsky & Lapatin (forthcoming).
6 See e.g. Le Goff (1992); Cubitt (2007).
7 See e.g. Geary (1994); Forty & Küchler (1999); Ricoeur (2004). On the cultural dynamics of "forgetting" in the Roman world, cf. e.g. Hedrick (2000); Flower (2006).
8 See e.g. Nelson & Olin (2003); Benoist *et al.* (2009). Specifically on Roman *damnatio memoriae*, cf. Varner (2004), along with the essays in Benoist & Daguet-Gagey (2007; 2008), with further bibliographies.
9 E.g. Rea (2007); Scarth (2008: 7–42); Behrwald (2009); Lamp (2011); Spencer (2011: esp. 66–78); Gallia (2012). Compare, too, Betts (2011), introducing an important "multi-sensory" dimension.
10 For the distinction – explored by the essays in H. Foster (1988b) – see the introduction to this volume.
11 For the passage, see Diels (1922: 2.345); cf. Yates (1966: 29–30); Carruthers (1990: 28); Small (1997: 113); Sorabji (2004: 30–1); Baroin (2007: 137–8; 2010: 204–5).

to prompt verbal words and concepts.[12] But it also drives home how, even by the end of the fifth century BCE, visual stimuli could be employed as useful mnemonic device.

Aristotle's fourth-century treatise *On Memory and Reminding Oneself* at once takes up and probes such thinking. According to Aristotle, the most effective way of remembering something was to devise a spatial system of "ordering" it (Aristotle's word is *taxis*, a term later translated into Latin as *ordo*).[13] What matters in this process is the successful harnessing of visual stimuli: "it is impossible to think without an image", as Aristotle strikingly puts it in the first chapter, "for the same phenomenon occurs in thinking as is found in the construction of geometrical figures" (καὶ νοεῖν οὐκ ἔστιν ἄνευ φαντάσματος· συμβαίνει γὰρ τὸ αὐτὸ πάθος ἐν τῷ νοεῖν ὅπερ καὶ ἐν τῷ διαγράφειν, 449b34–450a2).[14] For Aristotle, sight is explicitly introduced as the "most highly developed sense" (ἡ ὄψις μάλιστα αἴσθησίς ἐστι, *On the Soul* 3.3, 429a).[15] But his discussion of sight and memory simultaneously draws upon further-reaching Aristotelian ideas about the "mind's eye", and not least theories of *phantasia* or "cognitive impression": "it is possible for something to be brought before the eyes, as in the practice of mnemonics and by the formation of mental images", as Aristotle elsewhere puts it (πρὸ ὀμμάτων γὰρ ἔστι τι ποιήσασθαι, ὥσπερ οἱ ἐν τοῖς μνημονικοῖς τιθέμενοι καὶ εἰδωλοποιοῦντες, *On the Soul* 3.3, 427b). Memory, in other words, is understood as just one example of a deep-seated connection between seeing and knowing.

Classical Greek texts like these form the basis of later Roman rhetorical discussions. In line with the advice of the Greek *Dialexis*, Quintilian – writing at the end of the first century CE – likewise advises that images can be harnessed to remember particular names (*Training of the Orator* 11.2.30–1). Hidden within certain words, Quintilian argues, lie etymologies that can help visually bring the subject to mind. Just as one might summon up images so as to remember names like Cicero, Verrius or Aurelius (punning on the Latin words *cicer*/"chickpea", *uerres*/"boar" and *auris*/"ear"), so too are other onomastic words suffused with a visual impression: the names Aper, Ursus, Naso and Crispus, Quintilian writes, might be visually encoded, referring as they do to "Mr Boar", "Mr Bear", "Mr Nose" and "Mr Curly".

That visual artists could tap into similar ideas – and in the express attempt to preserve someone's memory – is clear from contemporary Roman funerary monuments. Consider, for example, a cinerary grave altar dedicated to a certain Titus Statilius

---

12 Nowhere more so, we might add, than when it comes to the depicted *episēmata* of shield devices, especially in Archaic and Classical Greek vase-painting: cf. Chase (1902); Vaerst (1980); Lissarrague (2009a).
13 For discussion, see e.g. Ross (1906: 269–70), discussing Aristotle, *On Memory* 452a14; cf. Sorabji (2004: 22–31, 104–5). Small (1997: 94) may be right to conclude that Aristotle consequently "provides the first full description of the system of places invented by Simonides".
14 For a review of Aristotle's meaning here, see Sorabji (2004: xi–xxi, 2–8); on Aristotle's influence on the formation of subsequent ancient memory systems, see Baroin (2005: esp. 203–5), along with the wide-ranging analysis of Bloch (2007).
15 On Aristotelian ideas of sight, see Nightingale (this volume); compare also Webb (this volume), on "sight and insight" in relation to Aristotelian ideas of *phantasia*.

Figure 9.1 Early Hadrianic marble funerary altar of T. Statilius Aper, *ca.* 120 CE. Rome, Musei Capitolini (Palazzo Nuovo): inv. MC0209 (photograph by M. J. Squire).

Aper and his wife Orcivia, erected at Rome in around 120 CE (Figure 9.1).[16] The altar's upper relief dresses the deceased in a Roman toga and places a scroll in his left hand. Beside him are the tools of Aper's architectural trade (as explained in a prose inscription at the altar's base), and to the left is an image of a young servant. But beside Aper's right foot is an animal that appears, at least in this setting, wholly incongruous: between the togate figure and the slave, a boar (*aper* in Latin) has been incorporated within the visual field. Playing on Aper's name – and in precisely the way that Quintilian had expounded – the emblem gives figurative form to an onomastic pun. In case viewers had overlooked the wordplay, an elaborate verse epitaph draws out the conceit, addressing "innocent Aper-Boar" (*innocuus Aper*), and contrasting Aper's own "silent death" (*mors tacita*) with the demise of Meleager (the mythological hero famously killed by a boar).[17] The visual emblematization of "Mr Boar" helps to preserve the deceased's memory from beyond the grave: it engraves his name in the mind of all who encounter the monument. No less importantly, the semantic interplay between image and text serves to overcome the perennial "silence" of the dead. With each commemorative inspection, Aper's legacy is made to live on in both word and image alike.[18]

Roman discussions about images visualizing names (and vice versa) take their place within broader rhetorical analyses about how to remember a verbal text.[19] As we have said, Greek orators and philosophers had long drawn an association between seeing and remembering. But it was in the Roman world – and above all, in the context of Roman rhetoric – that such ideas were explicitly introduced as pedagogical practice.[20] "Memory", writes Cicero, takes its part beside "invention", "disposition", "elocution" and "pronunciation" as one of the five pillars of rhetoric (*On Invention* 1.9). If the art of "artificial of memory" (*artificiosa memoria*) could be considered the monumental "treasury" of ideas supplied by invention (*thesaurus inuentorum*), in the words of an anonymous first-century BCE rhetorical treatise addressed "to Herennius", it was also "the guardian of all parts of rhetoric" (*omnium partium rhetoricae custodem*: *To Herennius* 3.28).

Since education in rhetoric was central to the self-respect and self-promotion of the elite, the role of memory – and vision within memory – served both a pragmatic

---

16 Rome, Musei Capitoloni (Palazzo Nuovo), inv. MC0209. On the monument, see Kleiner (1987: 213–16); Koortbojian (1996: 229–31); Elsner (2006b: 303–5); Squire (2009: 171–5). For other punning plays on the "boarishness" implied by the name "Aper" – in the context of the character in Tacitus' *Dialogue on Oratory*, for example, as well as in the *Letters* of the Younger Pliny and Martial's epigrams – see R. Edwards (2008).
17 For the inscription (= *Corpus Inscriptionum Latinarum* 6.1975/ *Carmina Latina Epigraphica* 441), see Courtney (1995: 374, no. 176); more generally on the importance of the Meleager myth in Roman funerary monuments, see Zanker & Ewald (2004: 346–55).
18 For related visual onomastic puns in Greek and Roman funerary monuments, see Ritti (1973–4; 1977); more generally on the intertwined thematics of "sight and death", see Turner (this volume).
19 There is a large bibliography on this theme. The classic discussion is that of Yates (1966: esp. 1–26), but see also Blum (1969); Rouveret (1982; 1989: 303–79); Carruthers (1990: 71–5; 1998); Coleman (1992: 39–59); Elsner (1995: 76–80); Small (1997: 81–137; 2007); Baroin (2007; 2010: 202–30); Scarth (2008: 43–63); Squire (2014: 401–17).
20 On rhetoric and education, see Marrou (1956: 194–216, 274–91 – on the Hellenistic world and Rome respectively); cf. T. Morgan (1998: 190–239, discussing memory on 250–1); Baroin (2010: 73–88); Webb (this volume).

and an ideological function. For Roman teachers and pupils of rhetoric, mnemonic techniques seem to have relied on familiar sequences of visual and spatial imagery, exploiting them as a mnemonic prompt to remember sequences of words and ideas: the visualized flow of movement from image to image is effectively exploited as a means to structure the paragraphs of a speech. Three Latin authors – all of them introduced in the preceding paragraph, and all writing between the first century BCE and late first century CE – are particularly important here. The first and earliest in-depth account of rhetorical memory is to be found in the *To Herennius* (3.28–40), attributed from late antiquity (until quite recently) to Cicero. Second comes Cicero himself: Cicero's *On the Orator* (composed *ca.* 55 BCE) contains a significant section on the centrality of memory within rhetorical education (2.350–60). The third and final author is Quintilian, writing at the end of the first century CE, and knowingly looking back to earlier texts: for Quintilian, memory-training is integral to the education of the ideal orator, and consequently occupies a large section in the penultimate book of his pedagogical treatise on the *Training of the Orator* (11.2.1–51).

There can be no doubting that these three Latin authors understood their methods of visual memory in relation to much earlier Greek paradigms. Revealingly, they also trace the origins back to the deep past of late Archaic Greece. For both Cicero and Quintilian, the figure of Simonides could provide an aetiology for their own practised method (Cicero, *On the Orator* 2.353–4; Quintilian, *Training of the Orator* 11.2.11–17). Simonides, the story goes, was once feasting at a private house when he was suddenly summoned outside. At that moment, the building collapsed, killing and disfiguring all those present – so much so, that the relatives of the dead were unable to recognize their bloody bodies. Through his ability to remember the layout of the room and the placement of the individual banqueters, Simonides could identify the corpses and return each cadaver to its respective family for burial. Here is Cicero's commentary on the episode (*On the Orator* 2.353–4):

> *Simonides dicitur ex eo, quod meminisset quo eorum loco quisque cubuisset, demonstrator unius cuiusque sepeliendi fuisse; hac tum re admonitus inuenisse fertur ordinem esse maxime qui memoriae lumen adferret. itaque eis qui hanc partem ingeni exercerent, locos esse capiendos et ea quae memoria tenere uellent effingenda animo atque in eis locis conlocanda; sic fore ut ordinem rerum locorum ordo conseruaret, res autem ipsas rerum effigies notaret atque ut locis pro cera, simulacris pro litteris uteremur.*

By his recollection of the place in which each of them had been reclining Simonides is said to have been able to identify each one individually for burial. This is the circumstance that prompted his discovery that order (*ordinem*) is the best way of achieving clarity of memory. The inference followed that those who wish to develop this aspect of their intellect must first select places/backgrounds (*locos*), second form mental images (*effingenda animo*) of the things which they wish to remember, and third store these images in the aforementioned places. The result is that the arrangement (*ordo*) of the backgrounds would preserve the order of things to be remembered, and the images (*effigies*) of the things would designate the things themselves. We should therefore, he realized, employ the places (*locis*) as we would a wax tablet, and the images as we would its letters.

Cicero's closing comparison between Simonides' mnemonic system and a "wax tablet" is revealing. For Cicero, seeing, remembering, reading and speaking go hand-in-hand; not for nothing, indeed, does he describe the orator as a figurative "painter".[21] The point sheds light on the conceptual connection with the figure of Simonides. In antiquity, Simonides was famous (among numerous other aphorisms) for his analogy between painting as "silent poetry" and poetry as "talking painting".[22] When it comes to the mnemonic method attributed to him, then, the figurative "visuality" of speech is (quite literally) literalized: the very act of speaking makes an imagined sequence of images "talk". This also explains the recurrent comparison between the visual props of memory and the implements used for writing a readable text: "the backgrounds are very similar to a wax tablet or papyrus, the images to the letters", declares the author of *To Herennius*, adding that "the rhetorical arrangement and structuring of images is very similar to the script, and the delivery to the act of reading" (*dispositio et conlocatio imaginum scripturae, pronuntiatio lectioni* [*sc. simillimae sunt*]: 3.30).[23]

For our purposes in this chapter, what is most important about this Simonidean story is its structural mode of organizing and recalling imagined visual stimuli. The visual faculty is harnessed for mnemonic ends in three particular ways. First, the orator must determine pre-established visual "sites" or "backgrounds" (*loci*), using these as spatial anchors. Second, he must create "images" of what needs to be remembered (labelled *effingenda* and *effigies* in the above passage, but most often referred to as *imagines*): once devised, these "images" were then to be placed against the spatial background *loci*. Third and finally, in order to be in command of how *loci* relate to the images contained within them, the rhetorician must have a visual sense of their "arrangement" or "disposition" (*ordo*). Throughout this process, rhetorical theory marshals vision in relation to both an object and its context, while also suggesting an acute sensitivity to the ways in which a viewing subject could take in a series of objects as it moves through space. In its appeal to the imagination, sight can not only facilitate memory but also, through the judicious use of that memory, enable the articulation of a polished rhetorical performance.

Despite the differences between their respective accounts, Quintilian, Cicero and the author of the treatise *To Herennius* offer a remarkably consistent analysis of how visual memory might operate. Fundamental to all three discussions, moreover, is an assumption about sight's capital currency within the broader sensory economy.

---

21 For one example, see Cicero, *On the Orator* 2.358, discussing "the representation of a whole concept by the image of a single word, according to the rationale and method of some virtuoso painter who distinguishes positions of objects by varying their shapes" (*unius uerbi imagine totius sententiae informatio pictoris cuiusdam summi ratione et modo formarum uarietate locos distinguentis*).

22 For the Simonidean analogy (Simonides, frg. 190b Bergk = Plutarch, *Moralia* 346f), see Squire's introduction to this volume (p. 12, with n. 39, and p. 1, n. 1): according to Plutarch, the aphorism was "frequently repeated" by the second century CE (*Moralia* 17e). On the connection between this Simonidean aphorism and the mnemonic system attributed to the sage, see Yates (1966: 28).

23 Cf. Cicero, *On the Orator* 2.354, itself quoted by Quintilian, *Training of the Orator* 11.2.21: Carruthers (1990: 16–32) provides the best discussion.

Cicero frames his discussion by explicitly reminding his readers that the sense of seeing is the sharpest of all our senses (*acerrimum autem ex omnibus sensibus esse sensum uidendi*: *On the Orator* 2.357), just as Quintilian recalls that "the sense of the eyes is sharper than that of the ears" (*acrior est oculorum quam aurium sensus*: *Training of the Orator* 11.2.34; cf. ibid. 11.2.10). The very recourse to seeing as mnemonic tool, in other words, is founded upon a deeply ocularcentric cultural understanding of the senses at large.[24] While all of our three authors provide a slightly different spin, each rhetorician likewise falls back on the same essential method of laying mnemonic emblems (*imagines*) against a prefabricated series of backgrounds (*loci*): ideas can be grasped by means of the emblems, as Cicero concisely puts it, and their "order" (*ordo*) by way of their backgrounds (*ut sententias imaginibus, ordinem locis comprehendamus*: *On the Orator* 2.359).

What, though, should the orator's imagined mnemonic *imagines* and *loci* look like? For the author of the *To Herennius*, *loci* are said to be exemplified by "a house, an intercolumnar space, a recess, an arch, etc." (*aedes, intercolumnium, angulum, fornicem et alia quae his similia sunt*, 3.29). Quintilian offers a slightly expanded list. After discussing the example of a large house divided into separate rooms, he explains that "what I have said about a house can be done also with public buildings, a long road, a town perambulation, or pictures" (*quod de domo dixi, et in operibus publicis et in itinere longo et urbium ambitu et picturis fieri potest*: *Training of the Orator* 11.2.21). As for the images laid out against these backgrounds, considerably less attention is paid to the *imagines* than to their spatially determined contexts. What is important, however, is the perceived capacity of the *imago* to spur the orator's visual recall (*To Herennius* 3.29):

> *imagines sunt formae quaedam et notae et simulacra eius rei quam meminisse uolumus: quod genus equi, leonis, aquilae memoriam si uolemus habere, imagines eorum locis certis conlocare oportebit.*

> An image is a sort of figure, mark or portrait of the object we wish to remember; for example, if we wish to recall a horse, a lion, or an eagle, we must place its image in a definite background.

For the author of the treatise *To Herennius*, the *imago* is here imagined to have a direct mimetic relationship to the thing remembered. But, as Quintilian suggests, *imagines* could also operate more symbolically – to function as signs or *signa* which, laid out in space, jog the memory (*Training of the Orator* 11.2.18–20):[25]

> *loca discunt quam maxime spatiosa, multa uarietate signata, domum forte magnam et in multos diductam recessus. in ea quidquid notabile est animo diligenter adfigunt, ut sine cunctatione ac mora partis eius omnis cogitatio possit percurrere. et primus hic labor est, non haerere in occursu: plus enim quam firma debet esse memoria quae aliam memoriam adiuuet. tum quae*

---

24 On Greek and Roman "ocularcentrism", see Squire's introduction to this volume.
25 Our translation here adapts that of Russell (2001: 5.67).

SIGHT AND MEMORY

scripserunt uel cogitatione complectuntur [et] aliquo signo quo moneantur notant, quod esse uel ex re tota potest, ut de nauigatione, militia, uel ex uerbo aliquo: nam etiam excidentes unius admonitione uerbi in memoriam reponuntur. sit autem signum nauigationis ut ancora, militiae ut aliquid ex armis. haec ita digerunt: primum sensum uestibulo quasi adsignant, secundum puta atrio, tum inpluuia circumeunt, nec cubiculis modo aut exhedris, sed statuis etiam similibusque per ordinem committunt...

[Students] learn sites (*loca*) which are as extensive as possible and are marked (*signata*) by a variety of objects – perhaps a large house divided into many separate areas. They carefully fix in their mind everything there which is notable, so that their thoughts can run over all the parts of it without any hold-up or delay. The first task is to make sure that it all comes to mind without any hold-up, because a memory which is to help another memory has to be something more than secure. The next stage is to mark what they have written or are mentally preparing with some sign (*signo*) which will jog their memory. This may be based on the subject as a whole (on navigation or warfare, for example) or on a word, because even people who lose the thread of what they are saying can have their memory put on track by the cue of a single word. Let us suppose a sign (*signum*) of navigation – such as an anchor, or of warfare, such as a weapon. They place the first idea, as it were, in the vestibule, the second, in the atrium (let us say), and then they go round the open areas, assigning (*committunt*) ideas in order not only to bedrooms and bays but to statues and the like...

Irrespective of the images chosen, and regardless of whether or not those images refer to words (*uerba*) or things (*res*),[26] the ingenuity of this system is said to lie in its implicit flexibility.[27] Walking around his mental stage-set, decoding each and every visual cue that he figuratively encounters, the orator has at once a fixed visual order for remembering something and a series of spatially arranged images that facilitate *ex tempore* innovation. That fundamental association between memory and rhetorical creativity is hugely important. As Mary Carruthers has argued,[28] Roman rhetoricians, like their mediaeval monastic successors,

---

26 Cf. Yates (1966: 8), paraphrasing the treatise *To Herennius*: "'memory of things' makes images to remind of an argument, a notion, or a 'thing'; but 'memory for words' has to find images to remind of a single word". More detailed is Blum (1969: 12–32).

27 Cf. Elsner (1995: 79) on "Roman speech" as "a rhetorisation of a prior and visually re-lived view": "unlike ekphrasis which necessarily freezes the speaker's *phantasia* in a particular order or structure, the range of possibilities for the ordering of paragraphs in a speech allows a much greater flexibility and freedom to the orator's use of his memorised vision, his *phantasia*".

28 Carruthers (1998: 4, her emphasis). Cf. Carruthers (1998: 8): "Thus the orator's 'art of memory' was not an art of recitation and reiteration but an art of invention, an art that made it possible for a person to act competently within the 'arena' of debate..., to respond to interruptions and questions, or to dilate upon the ideas that momentarily occurred to him, without becoming hopelessly distracted, or losing his place in the scheme of his basic speech." Compare also Dupont (2000: 27) on *memoria* "qui consiste non seulement à se souvenir de ce qu'on a préparé pour ce discours précis mais qui est

conceive of memory not only as "rote", the ability to reproduce something (whether a text, a formula, a list of items, an incident), but as the matrix of a reminiscing cogitation, shuffling and collating "things" stored in a random-access memory scheme, or set of schemes – a memory *architecture* and a library ... with the express intention that it be used inventively.

Despite their imagined visual objectivity, the memory of visual *imagines* and *loci* serve as sites of subjective invention: they are to be used creatively, according to the changing needs of a given oratorical performance.

Sight, memory and viewer response in Roman visual culture

Quite apart from their intrinsic interest for approaching Roman education and mental coaching, Roman rhetorical discussions of sight and memory are crucial for approaching how Romans (or at least a schooled Roman elite) *saw*. If Roman rhetoric schooled particular ways of seeing, it also prescribed certain modes of making sense of sight – of turning visual stimuli back into verbal discourse. As a result, we know better for this culture than for many others how the visual faculties of the elite were trained: the "virtual" visions of Roman mnemonics – structured around first environmental or contextual backgrounds, second specific images or symbols placed within them, and third an imagined spatial progression – represent an extraordinarily articulate cultural rationalization of what it meant to view.

From this perspective, Roman rhetorical texts also have a key importance for making historical sense of the actual visual materials seen in ancient Rome. So far in this chapter, we have talked about the "imaginary" visions of Roman rhetoric. Crucially, though, our rhetorician-authors draw on types of real visual stimuli. One of the most interesting aspects of these passages is the wide range of backdrops introduced: the *loci* that Roman rhetoricians cite encompass all manner of spatial sites and sights – from public buildings and urban landscapes, through intercolumnar spaces and recesses, to arches, the rooms of a house and individual paintings. In each case, the sets of background sites are also drawn from the experienced sights of Roman daily life.

So what might rhetorical discussions of sight and memory mean for approaching the objects that Romans viewed? Of course, it is often difficult to reconstruct the precise configurations of the visual stimuli that Roman orators discuss. It takes a remarkable archaeological accident – the catastrophic eruption of Vesuvius in 79 CE, for example, covering great swathes of Campania in its at once destructive and preservative volcanic upsurge – to render such sights visible in all their original complexity. But in the case of those archaeological survivals in Campania, and above all in the provincial towns of Pompeii and Herculaneum, we have a pretty good sense of the articulation and adornment of domestic housing and urban streets. As a result, art historians have been able to map discourses of sight and memory in Roman rhetorical texts against surviving archaeological realities (in particular, the axial vistas

---

plus généralement la capacité de mobiliser tout son savoir, toute son expérience en même temps que de souvenir de ce que l'adversaire vient de dire et qui n'était pas nécessairement prévu".

exploited in the disposition of Roman houses and their construction around a series of carefully managed views).[29] Such concern with views and vistas, steeped as it is in Roman rhetorical training and practice, can also be found in a range of other texts: one thinks, for example, of major didactic treatises on Roman architecture like that of Vitruvius in the late first century BCE, as well as of extant letters, such as those of the Younger Seneca in the mid-first century, the Younger Pliny in the early second and not least Sidonius Apollinaris much later in the mid-fifth century CE.[30] What archaeology sometimes allows us to do here is to map extant Roman architectural structures against such frameworks of "seeing", generated at least in part through mnemonic training: the very construction of buildings could serve to yield background *loci*, focal *imagines* and pathways of ordered movement. Moving from domestic and more private spaces to the public arena of the Roman city, the "visual" and "spatial rhetoric" of urban topography (in both the eastern and the western stretches of the Roman empire) might be approached in related terms: according to some scholars, the very layouts of Roman cities are indebted to the educational model of vision within rhetorical memory.[31]

In the remainder of this chapter, we explore the implications of Roman rhetorical ideas about sight and memory in relation to just one medium of Roman art: namely, Pompeian mural decoration. Preserved *in situ* within their domestic settings, wall-paintings offer a particularly rich case study for thinking about visual stimuli not only as *imagines*, but also in relation to their spatial settings (*loci*) and arrangement (*ordo*) within a room or house. Of course, the objection might be made here that Pompeian paintings preserve the interior decoration of sub-elite groups – and hence have only a limited connection with the elite voices of contemporary Roman rhetorical texts.[32] As Bettina Bergmann has shown in her classic 1994 discussion of Campanian wall-painting as "Roman memory theatre",[33] however, there are important connections to be drawn between the mechanics of imagined *loci* and *imagines* and the arrangements of paintings in the Pompeian house: rhetorical ideas about sight and memory filter all the way across Rome's social spectrum.

On the level of self-contained *imagines*, Roman rhetoric can help us to appreciate responses to single framed mural panels within the wall. One assumption that we have seen to underlie Roman rhetorical mnemonics is that, before an image can

---

29 See e.g. Bek (1980: 164–203); Jung (1984); Wallace-Hadrill (1994: 38–61); Hales (2003: 97–163).
30 Cf. Elsner (1995: 74–85). The principal texts in prose are: the sixth and seventh books of Vitruvius' *On Architecture*; Seneca, *Moral Letters* 55.6–7 and 86; Pliny the Younger, *Letters* 2.17 and 5.6, with Whitton (2013: 218–55) for commentary and bibliography; Sidonius Apollinaris, *Letters* 2.2. No less revealing are verse texts – not least Statius, *Silvae* 1.3 and 2.2, with Newlands (2011: 120–57) for commentary and bibliography.
31 On visual rhetoric, see Kjeldsen (2003), Lauer (2004: 437–9) and above all now the essays in Elsner & Meyer (2014). On spatial rhetoric, see Eidson (2013); Thomas (2014).
32 Compare e.g. Clarke (2003: 235–75) and Mayer (2012: 166–212) – although Mayer's case for an art of the "middle classes" starts out from a wholly flawed set of assumptions.
33 Bergmann (1994), arguing of Pompeii's Casa del Poeta Tragico (VI.8.3–5) that the "sustained contemplation of the arrangements exercised the educated viewer's memory by unlocking a variety of associations and inviting a sequence of reasoned calculations" (255); cf. Baroin (1998), and the more detailed, archaeologically oriented analyses of K. Lorenz (2008); compare also Muth (1998) on the poignant juxtapositions of mosaic images.

kick-start the memory to reveal what is prompted by it, that initial image must be recognized. If we add to this necessary emphasis on recognition the formulaic nature of Roman art – its limited range of iconographic types, showing particular dispositions of the body in different contexts and with different attributes to determine specific myths[34] – then Pompeian painting reveals something still more profound about the interconnected workings of sight and memory. In extant paintings, we frequently find a single repeated bodily schema being used in relation to different mythological figures: a reclining nude male youth (most often with a cloak draped over his lower body and arranged so as to reveal the genitals) is shown carrying one or more spears, and set either in a rural landscape or else in a more acculturated environment.[35] Within a long-standing Greek and Roman cultural imaginary, this figure of the resting hunter was replete with erotic overtones,[36] and in some contexts, that erotically charged aspect was further emphasized by the accompaniment of small cupid figures.[37]

But the precise narrative associations depend in each case on the artist's embellishing of the repeated bodily schema with additional attributes and figures. In the company of a female (clothed or nude), the male figure is often identified as Adonis (e.g. Figure 9.9);[38] reclining alone, with a pool beneath him (and above all with his face reflected in the pool's water), he is seen as Narcissus (e.g. Figures 9.3, 9.5; cf. Figure I.2);[39] seated with a stag beneath him, the figure might bring to mind Cyparissus (e.g. Figure 9.8),[40] but where Selene is shown approaching we are instead led to Endymion (e.g. Figure 9.2).[41] If the figure is situated beside a standing female who also carries hunting spears, the same schema might bring to mind Meleager with Atlanta,[42] but if an eagle is introduced into the scene, and especially when the male figure wears a Phrygian cap, we might now see him as Ganymede (e.g. Figure 9.6);[43] then again, accompanied by a dog and sandwiched between figures who may be Phaedra and her nurse, the figure might be understood as Hippolytus.[44] Given the damaged state of the frescoes on so many Campanian walls, the figure (perhaps with cupids but with no extra distinguishing attributes, or at any rate attributes that have survived) is often not easily identifiable at all.[45] But that is precisely what makes the visual schema so interesting: one bodily formula can serve to summon up all manner of narrative associations, dependent as it is on particular details within the image.

---

[34] More generally on the semantics of "nudity" in Roman bodily statuary, see Hallett (2005); for clothed female statuary, see Trimble (2011).
[35] Interest in these mythological panels has revived only relatively recently, after a century of focus on the architectural illusion of their frames in terms of the so-called "Four Styles" of Campanian wall-painting: see, amongst other treatments, Romizzi (2006); Hodske (2007); K. Lorenz (2008).
[36] Cf. e.g. Schnapp (1997: 318–54).
[37] Cf. Elsner (2007b: 153–4), on the addition of such figures in the context of Narcissus imagery.
[38] See Hodske (2007: 146–9, perhaps also 152–3).
[39] See Hodske (2007: 166–71).
[40] See Hodske (2007: 186, 251).
[41] See Hodske (2007: 210–12).
[42] See Hodske (2007: 223–5).
[43] See Hodske (2007: 231–2).
[44] See Hodske (2007: 233, no. 614).
[45] For instance, see Hodske (2007: 225, 231 no. 719, 270 no. 273) – suggesting Adonis, Ganymede and Paris. On such ephebic ambiguities, cf. S. Pearson (2015: esp. 158–62), published while this book was in proofs.

Roman rhetorical discussions of sight and memory help us to understand the importance of such seemingly small attributes alongside the recurring bodily schema. Quintilian, as we have said, explicitly introduces the example of "paintings" within his list of potential *loci* (*picturae*: *Training of the Orator* 11.2.21). From a Roman rhetorical perspective, then, each visual detail within the picture could subsequently serve to open up narrative vistas – to provide the viewer with prompts to turn the image into verbal interpretation or response. For the viewer accustomed to using paintings as mnemonic tools, relatively minor differences in attributes could serve to connote major differences of subject matter. As *aide-mémoire*, each picture might serve as a spatial *locus* in its own right: it could bring to mind words and ideas that could then be rhetorically elaborated at whim.

At the same time, the iconographic relationship between different subjects might spur the memory to draw semantic interconnections between different paintings. Just as, in our opening passage, Pausanias related one statue of Apollo to the memory of another seen elsewhere (albeit to tease out something about artistic attribution), so too could a shared schematic body type prompt the viewer to approach different visualized myths in association with one other. No less important is the connection between an individual painting and its frame. With each image, the tableau demands to be understood in spatial relationship with its mural surround – that is, in association with the illusory and sometimes surrealistic play of those architectural framing devices that determine the so-called "Four Styles" of Pompeian painting.[46] The relationship of these mythological panels to their mural frames, we might say, is directly analogous to the relationship of *imagines* to *loci* in the rhetorically trained Roman rhetorical art of memory.

Particularly intriguing here are the repetitions of framed tableaux within one and the same Roman house.[47] In this scenario, the domestic spaces could themselves serve as *loci* for interrelated schematic *imagines*; indeed, the nexus of visual associations, drawn out as one passes through different rooms within the house, could bestow the viewer with a physical and conceptual *ordo* for progressing through the house as a *locus* in its own right.[48] To explain what we mean here, consider first the Casa dei Dioscuri (Pompeii VI.9.6,7). This house is furnished with two decorated *triclinia* spaces for dining (rooms 38 and 49), and both are decorated with (admittedly poorly surviving) images that draw on the same bodily type of reclining male youth; in both rooms, we are likewise dealing with the so-called "Fourth Style" of Pompeian painting (roughly dating from between *ca.* 60 CE and the Vesuvian eruption of 79 CE). In *triclinium* 38, the north wall shows Endymion with dog and two spears seated seminaked, facing right and looking up at the arrival of Selene (Figure 9.2).[49] This scene survives because it was cut out of its mural context in the nineteenth century and

---

46 For introductions to August Mau's "Four Styles", see Ling (1991); Leach (2004); P. Stewart (2004: 74–92); Croisille (2005). More generally on the importance of such "framing" devices, especially in Roman wall-painting, see Platt & Squire (forthcoming b).
47 For explorations of the theme, see the classic discussions of Bergmann (1994; 1999); cf. Schefold (1952); Thompson (1961); Brilliant (1984: 53–89); Leach (1988: 361–408); K. Lorenz (2008). Cf. Morales (2004: 174–7) and Tanner (2006: 252–3) on Achilles Tatius, *Leucippe and Clitophon* 3.6–7.
48 For the argument, see especially Baroin (1998).
49 On the house as a whole, see Baldassare (1993: 860–1004). On *triclinium* 38, see Baldassare (1993: 893–7) and Romizzi (2006: 383–4).

Figure 9.2 "Fourth Style" panel-painting from the north wall of *triclinium* 38 in the Casa dei Dioscuri (Pompeii VI.9.6,7 = Baldassare 1993: 894, no. 65) (photograph reproduced by kind permission of the Archiv, Institut für Klassische Archäologie und Museum Klassischer Abgüsse, Ludwig-Maximilians-Universität, Munich).

removed to the National Archaeological Museum in Naples (inv. 9240). The south wall probably also featured a mythological picture, but this one has been lost and appears to have gone unrecorded. The west wall (whose central panel was not excised for museum display and has subsequently vanished in its entirety) was reproduced in more than one nineteenth-century drawing: it showed a seated Narcissus, with his body once again turned to the right, and with a dog and two spears (Figure 9.3). If the figure on the west wall clearly mirrors that of Endymion on the adjoining north wall,

Figure 9.3 Nineteenth-century reproduction drawing of a "Fourth Style" panel-painting from the west wall of *triclinium* 38 in the Casa dei Dioscuri (Pompeii VI.9.6,7 = Baldassare 1993: 896, no. 68) (photograph reproduced by kind permission of the Archiv, Institut für Klassische Archäologie und Museum Klassischer Abgüsse, Ludwig-Maximilians-Universität, Munich).

there are nonetheless some poignant differences. For one thing, the protagonist's face is turned away to the left, inspecting the pool below. For another, several other figures are included beside him: observe how a winged cupid is shown sleeping by his right shoulder, betokening his erotic self-immersion; notice too how a female figure (usually identified as Echo) and another winged cupid look towards him, while the cupid raises his hand to gesture in Narcissus' direction.

Whatever else we make of this pairing of near-nude youths in room 38 (and their relation to the lost image of the south wall), the tableaux are clearly related both in the iconography of the male protagonists and in their attributes: they ask to be put together, so that each image is understood in association with the other. No less importantly, that pairing also works in collaboration with related "Fourth Style"

Figure 9.4 Nineteenth-century reproduction drawing of a "Fourth Style" panel-painting from the east wall of *triclinium* 49 in the Casa dei Dioscuri (Pompeii VI.9.6,7 = Baldassare 1993: 951, no. 177) (photograph reproduced by kind permission of the Archiv, Institut für Klassische Archäologie und Museum Klassischer Abgüsse, Ludwig-Maximilians-Universität, Munich).

pairings elsewhere in the house, and not least those in a second *triclinium* (room 49). Although very little of room 49's painted mural panels survives, two of its pictures were recorded in the nineteenth century (Figures 9.4 and 9.5).[50] One showed Apollo with his lyre, a cow and a nude seated figure with cloak and Phrygian cap (but without a spear): although uncertain, the figure has been identified as either Laomedon or Admetus. In the second painting, we see another version of the Narcissus myth, which portrays the protagonist in a similar posture to the painting found in room 38. This time Narcissus is shown with only one spear and without the sleeping

50 On *triclinium* 49, see Baldassare (1993: 950–3) and Romizzi (2006: 385).

Figure 9.5 Nineteenth-century reproduction drawing of a "Fourth Style" panel-painting from the south wall of *triclinium* 49 in the Casa dei Dioscuri (Pompeii VI.9.6,7 = Baldassare 1993: 952, no. 179) (photograph reproduced by kind permission of the Archiv, Institut für Klassische Archäologie und Museum Klassischer Abgüsse, Ludwig-Maximilians-Universität, Munich).

cupid to his right. Although a cupid once again accompanies the figure, he is here portrayed pouring water into the very pool on which Narcissus fixes his gazes, while two female figures (one of them plausibly identified as Echo) stand in the background.

How should we approach the connections between the paintings in these two rooms of the Casa dei Dioscuri? It is impossible to develop an argument of great precision, of course. In both rooms we have no information about the third triangulating picture; even where we can reconstruct the iconography, we must rely on nineteenth-century copies (our interpretations are dependent not only on archaeological survival, but also on the long and chequered history of excavation, reproduction and reconstruction from the eighteenth to the twenty-first century). Still, we can

Figure 9.6 Nineteenth-century reproduction drawing of a "Fourth Style" panel-painting from the north wall of *oecus* 17 in the Casa dei Capitelli Colorati (Pompeii VII.4.31,51 = Baldassare 1996: 1017, no. 27) (photograph reproduced by kind permission of the Archiv, Institut für Klassische Archäologie und Museum Klassischer Abgüsse, Ludwig-Maximilians-Universität, Munich).

be sure that, through their iconographic and formal resonances, the paintings invited viewers (whether consciously or unconsciously) to draw out associations both within and between the parallel dining spaces. Both the images and their settings appeal to a rhetorically trained – and highly visually attuned – memory: together, they provide the viewer with a visual matrix, and one that had the potential to structure the viewer's social experience of the house.

Turning to a second case study, the Casa dei Capitelli Colorati (Pompeii VII.4.31,51), we find further examples of the nude-boy type repeated in different

SIGHT AND MEMORY

Figure 9.7 "Fourth Style" panel-painting from the west wall of *oecus* 17, Casa dei Capitelli Colorati (Pompeii VII.4.31,51 = Baldassare 1996: 1020, no. 30) (photograph reproduced by kind permission of the Archiv, Institut für Klassische Archäologie und Museum Klassischer Abgüsse, Ludwig-Maximilians-Universität, Munich).

configurations in different places across the house.[51] In the "Fourth Style" mural decoration of *oecus* 17, we find three formally related subjects (juxtaposed, on the south wall, with a central figure of Venus riding a marine centaur): on the north wall (in a panel which is today lost, but which was drawn in the nineteenth century), Ganymede is shown alongside the eagle of Zeus (Figure 9.6); on the west wall (in a panel preserved in the National Archaeological Museum at Naples, inv. 8996), a semi-nude Perseus is portrayed, but this time shown alongside Andromeda and holding the Gorgon's head in his left hand (Figure 9.7; compare also Figure 7.6); in a third picture, on the east wall, Apollo appears beside Cyparissus, who reclines with

---

51 On the house as a whole, see Baldassare (1996: 996–1106); K. Lorenz (2008: 582–6).

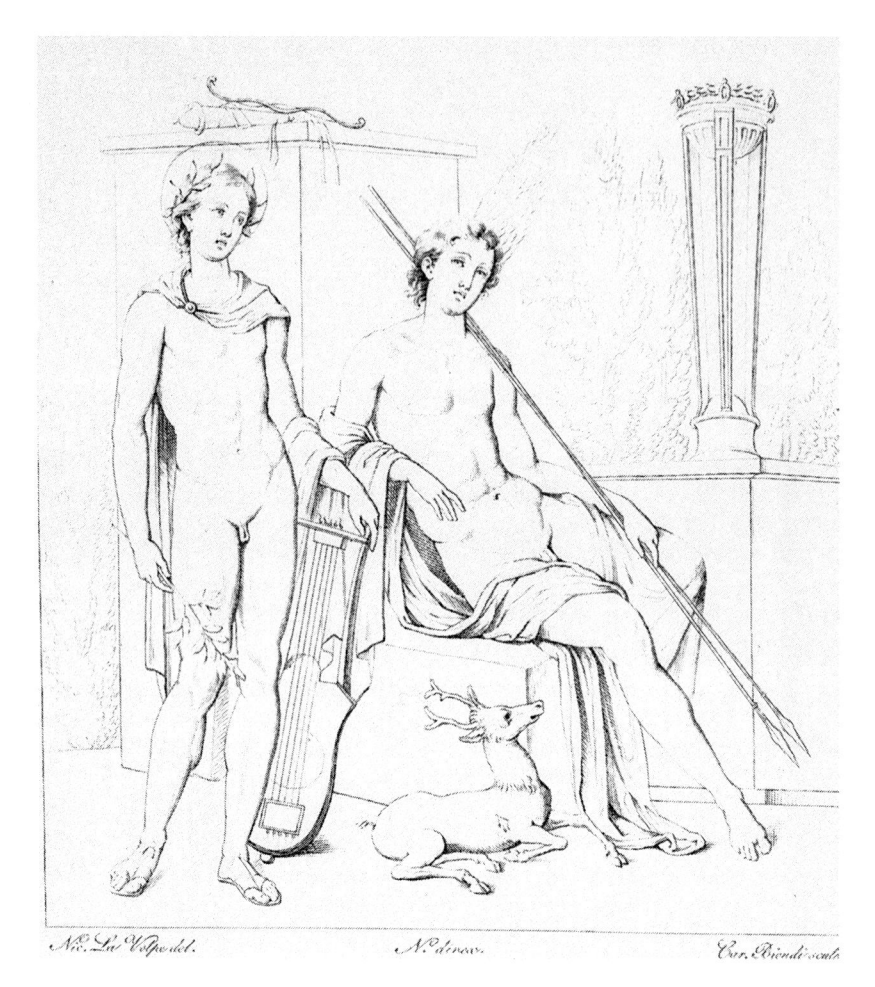

Figure 9.8 Nineteenth-century reproduction drawing of a "Fourth Style" panel-painting from the east wall of *oecus* 17, Casa dei Capitelli Colorati (Pompeii VII.4.31,51 = Baldassare 1996: 1024, no. 37) (photograph reproduced by kind permission of the Archiv, Institut für Klassische Archäologie und Museum Klassischer Abgüsse, Ludwig-Maximilians-Universität, Munich).

spears and beside a stag (Figure 9.8).[52] The motif of the semi-nude reclining youth recurs as Adonis beside Venus in the "Fourth Style" painting of *exedra* 22 (Figure 9.9),[53] and as a figure that may be Helios or Apollo with a female figure ("Rhodes") in a "Fourth Style" panel in *oecus* 24 (Figure 9.10).[54] Crucially, all of these spaces (rooms 17, 22 and 24) are accessible from the main peristyle at the house's centre (room 18). As such, the formal resemblances between the panels weave a nexus of possible interconnections, spatially structuring the viewer's progression from, to or

52 On *oecus* 17, see Baldassare (1996: 1009–25); Romizzi (2006: 426).
53 On *exedra* 22, see Baldassare (1996: 1040); Romizzi (2006: 426–7).
54 On *oecus* 24, see Baldassare (1996: 1048–9); Romizzi (2006: 427).

Figure 9.9 "Fourth Style" panel-painting from the north wall of *exedra* 22 in the Casa dei Capitelli Colorati (Pompeii VII.4.31,51 = Baldassare 1996: 1040, no. 59) (photograph reproduced by kind permission of the Archiv, Institut für Klassische Archäologie und Museum Klassischer Abgüsse, Ludwig-Maximilians-Universität, Munich).

through a central reception area. The repetition and subtle variation of iconographic forms might bring to mind myths that are formally and thematically related. But they also construct a symbolic world to be experienced in relation to the social realities of the house. By providing viewers with a mythological fantasy-land, and one that depends on the visual flow from image to image and from one background to the next, the paintings offer material counterparts to the visual stimuli discussed by rhetoricians: they materialize the mental world of imagined visual stimuli that lies at the heart of Roman mnemonics.

Rhetorical discussions of sight and memory can certainly help us to reconstruct some structures of visual response to such tableaux. Ultimately, however, they also

Figure 9.10 Nineteenth-century reproduction drawing of a "Fourth Style" panel-painting from the south wall of *oecus* 24 in the Casa dei Capitelli Colorati (Pompeii VII.4.31,51 = Baldassare 1996: 1049, no. 72) (photograph reproduced by kind permission of the Archiv, Institut für Klassische Archäologie und Museum Klassischer Abgüsse, Ludwig-Maximilians-Universität, Munich).

drive home the importance of individual subjective engagement. According to our Latin rhetorical texts, we have emphasized, the most powerful aspect of visual memory is its manipulation of a familiar visual space to creative personal ends. *Imagines* might be laid out in all manner of different *loci* – whether a house or urban setting (that is, something to be socially experienced, by way of bodily movement), or else a wholly more two-dimensional space (a painting, for example, that is to be experienced from outside the pictorial frame). Yet what matters in each case is less the visual prompts themselves than what the orator imaginatively does with them: the sights summoned up in the memory are designed to provide rhetorical speech with an *ordo* that can then be retraced at personal whim.[55] From this perspective, the function of vision in relation to memory might be said to be twofold. On the one hand, orators rely on familiar visual stimuli in order to create a mnemonic prompt. On the other, they learn to codify those visual stimuli, making them do symbolic duty for the particular purpose of a given oratorical performance. In turning images into symbols, there is no outside controlling mechanism: for all its reliance on visual stimuli, the symbolic world of Roman memory operates in the private subjective experience of the orator. Crucially, moreover, Roman rhetorical discussions of memory fuse *objective* visual stimuli with *subjective* visual response: the objective reality of a remembered space (whether a house, city or picture), subjectively manipulated by the visual movement of memory and occupied by the symbols the orator places in it, is used to fabricate the framework of an imagined speech – which can itself then be instantiated as objective reality before an audience.

Such creative subjectivity, we suggest, is also fundamental when it comes to visually responding to paintings like the ones laid out in the Pompeian home. Set within their framing mural surrounds, but nonetheless demarcated from those spatial backgrounds, the mythological panels of Pompeian murals have the potential to function symbolically: they are effectively placed *outside* the space of social allusion to which so much of Campanian mural painting referred.[56] As such, they materialize the sorts of visual stimuli discussed by Roman rhetoricians. The range of potential meanings that could be associated with these images was as diverse as the viewers who looked at them. But the point to emphasize is that the doubling of image (*imago*) and background (*locus*) in relation to a visual flow that enabled a painting to be both part of its background and symbolic of something else – which is the heart of the rhetorical memory system – also lies at the heart of Roman mural decoration, and may even be said to have been visually instantiated by it.

Conclusion: the Roman art of memory

This chapter has attempted to do two things. First, we explored some of the visual ways in which memory came to be theorized in the ancient world. Roman rhetoricians, we have argued, systematized earlier Greek associations between seeing and remembering: by advocating a particular mnemonic method founded on *loci*, *imagines* and *ordo*, Roman rhetoric at once rationalized the connection between sight and memory and incorporated such thinking within pedagogical programmes of rhetorical training. In turning to domestic Roman mural painting, the second part of the chapter argued that such mnemonic approaches to "sight and the ancient senses" might also shed light on the mechanics of viewing in the Roman world. Seen from the perspective of Roman rhetoric, Campanian wall-paintings can be understood in relation to both mnemonic *loci* and *imagines*: as visual stimuli, these tableaux offer a material instantiation of the visual memory as it was trained and operated by the Roman elite.

---

55 Cf. Carruthers (1990: 19): "the proof of a good memory lies not in the simple retention even of large amounts of material; rather, it is the ability to move it about instantly, directly, and securely that is admired".
56 See Wallace-Hadrill (1994: 17–28), with discussion of "allusion" and "illusion" by Elsner (1995: 74–6).

We end this chapter by tendering a still stronger version of our argument. In thinking about rhetorical theories of visual memory and their ramifications for approaching Roman visual culture, this chapter has restricted itself to the medium of wall-painting. Had we more space, however, a broader array of Roman materials might have been introduced.[57] After all, the claim that Roman images operate as a kind of "semantic system" – that is, almost as a "language" of forms and styles, with distinct and meaningful allusions to earlier precedents (above all from the Greek world, but also from e.g. Egypt and indeed earlier Italic models)[58] – is ultimately an argument about sight and memory. It is only in a culture with an acute historical and aesthetic awareness of stylistic differences that free and widespread creative usage, replication and play with different models is possible.[59] Such recourse to earlier paradigms, whether as something systematic (as most often suggested), or perhaps instead as simply the normative idiom of visual creation within Roman culture,[60] does not require the full commanding control of memory that Roman rhetoric taught. But it does depend on a broad and deep cultural memory-bank of images and visual types: it requires the visual memory to be triggered through recognition, and the viewer to register the reference to (and difference from) prior models. So much of Roman art – the iconography of sarcophagi,[61] the kinds of bodies used in honorific portraiture,[62] the play with recutting portrait heads (whether as *damnatio memoriae* or, as apparently in the Arch of Constantine, as a form of encomium)[63] – belongs within the broad range of functions that depend, in a variety of creative ways, on the art of visual memory. Better, perhaps, the very workings of replication in Roman art – and on a variety of levels – come down to ideas about seeing and remembering.

This observation returns us full circle to the Pausanian passage with which this chapter began. For all his apparent remove from the sorts of rhetorical texts that we have discussed, Pausanias, too, testifies to a culture that inculcated and trained a remarkable facility of remembering through seeing and seeing through remembering. This visual memory – with its particular qualities of movement and doubling – proved a fundamental cultural conditioning in its own right for the making and reception of Roman art. In the public arena of the urban landscape, the funerary contexts of the tomb and the domestic spaces of the Roman household, certainly. But also when it came to the hallowed images of the distant Greek past.

---

57 See in particular here arguments about the so-called *Tabulae Iliacae*, or "Iliac tablets", functioning as "véritables 'tablettes à mémoriser'": Rouveret (1988: 168); cf. Rouveret (1982; 1989: 359–69), with response in Squire (2011a: 71–2; 2014: 412–16).
58 See especially Hölscher (2004), with elaboration and extension by Elsner (2006a: 274–6); cf. also Trimble (2011: 32–6).
59 For a recent championing of the point, see Anguissola (2014).
60 Here we distance ourselves from the strongest form of Hölscher's argument about Roman art as a *semantic system* – that is, as something analogous to language and hence able to "communicate" clearly definable "messages": for critique, see e.g. Squire (2009: 83–7); Elsner (2010: 54–6).
61 For memory and sarcophagi, see e.g. Koortbojian (1995: 114–26); on commemorative mourning compare also e.g. Zanker & Ewald (2004: 62–115); on consolatory memory, see e.g. Newby (2014).
62 For bodies in statuary, see e.g. Hallett (2005); Fejfer (2008: 181–227, 331–50); Trimble (2011); Squire (2015c); cf. Ma (2013: 267–73) on Hellenistic precedents.
63 For recut heads, see e.g. Varner (2004) and Prusac (2011). On the Arch of Constantine and the art of memory, see most recently Hughes (2014), with overview of the vast bibliography.

10

SIGHT AND INSIGHT

Theorizing vision, emotion and imagination in ancient rhetoric

Ruth Webb

Sometime in the second century CE, somewhere in the eastern regions of the Roman empire, Lucian, a Greek-speaking sophist, purportedly made a speech in a magnificent lecture hall. The room was decorated with gold and with painted scenes but, rather than using this opulent setting as a background for a speech or simply praising it, he made a choice that was as unusual as it was typical of his self-reflexive style: he decided to talk about the very possibility of speaking in such a place. The speech as we have it (under the title "The Hall") asks whether the visual beauty of the setting was a help or a hindrance to the speaker in his task of finding things to say, and to the audience in their task of listening attentively. In his characteristic manner, Lucian sets out one side of the argument in his own voice before presenting the speech made by an imaginary dissenting voice explaining why the hall could only detract from the performance, distracting the audience and overwhelming the orator.

The first of these two opposing voices treats the hall as a spur to eloquence, an inspiration to the orator who feels moved to respond in words to the beauty of the sight, just as a warrior is inspired by the sight of splendid armour. Lucian provides a physiological justification, claiming that "no doubt something beautiful flows through the eyes into the soul (εἰσρεῖ τι διὰ τῶν ὀφθαλμῶν ἐπὶ τὴν ψυχὴν καλόν), then, having fashioned them in accordance with itself (πρὸς αὐτό) it sends out the words" (*The Hall* 4).

Sight and speech

I take this claim as my starting point because it indicates how widely philosophical ideas about sight and its impact were disseminated, leading us to the relationship between the sense of sight, the mind and the production and reception of language. It is possible to find in all sorts of texts from the Imperial period and from late antiquity allusions to the intimate connections that existed between the visual and the verbal. These connections, I will argue, go far beyond the practice of describing, of translating the visual into verbal form, in that the interface between the two lies in the human mind, more precisely in the faculty of the imagination that allows us to "see" in the mind's eye. Such virtual visions are intimately connected with language in that they can both be produced by and give rise to words; moreover, they serve complex functions that may be psychological, emotional and cognitive, moving the listeners, making them share experiences that they have not lived through themselves (and understand phenomena that are remote from normal human experience).[1] So all-pervasive are these ideas that it is difficult to find a single source that sets them out clearly and succinctly, making it necessary to examine a wide range of texts from the Roman Imperial (as indeed earlier) periods. Since rhetoric was the main communication technology of the ancient world, rhetorical treatises are our fullest sources and we will look in particular at what the Roman rhetorician, Quintilian, had to say. Different perspectives on the question are to be found in the treatise *On the Sublime* attributed to Longinus and in St Augustine, a church father who was steeped in classical philosophy and rhetoric.[2] These ideas also have their roots in the writings of Plato and Aristotle (particularly the latter).

To return, for a moment, to Lucian and his hall, the language he uses in the passage quoted above is close in places to that of Plato in the *Timaeus* (45b). Like Lucian, Plato also speaks of vision "flowing through the eyes" (*dia tōn ommatōn rhein*) – although, in Plato's case, the flow is primarily in the opposite direction, from inside out, as Andrea Nightingale has explained earlier in this book. However, both Plato and Lucian's understanding of sight share in common the absence of boundary between the perceiving subject and the world perceived: in Lucian's formulation, it is not an image or a simulacrum of beauty that penetrates into the soul, but "something beautiful" (*ti ... kalon*) which does not just reside in the soul of the viewer but adapts the words that he sends out to his listening audience.

Lucian points to a link between sight and the desire – or impulse – to respond to that sight immediately in words that we find in other contemporary authors. One example comes in literary *ekphraseis* (vivid "evocations") of paintings and statues, presented as immediate responses to the beauty and complexity of the art object that offers itself to the viewer's gaze. It is unlikely that the Elder Philostratus' *Imagines* were improvised inside the gallery they claim to describe (if this gallery even existed), but they are framed as extempore responses by a sophist skilled in the art of speaking.[3] In a different context, the sophist Aelius Aristides, asking the Emperors Marcus Aurelius and Lucius Verus for help after the city of Smyrna was devastated by an earthquake, recalls their earlier visit to the city asking them "what did you look at in

---

1 On the history of the imagination in antiquity, see Watson (1988) and (with special reference to poetics) Sheppard (2014). On Aristotle, see Schofield (1979) and D. Frede (1992), along with Nightingale's chapter in this volume; on Stoic conceptions of *phantasia*, see Long (1996a); Gourinat (1996). Much has been written on the role of appeals to the imagination in ancient poetry: e.g. Zanker (1981; 1987); Meijering (1987: 29–72); Manieri (1998); Otto (2009); Squire (2010a). On the imagination and its uses in rhetoric and Imperial prose, see Webb (1997a; 1997b); Hirsch-Luipold (2002); Goldhill (2007); Webb (2009a); on historiography, see Zangara (2007). Specifically on these themes in the Imperial period and late antiquity, see Boeder (1996), while Plett (2010) gives a survey up to the Early Modern period, and the essays in Lévy & Pernot (1997) treat philosophy, poetry and rhetoric from antiquity to the eighteenth century. There is a close connection between appeals to the imagination in language and the nature and function of the visual arts: on this aspect, see, for example, Zeitlin (1994); Elsner (1995); Newby (2002).
2 More generally on the importance of vision in early Christian thought, see Heath (this volume).
3 For a stimulating recent analysis of the *Imagines*, see Squire (2013a).

silence without the words of praise (*euphēmia*) that befit you?"[4] A verbal response was therefore considered to be the norm for the educated viewer faced with a beautiful or impressive sight.[5] The difference in Lucian's remark lies in the emphasis on the beauty of the resulting speech, an emphasis that is entirely fitting to the context and, elsewhere, there is no shortage of evidence linking the sense of sight to the production of words. In most cases, though, the link between sight and language (or sight and sound – Lucian is not clear whether the beauty of the speech is thought to lie in the content or its aural qualities or both) is not direct, as implied by Lucian, but passes through the intermediary of the mind or soul and the mental images that are stored or created there.

The way in which Aristides' *Letter* uses memories of past sights (the city of Smyrna before its destruction) to spur action in the present (financial support for the reconstruction of the city)[6] also draws our attention to the way in which images of things seen were thought to linger in the mind of the viewer. Aristides, after all, goes on to say that "nothing of this [i.e. what the Emperors saw in Smyrna] has left your memory", before inviting his addressees to contemplate the contrast with the city's present state. He reflects here the pervasive idea that perception left impressions on the soul, likened by Aristotle to the impressions left in wax by signet rings.[7] In the literature of the Roman period, this idea finds its clearest expression in the accounts of lovers obsessed with the image of the beloved that has lodged in their minds.[8]

In his treatise *On the Soul*, Aristotle describes these impressions (termed *phantasiai*) as being like an internal painting (3.3, 427b 23–4). But what is most interesting for us is that he points to a necessary link between *phantasia* and perception (*aisthēsis*) on the one hand, and supposition (*hupolēpsis*) on the other (*On the Soul* 3.3, 427b 15–16).[9] These traces left by sensation (primarily, but not exclusively, the sense of sight) both lingered as memory images and functioned as the raw material for thought and language. Following on from and developing Aristotle's ideas, Stoic philosophers, according to Diogenes Laertius, spoke of impressions (*phantasiai*) in the following terms: "the impression arises first, and then thought (*dianoia*), which has the power of talking, expresses in language what it experiences by the agency of the impression".[10] It is unclear whether this *phantasia* in Stoic thought was primarily

---

4 Aelius Aristides, *Oration* 19; cf. *Letter to the Emperors* 2. Further discussion can be found in Webb (1997a).
5 Cf. Newby (2002).
6 In this, Aristides' speech corresponds to the advice given on such speeches by Menander Rhetor, *On Epideictic* 2.423; one might also compare the ways in which images are used in modern charity appeals.
7 Aristotle, *On Memory* 1, 450a30–2. On this image in Democritus and Aristotle, see the chapters by Rudolph and Nightingale in this volume. Nightingale's chapter offers a much more detailed discussion of Aristotle's theories of vision; compare also Marmodoro (2014) for a comprehensive treatment of Aristotelian ideas about perception at large.
8 See, for example, Chariton, *Callirhoe* 6.5–7 and Achilles Tatius, *Leucippe and Clitophon* 1.9. On this phenomenon, see Bettini (1999).
9 On *phantasia*, see Sheppard (2014); on Aristotle, see D. Frede (1992). Plato had also used the term *phantasia* in the *Sophist* 263e10–264b4 to designate an illusory kind of opinion (*doxa*) based on sense perception (cf. also *Theaetetus* 152c1–2). At *On the Soul* 3.3, 428 a24–b2, Aristotle seems to be responding to Plato.
10 Diogenes Laertius 7.49: my translation follows that of Long & Sedley (1987: 33D).

visual or whether it was a more abstract phenomenon.[11] However, outside the writings of pure Stoic philosophers, and particularly in the work of authors involved in the teaching and study of rhetoric, we can find very clear examples of the use of the term to mean "mental image". The clearest example – and the most explicit statement of the relationship between mental images and language in everyday life – is to be found in the writings of Augustine, the fourth-/fifth-century church father from North Africa who had both trained in and taught the traditional rhetorical curriculum. He explains that when he wishes to say a word, an internal mental phenomenon precedes the utterance and that this phenomenon is particular to each word. The example he chooses is a very concrete one that serves to illustrate the visual nature of these mental phenomena and their origin in bodily sensation. He explains that when he wishes to speak the name of his own city of Carthage he looks inside himself (*apud me ipsum*) and finds (*inuenio*) a *phantasia* of Carthage.[12] Augustine makes clear that this *phantasia* results from direct sensory experience of the city acquired through the body (*per corporis sensum*) while he was present in body (*corpore*) within the city. This sensation, he explains, is retained in memory and it is this that he finds within himself when he wishes to pronounce the name of the city.

Mental images deriving from sensation are therefore at the root of knowledge, thought and language and this seems to be the model that Lucian had in mind when he made his claim about beauty flowing in through the eyes of the viewer and prompting speech. Such ideas may seem strange to modern readers, accustomed as they are to a strict division between the mind that thinks and the body that perceives. But the most unusual aspect of Lucian's claim is the fact that, in this particular case, the reception of the sight and the production of the words are almost simultaneous and not separated in time and space.

With all this in mind, we can move on to explore more fully some of the uses of mental images in the production of language and in communication. In the examples we have looked at so far, a sight (Lucian's hall, the city of Smyrna or the city of Carthage) had an impact on the mind that gave rise to language, even if the particulars of each case are rather different: Lucian evokes a situation in which the sight simultaneously prompts speech as its influence flows through the orator, while Augustine speaks of a situation in which the imprinted image is summoned when he speaks the mere name of Carthage. Aristides combines both, recalling the words prompted by the sight when it was still present to the emperors' senses, and then inviting them to recall the image left behind. The examples offered by Augustine and Aristides show that the interaction between the individual and the mental images stocked in his or her mind was a dynamic one. Both speakers and their audiences were thought of as constantly engaged in a process of calling up, developing and reflecting on these images. The examples we will examine next move still further in this direction: they illustrate the potential uses of mental image in conceiving, creating and communicating images of experiences of various kinds, and thus in providing insight into the minds and lives of others as well as into experiences that surpass normal human perception.

---

11 In some contexts, the term is used of concepts that are not perceptible to the senses: see Long (1996a: 271).
12 Augustine, *On the Trinity* 8.6.9: see O'Daly (1987: 117).

Creating images

The area in which mental imagery is most fully discussed by ancient authors is that of vivid language. While Augustine spoke about the mental processes involved in simply naming an entity and Aristides was able to rely on the existence of a memory image in the minds of his addressees which he could then exploit, it was more often necessary to use words to conjure up a scene in the listener's mind. This ability of language (something which is often neglected in modern literary criticism with its emphasis on formal phenomena) had various names in antiquity: *enargeia, euidentia, diatupōsis, hupotupōsis, ekphrasis* and *descriptio*. It was seen as belonging to various types of written and oral communication, oratory, poetry and historiography in particular,[13] but it was orators, in composing practical manuals on how to move and persuade an audience, who discussed this powerful effect in the greatest detail and who gave instructions on how to achieve it.

One of the richest sources on mental imagery and its interaction with the word is the work of the first-century CE Roman orator Quintilian. Quintilian distilled his considerable experience as a speaker and as a teacher (to the Emperor Domitian's nephews, among others) into the 12 books of his *Training of the Orator*. His most revealing discussion of the relationship between sight and words comes in the sixth book of this work where he is talking about the emotions and how to harness them in a speech. My interest in his discussions lies in the fact that Quintilian was not speculating about abstract principles but giving very practical advice to his readers about what worked (and what did not work) in front of an audience.

The particular problem that Quintilian needed to address was that emotion was a vital aspect of rhetorical effectiveness even though, in court cases, the Roman orator was usually speaking as an advocate for someone else. This was a very different situation from that of Classical Athens, where victims of crime brought their own cases before the court and spoke for themselves, as did defendants (even if both may have had professional help in composing their speeches). It was relatively easy to show emotion when speaking about the injustices suffered (though, even then, not everyone was equally gifted in expressing their own emotions and inducing others to share them). The fact that, in the Roman system, the speaker was nearly always at one remove from the crime made it vitally important to find artificial ways of expressing emotion with conviction, like an actor. For Quintilian, this is where mental images – which he refers to by the Greek term *phantasiai*, as well as the Latin *uisiones* – come in: they serve both to arouse emotion in the speaker and to evoke mental images and the appropriate emotions and virtual sensations in the listener, bringing about seeing (and feeling) through the sense of hearing. This aim of "turning listeners into spectators" was identified as the effect of *ekphrasis* in the Greek rhetorical exercises (*progymnasmata*) that provided a practical introduction to all the skills needed by the future orator, including that of making the audience "see".[14]

---

13 See Zanker (1981); Manieri (1998); Hirsch-Luipold (2002); Zangara (2007); Webb (2009a).
14 This formulation is used by Nicolaus (probably fifth century CE) in his *Progymnasmata*. The text is to be found in Felten (1913), translations in Kennedy (2003); an appendix in Webb (2009a) offers both the Greek text and a translation. For the underlying idea of turning the hearing audience into "viewers", see Felten (1913: 68, 70) and Webb (2009a: 203–5).

Quintilian starts by referring to the mental images (*phantasiai, uisiones*) "by means of which images (*imagines*) of absent things are represented to the mind with the result that we seem to see them with our eyes (*cernere oculis*) and to be in their presence" (*Training of the Orator* 6.2.29).[15] Quintilian speaks (as he does elsewhere in discussing mental images and the imagination) as if this experience was common to everyone and, in the passage that follows, he uses the phenomenon of the idle daydreams of students of rhetoric (dreams of travelling, fighting, addressing crowds or owning vast wealth) to make his point (*Training of the Orator* 6.2.30). This is a natural ability, he explains, which the effective orator needs to be able to harness and develop. Again we can see a link between mental images (and these *uisiones* are unmistakably visual in nature) and speech, which is developed by Quintilian in two closely interconnected but distinct directions. The first relates to the speaker's own involvement in the case in question (and does not involve speech), while the second relates to his task of verbally communicating a particular vision of things to his audience and inducing them to share this vision.

When talking about a murder, for example, the speaker should play through in his imagination a sort of virtual film of the brutal act. Quintilian describes how the orator should have "before his eyes" (*in oculis* – i.e. in his mind's eye) everything that could be credibly thought to have happened (*Training of the Orator* 6.2.31). He goes on to describe the scene that might play itself out in the orator's imagination in a series of dramatic rhetorical questions (6.2.31):

> *non percussor ille subitus erumpet? non expauescet circumuentus, exclamabit uel rogabit uel fugiet? non ferientem, non concidentem uidebo? non animo sanguis et pallor et gemitus, extremus denique expirantis hiatus insidet?*

> Will the murderer not spring out suddenly? Will the victim not be terrified when he finds himself surrounded and cry out or plead or run away? Will I not see the blow and the victim falling to the ground? Will his blood, his pallor, his dying groans not be impressed on my mind?

From the perspective of the orator, then, it is possible to see how the manipulation of his own mental images could prompt an intense emotional identification with (in this case) the victim. The sense of empathy created by the simulacrum of presence is twofold: the orator puts himself in the place of an eyewitness but it is the suffering of the victim that is clearly evoked.

The remarkable feature in Quintilian's discussion here is precisely the link between this virtual film of the murder and the orator's hypothetical speech: by simply verbalizing the process, Quintilian finds himself in the very act of communicating his image, and thus his sense of involvement, to his imaginary audience. He steps out of the role of distanced commentator, describing in didactic terms how

---

15 There is an ambiguity in Quintilian's use of the terms *phantasia* and *uisio* here: although the use of the plural would seem to imply that he is speaking about individual mental images, the rest of the sentence suggests that he is thinking of them as a type of faculty which enables the creation of such images.

emotional involvement can be achieved, and back into the role of orator in mid-flow, able not only to feel involved himself but also to work the same effect on his listeners through the vividness (*enargeia*) of his speech. It seems that there is no clear distinction in his mind between imagining a scene, putting that image into words and communicating it to a third party; moreover, it would appear all but impossible to give an outsider's account of this kind of image that does not itself participate in the process of visualizing. The author of the Imperial Greek treatise *On the Sublime*, conventionally attributed to Longinus (but who may have been a contemporary of Quintilian),[16] takes even further this conflation of the stages of imagining, verbalizing and prompting an image in the mind of the listener, when he offers his own definition of the term *phantasia*. He explains that he will use the term to designate what happens "when under the influence of inspiration and emotion you seem to see what you are talking about and place it before the eyes of your listeners".[17] For the specialists of ancient rhetoric, then, mental images, their verbal communication, and their impact on the audience were difficult to separate. The whole was conceived as a single process binding together speaker and audience in a shared process of imagining.

This same sense of presence was sought by readers of all kinds of texts in antiquity, including historiography. For Plutarch, for example, Thucydides' battle narratives were understood to show him as a master of this type of effect, inducing in his readers an impression that they were there alongside the people of the past and, most importantly, inducing them to feel similar emotions (*Moralia* 347a). Although our authors place great emphasis on the visual nature of such scenes and on their emotional impact, it is clear from their examples that the processes they are describing are more complex.

Quintilian's discussion and its echoes in pseudo-Longinus and others reveal several different aspects of mental images and their verbal expressions. For one thing, it is clear that the mind is not simply a passive receiver of impressions but can use the knowledge acquired through sensation to arrive at fresh images of things that have never been seen by the listener. Second, it is possible to transmit these images, through words, to a listener. Third, the sense of vision is far from being the only sense involved.

Regarding the last of these points, it is worth adding that many *uisiones* come complete with sounds or tactile sensations. The *Imagines* of Philostratus, to take just one striking example, foreground this multi-sensory aspect of *phantasia* by attributing to the paintings in the imaginary gallery the ability to appeal to these different senses.[18] Most importantly, there is a bodily sense of presence – of being in the same space as the thing or event described. Augustine alludes to this in relation to knowledge acquired through perception when he explains that his corporeal presence in

---

16 The treatise is usually dated to the first century CE: for a supposed later dating, see M. Heath (1999).
17 Pseudo-Longinus' definition here is a good example of the fluidity of ancient terminology: the author is clearly discussing the same phenomenon as Quintilian, but uses the term *phantasia* to designate the whole process rather than the mental images alone. In the same passage, pseudo-Longinus also shows that he is aware of the specialized Stoic definition of *phantasia* as "thought productive of speech", as he cites this as an alternative sense of the word to the one he is using.
18 See Manieri (1999); Squire (2009: 416–27; 2013a).

Carthage is the source of the *phantasia* of the city that is imprinted in his mind.[19] When Quintilian's orator imagines the scene of the crime, then, his understanding is not purely emotional. He gains through his act of placing himself within the scene an empathy that extends to the knowledge of what it might be like to witness or even experience such a crime.

The appeal to the imagination therefore encouraged readers to put themselves in the *place* of another person, both literally and metaphorically. Despite the repeated emphasis on *sight* in the discussions of *enargeia*, it is striking how often the spatial relations between viewer and viewed (or imaginer and imagined) are invoked as part of the process. To drive home the point, it is worth turning here to some examples from real speeches from the heyday of Greek oratory in fourth-century BCE Athens. These speeches predate most of the theoretical rhetorical treatises that have survived, but they were the foundation stone on which later theorists built their work.

Lysias, who was praised for his ability to make the people and incidents he talks about in his speeches seem present to the audience, provides many examples of this.[20] As a *metoikos*, a resident foreigner (his family was originally from Sicily), Lysias was not usually allowed to speak in court and instead wrote speeches for Athenians to memorize and use. But a series of particular historical circumstances (that brought about the restoration of democracy in Athens) allowed Lysias to prosecute the man whom he held responsible for the death of his brother under the régime of the Thirty tyrants in 404/3 BCE (in what is now known as speech 12, *Against Eratosthenes*). Here Lysias tells what he himself lived through during the round-up of wealthy metics that led to his brother's summary execution. He does not just give a plain account or simply relate the conversations he had with the tyrants' henchmen but instead gives a very detailed account of the various stages of the action and the locations within which they occurred, as he was taken from his own house to the house of a third party from which he finally managed to escape.

The climax of the story gives an impression of the whole effect. Lysias first recounts his thoughts as he wondered whether to risk an escape attempt or to trust his fate to the unscrupulous character who was responsible for guarding him; he then tells his audience how he fled into the street through three doors while his captors were guarding the entrance to the courtyard (12.8–16). The whole speech builds up suspense, as the listener accompanies Lysias in imagination, hearing his internal deliberations about what he should do (12.15), seeing deft sketches of the behaviour of his enemies ("I asked him if he would be willing to help me for a sum of money, he said he would if the sum was large", 12.9). Similar effects can be found throughout Lysias' speeches, and they certainly add to the *effet de réel* necessary for

---

[19] Augustine, *On the Trinity* 8.6.9: *praesens in ea corpore fui et eam uidi atque sensi memoriaque retinui* ("I was present in [Carthage] in body and saw it and felt it and retained it in memory"). For a broader discussion of "sight and memory", above all in the context of Roman rhetoric, see Elsner & Squire (this volume).

[20] See, in particular, the famous assessment in Dionysius of Halicarnassus, *Lysias* 7: "No one can be so clumsy, difficult to please or slow-witted that he will not feel that he can see what is being shown actually happening and that he is conversing with the characters introduced by the orator as if they were present." For discussion of this passage and others, see Zanker (1981).

persuasion. But they also do much more, making the listeners share the speaker's experience and his perspective on that experience through the use of focalization.

Another passage celebrated by later readers in antiquity is Demosthenes' brief evocation of the region of Phocis after it had been devastated and depopulated by war. This sketch, occupying just a few lines, is cited as an example of *diatupōsis* (another term designating passages that "place before the eyes") and also as a model of *ekphrasis*.[21] Like Lysias in the passage quoted above, he presents this image as something that he himself has witnessed, establishing his own spatial relationship to the sight before he evokes it (Demosthenes 19.65):

> Just now when we were travelling to Delphi, we could not help but see (*horan*) all of it: ruined houses, defensive walls razed to the ground, the land bereft of young men, just women, a few little children and some pitiful old men.

In both, we can notice the focus on a few salient details and, most importantly, the way in which the speaker situates himself in each case within the scene described (Lysias as an active participant making his way through the house, Demosthenes as an observer passing through).[22] By situating themselves as participants or observers, these speakers invite us to step into their shoes in our own imagination, seeing the scene not simply as in a distanced, disembodied photograph, but as if we were present ourselves within the same space, in bodily contact with the place and its happenings. This embodied perception mimics the original experience of the viewer, but it may well be more than a simple question of reproducing a "point of view". Recent work on the ways in which the brain perceives objects (and, more importantly still, remembers them) emphasizes the importance of our physical relationship to the object remembered (not just the visual stimuli in isolation).[23] These vivid evocations of situated events thus mimic both experience and memory and were a powerful tool in creating empathy and insight, giving a sense of contact with the experiences of another person. The listener does not simply learn facts about what happened (or may have happened) but experiences them in a quasi-physical way.[24] Although sight remains the chief sense appealed to and spoken by theorists, it is clear that all the senses are potentially involved and that these virtual sensations play a cognitive role.

---

21 For the scholion and Nicolaus passage, see Dilts (1983–6: 2.28, 157c) and Felten (1913: 71 = Webb 2009a: 204–5). The passage from Demosthenes' speech seems to have gained almost instant fame: within a few years of its deliver, Demosthenes' rival, Aeschines, included his own version of it in a speech (*Against Ctesiphon* 157), this time evoking the destruction of Thebes; cf. Webb (2009b).

22 In this particular case, the choice of the imperfect tense for the verb "to travel" and of the present infinitive with its imperfective aspect emphasize the act of witnessing as *process*.

23 See Damasio (2012: 132).

24 The insights offered by cognitive science, which suggest that imagining an action involves the same parts of the brain as actually performing that action, suggest that the association between imagination and actual experience is not so fanciful. See Jeannerod (2006: esp. 23–44), who argues that "the mental action can be considered as a *simulation* of the physical action" (24, his italics).

Imagining things unseen

This role of mental images in enabling individuals to understand things that they have not experienced themselves through a form of virtual embodied perception raises a further question. If mental images are the result of traces of sensation, how do we summon up images of things that we have not seen? The link between Augustine's mental image of Carthage and his own experience is clear, but the mental image of the murder that is summoned up and put into words by Quintilian is rather less likely to have been the direct result of his personal experience. Augustine has the answer to this question. His explanation of his own mental image of Carthage is part of a contrast between our knowledge of things that we have perceived through the senses and our knowledge of things that we have not seen. This category is represented by Alexandria – a city that Augustine claims not to have visited himself, but which he has heard about from others. Augustine explains that, in the absence of direct knowledge, he has shaped (*fingere*) an image in his mind as best he could (*finxi animo imaginem eius quam potui*). Like the Greek *phantasia*, the Latin word *imago* does not necessarily mean a visual representation, but Augustine strongly suggests that he has an image, rather than an abstract concept, in mind when he goes on to say that if he were able to "bring out" (*profero*) this *imago* of Alexandria and place it before the eyes (*ad oculos*) of someone who knew the city, he would be astonished if they said that it resembled the real sight.

Augustine's example is especially valuable because it shows how new mental images could be put together out of existing knowledge and be used to stand for things or concepts of which the individual had no direct experience. The verb used by Augustine here (*fingere*) is significant, as it means, like the Greek *plassō*, to "model" – to make a new shape from existing material (hence lying at the root of our English term "fiction").[25] Old images can therefore be marshalled, transformed and put together in fresh combinations to produce an image that has no direct basis in sense perception but which can still be a valuable tool "to think with".

This all helps, I think, to explain the unspoken steps in the process that leads Quintilian to come up with a convincing image of a murder that he has not witnessed himself.

One key element in Quintilian's account of how he uses imagery to arouse emotion in himself and in his listeners is his advice to imagine "what might *credibly* have happened" (*omnia quae … accidisse credibile est*: *Training of the Orator* 6.2.31). The image of the murder is a composite made from sensual knowledge of analogous events, and informed by common expectations of what might be expected to happen in such a case. In fact, Quintilian's image of the murder corresponds in several details to an example from a contemporary Greek textbook.[26] The image therefore uses stock material, familiar to both the speaker and his audience, which corresponded to images they had acquired from culture and from experience.

None of this, however, is made explicit by Quintilian. Although his *Training of the Orator* is the fullest source on the production and reception of vivid language, it

---

25 Cf. Romm (1990); on the Latin vocabulary, see Sznajder (2013).
26 Theon, *Progymnasmata*, 109.1–11 discussing the things one can say about a murderer in the exercise of common place. For the text – with translation – see Webb (2009a: 77).

remains, like all rhetorical manuals, essentially *practical* in its orientation and tends to focus on the effect rather than its philosophical implications. Once again, it is Augustine who makes things more explicit when he explains how he can imagine what he has never seen, so we will look again briefly at his discussion before returning to Quintilian. The distinction that Augustine makes between his *phantasia* of Carthage, derived from sensation and exact in every particular, and his invented *phantasma* of Alexandria seems to echo the distinction made by the Stoics between accurate representations of things and the misleading *phantasma* that derives from misperception (as when the mad Orestes saw his sister Electra and took her for one of the Furies pursuing him in Euripides, *Orestes* 255–7).[27] Augustine and the orators both seem to attribute a different status to these invented images: for Augustine, they have a heuristic function, enabling us to move onwards from knowledge of the appearance of physical objects acquired through the senses to knowledge of the appearance of things we have never seen. An important aspect of this heuristic function is the clear-sighted recognition that the *phantasma* is precisely that: as Augustine states, he knows perfectly well that his *phantasma* probably does not bear a precise resemblance to the city itself. In the immediate context of the argument Augustine distinguishes true knowledge of the just man from both of these sense-derived images, but earlier on in the same book he had explained how our experience of life (through our own lives) and death (through seeing others die) could inform our understanding of the Christian Resurrection (*On the Trinity* 8.5.8).

For an orator like Quintilian, concerned above all with persuasion rather than with distinguishing true impressions from false ones, what was important was that the images conceived and transmitted be *like* truth, that is, that they conform to expectations. This enabled the listeners (who were certainly aware, in the context of a court case, that any images were only likenesses) to respond easily by drawing on their own knowledge in turn, as we see Quintilian himself doing in his remarkable reading of a verbal sketch by Cicero of the corrupt governor, Verres. Cicero describes in a few words the position (on the shore), dress (a Greek-style cloak and long robe) and posture (leaning on his girlfriend) and, from this, Quintilian the reader (or listener) builds up a mental image containing details (including the emotional responses of imagined internal observers) that are not mentioned by Cicero (*Against Verres* 8.3.64–5).

Quintilian thus embroiders the details presented by the written text as he creates his own vision of the scene in his imagination. Such reactions, which Quintilian presents as entirely normal, are at least partly enabled by the general nature of the image conceived by the orator and put into words. There is a paradox here in that a certain amount of specific detail was clearly necessary to achieve the desired effect. But there also needed to be a sufficient degree of generalization, or openness, to allow the audience to conceive and elaborate a corresponding image. This generalized quality has further implications for, as Dorothea Frede has noted of Aristotle's conception of *phantasia*, the mental images deriving from sensation can possess a degree of generality that explains their role in reflection and understanding: "Thanks

---

27 On the Stoic use of this passage, see Sextus Empiricus, *Against the Mathematicians* 7.242–6 (= Long & Sedley 1987: 39 G).

to imagination ... we get a fuller picture of a situation or a sequence of situations."[28] *Phantasiai*, at one remove from the objects from which they derive, may not correspond with complete accuracy to any particular entity and may not be "true" in any strict sense of the word, but this does not mean that they have no epistemological value.

Transcendent visions

Whereas the images conjured up by orators had to fall within the bounds of credibility and needed only to create the necessary impact during the moment of the trial, poets and visual artists had far more license to evoke visions of phenomena beyond normal human experience and perception. In such cases the imagination might provide insight not only into situations that exist in the physical world but even into entities and events that belong outside, particularly in the domain of the divine. It is sometimes claimed, on the basis of a passage in Philostratus' *Life of Apollonius* (6.19), that the conception of *phantasia* as a faculty able to provide access to things that have not been perceived directly through the bodily senses – that is, as a creative type of imagination – was an innovation of Philostratus' period (the late second and early third centuries CE). It is true that Apollonius, within Philostratus' text, sets up a contrast between *mimesis* ("imitation"), which will produce (*dēmiourgēsei*) what it has seen, and *phantasia*, which is able to represent what it has not seen (*kai ho mē eiden*). However, from what we have just seen, it would appear that this creative form of *phantasia* may not be such a revolutionary idea. Instead, it results from the same sort of effort of re-combination and adjustment of knowledge previously acquired from the senses and from tradition, as disseminated in text as image, as did Quintilian's account of the murder.[29] This is suggested by the fact that Apollonius' *phantasia* "hypothesizes [what it has not seen] by reference to reality" (or, more literally, "by reference to what is": ὑποθήσεται γὰρ αὐτὸ πρὸς τὴν ἀναφορὰν τοῦ ὄντος). What is different is the status of the end result: Apollonius' discussion relates here to cult images, i.e. representations of persons generally agreed to exist but on a different level to that inhabited by mere mortals.

A similar power is attributed to poetry by the author of the treatise *On the Sublime*. Just after the definition of *phantasia* mentioned above, the author cites some passages from tragedy which evoked precisely such sights beyond normal human experience. The first, drawn from Euripides' *Orestes*, is an evocation of the appearance and actions of the Furies voiced by Orestes himself in his madness (Euripides, *Orestes* 255–7):

ὦ μῆτερ, ἱκετεύω σε, μὴ 'πίσειέ μοι
τὰς αἱματωποὺς καὶ δρακοντώδεις κόρας·
αὗται γάρ, αὗται πλησίον θρώσκουσί μου.

---

28 D. Frede (1992: 286). Compare Hirsch-Luipold (2002) on Plutarch's thinking about images.
29 See Babut (1985): Babut argues that this passage does not represent a break from the idea of *phantasia* as a mental image left by sensation, since these images were always understood as liable to give rise to new conceptions through various mental manipulations; cf. Halliwell (2002: 308–9).

> Mother, I beg you, do not rouse up against me
> These gore-faced and maidens with their snakes!
> Here they are, here they are rushing upon me!

The importance of this passage for us lies in the fact that the sight of the Furies to which Orestes responds is an illusion. In Euripides' play, in contrast to Aeschylus' *Eumenides*, the Furies are a figment of Orestes' imagination: in reality he is looking at his sister, Electra, but in his imagination he sees his mother's avengers. The words therefore are understood to portray the content of the character's mind as he expresses verbally what he (thinks he) sees, drawing the spectators of the play and the other characters in the drama into the world as he sees it (and here again we can notice the importance of the spatial relationship between Orestes and his pursuers that injects added urgency into his exclamation).

As we saw above, for Stoics this was a textbook example of false perception (*phantasma*) in that Orestes took his sister Electra for one of the Furies – or Erinyes – who were pursuing him.[30] Pseudo-Longinus, however, takes a different approach, claiming that the scene has further value as a sign of the poet's own powers of visualization (*On the Sublime* 15.2):

> ἐνταῦθ' ὁ ποιητὴς αὐτὸς εἶδεν Ἐρινύας, ὃ δ' ἐφαντάσθη μικροῦ δεῖν θεάσασθαι καὶ τοὺς ἀκούοντας ἠνάγκασεν.
>
> Here the poet has seen the Erinyes himself and has almost made the listeners see what he imagined (*phantazomai*).

It is difficult to know in what sense we are intended to understand the verbs translated as "see" here. The first is *eiden*, which is etymologically related to the verb meaning "to know" (*oida*), and the relative clause that follows, with its use of the verb *phantazomai*, indicates that the act of vision is an internal one. The poet has created in his own mind the knowledge-through-vision that the character Orestes might have had and used it to imagine the words that a character in such an eventuality might utter, just as Quintilian's orator was supposed to do. The audience, in turn, become spectators (*theatai*): the formulation used here is almost identical to that used by Nicolaus to describe the effect of *ekphrasis* in making "listeners into spectators".[31] If there is a difference in nuance here between the poet's knowing seeing and the audience's spectatorship, it is perhaps related to the theatrical context in which the audience are stunned by what the poet induces them to imagine (for pseudo-Longinus, *ekplēxis* – being struck – is the result of *phantasia* in poetry).

Pseudo-Longinus' remarks here also add a further type of insight to those offered by the internal visions of *phantasia*: the reader (if not the audience caught up in the moment of the performance and experiencing its effects) gains knowledge of the contents of the writer's or speaker's mind, for the ability to describe and evoke implies

---

30 On this passage, see Labarrière (2006: 12).
31 Nicolaus, *Progymnasmata* (= Felten 1913: 68); text and translation also in Webb (2009a: 203–4).

(working backwards up the chain) the ability to imagine, which in turn depends on some type of experience.

If seeing is knowing, it seems that the sight in question is not necessarily the physical sense: the mental images or *phantasiai* derived from sight and (perhaps most importantly) the fresh imaginings based on experience which go further than a particular experience (whether they are of a murder or of an escape from the enemy's clutches or of a divine being) can offer access to knowledge of a different type. They can help us to understand phenomena that are beyond the normal grasp of an individual human's perception, whether they be the experiences of another person (as experienced by that person), experience of the divine or (as implied by pseudo-Longinus) of transcendental phenomena.

A little further on, pseudo-Longinus discusses a passage from Euripides' play *Phaethon* (which has only come down to us in fragments). Commenting on the messenger speech that told how Phaethon mounted his father's chariot and, ignoring his father's frantic instructions, lost control and plunged to his death, the critic asks his reader (15.4):

ἆρ' οὐκ ἂν εἴποις, ὅτι ἡ ψυχὴ τοῦ γράφοντος συνεπιβαίνει τοῦ ἅρματος καὶ συγκινδυνεύουσα τοῖς ἵπποις συνεπτέρωται; οὐ γὰρ ἄν, εἰ μὴ τοῖς οὐρανίοις ἐκείνοις ἔργοις ἰσοδρομοῦσα ἐφέρετο, τοιαῦτ' ἄν ποτε ἐφαντάσθη.

Would you not say that the writer's soul has mounted the chariot as well and shared in the dangers? For if it had not been carried along keeping pace with those actions in the heavens he would never have imagined (*phantazomai*).

The claim is not (I think) to be taken literally but it shows how closely the capacity to imagine-and-place-before-the-eyes-of-the-audience (identified by pseudo-Longinus as *phantasia*) is linked to the *idea* of sense perception. To be able to put across these events with such vividness that the audience see them too, the soul of the poet must have somehow experienced them. What is particularly striking here is the word-picture that pseudo-Longinus himself creates of the poet being present on the chariot with Phaethon for, once again, the visual imagination is closely linked to the idea of bodily presence (note the repeated preposition *sun*, meaning "along with").

Conclusion

Looking back, then, we can see that Lucian's striking claim in his *On the Hall* offered us a very simple model of the relationship between sight, perception and words: the beauty present in the hall flows in through the eyes and fashions speech in its image, which is then sent out in the form of words. The speaker in this model serves as a channel through which the sight flows. Given Lucian's habitual trickiness, it is tempting to see this as a deliberate irony. What he does signal, as we saw, is the lack of strict boundary between perceiver and perceived and the widespread idea (so widespread that it is not always fully articulated) that the mind is a receptacle for sense impressions.

The other sources examined show that many other phenomena may come into play. A stored image, along with its emotional associations, may be revived and revivified by words (as Aelius Aristides does), or it may serve as a basis for a speaker to transmit his own experience to an audience (as do Lysias and Demosthenes) who, through the vividness of the resulting speech, conceive an analogous image in their minds. "Image", however, is a slightly misleading term: although vision is always the prime sense, what the reader or listener "witnesses" in his or her mind is a fully rounded and embodied virtual experience, one which brings with it knowledge, both intellectual and sensory, of the experience.

We have also seen how the images stored in the mind can be just a starting point for the elaboration of new images which, according to the context and aims of the speaker or author, can place them in and bring them to understand new situations and entities that they have not seen. These might be occurrences in the real world of the listener/viewer (a murder, a dramatic escape from danger), in which case he or she gains access to knowledge, to the experiences of another and, more than that, is made to all-but-live through these experiences. Alternatively, the mental image, built on sense perception and evoked by speech, has the capacity to make present things that do not exist in this world (Furies, the chariot of the sun, etc.), but that are accessible to the imagination.

11

SIGHT AND CHRISTIANITY
Early Christian attitudes to seeing

Jane Heath

"If Christ has not been raised, then vain is our proclamation, and vain your faith" (1 Corinthians 15:14). Writing in the mid-first century CE, before the term "Christianity" had even been coined, Paul sums up one of Christianity's central claims. From his perspective, the resurrection is a defining event: without it, the Christian message would be null and void.[1]

Paul's encapsulation of the grounds for Christian faith is well known. Less widely observed, however, is that the resurrection is not just the event but also the *sight* that defined Christianity. From the very beginnings, the resurrection was known and verified through the sense of vision. Indeed, Paul's words on the centrality of the resurrection are closely preceded by his declaration of the tradition which he had received and passed on as the content of his gospel, namely (1 Corinthians 15:3–8):

> that Christ died for our sins according to the Scriptures, that he was buried, and that he has been raised on the third day according to the Scriptures; that he *was seen* (*ōphthē*) by Cephas, then by the Twelve, and then that he *was seen* (*ōphthē*) by over five hundred brothers all at once (of whom most still remain, but some have fallen asleep); and that he then *was seen* (*ōphthē*) by James, then by all the apostles; and last of all, as if by one untimely born, that he *was seen* (*ōphthē*) also by me.

According to Paul's testimony, the appearances of the resurrected Christ, eyewitnessed by a series of different spectators, underpin the tradition of faith: the visual nature of the resurrection plays a key role in the significance of Christ's death and resurrection. Similarly, since to the early Christians Jesus' resurrection was a historical event, their narrative accounts of his life, death and resurrection drew on Greek forms of historiography and biography,[2] privileging the idea of autopsy.[3] Like earlier Greek texts, the single-authored double-work Luke-Acts and the gospel of John

---

1 The centrality of the resurrection to Christianity is consistent with the witness of the New Testament, but was disputed in the second century (as it has been in some modern liberal forms of Christianity). For discussion, see e.g. J. M. Robinson (1982); Lalleman (1996); Bobonich (2001). This chapter begins from the resurrection as a way to explore Christianity's distinctive thinking about sight; for a different approach to Christianity and the senses – focussing above all on the sense of smell – see Toner (2015).
2 Cf. Luke 1:1–4, with Burridge (1992); Byrskog (2000).
3 See Marincola (2003: 63–127). On the importance of "autopsy" within ancient historiography, see

(both late first/early second century CE) give particular prominence to eyewitness authority (Luke 1:2; John 1:14; 19:35 and *passim*).[4]

From the Christian point of view, the sequence of resurrection appearances described by Paul is a set of visual events without close analogies, for Jesus' resurrection is (in historical terms) strictly unique.[5] But such appearances could not be described except in the language of epiphanic seeing familiar from contemporary cultural discourse, in which Graeco-Roman ideas about sight had already shaped Hellenistic Jewish traditions.[6] How early Christians engaged with this powerful, strange and properly indescribable visual encounter of their risen Lord will be the subject of the first two sections of this chapter, which examine both the resurrection appearances and the closely allied issue of what it meant to "see" Jesus in the flesh. The chapter's third and fourth parts then consider how Christian faith shaped distinctive attitudes to sight, focussing on the two central commands of discipleship: love (more specifically, Christian *agapē*), and suffering even unto death. Together, I hope that these thoughts will offer the beginnings of a systematic analysis of sight's importance in the early church: long before this religion acquired a strong visible presence in the form of material images and objects, the sense of sight was endowed with special theological significance.

Faith through eyewitnesses: Christ's resurrection

"Am I not free? Am I not an apostle? Have I not *seen* Jesus, our Lord?" (1 Corinthians 9:1). With these questions Paul challenges his Corinthian readership: the Corinthians must appreciate, he suggests, his special authority to teach among them, something that is divinely ordained through his actual *seeing* of Jesus. Paul's visual encounter with Jesus is in fact the most frequently narrated episode of seeing within the New Testament. Paul mentions it at least twice,[7] and in Acts it is told on three separate occasions. The encounter had dramatic consequences in Paul's own life, converting him from a zealous persecutor of the Christians (on behalf of the Pharisees) to the renowned "apostle to the gentiles". In this role, Paul became one of the

---

Squire's introduction to this volume; one of the most important passages – and one well known by Imperial Greek writers – was Thucydides, *History of the Peloponnesian War* 1.22.

4 See e.g. Lincoln (2002); Rothschild (2004: 213–90); Bauckham (2006).

5 There were nonetheless comparanda: in Judaism, ascensions such as those of Moses and Elijah were believed to have been seen, and the early church found in them prototypes for Jesus' own ascension. People were raised from the dead even during the time of Jesus' ministry. In the Graeco-Roman world, there were many myths about those who descended to the underworld and returned alive (Orpheus, Odysseus, Alcestis, Persephone, Protesilaus, Aeneas etc.: cf. Turner in this volume). But none of these approaches the Christian claim to have witnessed Jesus' *resurrection* to a new kind of body and a new kind of life, and one in which humanity is to share. For further discussion, see Wright (2003: 32–206).

6 On "sight and the gods" in the Greek and Roman cultural imagination, see Platt (this volume). For the erosion of the dichotomy between "Judaism" and "Hellenism", see Hengel (1974); Engberg-Pedersen (2001), along with Jane Heath (2005; 2013a) in the context of sight specifically. On Christian appropriations of Jewish and Graeco-Roman discourses of seeing, cf. M. M. Mitchell (2004); Rowe (2005); Balch (2008); Nasrallah (2008; 2010); Squire (2009: 19–23); Platt (2011: 22–3); Jane Heath (2013b).

7 1 Corinthians 9:1; 15:8. Also relevant are Galatians 1:16; 1 Corinthians 13:12; 2 Corinthians 3:18, 4:6. For a "maximalist" interpretation of allusions to Paul's Christophany, see Kim (1984).

most widely travelled and influential missionaries in Christian history; indeed letters by Paul (or else traditionally attributed to him) comprise more than half of the documents in the New Testament canon.

The visual encounter between Paul and Jesus would change Paul's life – and through it, the course of western history. Yet the encounter was not a matter of seeing in the way that one sees letters written on a page. Though Paul writes simply "Have I not seen (*heoraka*) Jesus, our Lord?", there is no claim that he ever saw Jesus *before* Jesus died. Nor would having done so have had such dramatic consequences. Seeing the risen Lord, rather, was by all accounts a distinctive kind of seeing. The three versions of Paul's visual encounter with him in Acts all include a resplendent light – something that literally leaves him blind; in one, it is implied that Paul saw Jesus' form (Acts 9:7); in another, Jesus himself uses the language of epiphany (*ōphthēn*) so that Paul describes the event as a "heavenly vision" (*ouranios optasia*) (Acts 26:16, 19). Such epiphanic phraseology recurs in Paul's own list of resurrection appearances.[8] But it is particularly prominent at the start of Acts, relating how Jesus "presented himself alive after his suffering with many proofs, *being seen* (*optanomenos*) by them and speaking things about the kingdom of God" (Acts 1:3). The rare verb for "being seen" here (*optanomai*) is cognate with the word for "vision" (*optasia*); it is the same verb as Moses uses to recall God's reputation for *being seen* with the eyes in Israel, and on that basis to ask Him to continue protecting them (Numbers 14:14). In line with Greek and Roman accounts of divine epiphany, Christ's visual appearance is not only made credible through emphasis on autopsy, but occurs within a longer Jewish tradition of visionary seeing. "Epiphanic citation" of earlier visual encounters likewise helps to make sense of later narratives.[9] For those attuned to pagan literature, the many verbal and thematic connections between Acts and the *Bacchae* would likely encourage comparison between Jesus' appearances and Dionysus' epiphanies, coaxing readers by implicit comparison to trust the risen Lord's divine power.[10]

Luke and John further develop the sensory dimensions of encountering the resurrected Christ. Telling how two of Jesus' companions met him on the Road to Emmaus, Luke explains that "their eyes were overcome (οἱ δὲ ὀφθαλμοὶ αὐτῶν ἐκρατοῦντο) so as not to recognize him"; when Jesus spoke to them, they likewise remained melancholically "sullen in their eyes (*skythrōpoi*)". The companions tell Jesus the sorry tale of the women finding the empty tomb, seeing (*heōrakenai*) the "vision (*optasia*) of angels", and of others going afterward who found the same, "but *him* they did not see (*ouk eidon*)". At this point, the risen Christ, visually present all along, explains to them the Law and the Prophets; reclining with them in the village – taking bread, blessing it, breaking it – he gives the bread to them, "and their eyes were opened (*diēnoichthēsan hoi ophthalmoi*) and they recognized him, and he himself vanished (*aphantos egeneto*) from them" (Luke 24:13–32).

---

8 *Ōphthē* + dative: "was seen by" or "appeared to": the point is discussed in Origen, *Homilies on Luke* 3.
9 For "epiphanic autopsy", see Platt (2011: esp. 7, 12, 237, 251–2, 256); for "epiphanic citation", see Platt (2011: 8, 133, 136–7, 383, 392). For further discussion of the relationship between Paul and Graeco-Roman epiphany, cf. Versnel (1987); Brenk (1994).
10 For discussion, see Moles (2006).

Unlike the angels, the risen Jesus is not immediately recognized in this story. But unlike an ordinary, earthly companion, he disappears from sight the moment he is known. Throughout, sight remains the crucial sense in depicting the moment of recognition. As with Graeco-Roman epiphanic accounts and visual representations, this is a tantalizing, paradoxical kind of viewing that depends on instability between presence and absence, visibility and invisibility, recognition and misrecognition.[11]

John's accounts of Jesus' resurrection appearances exploit motifs similar to Luke's, even though they appear in the context of rather different stories. Like Luke, John highlights the sense of sight repeatedly: the disciple who ran first to the tomb *sees* (*blepei*) the grave-clothes lying there, Peter follows and also *sees* (*theōrei*) them and the other disciple *saw and believed* (*eiden kai episteusen*). Likewise, in the garden, Mary *sees* (*theōrei*) two angels, then turns and *sees* (*theōrei*) Jesus – even though she did not know his identity, thinking him to be a gardener (it is only when Jesus calls her by name that she turns and addresses him as "my teacher"). Later, when the disciples are in a locked room, Jesus suddenly stands in their midst and shows (*edeixen*) them his hands and his side so that the disciples are said to rejoice when they *see* (*idontes*) the Lord. John's story of "Doubting Thomas" further emphasizes the visual stakes. When Thomas (absent from the earlier disciples' gathering) receives only their message that "we have seen (*heōrakamen*) the Lord", he declares that unless he sees (*idō*) the imprint of nails in his hands and puts his finger into the imprint of nails and his hand into his side, he will not believe. A little later, Jesus appears once again – and again in a locked room – offering Thomas the opportunity to do just as he had proposed. John does not tell us whether Thomas actually did grope into Jesus' wounded side (availing himself of the sense of touch to confirm his vision). But Thomas is said to have uttered a cry of faith: "My Lord and My God".[12] This provides the context for Jesus' famous comment to Thomas: "Is it because you have seen (*heōrakas*) me that you have believed? Blessed are those who have not seen (*hoi mē idontes*) and have believed" (John 20:5–29).[13]

In all the accounts discussed here, the appearance of the risen Lord defies normal categories of sense perception. Jesus can be unrecognizable to his close acquaintances at one moment, and yet easily known by sight the next; he can vanish in an instant, or suddenly appear in a locked chamber. What is important, though, is that the senses – and the sensory perceptions of sight in particular – are a primary means by which the reality of his resurrection is tested and established. Whether it is the men on their way to Emmaeus, or the disciples in the sealed room, it is through seeing and even touching Jesus that those who were not expecting him (despite his best efforts to advise them ahead of time) are nonetheless brought to recognize and believe in the risen Christ. Throughout, sight is the sense that dominates these accounts, both in depicting their ambiguities and in asserting their reliability.

How are we to make sense of this Christian reliance on vision? If the epistemic value of sight is rooted in human physiology, the importance of seeing was widely thematized and problematized in classical culture – from historians' emphasis on

---

11 Petridou (2006); Platt (2011); Cioffi (2013).
12 This is also how Domitian (plausibly contemporary with John) demanded to be addressed: Suetonius, *Domitian* 13, cited in e.g. Bruner (2012: 1192).
13 Cf. Most (2005).

autopsy to the heightened visuality of many epiphanic encounters. Crucially, though, the Christian emphasis on eyewitnessing the resurrection (and the importance of those eyewitnesses to Christian faith) engaged this discourse of visual epistemology. Still more importantly, such ocularcentric accounts led to retrospective and prospective reflection about the nature, significance and possibility of seeing Jesus – and indeed of seeing God in seeing Jesus.

Retrospect and prospect: the spectacle of Jesus and the vision of God

"Blessed are your eyes because they see and your ears because they hear. Truly I say to you that many prophets and righteous men longed to see what you see and did not see it, to hear what you hear and did not hear it" (Matthew 13:17, late first century CE). In these words, the Matthean Jesus explains to his close disciples how blessed they are in having insight to understand the deeds they see and the words they hear from him during his ministry. But the words carry a further nuance besides. Jesus, after all, is talking to his disciples face-to-face: their eyes are locked on him at the very moment that he pronounces them blessed for seeing what they see. If Jesus' blessing is focussed on the act of beholding Jesus in the flesh, it raises an important question for later Christian followers: how and why did the spectacle of the earthly Jesus matter?

For Luke, such excitement about seeing Jesus commences long before his mature ministry of word and deed: it begins from the moment he appears from Mary's womb, a baby to be seen and held. According to Luke, angels promised the shepherds that they would find a "sign" (*sēmeion*) – a babe wrapped in swaddling clothes and lying in a manger. The shepherds say to each other, "Let us go to Bethlehem and *see* (*idōmen*) this word/thing (*rhēma*) which has happened", and when they *saw* (*idontes*) they understood about the word/thing (*rhēma*) spoken to them, and they went away praising God about all the things they had heard and *seen* (*eidon*) (Luke 2:12, 15, 17, 20).[14] When Mary and Joseph take the baby to be circumcised in the Temple, they are likewise immediately met by the elderly Simeon, who had received an oracle from the Holy Spirit that "he would not *see* (*idein*) death until he had *seen* (*idēi*) the Lord's anointed". Simeon takes the child into his arms and utters words still prominent in Christian liturgy: "Lord, now lettest thou thy servant depart in peace, according to thy word (*rhēma*), for *mine eyes have seen* (*eidon hoi ophthalmoi mou*) thy salvation, which thou hast promised *before the face* (*kata prosōpon*) *of all people*, a light to lighten the gentiles, and the glory of thy people Israel" (Luke 2:29–32, KJV). The baby himself appears to be the salvation that Simeon sees.

Luke's narrative is framed in such a way as to suggest that seeing Jesus meant more than just seeing a baby: to see the child was to see in the flesh what until then had been promised in words alone; more importantly, it was to see the human being through whom salvation would come for all peoples. But Luke never articulates a doctrine of incarnation in so many words. The situation is very different with John:

---

14 As a Hebraicism, Luke's choice of the word *rhēma* (translated as "word/think") is decidedly ambiguous here.

"The Word (*logos*) was made flesh", to quote the famous beginning of John's gospel (in which the "Word" is the Logos that was in the beginning with God and who was God, through whom all things were made: John 1:1–3, 14). John opens with a much more abstract image of the incarnation. Still, he cannot speak of the incarnation without speaking at once of its imbrication with vision: "The Word became flesh and tabernacled among us, and we *beheld* his glory, glory as of the one and only from the Father, full of grace and truth" (John 1:14). Not only was the incarnation apprehended through sight, but this was how God was made known to humanity, to mortals who could not see God's "Godself": "No-one has ever seen God (except) the only-begotten God [some manuscripts read "son"], who was in the bosom of the Father: he has exegeted (*exēgēsato*) him" (John 1:18). The unusual choice of vocabulary, "exegeted" (*exēgēsato*), assigns Jesus a role of exegete for less knowledgeable viewers. This role was attributed to angels in Jewish literature of apocalyptic visions, but was also prominent in Graeco-Roman accounts of inducting viewers to interpret spectacles of divine truth (by explaining cultic sites, images or experiences).[15]

John's depiction of Jesus' "exegesis" of God during his ministry focusses on the presentation of the words and deeds of God before the eyes of the people. The earlier accounts of Matthew, Mark and Luke, by contrast, offer a more spectacular account of seeing Jesus' body as the site (and sight) of God's glory. The Synoptic gospels tell how Jesus took three disciples (Peter, James and John) up a mountain to be "metamorphosed" before them until his face shone and his garments became radiant. The vocabulary of "metamorphosis" found in Mark (9:2) and Matthew (17:2) invites comparison with pagan stories of metamorphosis (and in a way which Luke's paraphrase may have intended to avoid, stating merely that "his appearance (*eidos*) became other", 9:29).[16] In many apocryphal traditions, the drama of Jesus' shape-shifting bodily quality is accentuated, and nowhere more so than in the apocryphal *Acts of John* (late second/early third century CE), where John recounts how he was called to Jesus' service (*Acts of John* 88–9):[17]

> [Jesus] came to me and to my brother James, saying "I need you; come to me!" And my brother <when he heard> this said: "John, what does he want, this child on the shore who called us?" And I said, "Which child?" And he answered me, "The one who is beckoning to us". And I replied: "Because of the long watch we have kept at sea, you are not seeing well, brother James. Do you not see the man standing there who is handsome, fair and cheerful-looking?" But he said to me, "I do not see that man, my brother. But let us go, and we shall see what this means". And when we had brought the boat *to land* we saw how he also helped us to beach the boat. And as we left the place, wishing to follow him, he appeared to me again as rather

---

15 E.g. Strabo 17.1.29, Dio Chrysostom, *Oration* 12.33; cf. Whitmarsh (2011: 99–100). The *exēgētēs* can also be the *maker* of the image – see Philostratus, *Heroicus* 7.1, with Platt (2011: 235, 244–5); cf. Elsner (1995: 40–6) and Squire & Grethlein (2014) for exegetical viewing in the *Tablet of Cebes*. For the Jewish *angelus interpres*, see Ezekiel 40–48; Zechariah 1–6; Daniel 7–8; 1 Enoch 17–36; 72–82; cf. Melvin (2013).
16 The key text here is Ovid's *Metamorphoses*: cf. McGuckin (1986: 57–65); S. Lee (2009: 25–30).
17 I take my translation from Schneemelcher (Wilson, trans.) (2003: 180).

bald-headed but with a thick flowing beard, but to James as a young man whose beard was just beginning. So we were both puzzled about the meaning of what we had seen.

Over the next few chapters this apocryphal John continues to elaborate the paradoxes and surprises of Jesus' polymorphic body even during the time of his earthly ministry. Some of the shapes taken on by Jesus are typically at odds with those of deities (small and ugly, for instance), while others draw on motifs associated with the divine – never-closing eyes (sometimes associated with Graeco-Roman cult statues), for example, and a focus on his hinder-parts (as when Moses at the Exodus was granted the opportunity to see God's back but not his face: Exodus 33). This dramatic, physical polymorphism contrasts with the depiction of the "Word made flesh" in John's gospel: according to John's gospel, scholars have argued, Jesus' earthly ministry is itself an extended transfiguration, focussed not on the external character of Jesus' body, but on how God is seen and known through him (in the eyes of those who "abide with" him in his words and works).[18]

While the early church took diverse positions on the relationship between the earthly Jesus and God, debates often clustered around ideas of sight and visibility: the very issue of Jesus' bodily form cultivated a new social and religious context for tackling questions of whether and how God could be seen. Christianity's Jewish heritage also plays a key role here. Where Greek and Roman religion routinely emphasized visual encounters with deities through images and epiphanies, in Jewish tradition, the desire to see God had been cherished but rarely consummated. Stories of apocalyptic visions of the divine throne whetted the appetite, but these were vouchsafed only to famous and exceptional prophets (themselves long since dead) like Moses, Ezekiel or Enoch.[19] Philo, the Alexandrian Jewish philosopher (early first century CE), insisted that the name "Israel" meant "the one who sees God".[20] In practice, however, the only occasion when ordinary Israelites might regularly have expected the chance to behold God was if they attended the annual Feast of Tabernacles in Jerusalem, where the display of the sacred vessels was so intensely experienced in the liturgy that it was tantamount to seeing God.[21] For Christian believers, Jesus' appearance demanded fresh reflection on how, to whom and in what circumstances God could become visible to humanity. This swiftly implicated issues of both ethics and eschatology.

As in Graeco-Roman portrayals of divine epiphanies, Christian authors emphasize the importance of the relationship between the one seen and those who were looking at him. Some writers underscored God's accommodation to human eyes in taking

---

18 The classic statement of this is Käsemann (1968). On polymorphism, see P. Foster (2007).
19 E.g. Ezekiel 1; 1–3 Enoch; *Apocalypse of Abraham* etc. The literature on Jewish apocalypticism is vast: see e.g. Gruenwald (1980); Rowland (1982); Halperin (1988). Translations of many relevant primary texts are handily collected in Charlesworth (1983).
20 E.g. *On the Life of Abraham* 57; *On the Preliminary Studies* 51; *On Flight and Finding* 128; *Who is the Heir?* 78; *On the Migration of Abraham* 39; *On the Change of Names* 81; Delling (1984). Note that even in this context, divine law ordained that only healthy Jewish males could participate.
21 See Anderson (2009). However, tracing this to the Second Temple period remains controversial. For the growth in significance of seeing God in Judaism after the destruction of the Temple, see Neis (2013).

flesh, "for if he had not come in the flesh, how would people be able to survive seeing him?" (Barnabas 5.9).[22] Such ideas about the danger of visually experiencing the divine likewise had a related conceptual archaeology in both Jewish and classical traditions: just as God said to Moses, "You cannot see my face, for no-one may see me and live" (Exodus 33:20), Homer observed that "the gods are hard to cope with when seen very clearly" (*Iliad* 20.131).[23] Other authors drew on an old trope in Greek philosophy, where perception, as well as cognition and attraction, is explained through *likeness* (*to homoion*) between subjects and objects.[24] The argument follows that to be able to see Jesus at all, one had to become like him[25] – or at least to be purified in heart (as Jesus put it in the Sermon on the Mount, "Blessed are the pure in heart, for they shall see God": Matthew 5:8). Those who were not pure or holy enough could not see Christ, at least not properly.[26] All of this has an impact on Christian liturgy too. For some, Christian worship invited, indeed even required, all the faithful to "gaze upon the blood of Christ" (1 Clement 7.4).[27] For others, true worship was deemed invisible to all but God (Matthew 6:5–6; *Diognetus* 6.4). Ignatius (early second century CE) speeds to his martyrdom to be fed to the beasts with a related aspiration: "Then I will truly be a disciple of Christ, when the world does not see even my body" (Ignatius, *To the Romans* 4.2).

The longing for a direct vision of God also shaped eschatological hopes of seeing Christ at the world's end. "Now we see through a glass darkly", Paul writes, "but then we will see face-to-face" (1 Corinthians 13:12). Paul's is a mystical image, albeit simultaneously a deeply visual one.[28] But it too is grounded in patterns of life forged in the present, requiring perfection of the kind of knowledge that is rooted in faith, hope and love (1 Corinthians 13:12–13). Those who now behold Christ through the metaphorical looking-glass are being transformed into the very image that they see (2 Corinthians 3:18): they express a physical hope one day to rise from the dead with spiritual bodies, "bearing the image of the heavenly man" (1 Corinthians 15, esp. vv.19, 23, 44–9). At the same time, though, this physical hope takes on a figurative dimension: theirs will be a transformation from a veiled and dim-sighted hard-heartedness to a spiritual life that manifests Christ (2 Corinthians 2:14–4:10).[29]

The ethical imperatives consequent upon seeing and recognizing God's manifestation in Jesus were, in the canonical gospels, focussed on two key commands of discipleship. In John's later gospel, Jesus gives the command to "love one another, as I have loved you" (John 13:34; 15:12, 17). In the Synoptics, Jesus commanded anyone who wished to be a disciple to take up their cross (Luke adds "daily") and follow him (Matthew 16:24//Mark 8:34//Luke 9:23). These central two instructions lead on

---

22 See further Novatian, *The Trinity* 18; Anderson (2009: 187–92).
23 Cf. Feeney (1998: 105).
24 Theophrastus, *On the Senses* 1 (as cited by Peters 1967: 9) lists among those who explain perception in this way Parmenides, Empedocles and Plato.
25 Cf. *Gospel of Philip* 44; *Acts of Thomas* 35–7. For the philosophical trope, see Schneider (1923). For *Gottähnlichkeit* and epiphany, see Cioffi (2013: 6).
26 Cf. Origen, *Homilies on Luke* 3.21. See also Hauck (1988); Coakley (2002).
27 Fisher (1980).
28 Seaford (1984).
29 E.g. Hafemann (1995).

directly to the following two sections of my chapter. For, as we shall see, both commandments had significant implications for the role of sight among early Christians.

Discipleship through love: chastity and the lover's gaze

Right at the beginning of this volume, Michael Squire's introduction emphasized the close relationship between sight and erotics in Graeco-Roman antiquity, arguing that the character of desiring (*eran* in Greek) was widely thematized in relation to the ocular act of looking (*horan*).[30] Within this cultural setting, Jesus' words in the Sermon on the Mount must have had a particular resonance (Matthew 5:28): "You have heard it said, 'Thou shalt not commit adultery'. But I say to you that everyone who looks at a woman so as to desire her has already committed adultery with her in his heart." Jesus' command here works against a Graeco-Roman cultural understanding of vision in which the overwhelming power of Eros/Amor was understood to operate through the eyes: Jesus challenges a power that was both feared and celebrated in beautiful images of Aphrodite, not to mention countless Greek and Roman narratives of irresistible "love at first sight".[31]

Jesus' words on the commandment "Thou shalt not commit adultery" are among the most frequently cited verses of the New Testament in early Christian literature:[32] even where the dominical command was not actually cited, the asceticism that it instructed was celebrated and encouraged through related stories. Among the earliest and most widely circulated is the tale of Thecla, recounted in the *Acts of Paul and Thecla* (second century CE), prominently subverting the pagan celebration of love at first sight.[33] Thecla is the virgin betrothed to Thamyris. And yet, we are told, she used to sit day and night at her window listening (*epi ... thyridos ... ēkouen*) to Paul. Paul's preaching began with Jesus' benediction ("Blessed are the pure in heart, for they shall see (*opsontai*) God": Matthew 5:8=*Acts of Paul* 5), but continued with benedictions of his own (which developed the notion of "purity in heart" through a focus on "purity in flesh").

In the *Acts of Paul and Thecla*, Thecla is depicted as falling in love with Paul, and thus being lost to her betrothed – who is duly outraged at the turn of events. At the same time, the correspondences between these two kinds of love – Thecla's love for the apostle, and her love for the betrothed – are underscored only to draw out their differences. In loving Paul, the sense of sight is for some time avoided: Thecla's longing grows only from hearing Paul's words (*Acts of Paul* 7). Likewise, she sits with downcast eyes (*katō blepousa*) when questioned by her disgruntled mother, all

---

30 See Squire (introduction to this volume); cf. also Nightingale's discussion in this volume of sight and *erōs* in Plato's *Timaeus*, *Republic* and *Phaedrus*.
31 Cf. Donaldson-Evans (1980: 9–26). For "love at first sight", see e.g. Homer, *Iliad* 14.293–5; *Homeric Hymn to Aphrodite* 56–7; Menander, *The Bad-Tempered Man* 50–3; Virgil, *Eclogues* 8.37–41; Propertius 1.1.1–2; Ovid, *Amores* 3.10.25–30; Apuleius, *Metamorphoses* 2.5; Chariton, *Callirhoe* 1.6. On a related topos in Second Sophistic Greek novels, see Cioffi (2013: 25); Chew (2014: 66–7).
32 E.g. Justin, *Apology* 1.15.1, 5; Tertullian, *Modesty* 6.6; Clement of Alexandria, *Miscellanies* 2.14.61.3; *Sentences of Sextus* 12; Origen, *Homilies on the Song of Songs* 4, 12; *Homilies on Joshua* 10; *Homilies on Luke* 2; Novatian, *The Spectacles* 6.4. A search using www.biblindex.mom.fr/ lists 36 citations in the first three centuries alone.
33 See further the excellent analysis in Eyl (2012).

the while "gazing (*atenizousa*) at the word of Paul" (*Acts of Paul* 10). Even when Thecla visits Paul in prison, she is not said to look at him; instead, she gives away her mirror on entering the prison – she sits at his feet to listen to him and kisses his chains. Only when put on trial does she gaze at Paul himself (*atenizousa*: *Acts of Paul* 20), and when about to be burnt to death she sees the Lord sitting in the form of Paul (*emblepsasa ... eiden*: *Acts of Paul* 21). Miraculously saved from death, she later finds Paul in a tomb, praying for her release; she pipes up behind him with a prayer of thanks that the Father of Jesus Christ saved her from the fire, "so that I might *see* (*idō*) Paul" (*Acts of Paul* 24). Paul rose up and *saw* (*eiden*) her and blessed God. In a poignant subsequent image, the narrator adds that "there was much love in the tomb" (*Acts of Paul* 25).

But what kind of "love"? For all the erotic charge of Thecla's encounter for Paul, and for all its parallel orientation around the sense of seeing, Thecla's love is called *agapē*, not *erōs*.[34] *Agapē* is what Paul in the letter to the Corinthians placed at the ethical core of his gospel, translated in the King James Version as "charity" (1 Corinthians 13). The tomb episode in *Acts of Paul and Thecla* emphasizes this distinctive character: the man and woman first address not one another, but rather God. Before laying eyes on Thecla, moreover, Paul declares her to be God's own. They celebrate with loaves and fish (a meal that was probably intended to evoke the Christian meal that was itself known as the *agapē*). It is only at this point that Thecla's beauty is mentioned, let alone thematized. Even then, moreover, Paul sees that beauty not because he desires it, but because he fears lest temptation take hold of Thecla. The remaining episodes in Thecla's story draw out the theme, charting various adventures in which men long for Thecla on account of her beauty (whether desiring her erotically, or simply desiring to protect her from death).[35] Thecla herself, however, is miraculously preserved: after receiving baptism, she next meets Paul only to be sent out to preach in her own right (something she gladly does). By this time, her original fiancé, Thamyris, has had his comeuppance: his literal death may be thought to allude to a spiritual death on the one hand, and physical decease on the other.

The story of Thecla is a tale of how Graeco-Roman *erōs* could be defeated and surpassed by Christian *agapē*. But, for our purposes, what is particularly significant about the opposition is the different roles each ascribes to sight. In the Christian conversion, love comes not first via the eyes but through words; it leads to seeing Jesus in the beloved, and to seeing the beloved through the mercy of the Father. *Agapē* undoes the desires of those who value the flesh; indeed, when Thecla is thrown naked to the seals, a cloud not only protects her from the animals, but also prevents her from being seen (*theōreisthai*) naked.

The relationship between Christian *agapē* and sight also came to be treated in other contexts. Because "love" was a central theme of discipleship, the affection that

---

34 The classic discussion is Nygren (1953). However, *erōs* as sexual love is to be distinguished from *erōs* as a language for desire for God. Christians were as comfortable with the latter as Plato had been before them: they had no trouble, for example, reading Canticles as an allegory of this kind of love (see further Zimmermann 2001).
35 This may also be conceived as a kind of erotic desire for the flesh, just as Ignatius warned the churches not to desire his flesh erotically so as to keep him from the beasts (Ignatius, *To the Romans* 2.1).

members of the Christian community (irrespective of gender) bore towards one another often received explicit attention. "See how they love one another!", as Tertullian (second to third century CE) envisaged critical spectators to observe when pondering the behaviour of the Christian community. In the novelistic *Clementine Recognitions* (fourth century CE), those who were brought to faith by Peter's preaching "could scarcely bear to be separated from him, but walked along with us again and again, gazing (*uidere*) upon him, again and again embracing him, again and again conversing with him" (*Clementine Recognitions* 4.1.2). In this story, Peter has a band of 12 disciples; when they hear he is to leave them, they declare that they will always retain the remembrance of his face in their hearts (*Clementine Recognitions* 3.70.2). The motif of retaining distinct, visual remembrance of a beloved teacher or companion in the faith is found in several other early Christian sources, both autobiographical and fictional. Irenaeus (late second century CE) exclaims that he can even describe the place where Polycarp sat, his mode of life and personal appearance, as well as his words – for he has these things "noted for remembrance not on papyrus but in my heart" (*Fragment* 2.24–5). Minucius Felix (second/third century CE) likewise contemplates with sweet affection his faithful companion, Octavius: "the contemplation of him, though removed from my eyes, was nonetheless entwined in my breast and practically in my innermost senses" (*Octavius* 1.1–2). These authors keep their beloved teachers in the tablets of memory. In the *Acts of John*, however, a certain Lycomedes, dared to try to put the same thing on another kind of tablet. He asked a painter secretly to paint the apostle's image for him so that he could then set it up in a private sanctuary, replete with garlands, altars, lamps and candles. This gives the author an opportunity explicitly to critique the artistic imitation of exterior forms. When John discovers the portrait of the old man in the bedroom sanctuary, he does not recognize it until someone brings a mirror: upon recognizing his own likeness in the image, he is appalled at the pagan gesture – Lycomedes should be painting his image in his soul, using colours such as faith, knowledge, reverence, kindness and fellowship (*Acts of John* 26).[36]

Christian "love" could also extend to other visual forms. Take Ignatius, writing in the second century CE. So focussed could his imagination be on the life of the church, that he writes of seeing "in faith" the congregation in the person of the bishop (and sometimes also in presbyters and deacons). Seeing them there, Ignatius says that he delights in and loves them (Ignatius, *To the Magnesians* 2, 6.1; *To the Trallians* 1.1, 3.2). Conversely, Ignatius insists that one should look to the bishop as to the Lord himself (Ignatius, *To the Magnesians* 6.1, 7.2), thus locating in a structured, ecclesial context a relationship construed through sight, and one that could resonate with the epiphanies told of in Christian romances (in which the devout/loving woman beholds the Lord in the form of the apostle who has won her trust: cf. *Acts of Paul* 21, above; *Acts of Andrew* 46.12–13; *Acts of Thomas* 11).

Christianity's emphasis on love drew on the language of the eyes in many ways. Yet it also challenged prevailing cultural ideas and ideologies. Thecla's was not the

---

36 The story closely resembles tales told about one of Plotinus' disciples attempting to get his portrait: see M. Edwards (1993). More generally on "sight and insight" – including its thematization in the works of St Augustine – see Webb (this volume).

only Christian love story to show how Christian *agapē* could be pitted against (and triumph over) sexual love. In these stories, though, sexual *erōs* did not just amount to extra-marital "desire"; instead, *agapē* could also be pitted against the *erōs* within legal marriage. Thecla, we remember, was snatched away from her betrothed through love of Paul, just as other beautiful heroines of Christian *agapē* were from their husband's embrace (*Acts of Thomas* 82–118). The love between Christians in the wider ecclesial community, strengthened by visual memory (and later by painted and sculpted images of holy people),[37] was the force that bound them together in the face of an often hostile outside world. In that world, Christian love was often to be manifested in suffering – the second of the two great commandments of discipleship, and the next subject of my chapter.[38]

Discipleship through suffering and death: transvaluation of things seen

"If anyone wishes to follow me, let him deny himself, take up his cross and follow me": such is Jesus' command to his disciples according to Mark (8:34). Suffering was not only central to the gospel, but was in practice a significant part of early Christian experience – when it came to internal battles against desires and temptations, certainly, but also in relation to social conflicts with both Jews and Romans. Once again, this thematic of Christian suffering was constructed in overtly visual terms. The very suffering of Christians was frequently understood to present horrific spectacles; those spectacles, moreover, could themselves offer images for Christian visual contemplation.

The idea of suffering – and of suffering made visible through the body – is already manifest in the writing of Paul. To be a Christian could entail subjecting one's body to trial and torment no less than to changing its outward appearance. "Five times I received from the Jews forty stripes save one", writes Paul – before listing many of the other sufferings he had endured ("thrice beaten with rods, once stoned, thrice shipwrecked", not to mention various other dangers: 2 Corinthians 11:24–7). In listing his bodily sufferings for the Corinthians, Paul poignantly begins with those that are most visible – with sufferings written in the flesh, as it were.

When the Christian life was but a spectacle of suffering, there was always a danger that onlookers might argue that this was all there was to see of salvation (that is, that there was no salvation at all to be seen). This spectre of "simply nothing there" presents itself repeatedly to the eyes of early Christian writers, as one martyr after another is sent to the lions. Such suffering could appear to signal not nearness to God and Christ, but rather abandonment by both. The so-called "Alexamenos graffito", which is plausibly the earliest visual representation of Christ's crucifixion, quite literally visualizes this visual perspective (Figure 11.1). Etched in apparent ridicule, a man raises his arm to salute a figure with a donkey's head hanging from a

---

37 For the beginnings of Christian art, see Ladner (1953); Mathews (1993); Finney (1994); Lowden (1997); Besançon (2000); Jensen (2000; 2005); Spier (2008).
38 For further discussions, see Perkins (1995: 26–30); Cooper (1996: 55–9); Konstan (1998); Schroeder (2000).

Figure 11.1 Drawing of the "Alexamenos graffito" from the Palatine Hill in Rome, most likely from the third century CE: the scrawled text reads *Alexamenos sebete theon* ("Alexamenos worships [his] god") (drawing provided by M. J. Squire).

cross. *Alexamenos sebete theon*, as the inscription reads: "Alexamenos worships [his] god".

How, then, were Christians to react to such a charge – and how were they to do so visually? Christian responses took several different forms, but they repeatedly found their focus in Christ's death and resurrection. At times, Paul indicates how he regards his own suffering as manifesting the death and life of Jesus: through that manifestation, Jesus' death works life in those who believe (2 Corinthians 4:10–12). It is the stigmata of Jesus that Paul claims to bear in his body (contrasting this to Jewish circumcision, practised by those who "seek to make a fine face in the flesh": Galatians 6:18, cf. v.12). Likewise, the chains that Paul wore in prison become "manifest in Christ in the whole praetorium and among all the others": they encourage those who have trusted in the Lord, while prompting others to aggravate his suffering (Philippians 1:13–17). By manifesting Christ's own suffering, the tokens of Paul's bodily trials – whether scars or chains – strengthen believers. But they also work the opposite effect. There are two ways of looking at such visual signs: to look upon them in faith is to be built up, whereas to look without faith is to have one's faith opposed. Physiological sight does not differentiate the one from the other: it is the eyes of faith that draw the distinctions.

Paul's chains soon developed a metaphorical and literary life of their own. Letters, whether authentic or not, were composed in the persona of "Paul, enchained of Christ" (Philemon 1, 9; Ephesians 3:1). The chains, according to this delineation, became an image associated with the bonds between Paul and his faithful addressees, to the extent that the letter to the Colossians closes with an enjoinder to "remember my chains" (Colossians 4:18; cf. Ephesians 4:1; Philemon 10; Hebrews 13:3). While Paul suffered to the point of chains, God's word remained unchained, thus grounding his endurance for the elect (2 Timothy 2:8–9). In his parting speech to the Ephesians, as portrayed in Acts, Paul likewise presents himself as "enchained in spirit" as he goes to Jerusalem, where "chains and suffering await me" (22:22–3). Hauled before the authorities there, Paul dramatically holds up his chains in a rhetorical gesture:[39] "I pray that not only you but all those who are listening today may become what I am, except for these chains!" (Acts 26:29). We should hear a nod in these words to the Acts' own readership. In the late first century, Clement urges his Roman audience to set before their eyes the good apostles, among whom he counts Paul who "seven times bore chains" (1 Clement 5:6). Likewise, in the account of Thecla's life, the protagonist was also envisaged as kissing Paul's chains in prison. Ignatius, known to be an admirer of Paul, thematized his own chains in a manner imitative of his saintly predecessor (Ignatius, *To the Smyrnaeans* 8, 10.2; *To the Trallians* 12.2; *To the Ephesians* 1.2, 21.2; *To the Magnesians* 1.2).

All this bestows upon the chains a grander visual significance: through their creative imagination, the very instrument of torture, physically restraining Paul, brought life to early Christians who could invoke them in whatever manner most befitted their situation. The same would also hold true of the cross. The cross on which Christ was crucified in weakness soon became in early Christian thought a locus and means of power. Apocryphal narratives of crucifixion, both that of Christ and those of certain apostles, depicted it in luminous radiance (e.g. *Acts of John* 98). The visual sign of the cross becomes a gesture used frequently in Christian prayer (Tertullian, *The Crown* 3.4), and elaborate allegories of the significance of the cross were written in pious contemplation of its mystical meaning (*Acts of John* 97–102; *Acts of Peter* 37.8–39.10). Such engagement with key symbols of Christianity's sacred narratives is one of the most significant ways in which Christianity had an implicit iconography before it ever had an extensive material art. These focal images were derived from real sights, of course. And yet – through creative, prayerful imagination – such material images could frame and anchor the Christian's experiences (and relationships with God), situating them in the immaterial arena of the heart.

Something similar can be said of the literal arena too. The most spectacular way in which Christian suffering was literally displayed before the eyes in the early centuries, after all, was the practice of throwing Christians to the beasts in Roman spectatorial contexts. Once again, Christians turned this practice to creative imaginary advantage. Roman culture was one in which such spectacles of death were relished as a well-known form of entertainment.[40] Christian moral teaching abhorred the practice: the passion for watching violence simply for pleasure should never be

---

39 I infer this from the demonstrative "these chains", as well as from the rhetorical context.
40 From the large bibliography, see e.g. Barton (1993).

indulged (Tertullian, *The Spectacles*; Novatian, *The Spectacles*).[41] However, in a religion focussed on life won through Christ's own violent (and spectacular) death, seeing the suffering and death of those punished in the arena for following Christ proffered a vivid invitation: it allowed onlookers to enter personally and emotionally into the Christian narrative of life through Christ's own death. Paul perceived this when he depicted himself (and the other apostles) as being metaphorically "put on show" by God, like "those condemned to die (*epithanatioi*), because we have become a spectacle (*theatron*) for the world and for angels and for human beings" (1 Corinthians 4:9). From this perspective, visual spectacles of Christians being put to death became an important setting for winning converts and strengthening the faithful; indeed, it was celebrated in various narratives, where the divine and heavenly side of the action could be made visible to the imagination, alongside (and despite) the violent drama of the arena.[42]

But the spectacle of Christian suffering came to have still greater significance within the Christian imaginary, transfiguring apparent tokens of trial into images of blessing and joy. Ignatius, for example, calls his chains "spiritual pearls" (Ignatius, *To the Ephesians* 11.2), just as Polycarp discusses "diadems of those truly chosen by God and by our Lord" (1.1). Among earlier Stoic thinkers, there was a similar "relabelling" technique for dealing with disturbing sense-impressions.[43] For them, as for the Christians, a radical (and subversive) reinterpretation of reality was required, adopting society's language of treasure and value only to reapply it in a set of profoundly new ways.

The apocryphal story of Thomas' trip to India offers an extended narrative intervention after the same fashion, emphasizing in particular the role of sight. Arriving in India, Thomas is said to have presented himself to the king as a builder, accepting a contract to build the king a new palace. When the king shows him the site, Thomas promises to begin work – but to do so in the winter. Disconcerted at the delay, the king demands to see an architectural plan, and Thomas duly obliges (sketching a splendid design with a reed-pen). When the king sees the plan, his mind is put to rest: he departs, and sends instalments of money as required.

But what of Thomas' palace? Removed from the king's direct surveillance, and unbeknown to the king himself, Thomas distributes the royal budget among the poor, spending the final instalment (intended for the roof) in similar almsgiving. Upon asking his friends about the awaited palace, the king finally discovers what has happened. "Have you built me the palace?" he asks. "Yes", comes Thomas' reply. "Then when shall we go and see (*blepomen*) it?" To the king's question, Thomas offers a poignant reply: "Now you cannot see (*idein*) it, but when you depart this life, that is the time when you see (*blepeis*)" (*Acts of Thomas* 21). Unsurprisingly, perhaps, the apostle is enchained and sent to prison, awaiting the grisly death designed by the king. But before these plans are carried out, the king's beloved brother falls ill: unbeknown to the grieving king, angels take his brother's soul to

---

41 Cf. Seneca, *Moral Letters* 95.33. However, Seneca's attitude is ambivalent: Wistrand (1990); Kyle (1998: 3–4).

42 One thinks of numerous examples in the writings of Ignatius – as well as in the *Acts of Paul* and *Passion of Perpetua and Felicity*: for further discussion, see Kyle (1998: esp. 242–64).

43 Cf. Sorabji (2000: 115, 179, 222).

heaven and show him the palace that Thomas had built there. Implored by the brother, the angels let him return to his body and beg the king to sell him the palace in heaven. At this point, the penny finally drops: realizing what has happened, the king releases the apostle and tries to become worthy of the palace for which he had not laboured.

The important point, at least in the context of this chapter, is that the "treasure in heaven" is financed, described and visualized in the same way as corresponding palaces on earth, even though – socially, politically, ethically and theologically – the palace's relationship to earthly realities is radically reconfigured through the Christian gospel (cf. Mark 10:21 parr.). Throughout the narrative, seeing the palace takes on a central resonance, both at the planning stage (through architectural drawings) and upon completion (where the difference between seeing it on earth and in heaven becomes manifest). Thomas does not offer the spectacle of the happy paupers as a visible palace on earth; rather, he says that the palace will only be seen after his life's end. This is not to say that there is "nothing there" in the realm of the living; rather, the happy paupers are but the visible token of what is promised in the invisible realm.

Insight as sight to the blind

This chapter has addressed just some of the ways in which sensory seeing – and above all, Greek and Roman ideologies of vision in particular – came to be appropriated within early Christian culture. Christianity, I suggested, depended on the unprecedented sight of the resurrected Jesus.[44] But it also came to focus on the contemplation of Jesus' visual body, exploring what God's physical manifestation signified for others in this life and the next. The visual implications have been discussed with particular attention to the themes of love and of suffering (that is, two of Jesus' most important general commands of discipleship).

In concluding this chapter, I want to recall one final vignette from the gospels – a vignette that draws out the significance of sight for early Christians, both as a discourse and as a reality. All four canonical gospels narrate at least one story of a blind man who received or regained sight through Jesus. Now, there are many miracle stories in the gospels where sight is important: Jesus' watching crowds were regularly said to have been prompted to wonder and sometimes to believe through the powerful deeds they beheld. But the healing of a blind man stands out because it concerns the gift of sight in a direct – and highly self-conscious – way.

Beyond the literal bestowal of sight in such stories, each of the gospels also emphasizes the metaphorical significance of this act.[45] In Mark, the physical healing of the blind man is narrated immediately after Jesus has rebuked his close disciples for their dim-wittedness (that is their incapacity to see): "having eyes, do you not see (*ophthalmous echontes ou blepete*)?", he asks them (in a poignant echo of Old Testament scripture), and "having ears, do you not hear?" (Mark 8:18; cf. Jeremiah 5:21). The juxtaposition encourages reflection on the relationship between spiritual

---

44 See n.5, above.
45 Cf. Hamm (1986).

and physical seeing – between the sight that Jesus bestows on the blind man, and the insight bestowed through Jesus for those who read the gospel.[46] Furthermore, the blind man of Mark's gospel is healed not all at once, but in stages: there is an intermediate step where he sees men but they look like trees walking around. Does this offer a figure, we might ask, for an intermediate stage in the journey towards spiritual insight?

John draws out the levels of meaning more explicitly in narrating how a man born blind was healed. When the healed man confesses his faith in Jesus, Jesus delivers the important lesson: "for judgement I came into this world, so that those who see not may see, and those who see may become blind (ἵνα οἱ μὴ βλέποντες βλέπωσιν καὶ οἱ βλέποντες τυφλοὶ γένωνται)". To the Pharisees, he adds this warning: "if you were blind (*tuphloi*), you would not have sin, but now you say, 'We see (*blepomen*)', your sin abides" (John 9:39–41). If the tension between sight and insight is critical to the gospel message of life through Christ, it is also set against death for those who do not see. Still more importantly, this metaphorical figure is allied to a message of real physical restoration – of sight being restored amongst other senses.

The following chapter will return to the theme of "blindness" in the ancient cultural imagination. For our immediate purposes, my closing vignette encapsulates what the rest of the chapter has sought to show: namely, that long before there was an articulate teaching on "spiritual senses", and long before Constantine lifted a ban on Christian worship (thereby effectively enabling the large-scale development of public Christian art from the fourth century onwards), Christians were recognizing the importance of vision as something foundational to their faith. Ideas of sight were – and would remain – crucial to the Christian message: it was through the figure of vision that Christianity set its challenge for those who had eyes, but who were still (at least from a Christian perspective) learning to see.[47]

---

[46] These tropes, of course, once again follow in the wake of longer-standing classical ideas about both "sight and insight" and "sight and blindness": see the chapters by Webb and Coo in this volume.

[47] For helpful comments on earlier versions of this paper, warm thanks to Stephen Barton, Jaś Elsner, Paul Foster, John Moles and Michael Squire, as well as to the Durham New Testament Research Seminar.

12

SIGHT AND BLINDNESS
The mask of Thamyris

Lyndsay Coo

As numerous contributors to this book have emphasized, ancient Greek culture was obsessed with vision as the primary sensory means of accessing the world. Such "ocularcentrism" was encoded in the Greek language itself: the most common word for "I know", *oida*, is a perfect form from the verbal root *id-*, which means "to see". Likewise, the expression "to look upon the light" was a euphemism for simply being alive, in the same way that (as Jeremy Tanner and Susanne Turner have already noted in this book) the underworld was characterized by darkness and obscurity – a place where one could no longer see or be seen.[1] In Greek linguistic and cultural parlance, to know is to have seen, to live is to look and to die is to be overcome by darkness.

But what about those *unable* to see? For Greek and Roman thinkers alike, the state of blindness held a special fascination, providing a way to explore and define different forms of sight itself. As the previous chapter has emphasized, such thinking lies behind the later Christian interest in "seeing" to define the theological, social and cultural parameters of Christianity in the first centuries after Jesus' death. But in earlier Greek mythology and literature too, the negation of this fundamental sense is a recurrent theme, most often associated with a significant change in some other ability, such as music, poetry, prophecy or true and insightful knowledge. This often-noted phenomenon will be at the centre of my investigation into the construction of blindness in the ancient Greek cultural imagination.[2]

---

1 In antiquity, the etymology of Hades (Ἅιδης) as "the Unseen" (privative ἀ + ἰδεῖν, "to see") was debated: see e.g. Plato, *Phaedo* 80d, *Cratylus* 403a. In this chapter, I use the following abbreviations: *FGrH* (= Jacoby 1923–); *LIMC* (= *Lexicon Iconographicum Mythologiae Classicae*, 1981–97, Zurich: Artemis); *PCG* (= Kassel & Austin 1983–2001).

2 A seminal discussion of ancient blindness, particularly in Sophocles, is Buxton (1980) (reprinted with additional material as Buxton 2013: 173–200): Buxton demonstrates how the "special defect" of blindness is often bestowed on mythological characters who would otherwise threaten to exceed human limits, whether through poetic or prophetic powers or transgressive actions. Bernidaki-Aldous (1990) is an extended study of blindness in Greek literature, with focus on Sophocles' *Oedipus at Colonus*. See also the wide-ranging study of Esser (1961), general overview of Barasch (2001: 7–44) and shorter discussions by Létoublon (2010) and Tatti-Gartziou (2010). On the blindness of Homer specifically, see particularly Graziosi (2002: 125–63). Scholars have tended to focus on Homer and Sophocles, but see also Lovatt (2013: 149–54), who uses Kristeva's concept of the "abject" to offer concise but thought-provoking discussion of blindness in Apollonius, Statius and Quintus of Smyrna. Due to constraints of space, this chapter considers only Greek representations.

Studies of blindness in antiquity have frequently taken their cue from three paradigmatic figures who fit into this pattern, namely the blind bard Homer, Oedipus who blinds himself at the moment of self-recognition and the blind seer Tiresias. My chapter offers a new focal figure for this enquiry: the Thracian musician Thamyris, who dared to boast that he could compete with the Muses in song, and was punished by being stripped of his sight. Thamyris' story exemplifies elements of the broader conceptualization and construction of blindness in ancient Greece, and his representation on the Athenian tragic stage offers a starting-point for thinking about the implications of depicting blindness visually. These interlinked investigations provide an overview of the symbolism of blindness in the ancient Greek world, and explore ways in which such constructions of blindness are always inseparable from forms and hierarchies of sight.[3]

Blindness and song

Our earliest encounter with Thamyris comes in the Catalogue of Ships in the second book of the *Iliad* (2.594–600), where a succinct but chilling account of his punishment is narrated as a brief digression from mention of the city of Dorion:

> ...where the Muses, meeting with Thamyris the Thracian, put a stop to his singing, as he was coming from Oechalia, from the house of Eurytus the Oechalian; for, boasting, he proclaimed that he would win even if the Muses themselves were to sing against him, the daughters of aegis-bearing Zeus. But they, in their anger, made him disabled (*pēron*), and took away his marvellous art of song and made him forget utterly the art of the *cithara*.

The Muses punish this arrogant musician by disabling him – but how? The adjective *pēros* (2.599) appears only here in Homeric epic, and later authors use it to mean "maimed", specifying the location of the injury. It is unclear exactly what aspect of physical or emotional damage is implied by this word in its Iliadic context. Thamyris is stripped of his power to make music with either his voice or his *cithara*, and this comprehensive deprivation of musical ability is emphasized by the positioning of *aoidēn* ("the art of song") and *kitharistun* ("the art of *cithara*-playing") at the ends of consecutive lines. The destruction of some aspect of Thamyris' physical or emotional identity, as indicated by *pēron*, is thus paralleled by the destruction of his poetic and musical identity.

Scholars, both ancient and modern, have argued that *pēron* at *Iliad* 2.599 cannot mean that Thamyris was blinded by the Muses, since this would have been no handicap to a bard.[4] Indeed, the role of singer or story-teller was one of the few

---

[3] I use the word "symbolism" because my focus here is on the conceptualization of blindness in Greek mythology and literature, where it is usually a marker of exceptional personal circumstances. Of course, in reality blindness and visual impairment would have affected very many people: on relating the evidence to real-life experience in the ancient world, see particularly Rose (2003: 79–94), and – in the context of ancient Rome – Trentin (2013).

[4] E.g. Σ A *Iliad* 2.599; Whallon (1964); Kirk (1985: 217). Throughout this chapter, my references to ancient Greek scholia are taken from Erbse (1969–88).

professions available to a blind person in the ancient world: the *Odyssey* features the sightless singer Demodocus, and according to the ancient biographical tradition, Homer himself was blind.⁵ Yet despite the imprecise meaning of *pēron* and the academic debate that this aroused (with Hellenistic scholars arguing that the word must denote lameness, muteness or madness), subsequent literary and artistic traditions are almost unanimous in representing the punishment of Thamyris as that of blindness.⁶

According to Stephanus of Byzantium, Hesiod stated in the *Catalogue of Women* that Thamyris was blinded by the Muses on the Dotian plain in Thessaly.⁷ It seems certain that the singer was blinded in Sophocles' now-fragmentary tragedy *Thamyras* (the Attic spelling of his name), and in the pseudo-Euripidean *Rhesus* the Muse recalls how she and her sisters, after competing against him in a contest of song, "blinded (*katuphlōsamen*) Thamyris, who had many times insulted our art" (*Rhesus* 924–5). We find the punishment strikingly depicted on a red-figure *hydria* attributed to the group of Polygnotus and dated to the 440–420s BCE, now in the Ashmolean Museum in Oxford (Figure 12.1) – the only surviving ancient vase to show the moment of blinding rather than the contest with the Muses. Thamyris sits with his eyes closed and his *cithara* cast onto the ground beside him, flanked on the left by his mother, who tears her hair in grief, and on the right by a Muse.⁸ The ambiguity of the Iliadic *pēron* thus transforms into a certainty that Thamyris must have been blinded, fitting him into a wider mythological network in which there is a deep and pervasive association between poetry and blindness. In Dio Chrysostom's thirty-sixth *Oration*, the narrator and his interlocutor even joke that blindness is a prerequisite for becoming a poet, and that poets catch their blindness from Homer, as though from *ophthalmia* (*Oration* 36.10–11).

Through his appearance in the *Iliad*, Thamyris becomes the first example of a blind person in classical literature. Yet this very identification hinges on an ambiguous and contested word into which both ancient and modern audiences have projected the disability of blindness, because of its strong association with poetic ability – a tradition to which the Iliadic Thamyris then contributes in turn. The earliest explicit example of this association is the bard Demodocus. In *Odyssey* 8 we are told that he was given musical ability alongside his blindness: "The Muse loved him [Demodocus] exceedingly, but she gave him both good and evil: she deprived him of his eyesight, but gave him the sweet gift of song" (*Odyssey* 8.63–4). Here, the bard's blindness is emblematic of his quasi-supernatural status and impartiality. Divorced from direct visual contact with the world around him, he relies instead on the divine inspiration of the Muse, which enables him to "see" the subjects of his songs, events to which he was not himself an eyewitness. Demodocus thus exemplifies the mythological pattern whereby

---

5 On Homer's blindness, see Graziosi (2002: 125–63); Beecroft (2011).
6 In Statius, Thamyris is mute rather than blind (*Thebaid* 4.182–6). Jakobi (1995) suggests that Statius is responding specifically to the Homeric scholia that interpreted *pēron* at *Iliad* 2.599 as "lame"; see also Parkes (2012: 133–4).
7 Hesiod, frg. 65 MW (= frg. 66 Most).
8 Oxford, Ashmolean Museum G 291: see Beazley (1963: 2.1061, no. 152), with further bibliography collected in Carpenter (1989: 323); cf. *LIMC*, s.v. "Thamyris", no. 16. On artistic depictions of this myth, see further *LIMC*, s.v. "Thamyris"; Bundrick (2005: 126–31); Wilson (2009: 70–7).

Figure 12.1 Detail of an Attic red-figure *hydria* attributed to the Group of Polygnotus, ca. 440–420 BCE. Oxford, Ashmolean Museum: inv. G 291 (© Ashmolean Museum, University of Oxford).

a particular gift is bestowed alongside, or in compensation for, blindness; by contrast, the unfortunate Thamyris loses both sight and song. The sequence of events is different, but in both cases the association between poetry and blindness is evident.[9]

Another well-known example of this is the lyric poet Stesichorus, who is said to have been blinded by Helen, but had his eyesight restored after appeasing her anger. The story is recounted by Socrates in Plato's *Phaedrus* (243a–b):

> There is, for those who have erred in their telling of myth, an ancient purification, which Homer did not know, but Stesichorus did. For when he had been stripped of his eyesight for his slander of Helen, he was not, like Homer, unaware of the reason, but since he was inspired by the Muses (*mousikos*), he recognized the reason, and straightaway he composed:
> "It is not true, this saying,
> You neither went on the well-benched ships,
> Nor did you reach the towers of Troy."
> And after composing the entire *Palinode*, as it is called, he recovered his eyesight on the spot.

9 See particularly Buxton (1980).

The story of Stesichorus is one of sight and song, since his musical skill is the reason for both his blinding and the restoral of his eyesight. Having offended Helen in his previous poetry, Stesichorus composes a work that absolves her of blame for the Trojan War, and is healed. At stake is not just his vision but also his poetic standing, since by recognizing both the reason for his affliction and its cure he reveals himself to be more *mousikos* ("inspired by the Muses"/"musical") than Homer. Crucially, even though he is blind, Stesichorus' healing relies on the true recognition of a deceptive visual phenomenon. In the account of his *Palinode*, the real Helen did not go to Troy but was replaced there by her *eidōlon* ("image" or "phantom"), a word containing the *id-* root that denotes seeing. While everyone else is duped by Helen's *eidōlon*, Stesichorus – even when blinded – is able to "see" past the deceptive outer appearance to the reality beneath and hence compose a more accurate poem, thereby demonstrating his superiority to Homer.[10]

The themes of sight and blindness are thus intimately bound up not just with song and poetry, but with artistic antagonism and competition. Just as Stesichorus' recovery of his sight allows him to claim superiority over Homer, so the narration of Thamyris' story in *Iliad* 2 offers a negative *exemplum* of poetic practice. Unlike the narrator of the *Iliad*, who has established a productive and benevolent relationship with the Muses, Thamyris antagonizes the very divinities on whom his musical gifts depend.[11] The stories of Thamyris and Stesichorus reflect a common pattern in Greek mythology where blindness is represented as a punishment inflicted by the gods, in response to a specific offence. Our earliest explicit example of this is also found in the *Iliad* (Lycurgus, who persecuted the nurses of Dionysus, is blinded by Zeus),[12] and as Buxton has demonstrated, blindness is typically inflicted as the consequence of over-stepping the limits that are proper to a mortal.[13] The act of singing successfully about the blinded Thamyris, who was himself deprived of the ability to sing because of a transgression, thus becomes a means of asserting one's own poetic, intellectual and religious superiority.[14] The traditions of Homer, Thamyris and Stesichorus play with the interconnection of physical, intellectual and artistic sight and blindness. Their blindness is not incidental, but symbolizes some deeper connection to their poetic ability, which is itself a kind of "sight".

---

10 On the connotations of *eidōlon*, see the discussions (with further references) by both Tanner and Turner (this volume).
11 Wilson (2009: 56–7), noting well how the Catalogue of Ships, into which Thamyris' story is set, starts with the narrator's respectful invocation of the Muses at *Iliad* 2.484–92.
12 *Iliad* 6.139.
13 Buxton (1980: 26–35). See also Bernidaki-Aldous (1990: 57–93); Steiner (1995); Tatti-Gartziou (2010). Scholars have noted that many examples of punitive blinding in the ancient Greek world, both mythological and historical, are in response to sexual transgression. A sexual element is also introduced into the mythology of Thamyris in later versions that record how Thamyris demanded, were he to be victorious in his musical contest against the Muses, the sexual favours of one or all of them. Devereux (1973: 41; 1987) offers a psychoanalytical reading of this material, but on the limitations of such approaches, especially the equation of blindness with castration, see Buxton (1980: 34–5).
14 On the agonistic dynamics of Thamyris' appearance in the *Iliad*, see R. P. Martin (1989: 229–30); Ford (1992: 93–101); Wilson (2009); Power (2010: 254–7); Biles (2011: 12–22).

Blind insight

The ancient Greek word *opisō* means "behind" or "backwards" when applied spatially, but "in the future" when used temporally. In this conceptual mapping, the future lies behind rather than ahead of us: we face the past, and walk blindly backwards into the unseen future. Blindness appears throughout ancient literature as one of the primary metaphors for uncertainty, inaccurate belief, ignorance and madness. To fail to see something clearly (or at all) is to possess incomplete or inauthentic knowledge of it. A verse from an unknown play of Sophocles employs sensory deprivation, including lack of perceptive vision, as a metaphor for human suffering: "But the unfortunate are not only dumb, but, possessing sight, do not see that which is visible" (Sophocles, frg. 923). This imagery also applies to the gods. Another Sophoclean fragment states that Ares, the raging god of war who kills indiscriminately, is "blind ... and cannot see" (Sophocles, frg. 838.1), and a verse possibly to be attributed to Euripides' tragedy *Oedipus* expresses the commonplace that "Justice can see even in darkness" (Euripides, frg. 555).

However, just as with poetic and musical ability, a deep association also exists between blindness and intellectual insight, especially with regard to genuine understanding of one's own circumstances and/or the power of prophecy. Along with poets, prophets and seers are frequently represented as blind in ancient mythology and literature, with Tiresias as a paradigmatic figure.[15] Similarly, in the *Iliad* Thamyris undergoes a journey from poetic knowledge to poetic ignorance when the Muses make him "forget utterly" (*eklelathon*: *Iliad* 2.600) his art. Yet simultaneously he moves from personal ignorance – mistakenly believing, and foolishly professing, himself to be more skilled than the Muses themselves – to personal knowledge, through a sudden and stark recognition of his own mortal limitations. The punishment of Thamyris literalizes his mental blindness, even as it is replaced by insight.

This coincidence of blindness with self-revelation is a pattern that is repeated throughout ancient Greek literature. In *Odyssey* 9, for example, it is only after being blinded by Odysseus that the one-eyed Cyclops Polyphemus recalls how this act had been foretold by a prophecy. His realization is especially ironic since it was precisely a lack of visual perception that stopped Polyphemus from recognizing Odysseus in the first place: he had been expecting someone more conspicuously powerful, and had failed to see what was right in front of his eye (*Odyssey* 9.506–16).[16]

A paradigmatic and much-analysed treatment of this theme comes in Sophocles' *Oedipus Tyrannus*, performed in Athens in around 429 BCE. Sophocles' tragedy presents an inverse correlation between physical and "true" sight, and it is standard for critical readings of the play to concentrate on this dichotomy.[17] Oedipus begins

---

15 Different traditions exist as to the reason for Tiresias' blinding: he offended Hera by claiming that women take greater pleasure than men from sexual intercourse (e.g. Hesiod, frg. 275 MW = frg. 211a Most), or saw Athena naked while she was bathing (e.g. Callimachus, *Hymn* 5). In both versions he is compensated with the gift of prophecy. On the associations between blindness and prophetic knowledge, see Buxton (1980: 27–30); Ustinova (2009: 168–72).

16 For Greek artistic representations of the story – themselves *visually* mediating the underlying themes of seeing and not seeing, and often in highly reflexive ways – see Grethlein (this volume).

17 See, for example, the following chapter-titles devoted to the *Oedipus Tyrannus*: "blindness and

the play with his eyesight but ignorant of his own identity, blinding himself after the discovery of his true parentage and horrific deeds. Conversely, the seer Tiresias, although physically blind, is the only character who possesses authentic knowledge and insight. The tragedy is dense with the language of sight and seeing. Oedipus mistakes Tiresias' physical blindness for mental blindness, accusing him of being blind "in the ears and the mind and the eyes" (*Oedipus Tyrannus* 371) as well as in his art (*Oedipus Tyrannus* 389), to which the prophet responds that Oedipus has sight, but cannot see his evil situation, nor where he is living, nor with whom he lives (*Oedipus Tyrannus* 413–14). The king sees, but lacks true sight of even these most basic of facts about his own situation. By the end of the play, when his metaphorical blindness has been literalized, the chorus state in horror that it would have been better for Oedipus to have died than to live blinded (*Oedipus Tyrannus* 1369). However, Oedipus wishes that he could have gone even further by destroying his hearing as well as his eyes (*Oedipus Tyrannus* 1386–90) – thus divorcing himself from the two senses integral to the theatrical experience itself.

Viewing blindness

The blind characters of ancient Greek theatre present a paradoxical phenomenon: blindness must be accessed by vision itself. The very performance context is articulated through the vocabulary of seeing. The audience were called *hoi theatai* or *hoi theōmenoi* ("the spectators", "the ones looking"), and sat in the *theatron* ("theatre", from the verb *theaomai*, "I look at"), literally a "place of seeing", where they could observe not only the drama, but also each other.[18] And yet, with characters such as Polyphemus, Oedipus, Tiresias, Polymestor, Phineus, Phoenix and Thamyris, ancient drama frequently placed an unseeing figure at the heart of what was conceptualized as a visual experience.[19]

Greek actors performed fully masked, and the word for the mask, *prosōpon*, was the same as that commonly used for the face, its etymology suggesting both that which is near to (one's own) eyes, and that which is opposite the eyes (of another).[20] In performance, the theatrical mask, and in particular its eyes, acted as a physical

---

vision" – Musurillo (1967: 80–93); "blindness and sight" – Seale (1982: 215–60); "blindness and insight" – Goldhill (1986: 199–221). Most recently, on the relationship of vision, blindness and knowledge in the play, see Thumiger (2013: 227–30).

18 There is ample bibliography on the *theatron* as a site of viewing. On the meaning of theatrical space and stagecraft, see e.g. Taplin (1978); Wiles (1997); Meineck (2013). On the audience's modes of viewing, see Zeitlin (1994); Goldhill (2000b). Cf. also Tanner (this volume).

19 Blind(ed) characters in extant Attic tragedies: Oedipus (Sophocles' *Oedipus Tyrannus, Oedipus at Colonus*; Euripides' *Phoenician Women*); Tiresias (Sophocles' *Antigone, Oedipus Tyrannus*; Euripides' *Bacchae*); Polymestor (Euripides' *Hecuba*). Known or probable blind(ed) characters in fragmentary and lost tragedies: Oedipus (Aeschylus' *Oedipus*; Euripides' *Oedipus*); Tiresias (Aeschylus' *Soul-Raisers*; possibly Euripides' *Alcmene*); Phineus (Aeschylus' *Phineus*; Sophocles' two *Phineus* plays, one of which also featured the blinded sons of Phineus); Thamyris (Sophocles' *Thamyras*); Phoenix (Euripides' *Phoenix*). The daughters of Phorcys (Aeschylus' *Daughters of Phorcys*) shared a single eye between them. One should also mention here the blinding of the central character in our sole fully extant satyr-play: Polyphemus (Euripides' *Cyclops*). Sophocles' satyric *Cedalion* may have featured the blinding and/or subsequent healing of Orion.

20 See Beekes (2010: 1240, s.v. "πρόσωπον").

conduit for the actor's line of vision and a natural focus for the gazes of the audience.[21] How, then, does the phenomenon of the "blind mask" – the mask worn by sightless dramatic characters – fit into the dynamics of viewing at work in this "place of seeing"? One approach emphasizes that the theatrical mask is a primary mediator of meaning between actor and audience, and so the blind mask entails a breaking or blocking of an essential visual communicative channel. In relation to the appearance of the blind Oedipus in Euripides' *Phoenician Women*, Zeitlin has written of "the confrontation of the audience with the rupture of a reciprocal gaze between spectator and actor, by which in the theatrical setting an unseeing figure is a spectacle for others' eyes".[22] Calame in particular has argued that the king's self-blinding in *Oedipus Tyrannus* is an act that threatens the very foundations of tragic discourse: "In appearing on stage masked but deprived of sight, Oedipus negates the possibility of visual (though mediated) communication between actor and spectator."[23] On these readings, the blind mask of tragedy functions by dissolving a pre-existing visual bond with its audience.

However, we might question to what extent the visual relationship between actor and audience is indeed reciprocal. Despite the strong likelihood that the ancient performance style favoured frontality, i.e. with the gaze of the speaking actor directed outwards towards that of the audience,[24] it is possible to argue that a form of "blindness" is inherent in the very form of tragic performance itself, since the audience is watching characters who, within the world of the play, cannot watch back. The masked gaze of the actor meets that of the audience, but the latter's physical and intellectual "vision" is superior to that of the characters, who cannot see beyond their fictional dramatic world.[25] There is already a hierarchy at work in the *theatron* where the spectator is placed on the highest level of vision, both literal and metaphorical, and the blind dramatic character on the lowest.[26]

There is a further important distinction to be drawn between the blind masks of ancient theatre. Some characters are blind throughout the duration of their plays, while others undergo a violent (self-)blinding that transforms them during the course

---

21 We seem neurologically "hard-wired" to be attracted to human faces and features, especially the eyes: for discussion of the Greek tragic mask in light of these findings from cognitive neuroscience, see Meineck (2011). There is extensive bibliography on the origin, function, effect and practical use of the ancient tragic mask: for a range of approaches, see Calame (1986a: 85–100) (translated in Calame 1986b = 1995: 97–115); Halliwell (1993); Marshall (1999); Hall (2006: 99–141); Wiles (2007).
22 Zeitlin (1994: 194–5).
23 Calame (1996: 28), restated in Calame (2005: 115). But see also the response of Buxton (1996: 38–9), who questions whether all blind characters are meant to be metatheatrically subversive in this way.
24 See Meineck (2011: 139–41).
25 The situation is different in comedy, where the actors may explicitly acknowledge the nature of their performance by addressing the audience directly (or else knowingly allude to theatrical conventions: cf. Bielfeldt in this volume). This divide between actor and audience is often termed the "fourth wall", based on the effect of the modern proscenium arch. The term is less appropriately applied to the outdoor ancient Greek theatre, where rather than conveying the impression that the audience was eavesdropping on a private event, the gaze and gestures of the actors "incorporated the audience in the spatial field of the performance" (Wiles 1997: 212).
26 The actors may also be fitted into this scheme, since the wearing of a theatrical mask, with its small eye-holes and severely restricted peripheral vision, is an experience of sensory deprivation: see Walton (1996: 43); Meineck (2011: 139–41).

of the drama from seeing into non-seeing figures. It seems certain that this latter change in status was marked by an off-stage change of mask.[27] In our extant plays, the characters of Oedipus, Polymestor and Polyphemus are all blinded off-stage, which would have allowed the actors in question to don special blind masks, presumably made even more striking by the visible presence of "blood" streaming from the ruined eye-sockets. Such gory masks would draw attention not only to the characters' blindness but also to their sudden and violent change in status. With Thamyris, we are faced with a different situation. Sophocles wrote a tragedy of this name of which 11 fragments survive, none of which provide any evidence for how the singer's blinding and blindness were represented.[28] However, this play must have differed significantly from those listed above, since its central figure was struck blind by divine power rather than by having his eyes violently burnt, stabbed or gouged out. This would have opened up new possibilities, both for the staging of the blinding itself and for the way in which its representation might have engaged the creative gaze of its theatrical audience.

In his work the *Onomasticon*, the second century CE rhetorician Pollux includes a long descriptive catalogue of different kinds of dramatic masks. After detailing the appearance of various stock types, he turns his attention to the special masks, intended primarily for tragedy, which were required to produce certain theatrical effects. Among these we find the mask of "Thamyris with one eye grey and the other eye black".[29] The mismatched eyes of Thamyris also appear in the Homeric scholia (Σ B *Iliad* 2.595), and were known to the fourth-century BCE mythographer Asclepiades of Tragilos, who wrote that "Thamyris was marvellous in his appearance; the right one of his eyes was white and the left one black, and he thought himself superior to all others in song" (*FGrH* 12 F 10). In this version, Thamyris goes on to challenge the Muses to a singing contest, after which the victorious goddesses take away his eyesight. Asclepiades thus knew of a version in which the singer's eyes were naturally heterochromial even before his blinding. However, Lessing posited an alternative explanation for the design of Thamyris' mask, arguing that its function was to enable the act of blinding to occur on-stage: before the event, the actor playing Thamyris would have performed turning only his profile with the dark seeing eye to audience, and after the blinding, the grey sightless one.[30]

Pollux does not associate this mask with any particular production, but since Sophocles is the only tragedian known to have produced a *Thamyras*,[31] this passage has often been taken as evidence for his staging, and many critics have followed

---

27 See e.g. Taplin (1978: 89) on Oedipus; cf. Marshall (1999: 192), *contra* Halliwell (1993: 206 n. 36).
28 Sophocles, frg. 236a–245. For discussion of the fragments, see A. C. Pearson (1917: 1.176–84); on the play's content and themes, see Wilson (2009). Sophocles is supposed to have played the *cithara* himself when he produced *Thamyras* (Athenaeus 1.20e–f), and the *Vita* claims that as a result he was depicted with this musical instrument on the *Stoa Poikilē* in Athens (*Vita* 5). These sources are often taken to imply that Sophocles actually played the role of Thamyris, but this is by no means a certain inference: see Wilson (2009: 60–1).
29 Pollux, *Onomasticon* 4.141: ἢ Θάμυρις τὸν μὲν ἔχων γλαυκὸν ὀφθαλμὸν τὸν δὲ μέλανα.
30 Lessing (1790: 104–7), drawing on the earlier work of Jean-Baptiste du Bos.
31 The scholion on pseudo-Euripides, *Rhesus* 916 (= Aeschylus, frg. 376a = *FGrH* 12 F 10) that preserves this fragment of Asclepiades used to also be taken as evidence for the existence of an Aeschylean *Thamyras* (see e.g. Hall 1989: 135–6), but this theory has now been debunked: see Merro (2006) and

Lessing in concluding (or at least admitting the possibility) that this mask enabled the blinding to occur on-stage in Sophocles' play.[32] In fact, this hypothesis poses considerable difficulties, not least since the physical and acoustical logistics of masked performance mean that it favours frontal delivery; moreover, it is doubtful that such miniscule detail as iris colour would have been perceptible from most seats in the *theatron*. However, the tradition of Thamyris' heterochromial eyes is so bizarre that it is difficult not to posit that it must have its roots in some conception of the singer as simultaneously blind and seeing. This confusion may be latent in an Iliadic scholion (Σ B *Iliad* 2.595), which records that Thamyris had one grey and one black eye, but that after his defeat by the Muses he lost only the latter. Additionally, Pollux's list places the mask of Thamyris in between those of "blind Phineus" (*Phineus tuphlos*) and "many-eyed Argos" (*Argos poluophthalmos*), so we might discern a linear progression in the compilation of the catalogue, from blind Phineus to half-blind Thamyris, to the supernaturally sighted Argos. Perhaps the detail of Thamyris' eyes arose from precisely the phenomenon that this chapter has been exploring, namely that the blind more often than not possess some kind of "sight" in Greek mythology and literature.

Although any reconstruction of the staging can only be speculative, we might also argue that the use of a single, unchanging mask with matching eyes would engage more subtly with the themes of sight and blindness that were evidently at the heart of this tragedy. If Thamyris were blinded on-stage, but without changing his mask (or profile and eye-colour), then the visual onus falls on the audience itself to "see" the instantaneous move from seeing to sightless.[33] Scholars have argued, and performances have demonstrated, that skilful use of the mask stimulates an active and creative viewing, where the spoken words and expressive gestures of the actor's body allow a viewer to project emotion and movement onto the mask's unchanging features. In the fifth century, the tragic mask seems to have been of indeterminate expression precisely to allow this kind of emotional visualization.[34] In the case of the blind mask of tragedy, the gaze of the onlooker is made to be engaged and active in constructing the different layers of sight and blindness inherent in the open-eyed yet sightless mask worn by a seeing actor playing a blind role, and this action replicates, in an intensified form, the essential tragic experience of watching a dramatic character

---

Wilson (2009: 59). The fourth century BCE comic poet Antiphanes wrote a *Thamyras*, of which only one fragment survives (*PCG* 104).

32 See e.g. A. C. Pearson (1917: 1.177–8); Calder (1959: 301, n. 2); Marshall (1999: 200, n. 41); Brillante (2009: 111–13); Wilson (2009: 61). On this mask more generally, see Lesky (1951), reprinted in Lesky (1966: 169–75).

33 Sophocles may also provide the only known example of the reverse, namely blindness being healed during the course of a tragedy. He wrote two plays entitled *Phineus*, one of which seems to have dramatized how Phineus was punished for blinding his sons by being struck blind himself. A fragment quoted in Aristophanes' *Wealth* and attributed to Sophocles' *Phineus* by the scholia may well refer to one son's healing by Asclepius (Sophocles frg. 710, "his sight has been restored and his eyeballs have been made bright, having met with a kindly healer in Asclepius"; cf. Phylarchus, *FGrH* 81 F 18), but this is not certain, and in any case we do not know whether this particular act of healing occurred on-stage.

34 Meineck (2011); see also Martha B. Johnson (1992), who compares Greek tragedy to the masked performance of Japanese Noh theatre.

who cannot watch you back. Perhaps, then, the tragic blinded mask absorbs the spectator, not so much because it ruptures what was previously a reciprocal relationship, but because it exemplifies the hierarchy of vision inherent in the theatrical experience itself. Add to this the fact that figures are often blinded at the moment they achieve a form of true "sight", usually by learning facts of which the audience is already aware, and the phenomenon of watching theatrical blindness becomes a particularly complex nexus of these different levels of physical, intellectual and metaphorical sight and blindness.

The same issues are at stake when we consider the depiction of blind figures in the visual arts.[35] Once again let us turn to Thamyris, and examine his representation in statuary and painting. Pausanias preserves a description of the famous underworld mural on the Cnidian Lesche at Delphi by the fifth-century artist Polygnotus, which featured Thamyris: "his vision is completely destroyed, and his attitude is utterly dejected ... a lyre is hurled down by his feet, with its horns shattered and its strings broken" (Pausanias 10.30.8). Pausanias also mentions a sculptural group of various ancient poets and musicians at Helicon, including Thamyris "already blind, and holding his broken lyre" (9.30.2).[36]

In both of these descriptions, the artist replicated the *Iliad*'s close identification of Thamyris' musical identity with that of his physical identity, represented by the parallelism of his smashed lyre and useless eyes. The symbol of the broken or abandoned *cithara* becomes Thamyris' special token of identity, and Pausanias (4.33.3) even writes of a Messenian river called Balyra, so named because it was there that Thamyris threw away his lyre (*ballein luran*) after his blinding. The breaking of the lyre was probably a significant moment in Sophocles' *Thamyras*: a lyric fragment assigned to the play speaks of someone "breaking the horn set with gold, breaking the harmony of the strung lyre".[37] Similarly, on the Ashmolean *hydria* (Figure 12.1) Thamyris is portrayed in the act of casting away his *cithara*, in contrast to the victorious Muse who stands upright still holding her musical instrument. Thamyris is depicted in profile with a closed eye, and interpretation of the surrounding details confirms to the viewer that this is indeed Thamyris, and that his eyes are shut in blindness, rather than in sleep, pain or mental distress. Thus, in order to "see" Thamyris' blindness on this vase or in the artistic works described by Pausanias, the viewer must work through a series of visual clues, so that the very act of identifying blindness draws attention to the vital importance of the faculty of sight and the active, creative nature of the process of viewing. And yet, such viewing of Thamyris' blindness – the deprivation of sight that once existed – is itself a multi-layered optical illusion: as with the tragic mask, the

---

35 Here I touch briefly upon a vast topic, and one treated in more depth by Grethlein (this volume). See especially the artistic representation of Oedipus and Polyphemus (cf. *LIMC*, s.v. "Oidipous", "Polyphemos I"), and R. Osborne (1988: 1–5) on the dynamics of viewing such images.
36 The location is especially pointed, since Mount Helicon was sacred to the Muses and hence associated with poetic inspiration. Garland (1995: 112) wonders if Thamyris' statue "perhaps served as a warning to over-ambitious bards". On Polygnotus' *Nekuia* painting at Delphi, cf. Turner (this volume).
37 Sophocles, frg. 244. The verses are recorded by Plutarch (*Moralia* 5.455c) as spoken by Thamyris and the assignment to Sophocles is plausible, since we know of no other tragic version of his story.

viewer must project the construction of lost sight onto an already blind, unseeing surface.[38]

Just as the narrator of the *Iliad* implicitly asserts his own poetic superiority by singing about the boast and blinding of Thamyris, so by construing the visual tokens of Thamyris' identity, or by parsing the layers of sight and blindness at work in the tragic blind mask or a painted image, the spectator is made to employ and to consider the very sense of which the bard himself was deprived. These examples of blindness cannot be construed without, or separately from, forms of physical, intellectual and artistic sight. In this way, the depiction of blindness, whether in poetry, performance or the visual arts, engages these forms of sight in a manner which itself draws attention to what is at stake, and to what is both lost and gained in blindness.

Although necessarily a limited and selective treatment of this vast topic, this chapter has explored some of the complex associations of blindness with music, poetry, transgression, punishment, insight and self-recognition, which are deeply ingrained in the ancient Greek cultural imagination. Blindness may lead to, coincide with or result from either the bestowal or the removal of special abilities or knowledge, but it is always marked in some way: mythological figures are never "just" blind. I have also suggested that when blindness appears in contexts that are themselves accessed by an act of vision, the phenomenon of engaging the faculty of sight in order to view blindness provides fertile ground for thinking through the complex dynamics of the relationship between viewer and viewed. The hypothetical mask of Thamyris, with its one dark and one grey eye, is a concrete representation of this simultaneous existence of blindness and sight: a single face that both sees and does not see (depending on how you look at it), and an empty, sightless object until placed over the seeing eyes of its wearer and viewed and interpreted by its spectators. In this sense, the enigmatic mask of Thamyris provides an evocative and fitting symbol for thinking about the double-sided nature of blindness and sight.[39]

---

[38] Indeed, in ancient Greece, statues were proverbial for their lack of sense and sensation, including sight: see Steiner (2001: 136–45).

[39] I am very grateful to Richard Buxton, William Kynan-Wilson and Michael Squire for their acute comments on drafts of this chapter.

13

SIGHT IN RETROSPECTIVE
The afterlife of ancient optics

A. Mark Smith

Although this volume has examined "sight and the ancient senses" from a variety of disciplinary perspectives, its primary concern has been to examine the sensory history of vision from *within* the intellectual, social and cultural parameters of classical antiquity, stretching from Archaic Greece (e.g. the chapters by Rudolph, Grethlein and Bielfeldt) all the way through to late antiquity (e.g. the chapters by Webb and Heath). In this final retrospective, my aim is somewhat different. Broadening the chronological remit, I venture beyond the "classical" frame, exploring the afterlife of ancient thinking in a range of different cultural contexts (and among a series of decidedly "non-classical" authors). Because, as we shall see, one of the most important aspects of this legacy lay in mathematical approaches to the mechanics of seeing, I will focus specifically on the reception of ancient optics (developing some of Reviel Netz & Michael Squire's observations in the third chapter). As for my chronological frame, I will likewise restrict myself to the period between the third and seventeenth centuries CE: for reasons explained towards the end of my chapter (and already hinted at in Michael Squire's introduction), the seventeenth century marks a decisive turning-point here, effectively bisecting what we might label "ancient" from "modern" traditions of theorizing about the sense of sight.

Let me begin by laying out – and critiquing – the conventional narrative told of (late) ancient optics. By the early third century CE, or so the story goes, ancient optics (and, more specifically, visual theory) had reached its culmination with the likes of Ptolemy and Galen, the former having provided the theory with its mathematical bones in the form of visual rays, the latter with its anatomical and physiological flesh. Meanwhile, the resulting body of optical theory was animated by an Aristotelian soul within which sensation, perception and cognition were thought to produce increasingly general "images", from *phantasmata* in the imagination to *eidē* in the intellect, of the external world and its constituent objects. Vision, in short, was assumed to yield a faithful picture of external reality and its ordering principles. And it was assumed to do so on the basis of primal colour impressions accompanied by secondary impressions of the so-called common sensibles – that is, such things as size, shape and distance.

For all its promise (the standard account continues) the ancient science of optics went into a sharp slump during the third century CE, a slump that lasted until the intellectual efflorescence of Baghdad in the ninth century. As part of this efflorescence, a range of Arabic thinkers from Ḥunayn ibn 'Isḥāq (d. 873) and Yaʿqūb al-Kindī (d. 873) to Qusṭā ibn Lūqā (d. 912) took up the traces of ancient visual theory and reworked them in various innovative ways. Moreover, although these thinkers clung to the theory of visual radiation that harked back to the Platonic and Stoic traditions, it was not long before the idea of visual radiation was superseded by that of light radiation. Accordingly, sight was understood to be a function not of something emitted from the eye to external objects in order to apprehend them visually, but of something radiating from those objects into the eye. Instrumental in the articulation of this new intromissive theory, Ibn al-Haytham (or Alhacen, in his Latin incarnation: d. 1040/1) rewrote the science of optics on the basis of light rays in his monumental, seven-book treatise, *Kitāb al-Manāẓir* ("Book of Optics"). In the process (the standard account concludes) he razed the entire edifice of ancient optics and laid the foundations of modern optics on its ruins. Alhacen, in other words, revolutionized the science of optics.[1]

The legacy of ancient optics in late antiquity

The standard account just outlined is not entirely without foundation, especially if one focusses exclusively on the development of geometrical optics from roughly 300 BCE to 160 CE, when Ptolemy brought classical visual ray-analysis to its peak.[2] Yet all indications are that by the beginning of the third century, not long after Ptolemy's death, interest and competence in geometrical optics had declined dramatically. Just how dramatically is indicated by Galen's reluctance, in the tenth book of *On the Usefulness of the Parts of the Body*, to explain the geometry of the visual cone for fear of daunting his audience, most of whom by his account were too ignorant to follow even the most rudimentary mathematical analysis.[3] Nor had things improved by the later fourth century, at least not if we are to judge by Theon of Alexandria's recension of the Euclidean *Optics*, which bears no comparison to Ptolemy's *Optics* in mathematical sophistication or scope.[4] In fact, the very failure of Ptolemy's *Optics* to survive in Greek suggests how far into disuse it, and the ray-analysis it contains, had fallen by late antiquity.

But there was more to ancient optics than ray-analysis. Unlike such "mathematicians" as Euclid, Hero of Alexandria and Ptolemy, a host of Classical and Hellenistic thinkers took a "philosophical" approach to visual theory, addressing the physical, physiological and psychological grounds of sight and light. In *Timaeus* 45b–46c, for instance, Plato supposedly followed the Pythagoreans in proposing a quasi-"extramissionist" theory based on the emission of a gentle, non-caustic visual fire

---

1 The lineaments of what I call the standard account can be found in Lindberg (1976). Whereas Lindberg makes no explicit reference to the revolutionary or modern nature of Alhacen's optical synthesis, a number of more recent scholars do: see, for example, Bellosta (2002), Sabra (2003) and G. Simon (2003), along with Netz & Squire (this volume). For a brief discussion of these claims, see A. M. Smith (2010a: xcvii–civ).
2 As Netz & Squire have already explained, Ptolemy's *Optics* currently exists only in a Latin translation from a lost Arabic translation of a lost Greek original. For the critical Latin text with an accompanying French translation, see Lejeune (1989). For a more recent English translation, see A. M. Smith (1996).
3 Galen, *On the Usefulness of the Parts of the Body* 10, 12: cf. May (1968: 492).
4 For the critical Greek text, with Latin translation, of the Theonine recension of Euclid's *Optics*, see Heiberg (1895: 142–284).

from the eyes that coalesces with external fire to put us into visual contact with things. Aristotle, on the other hand, plumped for an "intromissionist" alternative in which visual information is conveyed from external objects into the eye on the basis of colour impressions transmitted through transparent media.[5] In addition, he devoted considerable effort in the third book of *On the Soul* to making sense of sight on physical and psychological grounds, with special emphasis on the perceptual and cognitive results of visual sensation. Galen, too, paid close attention to sight, focussing on the anatomy and physiology of the visual system from the cornea all the way through the ventricles of the brain. Stoic in inspiration, the resulting account of visual perception was based on *pneuma*, a form of fire assumed to permeate the entire optic system from the brain to the front surface of the cornea and to provide the physical and physiological pathway for visual perception.[6]

Whether by coincidence or in compensation, just as interest in geometrical optics waned by the beginning of the third century CE, interest in its philosophical counterpart appears to have surged. In short, the science of optics seems to have undergone a shift of focus rather than a decline during late antiquity. This shift is manifested in the approach of various Late Platonist thinkers between the time of Plotinus (d. *ca.* 270) and that of John Philoponus (d. *ca.* 570), all of whom focussed on the physical, psychological and epistemological foundations of sight. Working primarily in the Greek and near eastern reaches of the late Roman empire, these thinkers wrote commentaries on, or paraphrases of, Aristotelian works from an interpretive slant dictated by the belief that, despite appearances, Plato and Aristotle were in basic agreement about virtually everything and therefore had to be reconciled. As far as visual theory is concerned, this meant that Aristotle's intromissionist account of sight in the *On the Soul* and *Parua naturalia* had somehow to be harmonized with Plato's extramissionist account in the *Timaeus*.[7]

The theoretical reconciliation that evolved out of this effort was marked by several salient features. Perhaps the most obvious of these has to do with the status of light. Plato had assumed two sorts of light (or fire), one emanating from the eye, the other suffusing the surrounding air, and both together conspiring to put us in visual touch with external objects. Galen and the Stoics proposed a similar theory on the basis of ocular and aerial *pneuma*.[8] Aristotle, on the other hand, supposed that light renders potentially transparent media actually transparent so that external objects – or, rather, their colours – can manifest themselves to us through them. According to him, then, light can be thought of as the "colour" of transparency.[9] In all these cases, external light serves as a sort of catalyst for sight rather than something visible in its own right,

---

5 It should be noted, however, that, although he adamantly supports an intromissionist theory in the *On the Soul* and in the works anthologized as *Short Treatises on Nature*, Aristotle falls back on visual radiation in the *On Meteorology*, and visual radiation is also at play in the pseudo-Aristotelian *Problems*. For introductions to Presocratic and Classical Greek paradigms of conceptualizing vision, see the chapters by Rudolph and Nightingale (this volume).
6 Galen spells his theory out in several works, among which *On the Usefulness of the Parts of the Body* and *On the Doctrines of Hippocrates and Plato* are particularly significant. On Stoic models – and literary critical takes on "sight and insight" more generally – cf. Webb (this volume).
7 On the late antique tendency to conflate Plato and Aristotle, see Blumenthal (1990).
8 See e.g. *On the Doctrines of Hippocrates and Plato* 7, 5.33: De Lacy (1980: 461).
9 See Aristotle, *On the Soul* 2.7, 418b6–13, with Barnes (1984: 666).

and it is precisely at this point that the Late Platonist commentators parted ways with both Plato and Aristotle. They regarded light not as a catalyst but as something manifesting itself directly to sight through transparent media. Conversely, the transparency of such media is manifested, and thus "actualized", by light's being seen through it. Not just per se visible, though, light also serves to render colours visible by illuminating them and thus enabling them to manifest themselves directly through transparent media. In essence, then, the Late Platonists treated *both* light and luminous colour as intrinsically visible.

By rendering light and colour per se visible, these thinkers emphasized intromission over extramission in the visual process and therefore favoured Aristotle over Plato. This is clearly demonstrated in John Philoponus' argument against extramission on the grounds that everything visual radiation explains can be accounted for better and more efficiently on the basis of light radiation. In short, Ockham's Razor dictates a preference for light radiation over visual radiation in accounting for sight. Furthermore, Philoponus continues, light is immaterial and qualitative, not material, so, rather than push its way physically into or through transparent media, as Plato and the Stoics would have it, light is conveyed by those media, spot-by-spot, in a rectilinear succession of qualitative alterations. From the perspective of the eye, such straight lines, or rays, when taken as a whole, form a cone with its base in the luminous object and its vertex at the centre of the eye. This, of course, is the visual cone of Euclid and Ptolemy transformed into a cone of radiation.[10]

As to the visual process arising from the eye's reception of light, the Late Platonist commentators followed Aristotle's lead fairly closely. They therefore assumed that the visual process occurs at three levels, starting with mere sensation, progressing to perception and culminating with cognition. Like Aristotle, they associated these stages with specific psychological faculties. At the level of sensation, the eye apprehends things visually insofar as it is affected by colour impressions. Perception of these sense impressions is carried out by the common sense and the imagination, through which the special and common sensibles arriving from the five external senses are combined into a single representation of the originally sensed object and stored for mnemonic recall. Apprehended in all its physical particularity at this stage, the represented object is then judged by discursive reason according to its intelligible aspects. The result is a cognitive grasp of what kind of thing is being represented both specifically and generically: a mule, a human, a triangle, a square, a polygon and so forth. In other words, the object is comprehended according to the Universal, or exemplar, that it instantiates.

This entire process takes place in the brain and the *pneuma* pervading its ventricles, so it unfolds in a material substrate. The problem is that, being material, this substrate is imperfect and subject to continual change, whereas the objects of cognition, the so-called Universals, are perfect and unchangeable. How, then, can the psychological faculties embodied in the cerebral ventricles yield such perfect exemplars? In response to this question, the Late Platonists took their cue from Plato by adducing two distinct levels of intellect. At the lower level is the embodied intellect, which is passive but has the potential to know. At the higher level is the actual or active

---

10 On Philoponus, see De Groot (1991).

intellect, which has fulfilled the potential to know and thus actually knows.[11] The passive intellect cannot make the transition from potential to actual knowledge on its own, however. It needs an ulterior agent (i.e. acting) intellect to help it, either by giving it the Universal it seeks or by showing it the Universal implicit in the perceived representations that it is thinking about. The mechanism most commonly appealed to in this context is intellectual illumination, which helps the mind "see" Universals in perceptual (or conceptual) representations by analogy to how physical illumination enables the eye to see the individual objects that are represented by them.[12]

The Arabic heritage

In a certain sense, the intellectual efflorescence that occurred in the Arabic East during the ninth and tenth centuries represented a continuation of the late antique Greek commentary tradition. Thus, along with translations from Greek into Syriac and Arabic of the primary Greek sources and late antique commentaries came a variety of original commentaries, paraphrases and studies at the hands of such well-known thinkers as al-Kindī, al-Fārābī (d. 950/1) and Ibn Sīnā (Avicenna: d. 1037), all of whom subscribed to essentially the same Platonized Aristotelian model of visual perception.[13] Accordingly, they distinguished potential from actual intellect and lodged the former in the ventricles of the brain with its charge of animal *pneuma*. Furthermore, they broke the potential intellect down into specific psychological faculties, each associated with a particular cerebral ventricle.[14] They also explained the process of perception and cognition in terms of formal representations or "images" yielded by these faculties. And, finally, they appealed to a supervening agent intellect that effects the transition from perception to cognition by providing intellectual illumination or by supplying the Universals themselves as templates.

The resulting account of visual perception and cognition took more or less canonical form in the model of five "internal senses" detailed by Avicenna in the sixth part of his *Shifā'* ("Healing").[15] Consisting of five psychological faculties, these internal senses are arrayed front to back in the cerebral ventricles. The first two, common sense and imagination, are associated with the frontmost ventricle, which in fact consists of a twinned pair. The third and fourth internal senses, which comprise compositive imagination (or fantasy) and the estimative faculty, are associated with the second, central ventricle, and the fifth and final internal sense, intellectual memory, is associated with the occipital ventricle. For their part, the five external

---

11 Sensation and cognition were commonly understood as acts of assimilation, the sense-organ or the intellect "becoming" its proper object (that is, colour for sight or the Universal for intellect). For a clear articulation of this notion, see Aristotle, *On the Soul* 2.5, 418a3–6; 3.4, 429b6–9 and 3.4, 430a14: Barnes (1984: 665, 682–4).
12 This notion harks back to Plato's allegory of the cave in the seventh book of the *Republic*: see Nightingale (this volume).
13 On the Arabic translation movement of the ninth and tenth centuries, see Gutas (1998).
14 For a late antique example of this model, see Nemesius, *On the Nature of Man*: Sharples & van der Eijk (2008). For an early Arabic example, see Ḥunayn ibn 'Isḥāq's *Ten Treatises on the Eye*: Meyerhof (1928).
15 For an excellent overview of Avicenna's internal senses model, see McGinnis (2010: esp. 89–116).

senses are all connected to the brain through particular neural pathways, the optic nerves forming such pathways for the eyes. Being hollow, they conduct psychic *pneuma* from the brain into the eyes and thence to the crystalline lens, which is rendered visually sensitive to impinging light and luminous colour by the charge of *pneuma* that permeates it. The impinging light and colour, in turn, reach the eye within a cone of radiation that has its base in the field of view and its vertex deep inside the eye.

The act of sight starts with the sensitive reception of light and colour by the area on the surface of the crystalline lens cut by the cone of radiation. Thus abstracted by the pneumatized lens, the resulting sensible representation or "image" passes through the eye and the *pneuma* pervading the optic nerve. On reaching the optic chiasma, where the two nerves intersect, the sensible representations from both eyes are fused. Bifurcating again after this intersection, the nerves convey the fused image to the front of the brain. There, the common sense abstracts a perceptible representation from the fused image and remands it to the imagination, where it is stored for short-term mnemonic recall. Passed to the compositive imagination, this perceptible representation is discursively analysed by association and dissociation according to its intelligible characteristics, which are virtually or implicitly, but not actually, present in it. Avicenna refers to such implications as intentions, and it is up to the estimative faculty to infer them. On that basis, the soul abstracts a conceptual representation, in the form of what Avicenna calls a "vague individual".[16] Not a true Universal, this conceptual representation can nonetheless be read as such in the right light, which is provided by the agent intellect. Once properly read, this representation is sent to the occipital ventricle of the brain to be stored for long-term intellectual memory.

The syncretic nature of Avicenna's model of visual perception is evident from the sources he drew upon. His emphasis on faculty psychology, for instance, clearly stems from Aristotle's account in the second and third books of the *On the Soul*, albeit refracted through the interpretive lens of his Late Platonist and Arabic predecessors. Likewise, his reliance on intromission puts him squarely in the Aristotelian camp. In adducing the radiant cone with its base on external objects and its vertex in the eye, moreover, Avicenna seems to have drawn directly from John Philoponus, whose vindication of intromission clearly influenced Avicenna's defence of that alternative.[17] At the same time, Galen figures prominently in Avicenna's account of the anatomy and physiology of the optic complex extending from the surface of the cornea, through the humours of the eye, to the occipital ventricle of the brain. This, of course, comes as no surprise, since Avicenna's main claim to fame in both the mediaeval Islamic East and the Latin West was as author of the monumental *Canon of Medicine*, which is thoroughly Galenic in inspiration.

Like Galen in the tenth book of the *On the Usefulness of the Parts of the Body*, Avicenna gave at least a nod to geometrical optics by adducing the cone of radiation and using its mathematical properties to explain such basic things as the visual angle. Whether that nod was inspired by a more profound grasp of geometrical optics is

---

16 See Black (2012).
17 See Gutas (2004).

unclear. That it could have been is borne out by the fact that optics had found a home among several Arabic thinkers a century or more before Avicenna was born. Foremost among thinkers were al-Kindī, Qusṭā ibn Lūqā, and Aḥmad ibn ʿĪsā, all of whom benefited to some degree from Arabic versions of the Euclidean *Optics* and *Catoptrics*.[18] All three therefore subscribed to the visual ray model in some form or another and, on that basis, attempted to explain various phenomena pertaining to direct, unimpeded vision, as well as to vision mediated by reflection and refraction.

Even a cursory look at the optical analyses of all three of these thinkers reveals some astonishing lapses. Perhaps the most remarkable is found in al-Kindī's account of image magnification in refraction, which is based on the assumption that light refracts at an angle equal to the angle of incidence.[19] That al-Kindī could have even entertained this assumption makes it virtually certain that he was unaware of Ptolemy's *Optics*, and there are indications elsewhere in his optical *oeuvre* that he, as well as his ninth-century confrères, either did not have access to or did not fully understand the Euclidean *Catoptrics*. Consequently, with some exceptions *à propos* of burning mirrors, the ray-analysis developed and applied by these ninth-century thinkers was fairly primitive in comparison not only to that of Ptolemy but also to that of Euclid.[20]

However unsure the grasp of geometrical optics was among this first cadre of Arabic thinkers, that grasp became considerably surer a century later. Thus, by the 980s, the Baghdadi mathematician Ibn Sahl was able to demonstrate that parallel light rays refracting out of a plano-hyperboloidal glass lens will be brought to point-convergence at the focus of the opposite branch of the hyperbola, and he did so on the basis of what amounts to the sine-law of refraction.[21] To be sure, much of the sophistication of Ibn Sahl's proof is due to an increasingly profound understanding of the mathematics of conic sections during the tenth century. Some of it, however, can be explained by the fact that Ibn Sahl had actually read and understood Ptolemy's account of refraction in the fifth book of the *Optics*. As far as we know, in fact, Ibn Sahl is the first Arabic thinker to have had access to, or at least to have assimilated the analysis in, Ptolemy's *Optics*.

The recovery of Ptolemy's *Optics* towards the very end of the tenth century takes on true significance with Alhacen's monumental *Kitāb al-Manāẓir*, which was likely composed in the later 1020s. So clear is Ptolemy's influence in this work, that the *Kitāb al-Manāẓir* can be fairly characterized as a critical evaluation of, and elaboration on, the *Optics*. At the level of gross organization, for instance, Alhacen follows Ptolemy virtually to the letter. Accordingly, he devotes the first part of the treatise (books 1–3) to how things are perceived and misperceived in direct, or unimpeded, vision. He then turns in the second part (books 4–6) to an account of how things are visually perceived and misperceived when the radiation is fully impeded by mirrors and thus reflected. Finally, in the third and last part (book 7), he analyses refracted or partially broken vision in order to explain a variety of misperceptions ranging

---

18 On the dissemination of the Euclidean *Optics* into the Arabic East, see Kheirandish (1999).
19 See Rashed (1997: 424–7).
20 On the analysis of burning mirrors among early mediaeval Arabic thinkers, see Rashed (2000); for the earlier intellectual archaeology, see Netz & Squire (this volume).
21 See Rashed (1990).

from the apparent upward displacement of stars when viewed at or near horizon to the apparent magnification of objects seen underwater.[22]

But what about the radiation itself? Does Alhacen's explicit rejection of visual radiation in favour of light radiation not imply a radical break with the Ptolemaic past? Not really, because Alhacen's theory of visual sensation and its physical basis is as firmly grounded as Ptolemy's in a cone of radiation, albeit one consisting of light propagated into the eye rather than of visual flux emanating from the eye. Alhacen, in short, merely substituted light rays for visual rays. Nor was he out to overthrow the "mathematicians" – i.e. the proponents of visual radiation – in support of the "natural philosophers", who accept light radiation. Quite the contrary, Alhacen explains, since "both parties have something true to say ... but neither is wholly satisfactory without the other [to complement it]" he will provide the proper reconciliation between the two.[23] The mathematical equivalence between the visual cone and the cone of radiation is, of course, what makes this reconciliation feasible. Hence, as far as the resulting optical analysis is concerned, Alhacen's *Kitāb al-Manāẓir* is essentially a mirror of Ptolemy's *Optics*.

To some extent this point is exemplified in Alhacen's theory of visual sensation. For a start, he follows Galen in assuming that the two spherical eyes are linked to the brain via the optic nerves, which intersect at the optic chiasma and then enter the brain after bifurcating. Being hollow, they convey visual spirit from the brain to the eye and thence to the lens, which is thereby sensitized to impinging light and colour. But the inspirited lens is not properly sensitive to *all* the light and luminous colour reaching it, only to the light and colour that radiate to it along the perpendiculars. The rest it effectively ignores. Passing through the round pupil and thus circumscribed by it, the full bundle of such incoming perpendicular rays forms a cone with its base in the field of view and its vertex at the centre of the eye. This point constitutes the "centre of sight" from which everything is visually judged.[24]

Each of the rays within the cone makes a formal impression of itself on the lens, and the sum of all such impressions on the surface of the lens constitutes a sort of pointillist image (or "form" in Alhacen's parlance) of the field of view. Abstracted visually by the lens, this form passes straight to the lens' posterior surface, where it is funnelled by refraction into the hollow optic nerve at the back of the eye (Figure 13.1). Continuing through the spirit-infused nerve to the optic chiasma, it coalesces with its mate from the other eye, after which the resulting amalgam continues to the front of the brain in order to be perceptually apprehended and judged. Such perceptual judgement is based on particular clues that indicate what the form represents. Numbering 22 and styled "visible intentions" by Alhacen, these clues range from light and colour, which are primal, to such secondary characteristics as size, shape, motion, rest and so forth. Alhacen's visible intentions, in short, are equivalent to Aristotle's common sensibles.

---

22 In Ptolemy's *Optics*, the first and second books are devoted to direct vision, whereas the third and fourth treat reflection, and the fifth book examines refraction: cf. Netz & Squire (this volume).
23 A. M. Smith (2001: 373–4).
24 For an overview of Alhacen's theory, with appropriate textual references, see A. M. Smith (2001: lii–lxxviii).

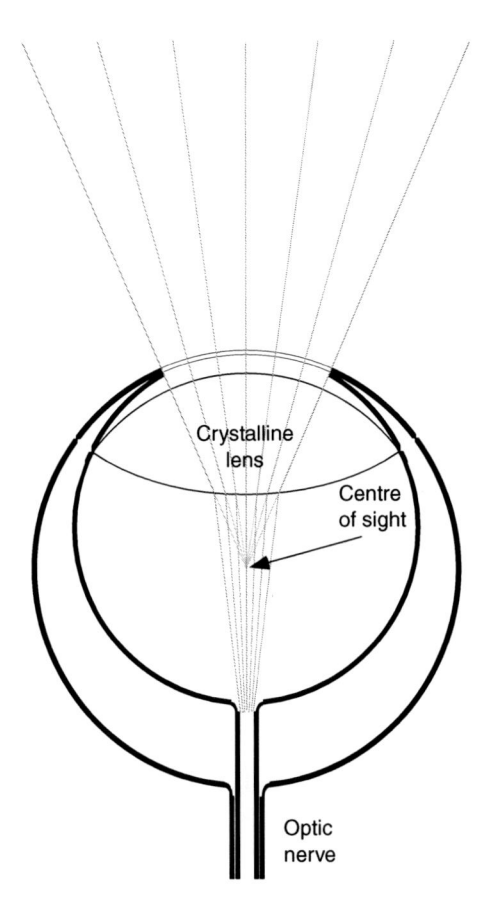

Figure 13.1 The eye according to Alhacen, based on his description in the first book of *De aspectibus* (*ca.* 1030 CE) (diagram supplied by the author).

Much like a portrait, therefore, the visual form abstracted by the lens implies a variety of spatial and non-spatial characteristics, such as depth, mass, and distance, or similarity and difference, that are virtually but not actually in it. Properly inferred by the "faculty of discrimination", these intentional characteristics yield a "particular form" of the original object that represents it in all its physical individuality: i.e. the particular, dull shade of red in the cushion I am sitting on; the particular schnauzer I see running through my lawn, etc. Continual experience of such individual instances and recollection of them through their particular forms leads to a more general grasp of what the objects they represent are according to type. This in turn yields the so-called universal form, which represents "red" in all its shades, "dog" in all its varieties and so forth.

Depending, as it does, on a cone of radiation with its vertex at the eye's centre, this visual model obviously mirrors Ptolemy's insofar as it is mathematically identical; only the direction of radiation has changed. But Alhacen takes Ptolemy a step further by adapting this mathematical model to a Galenic, or at least Galen-inspired, anatomical and physiological model. Consequently, Alhacen's account is based on a pneumatic medium that not only imbues the lens with its peculiar visual sensitivity but also supports the passage and abstraction of a succession of images or forms. Starting with the visual form, the succession continues at the perceptual level with the particular form abstracted from it, and the process culminates with the universal form, which represents the object at the conceptual level. Much like Avicenna's vague individual, however, Alhacen's universal form is not truly universal, although it certainly points to the Universal. In short, it is a crucial intermediary between potential and actual cognition. This point of similarity between Alhacen and Avicenna reflects a broader similarity between the two insofar as Alhacen's overall model of visual perception and cognition is, if not based on, at least fully consistent with Avicenna's internal senses model.

Whereas Alhacen looked to a variety of thinkers besides Ptolemy in articulating his fundamental account of visual perception, he looked exclusively to Ptolemy for his detailed ray-analysis of reflection and refraction in the fourth to seventh books of the *Kitāb al-Manāẓir*. A clear instance of such borrowing can be found in Alhacen's solution to what became known as "Alhacen's Problem" in the later seventeenth century.[25] This problem can be distilled to the following. Assume that two points lie within a completely enclosed concave spherical mirror, one being a point-source of light and the other a centre of sight. Posed thus, the problem is actually twofold: first, to determine how many rays from the point-source will reflect from the mirror to the centre of sight; second, to establish precisely where the point or points of reflection will lie on the mirror's surface.

For the first determination, Alhacen falls back on a simple but elegant expedient. Let the large circle centred on C in Figures 13.2 and 13.3 represent the mirror, and let A and B be the point-source of light and the centre of sight, respectively, within a given plane of reflection. Draw a circle through points A, B and C. Depending on whether and where that circle intersects the mirror, there can be as many as three reflections and as few as none from the facing arc. Thus, in the case illustrated in Figure 13.2, where circle ACB cuts the mirror at D and E on each side of line DX, which is perpendicular to line AB, there will be three reflections altogether, two from arc XD and one from arc EF. On the other hand, if circle ACB fails to cut the mirror at all, as in Figure 13.3, there can be no more than one reflection, and it must occur from arc EF cut off by line CBF and line CE, which bisects AB.[26]

Having thus isolated the arc or arcs within which reflection will occur, Alhacen is in a position to determine exactly where the point(s) of reflection will lie within the specified arc(s). How he does this need not detain us. The point is that he could not have done it without first establishing the arc(s) within which the point(s) of reflection would lie, and the method he employed to that end was developed not by him but by Ptolemy in the fourth book of the *Optics*.[27] In other words, neither Alhacen's eponymous problem nor his solution to it was entirely original to him; the former was implicit, and obviously so, in Ptolemy's treatment of concave spherical mirrors

---

25 See A. M. Smith (2008b).
26 This is a simplification of Alhacen's analysis in the fifth book of the *De aspectibus*; see A. M. Smith (2008a: 462–74, esp. 472–4).
27 See A. M. Smith (1996: 182–9).

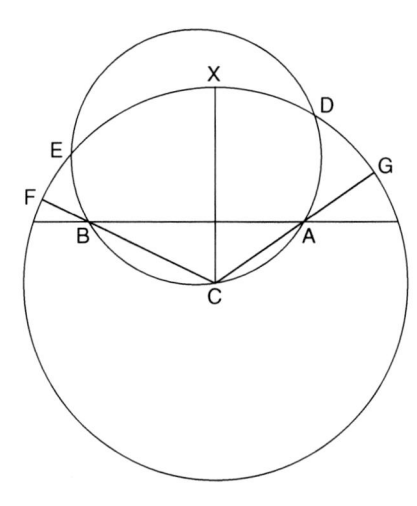

Figure 13.2 Two reflections from arc XD and one from arc EF; diagram after a passage in the fifth book of Alhacen's *De aspectibus* (*ca.* 1030 CE) (diagram supplied by the author).

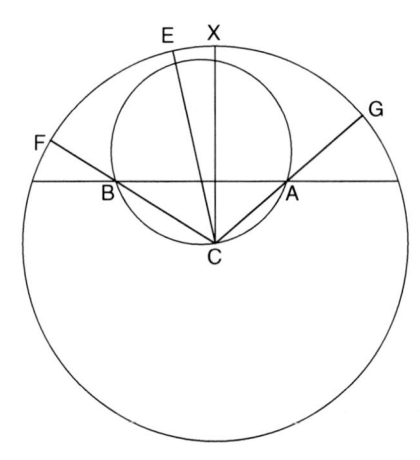

Figure 13.3 One reflection only, from arc EF; diagram after a passage in the fifth book of Alhacen's *De aspectibus* (*ca.* 1030 CE) (diagram supplied by the author).

in the fourth book of the optics, and the latter was constructed on foundations laid in that book. In a sense, then, Alhacen merely tied up loose ends left in Ptolemy's treatment of concave spherical mirrors, and although he did so brilliantly, he did not forge off in a new direction. On the contrary, he followed a path already clearly blazed by Ptolemy, and the same applies to the ray-analysis throughout the *Kitāb al-Manāẓir*: there are myriad points of convergence both topically and methodologically between it and the analysis in Ptolemy's *Optics*. Even the numerous experiments designed by Alhacen and cited as examples of his originality and modernity are derived from the *Optics*, although reconfigured in obvious ways to accommodate light rays rather than visual rays.[28]

Alhacen's account of light and visual perception was thus deeply rooted in Classical, Hellenistic, late antique and Arabic sources, and Ptolemy's *Optics* held pride of place among those sources.[29] This is not to say that Alhacen was slavishly unoriginal, but his originality did not lie in creating radically new concepts or methods. It lay in honing tried-and-true ones and, on that basis, resynthesizing them as seamlessly as possible. Consequently, although far more rigorous, sophisticated, coherent and comprehensive than any of its predecessors, Alhacen's theory of visual perception in the *Kitāb al-Manāẓir* represents an advance in degree rather than in kind. Far from overthrowing ancient optics, in short, Alhacen brought it to perfection.

The Latin Western passage

Alhacen's *Kitāb al-Manāẓir* was translated into Latin around 1200 under the title *De aspectibus*, the authorial attribution "Alhacen" being a transliteration of Ibn al-Haytham's given name, al-Ḥasan. It has long been fashionable to interpret the assimilation of the *De aspectibus* between roughly 1230 and 1280, particularly at the hands of the so-called Perspectivists – Roger Bacon (d. *ca.* 1290), Witelo (d. *ca.* 1300) and John Pecham (d. 1292) – as marking a sharp turn towards the evolution of modern optics. But that interpretation is simplistic at several levels. For one thing, Alhacen's *De aspectibus* was not assimilated in an intellectual vacuum; the way to its assimilation was prepared by the translation of other works from Arabic to Latin in the twelfth century. Key among these works were the sixth part of Avicenna's *Healing* on psychology and the *Canon of Medicine*, both of which provided an explicit anatomical and physiological context for Alhacen's mostly operational account of visual perception. As we saw, this account is fully consistent with Avicenna's internal senses model of perception and cognition. Recognizing this fact, Roger Bacon melded the two explicitly in his *Perspectiva* of *ca.* 1265. Alhacen's account of visual perception was thus quickly assimilated to Aristotelian faculty psychology, as mediated by Avicenna's internal senses model. It was also assimilated to the scholastic theory of intentional species that became an integral part of that model. Accordingly, the succession of Alhacenian forms was transformed into a succession of intentional species, Alhacen's visual form now converted into the visible species, his particular form into the sensible species and his universal form into the intelligible species.[30]

For another thing, Alhacen's theory did not sweep the field during the later Middle Ages and Renaissance. The idea that sight depends either in whole or in part on something radiating out from the eye was still entertained by a large number of physicians, whose adherence to Galenic anatomical and physiological principles led them to endorse an extramissionist account of vision. Roger Bacon himself, an avowed proponent of Alhacen's visual theory, nonetheless argued that vision was

---

28 See A. M. Smith (2007); G. Simon (2004).
29 For detailed support of this claim, see A. M. Smith (2015: 181–227).
30 On the process of translation and assimilation in the twelfth- and thirteenth-century Latin West, see A. M. Smith (2015: 242–5).

due both to species radiated into the eye and to species radiated out from the eye, this latter radiation necessary for the completion of the visual act. Small wonder that such late mediaeval and Renaissance figures as Leon Battista Alberti (d. 1472) and Leonardo da Vinci (d. 1519) could express ambivalence about which model of vision, intromissionist or extramissionist, was the correct one, or even whether a definitive choice between the two could be made on empirical or logical grounds.

Despite its failure to put paid to extramission, Alhacen's theory of visual perception was integrated into the university curriculum, as the *De aspectibus* and its Perspectivist derivatives filtered into scholastic circles from the late thirteenth century on. Thus, by the late Renaissance, that theory, duly incorporated into the Galeno-Avicennian model of internal senses and interpreted in terms of intentional species, was accepted almost universally by those with formal education. Its appeal lay in that fact that it offered a systematic justification of the prevailing supposition that the world is represented to us subjectively in mental "pictures" that are somehow like the objective reality they portray. After all, Aristotle himself insisted that we cannot think without images,[31] and our own experience with imagining seems to bear this point out. In the form of species, these images were thought to replicate one another *seriatim* in a train of increasingly abstract and general representations, as the process of perception unfolds from object to intellect, from the physical species in the transparent medium to the intelligible species in the mind.

The persistence of this pictures-in-the-mind model of visual perception and cognition is a testament both to its apparent explanatory power and to the continuing sway of ancient optical sources from Aristotle and Plato to Ptolemy and Galen. The model itself rested on two central assumptions harking back to the ancient optical tradition: first, that the selection of visual images by the lens is physiologically rather than optically determined, and second, that the key analytic device for evaluating this selection process and its perceptual ramifications is a cone of radiation with its vertex at the centre of sight in the middle of the eye. As long as these two assumptions shaped the way visual perception was understood and analysed, the science of optics would remain rooted in its ancient past. And so it did remain until the beginning of the seventeenth century, when Johannes Kepler (1571–1630) proposed his theory of retinal imaging, which recast the lens as a purely optical device and did away with both the cone of radiation and the centre of sight as an analytic reference-point.[32]

In great part it was the adoption of this theory with all its entailments during the seventeenth century that marked the definitive turn from ancient to modern optics – and hence to entirely new ways of theorizing about sensory seeing. To start with, by reducing the lens of the eye to an insensate projector of real, physical images on the retina, Kepler broke the chain of species so carefully wrought during the Middle Ages and Renaissance, each species somehow replicating its predecessor. Unlike these replicas, which are virtual and thus perceiver-dependent, Kepler's retinal images are real and perceiver-independent. Furthermore, by differentiating the physical cause of

---

31 For the Aristotelian thinking here, cf. the chapters by Nightingale and Elsner & Squire (this volume); on Renaissance ideas of "perspective" and their relation to antiquity, see Tanner (this volume).
32 On Kepler and his new theory of retinal imaging, see A. M. Smith (2015: 322–72, developing e.g. 1998, 2010b); cf. Squire's introduction to this volume.

vision, in the mere focussing of light and colour, from its psychological effect, in the production of mental "images", Kepler effectively divorced light theory from sight theory. Thus freed from the need to accommodate light to sight, such seventeenth-century thinkers as René Descartes (1596–1650), Christiaan Huygens (1620–95) and Isaac Newton (1643–1727) took a mechanistic approach to light theory, explaining light and colour in terms of microscopic particles interacting with one another according to a small set of dynamic and kinematic principles. In doing so, they stripped light and colour of all qualitative existence. No longer assumed to exist "in" external objects, light and colour were now distilled to mere figments of our imagination, totally unlike the objective reality that generates them and that they supposedly depict. This sharp rift between objective cause and subjective effect – and the consequent assumption of total dissimilarity between the two – would herald the beginning of a very different philosophical paradigm: it would give rise to the notorious mind–body dichotomy championed by Descartes, and thereby to new modes of theorizing about both the senses *tout court* and the sense of sight in particular.[33]

The seventeenth century marks a defining crossroads in the intellectual history of theorizing about vision. But for our purposes in this chapter – as indeed this book – it also marks a poignant end to "ancient" thinking about sight. Of course Greek and Roman art, literature and philosophy would continue to influence how the western world made sense of what it saw – in a process that endures right up to the present day. Within the field of optics specifically, though, something had changed. And it had changed profoundly.

---

33 For further discussion of this point, see A. M. Smith (2015: 373–416).

BIBLIOGRAPHY

Adams, J. N. 1999. "The Poets of Bu Njem: Language, Culture and the Centurionate". *Journal of Roman Studies* 89: 109–34.
Adler, A. (ed.) 1928–38. *Suidae Lexicon*, 5 vols. Leipzig: Teubner.
Akbari, S. C. 2004. *Seeing Through the Veil: Optical Theory and Medieval Allegory*. Toronto: University of Toronto Press.
Alcock, S. 2002. *Archaeologies of the Greek Past: Landscape, Monuments, and Memories*. Cambridge: Cambridge University Press.
Alden Smith, R. 2005. *The Primacy of Vision in Virgil's Aeneid*. Austin: University of Texas Press.
Alexander, C. 1955. "A Roman Sarcophagus From Badminton House". *Metropolitan Museum of Art Bulletin* 14(2): 39–47.
Alexiou, M. 2002. *The Ritual Lament in Greek Tradition*, 2nd edn., D. Yatromanolakis & P. Roilos (rev.). Lanham: Rowman & Littlefield.
Alpers, S. 1983. *The Art of Describing: Dutch Art in the Seventeenth Century*. Chicago: University of Chicago Press.
Andersen, K. 1987. "Ancient Roots of Linear Perspective". *Acta Historica Scientiarum Naturalium et Medicinalium* 39: 75–89.
Anderson, G. A. 2009. "Towards a Theology of the Tabernacle and Its Furniture". In *Text, Thought, and Practice in Qumran and Early Christianity*, R. Clements & D. R. Schwartz (eds), 161–94. Leiden: Brill.
Andò, V. 1996. "'Nymphe': la sposa e le Ninfe". *Quaderni Urbinati di Cultura Classica* 52: 47–79.
Andreae, B. 1962. "Herakles and Alkyoneus". *Jahrbuch des Deutschen Archäologischen Instituts* 77: 130–210.
—— 1996. *Ulisse: il mito e la memoria*. Rome: Progetti Museali.
Andriopoulos, D. Z. 2014. "Alcmaeon's Epistemological Framework". *Philosophical Inquiry* 38: 42–60.
Anguissola, A. 2014. "Remembering with Greek Masterpieces: Observations on Memory and Roman Copies". In *Memoria Romana: Memory in Rome and Rome in Memory*, K. Galinsky (ed.), 117–34. Ann Arbor: University of Michigan Press.
Annas, J. 1981. *An Introduction to Plato's Republic*. Oxford: Oxford University Press.
—— 1982. "Plato's Myths of Judgement". *Phronesis* 27: 119–43.
—— 1992. *Hellenistic Philosophy of Mind*. Berkeley: University of California Press.
—— 1995. "Understanding the Good: Sun, Line and Cave". In *Critical Essays on Plato's Republic*, R. Kraut (ed.), 143–68. Lanham: Rowman & Littlefield.
Arias, P. E. 1962. *A History of Greek Vase Painting*. London: Thames & Hudson.
Arnheim, R. 1954. *Art and Visual Perception: A Psychology of the Creative Eye*. Berkeley: University of California Press.

Arrington, N. 2010. "Topographic Semantics: The Location of the Athenian Public Cemetery and Its Significance for the Nascent Democracy". *Hesperia* 79: 499–539.

—— 2015. *Ashes, Images, and Memories: The Presence of the War Dead in Fifth-Century Athens*. Oxford: Oxford University Press.

Assmann, A. 2006. *Religion and Cultural Memory: Ten Studies*, R. Livingstone (trans.). Stanford: Stanford University Press.

—— 2011. *Cultural Memory and Western Civilization: Functions, Media, Archives*. Cambridge: Cambridge University Press.

Assmann, J. 2011. *Cultural Memory and Early Civilization*. Cambridge: Cambridge University Press.

Austin, C. & D. S. Olson (eds) 2004. *Aristophanes:* Thesmophoriazusae, *Edited with Introduction and Commentary*. Oxford: Oxford University Press.

Babut, D. 1985. "Sur la notion d'imitation dans les doctrines esthétiques de la Grèce classique". *Revue des études grecques* 98: 72–92.

Back, F. 1883. *De Graecorum caeremoniis in quibus homines deorum vice fungebantur*. Berlin: G. Schade.

Bal, M. 2003. "Visual Essentialism and the Object of Visual Culture". *Journal of Visual Culture* 2: 5–32.

Balch, D. L. 2008. *Roman Domestic Art and Early House Churches*. Tübingen: Mohr Siebeck.

Baldassare, I. (ed.) 1993. *Pompeii. Pitture e mosaici*, vol. 4. Rome: Istituto della Enciclopedia Italiana.

—— (ed.) 1996. *Pompeii. Pitture e mosaici*, vol. 6. Rome: Istituto della Enciclopedia Italiana.

Baldes, R. W. 1975. "Democritus on Visual Perception: Two Theories or One?" *Phronesis* 20: 93–105.

—— 1978. "Democritus on the Nature of Perception of 'Black' and 'White'". *Phronesis* 23: 87–100.

Balensiefen, L. 1990. *Die Bedeutung des Spiegelbildes als ikonographisches Motiv in der antiken Kunst*. Tübingen: Wasmuth.

Balland, A. 1976. "Sur la nudité des nymphes". In *L'Italie préromaine et la Rome républicaine: Mélanges offerts à Jacques Heurgon*, vol. 1, 1–11. Rome: Publications de l'École française de Rome.

Baltussen, H. 2000. *Theophrastus Against the Presocratics and Plato: Peripatetic Dialectic in the* De sensibus. Leiden: Brill.

—— 2015. "Ancient Philosophers on the Sense of Smell". In *Smell and the Ancient Senses*, M. Bradley (ed.), 30–45. London: Routledge.

Barasch, M. 2001. *Blindness: The History of a Mental Image in Western Thought*. New York: Routledge.

Bardel, R. 2000. "*Eidola* in Epic, Tragedy and Vase-painting". In *Word and Image in Ancient Greece*, N. K. Rutter & B. A. Sparkes (eds), 140–60. Edinburgh: Edinburgh University Press.

Barker, A. & M. Warner (eds) 1992. *The Language of the Cave*. Edmonton: Academic Printing and Publishing.

Barnes, J. 1982. *The Presocratic Philosophers*. London: Routledge.

—— (ed.) 1984. *The Complete Works of Aristotle*. Princeton: Princeton University Press.

Barnouw, J. 2002. *Propositional Perception:* Phantasia, *Predication and Sign in Plato, Aristotle and the Stoics*. Lanham: University Press of America.

Baroin, C. 1998. "La maison romaine comme image et lieu de mémoire". In *Images romaines*, C. Auvray-Assayas (ed.), 177–91. Paris: Presses de l'École normale supérieure.

—— 2005. "Le rôle de la vue dans les arts de la mémoire latins". In *Études sur la vision dans l'antiquité classique*, L. Villard (ed.), 199–214. Rouen: Publications des universités de Rouen et du Havre.

—— 2007. "Techniques, arts et pratiques de la mémoire en Grèce et à Rome". *Mètis* 5: 135–60.
—— 2010. *Se souvenir à Rome: formes, représentations et pratiques de la mémoire*. Paris: Belin.
Barthes, R. 1981. *Camera Lucida: Reflections on Photography*. New York: Hill & Wang.
Barton, C. A. 1993. *The Sorrows of the Ancient Romans: The Gladiator and the Monster*. Princeton: Princeton University Press.
—— 2002. "Being in the Eyes: Shame and Sight in Ancient Rome". In *The Roman Gaze: Vision, Power and the Body*, D. Fredrick (ed.), 216–35. Baltimore: Johns Hopkins University Press.
Bartsch, S. 1989. *Decoding the Ancient Novel: The Reader and the Role of Description in Heliodorus and Achilles Tatius*. Princeton: Princeton University Press.
—— 2000. "The Philosopher as Narcissus: Vision, Sexuality and Self-Knowledge in Classical Antiquity". In *Visuality Before and Beyond the Renaissance: Seeing as Others Saw*, R. S. Nelson (ed.), 70–97. Cambridge: Cambridge University Press.
—— 2006. *The Mirror of the Self: Sexuality, Self-Knowledge, and the Gaze in the Early Roman Empire*. Chicago: University of Chicago Press.
—— 2007. "Wait a Moment, *phantasia*: Stoic Ekphrasis". *Classical Philology* 102: 83–95.
Bassi, K. 2005. "Things of the Past: Objects and Time in Greek Narrative". *Arethusa* 38: 1–32.
Bauckham, R. 2006. *Jesus and the Eyewitnesses: The Gospels as Eyewitness Testimony*. Cambridge, MA: Eerdmans.
Baxandall, M. 1972. *Painting and Experience in Fifteenth-Century Italy: A Primer in the Social History of Pictorial Style*. Oxford: Clarendon Press.
—— 1985. *Patterns of Intention: On the Historical Explanation of Pictures*. New Haven: Yale University Press.
Beare, J. I. 1906. *Greek Theories of Elementary Cognition from Alcmaeon to Aristotle*. Oxford: Clarendon Press.
Beazley, J. D. 1956. *Attic Black-Figure Vase-Painters*. Oxford: Clarendon Press.
—— 1963. *Attic Red-Figure Vase-Painters*, 2nd edn. Oxford: Clarendon Press.
Becker, A. S. 1990. "The Shield of Achilles and the Poetics of Homeric Description". *American Journal of Philology* 111: 139–53.
—— 1995. *The Shield of Achilles and the Poetics of Ekphrasis*. Lanham: Rowman & Littlefield.
Beecroft, A. 2011. "Blindness and Literacy in the Lives of Homer". *Classical Quarterly* 61: 1–18.
Beekes, R. 2010. *Etymological Dictionary of Greek*, 2 vols. Leiden: Brill.
Behrwald, R. 2009. *Die Stadt als Museum? Die Wahrnehmung der Monumente Roms in der Spätantike*. Berlin: Akademie Verlag.
Beja, M. 1971. *Epiphany in the Modern Novel*. London: Peter Owen.
Bek, L. 1980. *Towards Paradise on Earth. Modern Space Conception in Architecture: A Creation of Renaissance Humanism*. Odense: Odense University Press.
Belayche, N. 2009. "'Un dieu est né…': à Stratonicée de Carie (*I. Stratonikeia* 10)". In *Manières de penser dans l'antiquité méditerranéenne et orientale*, C. Batsch & M. Vârtejanu-Joubert (eds), 193–212. Leiden: Brill.
Bellosta, H. 2002. "Burning Instruments from Diocles to Ibn Sahl". *Arabic Sciences and Philosophy* 12: 285–303.
Belting, H. 2011a. *Florence and Baghdad: Renaissance Art and Arab Science*. Cambridge, MA: Harvard University Press.
—— 2011b. *An Anthropology of Images: Picture, Medium, Body*, T. Dunlop (trans.). Princeton: Princeton University Press.
Benediktson, D. T. 2000. *Literature and the Visual Arts in Ancient Greece and Rome*. Norman: University of Oklahoma Press.

Benoist, S. & A. Daguet-Gagey 2007. *Mémoire et histoire: les procédures de condamnation dans l'antiquité romaine*. Metz: Centre régional universitaire lorrain d'histoire.

—— (eds) 2008. *Un discours en images de la condamnation de mémoire*. Metz: Centre régional universitaire lorrain d'histoire.

Benoist, S., A. Daguet-Gagey, S. Lefebvre & C. Hoët-van Cauwenberghe (eds) 2009. *Mémoires partagées, mémoires disputées: écriture et réécriture de l'histoire*. Metz: Centre régional universitaire lorrain d'histoire.

Benson, J. L. 1987. "The Central Group of the Corfu Pediment". *Antike Kunst* 4: 48–60.

Bérard, C. 1974. *Anodoi: essai sur l'imagerie des passages chthoniens*. Rome: Institut Suisse de Rome.

—— 1984. *Le cité des images: religion et société en Grèce antique*. Paris: Éditions de la Tour.

Bergemann, J. 1997. *Demos und Thanatos: Untersuchungen zum Wertsystem der Polis im Spiegel der attischen Grabreliefs des 4. Jahrhunderts v. Chr. und zur Funktion der gleichzeitigen Grabbauten*. Munich: Biering & Brinkmann.

Berger, J. 1972. *Ways of Seeing*. London: Penguin.

Bergmann, B. 1994. "The Roman House as Memory Theater: The House of the Tragic Poet in Pompeii". *Art Bulletin* 76: 225–56.

—— 1999. "Rhythms of Recognition: Mythological Encounters in Roman Landscape Painting". In *Im Spiegel des Mythos: Bilderwelt und Lebenswelt*, F. de Angelis & S. Muth (eds), 81–107. Wiesbaden: Reichert.

Bernidaki-Aldous, E. A. 1990. *Blindness in a Culture of Light: Especially the Case of Oedipus at Colonus of Sophocles*. New York: Peter Lang.

Besançon, A. 2000. *The Forbidden Image: An Intellectual History of Icononclasm*, J. M. Todd (ed.). Chicago: University of Chicago Press.

Besig, H. 1937. *Gorgo und Gorgoneion in der archaischen griechischen Literatur*. Berlin: H. Markert.

Bethe, E. 1935. *Ahnenbild und Familiengeschichte bei Römern und Griechen*. Munich: C. H. Beck.

Bettini, M. 1999. *The Portrait of the Lover*, L. Gibbs (trans.). Berkeley: University of California Press.

—— 2000. "Einander ins Gesicht sehen im antiken Rom: Begriffe der körperlichen Erscheinung in der lateinischen Kultur". *Saeculum* 51: 1–21.

—— 2005. "Death and its Double: *Imagines*, *ridiculum* and *honos* in the Roman Aristocratic Funeral". In *Hoping for Continuity: Childhood, Education and Death in Antiquity and the Middle Ages*, K. Mustakallio, J. Hanska, H.-L. Sainio & V. Voulanto (eds), 190–202. Rome: Institutum Romanum Finlandiae.

Betts, E. 2011. "Towards a Multisensory Experience of Movement in the City of Rome". In *Rome, Ostia and Pompeii: Movement and Space*, R. Laurence & D. J. Newsome (eds), 118–32. Oxford: Oxford University Press.

Betz, H. D. (ed.) 1992. *The Greek Magical Papyri in Translation, Including the Demotic Spells*, 2nd edn. Chicago: University of Chicago Press.

Beyen, H. G. 1957. "The Wall Decoration of the Villa of P. Fannius Synistor near Boscoreale in its Relations to Ancient Stage Painting". *Mnemosyne* 10: 147–53.

Bielfeldt, R. 2014. "Lichtblicke – Sehstrahlen: Zur Präsenz von römischen Figuren- und Bildlampen". In *Ding und Mensch in der Antike*, R. Bielfeldt (ed.), 195–238. Heidelberg: Universitätsverlag Winter.

Bierl, A. 2004. "'Turn on the Light!' Epiphany, the God-Like Hero Odysseus, and the Golden Lamp of Athena in Homer's *Odyssey* (especially 19.1–43)". *Illinois Classical Studies* 29: 43–61.

Biles, Z. P. 2011. *Aristophanes and the Poetics of Competition*. Cambridge: Cambridge University Press.

BIBLIOGRAPHY

Binford, L. R. 1971. "Mortuary Practices: Their Study and their Potential". In *Approaches to the Social Dimensions of Mortuary Practices*, J. Brown (ed.), 6–29. Washington, DC: Society for American Archaeology.

Bing, P. & J. S. Bruss (eds) 2007. *Brill's Companion to Hellenistic Epigram down to Philip*. Leiden: Brill.

Björck, G. 1946. "ONAPIΔEIN: de la perception de rêve chez les anciens". *Eranos* 44: 306–14.

Black, D. 2012. "Avicenna's 'Vague Individual' and Its Impact on Medieval Latin Philosophy". In *Vehicles of Transmission, Translation, and Transformation in Medieval Textual Culture*, R. Wisnovsky, F. Wallis, J. Furno & C. Fraenkel (eds), 269–302. Turnhout: Brepols.

Blake, M. E. 1936. "Roman Mosaics of the Second Century in Italy". *Memoires of the American Academy in Rome* 13: 67–214.

Bloch, D. 2007. *Aristotle on Memory and Recollection: Text, Translation, and Reception in Western Scholasticism*. Leiden: Brill.

Bloch, M. & J. P. Parry 1982. *Death and the Regeneration of Life*. Cambridge: Cambridge University Press.

Block, E. 1981. *The Effects of Divine Manifestations on the Reader's Perspective in Vergil's Aeneid*. New York: Arno Press.

Blok, J. H. 2006. "Solon's Funerary Laws: Questions of Authenticity and Function". In *Solon of Athens: New Historical and Philological Approaches*, J. H. Blok & A. Lardinois (eds), 197–249. Leiden: Brill.

Blum, H. 1969. *Die antike Mnemotechnik*. Hildesheim: G. Olms.

Blumenthal, H. J. 1990. "Neoplatonic Elements in the de Anima Commentaries". In *Aristotle Transformed*, R. Sorabji (ed.), 305–24. Ithaca: Cornell University Press.

Blundell, S., D. Cairns, E. Craik & N. S. Rabinowitz 2013. "Introduction". In *Vision and Viewing in Ancient Greece* (= *Helios* 40(1–2)), S. Blundell, D. Cairns & N. S. Rabinowitz (eds), 3–37. Luboch: Texas Tech University Press.

Blundell, S., D. Cairns & N. S. Rabinowitz (eds) 2013. *Vision and Viewing in Ancient Greece* (= *Helios* 40(1–2)). Luboch: Texas Tech University Press.

Boardman, J. 1955. "Painted Funerary Plaques and Some Remarks on Prothesis". *Annual of the British School at Athens* 50: 51–66.

—— 1976. "A Curious Eye-Cup". *Archäologischer Anzeiger* 1976: 281–90.

Bobonich, C. 2001. "Resurrection". In *The Cambridge Companion to Jesus*, M. Bockmuehl (ed.), 102–18. Cambridge: Cambridge University Press.

—— 2002. *Plato's Utopia Recast: His Later Ethics and Politics*. Oxford: Clarendon Press.

Bodel, J. 1999. "Death on Display: Looking at Roman Funerals". In *The Art of Ancient Spectacle*, B. Bergmann & C. Kondoleon (eds), 259–81. New Haven: Yale University Press.

Boeder, M. 1996. *Visa est vox: Sprache und Bild in der spätantiken Literatur*. Frankfurt am Main: Peter Lang.

Boehm, G. 1995. "Die Wiederkehr der Bilder". In *Was ist ein Bild?*, G. Boehm (ed.), 2nd edn., 11–38. Munich: Fink.

Böhr, E. 1997. "A Rare Bird on Greek Vases: The Wryneck". In *Athenian Potters and Painters*, J. H. Oakley, W. D. E. Coulson & O. Palagia (eds), 109–23. Oxford: Oxford University Press.

Borgeaud, P. 1988. *The Cult of Pan in Ancient Greece*, K. Atlass & J. Redfield (trans.). Chicago: University of Chicago Press.

Bowen, Z. R. 1979. "Epiphanies, Stephen's Diary, and the Narrative Perspective of *A Portrait of the Artist as a Young Man*". *James Joyce Quarterly* 16(4): 485–8.

Bowie, E. & J. Elsner (eds) 2009. *Philostratus*. Cambridge: Cambridge University Press.

Boyer, P. 1994. *The Naturalness of Religious Ideas: A Cognitive Theory of Religion*. Berkeley: University of California Press.

Bradley, M. 2009. *Colour and Meaning in Ancient Rome*. Cambridge: Cambridge University Press.
—— 2013. "Colour as Synaesthetic Experience in Antiquity". In *Synaesthesia and the Ancient Senses*, S. Butler & A. Purves (eds), 127–40. Durham: Acumen.
—— 2015a. "Introduction: Smell and the Ancient Senses". In *Smell and the Ancient Senses*, M. Bradley (ed.), 1–16. London: Routledge.
—— (ed.) 2015b. *Smell and the Ancient Senses*. London: Routledge.
Brancacci, A. 1995. "Ethos e pathos nella teoria delle arti". *Elenchos* 16: 103–27.
Bravo, J. 2004. "Heroic Epiphanies: Narrative, Visual, and Cultic Contexts". *Illinois Classical Studies* 29: 63–84.
Brécoulaki, H. 2006. *La peinture funéraire de Macédoine: emplois et fonctions de la couleur, IVe–IIe s. av. J.-C.* Paris: Publications de l'École française de Rome.
Bredekamp, H. 2003. "A Neglected Tradition? Art History as *Bildwissenschaft*". *Critical Inquiry* 29: 418–28.
Bremmer, J. N. 1995. "Religious Secrets and Secrecy in Classical Greece". In *Secrecy and Concealment. Studies in the History of Mediterranean and Near Eastern Religions*, H. G. Kippenberg & G. G. Stroumsa (eds), 61–78. Leiden: Brill.
Brenk, F. E. 1994. "Greek Epiphanies and Paul on the Road to Damaskos". In *The Notion of "Religion" in Comparative Research*, U. Bianchi, F. Mora & L. Bianchi (eds), 415–24. Rome: L'Erma di Bretschneider.
Brennan, T. & M. Jay (eds) 1996. *Vision in Context: Historical and Contemporary Perspectives on Sight*. London: Routledge.
Brillante, C. 2009. "Le Muse di Thamyris". In *Il cantore e la musa: poesia e modelli culturali nella Grecia arcaica*, C. Brillante (ed.), 91–120. Pisa: Edizioni ETS.
Brilliant, R. 1984. *Visual Narratives: Story-Telling in Etruscan and Roman Art*. Ithaca: Cornell University Press.
Brink, C. O. 1982. *Horace on Poetry. Vol. 3. Epistles, Book II: The Letters to Augustus and Florus*. Cambridge: Cambridge University Press.
Brisson, L. 1998. "Plato's Theory of Sense Perception in the *Timaeus*: How it Works and What it Means". *Proceedings of the Boston Area Colloquium in Ancient Philosophy* 12: 147–74.
Broadie, S. 1993. "Aristotle's Perceptual Realism". *The Southern Journal of Philosophy* 31: 137–59.
—— 2011. *Nature and Divinity in Plato's Timaeus*. Cambridge: Cambridge University Press.
Bronfen, E. 1992. *Over Her Dead Body: Death, Femininity and the Aesthetic*. Manchester: Manchester University Press.
Bronfen, E. & S. W. Goodwin 1993. "Introduction". In *Death and Representation*, S. W. Goodwin & E. Bronfen (eds), 3–25. Baltimore: Johns Hopkins University Press.
Bruit, L. 1989. "Les dieux aux festins des mortels: théoxénies et xeniai". In *Entre hommes et dieux: le convive, le héros, le prophète*, A. F. Laurens (ed.), 13–25. Paris: Annales littéraires de l'université de Besançon.
—— 2004. "Banquet des dieux". In *Thesaurus Cultus et Rituum Antiquorum*, V. Lambrinoudakis & J. C. Balty (eds), vol. 2, 220–9. Los Angeles: Getty Publications.
Bruner, F. D. 2012. *The Gospel of John: A Commentary*. Grant Rapids: Eerdmans.
Bruno, V. J. 1977. *Form and Colour in Greek Painting*. London: Thames & Hudson.
—— 1981. "The Painted Metopes at Lefkadia and the Problem of Color in Doric Sculpted Metopes". *American Journal of Archaeology* 85: 3–11.
Bryan, J. 2012. *Likeness and Likelihood in the Presocratics and Plato*. Cambridge: Cambridge University Press.
Bryson, N. 1983. *Vision and Painting: The Logic of the Gaze*. London: Macmillan.
—— 1988. "The Gaze in the Expanded Field". In *Vision and Visuality*, H. Foster (ed.), 86–113. Seattle: Bay Press.

Bryson, N., M. A. Holly & K. Moxey (eds) 1994. *Visual Culture: Images and Interpretations*. Hanover: University Press of New England.
Bundrick, S. D. 2005. *Music and Image in Classical Athens*. Cambridge: Cambridge University Press.
Burgess, J. S. 2001. *The Tradition of the Trojan War in Homer and the Epic Cycle*. Baltimore: Johns Hopkins University Press.
Burke, P. 2001. *Eyewitnessing: The Uses of Images as Historical Evidence*. London: Reaktion.
Burkert, W. 1977. "Air-Imprints or Eidola: Democritus' Aetiology of Vision". *Illinois Classical Studies* 2: 97–109.
Burnyeat, M. 1992. "Is an Aristotelian Philosophy of Mind Still Credible? A Draft". In *Essays on Aristotle's De Anima*, M. Nussbaum & R. Rorty (eds), 15–26. Oxford: Clarendon Press.
—— 2005. "Archytas and Optics". *Science in Context* 18: 35–53.
Burridge, R. A. 1992. *What are the Gospels? A Comparison with Graeco-Roman Biography*. Cambridge: Cambridge University Press.
Burton, D. 2003. "Public Memorials, Private Virtues: Women on Classical Athenian Grave Monuments". *Mortality* 8: 20–35.
—— 2005. "The Gender of Death". In *Personifications in the Greek World: From Antiquity to Byzantium*, E. Stafford & J. Herrin (eds), 45–68. Aldershot: Ashgate.
Butler, H. E. & A. S. Owen 1914. *Apulei Apologia sive pro se de magia liber*. Oxford: Clarendon Press.
Butler, S. & A. Purves 2013a. "Introduction: Synaesthesia and the Ancient Senses". In *Synaesthesia and the Ancient Senses*, S. Butler & A. Purves (eds), 1–8. Durham: Acumen.
—— (eds) 2013b. *Synaesthesia and the Ancient Senses*. Durham: Acumen.
Buxton, R. G. A. 1980. "Blindness and Limits: Sophokles and the Logic of Myth". *Journal of Hellenic Studies* 100: 22–37.
—— 1996. "What Can You Rely on in *Oedipus Rex*? Response to Calame". In *Tragedy and the Tragic: Greek Theatre and Beyond*, M. Silk (ed.), 38–48. Oxford: Clarendon Press.
—— 2000. "Les yeux de Médée: le regard et la magie dans les *Argonautiques* d'Apollonius de Rhodes". In *La Magie*, A. Moreau (ed.), 265–75. Montpellier: Université Paul Valéry.
—— 2009. *Forms of Astonishment: Greek Myths of Metamorphosis*. Oxford: Oxford University Press.
—— 2013. *Myths and Tragedies in their Ancient Greek Contexts*. Oxford: Oxford University Press.
Byrskog, S. 2000. *Story as History – History as Story: The Gospel Tradition in the Context of Ancient Oral History*. Tübingen: Mohr Siebeck.
Cagnat, R. & M. Besnier 1929. "Périodiques". *L'Année épigraphique* 1928: 1–44.
Cahoon, J. W. 1939. *Dio Chrysostom*. Cambridge, MA: Harvard University Press.
Cairns, D. 1993. *Aidos: the Psychology and Ethics of Honour and Shame in Ancient Greek Literature*. Oxford: Clarendon Press.
—— 2005. "Bullish Looks and Sidelong Glances: Social Interaction and the Eyes in Ancient Greek Culture". In *Body Language in the Greek and Roman Worlds*, D. Cairns (ed.), 123–55. Swansea: Classical Press of Wales.
—— 2011. "Looks of Love and Loathing: Cultural Models of Vision and Emotion in Ancient Greek Culture". *Mètis* 9: 37–50.
—— 2013. "The Imagery of *erôs* in Plato's *Phaedrus*". In *Erôs in Ancient Greece*, E. Sanders, C. Thumiger, C. Carey & N. J. Lowe (eds), 233–50. Oxford: Oxford University Press.
Calabi Limentani, I. 1958. *Studi sulla società romana: il lavoro artistico*. Milan: Istituto Editoriale Cisalpino.
Calame, C. 1986a. *Le récit en Grèce ancienne: énonciations et représentations de poètes*. Paris: Méridiens Klincksieck.

—— 1986b. "Facing Otherness: The Tragic Mask in Ancient Greece", A. Hobart (trans.). *History of Religions* 26: 125–42.
—— 1992. *The Poetics of Eros in Ancient Greece*, J. Lloyd (trans.). Princeton: Princeton University Press.
—— 1995. *The Craft of Poetic Speech in Ancient Greece*, J. Orion (trans.). Ithaca: Cornell University Press.
—— 1996. "Vision, Blindness, and Mask: The Radicalization of the Emotions in Sophocles' *Oedipus Rex*". In *Tragedy and the Tragic: Greek Theatre and Beyond*, M. Silk (ed.), 17–37. Oxford: Clarendon Press.
—— 2005. *Masks of Authority: Fiction and Pragmatics in Ancient Greek Poetics*, P. M. Burk (trans.). Ithaca: Cornell University Press.
Calder, W. M. 1959. "The Blinding, *Oedipus Tyrannus*, 1271–4". *American Journal of Philology* 80: 301–5.
Camerota, F. 2002. "Optics and the Visual Arts: The Role of 'Skenographia'". In *Homo Faber: Studies on Nature, Technology and Science at the Time of Pompeii*, J. Renn & G. Castagnetti (eds), 121–41. Rome: L'Erma di Bretschneider.
Camille, M. 1996. *Master of Death: The Lifeless Art of Pierre, Illustrator*. New Haven: Yale University Press.
Carpenter, T. H. 1989. *Beazley Addenda: Additional References to ABV, ARV² & Paralipomena*. Oxford: Oxford University Press.
Carruthers, M. 1990. *The Book of Memory*. Cambridge: Cambridge University Press.
—— 1998. *The Craft of Thought: Meditation, Rhetoric, and the Making of Images, AD 400–1200*. Cambridge: Cambridge University Press.
Carson, A. 1992. "Simonides Painter". In *Innovations of Antiquity*, R. Hexter & D. Seldon (eds), 51–64. London: Routledge.
Carson, D. N. 2009. "Seeing the Sea: Ships' Eyes in Classical Greece". *Hesperia* 78: 347–65.
Caston, V. 2004. "The Spirit and the Letter: Aristotle on Perception". In *Metaphysics, Soul, and Ethics: Themes from the Work of Richard Sorabji*, R. Salles (ed.), 245–320. Oxford: Oxford University Press.
Castriota, D. 1992. *Myth, Ethos and Actuality: Official Art in Fifth-Century Athens*. Madison: University of Wisconsin Press.
Catoni, M. L. 2010. *Bere vino puro: immagini del simposio*. Milano: Feltrinelli.
Chaniotis, A. 2005. *War in the Hellenistic World. A Social and Cultural History*. Oxford: Oxford University Press.
Charlesworth, J. H. 1983. *The Old Testament Pseudepigrapha, Volume One: Apocalyptic Literature and Testaments*. Garden City: Doubleday.
Chase, G. H. 1902. "The Shield Devices of the Greeks". *Harvard Studies in Classical Philology* 13: 61–127.
Cherry, D. 2004. "Art History, Visual Culture". *Art History* 27: 479–93.
Chew, K. S. 2014. "Achilles Tatius, Sophistic Master of Novelistic Conventions". In *A Companion to the Ancient Novel*, E. P. Cueva & S. N. Byrne (eds), 62–75. Oxford: Wiley-Blackwell.
Chinn, C. M. 2007. "Before Your Very Eyes: Pliny *Epistulae* 5.6 and the Ancient Theory of Ekphrasis". *Classical Philology* 102: 265–80.
Christensen, J. 1999. "Vindicating Vitruvius on the Subject of Perspective". *Journal of Hellenic Studies* 119: 161–6.
Cioffi, R. 2013. "Seeing Gods: Epiphany and Narrative in the Greek Novels". *Ancient Narrative* 11: 1–42.
—— 2014. "Epiphany". In *The Virgil Encyclopedia*, R. F. Thomas & J. M. Ziolkowski (eds). Chichester: Wiley-Blackwell.
Cixous, H. 1976. "The Laugh of the Medusa". *Signs* 1(4): 875–93.

BIBLIOGRAPHY

Clairmont, C. W. 1993. *Classical Attic Tombstones*, 9 vols. Kilchberg: Akanthus.
Clark, S. 2007. *Vanities of the Eye: Vision in Early Modern European Culture*. Oxford: Oxford University Press.
Clarke, J. R. 2003. *Art in the Lives of Ordinary Romans*. Berkeley: University of California Press.
—— 2007. *Looking at Laughter: Humor, Power, and Transgression in Roman Visual Culture, 100 B.C.–A.D. 250*. Berkeley: University of California Press.
Classen, C. (ed.) 1993. *Worlds of Sense: Exploring the Senses in History and Across Cultures*. London: Routledge.
Clauss, M. 1996. "*Deus Praesens*: Der römische Kaiser als Gott". *Klio* 78: 400–33.
Clay, D. 2004. *Archilochos Heros: The Cult of Poets in the Greek Polis*. Cambridge, MA: Harvard University Press.
Clements, A. 2013. "'Looking Mustard': Greek Popular Epistemology and the Meaning of δριμύς". In *Synaesthesia and the Ancient Senses*, S. Butler & A. Purves (eds), 71–88. Durham: Acumen.
—— 2014. *Aristophanes' Thesmophoriazusae: Philosophizing Theatre and the Politics of Perception in Late Fifth-Century Athens*. Cambridge: Cambridge University Press.
—— 2015. "Divine Scents and Presence". In *Smell and the Ancient Senses*, M. Bradley (ed.), 46–59. London: Routledge.
Cline, R. H. 1972. "Heart and Eyes". *Romance Philology* 25: 263–97.
Clinton, K. 1992. *Myth and Cult: The Iconography of the Eleusinian Mysteries*. Stockholm: Svenska Institutet i Athen.
—— 2004. "Epiphany in the Eleusinian Mysteries". *Illinois Classical Studies* 29: 85–109.
Clostermann, W. E. 1999. "The Self-Presentation of the Family: The Function of Classical Attic Peribolos Tombs". PhD dissertation, Johns Hopkins University.
—— 2006. "Family Members and Citizens: Athenian Identity and the Peribolos Tomb Setting". In *Antigone's Answer: Essays on Death and Burial, Family and State in Classical Athens*, C. Patterson (ed.), 49–78. Lubbock: Texas Tech University Press.
—— 2007. "Family Ideology and Family History: The Function of Funerary Markers in Classical Attic Peribolos Tombs". *American Journal of Archaeology* 111: 633–52.
Coakley, S. 2002. "The Resurrection and the 'Spiritual Senses'". In *Powers and Submissions: Spirituality, Philosophy and Gender*, S. Coakley (ed.), 130–52. Oxford: Blackwell.
Coarelli, F. 2007. *Rome and Environs: An Archaeological Guide*. Berkeley: University of California Press.
Coleman, J. 1992. *Ancient and Medieval Memories: Studies in the Reconstruction of the Past*. Cambridge: Cambridge University Press.
Collins, R. 1998. *The Sociology of Philosophies: A Global Theory of Intellectual Change*. Cambridge, MA: Belknap Press.
Connelly, J. B. 2007. *Portrait of a Priestess: Women and Ritual in Ancient Greece*. Princeton: Princeton University Press.
Connerton, P. 1989. *How Societies Remember*. Cambridge: Cambridge University Press.
Connor, W. R. 1987. "Tribes, Festivals and Processions: Civic Ceremonial and Political Manipulation in Archaic Greece". *Journal of Hellenic Studies* 107: 40–50.
—— 1988. "Seized by the Nymphs: Nympholepsy and Symbolic Expression in Classical Greece". *Classical Antiquity* 7: 155–89.
Conticelli, V. 2008. *Medusa: il mito, l'antico e i Medici*. Florence: Polistampa.
Cooper, K. 1996. *The Virgin and the Bride: Idealized Womanhood in Late Antiquity*. Cambridge: Harvard University Press.
Cornford, F. M. 1937. *Plato's Cosmology: The Timaeus of Plato*. London: Routledge & Kegan Paul.
Courtney, E. 1995. *Musa Lapidaria: A Selection of Latin Verse Inscriptions*. Atlanta: Scholars Press.

Cox Miller, P. 1994. *Dreams in Late Antiquity: Studies in the Imagination of a Culture*. Princeton: Princeton University Press.
Craik, E. M. 2006. *Two Hippocratic Treatises:* On Sight *and* On Anatomy. Leiden: Brill.
Crary, J. 1991. *Techniques of the Observer: On Vision and Modernity in the Nineteenth Century*. Cambridge, MA: MIT Press.
—— 1999. *Suspensions of Perception: Attention, Spectacle, and Modern Culture*. Cambridge, MA: MIT Press.
Croisille, J.-M. 2005. *La peinture romaine*. Paris: Picard.
Cubitt, G. 2007. *History and Memory*. Manchester: Manchester University Press.
Curd, P. 2001. "A New Empedocles? Implications of the Strasburg Fragments for Presocratic Philosophy". *Proceedings of the Boston Area Colloquium in Ancient Philosophy* 17: 27–50.
—— 2007. *Anaxagoras of Clazomenae: Fragments and Testimonia*. Toronto: University of Toronto Press.
Damasio, A. 2012. *The Self Comes to Mind: Constructing the Conscious Brain*. London: Vintage.
Darrigol, O. 2012. *A History of Optics: From Greek Antiquity to the Nineteenth Century*. Oxford: Oxford University Press.
Davies, G. 1985. "The Significance of the Handshake Motif in Classical Funerary Art". *American Journal of Archaeology* 89: 627–40.
—— 1986. "The Rape of Proserpina on Roman Grave Altars and Ash Chests". *Shadow: The Newsletter of the Traditional Cosmology Society* 3(2): 51–60.
Davies, P. 2000. *Death and the Emperor: Roman Imperial Funerary Monuments from Augustus to Marcus Aurelius*. Cambridge: Cambridge University Press.
Day, J. W. 1989. "Rituals in Stone: Early Greek Grave Epigrams and Monuments". *Journal of Hellenic Studies* 109: 16–28.
De Griño, B. & R. Olmos 1986. "Atlas". In *Lexicon Iconographicum Mythologiae Classicae* 3(1): 2–16.
De Groot, J. 1991. *Aristotle and Philoponus on Light*. New York: Garland.
De Jong, I. J. F. 2004. *Narrators and Focalizers: The Presentation of the Story in the Iliad*, 2nd edn. London: Bristol Classical.
De Lacy, P. (trans.) 1980. *Galen: On the Doctrines of Hippocrates and Plato*. Berlin: Akademie Verlag.
Delatte, A. 1932. *La catoptromancie grecque et ses dérivés*. Paris: Droz.
Delling, G. 1984. "The 'One Who Sees God' in Philo". In *Nourished with Peace: Studies in Hellenistic Judaism in Memory of Samuel Sandmel*, F. E. Greenspahn, E. Hilgert & B. L. Mack (eds), 27–41. Chico: Scholars Press.
Deonna, W. 1965. *Le symbolisme de l'œil*. Berne: Éditions Francke.
Descamps-Lequime, S. (ed.) 2007. *Peinture et couleur dans la monde Grec antique*. Paris: Louvre.
Devereux, G. 1973. "The Self-blinding of Oidipous in Sophokles' *Oidipous Tyrannos*". *Journal of Hellenic Studies* 93: 36–49.
—— 1987. "Thamyris and the Muses". *American Journal of Philology* 108: 199–201.
Dickie, M. W. 1991. "Heliodorus and Plutarch on the Evil Eye". *Classical Philology* 86: 17–29.
—— 1995. "The Fathers of the Church and the Evil Eye". In *Byzantine Magic*, H. Maguire (ed.), 9–34. Washington DC: Dumbarton Oaks Research Library and Collection.
Diels, H. 1879. *Doxographi graeci*. Berlin: Reimer.
—— (ed.) 1922. *Die Fragmente der Vorsokratiker*, 2 vols. Berlin: Weidmann.
Diels, H. & W. Kranz (eds) 1951–2. *Die Fragmente der Vorsokratiker*, 3 vols. Berlin: Weidmann.

Diez De Velasco, F. 1998. *Termalismo y religión: la sacralización del agua termal en la Península Ibérica y el norte de África en el mundo antiguo*. Madrid: Universidad Complutense, Servicio de Publicaciones.

Dilts, M. R. (ed.) 1983–6. *Scholia Demosthenica*, 2 vols. Leipzig: Teubner.

Dodds, E. R. 1951. *The Greeks and the Irrational*. Berkeley: University of California Press.

Dodge, H. 2011. *Spectacle in the Roman World*. London: Bristol Classical Press.

Donaldson-Evans, L. K. 1980. *Love's Fatal Glance: A Study of Eye Imagery in the Poets of the École Lyonnaise*. University, Mississippi: Romance Monographs.

Donohue, A. A. 1988. *Xoana and the Origins of Greek Sculpture*. Atlanta: Scholars Press.

—— 1997. "The Greek Images of the Gods: Considerations on Terminology and Methodology". *Hephaistos* 14: 31–45.

Downie, J. 2013. *At the Limits of Art. A Literary Study of Aelius Aristides' Hieroi Logoi*. Oxford: Oxford University Press.

Drerup, H. 1980. "Totenmaske und Ahnenbild bei den Römern". *Mitteilungen des Deutschen Archäologischen Instituts (Römische Abteilung)* 87: 81–129.

Dunbabin, K. 1978. *The Mosaics of Roman North Africa*. Oxford: Oxford University Press.

Dunbabin, K. & M. W. Dickie 1983. "*Invida rumpantur pectora*: The Iconography of *Phthonos/Invidia* in Graeco-Roman Art". *Jahrbuch für Antike und Christentum* 26: 7–37.

Dundes, A. (ed.) 1981. *The Evil Eye: A Folklore Casebook*. Madison: University of Wisconsin Press.

Dupont, F. 2000. *L'orateur sans visage: essai sur l'acteur romain et son masque*. Paris: Presses universitaires de France.

Edelstein, E. J. & L. Edelstein 1945. *Asclepius. A Collection and Interpretation of the Testimonies*. 2 vols. Baltimore: Johns Hopkins Press.

Edwards, C. 2007. *Death in Ancient Rome*. New Haven: Yale University Press.

Edwards, E. & K. Bhaumik 2008a. "Visual Sense and Cultures of Sight: An Introduction". In *Visual Sense: A Cultural Reader*, E. Edwards & K. Bhaumik (eds), 3–16. London: Bloomsbury.

—— (eds) 2008b. *Visual Sense: A Cultural Reader*. London: Bloomsbury.

Edwards, M. 1993. "A Portrait of Plotinus". *Classical Quarterly* 43: 480–90.

Edwards, R. 2008. "Hunting for Boars with Pliny and Tacitus". *Classical Antiquity* 27: 35–58.

Ehrhardt, W. 2004. "Zu Darstellung und Deutung des Gestirngötterpaares am Parthenon". *Jahrbuch des Deutschen Archäologischen Instituts* 119: 1–39.

Eidson, D. 2013. "The Celsus Library at Ephesus: Spatial Rhetoric, Literacy, and Hegemony in the Eastern Roman Empire". *Advances in the History of Rhetoric* 16: 189–217.

Elkins, J. 1994. *The Poetics of Perspective*. Ithaca: Cornell University Press.

Elsner, J. 1990. "Significant Details: Systems, Certainties and the Art Historian as Detective". *Antiquity* 64: 950–2.

—— 1995. *Art and the Roman Viewer: The Transformation of Art from the Pagan World to Christianity*. Cambridge: Cambridge University Press.

—— 1996. "Image and Ritual: Reflections on the Religious Appreciation of Classical Art". *Classical Quarterly* 46: 515–31.

—— 2006a. "Classicism in Roman Art". In *Classical Pasts: The Classical Traditions of Greece and Rome*, J. Porter (ed.), 270–97. Princeton: Princeton University Press.

—— 2006b. "Art and Text". In *A Companion to Latin Literature*, S. Harrison (ed.), 300–18. Oxford: Oxford University Press.

—— 2006c. "Reflections on the Greek Revolution in Art: From Changes in Viewing to the Transformation of Subjectivity". In *Rethinking Revolutions through Ancient Greece*, S. Goldhill & R. Osborne (eds), 68–95. Cambridge: Cambridge University Press.

—— 2007a. "Physiognomics: Art and Text". In *Seeing the Face, Seeing the Soul: Polemon's*

Physiognomy *from Classical Antiquity to Medieval Islam*, S. Swain (ed.), 203–24. Oxford: Oxford University Press.
—— 2007b. *Roman Eyes: Visuality and Subjectivity in Art and Text*. Princeton: Princeton University Press.
—— 2010. "Alois Riegl and Classical Archaeology". In *Alois Riegl Revisited: Beiträge zu Werk und Rezeption/Contributions to the Opus and its Reception*, P. Noever, A. Rosenauer & G. Vasold (eds), 45–57. Vienna: Verlag der österreichischen Akademie der Wissenschaften.
—— 2015. "Visual Culture and Ancient History: Issues of Empiricism and Ideology in the Samos Stele at Athens". *Classical Antiquity* 34: 33–73.
Elsner, J. & M. Meyer (eds) 2014. *Art and Rhetoric in Roman Culture*. Cambridge: Cambridge University Press.
Elsner, J. & I. Rutherford (eds) 2005. *Pilgrimage in Graeco-Roman and Early Christian Antiquity: Seeing the Gods*. Oxford: Oxford University Press.
Engberg-Pedersen, T. (ed.) 2001. *Paul Beyond the Judaism/Hellenism Divide*. Louisville: Westminster John Knox.
Erbse, H. (ed.) 1969–88. *Scholia Graeca in Homeri Iliadem (Scholia Vetera)*, 7 vols. Berlin: De Gruyter.
Erll, A. 2011. *Memory in Culture*, S. B. Young (trans.). Basingstoke: Palgrave Macmillan.
Erll, A. & A. Nünning (eds) 2010. *A Companion to Cultural Memory Studies*. Berlin: De Gruyter.
Esser, A. 1961. *Das Antlitz der Blindheit in der Antike*, 2nd edn. Leiden: Brill.
Everson, S. 1997. *Aristotle on Perception*. Oxford: Clarendon Press.
Ewald, B. C. 2004. "Men, Muscle, and Myth: Attic Sarcophagi in the Cultural Context of the Second Sophistic". In *Paideia: The World of the Second Sophistic*, B. E. Borg (ed.), 229–76. Berlin: De Gruyter.
Eyl, J. 2012. "Why Thekla Does not See Paul: Visual Perception and the Displacement of *erōs* in the *Acts of Paul and Thekla*". In *The Ancient Novel and Early Christian and Jewish Narrative: Fictional Intersections*, M. P. Futre Pinheiro, J. Perkins & R. Pervo (eds), 3–19. Groningen: Barkhuis Publishing.
Fattori, M. & M. Bianchi (eds) 1988. *Phantasia-imaginatio: Atti del V. colloquio internazionale (centro di studio per il lessico intellettuale europeo), Roma 9–11 gennaio 1986*. Rome: Edizioni dell'Ateneo.
Feeney, D. 1991. *The Gods in Epic*. Oxford: Oxford University Press.
—— 1998. *Literature and Religion at Rome: Cultures, Contexts, and Beliefs*. Cambridge: Cambridge University Press.
Fejfer, J. 2008. *Roman Portraits in Context*. Berlin: De Gruyter.
Felten, J. (ed.) 1913. *Nikolaos, Progymnasmata*. Leipzig: Teubner.
Fentress, J. & C. Wickham 1992. *Social Memory*. Oxford: Blackwell.
Ferrari, G. R. F. 1987. *Listening to the Cicadas: A Study of Plato's Phaedrus*. Cambridge: Cambridge University Press.
Ferrari, G. 1986. "Eye-Cup". *Revue archéologique* 1: 5–20.
—— 2002. *Figures of Speech: Men and Maidens in Ancient Greece*. Chicago: University of Chicago Press.
Fiedler, K. 1991. *Schriften zur Kunst. I–II*, G. Boehm (ed.). Munich: Fink.
Finney, P. C. 1994. *The Invisible God: The Earliest Christians on Art*. Oxford: Oxford University Press.
Fisher, E. 1980. "'Let Us Look Upon the Blood of Christ' (1 Clement 7:4)". *Vigiliae Christianae* 34: 218–36.
Fitzgerald, W. 1996. *Catullan Provocations: Lyric Poetry and the Drama of Position*. Berkeley: University of California Press.

Fletcher, R. 2014. *Apuleius' Platonism: The Impersonation of Philosophy*. Cambridge: Cambridge University Press.

Floren, J. 1977. *Studien zur Typologie des Gorgoneion*. Münster: Aschendorff.

Flower, H. 1996. *Ancestor Masks and Aristocratic Power in Roman Culture*. Oxford: Clarendon Press.

—— 2002. "Were Women Ever 'Ancestors' in Republican Rome?" In *Images of Ancestors*, J. Munk Højte (ed.), 159–84. Aarhus: Aarhus University Press.

—— 2006. *The Art of Forgetting: Disgrace and Oblivion in Roman Political Culture*. Chapel Hill: University of North Carolina Press.

Foley, H. P. 1993. "The Politics of Tragic Lamentation". In *Tragedy, Comedy and the Polis*, A. H. Sommerstein, S. Halliwell, J. Henderson & B. Zimmermann (eds), 101–44. Bari: Levante Editori.

—— 2001. *Female Acts in Greek Tragedy*. Princeton: Princeton University Press.

Ford, A. 1992. *Homer: The Poetry of the Past*. Ithaca: Cornell University Press.

Forty, A. & S. Küchler (eds) 1999. *The Art of Forgetting*. Oxford: Borg.

Foster, H. 1988a. "Preface". In *Vision and Visuality*, H. Foster (ed.), ix–xiv. Seattle: Bay Press.

—— (ed.) 1988b. *Vision and Visuality*. Seattle: Bay Press.

Foster, P. 2007. "Polymorphic Christology: Its Origins and Development in Early Christianity". *Journal of Theological Studies* 58: 66–99.

Foucault, M. 1980. *Power/Knowledge: Selected Interviews and Other Writings, 1972–1977*, C. Gordon (ed. & trans.). New York: Pantheon Books.

Frank, G. 2000. *The Memory of the Eyes: Pilgrims to Living Saints in Christian Late Antiquity*. Berkeley: University of California Press.

Frede, D. 1992. "The Cognitive Role of *Phantasia* in Aristotle". In *Essays on Aristotle's De Anima*, M. Nussbaum & A. O. Rorty (eds), 279–95. Oxford: Oxford University Press.

Frede, M. 1983. "Stoics and Skeptics on Clear and Distinct Impressions". In *The Skeptical Tradition*, M. Burnyeat (ed.), 65–93. Berkeley: University of California Press.

Fredrick, D. 1995. "Beyond the Atrium to Ariadne: Erotic Paintings and Visual Pleasure in the Roman House". *Classical Antiquity* 14: 266–303.

—— 2002. "Introduction: Invisible Rome". In *The Roman Gaze: Vision, Power and the Body*, D. Fredrick (ed.) 1–30. Baltimore: John Hopkins University Press.

—— (ed.) 2002. *The Roman Gaze: Vision, Power and the Body*. Baltimore: John Hopkins University Press.

Freedberg, D. 1989. *The Power of Images. Studies in the History and Theory of Response*. Chicago: University of Chicago Press.

Fried, M. 1980. *Absorption and Theatricality: Painting and Beholder in the Age of Diderot*. Berkeley: University of California Press.

Frontisi-Ducroux, F. 1986a. "La mort en face". *Mètis* 1: 197–213.

—— 1986b. "Les limites de l'anthropomorphisme: Hermès et Dionysos". In *Corps des dieux. Le temps de la réflexion* 7, C. Malamoud & J.-P. Vernant (eds), 193–211. Paris: Gallimard.

—— 1988. "Figures de l'invisible: stratégies textuelles et stratégies iconiques". *AION* 10: 27–40.

—— 1989. "In the Mirror of the Mask". In *A City of Images: Iconography and Society in Ancient Greece*, C. Bérard (ed.), 151–65. Princeton: Princeton University Press.

—— 1991. *Le dieu-masqué: une figure du Dionysos d'Athènes*. Paris: La découverte.

—— 1993. "La Gorgone: paradigme de création d'images". *Les Cahiers du College Iconique: communications et débats* 1: 71–86.

—— 1995. *Du masque au visage: aspects de l'identité en Grecè ancienne*. Paris: Flammarion.

—— 1996. "Eros, Desire and the Gaze". In *Sexuality in Ancient Art*, N. Kampen (ed.), 81–100. Cambridge: Cambridge University Press.

BIBLIOGRAPHY

Frontisi-Ducroux, F. & J.-P. Vernant 1997. *Dans l'œil du miroir*. Paris: Odile Jacob.

Futrell, A. 1997. *Blood in the Arena: The Spectacle of Roman Power*. Austin: University of Texas Press.

Gage, J. 1993. *Colour and Culture: Practice and Meaning from Antiquity to Abstraction*. London: Thames & Hudson.

Gaifman, M. 2008. "Visualized Rituals and Dedicatory Inscriptions on Votive Offerings to the Nymphs". *Opuscula: Annual of the Swedish Institute at Athens and Rome* 1: 85–103.

—— 2012. *Aniconism in Greek Antiquity*. Oxford: Oxford University Press.

Galinsky, K. 2014. "Introduction". In *Memoria Romana: Memory in Rome and Rome in Memory*, K. Galinsky (ed.), 1–12. Ann Arbor: University of Michigan Press.

—— (ed.) 2014. *Memoria Romana: Memory in Rome and Rome in Memory*. Ann Arbor: University of Michigan Press.

—— (ed.) (forthcoming). *Aspects of Memory in Ancient Rome and Early Christianity*. Oxford: Oxford University Press.

Galinsky, K. & K. Lapatin (eds) (forthcoming). *Cultural Memories in the Roman Empire*. Los Angeles: Getty Publications.

Gallia, A. 2012. *Remembering the Roman Republic*. Cambridge: Cambridge University Press.

Garber, M. & N. J. Vickers (eds) 2003. *The Medusa Reader*. London: Routledge.

Garland, R. 1982. "A First Catalogue of *peribolos* Tombs". *Annual of the British School at Athens* 77: 125–76.

—— 1992. *Introducing New Gods: The Politics of Athenian Religion*. Ithaca: Cornell University Press.

—— 1995. *The Eye of the Beholder. Deformity and Disability in the Graeco-Roman World*. London: Duckworth.

—— 2001. *The Greek Way of Death*, 2nd edn. Ithaca: Cornell University Press.

Gaskell, I. 1991. "History of Images". In *New Perspectives on Historical Writing*, P. Burke (ed.), 168–92. Cambridge: Cambridge University Press.

Geary, P. 1994. *Phantoms of Remembrance: Memory and Oblivion at the End of the First Millennium*. Princeton: Princeton University Press.

Gee, R. 2003. "The Vatican Necropolis: Ritual, Status and Social Identity in the Roman Chamber Tomb". PhD dissertation, University of Texas, Austin.

Geiger, J. 2009. *The Third Man Factor: Surviving the Impossible*. Harmondsworth: Weinstein Books.

Geurts, K. 2002. *Culture and the Senses: Bodily Ways of Knowing in an African Community*. Berkeley: University of California Press.

Gibson, J. J. 1979. *The Ecological Approach to Visual Perception*. Boston: Houghton Mifflin.

Giuliani, L. 2003. *Bild und Mythos: Geschichte der Bilderzählung in der griechischen Kunst*. Munich: C. H. Beck.

Giuman, M. 2013. *Archeologia dello sguardo: fascinazione e baskania nel mondo classico*. Rome: G. Bretschneider.

Gladigow, B. 1985–6. "Präsenz der Bilder, Präsenz der Götter: Kultbilder und Bilder der Götter in der griechischen Religion". *Visible Religion* 4–5: 114–33.

—— 1990. "Epiphanie, Statuette, Kultbild: Griechische Gottesvorstellungen im Wechsel von Kontext und Medium". *Visible Religion* 7: 98–121.

Gleason, M. W. 1995. *Making Men: Sophists and Self-Presentation in Ancient Rome*. Princeton: Princeton University Press.

Goldberg, B. 1985. *The Mirror and the Man*. Charlottesville: University Press of Virginia.

Goldhill, S. 1986. *Reading Greek Tragedy*. Cambridge: Cambridge University Press.

—— 1994. "The Naïve and Knowing Eye: Ecphrasis and the Culture of Viewing in the Hellenistic World". In *Art and Text in Ancient Greek Culture*, S. Goldhill & R. Osborne (eds), 197–223. Cambridge: Cambridge University Press.

—— 1996. "Refracting Classical Vision: Changing Cultures of Viewing". In *Vision in Context: Historical and Contemporary Perspectives on Sight*, T. Brennan & M. Jay (eds), 17–28. London: Routledge.

—— 1998. "The Seductions of the Gaze: Socrates and his Girlfriends". In *Kosmos: Essays in Order, Conflict and Community in Classical Athens*, P. Cartledge, P. Millett & S. von Reden (eds), 105–24. Cambridge: Cambridge University Press.

—— 2000a. "Viewing and the Viewer: Empire and the Culture of the Spectacle". In *The Body Aesthetic: From Fine Art to Body Modification*, T. Siebers (ed.), 41–74. Ann Arbor: University of Michigan Press.

—— 2000b. "Placing Theatre in the History of Vision". In *Word and Image in Ancient Greece*, N. K. Rutter & B. Sparkes (eds), 161–79. Edinburgh: Edinburgh University Press.

—— 2001. "The Erotic Eye: Visual Stimulation and Cultural Conflict". In *Being Greek Under Rome: Cultural Identity, the Second Sophistic, and the Development of Empire*, S. Goldhill (ed.), 197–223. Cambridge: Cambridge University Press.

—— 2007. "What is Ekphrasis For?" *Classical Philology* 102: 1–19.

Gombrich, E. W. 1960. *Art and Illusion: A Study in the Psychology of Pictorial Representation*. New York: Pantheon.

Gordon, R. 1979. "The Real and the Imaginary: Production and Religion in the Greco-Roman World". *Art History* 2: 5–34.

Gourinat, J.-B. 1996. *Les Stoïciens et l'âme*. Paris: Presses universitaires de France.

Graf, F. 2004. "Trick or Treat? Collective Epiphanies in Antiquity". *Illinois Classical Studies* 29: 111–30.

Granger, F. (ed. & trans.) 1931–4. *Vitruvius: On Architecture*, 2 vols. Cambridge, MA: Harvard University Press.

Graziosi, B. 2002. *Inventing Homer: The Early Reception of Epic*. Cambridge: Cambridge University Press.

Gregoric, P. 2007. *Aristotle on the Common Sense*. Oxford: Oxford University Press.

Gregory, R. L. 1998. *Eye and the Brain: The Psychology of Seeing*, 5th edn. Oxford: Oxford University Press.

Greifenhagen, A. 1962. *Corpus Vasorum Antiquorum Deutschland 22: Berlin Antiquarium 3, bearbeitet von A. Greifenhagen*. Munich: C. H. Beck.

Grethlein, J. 2015a. "Aesthetic Experiences, Ancient and Modern". *New Literary History* 46: 309–33.

—— 2015b. "Vision and Reflexivity in the *Odyssey* and Early Vase-Painting". *Word & Image* 31: 197–212.

Griswold. C. 1986. *Self-Knowledge in Plato's Phaedrus*. New Haven: Yale University Press.

Gros, P. 2008. "The Theory and Practice of Perspective in Vitruvius' *De Architectura*". In *Perspective, Projections and Design Technologies of Architectural Representation*, M. Carpo & F. Lemerle (eds), 5–18. London: Routledge.

Gross, K. 1992. *The Dream of the Moving Statue*. Ithaca: Cornell University Press.

Gross, N. 1989. *Senecas Naturales Quaestiones: Komposition, naturphilosophische Aussagen und ihre Quellen*. Stuttgart: Steiner.

Gruenwald, I. 1980. *Apocalyptic and Merkavah Mysticism*. Leiden: Brill.

Gunderson, E. 1996. "The Ideology of the Arena". *Classical Antiquity* 15: 113–51.

Gurd, S. 2008. "Meaning and Material Presence: Four Epigrams on Timomachus' Unfinished Medea". *Transactions of the American Philological Association* 137: 305–31.

Gutas, D. 1998. *Greek Thought, Arabic Culture*. London: Routledge.

—— 2004. "Avicenna's Marginal Glosses on *De anima* and the Greek Commentatorial Tradition". *Bulletin of the Institute of Classical Studies* 47: 77–88.

Guthrie, S. 2001. "Why Gods? A Cognitive Theory". In *Religion in Mind: Cognitive Perspectives on Religious Belief, Ritual, and Experience*, J. Andresen (ed.), 94–111. Cambridge: Cambridge University Press.

Guthrie, W. K. C. 1965. *A History of Greek Philosophy, Vol. 2: The Presocratic Tradition from Parmenides to Democritus*. Cambridge: Cambridge University Press.

—— 1975. *A History of Greek Philosophy, Vol. 4: Plato, the Man and His Dialogues (Earlier Period)*. Cambridge: Cambridge University Press.

—— 1978. *A History of Greek Philosophy, Vol. 5: The Later Plato and the Academy*. Cambridge: Cambridge University Press.

Gutzwiller, K. J. 2002. "Art's Echo: The Tradition of Hellenistic Ecphrastic Epigram". In *Hellenistic Epigrams*, M. A. Harder, R. Regtuit & G. C. Wakker (eds), 85–112. Leuven: Peeters.

—— 2004. "Seeing Thought: Timomachus' Medea and Ekphrastic Epigram". *American Journal of Philology* 125: 339–86.

Habicht, C. 1969. *Die Inschriften des Asklepieions: Altertümer von Pergamon*, vol. 8. Berlin: De Gruyter.

Hackett, P. M. W. 2014. *Fine Art and Neuroscience*. New York: Psychology Press.

Hafemann, S. J. 1995. *Paul, Moses, and the History of Israel: The Letter/Spirit Contrast and the Argument from Scripture in 2 Corinthians 3*. Tübingen: Mohr Siebeck.

Hägg, T. 2002. "Epiphany in the Greek Novels: The Employment of a Metaphor". *Eranos* 100: 51–61.

Halbwachs, M. 1936. *Les cadres sociaux de la mémoire*. Paris: F. Alcan.

—— 1941. *La topographie légendaire des évangiles en Terre Sainte: étude de mémoire collective*. Paris: Presses universitaires de France.

—— 1950. *La mémoire collective*. Paris: Presses universitaires de France.

—— 1992. *On Collective Memory*. Chicago: University of Chicago Press.

Hales, S. 2003. *The Roman House and Social Identity*. Cambridge: Cambridge University Press.

Hall, E. 1989. *Inventing the Barbarian*. Oxford: Clarendon Press.

—— 2006. *The Theatrical Cast of Athens: Interactions between Ancient Greek Drama and Society*. Oxford: Oxford University Press.

Hallett, C. 2005. *The Roman Nude*. Oxford: Oxford University Press.

Halliday, W. R. 1913. *Greek Divination: A Study of Its Methods and Principles*. London: Macmillan.

Halliwell, S. 1993. "The Function and Aesthetics of the Greek Tragic Mask". In *Intertextualität in der griechisch-römischen Komödie*, N. W. Slater & B. Zimmermann (eds), 195–211. Stuttgart: Metzlerche & Poeschel.

—— 2002. *The Aesthetics of Mimesis: Ancient Texts and Modern Problems*. Princeton: Princeton University Press.

—— 2011. *Between Ecstasy and Truth: Interpretations of Greek Poetics from Plato to Longinus*. Oxford: Oxford University Press.

Halperin, D. J. 1986. "Plato and Erotic Reciprocity". *Classical Antiquity* 5: 60–80.

—— 1988. *The Faces of the Chariot: Early Jewish Responses to Ezekiel's Vision*. Tübingen: Mohr.

Hamm, D. 1986. "Sight to the Blind: Vision as Metaphor in Luke". *Biblica* 67(4): 457–77.

Hampe, R. & H. Gropengiesser 1967. *Aus der Sammlung des Archäologischen Institutes der Universität Heidelberg. Werke der Kunst in Heidelberg*, vol. 2. Berlin: Springer.

Hansen, P. A. (ed.) 1989. *Carmina Epigraphica Graeca*. Berlin: De Gruyter.

Hanson, J. S. 1980. "Dreams and Visions in the Graeco-Roman World and Early Christianity". *Aufstieg und Niedergang der Römischen Welt* 2(23.2): 1395–427.

Hardie, P. 2002. *Ovid's Poetics of Illusion*. Cambridge: Cambridge University Press.

Harris, J. 2014. *Sensation and Perception*. London: Sage.

Harris, W. V. 2009. *Dreams and Experience in Classical Antiquity*. Cambridge, MA: Harvard University Press.
Harrison, T. 2000. *Divinity and History. The Religion of Herodotus*. Oxford: Oxford University Press.
Hartog, F. 1988. *The Mirror of Herodotus: The Representation of the Other in the Writing of History*, J. Lloyd (trans.). Berkeley: University of California Press.
Hauck, R. J. 1988. "'They Saw What They Said They Saw': Sense Knowledge in Early Christian Polemic". *Harvard Theological Review* 81(3): 239–49.
Haug, A. (2015). "Das Auge und der Blick: Zum Auftreten von Zuschauern in der griechischen Bilderwelt". In *Das Publikum im Bild*, B. Fricke & U. Krass (eds), 23–56. Zurich: Diaphanes.
Havelock, C. M. 1995. *The Aphrodite of Knidos and her Successors: A Historical Review of the Female Nude in Greek Art*. Ann Arbor: University of Michigan Press.
Havelock, E. A. 1963. *Preface to Plato*. Cambridge, MA: Harvard University Press.
Haynes, M. 2013. "Framing a View of the Unviewable: Architecture, Aphrodite, and Erotic Looking in the Lucianic *Erōtes*". In *Vision and Viewing in Ancient Greece* (= *Helios* 40(1–2)), S. Blundell, D. Cairns & N. S. Rabinowitz (eds), 71–95. Luboch: Texas Tech University Press.
Heath, Jane 2005. "Ezekiel Tragicus and Hellenistic Visuality: The Phoenix at Elim". *Journal of Theological Studies* 57: 23–41.
—— 2013a. "Greek and Jewish Visual Piety: Ptolemy's Gifts in the Letter of Aristeas". In *The Image and its Prohibition in Jewish Antiquity*, S. Pearce (ed.), 38–48. Oxford: Oxbow Books.
—— 2013b. *Paul's Visual Piety: The Metamorphosis of the Beholder*. Oxford: Oxford University Press.
Heath, John 1992. *Actaeon the Unmannerly Intruder: The Myth and its Meaning in Classical Literature*. New York: P. Lang.
Heath, M. 1999. "Longinus *On Sublimity*". *Proceedings of the Cambridge Philological Society* 45: 43–74.
Hedreen, G. 2007a. "Involved Spectatorship in Archaic Greek Art". *Art History* 30: 217–46.
—— 2007b. "Myths of Ritual in Athenian Vase-Painting of Silens". In *The Origins of Theater in Ancient Greece and Beyond: From Ritual to Drama*, E. Csapo (ed.), 150–95. Cambridge: Cambridge University Press.
Hedrick, C. 2000. *History and Silence: Purge and Rehabilitation of Memory in Late Antiquity*. Austin: University of Texas Press.
Heiberg, J. L. 1882. *Literaturgeschichtliche Studien über Euklid*. Leipzig: Teubner.
—— (ed.) 1895. *Euclidis Opera Omnia*, vol. 7. Leipzig: Teubner.
Henderson, I. 1991. "Quintilian and the Progymnasmata". *Antike und Abendland* 37: 82–99.
Henderson, J. (ed. & trans.) 2002. *Aristophanes: Frogs; Assemblywomen; Wealth*. Cambridge, MA: Harvard University Press.
Hendry, I. 1963. "Joyce's Epiphanies". In *James Joyce: Two Decades of Criticism*, S. Givens (ed.), 27–46. New York: Vanguard Press.
Hengel, M. 1974. *Judaism and Hellenism*, J. Bowden (trans.). Philadelphia: Fortress.
Herbert, J. D. 2003. "Visual Culture/Visual Studies". In *Critical Terms for Art History*, R. S. Nelson & R. Shiff (eds), 2nd edn., 452–64. Chicago: University of Chicago Press.
Herman, G. 2011. "Greek Epiphanies and the Sensed Presence". *Historia* 60: 127–57.
Herrmann, F. G. 2007. *Words and Ideas: The Roots of Plato's Philosophy*. Swansea: Classical Press of Wales.
—— 2013. "Dynamics of Vision in Plato's Thought". In *Vision and Viewing in Ancient Greece* (= *Helios* 40(1–2)), S. Blundell, D. Cairns & N. S. Rabinowitz (eds), 281–307. Luboch: Texas Tech University Press.
Himmelmann, N. 1956. *Studien zum Ilissos-Relief*. Munich: Prestel.

—— 1968. *Über einige gegenständliche Bedeutungsmöglichkeiten des frühgriechischen Ornaments*. Wiesbaden: Steiner.
Hirsch-Luipold, R. 2002. *Plutarchs Denken in Bildern: Studien zur literarischen, philosophischen und religiösen Funktion des Bildhaften*. Tübingen: Mohr-Siebeck.
Hodske, J. 2007. *Mythologische Bildthemen in den Häusern Pompejis: Die Bedeutung der zentralen Mythenbilder für die Bewohner Pompejis*. Ruhpolding: Franz Philipp Rutzen.
Holly, M. A. 1996. *Past Looking: Historical Imagination and the Rhetoric of the Image*. Ithaca: Cornell University Press.
Holmes, B. 2010. *The Symptom and the Subject: The Emergence of the Physical Body in Ancient Greece*. Princeton and Oxford: Princeton University Press.
Hölscher, T. 2004. *The Language of Images in Roman Art: Art as a Semantic System in the Roman World*, A. Snodgrass & A. M. Künzl-Snodgrass (trans.). Cambridge: Cambridge University Press.
Hope, V. 2003. "Remembering Rome: Memory, Funerary Monuments and the Roman Soldier". In *Archaeologies of Remembrance: Death and Memory in Past Societies*, H. Williams (ed.), 113–40. New York: Plenum Publishers.
—— 2009. *Roman Death: The Dying and the Dead in Ancient Rome*. London: Continuum.
—— 2010. "'The End is to the Beginning as the Beginning is to the End': Birth, Death, and the Classical Body". In *A Cultural History of the Human Body in Antiquity*, D. Garrison (ed.), 25–43. New York: Berg.
Houby-Nielsen, S. H. 1995. "'Burial Language' in Archaic and Classical Kerameikos". *Proceedings of the Danish Institute at Athens* 1: 129–91.
Houssay, H. 1912. "L'axe du médaillon intérieur dans les coupes grecques". *Revue archéologique* 19: 60–83.
Howe, T. P. 1954. "The Origin and Function of the Gorgon Head". *American Journal of Archaeology* 58: 209–21.
Howes, D. (ed.) 1991. *The Varieties of Sensory Experience: A Sourcebook in the Anthropology of the Senses*. Toronto: University of Toronto Press.
—— 2003. *Sensual Relations: Engaging the Senses in Culture and Social Theory*. Ann Arbor: University of Michigan Press.
—— (ed.) 2005. *Empire of the Senses: The Sensual Cultural Reader*. London: Bloomsbury.
Howes, D. & C. Classen 2014. *Ways of Sensing: Understanding the Senses In Society*. London: Routledge.
Howland, R. H. 1958. *The Athenian Agora: Results of Excavations Conducted by the American School of Classical Studies at Athens; Volume IV: Greek Lamps and their Survivals*. Princeton: The American School of Classical Studies at Athens.
Hubbard, T. 2002. "Pindar, Theoxenus and the Homoerotic Eye". *Arethusa* 35: 255–96.
Hubel, D. H. 1988. *Eye, Brain and Vision*. New York: Scientific American Library.
Hubel, D. H. & T. N. Wiesel 2005. *Brain and Visual Perception: The Story of a Fifteen-Year Collaboration*. Oxford: Oxford University Press.
Huffman, C. A. 2005. *Archytas of Tarentum: Pythagorean, Philosopher and Mathematician King*. Cambridge: Cambridge University Press.
Hug, A. 1927. "Lucerna". In *Paulys Realencyclopädie der classischen Altertumswissenschaft* 13(2): 1566–613.
Hughes, J. 2008. "Fragmentation as Metaphor in the Classical Healing Sanctuary". *Social History of Medicine* 21: 217–36.
—— 2014. "Memory and the Roman Viewer: Looking at the Arch of Constantine". In *Memoria Romana: Memory in Rome and Rome in Memory*, K. Galinsky (ed.), 103–15. Ann Arbor: University of Michigan Press.
Hurwit, J. M. 1977. "Image and Frame in Greek Art". *American Journal of Archaeology* 81: 1–30.

BIBLIOGRAPHY

Huxley, G. L. 1959. *Anthemius of Tralles: A Study of Later Greek Geometry*. Cambridge, MA: Eaton Press.
Ierodiakonou, K. 2005. "Empedocles on Colour and Colour Vision". *Oxford Studies in Ancient Philosophy* 29: 1–38.
Ilardi, V. 2007. *Renaissance Vision from Spectacles to Telescopes*. Philadelphia: American Philosophical Society.
Imbert, C. 1980. "Stoic Logic and Alexandrian Poetics". In *Doubt and Dogmatism: Studies in Hellenistic Epistemology*, M. Schofield, M. Burnyeat & J. Barnes (eds), 183–216. Oxford: Oxford University Press.
Ings, S. 2007. *The Eye: A Natural History*. London: Bloomsbury.
Innis, R. I. 1984. "Technics and the Bias of Perception". *Philosophy and Social Criticism* 10: 67–89.
Ioppolo, A.-M. 1990. "Presentation and Assent: A Physical and Cognitive Problem in Early Stoicism". *Classical Quarterly* 40: 433–49.
Irigaray, L. 1985. *This Sex Which is Not One*, C. Porter & C. Burke (trans.). Ithaca: Cornell University Press.
Ivins, W. M. 1946. *Art and Geometry: A Study in Space Intuitions*. Cambridge, MA: Harvard University Press.
Jackson, D. 1987. "Verism and the Ancestral Portrait". *Greece & Rome* 34: 32–47.
Jacobsthal, P. 1927. *Ornamente griechischer Vasen*. Berlin: Frankfurter Verlagsanstalt.
Jacoby, F. (ed.) 1923–. *Die Fragmente der griechischen Historiker*. Berlin/Leiden: Weidmann/Brill.
Jahn, O. 1885. "Über den Aberglauben des bösen Blickes bei den Alten". *Berichte über die Verhandlungen der Königlich Sächsischen Gesellschaft der Wissenschaften zu Leipzig* 7: 28–110.
Jakobi, R. 1995. "Statius, Homer und ihre antiken Erklärer". *Rheinisches Museum für Philologie* 138: 190–2.
Jameson, M. 1994. "Theoxenia". In *Ancient Greek Cult Practice from the Epigraphical Evidence. Proceedings of the Fourth International Seminar on Ancient Greek Cult*, R. H. Hägg (ed.), 35–57. Stockholm: Svenska institutet i Athen.
Janaway, C. 1995. *Images of Excellence: Plato's Critique of the Arts*. Oxford: Clarendon Press.
Jay, M. 1993. *Downcast Eyes: The Denigration of Vision in Twentieth-Century French Thought*. Berkeley: University of California Press.
—— 2011. "In the Realm of the Senses: An Introduction". *The American Historical Review* 116: 307–15.
Jeannerod, M. 2006. *Motor Cognition: What Actions Tell the Self*. Oxford: Oxford University Press.
Jeffrey, L. H. 1961. *The Local Scripts of Archaic Greece*. Oxford: Clarendon Press.
Jensen, R. M. 2000. *Understanding Early Christian Art*. London: Routledge.
—— 2005. *Face to Face: Portraits of the Divine in Early Christianity*. Minneapolis: Fortress.
Johansen, K. F. 1951. *The Attic Grave-Reliefs of the Classical Period: An Essay in Interpretation*, E. Jacobsen (trans.). Copenhagen: E. Munksgaard.
Johansen, T. K. 1997. *Aristotle on the Sense-Organs*. Cambridge: Cambridge University Press.
Johns, C. 1982. *Sex or Symbol: Erotic Images of Greece and Rome*. London: British Museum Press.
Johnson, Mark. 1987. *The Body in the Mind: The Bodily Basis of Meaning, Imagination, and Reason*. Chicago: University of Chicago Press.
Johnson, Martha B. 1992. "Reflections of Inner Life: Masks and Masked Acting in Ancient Greek Tragedy and Japanese Noh Drama". *Modern Drama* 35: 20–34.

BIBLIOGRAPHY

Jonas, H. 1982. "The Nobility of Sight: A Study in the Phenomenonology of the Senses". In *The Phenomenon of Life: Towards a Philosophical Biology*, 135–56. New York: Harper & Row.

—— 1994. "Homo Pictor: Von der Freiheit des Bildens". In *Was ist ein Bild?*, G. Boehm (ed.), 105–24. Munich: Fink.

Jones, A. 1994. "Peripatetic and Euclidean Theories of the Visual Ray". *Physis* 31: 47–76.

—— 2001. "Pseudo-Ptolemy *De Speculis*". *Sciamus* 2: 145–86.

Jonsson, E. M. 1995. *Le miroir: naissance d'un genre littéraire*. Paris: Belles Lettres.

Joyce, J. 1963. *Stephen Hero*. New York: New Directions.

Jung, F. 1984. "Gebaute Bilder". *Antike Kunst* 27: 71–122.

Jütte, R. 2004. *A History of the Senses: From Antiquity to Cyberspace*, J. Lynn (trans.). Cambridge: Polity Press.

Kaltsas, N. 2002. *Sculpture in the National Archaeological Museum, Athens*, D. Hardy (trans.). Los Angeles: Getty Publications.

Kambylis, A. 1965. *Die Dichterweihe und ihre Symbolik: Untersuchungen zu Hesiodos, Kallimachos, Properz und Ennius*. Heidelberg: Carl Winter.

Kamtekar, R. 2009. "Knowing by Likeness". *Phronesis* 54: 215–38.

Kanellou, M. 2013. "Lamp and Erotic Epigram: How an Object Sheds Light on the Lover's Emotions". In *Erôs in Ancient Greece*, E. Sanders, C. Thumiger, C. Carey & N. J. Lowe (eds), 277–92. Oxford: Oxford University Press.

Kansteiner, S., K. Hallof, L. Lehmann, B. Seidensticker, K. Stemmer (eds) 2014. *Der Neue Overbeck: Die antiken Schriftquellen zu den bildenden Künsten der Griechen*, 5 vols. Berlin: De Gruyter.

Käsemann, E. 1968. *The Testament of Jesus: A Study of the Gospel of John in the Light of Chapter 17*, G. Krodel (trans.). London: SCM.

Kassel, R. & C. Austin (eds) 1983–2001. *Poetae comici graecae*, 8 vols. Berlin: De Gruyter.

Kavoulaki, A. 1999. "Processional Performance and the Democratic Polis". In *Performance Culture and Athenian Democracy*, S. Goldhill & R. Osborne (eds), 293–320. Cambridge: Cambridge University Press.

Kearns, E. 1990. "Saving the City". In *The Greek City from Homer to Alexander*, O. Murray & S. Price (eds), 323–44. Oxford: Oxford University Press.

Kennedy, G. A. 2003. *Progymnasmata: Greek Textbooks of Prose Composition*. Atlanta: Society of Biblical Literature.

Kenney, E. J. (ed.) 2014. *Lucretius, De Rerum Natura III*, 2nd edn. Cambridge: Cambridge University Press.

Kessels, A. H. M. 1978. *Studies on the Dream in Greek Literature*. Utrecht: Hes Publishers.

Keuls, E. 1975. "Skiagraphia Once Again". *American Journal of Archaeology* 79: 1–16.

—— 1978a. "Rhetoric and the Visual Arts in Greece and Rome". In *Communication Arts in the Ancient World*, E. A. Havelock & J. P. Hershbell (eds), 121–34. New York: Hastings House.

—— 1978b. *Plato and Greek Painting*. Leiden: Brill.

Kheirandish, E. 1999. *The Arabic Version of Euclid's Optics*. New York: Springer.

Kim, S. 1984. *The Origin of Paul's Gospel*, 2nd edn. Tübingen: Mohr Siebeck.

Kindt, J. 2012. *Rethinking Greek Religion*. Cambridge: Cambridge University Press.

Kirk, G. S. 1985. *The Iliad: A Commentary. Volume I: Books 1–4*. Cambridge: Cambridge University Press.

Kirk, G. S., J. E. Raven & M. Schofield 2005. *The Presocratic Philosophers*. Cambridge: Cambridge University Press.

Kjeldsen, J. 2003. "Talking to the Eye: Visuality in Ancient Rhetoric". *Word & Image* 19: 133–7.

Kleiner, D. E. E. 1987. *Roman Imperial Funerary Altars with Portraits*. Rome: G. Bretschneider.

Knigge, U. 1988. *The Athenian Kerameikos: History – Monuments – Excavations*. Athens: Krene Editions.
Knorr, W. R. 1983. "The Geometry of Burning-Mirrors in Antiquity". *Isis* 74: 53–73.
—— 1985. "Archimedes and the Pseudo-Euclidean Catoptrics: Early Stages in the Ancient Geometric Theory of Mirrors". *Archives internationales d'histoire des sciences* 35: 28–105.
—— 1991. "On the Principle of Linear Perspective in Euclid's *Optics*". *Centaurus* 34: 193–210.
—— 1994. "Pseudo-Euclidean Reflections in Ancient Optics: A Re-examination of Textual Issues Pertaining to the Euclidean *Optica* and *Catoptrica*". *Physis* 31: 1–45.
Koch Piettre, R. 1996. "Le corps des dieux dans les épiphanies divines en Grèce ancienne". PhD dissertation, École Pratique des Hautes Etudes, Paris.
—— 1999. "Les dieux crèvent les yeux: l'*enargeia* dans la représentation du divin". In *Ateliers 21: la transmission de l'image dans l'antiquité*, D. Mulliez (ed.), 11–21. Lille: Cahiers de la Maison de la Recherche, Université Charles-de-Gaulle, Lille 3.
Konersmann, R. 1991. *Lebendige Spiegel: Die Metapher des Subjekts*. Frankfurt am Main: Fischer.
Konstan, D. 1998. "Acts of Love: A Narrative Pattern in the Apocryphal Acts". *Journal of Early Christian Studies* 6: 15–26.
Koortbojian, M. 1995. *Myth, Meaning and Memory on Roman Sarcophagi*. Berkeley: University of California Press.
—— 1996. "*In commemorationem mortuorum*: Text and Image along the 'Street of Tombs'". In *Art and Text in Roman Culture*, J. Elsner (ed.), 210–33. Cambridge: Cambridge University Press.
Korshak, Y. 1987. *Frontal Faces in Attic Vase Painting*. Chicago: Ares Publishers.
Korsmeyer, C. 1999. *Making Sense of Taste*. Ithaca: Cornell University Press.
Kost, K. 1971. *Musaios, Hero und Leander: Einleitung, Text, Übersetzung und Kommentar*. Bonn: Bouvier Verlag.
Kratzmüller, B. 2009. "The Sky as Hippodromos. Agonistic Motives within Astral Representations". In *Athenian Potters and Painters II*, J. H. Oakley & O. Palagia (eds), 108–15. Oxford: Oxbow Books.
Kraut, R. 1991. "Return to the Cave: *Republic* 519–521". *Proceedings of the Boston Area Colloquium for Ancient Philosophy* 7: 43–62.
—— (ed.) 1997. *Critical Essays on Plato's Republic*. Lanham: Rowman & Littlefield.
Kreilinger, U. 2007. *Körperpflege, Reinigungsriten und das Phänomen weiblicher Nacktheit im klassischen Athen*. Rahden: Verlag Marie Leidorf.
Kühn, W. 1971. *Götterszenen bei Vergil*. Heidelberg: Carl Winter.
Kunisch, N. 1990. "Die Augen der Augenschalen". *Antike Kunst* 33: 20–7.
Kunze-Götte, E. 1973. *Corpus Vasorum Antiquorum Deutschland 37: München Antikensammlungen 8*. Munich: C. H. Beck.
Kurtz, D. & J. Boardman 1971. *Greek Burial Customs*. London: Thames & Hudson.
Kyle, D. G. 1998. *Spectacles of Death in Ancient Rome*. London: Routledge.
—— 2007. *Sport and Spectacle in the Ancient World*. Oxford: Blackwell.
Labarrière, J.-L. (ed.) 2004. "Dossier: '*Phantasia*: apparaître, apparence, apparition'". *Mètis* 2: 189–272.
—— 2006. "Présentation". *Mètis* 4: 9–12.
Lacan, J. 1977. *The Four Fundamental Concepts of Psychoanalysis*, A. Sheridan (trans.). London: Hogarth Press.
Lacy, L. R. 1990. "Aktaion and a Lost 'Bath of Artemis'". *Journal of Hellenic Studies* 110: 26–42.
Ladner, G. B. 1953. "The Concept of the Image in the Greek Fathers and the Byzantine Iconoclastic Controversy". *Dumbarton Oaks Papers* 7: 1–34.

Lalleman, P. J. 1996. "The Resurrection in the Acts of Paul". In *The Apocryphal Acts of Paul and Thecla*, J. Bremmer (ed.), 126–41. Kampen: Kok.

Lamp, K. S. 2011. "'A City of Brick': Visual Rhetoric in Roman Rhetorical Theory". *Philosophy & Rhetoric* 44: 171–93.

Lane Fox, R. 1986. *Pagans and Christians*. Cambridge, MA: Harvard University Press.

Lapatin, K. D. S. 2001. *Chryselephantine Statuary in the Ancient Mediterranean World*. Oxford: Oxford University Press.

Larson, J. L. 1995. *Greek Heroine Cults*. Madison: University of Wisconsin Press.

—— 2001. *Greek Nymphs: Myth, Cult, Lore*. Oxford: Oxford University Press.

Latte, K. 2010. "Hesiods Dichterweihe". *Antike und Abendland* 2: 152–63.

Lauer, I. 2004. "Ritual and Power in Imperial Roman Rhetoric". *Quarterly Journal of Speech* 90: 422–45.

Lausberg, H. 1998. *Handbook of Literary Rhetoric: A Foundation for Literary Study*, M. T. Bliss, A. Jansen & D. E. Orton (trans.). Leiden: Brill.

Layton, R. 1977. "Naturalism and Cultural Relativity in Art". In *Form in Indigenous Art: Schematisation in the Art of Aboriginal Australia and Prehistric Europe*, P. J. Ucko (ed.), 33–43. London: Duckworth.

Leach, E. W. 1988. *The Rhetoric of Space: Literary and Artistic Representations of Landscape in Republican and Augustan Rome*. Princeton: Princeton University Press.

—— 2004. *The Social Life of Painting in Ancient Rome and on the Bay of Naples*. Cambridge: Cambridge University Press.

Leader, R. 1997. "In Death Not Divided: Gender, Family, and State on Classical Athenian Grave Stelae". *American Journal of Archaeology* 101: 683–99.

Lear, J. 1988. *Aristotle: The Desire to Understand*. Cambridge: Cambridge University Press.

—— 2006. "Allegory and Myth in Plato's *Republic*". In *The Blackwell Guide to Plato's Republic*, G. Santas (ed.), 25–43. Oxford: Blackwell.

Lee, E. N. 1976. "Reason and Rotation: Circular Movement as the Model of Mind (*Nous*) in Later Plato". In *Facets of Plato's Philosophy*, W. H. Werkmeister (ed.), 70–102. Assen: Van Gorcum.

Lee, S. 2009. *Jesus' Transfiguration and the Believers' Transformation: A Study of the Transfiguration and its Development in Early Christian Writings*. Tübingen: Mohr Siebeck.

Le Goff, J. 1992. *History and Memory*, S. Rendall & E. Clama (trans.). New York: Columbia University Press.

Lejeune, A. (ed. & trans.) 1989. *L'optique de Claude Ptolémée dans la version latine d'après l'arabe de l'émir Eugène de Sicile*. Leiden: Brill.

Lennon, J. J. 2014. *Pollution and Religion in Ancient Rome*. Cambridge: Cambridge University Press.

Lephas, P. 1998. "On Vitruvius' Concept of Scaenographia". *Quaderni ticinesi di numismatica e antichità classiche* 27: 261–71.

Lesky, A. 1951. "Die Maske des Thamyris". *Anzeiger der Akademie der Wissenschaften Wien* 88: 101–11.

—— 1966. *Gesammelte Schriften: Aufsätze und Reden zu antiker und deutscher Dichtung und Kultur*, W. Kraus (ed.). Bern: Francke Verlag.

Lessing, G. E. 1790. *Leben des Sophokles*. Berlin: Christian Friedrich Voß und Sohn.

Létoublon, F. 2010. "To See or Not to See: Blind People and Blindness in Ancient Greek Myths". In *Light and Darkness in Ancient Greek Myth and Religion*, M. Christopoulos, E. D. Karakantza & O. Levaniouk (eds), 167–80. Lanham: Lexington Books.

Levin, D. M. 1988. *The Opening of Vision: Nihilism and the Postmodern Situation*. New York: Routledge.

—— (ed.) 1993. *Modernity and the Hegemony of Vision*. Berkeley: University of California Press.

—— (ed.) 1997. *Sites of Vision: The Discursive Construction of Sight in the History of Philosophy*. Cambridge, MA: MIT Press.
Lévy, C. & L. Pernot (eds) 1997. *Dire l'évidence: philosophie et rhétorique antiques*. Paris: L'Harmattan.
Lincoln, A. 2002. "The Beloved Disciple as Eyewitness and the Fourth Gospel as Witness". *Journal for the Study of the New Testament* 85: 3–26.
Lindberg, D. C. 1976. *Theories of Vision from Al-Kindi to Kepler*. Chicago: University of Chicago Press.
—— 1978. "The Science of Optics". In *Science in the Middle Ages*, D. C. Lindberg (ed.), 338–68. Chicago: Chicago University Press.
Ling, R. 1979. "Hylas in Pompeian Art". *Mélanges de l'École française de Rome (antiquité)* 91: 773–816.
—— 1991. *Roman Painting*. Cambridge: Cambridge University Press.
Lissarrague, F. 1987. *Un flot d'image: une esthétique du banquet grec*. Paris: Adam Biro.
—— 2009a. "Les temps des boucliers". In *Traditions et temporalités des images*, G. Careri, F. Lissarrague, J.-C. Schmitt & C. Severi (eds), 21–31. Paris: Éditions de l'École des hautes études en sciences sociales.
—— 2009b. "L'image mise en cercle". *Mètis* 7: 13–41.
Livingstone, M. 2013. *Vision and Art: How the Eye Works*, 2nd edn. New York: Abrams.
Llewellyn-Jones, L. 2003. *Aphrodite's Tortoise: The Veiled Woman of Ancient Greece*. Swansea: Classical Press of Wales.
Lloyd, G. E. R. 1966. *Polarity and Analogy: Two Types of Argumentation in Early Greek Thought*. Bristol: Bristol Classical Press.
—— 1990. "Plato and Archytas in the Seventh Letter". *Phronesis* 35: 159–74.
—— 1991. *Methods and Problems in Greek Science: Selected Papers*. Cambridge: Cambridge University Press.
Lodge, R. C. 1953. *Plato's Theory of Art*. London: Routledge & Paul.
Long, A. A. 1996a. *Stoic Studies*. Cambridge: Cambridge University Press.
—— 1996b. "Theophrastus' *De Sensibus* on Plato". In *Polyhistor: Studies in the History and Historiography of Ancient Philosophy Presented to Jaap Mansfeld on his Sixtieth Birthday. Philosophia Antiqua*, K. A. Algra, P. W. van der Horst & D. T. Runia (eds), 345–62. Leiden: Brill.
—— (ed.) 1999. *The Cambridge Companion to Early Greek Philosophy*. Cambridge: Cambridge University Press.
Long, A. A. & D. Sedley (eds) 1987. *The Hellenistic Philosophers*. Cambridge: Cambridge University Press.
Lonsdale, S. H. 1989. "If Looks Could Kill: παπταίνω and the Interpenetration of Imagery and Narrative in Homer". *Classical Journal* 84: 325–33.
Lo Presti, R. 2009. "Between Distinction and Separation: Rethinking the Centrality of the Brain in Alcmaeon's Theory of Sense-Perception and Cognition". In *Antike Naturwissenschaft und ihre Rezeption* XIX, J. Althoff, S. Föllinger & G. Wöhrle (eds), 9–30. Trier: Wissenschaftlicher Verlag Trier.
Lorenz, H. 2006. *The Brute Within: Appetitive Desire in Plato and Aristotle*. Oxford: Oxford University Press.
Lorenz, K. 2007. "The Ear of the Beholder: Spectator Figures and Narrative Structure in Pompeian Wall-Painting". *Art History* 30: 665–82.
—— 2008. *Bilder machen Räume: Mythenbilder in pompeianischen Häusern*. Berlin: De Gruyter.
Lovatt, H. 2013. *The Epic Gaze: Vision, Gender and Narrative in Ancient Epic*. Cambridge: Cambridge University Press.
Lowden, J. 1997. *Early Christian and Byzantine Art*. London: Phaidon.

Lowenstam, S. 1992. "The Uses of Vase-Depictions in Homeric Studies". *Transactions of the American Philological Association* 122: 165–98.

Lührmann, D. 1975. "Epiphaneia: Zur Bedeutungsgeschichte eines griechischen Wortes". In *Tradition und Glaube: Das frühe Christentum in seiner Umwelt*, G. Jeremias, H. W. Kuhn & H. Stegemann (eds), 185–99. Göttingen: Vandenhoeck & Ruprecht.

Lyons, D. 1996. *Gender and Immortality: Heroines in Ancient Greek Myth and Cult*. Princeton: Princeton University Press.

Ma, J. 2013. *Statues and Cities: Honorific Portraits and Civic Identity in the Hellenistic World*. Oxford: Oxford University Press.

Mack, R. 2002. "Facing Down Medusa (An Aetiology of the Gaze)". *Art History* 25: 571–604.

Mackey, J. (forthcoming). *Cognitive Foundations of Roman Religion: Beliefs, Practices, and Institutions*. Princeton: Princeton University Press.

Macleod, C. W. 1983. *Collected Essays*. Oxford: Oxford University Press.

MacMullen, R. 1982. "The Epigraphic Habit in the Roman Empire". *American Journal of Philology* 103: 233–46.

Malamoud, C. & J.-P. Vernant (eds) 1986. *Corps des dieux: le temps de la réflexion* 7. Paris: Gallimard.

Maltby, P. 2002. *The Visionary Moment. A Postmodern Critique*. Albany: SUNY Press.

Malten, L. 1961. *Die Sprache des menschlichen Antlitzes im frühen Griechentum*. Berlin: De Gruyter.

Mandelbaum, D. G. 1965. "Social Uses of Funerary Rites". In *Death and Identity*, R. Fulton (ed.), 338–59. New York: Wiley.

Manieri, A. 1998. *L'immagine poetica nella teoria degli antichi: phantasia ed enargeia*. Pisa: Istituti editoriali e poligrafici internazionali.

—— 1999. "Colori, suoni e profumi nelle *Imagines*: principi dell'estetica filostratea". *Quaderni Urbinati di Cultura Classica* 63: 111–21.

Männlein-Robert, I. 2003. "Zum Bild des Phidias in der Antike: Konzepte zur Kreativität des bildenden Künstlers". In *Imagination – Fiktion – Kreation: Das kulturschaffende Vermögen der Phantasie*, T. Dewender & T. Welt (eds), 45–67. Munich: Saur.

—— 2007a. "Epigrams on Art: Voice and Voicelessness in Hellenistic Epigram". In *Brill's Companion to Hellenistic Epigram down to Philip*, P. Bing & J. S. Bruss (eds), 251–71. Leiden: Brill.

—— 2007b. *Stimme, Schrift und Bild: Zum Verhältnis der Künste in der hellenistischen Dichtung*. Heidelberg: Winter.

Mansfeld, J. 1975. "Alcmaeon: 'Physikos' or Physician? With Some Remarks on Calcidius' 'On Vision' compared to Galen, Plac. Hipp. Plat. VII". In *Kephalaion: Studies in Greek Philosophy and its Continuation Offered to Professor C. J. de Vogel*. J. Mansfeld & L. M. de Rijk (eds), 26–38. Assen: Van Gorcum.

—— 1986. "Aristotle, Plato, and the Preplatonic Doxography and Chronography". In *Storiografia e dossografia nella filosofia antica*, G. Cambiano (ed.), 1–59. Turin: Tirrenia Stampatori.

—— 1999. "Sources". In *The Cambridge Companion to Early Greek Philosophy*, A. A. Long (ed.), 22–44. Cambridge: Cambridge University Press.

Mansfeld, J. & D. T. Runia. 1997. *Aëtiana*. Leiden: Brill.

—— 2009. *Aëtiana. The Method and Intellectual Context of a Doxographer, Vol. II: The Compendium*. Leiden and Boston: Brill.

—— 2010. *Aëtiana. The Method and Intellectual Context of a Doxographer, Vol. III: Studies in the Doxographical Traditions of Ancient Philosophy*. Leiden: Brill.

Marconi, C. 2007. *Temple Decoration and Cultural Identity in the Archaic Greek World: The Metopes of Selinus*. Cambridge: Cambridge University Press.

Marin, L. 1977. *Détruire la peinture*. Paris: Édition de Minuit.
Marincola, J. 2003. *Authority and Tradition in Ancient Historiography*. Cambridge: Cambridge University Press.
Marmodoro, A. 2014. *Aristotle on Perceiving Objects*. Oxford: Oxford University Press.
Marrou, H. 1956. *A History of Education in Antiquity*. London: Sheed & Ward.
Marsden, E. W. 1971. *Greek and Roman Artillery: Technical Treatises*. Oxford: Clarendon Press.
Marshall, C. W. 1999. "Some Fifth-Century Masking Conventions". *Greece & Rome* 46: 188–202.
Martens, D. 1992. *Une esthétique de la transgression: le vase grec de la fin de l'époque géométrique au début de l'époque classique*. Brussels: Académie royale de Belgique.
Martin, A. & O. Primavesi 1999. *L'Empédocle de Strasbourg*. Berlin & New York: De Gruyter.
Martin, R. 1968. "Sculpture et peinture dans les façades monumentales au IVe siècle av J.-C.". *Revue archéologique* 1: 171–84.
Martin, R. P. 1989. *The Language of Heroes: Speech and Performance in the Iliad*. Ithaca: Cornell University Press.
Mathews, T. F. 1993. *The Clash of Gods: A Reinterpretation of Early Christian Art*. Princeton: Princeton University Press.
Mattusch, C. C. 1988. *Greek Bronze Statuary: From the Beginnings Through the Fifth Century B.C.* Ithaca: Cornell University Press.
May, M. T. (trans.) 1968. *Galen on the Usefulness of the Parts of the Body*. Ithaca: Cornell University Press.
Mayer, E. 2012. *The Ancient Middle Classes*. Cambridge, MA: Harvard University Press.
McCabe, M. M. 1992. "Myth, Allegory and Argument in Plato". In *The Language of the Cave*, A. Barker & M. Warner (eds), 47–68. Edmonton: Academic Printing and Publishing.
McCarty, W. 1989. "The Shape of the Mirror: Metaphorical Catoptrics in Classical Literature". *Arethusa* 22: 161–96.
McDiarmid, J. B. 1953. "Theophrastus on the Presocratic Causes". *Harvard Studies in Classical Philology* 61: 85–156.
McGinnis, J. 2010. *Avicenna*. Oxford: Oxford University Press.
McGowan, M. M. 2009. *Ovid in Exile: Power and Poetic Redress in the Tristia and the Epistulae Ex Ponto*. Leiden: Brill.
McGuckin, J. A. 1986. *The Transfiguration of Christ in Scripture and Tradition*. Lewiston: Mellen.
McHardy, F. 2004. "Women's Influence on Revenge in Ancient Greece". In *Women's Influence on Classical Civlisation*, F. McHardy & E. Marshall (eds), 92–114. London: Routledge.
McKenzie, J. 2007. *The Architecture of Alexandria and Egypt, 300 BC – AD 700*. New Haven: Yale University Press.
Meijering, R. 1987. *Literary and Rhetorical Theories in Greek Scholia*. Groningen: E. Forsten.
Meineck, P. 2011. "The Neuroscience of the Tragic Mask". *Arion* 19(1): 113–58.
—— 2013. "Under Athena's Gaze: Aeschylus' *Eumenides* and the Topography of *Opsis*". In *Performance in Greek and Roman Theatre*, G. W. M. Harrison & V. Liapis (eds), 161–79. Leiden: Brill.
Melion, W. S. & L. P. Wandel (eds) 2010. *Early Modern Eyes*. Leiden: Brill.
Melvin, D. P. 2013. *The Interpreting Angel Motif in Prophetic and Apocalyptic Literature*. Minneapolis: Fortress.
Merro, G. 2006. "Apollodoro, Asclepiade di Tragilo ed Eschilo in *Scholl. Eur. Rh.* 916 e 922". *Rivista di Filologia e di Instruzione Classica* 134: 26–51.

Metcalf, P. & R. Huntingdon 1991. *Celebrations of Death: The Anthropology of Funerary Ritual*, 2nd edn. Cambridge: Cambridge University Press.
Metz, C. 1974. *Film Language: A Semiotics of the Cinema*, M. Taylor (trans.). Oxford: Oxford University Press.
Meyer, D. 2007. "The Act of Reading and the Act of Writing in Hellenistic Epigram". In *Brill's Companion to Hellenistic Epigram down to Philip*, P. Bing & J. S. Bruss (eds), 187–210. Leiden: Brill.
Meyerhof, M. (trans.) 1928. *The Ten Treatises On the Eye*. Cairo: Government Press.
Mirzoeff, N. 1999. *An Introduction to Visual Culture*. London: Routledge.
Mitchell, M. M. 2004. "Epiphanic Evolutions in Earliest Christianity". *Illinois Classical Studies* 29: 183–204.
Mitchell, W. J. T. 1986. *Iconology: Image, Text, Ideology*. Chicago: Chicago University Press.
—— 1994. *Picture Theory: Essays on Verbal and Visual Representation*. Chicago: University of Chicago Press.
Mittag, P. F. 2006. *Antiochos IV Epiphanes: Eine politische Biographie*. Berlin: Akademie Verlag.
Moles, J. 2006. "Jesus and Dionysus in 'The Acts Of The Apostles' and Early Christianity". *Hermathena* 180: 65–104.
Montiglio, S. 2005. *Wandering in Ancient Greek Culture*. Chicago: University of Chicago Press.
Moore, M. B. 1997. *The Athenian Agora: Results of Excavations Conducted by the American School of Classical Studies at Athens; Volume XXX: Attic Red-figured and White-ground Pottery*. Princeton: The American School of Classical Studies at Athens.
Morales, H. 2004. *Vision and Narrative in Achilles Tatius' Leucippe and Cleitophon*. Cambridge: Cambridge University Press.
Morgan, K. 2000. *Myth and Philosophy from the Presocratics to Plato*. Cambridge: Cambridge University Press.
Morgan, T. 1998. *Literate Education in the Hellenistic and the Roman Worlds*. Cambridge: Cambridge University Press.
Morra, J. & M. Smith (eds) 2006. *Visual Culture: Critical Concepts in Media and Cultural Studies*, 5 vols. London: Routledge.
Morris, I. 1987. *Burial and Society: The Rise of the Greek City State*. Cambridge: Cambridge University Press.
—— 1992. *Death Ritual and Social Structure in Classical Antiquity*. Cambridge: Cambridge University Press.
—— 1992–3. "Law, Culture and Funerary Art in Athens, 600–300 BC". *Hephaistos* 11–12: 35–50.
—— 1993. "Poetics of Power: The Interpretation of Ritual Action in Archaic Greece". In *Cultural Poetics in Archaic Greece*, C. Dougherty & L. Kurke (eds), 15–45. Oxford: Oxford University Press.
—— 1998. "Remaining Invisible: The Archaeology of the Excluded in Classical Athens". In *Women and Slaves in Greco-Roman Culture: Differential Equations*, S. R. Joshel & S. Murnaghan (eds), 193–220. London: Routledge.
Morris, S. P. 1984. *The Black and White Style: Athens and Aigina in the Orientalizing Period*. New Haven: Yale University Press.
Morrison. J. S., J. E. Coates & N. B. Rankov 2000. *The Athenian Trireme: The History and Reconstruction of an Ancient Greek Warship*, 2nd edn. Cambridge: Cambridge University Press.
Morrison, J. V. 1999. "Homeric Darkness: Patterns and Manipulation of Death Scenes in the *Iliad*". *Hermes* 127: 129–44.

Moser von Filseck, K. 1996. *Blickende Bilder: Versuch zu einer hermeneutischen Archäologie*. [Bodelhausen: private publication].

Most, G. 2005. *Doubting Thomas*. Cambridge, MA: Harvard University Press.

Mugler, C. 1964. *Dictionnaire historique de la terminologie optique des Grecs: douze siècles de dialogues avec la lumière*. Paris: Klincksieck.

Mulvey, L. 1975. "Visual Pleasure and Narrative Cinema". *Screen* 16(3): 6–18.

—— 2009. *Visual and Other Pleasures*, 2nd edn. Basingstoke: Palgrave Macmillan.

Murray, O. 1990. *Sympotica: A Symposium on the Symposion*. Oxford: Oxford University Press.

Musurillo, H. 1967. *The Light and the Darkness: Studies in the Dramatic Poetry of Sophocles*. Leiden: Brill.

Muth, S. 1998. *Erleben von Raum – Leben im Raum: Zur Funktion mythologischer Mosaikbilder in der römisch-kaiserzeitlichen Wohnarchitektur*. Heidelberg: Verlag Archäologie und Geschichte.

Mylonas, G. E. 1961. *Eleusis and the Eleusinian Mysteries*. Princeton: Princeton University Press.

Naas, V. 2011. "La jeune fille de Corinthe: de l'anecdote à l'invention de l'art". In *Inventer la peinture grecque antique*, S. Alexandre, N. Philippe & C. Ribeyrol (eds), 71–93. Paris: ENS Éditions.

Nagy, G. 1990. *Greek Mythology and Poetics*. Ithaca: Cornell University Press.

Nasrallah, L. 2008. "The Earthen Human, The Breathing Statue: The Sculptor God, Greco-Roman Statuary, and Clement of Alexandria". In *Beyond Eden: The Biblical Story of Paradise (Genesis 2–3) and Its Reception History*, K. Schmid & C. Riedweg (eds), 110–40. Tübingen: Mohr Siebeck.

—— 2010. *Christian Responses to Roman Art and Architecture: The Second-Century Church Amid the Spaces of Empire*. Cambridge: Cambridge University Press.

Neer, R. 1997. "Beazley and the Language of Connoisseurship". *Hephaistos* 15: 7–30.

—— 2002a. "Space and Politics: On the Earliest Athenian Gravestones". *Apollo* 156: 20–7.

—— 2002b. *Style and Politics in Athenian Vase-Painting: The Craft of Democracy, ca. 530–460 B.C.E.* Cambridge: Cambridge University Press.

—— 2010. *The Emergence of the Classical Style in Greek Sculpture*. Chicago: University of Chicago Press.

—— 2012. *Art and Archaeology of the Greek World: A New History, c.2500 – c.150 BCE*. London: Thames & Hudson.

Neis, R. 2013. *The Sense of Sight in Rabbinic Culture: Jewish Ways of Seeing in Late Antiquity*. Cambridge: Cambridge University Press.

Nelson, R. S. (ed.) 2000. *Visuality Before and Beyond the Renaissance: Seeing as Others Saw*. Cambridge: Cambridge University Press.

Nelson, R. S. & M. Olin (eds) 2003. *Monuments and Memory, Made and Unmade*. Chicago: University of Chicago Press.

Nelson, R. S. & R. Shiff (eds) 2003. *Critical Terms for Art History*, 2nd edn. Chicago: University of Chicago Press.

Nenci, G. 1953. "Il motive dell'autopsia nella storiografia grec". *Studi Classici e Orientali* 3: 14–46.

Netz, R. 1999. *The Shaping of Deduction in Greek Mathematics: A Study in Cognitive History*. Cambridge: Cambridge University Press.

—— 2002. "Greek Mathematicians: A Group Picture". In *Science and Mathematics in Ancient Greek Culture*, C. J. Tuplin & T. E. Rihll (eds), 196–216. Oxford: Oxford University Press.

—— (forthcoming). "Ancient Greek Mathematics". In *Wiley-Blackwell Companion to Ancient Science, Medicine and Technology*, G. L. Irby-Massie (ed.). Malden: Wiley.

Neugebauer, O. 1938. "Über eine Methode zur Distanzbestimmung Alexandria-Rom bei Heron I". *Det Kongelige Danske Videnskabernes Selskab* 26: 3–26.
Neutsch, B. 1949. *Henkel und Schalenbild: Ein ästhetisches Problem der antiken Keramik.* Marburg: Verlag des Kunstgeschichtlichen Seminars der Universität Marburg.
Newby, Z. 2002. "Testing the Boundaries of Ekphrasis". *Ramus* 31: 126–35.
—— 2009. "Absorption and Erudition in Philostratus' *Imagines*". In *Philostratus*, E. Bowie & J. Elsner (eds), 322–42. Cambridge: Cambridge University Press.
—— 2014. "Poems in Stone: Reading Mythological Sarcophagi through Statius' *Consolations*". In *Art and Rhetoric in Roman Culture*, J. Elsner & M. Meyer (eds), 256–87. Cambridge: Cambridge University Press.
Newlands, C. 2011. *Statius, Silvae Book II*. Cambridge: Cambridge University Press.
Nichols, M. 2010. *Socrates on Friendship and Community: Reflections on Plato's* Symposium, Phaedrus *and* Lysis. Cambridge: Cambridge University Press.
Nightingale, A. W. 1995. *Genres in Dialogue: Plato and the Construct of Philosophy*. Cambridge: Cambridge University Press.
—— 2001. "On Wandering and Wondering: *Theôria* in Greek Philosophy and Culture". *Arion* 9(2): 23–58.
—— 2004. *Spectacles of Truth in Classical Greek Philosophy: Theoria in its Cultural Context*. Cambridge: Cambridge University Press.
—— 2005. "The Philosopher at the Festival: Plato's Transformation of Traditional *theôria*". In *Pilgrimage in Graeco-Roman and Early Christian Antiquity: Seeing the Gods*, J. Elsner & I. Rutherford (eds), 151–80. Oxford: Oxford University Press.
Nock, A. D. 1972. *Essays on Religion and the Ancient World*, 2 vols. Cambridge, MA: Harvard University Press.
Nora, P. 1984–92. *Les lieux de mémoire*, 4 vols. Paris: Gallimard.
—— 2001. *Realms of Memor*, A. Goldhammer (trans.). New York: Columbia University Press.
Noy, D. 2011. "'Goodbye Livia': Dying in the Roman House". In *Memory and Mourning: Studies on Roman Death*, V. Hope & J. Huskinson (eds), 1–20. Oxford: Oxbow Books.
Nünlist, R. 2009. *The Ancient Critic at Work: Terms and Concepts of Literary Criticism in Greek Schlolia*. Cambridge: Cambridge University Press.
Nussbaum, M. 1986. *The Fragility of Goodness: Luck and Ethics in Greek Tragedy and Philosophy*. Cambridge: Cambridge University Press.
Nussbaum, M. & H. Putnam 1992. "Changing Aristotle's Mind". In *Essays on Aristotle's De Anima*, M. Nussbaum & R. Rorty (eds), 27–56. Oxford: Clarendon Press.
Nussbaum, M. & R. Rorty (eds) 1992. *Essays on Aristotle's De Anima*. Oxford: Clarendon Press.
Nygren, A. 1953. *Agape and Eros*, 2nd edn., P. S. Watson (trans.). London: SPCK.
Oberhelman, S. M. 1987. "The Diagnostic Dream in Ancient Medical Theory and Practice". *Bulletin of the History of Medicine* 61: 47–60.
O'Brien, D. 1984. "Théories atomistes de la vision: Démocrite et le problème de la fourmi céleste". In *Proceedings of the First International Congress on Democritus*, L. Benakis (ed.), 27–57. Xanthi: Bouloukos.
O'Daly, G. 1987. *Augustine's Philosophy of Mind*. London: Duckworth.
Ogden, M. 2009. *Magic, Witchcraft, and Ghosts in the Greek and Roman Worlds: A Sourcebook*, 2nd edn. Oxford: Oxford University Press.
Ogle, B. 1920. "The Lover's Blindness". *American Journal of Philology* 41: 240–52.
Onians, J. 2007. *Neuroarthistory from Aristotle and Pliny to Baxandall and Zeki*. New Haven: Yale University Press.
O'Regan, J. K. & A. Noë 2001. "A Sensorimotor Account of Vision and Visual Consciousness". *Behavioral and Brain Sciences* 24: 939–73.

Osborne, C. 2000. "Rummaging in the Recycling Bins of Upper Egypt: A Discussion of A. Martin and O. Primavesi, *L'Empédocle de Strasbourg*". *Oxford Studies in Ancient Philosophy* 18: 329–56.

Osborne, R. 1988. "Death Revisited, Death Revised: The Death of the Artist in Archaic and Classical Greece". *Art History* 11: 1–16.

—— 1997. "Law, the Democratic Citizen and the Representation of Women in Classical Athens". *Past and Present* 155: 3–33.

—— 1998. *Archaic and Classical Greek Art*. Oxford: Oxford University Press.

—— 2010. "The Art of Signing in Ancient Greece". In *The Art of Art History in Graeco-Roman Antiquity* (= *Arethusa* 43(2)), V. J. Platt & M. J. Squire (eds), 231–51. Baltimore: Johns Hopkins Press.

—— 2011. *The History Written on the Classical Greek Body*. Cambridge: Cambridge University Press.

Otto, N. 2009. *Enargeia: Untersuchung zur Charakteristik alexandrinischer Dichtung*. Stuttgart: Steiner.

Pache, C. O. 2011. *A Moment's Ornament: The Poetics of Nympholepsy in Ancient Greece*. Oxford: Oxford University Press.

Padel, R. 1990. "Making Space Speak". In *Nothing to Do with Dionysos? Athenian Drama in its Social Context*, J. J. Winkler & F. Zeitlin (eds), 336–65. Princeton: Princeton University Press.

Palazzini, S. 1996. "Il vocabolario della vista nelle *Imagines* di Filostrato". *Annali della Facoltà di Lettere e Filosofia, Università di Macerata* 29: 113–28.

Palmer, J. A. 1999. *Plato's Reception of Parmenides*. Oxford: Oxford University Press.

Panofsky, E. 1991. *Perspective as Symbolic Form*, C. S. Wood (trans.). New York: Zone Books.

Park, D. 1999. *The Fire within the Eye: A Historical Essay on the Nature and Meaning of Light*. Princeton: Princeton University Press.

Parker Pearson, M. 1982. "Mortuary Practices, Society and Ideology: An Ethnographical Study". In *Symoblic and Structural Archaeology*, I. Hodder (ed.), 99–113. Cambridge: Cambridge University Press.

Parkes, R. (ed.) 2012. *Status, Thebaid 4. Edited with an Introduction, Translation, and Commentary*. Oxford: Oxford University Press.

Parisinou, E. 2000. *The Light of the Gods: The Role of Light in Archaic and Classical Greek Cult*. London: Duckworth.

Patillon, M. & G. Bolognesi (eds) 1997. *Aelius Théon, Progymnasmata*. Paris: Belles Lettres.

Patterson, J. R. 2000. "Living and Dying in the City of Rome: Houses and Tombs". In *Ancient Rome: The Archaeology of the Eternal City*, J. Coulston & H. Dodge (eds), 259–89. Oxford: Oxford University School of Archaeology.

Paul, A. J. 1994–5: "A New Vase by the Dinos Painter: Eros and an Erotic Image of Women in Greek Vase Painting". *Harvard University Art Museums* 3(2): 60–7.

Pax, E. 1955. *ΕΠΙΦΑΝΕΙΑ: Ein religionsgeschichtlicher Beitrag zur biblischen Theologie*. Munich: Zink.

Pearson, A. C. 1917. *The Fragments of Sophocles*, 3 vols. Cambridge: Cambridge University Press.

Pearson, S. 2015. "Bodies of Meaning: Figural Repetition in Pompeian Painting". In *Beyond Iconography: Materials, Methods, and Meaning in Ancient Surface Decoration*, S. Lepinksi & S. McFadden (eds), 149–66. Boston: Archaeological Institute of America.

Pekáry, T. 2002. *Imago res mortua est: Untersuchungen zur Ablehnung der bildenden Künste in der Antike*. Stuttgart: Steiner.

Pellitzer, E. 1990. "Outlines of a Morphology of Sympotic Entertainment". In *Sympotica: A Symposium on the Symposion*, O. Murray (ed.), 177–84. Oxford: Oxford University Press.

Pemberton, E. G. 1989. "The Dexiosis on Attic Gravestones". *Mediterranean Archaeology* 2: 45–50.

Perilli, L. 2001. "Alcmeone di Crotone tra filosofia e scienza". *Quaderni Urbinati di Cultura Classica* 69: 55–79.

Perkins, J. 1995. *The Suffering Self: Pain and Narrative Representation in the Early Christian Era*. London: Routledge.

Peters, F. E. 1967. *Greek Philosophical Terms: A Historical Lexicon*. New York: New York University.

Petersen Hackworth, L. 2003. "The Baker, His Tomb, His Wife and the Breadbasket: The Monument of Eurysaces in Rome". *Art Bulletin* 85: 230–57.

—— 2006. *The Freedman in Roman Art and Art History*. Cambridge: Cambridge University Press.

Petridou, G. 2006. "On Divine Epiphanies: Contextualising and Conceptualising Epiphanic Narratives in Greek Literature and Culture (Seventh Century BC – Second Century AD)". PhD dissertation, University of Exeter.

—— 2013. "'Blessed is He Who has Seen': The Power of Ritual Viewing and Ritual Framing in Eleusis". In *Vision and Viewing in Ancient Greece* (= *Helios* 40(1–2)), S. Blundell, D. Cairns & N. S. Rabinowitz (eds), 309–41. Luboch: Texas Tech University Press.

—— 2014. "Asclepius the Divine Healer, Asclepius the Divine Physician: Epiphanies as Diagnostic and Therapeutic Tools". In *Medicine and Healing in the Ancient Mediterranean*, D. Michaelides (ed.), 291–301. Oxford: Oxbow Books.

—— (forthcoming a). *Divine Epiphany in Ancient Greek Literature and Culture*. Oxford: Oxford University Press.

—— (forthcoming b). "Erotic Epiphanies: Divine Lovers and Aggressors in Greek Literature and Culture". In *Envisioning the Divine in Greco-Roman Cult and Culture*, G. Petridou, V. J. Platt & S. Turner (eds). Aldershot: Ashgate.

Petridou, G., V. J. Platt & S. Turner (eds) (forthcoming). *Envisioning the Divine in Graeco-Roman Antiquity*. Aldershot: Ashgate.

Petrovic, A. 2005. "Kunstvolle Stimme der Steine, sprich! Zur Intermedialität der griechischen epideiktischen Epigramme". *Antike und Abendland* 51: 30–42.

Petsalis-Diomidis, A. 2005. "The Body in Space: Visual Dynamics in Graeco-Roman Healing Pilgrimage". In *Pilgrimage in Graeco-Roman and Early Christian Antiquity: Seeing the Gods*, J. Elsner & I. Rutherford (eds), 183–218. Oxford: Oxford University Press.

—— 2006. "Amphiaraos Present: Images and Healing Pilgrimage in Classical Greece". In *Presence: The Inherence of the Prototype within Images and Other Objects*, R. Maniura & R. Shepherd (eds), 205–29. Aldershot: Ashgate.

—— 2008. "The Body in the Landscape: Aristides' *corpus* in the Light of the *Sacred Tales*". In *Aelius Aristides between Greece, Rome, and the Gods*, W. V. Harris & B. Holmes (eds), 130–50. Leiden: Brill.

—— 2010. *Truly Beyond Wonders: Aelius Aristides and the Cult of Asklepios*. Oxford: Oxford University Press.

Petsas, P. M. 1966. Ο Τάφος των Λευκαδίων. Athens: Archaeological Society.

Pfister, F. 1924. "Epiphanie". In *Realenzyklopädie der classischen Altertumswissenschaft*, W. Pauly & G. Wissowa (eds), suppl. 4, 277–323. Stuttgart: J. B. Metzler.

Pizlio, Y., Y. Li, T. Sawada & R. M. Steinman 2014. *Making a Machine That Sees Like Us*. Oxford: Oxford University Press.

Plantzos, D. 1997. "Crystals and Lenses in the Graeco-Roman World". *American Journal of Archaeology* 101: 451–64.

Platt, V. J. 2002. "Viewing, Desiring, Believing: Confronting the Divine in a Pompeian House". *Art History* 25: 87–112.

—— 2006. "Making an Impression: Replication and the Ontology of the Graeco-Roman Seal Stone". *Art History* 29: 233–57.

—— 2010. "Art History in the Temple". In *The Art of Art History in Graeco-Roman Antiquity* (= *Arethusa* 43(2)), V. J. Platt & M. J. Squire (eds), 197–213. Baltimore: Johns Hopkins Press.

—— 2011. *Facing the Gods: Epiphany and Representation in Graeco-Roman Art, Literature and Religion*. Cambridge: Cambridge University Press.

—— 2012. "Framing the Dead on Roman Sarcophagi". *RES: Anthropology and Aesthetics* 61-2: 213–27.

—— 2014. "Likeness and Likelihood in Classical Greek Art". In *Probabilities, Hypotheticals, and Counterfactuals in Ancient Greek Thought*, V. Wohl (ed.), 185–207. Cambridge: Cambridge University Press.

—— 2015. "Epiphanies". In *The Oxford Handbook of Greek and Roman Religion*, E. Edinow & J. Kindt (eds), 491–504. Oxford: Oxford University Press.

—— (forthcoming). "Double Vision: Epiphanies of the Dioscuri in Greece and Rome". In *Envisioning the Divine in Greco-Roman Cult and Culture*, G. Petridou, V. J. Platt & S. Turner (eds). Aldershot: Ashgate.

Platt, V. J. & M. J. Squire (eds) 2010. *The Art of Art History in Graeco-Roman Antiquity* (= *Arethusa* 43(2)). Baltimore: Johns Hopkins Press.

—— (forthcoming a). "Please Do Not Touch! The Art of Touching in Graeco-Roman Antiquity". In *Touch and the Ancient Senses*, A. Purves (ed.). London: Routledge.

—— (forthcoming b) (eds) *A Cultural History of the Frame in Graeco-Roman Art*. Cambridge: Cambridge University Press.

Plett, H. 2010. *Enargeia in Classical Antiquity and the Early Modern Age: The Aesthetics of Experience*. Leiden: Brill.

Pollini, J. 2007. "Ritualizing Death in Republican Rome: Memory, Religion, Class Struggle, and the Wax Ancestral Mask Tradition's Origin and Influence on Veristic Portraiture". In *Performing Death: Social Analyses of Funerary Traditions in the Ancient Near East and Mediterranean*, N. Laneri (ed.), 237–85. Chicago: Oriental Institution of the University of Chicago.

Pollitt, J. J. 1974. *The Ancient View of Greek Art: Criticism, History and Terminology*. New Haven: Yale University Press.

—— 1993. *The Art of Ancient Greece: Sources and Documents*. Cambridge: Cambridge University Press.

—— 2002. "*Peri chromaton*: What Ancient Greek Painters Thought About Colors". In *Color in Ancient Greece: The Role of Color in Ancient Greek Art and Architecture*, M. A. Tiverios & D. S. Tsifakis (eds), 1–8. Thessaloniki: Aristotle University.

—— (ed.) 2015. *The Cambridge History of Painting in the Classical World*. Cambridge: Cambridge University Press.

Porter, J. 2010. *The Origins of Aesthetic Thought in Ancient Greece: Matter, Sensation and Experience*. Cambridge: Cambridge University Press.

—— 2013. "Why Are There Nine Muses?" In *Synaesthesia and the Ancient Senses*, S. Butler & A. Purves (eds), 9–26. Durham: Acumen.

Potts, A. M. 1982. *The World's Eye*. Lexington: University Press of Kentucky.

Power, T. 2010. *The Culture of Kitharôidia*. Cambridge, MA: Harvard University Press.

Powers, N. 2002. "Magic, Wonder and Scientific Explanation in Apollonius' *Argonautica* 4.1638–93". *Proceedings of the Cambridge Philological Society* 48: 87–101.

Preisendanz, K. & A. Heinrichs (eds) 1973. *Papyri Graecae Magicae: Die Griechischen Zauberpapyri*. Stuttgart: Teubner.

Prier, R. A. 1989. *Thauma idesthai: The Phenomenology of Sight and Appearance in Archaic Greek*. Tallahassee: Florida State University Press.

Primavesi, O. & L. Giuliani 2012. "Bild und Rede: Zum Proömium der *Eikones* des zweiten Philostrat". *Poetica* 44: 25–79.

Prioux, É. 2007. *Regards alexandrins: histoire et théorie des arts dans l'épigramme hellénistique*. Leuven: Peeters.

Pritchett, W. K. 1974–91. *The Greek State at War*, 5 vols. Berkeley: University of California Press.

Prusac, M. 2011. *From Face to Face: Recarving of Roman Portraits and the Late-Antique Portrait Arts*. Leiden: Brill.

Pucci, P. 1998. *The Song of the Sirens: Essays on Homer*. Lanham: Rowman and Littlefield.

Purcell, N. 1987. "Tomb and Suburb". In *Römische Grabstraßen: Selbstdarstellung, Status, Standard*, H. von Hesberg & P. Zanker (eds), 25–42. Munich: Verlag der Bayerischen Akademie der Wissenschaften.

Purves, A. 2013. "Haptic Herodotus". In *Synaesthesia and the Ancient Senses*, S. Butler & A. Purves (eds), 27–41. Durham: Acumen.

Rackham, H. (ed. & trans.) 1949–52. *Pliny, Natural History*, 9 vols. Cambridge, MA: Harvard University Press.

Rakoczy, T. 1996. *Böser Blick, Macht des Auges und Neid der Götter: Eine Untersuchung zur Kraft des Blickes in der griechischen Literatur*. Tübingen: Gunter Narr.

Rashed, R. 1990. "A Pioneer in Anaclastics: Ibn Sahl on Burning Mirrors and Lenses". *Isis* 81: 464–91.

—— 1997. *Oeuvres Philosophiques et scientifiques d'al-Kindi. I: l'optique et la catoprique*. Leiden: Brill.

—— (ed.) 2000. *Les catoptriciens grecs I: Les miroirs ardents*. Paris: Les Belles Lettres.

Rausch, H. 1982. *Theoria: Von ihrer sakralen zur philosophischen Bedeutung*. Munich: Fink.

Rea, J. 2007. *Legendary Rome: Myth, Monuments and Memory on the Palatine and Capitoline*. London: Duckworth.

Rebuffat, R. 1965. "Les mosaïques du bain de Diana à Volubilis". *La mosaïque gréco-romaine I*, G. Picard & H. Stern (eds), 193–217. Paris: CNRS Éditions.

Reeve, M. D. 1989. "Conceptions". *Proceedings of the Cambridge Philological Society* 35: 81–112.

Reinach, A. 1981. *Textes grecs et latins relatifs à l'histoire de la peinture ancienne*, 2nd edn. Chicago: Ares.

Renberg, G. 2003. "'Commanded by the Gods': An Epigraphical Study of Dreams and Visions in Greek and Roman Religious Life". PhD dissertation, Duke University.

—— 2010. "Dream-Narratives and Unnarrated Dreams in Greek and Latin Dedicatory Inscriptions". In *Sub imagine somni: Nighttime Phenomena in the Greco-Roman World*, E. Scioli & C. Walde (eds), 33–61. Pisa: Edizioni ETS.

Rhomaios, K. A. 1911. "Arkadikoi ermai". *Archaiologike Ephemeris*: 149–59.

Richardson, N. J. 1974. *The Homeric Hymn to Demeter*. Oxford: Oxford University Press.

Ricoeur, P. 2004. *Memory, History, Forgetting*. Chicago: University of Chicago Press.

Ridgway, B. S. 2004. *Second Chance: Greek Sculptural Studies Revisited*. London: Pindar Press.

Riegl, A. 1901. *Die spätrömische Kunst-Industrie nach den Funden in Österreich-Ungarn*. Vienna: Druck und Verlag der Österreichischen Staatsdruckerei.

Rispoli, G. M. 1984. "φαντασία ed ἐνάργεια negli scolî all'*Iliade*". *Vichiana* 13: 311–39.

Ritti, T. 1973–4. "L'uso di 'immagini onomastiche' nei monumenti sepolcrali di età greca: alcune testimonianze epigrafiche, archeologiche e letterarie". *Archeologia Classica* 25–6: 639–60.

—— 1977. "Immagini onomastiche sui monumenti sepolcrali di età imperiale". *Atti dell'Accademia Nazionale dei Lincei (Rendiconti)* 21: 257–396.

Rivier, A. 1975. "Remarques sur les fragments 34 et 35 de Xénophane". *Revue de philosophie* 30: 37–61.

Rivière-Adonon, A. 2011. "Les 'grands yeux': une mise en scène visuelle". *Mètis* 9: 245–77.

Rizzini, I. 1998. *L'occhio parlante: per una semiotica dello sguardo nel mondo antico*. Venice: Istituto veneto di scienze, lettere ed arti.
—— 1999. "Gli occhi di Persuasione e la persuasione attraverso gli occhi". *Quaderni Urbinati di Cultura Classica* 62: 87–97.
Robert, C. 1919. *Bild und Lied: Anleitung zur Deutung klassischer Bildwerke*. Berlin: Weidmann.
Robert, R. 1992. "*Ars regenda amore*: séduction érotique et plaisir esthétique". *Mélanges de l'École française de Rome (antiquité)* 104: 373–437.
—— 1996. "Une théorie sans image? Le trompe l'œil dans l'antiquité classique". In *Le trompe l'œil, de l'antiquité au xx siècle*, P. Mauries (ed.), 17–61. Paris: Gallimard.
Robertson, M. 1976. *A History of Greek Art*. Cambridge: Cambridge University Press.
Robinson, J. M. 1982. "Jesus from Easter to Valentinus (or to the Apostles' Creed)". *Journal of Biblical Literature* 101: 5–37.
Robinson, T. M. 1970. *Plato's Psychology*. Toronto: University of Toronto Press.
Roby, C. (forthcoming). "Framing Technologies in Hero and Ptolemy". In *A Cultural History of the Frame in Graeco-Roman Art*, V. J. Platt & M. J. Squire (eds). Cambridge: Cambridge University Press.
Rodenwaldt, G. 1939. *Korkyra II: Die Bildwerke des Artemistempels*. Berlin: Mann.
Rome, A. (ed.) 1931–43. *Commentaires de Pappus et de Théon d'Alexandrie sur l'Almageste*, 3 vols. Rome: Biblioteca Apostolica Vaticana.
Romizzi, L. 2006. *Programmi decorativi di III e IV stile a Pompei: un'analisi sociologica ed iconologica*. Naples: Loffedo.
Romm, J. 1990. "Wax, Stone, and Promethean Clay: Lucian as Plastic Artist". *Classical Antiquity* 9: 74–98.
Rose, M. L. 2003. *The Staff of Oedipus: Transforming Disability in Ancient Greece*. Ann Arbor: University of Michigan Press.
Rosenmeyer, T. G. 1986. "*Phantasia* und Einbildungskraft: Zur Vorgeschichte eines Leitbegriffes der europäischen Ästhetik". *Poetica* 18: 197–248.
Ross, G. R. T. (ed.) 1906. *Aristotle: De sensu and De memoria*. Cambridge: Cambridge University Press.
Rothschild, C. K. 2004. *Luke-Acts and the Rhetoric of History: An Investigation of Early Christian Historiography*. Tübingen: Mohr Siebeck.
Rouveret, A. 1982. "Peinture et 'art de la mémoire': le paysage et l'allégorie dans les tableaux grecs et romains". *Comptes rendus des séances. Académie des Inscriptions et Belles Lettres* 126: 571–88.
—— 1984. "Peinture et théâtre dans les fresques de 'second style': à propos de Vitruve (*De architectura* VII, Préface 11)". In *Texte et Imag: Actes du Colloque International de Chantilly (13 au 15 Octobre 1982)*, 151–65. Paris: Belles Lettres.
—— 1988. "Tables iliaques et l'art de la mémoire". *Bulletin de la Société Nationale des Antiquaires de France* 1988: 166–76.
—— 1989. *Histoire et imaginaire de la peinture ancienne (V siècle av. J.-C. – I siècle ap. J.-C.)*. Rome: Publications de l'École française de Rome.
—— 2006. "Les yeux pourpres: l'expérience de la couleur dans la peinture classique entre réalités et fictions". In *Couleurs et matières dans l'antiquité: textes, techniques et pratiques*, A. Rouveret, S. Dubel & V. Naas (eds), 17–28. Paris: Éditions Rue d'Ulm.
—— 2007. "La couleur retrouvé: découvertes de Macédoine et textes antiques". In *Peinture et couleur dans la monde Grec antique*, S. Descamps-Lequime (ed.), 69–79. Paris: Louvre.
Rowe, C. K. 2005. "New Testament Iconography? Situating Paul in the Absence of Material Evidence". In *Picturing the New Testament: Studies in Ancient Visual Images*, A. Weissenrieder, F. Wendt & P. von Gemünden (eds), 289–312. Tübingen: Mohr Siebeck.
Rowell, H. T. 1940. "The Forum and Funeral *imagines* of Augustus". *Memoirs of the American Academy in Rome* 17: 131–43.

Rowland, C. 1982. *The Open Heaven: A Study of Apocalyptic in Judaism and Early Christianity*. London: SPCK.

Rückert, B. 1998. *Die Herme im öffentlichen und privaten Leben der Griechen: Untersuchungen zum Funktion der griechischen Herme als Grenzmal, Inschriftträger und Kultbild des Hermes*. Regensburg: Roderer.

Rudolph, K. 2011. "Democritus' Perspectival Theory of Vision". *Journal of Hellenic Studies* 131: 67–83.

—— 2012. "Democritus' Ophthalmology". *Classical Quarterly* 62: 496–501.

Runia, D. T. 2008. "The Sources for Presocratic Philosophy". In *The Oxford Handbook of Presocratic Philosophy*, P. Curd and D. Graham (eds), 27–54. Oxford: Oxford University Press.

Russell, D. A. (ed. & trans.) 2001. *Quintilian: The Orator's Education*, 5 vols. Cambridge, MA: Harvard University Press.

Rutherford, I. 1995. "Theoric Crisis: The Dangers of Pilgrimage in Greek Religion and Society". *Studi e materiali di storia delle religioni* 61: 276–92.

—— 2000. "*Theoria* and *Darsan*: Pilgrimage and Vision in Greece and India". *Classical Quarterly* 50: 133–46.

Rutter, N. K & B. Sparkes (eds) 2000. *Word and Image in Ancient Greece*. Edinburgh: Edinburgh University Press.

Saatoglu-Paliadele, C. 1978. "Marble Eyes from Piraeus". *Archaiologike Ephemeris* 1978: 119–35.

Sabra, A. I. 2003. "Ibn al-Haytham's Revolutionary Project in Optics: The Achievement and the Obstacle". In *The Enterprise of Science in Islam: New Perspectives*, J. P. Hogendijk & A. I. Sabra (eds), 85–118. Cambridge, MA: MIT Press.

Şahin, M. Ç. (ed.) 1981. *Die Inschriften von Stratonikeia. Teil I: Panamara*. Bonn: Habelt.

Salta, M. 2012. "Gliederweihungen in attischen Heiligtümern: Die Weihung des Praxias im Athener Aklepeion". *Hephaistos* 29: 87–120.

Sandbach, F. H. 1971. "Phantasia Kataleptikē". In *Problems in Stoicism*, A. A. Long (ed.), 9–21. London: Bloomsbury Academic.

Scarth, E. A. 2008. *Mnemotechnics and Virgil: The Art of Memory and Remembering*. Saarbruchen: VDM Publishing.

Schauenburg, K. 1955. *Helios: Archäologisch-mythologische Studien über den antiken Sonnengott*. Berlin: Gebrüder Mann Verlag.

—— 1960. *Perseus in der Kunst des Altertums*. Bonn: Habelt.

Schefold, K. 1952. *Pompejanische Malerei: Sinn und Ideengeschichte*. Basel: Schwabe.

—— 1993. *Götter- und Heldensagen der Griechen in der früh- und hocharchaischen Kunst*. Munich: Hirmer.

Schepens, G. 1971. "Ephore sur la valeur de l'autopsie". *Ancient Society* 1: 162–83.

—— 1975. "L'idéal de l'information complète chez les historiens grecs". *Revue des Études Grecques* 88: 81–93.

Schirren, T. 1998. *Aisthesis vor Platon: Eine semantisch-systematische Untersuchung zum Problem der Wahrnehmung*. Stuttgart & Leipzig: Teubner.

Schlam, C. C. 1984. "Diana and Actaeon: Metamorphoses of a Myth". *Classical Antiquity* 3.1: 82–110.

Schlesier, R. 1994. "Zauber und Neid: Zum Problem des bösen Blick in der antiken griechischen Tradition". In *Tradition und Translation: Festschrift C. Colpe*, C. Elsas (ed.), 96–112. Berlin: De Gruyter.

Schmaltz, B. 1983. *Griechische Grabreliefs*. Darmstadt: Wissenschaftliche Buchgesellschaft.

Schmidt, W. (ed.) 1900. *Heronis Alexandrini opera quae supersunt omnia*. Leipzig: Teubner.

Schmitt-Pantel, P. 1992. *La cité au banquet: histoire des repas publics dans les cités grecques*. Rome: Publications de l'École française de Rome.

Schnapp, A. 1997. *Le chasseur et la cité: chasse et érotique dans la Grèce ancienne*. Paris: A. Michel.

Schneemelcher, W. 2003. *New Testament Apocrypha, Volume Two: Writings Relating to the Apostles, Apocalypses and Related Subjects*, R. McL. Wilson (trans.). Louisville: Westminster John Knox.

Schneider, A. 1923. "Der Gedanke der Erkenntnis des Gleichen durch Gleiches in antiker und patristischer Zeit". In *Festgabe für Clemens Baeumker zum 70. Geburtstag (16. September 1923)*, F. Ehrle (ed.), 65–76. Münster: Aschendorff.

Schoerner, G. & H. R. Goette 2004. *Die Pan-Grotte von Vari*. Mainz am Rhein: Philipp von Zabern.

Schofield, M. 1979. "Aristotle on the Imagination". In *Articles on Aristotle 4: Psychology and Aesthetics*, J. Barnes (ed.), 103–32. London: Duckworth.

Scholz, B. 1998. "*Sub oculos subiecto*: Quintilian on Ekphrasis and Enargeia". In *Pictures into Words: Theoretical and Descriptive Approaches to Ekphrasis*, V. Robillard & E. Jongeneel (eds), 73–99. Amsterdam: VU University Press.

Schöne, R. (ed.) 1897. *Damianos Schrift über Optik, mit Auszugen aus Geminos*. Berlin: Reichsdrückerei.

—— (ed.) 1903. *Heronis Alexandrini opera quae supersunt omnia*. Berlin: Weidmann.

Schroeder, C. T. 2000. "Embracing the Erotic in the Passion of Andrew: The Apocryphal Acts of Andrew, the Greek Novel, and Platonic Philosophy". In *The Apocryphal Acts of Andrew*, J. N. Bremmer (ed.), 110–26. Leuven: Peeters.

Scott, M. 2013. *Space and Society in the Greek and Roman Worlds*. Cambridge: Cambridge University Press.

Seaford, R. 1984. "Through a Glass Darkly". *Journal of Theological Studies* 35: 117–20.

—— 2005. "In the Mirror of Dionysus". In *The Sacred and the Feminine in Ancient Greece*, S. Blundell & M. Williamson (eds), 101–17. London: Routledge.

Seale, D. 1982. *Vision and Stagecraft in Sophocles*. London: Croom Helm.

Sedley, D. N. 1988. "Epicurean Anti-Reductionism". In *Matter and Metaphysics: 4th Symposium Hellenisticum*, J. Barnes & M. Mignucci (eds), 297–327. Naples: Bibliopolis.

—— 1992. "Empedocles' Theory of Vision and Theophrastus' *De Sensibus*". In *Theophrastus: His Psychological, Doxographical and Scientific Writings*, W. W. Fortenbaugh & D. Gutas (eds), 20–31. New Brunswick, NJ: Transaction Books.

—— 1998. *Lucretius and the Transformation of Greek Wisdom*. Cambridge: Cambridge University Press.

—— 2009. *Creationism and its Critics in Antiquity*. Berkeley: University of California Press.

Segal, C. 1994. *Singers, Heroes, and Gods in the Odyssey*. Ithaca: Cornell University Press.

Senseney, J. R. 2011. *The Art of Building in the Classical World: Vision, Craftsmanship and Linear Perspective in Greek and Roman Architecture*. Cambridge: Cambridge University Press.

Serra, M. 2007. "La *phantasia* del sublime: genealogia di una categoria letteraria". *Testi e linguaggi* 1: 29–41.

Shapiro, H. A. 1985. "Greek Bobbins – A New Interpretation". *Ancient World* 11: 115–20.

—— 1991. "The Iconography of Mourning in Athenian Art". *American Journal of Archaeology* 95: 629–56.

Sharples, R. W. & P. J. van der Eijk (trans.) 2008. *Nemesius: On the Nature of Man*. Liverpool: Liverpool University Press.

Sheppard, A. 2014. *The Poetics of Phantasia: Imagination in Ancient Aesthetics*. London: Bloomsbury.

Sidoli, N. 2005. "Heron's *Dioptra* 35 and Analemma Methods: An Astronomical Determination of the Distance between Two Cities". *Centaurus* 47: 236–58.

Silverman, A. 1989. "Color and Color-Perception in Aristotle's *De Anima*". *Ancient Philosophy* 9: 271–92.

—— 1991. "Plato on *Phantasia*". *Classical Antiquity* 10: 123–47.
Silverman, K. 2009. *Flesh of My Flesh*. Stanford: Stanford University Press.
Simon, E. 1976. *Die griechischen Vasen*. Munich: Hirmer.
Simon, G. 1988. *Le regard, l'être, et l'apparence dans l'optique de l'antiquité*. Paris: Éditions du Seuil.
—— 1992. *Der Blick, das Sein und die Erscheinung in der antiken Optik*. Munich: Wilhelm Fink Verlag.
—— 2003. *Archéologie de la vision: l'optique, le corps, la peinture*. Paris: Éditions du Seuil.
—— 2004. "L'expérimentation sur la réflexion et la réfraction chez Ptolémée et Ibn al-Haytham". In *De Zénon d'Élée à Poincaré*, R. Morelon & A. Haznawi (eds), 335–75. Leuven: Peeters.
Simms, R. R. 1998. "Mourning and Community at the Athenian Adonia". *The Classical Journal* 93: 121–41.
Sinisgalli, R. 2012. *Perspective in the Visual Culture of Classical Antiquity*. Cambridge: Cambridge University Press.
Sinos, R. H. 1993. "Divine Selection: Epiphany and Politics in Archaic Greece". In *Cultural Poetics in Archaic Greece: Cult, Performance, Politics*, C. Dougherty & L. Kurke (eds), 73–91. Cambridge: Cambridge University Press.
Slater, W. J. 1991. *Dining in a Classical Context*. Ann Arbor: University of Michigan Press.
Small, J. P. 1997. *Wax Tablets of the Mind: Cognitive Studies of Memory and Literacy in Classical Antiquity*. London: Routledge.
—— 2007. "Memory and the Roman Orator". In *A Companion to Roman Rhetoric*, W. Dominik & J. Hall (eds), 195–206. Oxford: Wiley-Blackwell.
Smith, A. M. 1996. *Ptolemy's Theory of Visual Perception: An English Translation of the* Optics *with Introduction and Commentary*. Philadelphia: American Philosophical Society.
—— 1998. "Ptolemy, Alhazen, and Kepler and the Problem of Optical Images". *Arabic Sciences and Philosophy* 8: 9–44.
—— (ed. & trans.) 2001. *Alhacen's Theory of Visual Perception*. Philadelphia: American Philosophical Society.
—— 2007. "Le *De aspectibus* d'Alhacen: Révolutionnaire ou réformiste?" *Revue d'histoire des sciences* 60: 65–81.
—— (ed. & trans.) 2008a. *Alhacen on Image-Formation and Distortion in Mirrors*. Philadelphia: American Philosophical Society.
—— 2008b. "Alhacen's Approach to 'Alhazen's Problem'". *Arabic Sciences and Philosophy* 18: 143–63.
—— (ed. & trans.) 2010a. *Alhacen on Refraction*. Philadelphia: American Philosophical Society.
—— 2010b. "Alhacen and Kepler and the Origins of Modern Lens-Theory". In *Origins of the Telescope*, Huib Zuidervaart (ed.), 147–65. Amsterdam: Royal Netherlands Academy of Arts and Sciences.
—— 2015. *From Sight to Light: The Passage from Ancient to Modern Optics*. Chicago: University of Chicago Press.
Smith, J. Z. 1978. "Towards Interpreting Demonic Powers in Hellenistic and Roman Antiquity". *Aufstieg und Niedergang der Römischen Welt* 2(16.1): 425–39.
Smith, M. M. 2007. *Sensing the Past: Seeing, Hearing, Smelling, Tasting and Touching in History*. Berkeley: University of California Press.
Snell, B. 1975. *Die Entdeckung des Geistes: Studien zur Entstehung des europäischen Denkens bei den Griechen*, 4th edn. Göttingen: Vandenhoeck & Ruprecht.
—— (ed.) 1986. *Tragicorum Graecorum Fragmenta I: Didascaliae tragicae, catalogi tragicorum et tragoediarum testimonia et fragmenta tragicorum minorum*, 2nd edn., R. Kannicht (ed.). Göttingen: Vandenhoeck & Ruprecht.

Snodgrass, A. 1998. *Homer and the Artists: Text and Picture in Early Greek Art*. Cambridge: Cambridge University Press.
Sobchack, V. 1992. *The Address of the Eye*. Princeton: Princeton University Press.
Solmsen, F. 1942. *Plato's Theology*. Ithaca: Cornell University Press.
Sommerstein, A. H. (ed.) 1998. *Aristophanes, Ecclesiazusae*. Warminster: Aris & Phillips.
Sorabji, R. 1971. "Aristotle on Demarcating the Five Senses". *Philosophical Review* 80(1): 55–79.
—— 1972. "Aristotle, Mathematics and Colour". *Classical Quarterly* 22: 293–308.
—— 1974. "Body and Soul in Aristotle". *Philosophy* 49: 63–89.
—— 1992. "Intentionality and Physiological Processes: Aristotle's Theory of Sense-Perception". In *Essays on Aristotle's De Anima*, M. Nussbaum & R. Rorty (eds), 195–226. Oxford: Clarendon Press.
—— 2000. *Emotion and Peace of Mind: From Stoic Agitation to Christian Temptation*. Oxford: Oxford University Press.
—— 2004. *Aristotle on Memory*, 2nd edn. London: Duckworth.
Sourvinou-Inwood, C. 1981. "To Die and Enter the House of Hades: Homer, Before and After". In *Mirrors of Mortality: Studies in the Social History of Death*, J. Whaley (ed.), 15–39. New York: St. Martin's Press.
—— 1995. *"Reading" Greek Death: To the End of the Classical Period*. Oxford: Oxford University Press.
—— 2005. *Hylas, the Nymphs, Dionysos and Others: Myth, Ritual, Ethnicity*. Stockholm: Paul Aaström.
Speidel, M. A. 2012. "Being a Soldier in the Roman Imperial Army – Expectations and Responses". In *Le métier de soldat dans le monde romain*, C. Wolff (ed.), 175–86. Lyon: Cergr.
Spencer, D. 2011. "Movement and the Linguistic Turn: Reading Varro's *De Lingua Latina*". In *Rome, Ostia and Pompeii: Movement and Space*, R. Laurence & D. J. Newsome (eds), 57–80. Oxford: Oxford University Press.
Speyer, W. 1980. "Die Hilfe und Epiphanie einer Gottheit, eines Heroen und eines Heiligen in der Schlacht". In *Pietas: Festschrift für B. Kötting*, E. Dassmann & K. Suso Frank (eds), 55–7. Münster: Aschendorff.
Spier, J. (ed.) 2008. *Picturing the Bible: The Earliest Christian Art*. New Haven: Yale University Press.
Sprigath, G. K. 2004. "Das Dictum des Simonides: Der Vergleich von Dichtung und Malerei". *Poetica* 36: 243–80.
Squire, M. J. 2009. *Image and Text in Graeco-Roman Antiquity*. Cambridge: Cambridge University Press.
—— 2010a. "Reading a View: Poem and Picture in the *Greek Anthology*". *Ramus* 39: 73–103.
—— 2010b. "Making Myron's Cow Moo? Ecphrastic Epigram and the Poetics of Simulation". *American Journal of Philology* 131: 589–634.
—— 2011a. *The Iliad in a Nutshell: Visualizing Epic on the Tabulae Iliacae*. Oxford: Oxford University Press.
—— 2011b. *The Art of the Body: Antiquity and its Legacy*. Oxford: Oxford University Press.
—— 2013a. "Apparitions Apparent: Ekphrasis and the Parameters of Vision in the Elder Philostratus' *Imagines*". In *Vision and Viewing in Ancient Greece* (= *Helios* 40(1–2)), S. Blundell, D. Cairns & N. S. Rabinowitz (eds), 97–140. Luboch: Texas Tech University Press.
—— 2013b. "Ekphrasis at the Forge and the Forging of Ekphrasis: The Shield of Achilles in Graeco-Roman Word and Image". *Word & Image* 29: 157–91.
—— 2013c. "*Ars* in their I's: Authority and Authorship in Graeco-Roman Visual Culture". In *The Author's Voice in Classical and Late Antiquity*, A. Marmodro & J. Hill (eds), 357–414. Oxford: Oxford University Press.
—— 2014. "The *ordo* of Rhetoric and the Rhetoric of Order". In *Art and Rhetoric in Roman Culture*, J. Elsner & M. Meyer (eds), 353–417. Cambridge: Cambridge University Press.

—— 2015a. "Patterns of Significance: Publilius Optatianus Porfyrius and the Figurations of Meaning". In *Images and Texts: Papers in Honour of Professor E. W. Handley, CBE, FBA*, R. Green & M. Edwards (eds), 87–121. London: Institute of Classical Studies.

—— 2015b. "Roman Art and the Artist". In *A Companion to Roman Art*, B. E. Borg (ed.), 172–94. Malden: Wiley.

—— 2015c. "Roman Portraiture and the Semantics of Extraction". In *Gesicht und Identität/ Face and Identity*, G. Boehm, O. Budelacci, M. G. di Monte & M. Renner (eds), 79–106. Munich: Fink.

—— (forthcoming). "Framing Bodies". In *A Cultural History of the Frame in Graeco-Roman Art*, V. J. Platt & M. J. Squire (eds). Cambridge: Cambridge University Press.

Squire, M. J. & J. Elsner (forthcoming). "Homer and the Ekphrasists: Text and Picture in the Elder Philostratus' Scamander (*Imagines* I.1)". In *"In a Giant's Footsteps": Contributions to Greek, Roman and Wider Archaeology and History Inspired by the Life and Work of Anthony McElrea Snodgrass*, J. Bintliff & K. Rutter (eds). Edinburgh: Edinburgh University Press.

Squire, M. J. & J. Grethlein 2014. "Persuasive in Appearance but Deceitful in Character: Reviewing the *ainigma* of the *Tabula Cebetis*". *Classical Philology* 109: 285–324.

Stansbury-O'Donnell, M. 1990. "Polygnotos's *Nekyia*: A Reconstruction and Analysis". *American Journal of Archaeology* 94: 213–35.

—— 2006. *Vase Painting, Gender, and Social Identity in Archaic Athens*. Cambridge: Cambridge University Press.

Stears, K. 1993. "Women and the Family in the Funerary Ritual and Art of Classical Athens". PhD dissertation, King's College London.

—— 1995. "Dead Women's Society: Constructing Female Gender in Classical Athenian Funerary Sculpture". In *Time, Tradition and Society in Greek Archaeology: Bridging the "Great Divide"*, N. Spencer (ed.), 109–31. London: Routledge.

Steiner, D. T. 1995. "Stoning and Sight: A Structural Equivalence in Greek Mythology". *Classical Antiquity* 14: 193–211.

—— 2001. *Images in Mind: Statues in Archaic and Classical Greek Literature and Thought*. Princeton: Princeton University Press.

Steinhart, M. 1995. *Das Motiv des Auges in der griechischen Kunst*. Mainz am Rhein: Philipp von Zabern.

Stevens, A. 2002. "Telling Presences: Narrating Divine Epiphany in Homer and Beyond". PhD dissertation, Cambridge University.

Stewart, A. 1990. *Greek Sculpture: An Exploration*. New Haven: Yale University Press.

—— 1996. "Reflections". In *Sexuality in Ancient Art*, N. Kampen (ed.), 136–54. Cambridge: Cambridge University Press.

Stewart, P. 2004. *Roman Art*. Oxford: Oxford University Press.

Stieber, M. C. 2004. *The Poetics of Appearance in the Attic Korai*. Austin: University of Texas Press.

Stinson, P. 2011. "Perspective Systems in Roman Second Style Wall-Painting". *American Journal of Archaeology* 115: 403–26.

Stoichita, V. I. 1997. *A Short History of the Shadow*, A. M. Glasgeen (trans.). London: Reaction Books.

Stückelberger, A. 1994. *Bild und Wort: Das illustrierte Fachbuch in der antiken Naturwissenschaft, Medizin und Technik*. Mainz am Rhein: Philipp von Zabern.

Summers, D. 1987. *The Judgment of Sense: Renaissance Naturalism and the Rise of Aesthetics*. Cambridge: Cambridge University Press.

—— 2003. *Real Spaces: World Art History and the Rise of Western Modernism*. London: Phaidon.

—— 2007. *Vision, Reflection and Desire in Western Painting*. Chapel Hill: University of North Carolina Press.

Suter, A. 2003. "Lament in Euripides' *Trojan Women*". *Mnemosyne* 56: 1–28.

Svenbro, J. 1993. *Phrasiklea: An Anthropology of Reading in Ancient Greece*, J. Lloyd (trans.). Ithaca: Cornell University Press.

Sznajder, L. 2013. "Quelques pistes dans le champ lexical de la fiction en latin". In *Théories et pratique de la fiction à l'époque impériale*, C. Bréchet, A. Videau & R. Webb (eds), 49–62. Paris: Picard.

Tanner, J. 2006. *The Invention of Art History in Ancient Greece: Religion, Society and Artistic Rationalisation*. Cambridge: Cambridge University Press.

Taplin, O. 1978. *Greek Tragedy in Action*. London: Metheun & Co.

Tarlow, S. 1999. *Bereavement and Commemoration: An Archaeology of Mortality*. Oxford: Blackwell.

—— 2000. "Emotion in Archaeology". *Current Anthropology* 41: 713–46.

Tatti-Gartziou, A. 2010. "Blindness as Punishment". In *Light and Darkness in Ancient Greek Myth and Religion*, M. Christopoulos, E. D. Karakantza & O. Levaniouk (eds), 181–90. Lanham: Lexington Books.

Taylor, C. C. W. 1999. *The Atomists: Leucippus and Democritus*. Toronto: University of Toronto Press.

Taylor, R. 2008. *The Moral Mirror of Roman Art*. Cambridge: Cambridge University Press.

Thébert, Y. 2003. *Thermes romains d'Afrique du Nord et leur contexte méditerranéen*. Rome: Publications de l'École française de Rome.

Thomas, E. 2014. "Architecture, Rhetoric and the Sublime". In *Art and Rhetoric in Roman Culture*, J. Elsner & M. Meyer, 37–88. Cambridge: Cambridge University Press.

Thompson, M. L. 1961. "The Monumental and Literary Evidence for Programmatic Painting in Antiquity". *Marsyas* 9: 36–77.

Thumiger, C. 2013. "Vision and Knowledge in Greek Tragedy". In *Vision and Viewing in Ancient Greece* (= *Helios* 40(1–2)), S. Blundell, D. Cairns & N. S. Rabinowitz (eds), 233–45. Luboch: Texas Tech University Press.

Tobin, R. 1990. "Ancient Perspective and Euclid's *Optics*". *Journal of the Warburg and Courtauld Institutes* 53: 14–41.

Toner, J. (ed.) 2014. *A Cultural History of the Senses in Antiquity, 500 BCE – 500 CE*. London: Bloomsbury.

—— 2015. "Smell and Christianity". In *Smell and the Ancient Senses*, M. Bradley (ed.), 158–70. London: Routledge.

Toomer, G. J. 1976. *Diocles on Burning Mirrors*. New York: Springer.

Topper, K. 2007. "Perseus, the Maiden Medusa, and the Imagery of Abduction". *Hesperia* 76: 73–105.

Touchefeu-Meynier, O. 1968. *Thèmes odysséens dans l'art antique*. Paris: de Boccard.

—— 1992. "Odysseus". In *Lexicon Iconographicum Mythologiae Classicae* 6(1): 943–70.

Toynbee, J. M. C. 1977. "Greek Myth in Roman Stone". *Latomus* 36: 343–412.

Trapp M. 1990. "Plato's *Phaedrus* in Second-Century Literature". In *Antonine Literature*, D. A. Russell (ed.), 141–73. Oxford: Clarendon Press.

Tremlin, T. 2006. *Minds and Gods: The Cognitive Foundations of Religion*. Oxford: Oxford University Press.

Trentin, L. 2013. "Exploring Visual Impairment in Ancient Rome". In *Disabilities in Roman Antiquity: Disparate Bodies A Capite ad Calcem*, C. Laes, C. F. Goodey & M. L. Rose (eds), 89–114. Leiden: Brill.

Trimble, J. 2011. *Women and Visual Replication in Roman Imperial Art and Culture*. Cambridge: Cambridge University Press.

Trimpi, W. 1978. "The Early Metaphorical Uses of *skiagraphia* and *skenographia*". *Traditio* 34: 404–13.

Tsiafakis, D. 2003. "*ΠΕΛΩΡΑ*: Fabulous Creatures and/or Demons of Death". In *The Centaur's Smile: The Human Animal in Early Greek Art*, J. M. Padgett (ed.), 73–106. New Haven: Yale University Press.

Tueller, M. A. 2008. *Look Who's Talking: Innovations in Voice and Identity in Hellenistic Poetry*. Leuven: Peeters.

Turkeltaub, D. 2003. "The Gods' Radiance Manifest: An Analysis of the Narrative Pattern Underlying Homeric Divine Epiphany Scenes". PhD dissertation, Cornell University.

—— 2007. "Perceiving Iliadic Gods". *Harvard Studies in Classical Philology* 103: 1–28.

Turner, S. 2009. "Classical Attic Grave Stelai: Gender, Death and the Viewer". PhD dissertation, University of Cambridge.

—— 2012. "In Cold Blood: Dead Athletes in Classical Athens". *World Archaeology* 44: 217–33.

Tybout, R. A. 1989. "Die Perspektive bei Vitruv: Überlieferungen von *scaenographia*". In *Munus non ingratum: Proceedings of the International Symposium on Vitruvius' De Architectura and Hellenistic and Republican Architecture*, H. Geertman & J. J. de Jong (eds), 55–68. Leiden: Stichting Bulletin Antike Beschaving.

Tyler, S. A. 1984. "The Vision Quest in the West, or What the Mind's Eye Sees". *Journal of Anthropological Research* 40: 23–39.

Ussher, R. G. (ed.) 1973. *Aristophanes, Ecclesiazusae*. Bristol: Bristol Classical Press.

Ustinova, Y. 2009. *Caves and the Ancient Greek Mind: Descending Underground in the Search for Ultimate Truth*. Oxford: Oxford University Press.

Vaerst, A. 1980. "Griechische Schildzeichen vom 8. bis zum 6. Jh.". PhD dissertation, Universität-Salzburg.

van der Grinten, E. V. 1966. *On the Composition of the Medallions in the Interiors of Greek Black- and Red-figured Kylixes*. Amsterdam: Noord-Hollandsche Uitg. Maatschappij.

van Dyke, R. & S. Alcock (eds) 2003. *Archaeologies of Memory*. Oxford: Blackwell.

van Hoorn, W. 1972. *As Images Unwind: Ancient and Modern Theories of Visual Perception*. Amsterdam: University Press Amsterdam.

van Lieshout, R. G. A. 1980. *Greeks on Dreams*. Utrecht: Hes Publishers.

van Straten, F. 1976. "Daikrates' Dream: A Votive Relief from Kos, and Some Other *kat'onar* Dedications". *Bulletin Antieke Beschaving* 51: 1–38.

Varner, E. 2004. *Mutilation and Transformation: Damnatio Memoriae and Roman Imperial Portraiture*. Leiden: Brill.

Vasaly, A. 1993. *Representations: Images of the World in Ciceronian Oratory*. Berkeley: University of California Press.

Vermeule, E. 1979. *Aspects of Death in Early Greek Art and Poetry*. Berkeley: University of California Press.

Vernant, J.-P. 1975. "Image et apparence dans la théorie platonicienne de la *mimèsis*". *Journal de Pyschologie* 2: 133–60.

—— 1982. "La belle mort et le cadavre outragé". In *La mort, les morts dans les sociétés anciennes*, G. Gnoli & J.-P. Vernant (eds), 45–76. Paris: Éditions de la maison des sciences de l'homme.

—— 1985a. *La mort dans les yeux: figures de l'Autre en Grèce ancienne*. Paris: Hachette.

—— 1985b. "Figures féminines de la mort en Grèce". In *L'Individu, la mort, l'amour: soi-même et l'Autre en Grèce ancienne*, J.-P. Vernant (ed.), 131–52. Paris: Gallimard.

—— 1987. "Das l'œil du miroir: Méduse". In *Lo specchio e il doppio: dallo stagno di Narciso allo schermo televiso*, G. Macchi, M. Vitali & M. Antonelliana (eds), 26–32. Milan: Fabbri Editori.

—— 1990a. "Figuration et image". *Mètis* 5: 225–38.

—— 1990b. *Figures, idoles, masques*. Paris: Julliard.

—— 1991. *Mortals and Immortals: Collected Essays*, F. Zeitlin (ed. & trans.) Princeton: Princeton University Press.

—— 1998. *La mort dans les yeux. Figures de l'Autre en Grèce ancienne: Artémis, Gorgô*, 2nd edn. Paris: Hachette.
Vernant, J.-P. & F. Frontisi 1983. "Figures du masque en Grèce ancienne". *Journal de Psychologie Normale et Pathologique* 1–2: 53–69.
Versnel, H. S. 1987. "What did Ancient Man See When He Saw a God? Some Reflections on Greco-Roman Epiphany". In *Effigies Dei: Essays on the History of Religions*, D. van der Plas (ed.), 42–55. Leiden: Brill.
—— 2011. *Coping with the Gods: Wayward Readings in Greek Theology*. Leiden: Brill.
Vetta, M. 1995. *Poesia e simposio nella Grecia antica: guida storica e critica*. Bari: Laterza.
Villard, L. (ed.) 2005. *Études sur la vision dans l'antiquité classique*. Rouen: Publication Universités de Rouen et du Havre.
Vitrac, B. 2002. "Note Textuelle sur un (problème de) lieu géométrique dans les *Météorologiques* d'Aristote (III. 5, 375 b 16—376 b 22)". *Archive for the History of Exact Sciences* 56: 239–83.
Vlastos, G. 1975. *Plato's Universe*. Seattle: University of Washington Press.
—— 1980. "The Role of Observation in Plato's Conception of Astronomy". In *Science and the Sciences in Plato*, J. P. Anton (ed.), 1–31. New York: Eidos.
—— 1995. *Socrates, Plato and Their Tradition*. Princeton: Princeton University Press.
von den Hoff, R. 2009. "Odysseus in der antiken Bildkunst". In *Odysseus: Irrfahrten durch die Jahrhunderte*, H.-J. Gehrke & M. Kirschkowski (eds), 39–64. Freiburg: Rombach.
von Fritz, K. 1953. "Democritus' Theory of Vision". In *Science, Medicine and History: Essays on the Evolution of Scientific Thought and Medical Practice Written in Honour of Charles Singer*, vol. 1, E. A. Underwood (ed.), 83–99. Oxford: Oxford University Press.
Vout, C. 2003. "Embracing Egypt". In *Rome the Cosmopolis*, C. Edwards & G. Woolf (eds), 177–202. Cambridge: Cambridge University Press.
Wade, N. J. 1998. *A Natural History of Vision*. Cambridge, MA: MIT Press.
Wade, N. J. & M. Swanston 2013. *Visual Perception: An Introduction*, 3rd edn. Hove: Psychology Press.
Walde, C. 2001. *Antike Traumdeutung und moderne Traumforschung*. Düsseldorf: Artemis & Winkler.
—— 2004. "Dreams: Interpretation of Dreams. II. Classical Antiquity". In *Brill's New Pauly. Encyclopaedia of the Ancient World*, vol. 4, H. Cancik & H. Schneider (eds), 715–19. Leiden: Brill.
Walker, A. 1993. "*Erôs* and the Eye in the *Love-Letters* of Philostratus". *Proceedings of the Cambridge Philological Association* 38: 132–48.
Wallace-Hadrill, A. 1994. *Houses and Society in Pompeii and Herculaneum*. Princeton: Princeton University Press.
—— 2008. "Housing the Dead: The Tomb as House in Roman Italy". In *Commemorating the Dead: Texts and Artifacts in Context*, L. Brink & D. Green (eds), 39–77. Berlin: De Gruyter.
Walter-Karydi, E. 2002. "Color in Classical Painting". In *Color in Ancient Greece: The Role of Color in Ancient Greek Art and Architecture*, M. A. Tiverios & D. S. Tsifakis (eds), 75–88. Thessaloniki: Aristotle University.
Walters, B. 2013. "Reading Death and the Senses in Lucan and Lucretius". In *Synaesthesia and the Ancient Senses*, S. Butler & A. Purves (eds), 115–26. Durham: Acumen.
Walton, J. M. 1996. *The Greek Sense of Theatre: Tragedy Reviewed*, 2nd edn. Amsterdam: Harwood Academic Publishers.
Wardy, R. B. B. 1988. "Eleatic Pluralism". *Archiv für Geschichte der Philosophie* 70: 125–46.
Warren, J. 2007. *The Presocratics*. Durham: Acumen.
Wartofsky, M. W. 1979. "Picturing and Representing". In *Perception and Pictorial Representation*, C. F. Nodine & D. F. Fisher (eds), 272–83. New York: Praeger.

Watson, G. 1988. *Phantasia in Classical Thought*. Galway: Galway University Press.
—— 1994. "The Concept of 'Phantasia' from the Late Hellenistic Period to Early Neoplatonism". *Aufstieg und Niedergang der Römischen Welt* 2(36.7): 4765–810.
Webb, R. 1997a. "Imagination and the Arousal of the Emotions in Greco-Roman Rhetoric". In *The Passions in Roman Thought and Literature*, S. M. Braund & C. Gill (eds), 112–27. Cambridge: Cambridge University Press.
—— 1997b. "Mémoire et imagination: les limites de l'*enargeia* dans la théorie rhétorique grecque". In *Dire l'évidence: philosophie et rhétorique antiques*, C. Lévy & L. Pernot (eds), 229–48. Paris: L'Harmattan.
—— 2009a. *Ekphrasis, Imagination and Persuasion in Ancient Rhetorical Theory and Practice*. Aldershot: Ashgate.
—— 2009b. "Eschine et le passé athénien: narration, imagination et construction de la mémoire". *Cahiers des études anciennes* 46: 129–47.
Weber, G. 2000. *Kaiser, Träume und Visionen in Prinzipat und Spätantike*. Stuttgart: Steiner.
Webster, C. 2014. "Euclid's *Optics* and Geometrical Astronomy". *Apeiron* 47: 526–51.
Webster, T. B. L. 1939. "Tondo Composition in Archaic and Classical Greek Art". *Journal of Hellenic Studies* 59: 103–23.
Whallon, W. 1964. "Blind Thamyris and Blind Maeonides". *Phoenix* 18: 9–12.
White, J. 1956. *Perspective in Ancient Drawing and Painting*. London: Society for the Promotion of Hellenic Studies.
—— 1987. *The Birth and Rebirth of Pictorial Space*, 3rd edn. London: Faber.
Whitley, J. 1994. "Protoattic Pottery: A Contextual Approach". In *Classical Greece: Ancient Histories and Modern Archaeologies*, I. Morris (ed.), 51–70. Cambridge: Cambridge University Press.
Whitmarsh, T. 2011. *Narrative and Identity in the Ancient Greek Novel: Returning Romance*. Cambridge: Cambridge University Press.
Whitton, C. (ed.) 2013. *Pliny the Younger: Epistles Book II*. Cambridge: Cambridge University Press.
Wiles, D. 1997. *Tragedy in Athens: Performance Space and Theatrical Meaning*. Cambridge: Cambridge University Press.
—— 2007. *Mask and Performance in Greek Tragedy: From Ancient Festival to Modern Experimentation*. Cambridge: Cambridge University Press.
Wilson, P. 2009. "Thamyris the Thracian: The Archetypal Wandering Poet In *Wandering Poets in Ancient Greek Culture: Travel, Locality and Pan-Hellenism*, R. Hunter & I. Rutherford (eds), 46–79. Cambridge: Cambridge University Press.
Wiseman, T. P. 2004. *The Myths of Rome*. Exeter: University of Exeter Press.
Wistrand, M. 1990. "Violence and Entertainment in Seneca the Younger". *Eranos* 88: 31–46.
Wölfflin, H. 1932. *Principles of Art History: The Problem of the Development of Style in Later Art*, M. D. Hottinger (trans.). London: G. Bell & Sons.
Wollheim, R. 1980. *Art and its Objects*, 2nd edn. Cambridge: Cambridge University Press.
—— 1987. *Painting as an Art*. Princeton: Princeton University Press.
Wood, S. 2000. "Mortals, Empresses, and Earth Goddesses: Demeter and Persephone in Public and Private Apotheosis". In *I Claudia II. Women in Roman Art and Society*, D. E. E. Kleiner & S. B. Matheson (eds), 77–100. Austin: University of Texas Press.
Wright, N. T. 2003. *The Resurrection of the Son of God*. London: SPCK.
Wycherley, R. 1978. *The Stones of Athens*. Princeton: Princeton University Press.
Wypustek, A. 2013. *Images of Eternal Beauty in Funerary Verse Inscriptions of the Hellenistic and Graeco-Roman Periods*. Leiden: Brill.
Yalouris, N. 1990. "Helios". In *Lexicon Iconographicum Mythologiae Classicae* 5(1): 1005–34.

Yates, F. A. 1966. *The Art of Memory*. Chicago: University of Chicago Press.

Younger, J. G. 2002. "Women in Relief: 'Double Consciousness' in Classical Attic Tombstones". In *Among Women: From the Homosocial to the Homoerotic in the Ancient World*, N. S. Rabinowitz & L. Auanger (eds), 167–210. Austin: University of Texas Press.

Zadoks-Josephus Jitta, A. N. 1932. *Ancestral Portraiture in Rome and the Art of the Last Century of the Republic*. Amsterdam: Allard Pierson Stichting, Universiteit van Amsterdam.

Zagdoun, M.-A. 2000. *La philosophie stoïcienne de l'art*. Paris: CNRS Éditions.

Zajko, V. & M. Leonard (eds) 2006. *Laughing with Medusa: Classical Myth and Feminist Thought*. Oxford: Oxford University Press.

Zangara, A. 2007. *Voir l'histoire: théories anciennes du récit historique*. Paris: Éditions de l'École des hautes études en sciences sociales.

Zanker, G. 1981. "*Enargeia* in the Ancient Criticism of Poetry". *Rheinisches Museum* 124: 297–311.

—— 1987. *Realism in Alexandrian Poetry: A Literature and its Audience*. London: Croom Helm.

—— 2004. *Modes of Viewing in Hellenistic Poetry and Art*. Madison: University of Wisconsin Press.

Zanker, P. & B. C. Ewald 2004. *Mit Mythen leben: Die Bilderwelt der römischen Sarkophage*. Munich: Hirmer.

—— 2012. *Living with Myths: The Imagery of Roman Sarcophagi*, J. Slater (trans.). Oxford: Oxford University Press.

Zeitlin, F. I. 1994. "The Artful Eye: Vision, Ecphrasis and Spectacle in Euripidean Theatre". In *Art and Text in Ancient Greek Culture*, S. Goldhill & R. Osborne (eds), 138–96. Cambridge: Cambridge University Press.

—— 2001. "Visions and Revisions of Homer". In *Being Greek Under Rome: Cultural Identity, the Second Sophistic, and the Development of Empire*, S. Goldhill (ed.), 195–266. Cambridge: Cambridge University Press.

Zeki, S. 1999. *Inner Vision: An Exploration of Art and the Brain*. Oxford: Oxford University Press.

Zimmermann, R. 2001. *Geschlechtermetaphorik und Gottesverhältnis: Traditionsgeschichte und Theologie eines Bildfelds in Urchristentum und antiker Umwelt*. Tübingen: Mohr Siebeck.

Zografou, A. 2010. "Magic Lamps, Luminous Dreams: Lamps in *PGM* Recipes". In *Light and Darkness in Ancient Greek Myth and Religion*, M. Christopoulos, E. D. Karakantza & O. Levaniouk (eds), 276–94. Lanham: Lexington Books.

INDEX

"absorption" 85, 99–100
Achilles Tatius 25n93, 26n98, 193n47, 207n8
Actaeon 25, 165, 167, 169n30, 175, 177
Adonis 192, 200
Aelius Aristides 170n34, 174n58, 175n61, 206–7, 219
Aeneas 165, 221n5
Aeschines 213n21
Aeschylus 50, 110, 131n29, 217, 243n19, 245–6n31
aesthetics 8–9; *see also* senses; synaesthesia
agapē (Christian "love"/"charity") 25n94, 229–31
Agatharchus 50, 110–13
Agathon 25, 128–129n20, 130n24
Alberti, Leon Battista 261; *see also* perspective
Alcmaeon 16, 37, 39–44, 46, 49, 52
Alhacen (Ibn al-Haytham) 34–5, 80, 255–6, 257–61
"allegory of the cave" 15, 58–9, 61, 253n12; *see also* Plato; *skiagraphia*
Alxenor 10n36
Anaxagoras 37–8, 41–4, 50, 52–3, 110, 111, 113
Anaximander 129n22, 130, 131n28
Andromeda 25, 159, 199
angels 222–3, 225, 234, 234–5
aniconism 177, 179; *see also* gods
Anthemius of Tralles 71
anthropomorphism 162, 163, 172, 176, 177, 179; *see also* epiphany; gods
Anticlea 121, 144–5, 149, 155
Aper, T. Statilius 182–4
Aphrodite (Venus) 165n15, 165, 176, 199, 200, 228
Apollodorus (Classical Greek painter) 47, 116
Apollodorus (Imperial mythographer) 98n36, 156n58, 157n67, 166n17
Apollonius (Hellenistic poet) 28, 166n17, 237n2

Apollonius (Imperial philosopher) 216
Apuleius 43n33, 78, 228n31
Aquae Flavianae 161–79
Archimedes 69, 76, 77–8, 84n47; *see also* optics
Archinos 22–3, 173n56
Archytas 77–8, 83, 117; *see also* optics
Ares (Mars) 100, 182, 242
Argos 246
Aristophanes 40n15, 43n33, 112, 115, 126–33, 139–41, 176n66, 246n33
Aristotle 12, 17, 24, 62–6, 79–80, 183, 207, 215–16, 251–4; *Metaphysics* 12n9, 63n29; *On Dreams* 25n93; *On the Generation of Animals* 46n48, 64n30; *On the Heavens* 131n28; *On Memory* 13n49, 183, 207n7; *On Meteorology* 24, 40n15, 77, 78n31; *On the Parts of Animals* 65–6; *On Sense and the Sensible* 41n19, 46n48, 50n62, 63n29, 79n34, 117, 171n43; *On the Soul* 12, 13n49, 17, 24–5, 54n2, 58n14, 62–5, 171n43, 183, 207, 253n11, 254, 261; *Physics* 64n30; *Rhetoric* 48n54
art: and cultural "ways of seeing" 3–7; *see also* mosaics; naturalism (in art); painting; perspective; Pompeian wall-painting; vase-painting
Artemidorus 15, 175
Artemis (Diana) 25, 157, 165, 175n64
Asclepius 20–2, 169n31, 170n40, 174, 177n71, 246n33
astronomy 76–7, 80, 83, 112
Athena 25, 90, 97–100, 165, 169n30, 170n34, 171, 173, 242n15; Athena Parthenos 176
Athenaeus 139, 140, 245n28
Atlas 133–4
atomist theories of matter 16, 49–51, 55–6, 66, 116, 125–126n11; *see also* Democritus; "extramission"; sight
autopsy 12, 161, 163–4, 174–5, 220–4

INDEX

Augustine, St 13–14n51, 206, 208–9, 211–12, 214–15
Augustus 151, 169n31
Avicenna (Ibn Sīnā) 253–5, 258, 260

Bacon, Roger 260–1
"Badminton sarcophagus" 154–5
baskania see "evil eye"
Baxandall, Michael 3n11, 13
beauty 25, 60–1, 66, 176, 205–8, 229; *see also* Aristotle; Plato; sight
Beazley, Sir John 180
Belting, Hans 82n43, 108–109n8
Bergmann, Bettina 191
Biton 76
blindness 17, 18, 25, 90–6, 156–7, 222, 235–6, 237–48; in art 247–8 (*see also* Polyphemus); and death 10 (*see also* Hades); of Homer 18, 237–41, 248; and insight 235–6, 242–3, 248; as punishment 241; in theatre 243–8
"Bobbio fragment" 71n4, 72
body: of actor 246; body-votives 20; dead bodies 143–60 (*see also* death); embodied knowledge 208; and the eye 19–30; of the gods 179 (*see also* gods); of Jesus 225–7; and soul 54–61, 64, 66–7; suffering of 231–5
brain 13, 39, 43–4, 67, 79, 213, 251–4, 256; *see also* imagination; insight; mind; "mind's eye"; neuroscience
Bryson, Norman 4n15, 109
"burning mirrors" 70–4, 76, 82, 83–4, 255; *see also* mirrors
Butades 26
Buxton, Richard 241

Caesar, Julius 161, 163
Callimachus 242n15
camera obscura 14, 19
Camille, Michael 4
Canachus 180–1
Carruthers, Mary 189–90, 202–3
catoptrics 43n29, 72–4, 76–8, 81, 255; *see also* mirrors; optics
Catullus 165
Cestius, Gaius 151
Chardin, Jean-Baptiste-Siméon 87–8
Chariton 207n8, 228n31
Christianity 1–2n2, 26n100, 171, 215, 220–36, 237
Cicero 12, 18, 23n103, 28n103, 125, 147n8, 148n19, 169n31, 181–90, 215, 261–2
Clement of Alexandria 228n32
Clement of Rome 227, 233
Clementine Recognitions 230

colour 4n18, 24, 41–2, 44–52, 63n27, 107–8, 116–7; Anaxaogoras on 41–2; Aristotle on 48, 63n27, 79, 117, 253n11; Democritus on 49, 51–2, 116–17; Empedocles on 44–52; of eye 24, 46; in optics 74n19, 249, 251–2, 254, 256, 262; in painting 90, 107–8, 115–21 (*see also* painting; *skiagraphia*)
comedy 244n25; *see also* Aristophanes, Menander
"conic sections" 71, 255
Constantine 204, 236
Corfu 157–9
corpses 143–55; *see also* death
cupids 192, 195, 197
Cyclops *see* Polyphemus

Damianus of Larissa 74
damnatio memoriae 182n7, 204
death 10, 90–3, 120–1, 143–60, 237; as blindness 10, 156–7 (*see also* blindness; Gorgon; Hades); death-masks 148–9
deception: and sight 18–19, 53, 57–62, 108, 115, 117–18; *see also* "allegory of the cave"; *phantasmata*; Plato
Delphi 50n66, 144, 169, 170, 213, 247
Democritus 16, 37–8, 49–53, 54–6, 64n30, 66, 76n25, 111, 113, 116, 170n40
Demodocus 106, 239–40
Demosthenes 139n40, 145n8, 213, 219
depilation 140
Descartes, René 15, 19, 30, 262
desire *see eros*
dexiōsis ("handshake" motif) 152, 154
diagrams 70, 74–6
Dialexis (*Dissoi Logoi*) 182
Didyma 180
Dio Chrysostom 179, 225n15, 239
Diocles 71
Diogenes Laertius 43n32, 76n25, 111n19, 207
Dionysius of Halicarnassus 18n78, 212n20
Dionysus 59, 62, 154, 222, 241; *see also* theatre
dioptrics 15, 72–4, 76–7; *see also* Descartes; optics
Dipylon amphora 146
"Doubting Thomas" 171, 234–5
dreams 15, 121, 144, 168, 173–5; *see also* Aelius Aristides; epiphany
drunkenness 58; *see also* Polyphemus; symposium
Dtrūms 71

Egypt 28, 123, 204
eidē ("Forms") 14–15, 58; *see also* Plato

INDEX

eidōla ("images", "effluences", "phantoms") 14, 16, 49, 108, 118, 121, 144, 149, 155, 160, 241
ekphrasis 17–18, 19n80, 176–7, 206, 209, 213, 217; *see also enargeia*; hearing; *phantasia*; Philostratus; *Progymnasmata*; Theon
ekplēxis 217
Eleusinian Mysteries 168, 169n33
Eleusis amphora 89–96, 101, 105
emissionist theories of vision *see* "extramission"
Empedocles 37–8, 44–8, 52–3, 55n5, 57n11, 64n30, 124, 131n29, 227n24
emphasis see reflections
enargeia ("visual vividness") 17–18, 165, 170, 172, 209–12; *see also* Aristotle; *ekphrasis*; imagination; "mind's eye"; *phantasia*; sight; Stoics
Endymion 192, 193, 194
envy 26–8
entasis ("distention") 111
Epicureans 16, 44; *see also* Lucretius
epiphany 22–3, 157, 161–79, 221–4, 224–7, 230; *see also* gods; sight
episēmata (shield emblems) 97–9, 183n12
Erinyes 215–18
erōs (sexual "desire") 25–6, 59–61, 179, 228–31
Euclid 15, 16, 50, 72–5, 76–77n26, 81, 84, 110–12, 250, 252, 255; *see also* optics
Euphronios 100
Euripides 130–1, 215, 216–17, 218, 239, 242, 243n19, 244, 245n31
Eurydice 156–7
Eurysices, Marcus Vergilius 151
"evil eye" 22, 26–30; *see also* eye; "extramission"; gaze
eye 19–30; in ancient art 20–4 (*see also* eye-cups); artificial recreations of 5n22; colour of 24, 46; disease of 15–16, 25 (*see also* medicine); dissection of 15, 19, 24, 49n58; and ear 12, 17, 224, 235 (*see also* hearing); as embodied entity 19–30, 85 (*see also* body); "exosomatic" viewing devices 19n82; as fire 39–40, 41, 45–7, 57, 123–42; Greek languages of 29, 125; in Homer 123–4 (*see also* Homer); of inanimate objects 20–4, 126–7; and lamps 131–3 (*see also* lamps); and magic 28; and mind 13, 16, 17, 57–62 (*see also* imagination; mind; "mind's eye"; *phantasia*); as mirror 40, 43, 56 (*see also* mirrors); and nose 129 (*see also* smell); in optics 75–6, 110; in painting 29–30; as phallus 26; physiology of 2, 256–8; in sculpture 24; as sun 123, 125–6, 131 (*see also* sun); as water 42–3, 56; as "window of the soul" 29–30 (*see also* soul); of women 27–8; *see also* "evil eye"; "extramission"; gaze; "intromission"; "mind's eye"; "period eye"; sight
eye-cups 20, 87–8, 102–5, 126–7, 132, 136–9, 159
eye-witnessing *see* autopsy
ex uisu inscriptions 164, 167, 173
"extramission" 16–17, 36–7, 44–5, 62, 63n29, 65, 124–6, 130, 142, 156, 171–2, 250–2, 261

face 20, 29–30, 62, 88, 97, 102–5, 125–6, 130, 141, 148–9, 226–7, 243–4; *see also* eye; masks
fascinatio see "evil eye"
Fiedler, Konrad 85
foreshortening 110–14; *see also* optics; perspective
Foster, Hal 4, 182n9
Foucault, Michel 4n14
funerals 145–9; *see also* death
Fried, Michael 85, 99–100

Galen 16, 17n70, 79–80, 249–61
Ganymede 192, 199
gaze 4–5, 26, 28–30, 61–2, 66, 85, 89–106, 123–7, 154–9, 166, 228–9, 244; *see also* "evil eye"; eye; Gorgon; psychoanalysis; spectator figures (in ancient art)
gender 26; *see also* women
geometry 48, 49, 68–83, 110–14, 115, 183, 250–60; *see also* optics
Gestalt theory 3n9
gladiators *see* spectacles
gods 22–3, 33, 161–79, 220–36; *see also* epiphany
Gombrich, Ernst 109
Gorgias 13n48, 108, 120n65
Gorgon 25, 89–106, 132, 139, 157–60, 199
grave stelai 10, 151–5
Greek Anthology see Palatine Anthology; *Planudean Anthology*
"Greek Revolution" 109; *see also* naturalism (in art)

Hades 90, 104, 121, 237n1; *see also* death
hand: as metaphor for the eye 16; *see also* touch
haptic *see* touch
hearing 1, 8–9, 12, 17–18, 42n24, 142, 171, 187–8, 209–13, 224, 234; *see also* *ekphrasis*; senses
heaven 234–5

INDEX

Hecate 169–70
Helen 240–1
Heliodorus 25, 27n102
Helios 125, 129, 131n28, 134–6, 200; *see also* sun
Hephaestus (Vulcan) 124, 182
Hera (Juno) 165, 242n15
Heraclitus 12, 65, 127n17
Hero 15, 73, 81, 250
Herodotus 12, 169n29, 173, 176
Hesiod 11, 157n67, 167n20, 170n36, 239, 242n15
Hipparchus 17
Hippocrates/Hippocratic corpus 15–16, 39n13
Hippolytus 192
Hölscher, Tonio 204
Homer: Homeric attitudes to seeing 10, 19, 29, 39, 121, 123–5, 144–5, 156–7 (*see also thauma idesthai*); blindness of 18, 237–41, 248 (*see also* blindness); gods in Homer 165, 170, 172–3, 176, 227; and Late Geometric art 94; Plato's attitude towards 62; "visual" qualities of Homeric poetry 18 (*see also enargeia*); *Iliad* 18, 39n11, 40n15, 123n1, 124, 156n63, 165, 170n36, 172, 173n52, 227, 228n31, 238–47; *Odyssey* 10, 39n11, 106, 121, 124, 136n37, 144–5, 165, 170n36, 171, 239–40, 242; *see also* Anticlea; *Homeric Hymns*; Odysseys; Polyphemus; "shield of Achilles"; Thamyris
Homeric Hymns 39, 165n15, 176n67, 228n31
homosexuality 60
Horace 148n19, 169n31
Huygens, Christiaan 262
Hylas 166–7, 175

Ibn Sahl 255
idesthai ("to behold")13, 19–20n84, 121n69, 237n1; *see also* sight
Ignatius 227, 229n35, 230, 233, 234
Iliad see Homer
"Ilissos stele" 153–5
imagination 17, 179, 187, 205–19, 233–4, 249, 252–4; *see also* memory; mind; mind's eye; *phantasia*; "seeing as"/"seeing in"
imago 149, 188–9, 214
insight 205–19; *see also enargeia*; imagination; memory; mind; "mind's eye"; *phantasia*
"intromission" 16–17, 36–7, 51, 54–6, 64, 78, 125n11, 156, 171–2, 250, 252, 254, 261

invisibility 29–30, 55, 58–9, 227–8, 223; *see also* blindness; death; gods
Irenaeus 230

Jesus *see* Christianity
Jews *see* Judaism
John (Evangelist) 220–1, 222, 223, 224–6, 227, 236
Judaism 13–41n51, 26n100, 221, 225–7, 231, 232
Julius Africanus 76

Keats, John 18n78
Kepler, Johannes 15, 19, 35, 261–2
Kerameikos 150–1
Knidian Aphrodite 176–7
knowledge: and sight 10–15, 17–18, 36–67, 237; *see also* "mind's eye"; *phantasia*; senses; sight
kottabos (sympotic game) 102

Lacan, Jacques 5
lamps 45, 57n11, 123–42; as replications of the eye 131–3
Lefkadia 118–20
Leonardo da Vinci 261
Leontius 61–2
Lessing, Gotthold Ephraim 245–6
Leucippus 16
light: divine light of the gods 170–1, 222, 224; "seeing the light" (as metaphor for life) 10, 237 (*see also* blindness; death); theories of light and sight 39–53, 56, 57, 60–6, 123–6, 130; *see also* eye; lamps; optics; rays; shadows; sight
Livy 168n26
"Longinus" 18n78, 206, 211, 217–18
Longus 175
love *see agapē*; *erōs*
Lucan 98n36, 100n39
Lucian 18n78, 43n33, 98, 205–8, 218
Lucretius 16, 44, 125–126n11
Luke (Evangelist) 220–1, 222, 223, 224–5, 227
Luna *see* Selene
Lycurgus 241
Lysias 212–13, 219

Mack, Rainer 96–8
magic 28–9
Martins, Didier 87–8, 103n48
masks 20, 29n108, 96, 97, 102–5; death-masks 148–9; in theatre 87, 114, 243–8; *see also* eye-cups
mathematics 68–84; *see also* geometry; optics
Matthew (Evangelist) 224, 225, 227, 228

INDEX

Mau, August 183
Medea 28, 30n109
medicine 15–16, 20–1, 39, 111, 254, 260; *see also* eye; Galen; optic nerve
Medusa *see* Gorgon
Meleager 185, 192
memory 12, 144–51, 162, 180–204, 208–9, 212–13, 230, 231, 253–4
Menander 228n31
Meton 112, 115
Micon 114
mimesis 14, 52, 93, 100, 107–9, 216; *see also* Aristotle; Plato
mind 205–19; *see also* brain; imagination; "mind's eye"; *phantasia*; soul
"mind's eye" 13, 16–17, 45, 54, 57–62, 64–7, 149, 171, 183, 205–19, 252–3, 261; *see also* Aristotle; *enargeia*; imagination; memory; mind; *phantasia*; Plato; soul
Minucius Felix 230
mirrors 1–2, 6–7, 70, 78, 85, 97–100, 157; "burning mirrors" 70–4, 76, 82, 83–4, 255; in Christian thinking 230; as metaphor for eye 40, 43, 104, 142; spherical mirrors 258–9; *see also* catoptrics; gaze; Gorgon; Narcissus; optics
mnemonics 182–90; *see also* memory
moon *see* Selene
mosaics 22, 28, 175, 191n33
Mulvey, Laura 5n20, 26n99, 158n73
music 77, 79–80, 83, 117, 237–9, 241–2, 247; *see also* Thamyris
mysteries 163n4; *see also* Eleusinian Mysteries; religion

Nabus, Gaius Julius
Narcissus 6–7, 25–6, 192, 194–5, 196–7
naturalism (in art) 10n135, 109, 114, 121, 176, 177, 179; *see also* aniconism; "Greek Revolution"; mimesis; optics; perspective; Plato
Nemesius 253
Neoplatonists 14–15n58, 252–4; *see also* Plotinus
neuroscience 5, 85; *see also* brain
Newton, Isaac 262
nose 129; *see also* smell
Novatian 227n22, 228n32, 234
novels *see* Achilles Tatius; Chariton; *Clementine Recognitions*; Heliodorus; Longus; Petronius
nymphs 161–79

"Ockham's Razor" 252
ocularcentrism 8–10, 145, 160, 163, 171, 188, 224, 237; *see also* senses; sight

Odysseus 90–6, 121n68, 144–5, 221n5, 242
Odyssey see Homer
Oedipus 114, 131n29, 237–8, 242–3, 244, 245
optic nerve 15, 39, 253, 256–7; *see also* eye
optics 15, 16, 18, 46, 68–84, 108–14, 116–17, 125, 249–62; *see also* perspective
Orestes 215–17
Origen 222n8, 227n26, 228n32
Orpheus 156–7, 221n5
Ovid 26n96, 92, 98, 126n12, 149n23, 156–7, 169n31, 225, 228

painting: and colour 90, 118–21 (*see also* colour); and the eye 29–30; from Macedonia 115–21; as metaphor for sight 46–8; Pompeian/Roman wall-painting 6, 112n26, 159, 190–204; *see also* optics; perspective; *skēnographia*; *skiagraphia*; vase-painting
Palatine Anthology 1–2, 142n45
Pamphilus 112
Panofsky, Erwin 108–9, 112–13
Pappus of Alexandria 73, 76–77n26, 81
Parmenides 14–15n78, 227n24
Parrhasius 29–30, 107–8
Paul, Saint 220–2, 227, 228–9, 231, 232–4
Pausanias 43n33, 144n3, 169n30, 170n34, 180–1, 193, 204–5, 247
Pecham, John 260
perception: and sight 1–5, 13–16; *see also* brain; mind; "mind's eye"; senses; sight; soul
Pergamon 174–5
"period eye" 3
Perseus 90, 97–100, 157–9, 199
perspective 5, 32, 50–1, 72, 74, 81, 108–15, 121–2, 261; *see also* foreshortening; optics; painting
Petronius 144
phantasia (cognitive "impression") 17–18, 118, 179, 183, 189n27, 205–19; *see also* Aristotle; *enargeia*; imagination; mind; "mind's eye"; sight; Stoics
phantasmata ("apparitions") 118, 215, 217, 249
Philo 226
Philoponus, John 251, 252, 254
Philostratus the Elder 15, 18n77, 25n94, 30n109, 125n9, 170n34, 206, 211, 216, 225n15
Phineus 243, 246
Phoenix 243
Phorcys 243n19
Phrasikleia 146

310

INDEX

phthonos 26–8
Phye 173, 176
physiognomics 29–30
Pindar 39, 123, 127n17
Pitsa 115
Planudean Anthology 30n109, 176–7
Plato 14–15, 17, 57–62, 66–7, 83, 108, 113–14, 115, 117–18, 120–1, 124, 171, 206, 251–2; *Alcibiades* 43n30, 104, 142n46; *Cratylus* 121n69, 237n1; *Critias* 118n56; *Laws* 48n55, 58n14, 60n19, 139n40; *Meno* 46, 55n5, 57n11; *Parmenides* 48n54; *Phaedo* 48n56, 58, 121n69, 237n1; *Phaedrus* 14–15, 25, 60–1, 240–1; *Philebus* 48n56, 111n22; *Republic* 13n48, 14, 15, 44n36, 48n56, 58–62, 83, 108, 115, 117–18, 121n67, 139n40, 253n12; *Sophist* 13n48, 44n36, 207n9; *Symposium* 13n48; *Theaetetus* 48n54, 118n56, 207n9; *Timaeus* 16, 39n12, 40n15, 57–9, 60n19, 118n56, 120n65, 124, 206, 207n9, 250–1; *see also* "allegory of the cave"
pleasure 48, 59, 61–2, 65, 108, 118, 233–4; *see also* beauty
Pliny the Elder 26, 28n103, 30, 47–8, 107–8, 112n24, 116–17, 126n12, 148n20, 149, 154n54, 180n1
Pliny the Younger 191
Plotinus 14–15n58, 230n36, 251
Plutarch 26–8, 43n32, 168n26, 173n55, 187n22, 211, 247n37
pneuma (ocular emission) 16–17, 251–3, 254; *see also* "extramission"; Stoics
Pollux 245–6
Polybius 12, 147–9
Polyclitus 111–12
Polygnotus 144, 239, 247
Polymestor 243, 245
Polyphemus 89–96, 100–1, 242, 243, 245, 247n35
Pompeian wall-painting 6, 112n26, 159, 190–204
Porter, Jim 2n6, 9
Praxias 22n80
Presocratics 36–53, 55–6, 124, 131; *see also* Alcmaeon; Anaxagoras; Anaximander; Democritus; Empedocles
Progymnasmata 17–18, 204, 217; *see also* Theon
Propertius 166n17
prosōpon 29–30; *see also* face; masks
psychoanalysis 5, 96; *see also* gaze
Ptolemy 15, 16, 69, 72–4, 77–9, 83, 249, 250, 256–61; *see also* optics
Pythagoreans 16, 77, 113, 250–1

Quintilian 17, 47n51, 116, 183, 186–90, 193, 206, 209–12, 214–17

"rays" 16–17; *see also* Alcmaeon; Anaxagoras; Democritus; Empedocles; eye; "extramission"; gaze; "intromission"; light; mirrors; optics; Plato; *pneuma*; sun
reading 1, 8, 9, 75, 146–7, 187–8, 211, 215
reflections: as model for conceptualizing sight 39–44, 56, 123; *see also* Alcmaeon; Anaxagoras; Democritus; eye; Gorgon; light; mirrors; Narcissus; Presocratics; shadows; sight
religion 22–3, 161–79, 220–36; *see also* Christianity; epiphany; gods; Judaism
Renaissance 15, 261–2
rhetoric 17–18, 181–90, 201–3, 209–14; *see also* memory

sarcophagi 10, 144n3, 154–5, 166, 204
scene-painting *see* skēnographia
Sceptics 44
"scopic regime" 4
seals 16, 52, 63n27
"seeing in"/"seeing as" 89, 92, 101, 156
Selene 125, 135, 192, 193
Semele 25, 165, 169
Seneca the Younger 18–19, 149n23, 156n58, 191, 234n41
senses: in antiquity 1–35 (*see also* hearing; sight; smell; synaesthesia; taste; touch); and knowledge 12–15, 36–67; in mediaeval Arabic thought 253–4; "sensory history" 1–8, 142; sight as supreme sense in the ancient sensorium 8–19, 142, 183, 187–8, 212–13, 237 (*see also* ocularcentrism; sight)
sex: and sight 25–6, 228–31; *see also* erōs; sight
Sextus Empiricus 41–2, 42n23, 52n74, 215n27
shadows 26, 46–8, 111, 119–20, 144–5, 149; *see also* "allegory of the cave"; death; *skiagraphia*
shame 29
"shield of Achilles" 18n75, 106; *see also* ekphrasis
shields *see* episēmata
Sidonius Apolliniaris 191
sight: "ancient" attitudes towards (as compared with "modern") 3, 8, 15–16, 260–2 (*see also* eye; gaze); and art history 3–5; atomist theories of 16, 49–51, 55–6, 66, 116, 125–126n11; Christian attitudes towards 1–2n2, 26n100, 171, 215, 220–36, 237; as culturally constructed 1–8, 163; and death 10, 90–3, 120–1,

INDEX

sight *continued*
143–60, 237 (*see also* blindness; death; Hades); and deception 18–19, 53, 57–62, 108, 115, 117–18 (*see also* "allegory of the cave"; *phantasmata*; Plato); and desire 25–6, 228–31 (*see also agapē*; *erōs*); feminist attitudes towards 5 (*see also* Gorgon; women); and gender 26; Greek and Latin terminologies of 12, 13–14, 124–5, 170–1, 237; in Homer 10, 19, 123–5, 144–5, 156–7 (*see also* Homer); Judaic attitudes towards 226–7 (*see also* Judaism); and knowledge/perception/truth 4–5, 12–15, 17–18, 36–67, 149, 171, 173, 183, 205–19, 237, 253, 261 (*see also* memory; mind; "mind's eye"); in myth 25–6, 165 (*see also* Actaeon; Anticlea; Eurydice; Gorgon; Hylas; Lycurgus; Narcissus; Oedipus; Perseus; Phineus; Polymestor; Polyphemus; Semele; Thamyris; Tiresias); and philosophy 36–67 (*see also* Alcmaeon; Anaxagoras; Aristotle; Augustine; Cicero; Democritus; *enargeia*; Empedocles; Epicureans; Lucretius; medicine; "mind's eye"; Neoplatonists; optics; *phantasia*; Plato; Presocratics; Ptolemy; Seneca; Stoics; soul; Theophrastus); and sound 1, 8–9, 12, 17–18, 187–8, 209–13, 224 (*see also ekphrasis*; hearing; senses); "spiritual seeing" 235–6 (*see also* Christianity); and subjectivity 201–3; as supreme sense in the ancient sensorium 8–19, 142, 171, 183, 187–8, 212–13, 237 (*see also* eye; ocularcentrism; senses; synaesthesia); and touch 16–17, 144–5 (*see also* touch); wax analogy of 51–2, 55–6, 63n27, 207: *see also* blindness; epiphany; eye; "extramission"; "intromission"; invisibility; light; ocularcentrism; optics; senses
Simonides 12, 186–7
skēnographia ("scene-painting") 36–7, 50, 81, 110–16, 121–1; *see also* optics; perspective
skiagraphia ("shadow-painting") 36–7, 47–8, 115–21
smell 3, 8–9, 42n24, 151; epiphanic smell 170n34; *see also* senses
Snell, Bruno 124–5
Socrates 14, 29–30, 107; *see also* Plato
Solon 145–6
Sophocles 39n10, 39n12, 41, 130n24, 131n29, 237n2, 239, 242–3, 245, 246, 247
soul: and body 54n2; as instrument for "sight" 25, 27–8, 44, 54–67, 107–8, 118, 120–1, 205–7, 218, 230, 254; *see also* Aristotle; brain; death; imagination; mind; "mind's eye"; *phantasia*; Plato
sound *see* hearing
spectacles (Roman) 233–4
spectator figures (in ancient art) 86–9; *see also* gaze
Stansbury-O'Donnell, Mark 88–9
Statius 191n30, 237n2, 239n6
stelai *see* grave stelai
Stesichorus 240–1
Stoics 16–17, 179n74, 206n1, 207–8, 211n17, 215, 217, 234, 250, 251, 252; *see also enargeia*; *phantasia*; *pneuma*
sun 10, 39, 46n48, 51, 56, 57–8, 59n16, 119, 121n68, 123, 125–6, 129–33, 134; *see also* Helios
Strabo 163n4, 166n17, 170n40, 225n15
symposium 86, 88–9, 100–5, 126, 159
synaesthesia 8–9, 17–18, 157, 169; *see also* senses

Tabulae Iliacae 204n57
Tacitus 185n16
Taporley Painter 97–100
Tarentum 174
taste 9, 142; *see also* senses
Tertullian 228n32, 233, 234
Thales 111
Thamyris 238–48; in ancient art 239; in Homer 238–9; Sophocles' *Thamyris* 245–8
thauma 10n35, 18–19, 65–6
thauma idesthai ("wonder to behold") 10n35, 19–20n84; *see also* Homer
theatre 32, 34, 107–15, 119, 121–2, 242–8; as a place for seeing 13, 243; *see also* masks; *skēnographia*
Thecla 228–31
Theocritus 166n17
Theon (author of *Progymnasmata*) 18n75, 214n26
Theon (mathematician) 76–77n26, 250
Theophrastus 38, 39, 40, 41–52, 55–6, 124, 227n24
theōria 13–15, 60, 171
theoxenia 167–8
Thomas, St 171, 223, 227n25, 230, 231, 234–5
Thucydides 176n66, 211, 220–221n3
Timomachus 30n109
Tiresias 25, 121n68, 238, 242–4
tombs 149–55; *see also* death
touch: grasping the dead 144–5, 152, 154, 156–7, 160, 223; and vision 16–17, 27–8, 44–5, 49, 57n13, 62, 116, 124–5, 171–2, 179, 223 (*see also* "extramission"; "intromission"; "rays"; senses; sight)

INDEX

Valerius Flaccus 166n17
Valerius Maximus 149n23
Varro 12, 18
vase-painting 6, 50, 85–107, 110, 112–14, 126–7, 133–9, 146, 180, 183n12, 239
Verres 215
Vergina 117–18
Via Appia 150–1
Virgil 156n58, 165, 169n31, 228n31
vision *see* sight
"visual culture" 3–4
"visual turn" 3
"visuality" 4, 163
Vitruvius 50–1, 81n41, 110–11, 125n11, 191
Volubilis 175
votive offerings 20–3, 161–79

wall-painting *see* painting; perspective; Pompeian wall-painting

Wollheim, Richard 3n9, 89, 101, 156; *see also* "seeing as"/"seeing in"
women: in Aristophanes' *Assemblywomen* 126–42; Christian attitudes towards 228–31; eyes of 27–8; on grave stelai 151–3; as mourners 145–6; as visual objects 26, 157–8; *see also* Gorgon; Mulvey; nymphs

Xenocrates 116
Xenophon 12, 29–30, 107, 108n4, 120n65, 125n9, 139n40

Zeitlin, Froma 244
Zeus (Jupiter) 25, 127n17, 165, 199, 241
Zeuxis 47n51, 107–8, 114n32, 116, 119n62

Taylor & Francis eBooks

Helping you to choose the right eBooks for your Library

Add Routledge titles to your library's digital collection today. Taylor and Francis ebooks contains over 50,000 titles in the Humanities, Social Sciences, Behavioural Sciences, Built Environment and Law.

Choose from a range of subject packages or create your own!

Benefits for you
- Free MARC records
- COUNTER-compliant usage statistics
- Flexible purchase and pricing options
- All titles DRM-free.

Benefits for your user
- Off-site, anytime access via Athens or referring URL
- Print or copy pages or chapters
- Full content search
- Bookmark, highlight and annotate text
- Access to thousands of pages of quality research at the click of a button.

REQUEST YOUR FREE INSTITUTIONAL TRIAL TODAY

Free Trials Available
We offer free trials to qualifying academic, corporate and government customers.

eCollections – Choose from over 30 subject eCollections, including:

Archaeology	Language Learning
Architecture	Law
Asian Studies	Literature
Business & Management	Media & Communication
Classical Studies	Middle East Studies
Construction	Music
Creative & Media Arts	Philosophy
Criminology & Criminal Justice	Planning
Economics	Politics
Education	Psychology & Mental Health
Energy	Religion
Engineering	Security
English Language & Linguistics	Social Work
Environment & Sustainability	Sociology
Geography	Sport
Health Studies	Theatre & Performance
History	Tourism, Hospitality & Events

For more information, pricing enquiries or to order a free trial, please contact your local sales team: **www.tandfebooks.com/page/sales**

Routledge
Taylor & Francis Group
The home of Routledge books

www.tandfebooks.com